THE LOEB CLASSICAL LIBRARY

FOUNDED BY JAMES LOEB

EDITED BY

G. P. GOOLD

STRABO

VIII

LCL 267

STRABO

GEOGRAPHY

BOOK XVII
GENERAL INDEX

WITH AN ENGLISH TRANSLATION BY

HORACE LEONARD JONES

HARVARD UNIVERSITY PRESS
CAMBRIDGE, MASSACHUSETTS
LONDON, ENGLAND

First published 1932
Revised and reprinted 1935, 1949
Reprinted 1959, 1967, 1982, 1996

ISBN 0-674-99295-4

Printed in Great Britain by St Edmundsbury Press Ltd,
Bury St Edmunds, Suffolk, on acid-free paper.
Bound by Hunter & Foulis Ltd, Edinburgh, Scotland.

CONTENTS

THE

GEOGRAPHY OF STRABO

BOOK XVII

ΣΤΡΑΒΩΝΟΣ ΓΕΩΓΡΑΦΙΚΩΝ

IZ′

I

1. Ἐπεὶ δὲ τὴν Ἀραβίαν ἐφοδεύοντες καὶ τοὺς κόλπους συμπεριελάβομεν τοὺς σφίγγοντας αὐτὴν καὶ ποιοῦντας χερρόνησον, τὸν Περσικὸν καὶ τὸν Ἀράβιον, τούτῳ δέ τινα συμπεριωδεύθη καὶ τῆς Αἰγύπτου καὶ τῆς Αἰθιοπίας, τὰ τῶν Τρωγλοδυτῶν καὶ τῶν ἑξῆς μέχρι τῶν ἐσχάτων τῆς κινναμωμοφόρου, τὰ λειπόμενα καὶ συνεχῆ τοῖς ἔθνεσι τούτοις, ταῦτα δ' ἐστὶ τὰ περὶ τὸν Νεῖλον, ἐκθετέον· μετὰ δὲ ταῦτα τὴν Λιβύην ἔπιμεν, ἥπερ ἐστὶ λοιπὴ τῆς συμπάσης γεωγραφίας. κἀνταῦθα δ' Ἐρατοσθένους ἀποφάσεις προεκθετέον.

2. Φησὶ δὴ τοῦ Ἀραβίου κόλπου πρὸς τὴν ἑσπέραν ἐννακοσίους ἢ χιλίους[1] σταδίους διέχειν τὸν Νεῖλον, παραπλήσιον ὄντα κατὰ τὸ σχῆμα[2] τῷ γράμματι τῷ Ν[3] κειμένῳ ἀνάπαλιν· ῥυεὶς γάρ, φησίν, ἀπὸ Μερόης ἐπὶ τὰς ἄρκτους ὡς δισχιλίους καὶ ἑπτακοσίους σταδίους, πάλιν ἀναστρέφει πρὸς[4] μεσημβρίαν καὶ τὴν χειμερινὴν

C 786

---

[1] ἐννακοσίους ἢ χιλίους, Groskurd, for ἐννακισχιλίους (F has ‚α in margin); ἐννακοσίους, Corais; χιλίους, Kramer.

[2] σχῆμα, C. Müller, for στόμα. Meineke ejects κατὰ τὸ στόμα.

[3] τῷ νυ EFDr, though D has N above νυ.

2

THE GEOGRAPHY OF STRABO

BOOK XVII

I

1. SINCE, in my description of Arabia, I have also included the gulfs which pinch it and make it a peninsula, I mean the Persian and Arabian Gulfs, and at the same time have gone the rounds of certain parts both of Aegypt and of Aethiopia, I mean the countries of the Troglodytes and the peoples situated in order thereafter as far as the Cinnamon-bearing country, I must now set forth the remaining parts that are continuous with these tribes, that is, the parts in the neighbourhood of the Nile; and after this I shall traverse Libya, which is the last remaining subject of my whole geography. And here too I must first set forth the declarations of Eratosthenes.

2. Now according to him the Nile is nine hundred or a thousand stadia distant towards the west from the Arabian Gulf, and is similar in shape to the letter N written reversed; [1] for after flowing, he says, from Meroê towards the north about two thousand seven hundred stadia, it turns back towards the south and the winter sunset about three thousand

---

[1] *i.e.* И. This is true, roughly speaking, of the course of the Nile from Meroê to Syenê (see critical note).

---

[1] D*h* insert τήν after πρός.

δύσιν ὡς τρισχιλίους καὶ ἑπτακοσίους σταδίους,
καὶ σχεδὸν ἀντάρας τοῖς κατὰ Μερόην τόποις καὶ
εἰς τὴν Λιβύην πολὺ προπεσὼν[1] καὶ τὴν ἑτέραν
ἐπιστροφὴν ποιησάμενος πρὸς τὰς ἄρκτους φέρεται
πεντακισχιλίους μὲν καὶ τριακοσίους σταδίους
ἐπὶ τὸν μέγαν καταράκτην, μικρὸν παρεπι-
στρέφων πρὸς τὴν ἕω, χιλίους δὲ καὶ διακοσίους
τοὺς ἐπὶ τὸν ἐλάττω τὸν κατὰ Συήνην, πεντακισχιλίους δὲ ἄλλους καὶ τριακοσίους ἐπὶ τὴν
θάλατταν. ἐμβάλλουσι δ' εἰς αὐτὸν δύο ποταμοί,
φερόμενοι μὲν ἔκ τινων λιμνῶν ἀπὸ τῆς ἕω, περι-
λαμβάνοντες δὲ νῆσον εὐμεγέθη τὴν Μερόην· ὧν
ὁ μὲν Ἀσταβόρας καλεῖται κατὰ τὸ πρὸς ἕω
πλευρὸν ῥέων, ἅτερος δ' Ἀστάπους· οἱ δ' Ἀστα-
σόβαν καλοῦσι, τὸν δ' Ἀστάπουν ἄλλον εἶναι,
ῥέοντα ἔκ τινων λιμνῶν ἀπὸ μεσημβρίας, καὶ
σχεδὸν τὸ κατ' εὐθεῖαν σῶμα τοῦ Νείλου τοῦτον
ποιεῖν· τὴν δὲ πλήρωσιν αὐτοῦ τοὺς θερινοὺς
ὄμβρους παρασκευάζειν. ὑπὲρ δὲ τὰς συμβο-
λὰς τοῦ Ἀσταβόρα καὶ τοῦ Νείλου σταδίοις
ἑπτακοσίοις Μερόην εἶναι πόλιν ὁμώνυμον τῇ
νήσῳ· ἄλλην δ' εἶναι νῆσον ὑπὲρ τῆς Μερόης, ἣν
ἔχουσιν οἱ Αἰγυπτίων φυγάδες οἱ ἀποστάντες
ἐπὶ[2] Ψαμμιτίχου,[3] καλοῦνται δὲ Σεμβρῖται, ὡς
ἂν ἐπήλυδες· βασιλεύονται δὲ ὑπὸ γυναικός,
ὑπακούουσι[4] δὲ τῶν ἐν Μερόῃ. τὰ δὲ κατωτέρω
ἑκατέρωθεν Μερόης, παρὰ μὲν τὸν Νεῖλον πρὸς

[1] προπεσών D, προσπεσών other MSS.
[2] ἐπί, Corais emends to ἀπό, citing Herodotus 2. 30; and
so Meineke, but both ἐπὶ Ψαμμητίχου and ἀπὸ Ψαμμητίχου are
found in that passage.
[3] Ψαμμιτίχου CDFhiuz.
[4] ὑπακούουσι, Corais emends to ἐπαρχούσης (cp. 16. 4. 8).

seven hundred stadia, and after almost reaching the
same parallel as that of the region of Meroê and
projecting far into Libya and making the second
turn, flows towards the north five thousand three
hundred stadia to the great cataract, turning aside
slightly towards the east, and then one thousand
two hundred stadia to the smaller cataract at Syenê,
and then five thousand three hundred more to the
sea. Two rivers empty into it, which flow from
some lakes on the east and enclose Meroê, a rather
large island. One of these rivers, which flows on
the eastern side of the island, is called Astaboras [1]
and the other is called Astapus,[2] though some call it
Astasobas and say that another river, which flows
from some lakes from the south,[3] is the Astapus and
that this river forms almost all the straight part of
the body of the Nile, and that it is filled by the
summer rains. Above the confluence of the Astaboras and the Nile, he says, at a distance of seven
hundred stadia, lies Meroê, a city bearing the same
name as the island; and there is another island above
Meroê which is held by the Aegyptian fugitives
who revolted in the time of Psammitichus, and are
called "Sembritae," meaning "foreigners." [4] They
are ruled by a queen, but they are subject to the
kings of Meroê.[5] The lower parts of the country
on either side of Meroê, along the Nile towards the

[1] Now Atbara or Takazze.
[2] Now Bahr el-Abiad.   [3] Now Bahr el-Asrek.
[4] See 16. 4. 8. According to Herodotus (2. 30), the original
number of these fugitives was 240,000 (see Rawlinson's note,
Vol. II, p. 37).
[5] This statement is inconsistent with that in 16. 4. 8,
which, however, appears to have been taken from Artemidorus.

τὴν Ἐρυθρὰν Μεγάβαροι καὶ Βλέμμυες, Αἰθιόπων
ὑπακούοντες, Αἰγυπτίοις δ' ὅμοροι· παρὰ θάλατταν δὲ Τρωγλοδύται· διεστᾶσι δὲ εἰς δέκα ἢ
δώδεκα ἡμερῶν ὁδὸν οἱ κατὰ τὴν Μερόην Τρωγλοδύται τοῦ Νείλου. ἐξ ἀριστερῶν δὲ τῆς ῥύσεως
τοῦ Νείλου Νοῦβαι κατοικοῦσιν ἐν τῇ Λιβύῃ,
μέγα ἔθνος, ἀπὸ τῆς Μερόης ἀρξάμενοι μέχρι τῶν
ἀγκώνων, οὐχ ὑποταττόμενοι τοῖς Αἰθίοψιν, ἀλλ'
ἰδίᾳ κατὰ πλείους βασιλείας διειλημμένοι. τῆς δ'
Αἰγύπτου τὸ παρὰ τὴν θάλατταν ἐστιν ἀπὸ τοῦ
Πηλουσιακοῦ στόματος πρὸς τὸ Κανωβικὸν στάδιοι
χίλιοι[1] τριακόσιοι. Ἐρατοσθένης μὲν οὖν οὕτως.

3. Δεῖ δὲ ἐπὶ πλέον εἰπεῖν, καὶ πρῶτον τὰ περὶ
τὴν Αἴγυπτον, ὅπως ἀπὸ τῶν γνωριμωτέρων ἐπὶ
τὰ ἑξῆς προΐωμεν· κοινὰ μὲν γάρ τινα καὶ ταύτῃ
τῇ χώρᾳ καὶ τῇ συνεχεῖ καὶ ὑπὲρ αὐτὴν τῇ τῶν
Αἰθιόπων ὁ Νεῖλος παρασκευάζει, ποτίζων τε
αὐτὰς κατὰ τὰς ἀναβάσεις καὶ τοῦτ' οἰκήσιμον
αὐτῶν τὸ μέρος ἀπολείπων μόνον τὸ καλυπτό-
μενον ἐν ταῖς πλημμυρίσι, τὸ δ' ὑπερδέξιον καὶ
μετεωρότερον τοῦ ῥεύματος πᾶν ἀοίκητον διεξιὼν
ἑκατέρωθεν καὶ ἔρημον διὰ τὴν αὐτὴν ἀνυδρίαν.
C 787 ἀλλὰ τὴν μὲν Αἰθιοπίαν οὔτε πᾶσαν διέξεισιν ὁ
Νεῖλος οὔτε μόνος οὔτ' ἐπ' εὐθείας οὔτ' οἰκουμένην
καλῶς· τὴν δὲ Αἴγυπτον καὶ μόνος καὶ πᾶσαν καὶ
ἐπ' εὐθείας ἀπὸ τοῦ μικροῦ καταράκτου ὑπὲρ
Συήνης καὶ Ἐλεφαντίνης ἀρξάμενος, οἵπερ εἰσὶν
ὅροι τῆς Αἰγύπτου καὶ τῆς Αἰθιοπίας, ἕως τῶν ἐπὶ

---

[1] χίλιοι (as in 15. 1. 33 ; cp. 1. 4. 5), the editors, for τρισχίλιοι (E reads γσ').

6

Red Sea, are inhabited by Megabari and Blemmyes, who are subject to the Aethiopians and border on the Aegyptians, and, along the sea, by Troglodytes (the Troglodytes opposite Meroê are a ten or twelve days' journey distant from the Nile), but the parts on the left side of the course of the Nile, in Libya, are inhabited by Nubae, a large tribe, who, beginning at Meroê, extend as far as the bends of the river, and are not subject to the Aethiopians but are divided into several separate kingdoms. The extent of Aegypt along the sea from the Pelusiac to the Canobic mouth is one thousand three hundred stadia. This, then, is what Eratosthenes says.

3. But it is necessary to speak at greater length, and first of the parts about Aegypt, in order to proceed from those that are better known to those that come in order thereafter; for the Nile effects certain common results in this country and in that which is continuous with it and lies above it, I mean the country of the Aethiopians, in that it waters them at the time of its rise and also leaves only those parts of them habitable which have been covered during the overflows, and in that it merely passes through all the higher parts that are at a greater altitude than its current, leaving them uninhabited and desert on both sides because of the same lack of water. However, the Nile does not pass through the whole of Aethiopia, nor alone, nor in a straight line, nor through country that is well inhabited, but it alone passes through Aegypt, through the whole of it and in a straight line, beginning from the little cataract above Syenê and Elephantinê, which are the boundaries of Aegypt and Aethiopia, to its outlets on the sea-coast. And

7

θάλατταν ἐκβολῶν.[1] καὶ μὴν οἵ γε Αἰθίοπες τὸ
πλέον νομαδικῶς ζῶσι καὶ ἀπόρως διά τε τὴν λυπ-
ρότητα τῆς χώρας καὶ τὴν τῶν ἀέρων ἀσυμμετρίαν
καὶ τὸν ἀφ᾽ ἡμῶν ἐκτοπισμόν, τοῖς δ᾽ Αἰγυπτίοις
ἅπαντα τἀναντία συμβέβηκε· καὶ γὰρ πολιτικῶς
καὶ ἡμέρως ἐξ ἀρχῆς ζῶσι καὶ ἐν γνωρίμοις
ἵδρυνται τόποις, ὥστε καὶ αἱ διατάξεις αὐτῶν
μνημονεύονται. καὶ ἐπαινοῦνταί γε, δοκοῦντες
ἀξίως χρήσασθαι τῇ τῆς χώρας εὐδαιμονίᾳ, μερί-
σαντές τε εὖ καὶ ἐπιμεληθέντες· βασιλέα γὰρ
ἀποδείξαντες τριχῇ τὸ πλῆθος διεῖλον, καὶ τοὺς
μὲν στρατιώτας ἐκάλεσαν, τοὺς δὲ γεωργούς, τοὺς
δὲ ἱερέας· καὶ τοὺς μὲν τῶν ἱερῶν ἐπιμελητάς,
τοὺς δ᾽ ἄλλους τῶν περὶ τὸν ἄνθρωπον· καὶ τοὺς
μὲν τὰ[2] ἐν τῷ πολέμῳ, τοὺς δ᾽ ὅσα ἐν εἰρήνῃ, γῆν
τε καὶ τέχνας ἐργαζομένους,[3] ἀφ᾽ ὧνπερ καὶ αἱ
πρόσοδοι συνήγοντο τῷ βασιλεῖ. οἱ δ᾽ ἱερεῖς καὶ
φιλοσοφίαν ἤσκουν καὶ ἀστρονομίαν· ὁμιληταί τε
τῶν βασιλέων ἦσαν. ἡ δὲ χώρα τὴν μὲν πρώτην
διαίρεσιν εἰς νομοὺς ἔσχε, δέκα μὲν ἡ Θηβαΐς,
δέκα δ᾽ ἡ ἐν τῷ Δέλτα, ἑκκαίδεκα δ᾽ ἡ μεταξύ
(ὡς δέ τινες, τοσοῦτοι ἦσαν οἱ σύμπαντες νομοί,
ὅσαι αἱ ἐν τῷ λαβυρίνθῳ αὐλαί·[4] αὗται δ᾽ ἐλάττους τῶν τριάκοντα[5])· πάλιν δ᾽ οἱ νομοὶ τομὰς
ἄλλας ἔσχον, εἰς γὰρ τοπαρχίας οἱ πλεῖστοι

---

[1] τοῦ Νείλου, after ἐκβολῶν, Groskurd and later editors eject.
[2] τά, added from the Epitome.
[3] ἐργαζομένους, Kramer, for ἐργαζομένων.
[4] αὐλαί F, αὐταί other MSS.
[5] τριάκοντα, Meineke, following conj. of Groskurd, emends to τριάκοντα ἕξ.

indeed the Aethiopians lead for the most part a nomadic and resourceless life, on account of the barrenness of the country and of the unseasonableness of its climate and of its remoteness from us, whereas with the Aegyptians the contrary is the case in all these respects; for from the outset they have led a civic and cultivated life and have been settled in well-known regions, so that their organisations are a matter of comment. And they are commended in that they are thought to have used worthily the good fortune of their country, having divided it well and having taken good care of it; for when they had appointed a king they divided the people into three classes, and they called one class soldiers, another farmers, and another priests; and the last class had the care of things sacred and the other two of things relating to man; and some had charge of the affairs of war, and others of all the affairs of peace, both tilling soil and following trades, from which sources the revenues were gathered for the king. The priests devoted themselves both to philosophy and to astronomy; and they were companions of the king. The country was first divided into Nomes,[1] the Thebaïs containing ten, the country in the Delta ten, and the country between them sixteen (according to some, the number of the Nomes all told was the same as that of the halls in the Labyrinth, but the number of these is less than thirty[2]); and again the Nomes were divided into other sections, for most of them were divided into

---

[1] The Greek word (Nομοί) here means Districts or Provinces. Pliny (5. 9) refers to them as *praefecturae oppidorum.*

[2] Meineke and others unnecessarily emend the text to read "thirty-six" (see critical note).

9

διῄρητο, καὶ αὗται δ' εἰς ἄλλας τομάς· ἐλάχισται
δ' αἱ ἄρουραι μερίδες. ἐδέησε δὲ τῆς ἐπ' ἀκριβὲς
καὶ κατὰ λεπτὸν διαιρέσεως διὰ τὰς συνεχεῖς τῶν
ὅρων συγχύσεις, ἃς ὁ Νεῖλος ἀπεργάζεται κατὰ
τὰς αὐξήσεις, ἀφαιρῶν καὶ προστιθεὶς καὶ ἐναλ-
λάττων τὰ σχήματα καὶ τἆλλα σημεῖα ἀποκρύπ-
των, οἷς διακρίνεται τό τε ἀλλότριον καὶ τὸ
ἴδιον· ἀνάγκη δὴ ἀναμετρεῖσθαι πάλιν καὶ πάλιν.
ἐντεῦθεν δὲ καὶ τὴν γεωμετρίαν συστῆναί φασιν,
ὡς τὴν λογιστικὴν καὶ ἀριθμητικὴν παρὰ Φοινίκων
διὰ τὰς ἐμπορίας. τριχῇ δὲ διῄρητο, ὥσπερ τὸ
σύμπαν, καὶ τὸ ἐν ἑκάστῳ τῷ νομῷ πλῆθος, εἰς
τρία ἴσα μερισθείσης τῆς χώρας. ἡ δὲ περὶ τὸν
ποταμὸν πραγματεία διαφέρει τοσοῦτον, ὅσον τῇ
ἐπιμελείᾳ νικᾶν τὴν φύσιν. φύσει γὰρ πλείονα
φέρει καρπὸν καὶ ποτισθεῖσα μᾶλλον, φύσει καὶ
C 788 ἡ μείζων ἀνάβασις τοῦ ποταμοῦ πλείω ποτίζει
γῆν, ἀλλ' ἡ ἐπιμέλεια πολλάκις καὶ τῆς φύσεως
ἐξίσχυσεν ἐπιλιπούσης, ὥστε καὶ κατὰ τὰς ἐλάττους ἀναβάσεις τοσαύτην ποτισθῆναι γῆν, ὅσην
ἐν ταῖς μείζοσι, διά τε τῶν διωρύγων καὶ τῶν
παραχωμάτων· ἐπὶ γοῦν τῶν πρὸ Πετρωνίου
χρόνων ἡ μεγίστη μὲν ἦν φορὰ καὶ ἀνάβασις,
ἡνίκα ἐπὶ τεσσαρεσκαίδεκα πήχεις ἀνέβαινεν ὁ
Νεῖλος, ἡνίκα δ' ἐπ' ὀκτώ, συνέβαινε λιμός· ἐπ'
ἐκείνου δὲ ἄρξαντος τῆς χώρας καὶ δώδεκα μόνον

---

[1] By "arourae" Strabo refers to the Aegyptian land-measure,
which was 100 Aegyptian cubits square (Herodotus 2. 168),
i.e. about seven-elevenths of our acre. Each soldier was

toparchies, and these also into other sections; and
the smallest portions were the arourae.[1] There was
need of this accurate and minute division on account
of the continuous confusion of the boundaries caused
by the Nile at the time of its increases, since the Nile
takes away and adds soil, and changes conformations
of lands, and in general hides from view the signs by
which one's own land is distinguished from that of
another. Of necessity, therefore, the lands must be
re-measured again and again. And here it was, they
say, that the science of geometry[2] originated, just
as accounting and arithmetic originated with the
Phoenicians, because of their commerce.[3] Like the
people as a whole, the people in each Nome were also
divided into three parts, since the land had been
divided into three equal parts. The activity of the
people in connection with the river goes so far as to
conquer nature through diligence. For by nature
the land produces more fruit than do other lands, and
still more when watered; and by nature a greater rise
of the river waters more land; but diligence has often-
times, even when nature has failed, availed to bring
about the watering of as much land even at the
time of the smaller rises of the river as at the greater
rises, that is, through the means of canals and
embankments. At any rate, in the times before
Petronius[4] the crop was the largest and the rise
the highest when the Nile would rise to fourteen
cubits, and when it would rise to only eight a famine
would ensue; but in the time of his reign over the

granted the free use of twelve arourae of land without tax-
ation (Herodotus 2. 168).
  [2] Literally, "land-measuring."   [3] See 16. 2. 24.
  [4] C. Petronius (see 17. 1. 54).

πληρώσαντος πήχεις τοῦ Νείλου μέτρου,[1] μεγίστη ἦν ἡ φορά, καὶ ὀκτώ ποτε μόνον πληρώσαντος, λιμοῦ οὐδεὶς ἤσθετο. τοιαύτη μὲν ἡ διάταξις, τὰ δ' ἑξῆς λέγωμεν νυνί.

4. Ἀπὸ γὰρ τῶν Αἰθιοπικῶν τερμόνων ῥεῖ ἐπ' εὐθείας ὁ Νεῖλος πρὸς ἄρκτους, ἕως τοῦ καλουμένου χωρίου Δέλτα· εἶτ' ἐπὶ κορυφὴν σχιζόμενος ὁ Νεῖλος, ὥς φησιν ὁ Πλάτων, ὡς ἂν τριγώνου κορυφὴν ἀποτελεῖ τὸν τόπον τοῦτον, πλευρὰς δὲ τοῦ τριγώνου τὰ σχιζόμενα ἐφ' ἑκάτερα ῥεῖθρα καθήκοντα μέχρι τῆς θαλάττης, τὸ μὲν ἐν δεξιᾷ τῆς κατὰ Πηλούσιον, τὸ δ' ἐν ἀριστερᾷ τῆς κατὰ Κάνωβον καὶ τὸ πλησίον Ἡράκλειον προσαγορευόμενον, βάσιν δὲ τὴν παραλίαν τὴν μεταξὺ τοῦ Πηλουσίου καὶ τοῦ Ἡρακλείου. γέγονε δὴ[2] νῆσος ἔκ τε τῆς θαλάττης καὶ τῶν ῥευμάτων ἀμφοῖν τοῦ ποταμοῦ, καὶ καλεῖται Δέλτα διὰ τὴν ὁμοιότητα τοῦ σχήματος· τὸ δ' ἐπὶ τῇ κορυφῇ χωρίον ὁμωνύμως κέκληται διὰ τὸ ἀρχὴν εἶναι τοῦ λεχθέντος σχήματος, καὶ ἡ κώμη δὲ ἡ ἐπ' αὐτῷ καλεῖται Δέλτα. δύο μὲν οὖν ταῦτα τοῦ Νείλου στόματα, ὧν τὸ μὲν Πηλουσιακὸν καλεῖται, τὸ δὲ Κανωβικὸν καὶ Ἡρακλειωτικόν, μεταξὺ δὲ τούτων ἄλλαι πέντε εἰσὶν ἐκβολαὶ αἵ γε ἀξιόλογοι, λεπτότεραι δὲ πλείους· ἀπὸ γὰρ τῶν πρώτων μερῶν ἀπορρῶγες πολλαὶ καθ' ὅλην μερισθεῖσαι τὴν νῆσον πολλὰ καὶ ῥεῖθρα καὶ νήσους ἐποίησαν, ὥσθ' ὅλην γενέσθαι πλωτὴν διωρύγων ἐπὶ διώρυξι τμηθεισῶν, αἳ κατὰ ῥᾳστώνην πλέονται τοσαύτην,

---

[1] Νείλου μέτρου r; Νειλομετρίου, Corais; πηχέων . . . μέτρον conj. Villebrun.

[2] δή, Groskurd, for δ' ἡ.

country, and when the Nilometer registered only
twelve cubits, the crop was the largest, and once,
when it registered only eight cubits, no one felt
hunger. Such is the organisation of Aegypt; but
let me now describe the things that come next in
order.

4. The Nile flows from the Aethiopian boundaries
towards the north in a straight line to the district
called "Delta," and then, being "split at the head,"
as Plato says,[1] the Nile makes this place as it were
the vertex of a triangle, the sides of the triangle being
formed by the streams that split in either direction
and extend to the sea—the one on the right to the
sea at Pelusium and the other on the left to the sea
at Canobus and the neighbouring Heracleium, as it is
called,—and the base by the coast-line between
Pelusium and the Heracleium. An island, therefore,
has been formed by the sea and the two streams of
the river; and it is called Delta on account of the
similarity of its shape; and the district at the vertex
has been given the same name because it is the
beginning of the above-mentioned figure; and the
village there is also called Delta. Now these are two
mouths of the Nile, of which one is called Pelusiac
and the other Canobic or Heracleiotic; but between
these there are five other outlets, those at least that
are worth mentioning, and several that are smaller;
for, beginning with the first parts of the Delta, many
branches of the river have been split off throughout
the whole island and have formed many streams and
islands, so that the whole Delta has become navigable
—canals on canals having been cut, which are

---

[1] *Timaeus* 21 **E**.

ὥστε καὶ ὀστράκινα ἐνίοις εἶναι πορθμεῖα. τὴν
μὲν οὖν περίμετρον ὅσον τρισχιλίων σταδίων
ἐστὶν ἡ σύμπασα νῆσος· καλοῦσι[1] δ' αὐτὴν καὶ
τὴν κάτω χώραν σὺν ταῖς ἀπαντικρὺ ποταμίαις
τοῦ Δέλτα· ἐν δὲ ταῖς ἀναβάσεσι τοῦ Νείλου
καλύπτεται πᾶσα καὶ πελαγίζει πλὴν τῶν οἰκή-
σεων· αὗται δ' ἐπὶ λόφων αὐτοφυῶν ἢ χωμάτων
C 789 ἵδρυνται, πόλεις τε ἀξιόλογοι καὶ κῶμαι, νησίζου-
σαι κατὰ τὴν πόρρωθεν ὄψιν. πλείους δ' ἢ[2]
τετταράκοντα ἡμέρας τοῦ θέρους διαμεῖναν τὸ
ὕδωρ ἔπειθ' ὑπόβασιν λαμβάνει κατ' ὀλίγον,
καθάπερ καὶ τὴν αὔξησιν ἔσχεν· ἐν ἑξήκοντα δὲ
ἡμέραις τελέως γυμνοῦται καὶ ἀναψύχεται τὸ
πεδίον· ὅσῳ δὲ θᾶττον ἡ ἀνάψυξις, τοσῷδε θᾶττον
ὁ ἄροτος καὶ ὁ σπόρος· θᾶττον δέ, παρ' οἷς τὰ
μείζω θάλπη. τὸν αὐτὸν τρόπον καὶ τὰ ἐπάνω
τοῦ Δέλτα ποτίζεται, πλὴν ὅτι ἐπ' εὐθείας ὅσον
τετρακισχιλίοις σταδίοις δι' ἑνὸς ῥείθρου τοῦ
ποταμοῦ φερομένου, πλὴν εἴ πού[3] τις ἐντρέχει
νῆσος, ὧν ἀξιολογωτάτη ἡ τὸν Ἡρακλειωτικὸν
νομὸν περιέχουσα, ἢ εἴ πού τις ἐκτροπὴ διώρυγι
ἐπὶ πλέον εἰς λίμνην μεγάλην καὶ χώραν, ἢν
ποτίζειν δύναται, καθάπερ ἐπὶ τῆς τὸν Ἀρσινοΐτην[4]
νομὸν ποτιζούσης[5] καὶ τὴν Μοίριδος λίμνην καὶ
τῶν εἰς τὴν Μαρεῶτιν[6] ἀναχεομένων. συλλήβδην
δ' εἰπεῖν, ἡ ποταμία μόνον ἐστὶν Αἴγυπτος ἡ
ἑκατέρωθεν ἐσχάτη τοῦ Νείλου, σπάνιον εἴ που

---

[1] καλοῦσι, Brequigny, for κολποῦσι; κατοικοῦσι, Corais.
[2] δ' ἤ hmox, ἤ E, δέ other MSS.
[3] εἴ που EF; εἰ μή που other MSS.
[4] Ἀρσινοΐτην D; Ἀρσινοήτην other MSS.
[5] ποτιζούσης Letronne, for ποιούσης.

14

navigated with such ease that some people even use earthenware ferry-boats.[1] Now the island as a whole is as much as three thousand stadia in perimeter; and they also call it, together with the opposite river-lands of the Delta, Lower Egypt;[2] but at the rising of the Nile the whole country is under water and becomes a lake, except the settlements; and these are situated on natural hills or on artificial mounds, and contain cities of considerable size and villages, which, when viewed from afar, resemble islands. The water stays more than forty days in summer and then goes down gradually just as it rose; and in sixty days the plain is completely bared and begins to dry out; and the sooner the drying takes place, the sooner the ploughing and the sowing; and the drying takes place sooner in those parts where the heat is greater. The parts above the Delta are also watered in the same way, except that the river flows in a straight course about four thousand stadia through only one channel, except where some island intervenes, of which the most noteworthy is that which comprises the Heracleiotic Nome, or except where the river is diverted to a greater extent than usual by a canal into a large lake or a territory which it can water, as, for instance, in the case of the canal which waters the Arsinoïte Nome and Lake Moeris[3] and of those which spread over Lake Mareotis.[4] In short, Aegypt consists of only the river-land, I mean the last stretch of river-

[1] Cp. Juvenal 15. 126.
[2] Cp. 1. 2. 23 and 16. 2. 35.
[3] See Herodotus 2. 149 and Breasted's *A History of Egypt*, pp. 191–94.
[4] Now Lake Mariout.

---

[6] Μαρεῶτιν E, Μαραιῶτιν other MSS.

τριακοσίων σταδίων ἐπέχουσα συνεχῶς πλάτος
τὸ οἰκήσιμον, ἀρξαμένη ἀπὸ τῶν ὅρων[1] τῆς
Αἰθιοπίας, μέχρι τῆς κορυφῆς τοῦ Δέλτα. ἔοικεν
οὖν κειρίᾳ[2] ψυχομένη[3] ἐπὶ μῆκος, ὑπεξαιρου-
μένων τῶν ἐπὶ πλέον ἐκτροπῶν. ποιεῖ δὲ το
σχῆμα τοῦτο τῆς ποταμίας, ἧς λέγω, καὶ τῆς
χώρας τὰ ὅρη τὰ ἑκατέρωθεν ἀπὸ τῶν περὶ
Συήνην τόπων καταγόμενα μέχρι τοῦ Αἰγυπτίου
πελάγους· ἐφ' ὅσον γὰρ ταῦτα παρατείνει καὶ
διέστηκεν ἀπ' ἀλλήλων, ἐπὶ τοσοῦτον καὶ ὁ
ποταμὸς συνάγεταί τε καὶ διαχεῖται καὶ διασχη-
ματίζει τὴν χώραν διαφόρως τὴν οἰκήσιμον. ἡ δὲ
ὑπὲρ τῶν ὅρων ἐπὶ συχνὸν ἀοίκητός ἐστιν.

5. Οἱ μὲν οὖν ἀρχαῖοι στοχασμῷ τὸ πλέον, οἱ
δ' ὕστερον αὐτόπται γενηθέντες ᾔσθοντο ὑπὸ
ὄμβρων θερινῶν πληρούμενον τὸν Νεῖλον, τῆς
Αἰθιοπίας τῆς ἄνω κλυζομένης, καὶ μάλιστα ἐν τοῖς
ἐσχάτοις ὄρεσι, παυσαμένων δὲ τῶν ὄμβρων
παυομένην κατ' ὀλίγον τὴν πλημμυρίδα. τοῦτο
δ' ὑπῆρξε μάλιστα δῆλον τοῖς πλέουσι τὸν
Ἀράβιον κόλπον μέχρι τῆς κινναμωμοφόρου καὶ
τοῖς ἐκπεμπομένοις ἐπὶ τὴν τῶν ἐλεφάντων θήραν,
καὶ εἴ τινες ἄλλαι χρεῖαι παρώξυνον ἐκεῖσε ἄνδρας προχειρίζεσθαι τοὺς τῆς Αἰγύπτου βασιλέας
τοὺς Πτολεμαϊκούς. οὗτοι γὰρ ἐφρόντισαν τῶν
τοιούτων, διαφερόντως δ' ὁ Φιλάδελφος ἐπικλη-

[1] ὅρων, Corais, for ὀρῶν.
[2] κηρίᾳ CEFs (C adding υ above η), κειρίᾳ Dhimowxz (D
adding the ει above η), κυρίᾳ Ald.
[3] ψυχομένη, Corais (who conj. τεταμένη, however), for
ψυχομένη; ἀναπτυσσομένη or ἀνεπτυγμένη conj. Kramer.

[1] But the text seems corrupt (see critical note). Strabo
may have written, "Accordingly, it resembles length-wise an

land on either side of the Nile, which, beginning at the boundaries of Aethiopia and extending to the vertex of the Delta, scarcely anywhere occupies a continuous habitable space as broad as three hundred stadia. Accordingly, when it is dried, it resembles lengthwise a girdle-band,[1] the greater diversions of the river being excepted. This shape of the river-land of which I am speaking, as also of the country, is caused by the mountains on either side, which extend from the region of Syenê down to the Aegyptian Sea; for in proportion as these mountains lie near together or at a distance from one another, in that proportion the river is contracted or widened, and gives to the lands that are habitable their different shapes. But the country beyond the mountains is for a great distance uninhabited.[2]

5. Now the ancients depended mostly on conjecture, but the men of later times, having become eye-witnesses, perceived that the Nile was filled by summer rains, when Upper Aethiopia was flooded, and particularly in the region of its farthermost mountains, and that when the rains ceased the inundation gradually ceased. This fact was particularly clear to those who navigated the Arabian Gulf as far as the Cinnamon-bearing country, and to those who were sent out to hunt elephants[3] or upon any other business which may have prompted the Ptolemaic kings of Aegypt to despatch men thither. For these kings were concerned with things of this kind; and especially the Ptolemy surnamed Philadelphus, since he was of an

unwound girdle-band," or else, " Accordingly, it resembles a hand outstretched to full length," meaning both arm and hand, and thus referring to the Delta as well as to the stretch of river-land from Aethiopia to the vertex.

[2] See 1. 2. 25.   [3] See 16. 4. 7.

θείς, φιλιστορῶν καὶ διὰ τὴν ἀσθένειαν τοῦ
σώματος διαγωγὰς ἀεί τινας καὶ τέρψεις ζητῶν
καινοτέρας. οἱ πάλαι δὲ βασιλεῖς οὐ πάνυ
C 790 ἐφρόντισαν τῶν τοιούτων, καίπερ οἰκεῖοι σοφίας
γεγονότες καὶ αὐτοὶ καὶ οἱ ἱερεῖς, μεθ' ὧν ἦν
αὐτοῖς ὁ πλείων βίος· ὥστε καὶ θαυμάζειν ἄξιον
καὶ διὰ τοῦτο καὶ διότι Σέσωστρις τὴν Αἰθιοπίαν
ἐπῆλθεν ἅπασαν μέχρι τῆς κινναμωμοφόρου, καὶ
ὑπομνήματα τῆς στρατείας αὐτοῦ καὶ νῦν ἔτι
δείκνυται, στῆλαι καὶ ἐπιγραφαί. Καμβύσης τε
τὴν Αἴγυπτον κατασχὼν προῆλθε καὶ μέχρι τῆς
Μερόης μετὰ τῶν Αἰγυπτίων· καὶ δὴ καὶ τοὔνομα
τῇ τε νήσῳ καὶ τῇ πόλει τοῦτο παρ' ἐκείνου
τεθῆναί φασιν, ἐκεῖ τῆς ἀδελφῆς ἀποθανούσης
αὐτῷ Μερόης (οἱ δὲ γυναικά φασι)· τὴν ἐπωνυμίαν
οὖν ἐχαρίσατο αὐτῇ τιμῶν τὴν ἄνθρωπον. θαυ-
μαστὸν οὖν, πῶς ἐκ τῶν τοιούτων ἀφορμῶν οὐ
τελέως ἐναργὴς ἦν ἡ περὶ τῶν ὄμβρων ἱστορία
τοῖς τότε, καὶ ταῦτα τῶν ἱερέων φιλοπραγμονέσ-
τερον ἀναφερόντων εἰς τὰ ἱερὰ γράμματα καὶ
ἀποτιθεμένων, ὅσα μάθησιν περιττὴν ἐπιφαίνει.[1]
εἰ γὰρ ἄρα, τοῦτ' ἐχρῆν ζητεῖν, ὅπερ καὶ νῦν ἔτι
ζητεῖται, τί δή ποτε θέρους, χειμῶνος δὲ οὔ, καὶ
ἐν τοῖς νοτιωτάτοις, ἐν δὲ τῇ Θηβαΐδι καὶ τῇ περὶ
Συήνην οὐ συμπίπτουσιν ὄμβροι· τὸ δ' ὅτι ἐξ
ὄμβρων αἱ ἀναβάσεις μὴ ζητεῖν, μηδὲ τοιούτων
δεῖσθαι μαρτύρων, οἵους Ποσειδώνιος εἴρηκε.
φησὶ γὰρ Καλλισθένη λέγειν τὴν ἐκ τῶν ὄμβρων

¹ ὑποφαίνει *moz*, ἐπιτείνει E, marg. F, D first hand but
changed to ἐπιφαίνει.

---

¹ Diodorus Siculus (1. 33) says his mother.
² So 15. 1. 19.

inquiring disposition, and on account of the infirmity of his body was always searching for novel pastimes and enjoyments. But the kings of old were not at all concerned with such things, although they proved themselves congenial to learning, both they and the priests, with whom they spent the greater part of their lives; and therefore we may well be surprised, not only on this account, but also by the fact that Sesostris traversed the whole of Aethiopia as far as the Cinnamon-bearing country, and that memorials of his expedition, pillars and inscriptions, are to be seen even to this day. Further, when Cambyses took possession of Aegypt, he advanced with the Aegyptians even as far as Meroê; and indeed this name was given by him to both the island and the city, it is said, because his sister Meroê—some say his wife—[1] died there. The name, at any rate, he bestowed upon the place in honour of the woman. It is surprising, therefore, that the men of that time, having such knowledge to begin with, did not possess a perfectly clear knowledge of the rains, especially since the priests rather meticulously record in their sacred books, and thus store away, all facts that reveal any curious information; for they should have investigated, if they made any investigations at all, the question, which even to this day is still being investigated, I mean why in the world rains fall in summer but not in winter, and in the southernmost parts but not in Thebaïs and the country round Syenê;[2] but the fact that the rising of the river results from rains should not have been investigated, nor yet should this matter have needed such witnesses as Poseidonius mentions; for instance, he says that it was Callisthenes who states that the summer rains

αἰτίαν τῶν θερινῶν, παρὰ ᾿Αριστοτέλους λαβόντα,
ἐκεῖνον δὲ παρὰ Θρασυάλκου τοῦ Θασίου (τῶν
ἀρχαίων δὲ φυσικῶν εἷς οὗτος), ἐκεῖνον δὲ παρ᾿
ἄλλου,[1] τὸν δὲ παρ᾿ Ὁμήρου διπετέα φάσκοντος
τὸν Νεῖλον·

 ἂν δ᾿ εἰς Αἰγύπτοιο διιπετέος ποταμοῖο.

᾿Αλλ᾿ ἐῶ ταῦτα, πολλῶν εἰρηκότων, ὧν ἀρκέσει
δύο μηνῦσαι τοὺς ποιήσαντας καθ᾿ ἡμᾶς τὸ περὶ τοῦ
Νείλου βιβλίον, Εὔδωρόν τε καὶ ᾿Αρίστωνα τὸν
ἐκ τῶν περιπάτων· πλὴν γὰρ τῆς τάξεως τά γε
ἄλλα καὶ τῇ φράσει καὶ τῇ ἐπιχειρήσει ταῦτά[2]
ἐστι κείμενα παρ᾿ ἀμφοτέροις. ἐγὼ γοῦν ἀπορού-
μενος ἀντιγράφων εἰς τὴν ἀντιβολὴν ἐκ θατέρου
θάτερον ἀντέβαλον· πότερος δ᾿ ἦν ὁ τἀλλότρια
ὑποβαλλόμενος, ἐν ῎Αμμωνος εὕροι τις ἄν. Εὔδωρος
δ᾿ ᾐτιᾶτο τὸν ᾿Αρίστωνα· ἡ μέντοι φράσις ᾿Αρισ-
τώνειος μᾶλλόν ἐστιν.

Οἱ μὲν οὖν ἀρχαῖοι τὸ οἰκούμενον αὐτὸ καὶ
ποτιζόμενον ὑπὸ τοῦ Νείλου μόνον Αἴγυπτον
ἐκάλουν, ἀπὸ τῶν περὶ Συήνην τόπων ἀρξάμενοι
μέχρι τῆς θαλάττης· οἱ δ᾿ ὕστερον μέχρι νῦν
προσέλαβον ἐκ μὲν τῶν πρὸς ἔω μερῶν τὰ[3]
μεταξὺ τοῦ ᾿Αραβίου κόλπου καὶ τοῦ Νείλου
C 791 σχεδόν τι πάντα (οἱ δ᾿ Αἰθίοπες οὐ πάνυ χρῶνται
τῇ ᾿Ερυθρᾷ θαλάττῃ), ἐκ δὲ τῶν ἑσπερίων τὰ

---

[1] For ἄλλου C. Müller conj. παρὰ Θαλοῦ (citing 1. 1. 11).
[2] ταῦτά, Corais, for ταῦτα.
[3] τά, before μεταξύ, Corais inserts.

---

[1] Literally "antigraphs"; i.e., apparently, "copies" of
parallel passages from the two works.

are the cause of the risings, though Callisthenes took the assertion from Aristotle, and Aristotle from Thrasyalces the Thasian (one of the early physicists), and Thrasyalces from someone else, and he from Homer, who calls the Nile "heaven-fed": "And back again to the land of Aegyptus, heaven-fed river."

But I dismiss this subject, since it has been discussed by many writers, of whom it will suffice to report only the two who in my time have written the book about the Nile, I mean Eudorus and Ariston the Peripatetic philosopher; for except in the matter of arrangement everything found in the two writers is the same as regards both style and treatment. I, at any rate, being in want of copies [1] with which to make a comparison, compared the one work with the other;[2] but which of the two men it was who appropriated to himself the other's work might be discovered at Ammon's temple! Eudorus accused Ariston; the style, however, is more like that of Ariston.

Now the early writers gave the name Aegypt to only the part of the country that was inhabited and watered by the Nile, beginning at the region of Syenê and extending to the sea; but the later writers down to the present time have added on the eastern side approximately all the parts between the Arabian Gulf and the Nile (the Aethiopians do not use the Red Sea at all[3]), and on the western side the parts

[2] In the Alexandrian library, apparently.

[3] The other translators interpret πάνυ as meaning "much," or "to such an extent," or the like. But Strabo is speaking of Aethiopians in the strict sense of the term; for "the country between the Nile and Arabian Gulf is Arabia" (17.1. 21), and even Aegyptian Heliupolis (17. 1. 30) and Thebes (17. 1. 46) are in "Arabia."

μέχρι τῶν Αὐάσεων καὶ ἐν τῇ παραλίᾳ τὰ ἀπὸ
τοῦ Κανωβικοῦ στόματος μέχρι Καταβαθμοῦ καὶ
τῆς Κυρηναίων ἐπικρατείας. οἵ τε γὰρ ἀπὸ τοῦ
Πτολεμαίου βασιλεῖς ἴσχυσαν τοσοῦτον, ὥστε[1]
καὶ τὴν Κυρηναίαν αὐτὴν κατέσχον καὶ διενεί-
μαντο πρὸς τὴν Αἴγυπτον καὶ τὴν Κύπρον.
Ῥωμαῖοί τε οἱ διαδεξάμενοι τὴν ἐκείνων ἐπαρχίαν
κρίναντες τὴν Αἴγυπτον ἐν τοῖς αὐτοῖς ὅροις
διεφύλαξαν. Αὐάσεις δ' οἱ Αἰγύπτιοι καλοῦσι
τὰς οἰκουμένας χώρας περιεχομένας κύκλῳ μεγάλαις ἐρημίαις, ὡς ἂν νήσους πελαγίας. πολὺ δὲ
τοῦτ' ἔστι κατὰ τὴν Λιβύην, τρεῖς δ' εἰσὶν αἱ
πρόσχωροι τῇ Αἰγύπτῳ καὶ ὑπ'[2] αὐτῇ τεταγμέναι.
τὰ μὲν οὖν καθ' ὅλου καὶ ἀνωτάτω περὶ τῆς
Αἰγύπτου ταῦτα λέγομεν, τὰ καθ' ἕκαστα δὲ καὶ[3]
τὰς ἀρετὰς αὐτῆς νῦν διέξιμεν.

6. Ἐπεὶ δὲ τὸ πλεῖστον τοῦ ἔργου τούτου καὶ
τὸ κυριώτατον ἡ Ἀλεξάνδρειά ἐστι καὶ τὰ περὶ
αὐτήν, ἐντεῦθεν ἀρκτέον. ἔστι τοίνυν ἡ ἀπὸ
Πηλουσίου παραλία πρὸς τὴν ἑσπέραν πλέουσι
μέχρι μὲν τοῦ Κανωβικοῦ στόματος χιλίων που
καὶ τριακοσίων σταδίων, ὃ δὴ καὶ βάσιν τοῦ
Δέλτα ἔφαμεν· ἐντεῦθεν δ' ἐπὶ Φάρον τὴν νῆσον
ἄλλοι στάδιοι πεντήκοντα πρὸς τοῖς ἑκατόν. ἡ
δὲ Φάρος νησίον ἐστὶ παράμηκες, προσεχέστατον
τῇ ἠπείρῳ, λιμένα πρὸς αὐτὴν ποιοῦν ἀμφίστομον.

---

[1] ὥστε, Letronne and Groskurd, for οἵ γε.
[2] ὑπ' m for ἐπ'; so Corais and Meineke.
[3] The text of F from καί to Πτολεμαῖος (17. 1. 11) is lost.

---

[1] Ptolemy I (Soter), reigned 323–285 B.C.

extending as far as the oases, and on the sea-coast
the parts extending from the Canobic mouth to
Catabathmus and the domain of the Cyrenaeans.
For the kings after Ptolemy [1] became so powerful
that they took possession of Cyrenaea itself and even
united Cypros with Aegypt. The Romans, who
succeeded the Ptolemies, separated their three
dominions and have kept Aegypt within its former
limits.[2] The Aegyptians call "oases"[3] the inhabited
districts which are surrounded by large deserts, like
islands in the open sea. There is many an oasis in
Libya, and three of them lie close to Aegypt and are
classed as subject to it. This, then, is my general,
or summary, account of Aegypt, and I shall now
discuss the separate parts and the excellent attributes
of the country.

6. Since Alexandria [4] and its neighbourhood constitute the largest and most important part of this
subject, I shall begin with them. The sea-coast,
then, from Pelusium, as one sails towards the west,
as far as the Canobic mouth, is about one thousand
three hundred stadia—the "base" of the Delta, as
I have called it; [5] and thence to the island Pharos,
one hundred and fifty stadia more. Pharos is an
oblong isle, is very close to the mainland, and
forms with it a harbour with two mouths; for

[2] The Romans made Cyrenaea an "allied state" (*civitas
foederata*) in 96 B.C., a Roman province in 88 B.C., and later
(see 17. 3. 25) united it with Crete. Cypros was annexed to
the province of Cilicia in 47 B.C., presented by Antony to
Cleopatra in 32 B.C., made an imperial province in 27 B.C.,
and a senatorial province in 22 B.C.

[3] The Greek spelling is "auases."

[4] See Map of Alexandria at end of volume.

[5] 17. 1. 4.

ἠιὼν γάρ ἐστι κολπώδης, ἄκρας εἰς τὸ πέλαγος
προβεβλημένη δύο· τούτων δὲ μεταξὺ ἡ νῆσος
ἵδρυται κλείουσα τὸν κόλπον, παραβέβληται γὰρ
αὐτῷ κατὰ μῆκος. τῶν δ' ἄκρων τῆς Φάρου τὸ
μὲν ἑῷον μᾶλλόν ἐστι προσεχὲς τῇ ἠπείρῳ καὶ
τῇ κατ' αὐτὴν ἄκρα (καλεῖται δ' ἄκρα Λοχιάς),
καὶ ποιεῖ τὸν λιμένα ἀρτίστομον·[1] πρὸς δὲ τῇ
στενότητι τοῦ μεταξὺ πόρου καὶ πέτραι εἰσίν, αἱ
μὲν ὕφαλοι, αἱ δὲ καὶ ἐξέχουσαι, τραχύνουσαι
πᾶσαν ὥραν τὸ προσπῖπτον ἐκ τοῦ πελάγους
κλυδώνιον. ἔστι δὲ καὶ αὐτὸ τὸ τῆς νησῖδος
ἄκρον πέτρα περίκλυστος, ἔχουσα πύργον
θαυμαστῶς κατεσκευασμένον λευκοῦ λίθου πο-
λυόροφον, ὁμώνυμον τῇ νήσῳ. τοῦτον δ' ἀνέθηκε
Σώστρατος Κνίδιος, φίλος τῶν βασιλέων, τῆς
τῶν πλωϊζομένων σωτηρίας χάριν, ὥς φησιν ἡ
ἐπιγραφή·[2] ἀλιμένου γὰρ οὔσης καὶ ταπεινῆς
τῆς ἑκατέρωθεν παραλίας, ἐχούσης δὲ καὶ χοιρά-
δας καὶ βράχη τινά, ἔδει σημείου τινὸς ὑψηλοῦ

---

[1] ἀμφίστομον w, Corais.

[2] After ἐπιγραφή C, in the margin, adds: Ἐπίγραμμα.
Σώστρατος Κνίδιος Δεξιφάνους θεοῖς σωτῆρσιν ὑπὲρ τῶν πλωϊζο-
μένων· The same words are found in Dhirw, and also, with
Ἐπίγραμμα omitted, in moxz.

---

[1] This tower, one of the "Wonders of the World," cost
800 talents (Pliny 6. 18). According to Eusebius (*Chron. ad
Olymp.* 124. 1), it was built in the time of Ptolemy Philadelphus, but, according to Suidas, at the beginning of the
reign of Pyrrhus (299 B.C.), *i.e.* in the time of Ptolemy Soter.
According to Josephus (*Bell. Jud.* 4. 10. 5, or L.C.L. edition,
Vol. III, pp. 181 and 251), it was visible from the sea at
300 stadia ; according to Epiphanes (Steph. Byz., s.v. Φάρος),
it was 306 fathoms high ; and the *Schol.* Lucian *ad Icaro-
menippum*, § 12, says that it was visible 300 miles away ! See

the shore of the mainland forms a bay, since it
thrusts two promontories into the open sea, and
between these is situated the island, which closes
the bay, for it lies lengthwise parallel to the shore.
Of the extremities of Pharos, the eastern one lies
closer to the mainland and to the promontory
opposite it (the promontory called Lochias), and
thus makes the harbour narrow at the mouth; and
in addition to the narrowness of the intervening
passage there are also rocks, some under the water,
and others projecting out of it, which at all hours
roughen the waves that strike them from the open
sea. And likewise the extremity of the isle is a
rock, which is washed all round by the sea and has
upon it a tower that is admirably constructed of
white marble with many stories and bears the same
name as the island.[1] This was an offering made by
Sostratus of Cnidus, a friend of the kings, for the
safety of mariners, as the inscription says:[2] for since
the coast was harbourless and low on either side, and
also had reefs and shallows, those who were sailing
from the open sea thither needed some lofty and

A. M. de Zogheb, *Études sur L'Ancienne Alexandrie*, Paris,
1910 ; and Thiersch's restoration of the tower in Rostovtzeff's
A History of the Ancient World, Vol. I, p. 369.

[2] Some of the MSS. (see critical note) record the inscription,
which is preserved in Lucian, *How to Write History*, § 62
(but is obviously a gloss in Strabo): "Sostratus of Cnidus,
son of Dexiphanes, on behalf of mariners, to the Divine
Saviours." "The Divine Saviours" might refer to Ptolemy
Soter and Berenicê (see the Corais-Letronne edition, which
cites Spannheim, *De Praestantia et Usu Numismat.* I, p. 415,
and Visconti, *Iconographie Grecque* II, 18, p. 564), but it was
the Dioscuri (Castor and Pollux) who were known by "all"
as "guardians of the sea" and "the saviours of sailors"
(1. 3. 2 and 5. 3. 5).

STRABO

καὶ λαμπροῦ τοῖς ἀπὸ τοῦ πελάγους προσπλέου-
C 792 σιν, ὥστ᾽ εὐστοχεῖν τῆς εἰσβολῆς τοῦ λιμένος.
καὶ τὸ ἑσπέριον δὲ στόμα οὐκ εὐείσβολόν ἐστιν,
οὐ μὴν τοσαύτης γε δεῖται προνοίας. ποιεῖ δὲ
καὶ τοῦτο ἄλλον λιμένα τὸν τοῦ Εὐνόστου καλού-
μενον· πρόκειται δ᾽ οὗτος τοῦ ὀρυκτοῦ καὶ κλεισ-
τοῦ λιμένος· ὁ μὲν γὰρ ἐκ τοῦ λεχθέντος πύργου
τῆς Φάρου τὸν εἴσπλουν ἔχων ὁ μέγας ἐστὶ
λιμήν· οὗτοι δὲ συνεχεῖς ἐν βάθει ἐκείνῳ, τῷ
ἑπτασταδίῳ καλουμένῳ χώματι διειργόμενοι ἀπ᾽
αὐτοῦ, παράκεινται. τὸ δὲ χῶμά ἐστιν ἀπὸ τῆς
ἠπείρου γέφυρα ἐπὶ τὴν νῆσον κατὰ τὸ ἑσπέριον
αὐτῆς μέρος ἐκτεταμένη, δύο διάπλους ἀπολείπουσα μόνον εἰς τὸν Εὐνόστου λιμένα, καὶ αὐτοὺς
γεγεφυρωμένους· ἦν δ᾽ οὐ γέφυρα μόνον ἐπὶ τὴν
νῆσον τὸ ἔργον τοῦτο, ἀλλὰ καὶ ὑδραγώγιον, ὅτε
γε ᾠκεῖτο· νῦν δ᾽ ἠρήμωσεν αὐτὴν ὁ θεὸς Καῖσαρ
ἐν τῷ πρὸς Ἀλεξανδρέας πολέμῳ, τεταγμένην
μετὰ τῶν βασιλέων· ὀλίγοι δ᾽ οἰκοῦσι πρὸς τῷ
πύργῳ ναυτικοὶ ἄνδρες. ὁ γοῦν μέγας λιμὴν πρὸς
τῷ κεκλεῖσθαι καλῶς τῷ τε χώματι καὶ τῇ φύσει,
ἀγχιβαθής τέ ἐστιν, ὥστε τὴν μεγίστην ναῦν ἐπὶ
κλίμακος ὁρμεῖν, καὶ εἰς πλείους σχίζεται λιμένας.
οἱ μὲν οὖν πρότεροι τῶν Αἰγυπτίων βασιλεῖς,

---

[1] *i.e.* "Harbour of the happy return." This harbour might
have been so named after Eunostus, king of Soli in Cyprus
and son-in-law of Ptolemy Soter (C. Wachsmuth, *Göttinger
Festrede*, 1876, 4), the idea being inspired, perhaps, by the
fact that Eunostus was so good a harbour as compared with
the eastern.

[2] This harbour (called "Cibotus," *i.e.* "Chest" or "Box"),
which was fortified, was connected with Lake Mareotis by
a canal. Its shape and size are to-day problematical, for it

conspicuous sign to enable them to direct their course aright to the entrance of the harbour. And the western mouth is also not easy to enter, although it does not require so much caution as the other. And it likewise forms a second harbour, that of Eunostus,[1] as it is called, which lies in front of the closed harbour which was dug by the hand of man.[2] For the harbour which affords the entrance on the side of the above-mentioned tower of Pharos is the Great Harbour, whereas these two lie continuous with that harbour in their innermost recess, being separated from it only by the embankment called the Heptastadium.[3] The embankment forms a bridge extending from the mainland to the western portion of the island, and leaves open only two passages into the harbour of Eunostus, which are bridged over. However, this work formed not only a bridge to the island but also an aqueduct, at least when Pharos was inhabited. But in these present times it has been laid waste by the deified Caesar[4] in his war against the Alexandrians, since it had sided with the kings. A few seamen, however, live near the tower. As for the Great Harbour, in addition to its being beautifully enclosed both by the embankment and by nature, it is not only so deep close to the shore that the largest ship can be moored at the steps, but also is cut up into several harbours. Now the earlier kings of the

has been filled up and its site lies within that of the present Heptastadium.

[3] So called from its being "Seven Stadia" in length. It has been so much enlarged by alluvial deposits and debris from the old city that it is now, generally speaking, a mile wide, and forms a large part of the site of the city of to-day.

[4] Julius Caesar.

ἀγαπῶντες οἷς εἶχον καὶ οὐ πάνυ ἐπεισάκτων
δεόμενοι, διαβεβλημένοι πρὸς ἅπαντας τοὺς πλέον-
τας, καὶ μάλιστα τοὺς Ἕλληνας (πορθηταὶ γὰρ
ἦσαν καὶ ἐπιθυμηταὶ τῆς ἀλλοτρίας κατὰ σπάνιν
γῆς), ἐπέστησαν φυλακὴν τῷ τόπῳ τούτῳ, κελεύ-
σαντες ἀπείργειν τοὺς προσιόντας· κατοικίαν δ'
αὐτοῖς ἔδοσαν τὴν προσαγορευομένην Ῥακῶτιν,
ἣ νῦν μὲν τῆς Ἀλεξανδρέων πόλεώς ἐστι μέρος τὸ
ὑπερκείμενον τῶν νεωρίων, τότε δὲ κώμη ὑπῆρχε·
τὰ δὲ κύκλῳ τῆς κώμης βουκόλοις παρέδοσαν,
δυναμένοις καὶ αὐτοῖς κωλύειν τοὺς ἔξωθεν
ἐπιόντας. ἐπελθὼν δὲ Ἀλέξανδρος, ἰδὼν τὴν
εὐκαιρίαν, ἔγνω τειχίζειν ἐπὶ τῷ λιμένι τὴν πόλιν·
τῆς δ' ὕστερον ἐπηκολουθηκυίας εὐδαιμονίας τῇ
πόλει μνημονεύουσί τι σημεῖον κατὰ τὴν ὑπο-
γραφὴν τοῦ κτίσματος συμβάν· τῶν γὰρ ἀρχιτεκ-
τόνων γῇ[1] λευκῇ διασημαινομένων τὴν τοῦ
περιβόλου γραμμήν, ἐπιλιπούσης τῆς γῆς καὶ
τοῦ βασιλέως ἐπιόντος, οἱ διοικηταὶ τῶν ἀλφίτων
μέρος τῶν παρεσκευασμένων τοῖς ἐργάταις
παρέσχον, δι' ὧν καὶ αἱ ὁδοὶ κατετμήθησαν εἰς
πλείους·[2] τοῦτ' οὖν οἰωνίσθαι λέγονται[3] πρὸς
ἀγαθοῦ γεγονός.[4]

7. Ἡ δ' εὐκαιρία πολύτροπος· ἀμφίκλυστόν
τε γάρ ἐστι τὸ χωρίον δυσὶ πελάγεσι, τῷ μὲν[5]

[1] γῇ, Groskurd, for τῇ.
[2] εἰς πλείους, Tozer suspects as being a gloss.
[3] λέγεται moz.   [4] γεγονότος Dhi.
[5] τῷ μὲν . . . τῷ δέ E, τὸ μὲν . . . τὸ δέ other MSS.

---

[1] Literally, "white earth."
[2] According to Plutarch (*Alexander* 26), birds of all kinds
settled on the place like clouds and ate up all the barley-

Aegyptians, being content with what they had and not wanting foreign imports at all, and being prejudiced against all who sailed the seas, and particularly against the Greeks (for owing to scarcity of land of their own the Greeks were ravagers and coveters of that of others), set a guard over this region and ordered it to keep away any who should approach; and they gave them as a place of abode Rhacotis, as it is called, which is now that part of the city of the Alexandrians which lies above the ship-houses, but was at that time a village; and they gave over the parts round about the village to herdsmen, who likewise were able to prevent the approach of outsiders. But when Alexander visited the place and saw the advantages of the site, he resolved to fortify the city on the harbour. Writers record, as a sign of the good fortune that has since attended the city, an incident which occurred at the time of tracing the lines of the foundation: When the architects were marking the lines of the enclosure with chalk,[1] the supply of chalk gave out; and when the king arrived, his stewards furnished a part of the barley-meal which had been prepared for the workmen, and by means of this the streets also, to a larger number than before, were laid out. This occurrence, then, they are said to have interpreted as a good omen.[2]

7. The advantages of the city's site are various; for, first, the place is washed by two seas, on the

---

meal with which the area had been marked out, so that Alexander was greatly disturbed at the omen; but the seers assured him that the omen was good. The barley-meal betokened an abundance of food (Ammianus Marcellinus 22. 16. 7).

C 793 ἀπὸ τῶν ἄρκτων τῷ Αἰγυπτίῳ λεγομένῳ, τῷ
δ' ἀπὸ μεσημβρίας τῷ τῆς λίμνης τῆς Μαρείας,
ἢ καὶ Μαρεῶτις[1] λέγεται· πληροῖ δὲ ταύτην
πολλαῖς διώρυξιν ὁ Νεῖλος, ἄνωθέν τε καὶ ἐκ
πλαγίων, δι' ὧν τὰ εἰσκομιζόμενα πολλῷ πλείω
τῶν ἀπὸ θαλάττης ἐστίν, ὥσθ' ὁ λιμὴν ὁ λιμναῖος
ὑπῆρχε πλουσιώτερος τοῦ θαλαττίου· ταύτῃ δὲ
καὶ τὰ ἐκκομιζόμενα ἐξ Ἀλεξανδρείας πλείω τῶν
εἰσκομιζομένων ἐστί· γνοίη δ' ἄν τις ἔν τε τῇ
Ἀλεξανδρείᾳ καὶ τῇ Δικαιαρχίᾳ γενόμενος, ὁρῶν
τὰς ὁλκάδας ἔν τε τῷ κατάπλῳ καὶ ἐν ταῖς
ἀναγωγαῖς, ὅσον βαρύτεραί τε καὶ κουφότεραι
δεῦρο κἀκεῖσε πλέοιεν. πρὸς δὲ τῷ πλούτῳ τῶν
καταγομένων ἑκατέρωσε εἴς τε τὸν κατὰ θάλατταν
λιμένα καὶ εἰς τὸν λιμναῖον, καὶ τὸ εὐάερον ἄξιον
σημειώσεώς ἐστιν· ὃ καὶ αὐτὸ συμβαίνει διὰ τὸ
ἀμφίκλυστον καὶ τὸ εὔκαιρον τῆς ἀναβάσεως τοῦ
Νείλου. αἱ μὲν γὰρ ἄλλαι πόλεις αἱ ἐπὶ λιμνῶν
ἱδρυμέναι βαρεῖς καὶ πνιγώδεις ἔχουσι τοὺς ἀέρας
ἐν τοῖς καύμασι τοῦ θέρους· ἐπὶ γὰρ τοῖς χείλεσιν
αἱ λίμναι τελματοῦνται διὰ τὴν ἐκ τῶν ἡλίων
ἀναθυμίασιν· βορβορώδους οὖν ἀναφερομένης
τοσαύτης ἰκμάδος, νοσώδης ὁ ἀὴρ ἕλκεται καὶ
λοιμικῶν κατάρχει παθῶν· ἐν Ἀλεξανδρείᾳ δὲ
τοῦ θέρους ἀρχομένου πληρούμενος ὁ Νεῖλος
πληροῖ καὶ τὴν λίμνην καὶ οὐδὲν ἐᾷ τελματῶδες
τὸ τὴν ἀναφορὰν ποιῆσον[2] μοχθηράν· τότε δὲ
καὶ οἱ ἐτησίαι πνέουσιν ἐκ τῶν βορείων καὶ τοῦ
τοσούτου πελάγους, ὥστε κάλλιστα τοῦ θέρους
Ἀλεξανδρεῖς διάγουσιν.

---

[1] Μαρείας . . . Μαρεῶτις E, Μαρίας . . . Μαραιῶτις other
MSS.   [2] ποιῆσον moz, ποιῆσαν other MSS.

north by the Aegyptian Sea, as it is called, and on
the south by Lake Mareia, also called Mareotis. This
is filled by many canals from the Nile, both from
above and on the sides, and through these canals
the imports are much larger than those from the sea,
so that the harbour on the lake was in fact richer
than that on the sea; and here the exports from
Alexandria also are larger than the imports; and
anyone might judge, if he were at either Alexandria
or Dicaearchia [1] and saw the merchant vessels both
at their arrival and at their departure, how much
heavier or lighter they sailed thither or therefrom.
And in addition to the great value of the things
brought down from both directions, both into the
harbour on the sea and into that on the lake, the
salubrity of the air is also worthy of remark. And
this likewise results from the fact that the land
is washed by water on both sides and because of the
timeliness of the Nile's risings; for the other cities
that are situated on lakes have heavy and stifling
air in the heats of summer, because the lakes then
become marshy along their edges because of the
evaporation caused by the sun's rays, and, accordingly, when so much filth-laden moisture rises, the
air inhaled is noisome and starts pestilential diseases,
whereas at Alexandria, at the beginning of summer,
the Nile, being full, fills the lake also, and leaves
no marshy matter to corrupt the rising vapours.
At that time, also, the Etesian winds blow from
the north and from a vast sea,[2] so that the Alexandrians pass their time most pleasantly in summer.

[1] Now Puteoli.
[2] The Aegyptian monsoons, here called the "Etesian"
(*i.e.* "Annual") winds, blow from the north-west all
summer.

8. Ἔστι δὲ χλαμυδοειδὲς τὸ σχῆμα τοῦ ἐδάφους τῆς πόλεως· οὗ τὰ μὲν ἐπὶ μῆκος πλευρά ἐστι τὰ ἀμφίκλυστα, ὅσον τριάκοντα σταδίων ἔχοντα διάμετρον, τὰ δὲ ἐπὶ πλάτος οἱ ἰσθμοί, ἑπτὰ ἢ ὀκτὼ σταδίων ἑκάτερος, σφιγγόμενος τῇ μὲν ὑπὸ θαλάττης, τῇ δ' ὑπὸ τῆς λίμνης. ἅπασα μὲν ὁδοῖς κατατέτμηται ἱππηλάτοις καὶ ἁρματηλάτοις, δυσὶ δὲ πλατυτάταις, ἐπὶ πλέον ἢ πλέθρον ἀναπεπταμέναις, αἳ δὴ δίχα καὶ πρὸς ὀρθὰς τέμνουσιν ἀλλήλας. ἔχει δ' ἡ πόλις τεμένη τε κοινὰ κάλλιστα καὶ τὰ βασίλεια, τέταρτον ἢ καὶ τρίτον τοῦ παντὸς περιβόλου μέρος· τῶν γὰρ βασιλέων ἕκαστος ὥσπερ τοῖς κοινοῖς ἀναθήμασι προσεφιλοκάλει τινὰ κόσμον, οὕτω καὶ οἴκησιν ἰδίᾳ

---

[1] According to Plutarch (5. 11), the shape was like that of a *Macedonian* chlamys, or military cloak ; and the plan was designed by "Diochares" (probably an error for "Deinocrates"). Likewise, "the inhabited world is chlamys-shaped" (see Vol. I, p. 435 and footnote 3). See Tarbell, *Classical Philology*, I, p. 283, for a discussion of this passage as bearing on the shape of the chlamys.

[2] Strabo is thinking apparently of a line drawn from the centre of the skirt of the chlamys, which was circular, to the centre of the collar.

[3] According to Philo (*In Flaccum* 973 A) the city was divided into five sections, which were designated as Alpha, Beta, Gamma, Delta, and Epsilon. Beta apparently comprised the palaces, including the Museum, the Sema and many other buildings ; Delta, the Jewish quarter (Josephus, *Bell. Jud.* 2. 8) ; but the sites of the three others are doubtful. On the dimensions of the city, cp. Josephus, *Bell. Jud.* 2. 16. 4 (30 × 10 stadia) ; Philo, *In Flaccum* 757 (10 stadia in breadth) ; Stephanus Byzantinus, *s.v.* Ἀλεξάνδρεια (34 × 8,

8. The shape of the area of the city is like a chlamys;[1] the long sides of it are those that are washed by the two waters, having a diameter[2] of about thirty stadia, and the short sides are the isthmuses, each being seven or eight stadia wide and pinched in on one side by the sea and on the other by the lake.[3] The city as a whole is intersected by streets practicable for horse-riding and chariot-driving, and by two that are very broad, extending to more than a plethrum in breadth, which cut one another into two sections and at right angles.[4] And the city contains most beautiful public precincts and also the royal palaces, which constitute one-fourth or even one-third of the whole circuit of the city ; for just as each of the kings, from love of splendour, was wont to add some adornment to the public monuments, so also he would invest himself at his own expense with a residence, in addition to those

and 110 in circuit) ; Pliny 5. 10 (15 miles in circuit) ; and Diodorus Siculus 17. 59 (40 in breadth), who obviously means by " breadth " what others call "length," and seems to include suburban districts on east and west.

[4] The main longitudinal street ran straight through from the "Canobic Gate," or "Gate of the Sun," on the east to the "Gate of the Moon" on the west. Its site has been identified in part with that of the present Rosetta Street (see A. M. de Zogher, *Études sur L'Ancienne Alexandrie*, p. 11); but Dr. Botti (cited by Zogher) takes a different view. "The most important of the latitudinal streets was that of the Sema, which had on its right the tomb of Alexander the Great, and, on its left, very probably the Museum. Then it crossed the Canobic avenue, passed the Adrianum and Caesareum on the right, the temple of Isis-Plousia and the Emporium on the left, and ends on the quay of the great maritime port and the place of embarkation, near the two obelisks " (Neroutsos-Bey, quoted by Zogher, p. 15). See Map at end of volume.

περιεβάλλετο πρὸς ταῖς ὑπαρχούσαις, ὥστε νῦν
τὸ τοῦ ποιητοῦ,

ἐξ ἑτέρων ἕτερ᾽ ἐστίν·

ἅπαντα μέντοι συναφῆ καὶ ἀλλήλοις καὶ τῷ
λιμένι, καὶ ὅσα ἔξω αὐτοῦ. τῶν δὲ βασιλείων
μέρος ἐστὶ καὶ τὸ Μουσεῖον, ἔχον περίπατον καὶ
C 794 ἐξέδραν καὶ οἶκον μέγαν, ἐν ᾧ τὸ συσσίτιον τῶν
μετεχόντων τοῦ Μουσείου φιλολόγων ἀνδρῶν.
ἔστι δὲ τῇ συνόδῳ ταύτῃ καὶ χρήματα κοινὰ καὶ
ἱερεὺς ὁ ἐπὶ[1] τῷ Μουσείῳ, τεταγμένος τότε μὲν
ὑπὸ τῶν βασιλέων, νῦν δ᾽ ὑπὸ Καίσαρος. μέρος
δὲ τῶν βασιλείων ἐστὶ καὶ τὸ καλούμενον Σῆμα,[2]
ὃ περίβολος ἦν, ἐν ᾧ αἱ τῶν βασιλέων ταφαὶ καὶ
ἡ Ἀλεξάνδρου· ἔφθη γὰρ τὸ σῶμα ἀφελόμενος
Περδίκκαν ὁ τοῦ Λάγου Πτολεμαῖος, κατακομί-
ζοντα ἐκ τῆς Βαβυλῶνος καὶ ἐκτρεπόμενον ταύτῃ
κατὰ πλεονεξίαν καὶ ἐξιδιασμὸν τῆς Αἰγύπτου·

---

[1] ὑπό Dhi.
[2] Σῆμα, Tzschucke, for Σῶμα; so later editors.

---

[1] *Odyssey*, 17. 266 (concerning the palace of Odysseus).
[2] *i.e.* on the promontory called Lochias (see § 9 following).
[3] Cp. the structure described by Vitruvius, *De Architectura*
(5. 11 2): "Spacious exedras within three porticoes with
seats, where philosophers, rhetoricians and all others who
take delight in studies can engage in disputation." Suidas
(*s.v.* ἐξέδρα) seems to make the Exedra a building distinct
from the Museum.: "They live near the Museum and the
Exedra."
[4] *i.e.* "Tomb." However, the MSS. (see critical note)
read *Soma*, *i.e.* "Body." And so does the Greek version
of the Pseudo-Callisthenes (C. Müller, Didot Edition, *Scrip-
tores Rerum Alexandri Magni* III, 3. 4): "And Ptolemy
made a tomb in the holy place called 'Body of Alexander,'
and there he laid the body, or remains, of Alexander"; but

already built, so that now, to quote the words of the poet,[1] "there is building upon building." All, however, are connected with one another and the harbour, even those that lie outside[2] the harbour. The Museum is also a part of the royal palaces; it has a public walk, an Exedra with seats, and a large house,[3] in which is the common mess-hall of the men of learning who share the Museum. This group of men not only hold property in common, but also have a priest in charge of the Museum, who formerly was appointed by the kings, but is now appointed by Caesar. The Sema also,[4] as it is called, is a part of the royal palaces. This was the enclosure which contained the burial-places of the kings and that of Alexander; for Ptolemy,[5] the son of Lagus, forestalled Perdiccas by taking the body away from him when he was bringing it down from Babylon and was turning aside towards Aegypt, moved by greed and a desire to make that country his own.[6] Further-

the Syrian version (*Alexander the Great*, trans. by E. A. W. Budge, p. 142) reads: "and they call that place 'The tomb of Alexander' unto this day." But more important is the statement of Zenobius (*Proverbia* III, 94): "Ptolemy (Philopator) built in the middle of the city a *mnema* (μνῆμα οἰκοδομήσας), which is now called the *Sema*, and he laid there all his forefathers together with his mother, and also Alexander the Macedonian."

[5] Ptolemy Soter.

[6] The accounts vary. According to Diodorus Siculus (18. 26–28), Arrhidaeus spent two years making elaborate preparations for the removal of Alexander's body; and Ptolemy I went as far as Syria to meet him, and thence took the body to Aegypt for burial. Pausanias (1. 6. 3, 1. 7. 1) says that Ptolemy I buried it at Memphis and Ptolemy II transferred it to Alexandria. The Pseudo-Callisthenes (*l.c.*) says that the Macedonians were at first determined to take the body back to Macedonia, but later, upon consulting the

καὶ δὴ καὶ ἀπώλετο διαφθαρεὶς ὑπὸ τῶν στρατιωτῶν, ἐπελθόντος τοῦ Πτολεμαίου καὶ κατακλεί-
σαντος αὐτὸν ἐν νήσῳ ἐρήμῃ· ἐκεῖνος μὲν οὖν
ἀπέθανεν ἐμπεριπαρεὶς[1] ταῖς σαρίσσαις, ἐπελθόντων ἐπ' αὐτὸν[2] τῶν στρατιωτῶν, σὺν αὐτῷ
δὲ καὶ οἱ βασιλεῖς, Ἀριδαῖός τε καὶ τὰ παιδία
τὰ Ἀλεξάνδρου, καὶ ἡ γυνὴ Ῥωξάνη ἀπῆραν εἰς
Μακεδονίαν· τὸ δὲ σῶμα τοῦ Ἀλεξάνδρου κομίσας
ὁ Πτολεμαῖος ἐκήδευσεν ἐν τῇ Ἀλεξανδρείᾳ, ὅπου
νῦν ἔτι κεῖται· οὐ μὴν ἐν τῇ αὐτῇ πυέλῳ· ὑαλίνη
γὰρ αὕτη, ἐκεῖνος δ' ἐν χρυσῇ κατέθηκεν· ἐσύλησε
δ' αὐτὴν[3] ὁ Κόκκης καὶ Παρείσακτος ἐπικληθεὶς
Πτολεμαῖος, ἐκ τῆς Συρίας ἐπελθὼν καὶ ἐκπεσὼν
εὐθύς, ὥστ' ἀνόνητα αὐτῷ τὰ σῦλα γενέσθαι.

9. Ἔστι δ' ἐν τῷ μεγάλῳ λιμένι κατὰ μὲν τὸν
εἴσπλουν ἐν δεξιᾷ ἡ νῆσος καὶ ὁ πύργος ὁ Φάρος,
κατὰ δὲ τὴν ἑτέραν χεῖρα αἵ τε χοιράδες καὶ ἡ

---

[1] περιπαρείς Corais.   [2] ἐπ' αὐτῷ στρατιωτῶν Dhi.
[3] αὐτήν Emoz, αὐτόν other MSS.

---

oracle of the Babylonian Zeus, all agreed that "Philip
Ptolemy" (surely an error for "Philip Arrhidaeus," the
immediate successor of Alexander, or for "Ptolemy I")
should take it from Babylon to Aegypt and bury it at
Memphis; and that he took the body to Memphis, but, by
order of the chief priest of the temple there, immediately
took it to Alexandria. There, according to Diodorus Siculus
(*l.c.*), Ptolemy devised a sacred precinct (τέμενος), which in
size and construction was worthy of Alexander's glory.
When Augustus was in Alexandria, he saw the body, having
had the coffin and body brought forth from its shrine,
penetrali (Suetonius, *Augustus* 18); and "he not only saw the
body, but touched it, whereupon, it is said, a piece of nose
broke off" (Dio Cassius 51. 16).

[1] Perdiccas first attacked Ptolemy on the Pelusiac branch
of the Nile "not far from a fortress called 'Camel's Wall,'"

more, Perdiccas lost his life, having been slain by
his soldiers at the time when Ptolemy attacked him
and hemmed him up in a desert island.[1] So Perdiccas was killed, having been transfixed by his
soldiers' sarissae[2] when they attacked him; but the
kings who were with him, both Aridaeus[3] and the
children of Alexander, and also Rhoxanê, Alexander's
wife, departed for Macedonia; and the body of
Alexander was carried off by Ptolemy and given
sepulture in Alexandria, where it still now lies—not,
however, in the same sarcophagus as before, for the
present one is made of glass,[4] whereas the one
wherein Ptolemy laid it was made of gold. The
latter was plundered by the Ptolemy nicknamed
"Cocces"[5] and "Pareisactus,"[6] who came over
from Syria but was immediately[7] expelled, so that
his plunder proved unprofitable to him.

9. In the Great Harbour at the entrance, on the
right hand, are the island and the tower Pharos,
and on the other hand are the reefs and also the

where he was unsuccessful; and then later near Memphis,
where his soldiers mutinied (Diodorus Siculus 18. 33 ff.).

[2] Long Macedonian pikes.

[3] Also spelled Arrhidaeus.

[4] Or, possibly, "alabaster." Cp. the *so-called* "Sarcophagus
of Alexander" found at Sidon and now at the Ottoman
Museum in Constantinople.

[5] *i.e.* "scarlet."

[6] Literally, "Pareisactus" means "one who has been
brought in (*i.e.* upon the throne) privily," *i.e.* "usurper."
But scholars take the word to mean "Illegitimate" (*i.e.*
"Pretender") in this passage and identify this Ptolemy
with Ptolemy XI (so Tozer, *Selections*, p. 350).

[7] This must mean "immediately" after his violation of
the tomb, for Ptolemy XI mounted the throne in 80 B.C.
and, so far as is known, he was never expelled till 58 B.C.

Λοχιὰς ἄκρα, ἔχουσα βασίλειον. εἰσπλεύσαντι
δ᾽ ἐν ἀριστερᾷ ἐστι συνεχῆ τοῖς ἐν τῇ Λοχιάδι
τὰ ἐνδοτέρω βασίλεια, πολλὰς καὶ ποικίλας
ἔχοντα διαίτας καὶ ἄλση· τούτοις δ᾽ ὑπόκειται
ὅ τε ὀρυκτὸς λιμὴν καὶ κρυπτός,[1] ἴδιος τῶν
βασιλέων, καὶ ἡ Ἀντίρροδος, νησίον προκείμενον
τοῦ ὀρυκτοῦ λιμένος, βασίλειον ἅμα καὶ λιμένιον
ἔχον· ἐκάλεσαν δ᾽ οὕτως, ὡς ἂν τῇ Ῥόδῳ ἐνά-
μιλλον. ὑπέρκειται δὲ τούτου τὸ θέατρον· εἶτα
τὸ Ποσείδιον, ἀγκών τις ἀπὸ τοῦ Ἐμπορίου καλουμένου προπεπτωκώς, ἔχων ἱερὸν Ποσειδῶνος· ᾧ
προσθεὶς χῶμα Ἀντώνιος ἔτι μᾶλλον προνεῦον
εἰς μέσον τὸν λιμένα ἐπὶ τῷ ἄκρῳ κατεσκεύασε
δίαιταν βασιλικήν, ἣν Τιμώνιον προσηγόρευσε.
τοῦτο δ᾽ ἔπραξε τὸ τελευταῖον, ἡνίκα προλειφθεὶς
ὑπὸ τῶν φίλων ἀπῆρεν εἰς Ἀλεξάνδρειαν μετὰ
τὴν ἐν Ἀκτίῳ κακοπραγίαν, Τιμώνειον[2] αὑτῷ
κρίνας τὸν λοιπὸν βίον, ὃν διάξειν ἔμελλεν ἔρημος
τῶν τοσούτων φίλων. εἶτα τὸ Καισάριον καὶ τὸ
Ἐμπόριον καὶ αἱ[3] ἀποστάσεις· καὶ μετὰ ταῦτα
τὰ νεώρια μέχρι τοῦ ἑπτασταδίου. ταῦτα μὲν
τὰ περὶ τὸν μέγαν λιμένα.

10. Ἑξῆς δ᾽ Εὐνόστου λιμὴν μετὰ τὸ ἑπτα-
C 795 στάδιον· καὶ ὑπὲρ τούτου ὁ ὀρυκτός, ὃν καὶ
Κιβωτὸν καλοῦσιν, ἔχων καὶ αὐτὸς νεώρια. ἐνδο-
τέρω δὲ τούτου διῶρυξ πλωτὴ μέχρι τῆς λίμνης

---

[1] κρυπτός, the reading of all MSS., Jones restores, for
κλειστός, Corais and the later editors.
[2] Τιμώνειον E, Τιμώνιον other MSS.
[3] αἱ, Corais inserts ; καὶ ἀσποστάσεις E.

---

[1] Cp. § 6 above. [2] 31 B.C.

promontory Lochias, with a royal palace upon it; and on sailing into the harbour one comes, on the left, to the inner royal palaces, which are continuous with those on Lochias and have groves and numerous lodges painted in various colours. Below these lies the harbour that was dug by the hand of man and is hidden from view,[1] the private property of the kings, as also Antirrhodos, an isle lying off the artificial harbour, which has both a royal palace and a small harbour. They so called it as being a rival of Rhodes. Above the artificial harbour lies the theatre; then the Poseidium—an elbow, as it were, projecting from the Emporium, as it is called, and containing a temple of Poseidon. To this elbow of land Antony added a mole projecting still farther, into the middle of a harbour, and on the extremity of it built a royal lodge which he called Timonium. This was his last act, when, forsaken by his friends, he sailed away to Alexandria after his misfortune at Actium,[2] having chosen to live the life of a Timon[3] the rest of his days, which he intended to spend in solitude from all those friends.[4] Then one comes to the Caesarium and the Emporium and the warehouses; and after these to the ship-houses, which extend as far as the Heptastadium. So much for the Great Harbour and its surroundings.

10. Next, after the Heptastadium, one comes to the Harbour of Eunostus, and, above this, to the artificial harbour, which is also called Cibotus; it too has ship-houses. Farther in there is a navigable

---

[3] Timon the Athenian was nicknamed the "Misanthrope." Antony, like Timon, felt that he himself also had been wronged and treated with ingratitude, and therefore hated all men (Plutarch, *Antony* 69).

[4] He slew himself in 30 B.C.

τεταμένη τῆς Μαρεώτιδος.¹ ἔξω μὲν οὖν τῆς διώρυγος μικρὸν ἔτι λείπεται τῆς πόλεως· εἶθ' ἡ Νεκρόπολις ² τὸ προάστειον, ἐν ᾧ κῆποί τε πολλοὶ καὶ ταφαὶ καὶ καταγωγαὶ πρὸς τὰς ταριχείας τῶν νεκρῶν ἐπιτήδειαι. ἐντὸς δὲ τῆς διώρυγος τό τε Σαράπιον καὶ ἄλλα τεμένη ἀρχαῖα ἐκλελειμμένα πως διὰ τὴν τῶν νέων ³ κατασκευὴν τῶν ἐν Νικοπόλει· καὶ γὰρ ἀμφιθέατρον καὶ στάδιον καὶ οἱ πεντετηρικοὶ ἀγῶνες ἐκεῖ συντελοῦνται· τὰ δὲ παλαιὰ ὠλιγώρηται. συλλήβδην δ' εἰπεῖν ἡ πόλις μεστή ἐστιν ἀναθημάτων καὶ ἱερῶν· κάλλιστον δὲ τὸ γυμνάσιον, μείζους ἢ σταδιαίας ἔχον τὰς στοάς. ἐν μέσῳ δὲ τό τε⁴ δικαστήριον καὶ τὰ ἄλση. ἔστι δὲ καὶ Πάνειον, ὕψος τι χειροποίητον στροβιλοειδὲς ἐμφερὲς ὄχθῳ πετρώδει διὰ κοχλίου τὴν ἀνάβασιν ἔχον· ἀπὸ δὲ τῆς κορυφῆς ἔστιν ἀπιδεῖν ὅλην τὴν πόλιν ὑποκειμένην αὐτῷ πανταχόθεν. ἀπὸ δὲ τῆς Νεκροπόλεως ἡ ἐπὶ τὸ μῆκος πλατεῖα διατείνει παρὰ τὸ γυμνάσιον μέχρι τῆς πύλης τῆς Κανωβικῆς· εἶθ' Ἱππόδρομος καλούμενός ἐστι καὶ αἱ παρακείμεναι ⁵ ἄλλαι μέχρι τῆς διώρυγος τῆς Κανωβικῆς. διὰ

¹ Μαρεώτιδος Ε, Μαραιώτιδος other MSS.
² Emoz read καὶ after Νεκρόπολις.
³ νέων, Groskurd, for νεκρῶν s, νεῶν other MSS.
⁴ στοάς. ἐν μέσῳ δὲ τό τε, Corais, for στοὰς ἐν μέσῳ. τὸ δέ.
⁵ D (?) and the editors before Kramer add αἱ before ἄλλαι. Kramer conj. that κατοικίαι, or some word of similar meaning, has fallen out after ἄλλαι. Meineke conj. καλιαί ("wooden dwellings"), Vogel ἅλαι ("salt-works"), for ἄλλαι.

¹ Cp. the Nicopolis near Actium, and its sacred precinct, and its quinquennial games (7. 7. 6 and footnote 1).
² Of the *city*, not the *gymnasium*.

canal, which extends to Lake Mareotis. Now outside the canal there is still left only a small part of the
city; and then one comes to the suburb Necropolis,
in which are many gardens and graves and halting-
places fitted up for the embalming of corpses, and,
inside the canal, both to the Sarapium and to other
sacred precincts of ancient times, which are now
almost abandoned on account of the construction of
the new buildings at Nicopolis; for instance, there
are an amphitheatre and a stadium at Nicopolis, and
the quinquennial games are celebrated there; [1] but
the ancient buildings have fallen into neglect. In
short, the city is full of public and sacred structures;
but the most beautiful is the Gymnasium, which has
porticoes more than a stadium in length. And in
the middle [2] are both the court of justice and the
groves. Here, too, is the Paneium, [3] a "height," as
it were, which was made by the hand of man; it has
the shape of a fir-cone, resembles a rocky hill, and is
ascended by a spiral road; and from the summit one
can see the whole of the city lying below it on all
sides. The broad street that runs lengthwise [4]
extends from Necropolis past the Gymnasium to the
Canobic Gate; and then one comes to the Hippodrome, as it is called, and to the other (streets?) [5]
that lie parallel, extending as far as the Canobic

[3] Sanctuary of Pan.

[4] See § 8 above.

[5] Both the text and the interpretation are doubtful. ὁδοί
("streets") is not found in the MSS.; but, although it is the
natural word to supply, just as ὁδός *must* be supplied above
with πλατεῖα ("broad"), it hardly suits the context, as
Kramer, who conjectures κατοικίαι ("settlements"), insists.
Vogel (see critical note) simply emends ἄλλαι ("other") to
ἅλαι ("salt-works").

δὲ τοῦ Ἱπποδρόμου διελθόντι ἡ Νικόπολίς ἐστιν, ἔχουσα κατοικίαν ἐπὶ θαλάττῃ πόλεως οὐκ ἐλάττω· τριάκοντα δέ εἰσιν ἀπὸ τῆς Ἀλεξανδρείας στάδιοι. τοῦτον δὲ ἐτίμησεν ὁ Σεβαστὸς Καῖσαρ τὸν τόπον, ὅτι ἐνταῦθα ἐνίκα τῇ μάχῃ τοὺς ἐπεξιόντας ἐπ᾽ αὐτὸν μετὰ Ἀντωνίου· καὶ λαβὼν ἐξ ἐφόδου τὴν πόλιν ἠνάγκασε τὸν μὲν Ἀντώνιον ἑαυτὸν διαχειρίσασθαι, τὴν δὲ Κλεοπάτραν ζῶσαν ἐλθεῖν εἰς τὴν ἐξουσίαν· μικρὸν δ᾽ ὕστερον κἀκείνη ἑαυτὴν ἐν τῇ φρουρᾷ διεχειρίσατο λάθρα δήγματι ἀσπίδος ἢ φαρμάκῳ ἐπιχρίστῳ (λέγεται γὰρ ἀμφοτέρως), καὶ συνέβη καταλυθῆναι τὴν τῶν Λαγιδῶν ἀρχήν, πολλὰ συμμείνασαν ἔτη.

11. Πτολεμαῖος γὰρ ὁ Λάγου διεδέξατο Ἀλέξανδρον, ἐκεῖνον δὲ ὁ Φιλάδελφος, τοῦτον δὲ ὁ Εὐεργέτης, εἶθ᾽ ὁ Φιλοπάτωρ ὁ τῆς Ἀγαθοκλείας, εἶθ᾽ ὁ Ἐπιφανής, εἶθ᾽ ὁ Φιλομήτωρ, παῖς παρὰ πατρὸς ἀεὶ διαδεχόμενος· τοῦτον δ᾽ ἀδελφὸς διεδέξατο ὁ δεύτερος Εὐεργέτης, ὃν καὶ Φύσκωνα προσαγορεύουσι, τοῦτον δ᾽ ὁ Λάθουρος ἐπικληθεὶς C 796 Πτολεμαῖος, τοῦτον δ᾽ ὁ Αὐλητὴς ὁ καθ᾽ ἡμᾶς, ὅσπερ ἦν τῆς Κλεοπάτρας πατήρ. ἅπαντες μὲν οὖν οἱ μετὰ τὸν τρίτον Πτολεμαῖον ὑπὸ τρυφῆς διεφθαρμένοι χεῖρον ἐπολιτεύσαντο, χείριστα δ᾽ ὁ τέταρτος καὶ ἕβδομος καὶ ὁ ὕστατος, ὁ Αὐλητής· ὃς χωρὶς τῆς ἄλλης ἀσελγείας χοραυλεῖν[1] ἤσκησε,

_____

[1] χοραυλεῖν E, χοραύλην other MSS.

_____

[1] Josephus (*Bell. Jud.* 4. 11. 5) says "twenty."
[2] Cp. Plutarch, *Antony* 86.

canal. Having passed through the Hippodrome, one comes to Nicopolis, which has a settlement on the sea no smaller than a city. It is thirty [1] stadia distant from Alexandria. Augustus Caesar honoured this place because it was here that he conquered in battle those who came out against him with Antony; and when he had taken the city at the first onset, he forced Antony to put himself to death and Cleopatra to come into his power alive; but a little later she too put herself to death secretly, while in prison, by the bite of an asp or (for two accounts are given) by applying a poisonous ointment; [2] and the result was that the empire of the sons of Lagus, which had endured for many years, was dissolved.

11. For Ptolemy the son of Lagus succeeded Alexander; and he in turn was succeeded by Philadelphus, and he by Euergetes, and then he by Philopator the son of Agathocleia, and then he by Epiphanes, and then he by Philometor, a son always succeeding a father; but Philometor was succeeded by a brother, the second Euergetes, who is also called Physcon, and he by the Ptolemy nicknamed Lathurus, [3] and he by Auletes of our own time, who was the father of Cleopatra. Now all the kings after the third Ptolemy, being corrupted by luxurious living, have administered the affairs of government badly, but worst of all the fourth, seventh, and the last, Auletes, who, apart from his general licentiousness, practised the accompaniment of choruses with

[3] *i.e.* Ptolemy VII. Strabo here skips Ptolemy IX (Alexander I) and Ptolemy X (Alexander II), who apparently had no place in the official list of legitimate kings (cp. Letronne edition, note *ad loc.*).

καὶ ἐπ᾽ αὐτῷ γε [1] ἐσεμνύνετο [2] τοσοῦτον, ὥστ᾽ οὐκ
ὤκνει συντελεῖν ἀγῶνας ἐν τοῖς βασιλείοις, εἰς
οὓς παρῄει διαμιλλησόμενος τοῖς ἀνταγωνισταῖς.
τοῦτον μὲν οὖν οἱ Ἀλεξανδρεῖς ἐξέβαλον, τριῶν
δ᾽ αὐτῷ θυγατέρων οὐσῶν, ὧν μία γνησία ἡ
πρεσβυτάτη, ταύτην ἀνέδειξαν βασίλισσαν· οἱ
υἱοὶ δ᾽ αὐτοῦ δύο νήπιοι τῆς τότε χρείας ἐξέπιπτον
τελέως. τῇ δὲ κατασταθείσῃ μετεπέμψαντο ἄνδρα
ἐκ τῆς Συρίας Κυβιοσάκτην [3] τινά, προσποιησά-
μενον τοῦ γένους εἶναι τῶν Συριακῶν βασιλέων·
τοῦτον μὲν οὖν ὀλίγων ἡμερῶν ἀπεστραγγάλισεν
ἡ βασίλισσα, οὐ φέρουσα τὸ βάναυσον καὶ τὸ
ἀνελεύθερον. ἧκε δ᾽ ἀντ᾽ ἐκείνου προσποιησά-
μενος καὶ αὐτὸς εἶναι Μιθριδάτου υἱὸς τοῦ
Εὐπάτορος Ἀρχέλαος, ὃς ἦν μὲν Ἀρχελάου υἱὸς
τοῦ πρὸς Σύλλαν διαπολεμήσαντος καὶ μετὰ
ταῦτα τιμηθέντος ὑπὸ Ῥωμαίων, πάππος δὲ τοῦ
βασιλεύσαντος Καππαδόκων ὑστάτου καθ᾽ ἡμᾶς,
ἱερεὺς δὲ τῶν ἐν Πόντῳ Κομάνων. Γαβινίῳ δὲ
τότε συνδιέτριψεν ὡς συστρατεύσων ἐπὶ Παρ-
θυαίους, λαθὼν δὲ τοῦτον κομίζεται διά τινων
εἰς τὴν βασίλισσαν καὶ ἀναδείκνυται βασιλεύς.
ἐν τούτῳ τὸν Αὐλητὴν ἀφικόμενον εἰς Ῥώμην
δεξάμενος Πομπήιος Μάγνος συνίστησι τῇ συγ-

---

[1] γε, Corais, for δέ.   [2] Cx have ἐπί before τοσοῦτον.
[3] Κυβισάκτην C.

---

[1] Hence "Auletes" ("Flute-player").
[2] According to Dio Cassius (39. 13), this was Berenicê
(IV). She reigned with her mother Cleopatra Tryphaena for
one year (58–57 B.C.) and then alone for one year.
[3] Later, Ptolemy XII and XIII.
[4] A nickname, "Salt-fish Dealer." Dio Cassius (39. 57)
says, "a certain Seleucus."

the flute,[1] and upon this he prided himself so much
that he would not hesitate to celebrate contests
in the royal palace, and at these contests would
come forward to vie with the opposing contestants.
He, however, was banished by the Alexandrians;
and since he had three daughters, of whom one,
the eldest, was legitimate, they proclaimed her
queen;[2] but his two sons,[3] who were infants, were
completely excluded from service at the time.
When she had been established on the throne, they
sent after a husband for her from Syria, a certain
Cybiosactes,[4] who had pretended that he belonged
to the family of the Syrian kings. Now the queen
had this man strangled to death within a few days,
being unable to bear his coarseness and vulgarity;
but in his place came a man who likewise had
pretended that he was a son of Mithridates Eupator
—I mean Archelaüs, who was son of the Archelaüs
who carried on war against Sulla and afterwards was
honoured by the Romans, and was grandfather of
the man who was last to reign as king over the
Cappadocians in our time,[5] and was priest of Comana
in Pontus.[6] At that time he had been tarrying
with Gabinius,[7] in the hope of joining with him
on an expedition against the Parthians, but without
the knowledge of Gabinius he was brought by
certain agents to the queen and proclaimed king.[8]
In the meantime Pompey the Great, having received
Auletes, who had arrived at Rome, recommended

---

[5] 12. 1. 2.
[6] On this Archelaüs, see 12. 3. 34.
[7] Proconsul of Syria, 57 B.C.
[8] He reigned only six months, being slain in battle by
Gabinius (12. 3. 34).

κλήτῳ καὶ διαπράττεται κάθοδον μὲν τούτῳ, τῶν
δὲ πρέσβεων τῶν πλείστων, ἑκατὸν ὄντων, ὄλεθρον
τῶν καταπρεσβευσάντων αὐτοῦ· τούτων δ' ἦν καὶ
Δίων ὁ 'Ακαδημαϊκός, ἀρχιπρεσβευτὴς γεγονώς.
καταχθεὶς οὖν ὑπὸ Γαβινίου Πτολεμαῖος τόν τε
'Αρχέλαον ἀναιρεῖ καὶ τὴν θυγατέρα, χρόνον δ'
οὐ πολὺν τῇ βασιλείᾳ προσθεὶς τελευτᾷ νόσῳ,
καταλιπὼν δύο μὲν υἱεῖς, δύο δὲ θυγατέρας, πρεσ-
βυτάτην δὲ Κλεοπάτραν. οἱ μὲν οὖν 'Αλεξανδρεῖς
ἀπέδειξαν βασιλέας τόν τε πρεσβύτερον τῶν
παίδων καὶ τὴν Κλεοπάτραν, οἱ δὲ συνόντες τῷ
παιδὶ καταστασιάσαντες ἐξέβαλον τὴν Κλεοπάτραν, καὶ ἀπῆρε μετὰ τῆς ἀδελφῆς εἰς τὴν
Συρίαν. ἐν τούτῳ Πομπήιος Μάγνος ἧκε φεύγων
ἐκ Παλαιφαρσάλου πρὸς τὸ Πηλούσιον καὶ τὸ
Κάσιον [1] ὄρος. τοῦτον μὲν οὖν δολοφονοῦσιν οἱ
μετὰ τοῦ βασιλέως, ἐπελθὼν δὲ Καῖσαρ τόν τε
μειρακίσκον διαφθείρει καὶ καθίστησι τῆς Αἰγύπτου βασίλισσαν τὴν Κλεοπάτραν, μεταπεμ-
ψάμενος ἐκ τῆς φυγῆς· συμβασιλεύειν δ' ἀπέδειξε
τὸν λοιπὸν ἀδελφὸν αὐτῇ, νέον παντελῶς ὄντα.
C 797 μετὰ δὲ τὴν Καίσαρος τελευτὴν καὶ τὰ ἐν Φιλίπ-
ποις διαβὰς 'Αντώνιος εἰς τὴν 'Ασίαν ἐξετίμησεν
ἐπὶ πλέον τὴν Κλεοπάτραν, ὥστε καὶ γυναῖκα
ἔκρινε καὶ ἐτεκνοποιήσατο ἐξ αὐτῆς, τόν τε
'Ακτιακὸν πόλεμον συνήρατο ἐκείνη καὶ συνέφυγε·
καὶ μετὰ ταῦτα ἐπακολουθήσας ὁ Σεβαστὸς
Καῖσαρ ἀμφοτέρους κατέλυσε καὶ τὴν Αἴγυπτον
ἔπαυσε παροινουμένην.

---

[1] Κάσιον Dhx, κάσσιον other MSS.

---

[1] So Dio Cassius (39. 13).

him to the Senate and effected, not only his restoration, but also the death of most of the ambassadors, one hundred in number, who had undertaken the embassy against him,[1] and among these was Dion the academic philosopher, who had been made chief ambassador. Accordingly, on being restored by Gabinius, Ptolemy slew both Archelaüs and his own daughter. But before he had added much time to his reign, he died of disease, leaving behind two sons and also two daughters, the eldest daughter being Cleopatra.[2] Now the Alexandrians proclaimed as sovereigns both the elder of the boys and Cleopatra; but the associates of the boy caused an uprising and banished Cleopatra, and she set sail with her sister to Syria. In the meantime Pompey the Great had come in flight from Palaepharsalus to Pelusium and Mt. Casius. Now Pompey was treacherously slain by the king's party, but when Caesar arrived he put the lad to death, and, having summoned Cleopatra from exile, established her as queen of Aegypt; and he appointed her remaining brother to reign as king with her, although he was exceedingly young. After the death of Caesar and the battle of Philippi,[3] Antony crossed over to Asia and held Cleopatra in such extraordinary honour that he chose her as wife and had children by her; and he undertook the battle at Actium with her and fled with her; and after this Augustus Caesar pursued them, destroyed both, and put an end to Aegypt's being ruled with drunken violence.

[2] The famous Cleopatra. [3] 42 B.C.

12. Ἐπαρχία δὲ νῦν ἐστι, φόρους μὲν τελοῦσα ἀξιολόγους, ὑπὸ σωφρόνων δὲ ἀνδρῶν διοικουμένη τῶν πεμπομένων ἐπάρχων ἀεί. ὁ μὲν οὖν πεμφθεὶς τὴν τοῦ βασιλέως ἔχει τάξιν· ὑπ' αὐτῷ δ' ἐστὶν ὁ δικαιοδότης, ὁ τῶν πολλῶν κρίσεων κύριος· ἄλλος δ' ἐστὶν ὁ προσαγορευόμενος ἰδιόλογος,[1] ὃς τῶν ἀδεσπότων καὶ τῶν εἰς Καίσαρα πίπτειν ὀφειλόντων ἐξεταστής ἐστι· παρέπονται δὲ τούτοις ἀπελεύθεροι Καίσαρος καὶ οἰκονόμοι, μείζω καὶ ἐλάττω πεπιστευμένοι πράγματα. ἔστι δὲ καὶ στρατιωτικοῦ τρία τάγματα, ὧν τὸ ἓν κατὰ τὴν πόλιν ἵδρυται, τἆλλα δ' ἐν τῇ χώρᾳ· χωρὶς δὲ τούτων ἐννέα μέν εἰσι σπεῖραι Ῥωμαίων, τρεῖς μὲν ἐν τῇ πόλει, τρεῖς δ' ἐπὶ τῶν ὅρων τῆς Αἰθιοπίας ἐν Συήνῃ, φρουρὰ τοῖς τόποις, τρεῖς δὲ κατὰ τὴν ἄλλην χώραν. εἰσὶ δὲ καὶ ἱππαρχίαι τρεῖς ὁμοίως διατεταγμέναι κατὰ τοὺς ἐπικαιρίους τόπους. τῶν δ' ἐπιχωρίων ἀρχόντων κατὰ πόλιν μὲν ὅ τε ἐξηγητής ἐστι, πορφύραν ἀμπεχόμενος καὶ ἔχων πατρίους τιμὰς καὶ ἐπιμέλειαν τῶν τῇ πόλει χρησίμων, καὶ ὁ ὑπομνηματογράφος καὶ ὁ ἀρχιδικαστής, τέταρτος δὲ ὁ νυκτερινὸς στρατηγός. ἦσαν μὲν οὖν καὶ ἐπὶ τῶν βασιλέων αὗται αἱ ἀρχαί, κακῶς δὲ πολιτευομένων τῶν βασιλέων ἠφανίζετο καὶ ἡ τῆς πόλεως εὐκαιρία διὰ τὴν ἀνομίαν. ὁ γοῦν Πολύβιος γεγονὼς ἐν τῇ πόλει βδελύττεται τὴν

---

[1] ἰδιόλογος, Corais, for κύριος λόγος s, ἴδιος λόγος other MSS.

---

[1] e.g. Strabo's friend Aelius Gallus (2. 5. 12).
[2] Juri dicendo praefectus.

12. Egypt is now a Province; and it not only pays considerable tribute, but also is governed by prudent men [1]—the praefects who are sent there from time to time. Now he who is sent has the rank of the king; and subordinate to him is the administrator of justice,[2] who has supreme authority over most of the law-suits; and another is the official called Idiologus,[3] who inquires into all properties that are without owners and that ought to fall to Caesar; and these are attended by freedmen of Caesar, as also by stewards, who are entrusted with affairs of more or less importance. There are also three legions of soldiers, one of which is stationed in the city and the others in the country; and apart from these there are nine Roman cohorts, three in the city, three on the borders of Aethiopia in Syenê, as a guard for that region, and three in the rest of the country. And there are also three bodies of cavalry, which likewise are assigned to the various critical points. Of the native officials in the city, one is the Interpreter,[4] who is clad in purple, has hereditary prerogatives, and has charge of the interests of the city; and another the Recorder;[5] and another the Chief Judge;[6] and the fourth the Night Commander.[7] Now these officers existed also in the time of the kings, but, since the kings were carrying on a bad government, the prosperity of the city was also vanishing on account of the prevailing lawlessness. At any rate, Polybius, who had visited the city, is disgusted with the state of

---

[3] A kind of "Special Agent," or "Procurator," of Caesar.

[4] Interpres.　　　　　[5] Scriba publicus.
[6] Judicum praefectus.　　[7] Praetor nocturnus.

49

τότε κατάστασιν, καί φησι τρία γένη τὴν πόλιν
οἰκεῖν, τό τε Αἰγύπτιον καὶ[1] ἐπιχώριον φῦλον,
ὀξὺ καὶ ἀπολιτικόν,[2] καὶ τὸ μισθοφορικόν, βαρὺ
καὶ[3] πολὺ καὶ ἀνάγωγον· ἐξ ἔθους γὰρ παλαιοῦ
ξένους ἔτρεφον τοὺς τὰ ὅπλα ἔχοντας, ἄρχειν
μᾶλλον ἢ ἄρχεσθαι δεδιδαγμένους διὰ τὴν τῶν
βασιλέων οὐδένειαν· τρίτον δ᾽ ἦν γένος τὸ τῶν
Ἀλεξανδρέων, οὐδ᾽ αὐτὸ εὐκρινῶς πολιτικὸν διὰ
τὰς αὐτὰς αἰτίας, κρεῖττον δ᾽ ἐκείνων ὅμως· καὶ
γὰρ εἰ μιγάδες, Ἕλληνες ὅμως ἀνέκαθεν ἦσαν
καὶ ἐμέμνηντο τοῦ κοινοῦ τῶν Ἑλλήνων ἔθους.
ἠφανισμένου δὲ καὶ τούτου τοῦ πλήθους, μάλιστα
C 798 ὑπὸ τοῦ Εὐεργέτου τοῦ Φύσκωνος, καθ᾽ ὃν ἧκεν
εἰς τὴν Ἀλεξάνδρειαν ὁ Πολύβιος (καταστασιαζό-
μενος γὰρ ὁ Φύσκων πλεονάκις[4] τοῖς στρατιώταις
ἐφίει τὰ πλήθη καὶ διέφθειρε), τοιούτων δή,
φησίν, ὄντων τῶν ἐν τῇ πόλει, λοιπὸν ἦν τῷ ὄντι
τὸ τοῦ ποιητοῦ·

Αἴγυπτόνδ᾽ ἰέναι δολιχὴν ὁδὸν ἀργαλέην τε.

13. Τοιαῦτα δ᾽ ἦν, εἰ μὴ[5] χείρω, καὶ τὰ τῶν
ὕστερον βασιλέων.[6] Ῥωμαῖοι δ᾽ εἰς δύναμιν, ὡς
εἰπεῖν, ἐπηνώρθωσαν τὰ πολλά, τὴν μὲν πόλιν
διατάξαντες ὡς εἶπον, κατὰ δὲ τὴν χώραν

---

[1] Except F, the MSS. read τό before ἐπιχώριον.
[2] Before πολιτικόν (MSS.) Tyrwhitt conj. οὐ; Kramer conj.
ἀπολιτικόν; C. Müller ὀχλητικόν.
[3] The words βαρὺ καί are found only in C.
[4] πολλάκις moz.   [5] F has καί after μή.
[6] Except Fx, the MSS. have καί before Ῥωμαῖοι.

things then existing; and he says that three classes
inhabited the city: first, the Aegyptian or native
stock of people, who were quick-tempered and not [1]
inclined to civic life; and, secondly, the mercenary
class, who were severe and numerous and intractable
(for by an ancient custom they would maintain
foreign men-at-arms, who had been trained to rule
rather than to be ruled, on account of the worth-
lessness of the kings); and, third, the tribe of the
Alexandrians, who also were not distinctly inclined
to civil life, and for the same reasons, but still they
were better than those others,[2] for even though
they were a mixed people, still they were Greeks
by origin and mindful of the customs common to
the Greeks. But after this mass of people had also
been blotted out, chiefly by Euergetes Physcon, in
whose time Polybius went to Alexandria (for, being
opposed by factions, Physcon more often sent the
masses against the soldiers and thus caused their
destruction)—such being the state of affairs in the
city, Polybius says, in very truth there remained for
one, in the words of the poet, merely

" to go to Aegypt, a long and painful journey." [3]

13. Such, then, if not worse, was the state of
affairs under the later kings also; but the Romans
have, to the best of their ability, I might say, set
most things right, having organised the city as
I have said,[4] and having appointed throughout the

---

[1] The MSS. omit the negative ("not"), without which one
would naturally interpret ὀξύ as meaning "acute" rather
than "quick-tempered."
[2] *i.e.* the first class.
[3] *Odyssey* 4. 483.   [4] § 12 above.

ἐπιστρατήγους τινὰς καὶ νομάρχας καὶ ἐθνάρχας
καλουμένους ἀποδείξαντες, πραγμάτων οὐ μεγάλων ἐπιστατεῖν ἠξιωμένους. τῆς δ' εὐκαιρίας
τῆς κατὰ τὴν πόλιν τὸ μέγιστόν ἐστιν, ὅτι τῆς
Αἰγύπτου πάσης μόνος ἐστὶν οὗτος ὁ τόπος πρὸς
ἄμφω πεφυκὼς εὖ, τά τε ἐκ θαλάττης διὰ τὸ
εὐλίμενον, καὶ τὰ ἐκ τῆς χώρας, ὅτι πάντα
εὐμαρῶς ὁ ποταμὸς πορθμεύει συνάγει τε εἰς
τοιοῦτον χωρίον, ὅπερ μέγιστον ἐμπόριον τῆς
οἰκουμένης ἐστί.

Τῆς μὲν οὖν πόλεως ταύτας ἄν τις λέγοι τὰς
ἀρετάς· τῆς Αἰγύπτου δὲ τὰς προσόδους[1] ἔν
τινι λόγῳ Κικέρων φράζει, φήσας κατ' ἐνιαυτὸν
τῷ τῆς Κλεοπάτρας πατρὶ τῷ Αὐλητῇ προσ-
φέρεσθαι φόρον ταλάντων μυρίων δισχιλίων
πεντακοσίων. ὅπου οὖν ὁ κάκιστα καὶ ῥαθυμό-
τατα τὴν βασιλείαν διοικῶν τοσαῦτα προσω-
δεύετο, τί χρὴ νομίσαι τὰ νῦν, διὰ τοσαύτης
ἐπιμελείας οἰκονομούμενα καὶ τῶν Ἰνδικῶν
ἐμποριῶν καὶ τῶν Τρωγλοδυτικῶν ἐπηυξημένων
ἐπὶ τοσοῦτον; πρότερον μέν γε οὐδ' εἴκοσι πλοῖα
ἐθάρρει τὸν Ἀράβιον κόλπον διαπερᾶν, ὥστε ἔξω
τῶν στενῶν ὑπερκύπτειν, νῦν δὲ καὶ στόλοι
μεγάλοι στέλλονται μέχρι τῆς Ἰνδικῆς καὶ τῶν
ἄκρων τῶν Αἰθιοπικῶν, ἐξ ὧν ὁ πολυτιμότατος

[1] Except E, the MSS. have ἄς after προσόδους.

---

[1] Strabo seems not to have known that the office of
Epistrategus was in existence as far back as 181 B.C. (Victor
Martin, Les Epistratiges, pp. 11, 173, Geneva, 1911). But in
the time of the Ptolemies only the Thebaïs had an Epistra-
tegus (l.c. p. 22), and, as the title indicates, he was a
Military Governor. The several Epistrategi appointed by the

country officials called Epistrategi [1] and Nomarchs [2] and Ethnarchs,[3] who were thought worthy to superintend affairs of no great importance. Among the happy advantages of the city, the greatest is the fact that this is the only place in all Aegypt which is by nature well situated with reference to both things—both to commerce by sea, on account of the good harbours, and to commerce by land, because the river easily conveys and brings together everything into a place so situated—the greatest emporium in the inhabited world.

Now one might call these the excellent attributes of the city; and as for the revenues of Aegypt, Cicero tells about them in a certain speech,[4] saying that a tribute of twelve thousand five hundred talents [5] was paid annually to Auletes, the father of Cleopatra. If, then, the man who administered the kingdom in the worst and most careless way obtained so large a revenue, what should one think of the present revenues, which are managed with so much diligence, and when the commerce with the Indians and the Troglodytes has been increased to so great an extent? In earlier times, at least, not so many as twenty vessels would dare to traverse the Arabian Gulf far enough to get a peep outside the straits, but at the present time even large fleets are despatched as far as India and the extremities of Aethiopia, from which the most valuable cargoes

Romans, however, were given only administrative power, being wholly deprived of military power (*l.c.* p. 57).

  [2] " Rulers of Nomes " (on the " Nomes," see 17. 1. 3).
  [3] Rulers of Tribes.   [4] No longer extant.
  [5] Cp. Diodorus Siculus (17. 52), who says six thousand talents.

κομίζεται φόρτος εἰς τὴν Αἴγυπτον, κἀντεῦθεν
πάλιν εἰς τοὺς ἄλλους ἐκπέμπεται τόπους· ὥστε
τὰ τέλη διπλάσια συνάγεται, τὰ μὲν εἰσαγωγικά,
τὰ δὲ ἐξαγωγικά· τῶν δὲ βαρυτίμων βαρέα καὶ
τὰ τέλη. καὶ γὰρ δὴ καὶ μονοπωλίας ἔχει· μόνη
γὰρ ἡ Ἀλεξάνδρεια τῶν τοιούτων ὡς ἐπὶ τὸ
πολὺ καὶ ὑποδοχεῖόν ἐστι καὶ χορηγεῖ τοῖς
ἐκτός. ἔτι δὲ μᾶλλον κατιδεῖν ἔστι τὴν εὐφυΐαν
ταύτην περιοδεύοντι τὴν χώραν, καὶ πρῶτον τὴν
παραλίαν ἀρξαμένην ἀπὸ τοῦ Καταβαθμοῦ·
μέχρι δεῦρο γάρ ἐστιν ἡ Αἴγυπτος, ἡ δ᾽ ἑξῆς
ἐστι Κυρηναία καὶ οἱ περιοικοῦντες βάρβαροι
Μαρμαρίδαι.

14. Ἀπὸ μὲν οὖν Καταβαθμοῦ εἰς Παραιτόνιον[1]
εὐθυπλοοῦντι σταδίων ἐστὶν ἐννακοσίων ὁ δρόμος.
πόλις δ᾽ ἐστὶ καὶ λιμὴν μέγας τετταράκοντά που
C 799 σταδίων· καλοῦσι δ᾽ οἱ μὲν Παραιτόνιον τὴν
πόλιν, οἱ δ᾽ Ἀμμωνίαν. μεταξὺ δὲ ἥ τε Αἰγυπτίων
κώμη καὶ ἡ Αἰνησίσφυρα[2] ἄκρα, καὶ Τυνδάρειοι
σκόπελοι, νησίδια τέτταρα ἔχοντα λιμένα· εἶθ᾽
ἑξῆς ἄκρα Δρέπανον καὶ νῆσος Αἰνησίππεια[3]
ἔχουσα λιμένα καὶ κώμη Ἄπις, ἀφ᾽ ἧς εἰς μὲν
Παραιτόνιον στάδιοι ἑκατόν, εἰς δὲ Ἄμμωνος
ὁδὸς ἡμερῶν πέντε. ἀπὸ δὲ τοῦ Παραιτονίου εἰς
Ἀλεξάνδρειαν[4] χίλιοί που καὶ τριακόσιοι στάδιοι. μεταξὺ δὲ πρῶτον μὲν ἄκρα λευκόγειος,
Λευκὴ ἀκτὴ καλουμένη, ἔπειτα Φοινικοῦς λιμὴν

---

[1] Παραιτόμιον E, Παρατόνιον F, Παραιτόνιον *moxz*.

[2] Αἰνησίσφυρα, Xylander and later editors, following
Ptolemaeus (4. 5), for νησίφιρα F, νησισφύρα other MSS.

[3] ἐνισσίπεια DEF*hi*, ἐνισίσπεια C*xz*, ἐνισίσπια *r*, ἐνισίπεια *m*,
ἐνίσπεια *o*, Αἰνησίππη Ptolemaeus.

54

are brought to Aegypt, and thence sent forth again to the other regions; so that double duties are collected, on both imports and exports; and on goods that cost heavily the duty is also heavy. And in fact the country has monopolies also; for Alexandria alone is not only the receptacle of goods of this kind, for the most part, but also the source of supply to the outside world. And, further, one can perceive more clearly these natural advantages if one travels round the country, visiting first of all the part of the coast which begins at Catabathmus—for Aegypt extends as far as that place, though the country next thereafter belongs to the Cyrenaeans and to the neighbouring barbarians, the Marmaridae.

14. Now the run from Catabathmus to Paraetonium, if one sails in a straight course, is nine hundred stadia. It is a city and large harbour of about forty stadia.[1] Some call the city Paraetonium, but others Ammonia. In the interval, one comes to the village of the Aegyptians, to the promontory Aenesisphyra, and to the Tyndareian Rocks, which latter are four small islands with a harbour; then next to Drepanum, a promontory, and to Aenesippeia, an island with a harbour, and to Apis, a village, from which the distance to Paraetonium is one hundred stadia, and to the temple of Ammon, a five days' journey. The distance from Paraetonium to Alexandria is approximately one thousand three hundred stadia; and in the interval one comes first to a promontory of white earth, Leucê Actê, as it is called, and then to Phoenicus, a harbour, and to

---

[1] *i.e.* in circuit.

---

[4] εἰς ’Αλεξάνδρειαν, inserted by Mannert and the editors.

καὶ Πνιγεὺς κώμη· εἶτα νῆσος Πηδωνία[1] λιμένα
ἔχουσα, εἶτ' Ἀντίφραι μικρὸν ἀπωτέρω τῆς
θαλάττης. ἅπασα μὲν ἡ χώρα αὕτη οὐκ εὔοινος,
πλείω δεχομένου τοῦ κεράμου θάλατταν ἢ οἶνον,
ὃν δὴ καλοῦσι Λιβυκόν, ᾧ δὴ καὶ τῷ ζύθῳ[2] τὸ
πολὺ φῦλον χρῆται τῶν Ἀλεξανδρέων· σκώπτονται
δὲ μάλιστα αἱ Ἀντίφραι· εἶθ' ὁ Δέρρις[3] λιμήν,
καλούμενος οὕτως διὰ τὴν πλησίον πέτραν
μέλαιναν δέρρει ἐοικυῖαν· ὀνομάζουσι δὲ καὶ
Ζεφύριον τὸν πλησίον τόπον, εἶτ' ἄλλος λιμὴν
Λεύκασπις καὶ ἄλλοι πλείους· εἶτα Κυνὸς σῆμα·
εἶτα Ταπόσειρις,[4] οὐκ ἐπὶ θαλάττῃ, πανήγυριν
δεχομένη μεγάλην. (καὶ ἄλλη δ' ἐστὶ Ταπόσειρις
ἐπέκεινα τῆς πόλεως ἱκανῶς.) αὐτῆς δὲ πλησίον
πετρῶδες ἐπὶ τῇ θαλάττῃ χωρίον, καὶ αὐτὸ
δεχόμενον πολλοὺς τοὺς ἀκμάζοντας[5] ἅπασαν
ὥραν ἔτους· εἶθ' ἡ Πλινθίνη[6] καὶ Νικίου κώμη
καὶ Χερρόνησος φρούριον, πλησίον ἤδη τῆς
Ἀλεξανδρείας καὶ τῆς Νεκροπόλεως ἐν ἑβδομήκοντα σταδίοις. ἡ δὲ Μαρεία[7] λίμνη παρατεί-
νουσα μέχρι καὶ δεῦρο πλάτος μὲν ἔχει πλειόνων

---

[1] Σιδονία Cmoz.
[2] ζύθῳ, Xylander, for ζύγῳ.
[3] Δέρρις EF, Δέρις other MSS.
[4] Ταφόσειρις Ehi, Ταπόσειρις with φ above π, D.
[5] ἀκμάζοντας, the later editors, following conj. of Tyrwhitt,
emend to κωμάζοντας.
[6] Πλινθηνή DEh, Πλιθήνη CFx.
[7] Μαρεία E, Μαρίνα F, Μαρία other MSS.

---

[1] i.e. apparently, as distinguished from the two other
classes of people at Alexandria (see § 12 above), and not
"most of the people at Alexandria," as others interpret it.
[2] i.e. because of the bad wine.   [3] i.e. a "hide."
[4] i.e. like that mentioned in § 16 below.

Pnigeus, a village, and then to Pedonia, an island with a harbour, and then to Antiphrae, which is at only a little distance from the sea. The whole of this country is without good wine, since the wine-jars receive more sea-water than wine; and this they call "Libyan" wine, which, as also beer, is used by most of the tribe of Alexandrians;[1] but Antiphrae is ridiculed most.[2] Then one comes to the harbour Derrhis, so called because of the black rock near by, which resembles a "derrhis";[3] and the neighbouring place is also called Zephyrium.[4] Then to another harbour, Leucaspis[5] and several others; and then to Cynos-Sema;[6] and then to Taposeiris, not on the sea, which holds a great public festival. (There is also another Taposeiris on the other side of the city and quite far from it.) And near it[7] there is a rocky place on the sea where likewise crowds of people in the prime of life[8] assemble during every season of the year. And then[9] one comes to Plinthinê and to the village of Nicias, and to Cherronesus, a stronghold, where we are now near Alexandria and Necropolis, a distance of seventy stadia. Lake Mareia,[10] which extends even as far as this,[11] has a

---

[5] "White-shield."

[6] "Bitch's Monument" (cp. Vol. III, p. 377).

[7] The translator understands "it" to refer to the *first* Taposeiris, and parenthesises the preceding statement accordingly, though "it" might refer to the *second* (cp. §§ 16 and 17 below), in which case the parenthesis should end with "season of the year."

[8] The later editors, except Müller-Dübner, very plausibly emend the text to read, "crowds of 'revellers'" (see critical note, and cp. §§ 16 and 17 below).

[9] *i.e.* continuing from the first Taposeiris.

[10] Also called "Mareotis" (§ 7 above).

[11] *i.e.* Cherronesus.

ἢ πεντήκοντα καὶ ἑκατὸν σταδίων, μῆκος δ' ἐλαττόνων ἢ τριακοσίων. ἔχει δ' ὀκτὼ νήσους καὶ τὰ
κύκλῳ πάντ' οἰκούμενα καλῶς· εὐοινία τέ ἐστι
περὶ τοὺς τόπους, ὥστε καὶ διαχεῖσθαι πρὸς
παλαίωσιν τὸν Μαρεώτην[1] οἶνον.

15. Φύεται δ' ἐν τοῖς Αἰγυπτιακοῖς ἕλεσι καὶ
ταῖς λίμναις ἥ τε βύβλος καὶ ὁ Αἰγύπτιος κύαμος,
ἐξ οὗ τὸ κιβώριον, σχεδόν τι ἰσούψεις ῥάβδοι
ὅσον δεκάποδες. ἀλλ' ἡ μὲν βύβλος ψιλὴ ῥάβδος
ἐστὶν ἐπ' ἄκρῳ χαίτην ἔχουσα, ὁ δὲ κύαμος κατὰ
πολλὰ μέρη φύλλα καὶ ἄνθη ἐκφέρει καὶ καρπὸν
ὅμοιον τῷ παρ' ἡμῖν κυάμῳ, μεγέθει μόνον καὶ
γεύσει διαλλάττοντα. οἱ οὖν κυαμῶνες ἡδεῖαν
ὄψιν παρέχουσι καὶ τέρψιν τοῖς ἐνευωχεῖσθαι
βουλομένοις· εὐωχοῦνται δ' ἐν σκάφαις θαλαμη-
γοῖς, ἐνδύνοντες εἰς τὸ πύκνωμα τῶν κυάμων καὶ
C 800 σκιαζόμενοι τοῖς φύλλοις· ἔστι γὰρ σφόδρα
μεγάλα, ὥστε καὶ ἀντὶ ποτηρίων καὶ τρυβλίων
χρῆσθαι· ἔχει γάρ τινα καὶ κοιλότητα ἐπιτηδείαν
πρὸς τοῦτο· καὶ δὴ καὶ ἡ Ἀλεξάνδρεια μεστὴ
τούτων ἐστὶ κατὰ τὰ ἐργαστήρια, ὡς σκεύεσι
χρωμένων· καὶ οἱ ἀγροὶ μίαν τινὰ τῶν προσόδων
καὶ ταύτην ἔχουσι τὴν ἀπὸ τῶν φύλλων. ὁ μὲν
δὴ κύαμος τοιοῦτος· ἡ δὲ βύβλος ἐνταῦθα μὲν οὐ
πολλὴ φύεται (οὐ γὰρ ἀσκεῖται), ἐν δὲ τοῖς
κάτω μέρεσι τοῦ Δέλτα πολλή, ἡ μὲν χείρων,

---

[1] Μαραιώτην CDEλ, Μαρεῶτιν Fmoxz.

---

[1] *i. e.* drawn off from the lees, not merely once or twice, for
early consumption, but time and again, with a view to ageing it into old wine of superior quality. The special name

breadth of more than one hundred and fifty stadia and a length of less than three hundred. It contains eight islands; and all the shores round it are well inhabited; and the vintages in this region are so good that the Mareotic wine is racked off with a view to ageing it.[1]

15. The byblus[2] grows in the Aegyptian marshes and lakes, as also the Aegyptian cyamus,[3] from which comes the ciborium;[4] and they have stalks approximately equal in height, about ten feet. But whereas the byblus is a bare stock with a tuft on top, the cyamus produces leaves and flowers in many parts, and also a fruit like our cyamus, differing only in size and taste. Accordingly, the bean-fields afford a pleasing sight, and also enjoyment to those who wish to hold feasts therein. They hold feasts in cabin-boats, in which they enter the thick of the cyami and the shade of the leaves; for the leaves are so very large that they are used both for drinking-cups and for bowls, for these even have a kind of concavity suited to this purpose; and in fact Alexandria is full of these in the work-shops, where they are used as vessels; and the farms have also this as one source of their revenues—I mean the revenue from the leaves. Such, then, is the cyamus. As for the byblus, it does not grow in large quantities here (for it is not cultivated), but it grows in large quantities in the lower parts of the Delta, one kind

---

" Mareotic" indicates both the quality and the wide use of this wine.

[2] The Aegyptian papyrus.

[3] *i.e.* "bean."

[4] *i.e.* the "seed-vessel," of which drinking-cups were made (cp. Horace, *Carmina* 2. 7. 22).

ἡ δὲ βελτίων, ἡ ἱερατική· κἀνταῦθα δέ τινες τῶν
τὰς προσόδους ἐπεκτείνειν βουλομένων μετήνεγκαν
τὴν Ἰουδαϊκὴν ἐντρέχειαν,[1] ἣν ἐκεῖνοι παρεῦρον
ἐπὶ τοῦ φοίνικος (καὶ μάλιστα τοῦ καρυωτοῦ) καὶ
τοῦ βαλσάμου· οὐ γὰρ ἐῶσι πολλαχοῦ φύεσθαι,
τῇ δὲ σπάνει τιμὴν ἐπιτιθέντες τὴν πρόσοδον
οὕτως[2] αὔξουσι, τὴν δὲ κοινὴν χρείαν διαλυ-
μαίνονται.

16. Ἐν δεξιᾷ δὲ τῆς Κανωβικῆς πύλης ἐξιόντι
ἡ διῶρυξ ἐστιν ἡ ἐπὶ Κάνωβον συνάπτουσα τῇ
λίμνῃ· ταύτῃ δὲ καὶ ἐπὶ Σχεδίαν ὁ πλοῦς ἐπὶ τὸν
μέγαν ποταμὸν καὶ ἐπὶ τὸν Κάνωβον, πρῶτον δὲ
ἐπὶ τὴν Ἐλευσῖνα· ἔστι δ' αὕτη κατοικία πλησίον
τῆς τε Ἀλεξανδρείας καὶ τῆς Νικοπόλεως ἐπ'
αὐτῇ τῇ Κανωβικῇ διώρυγι κειμένη, διαίτας
ἔχουσα καὶ ἀπόψεις τοῖς καπυρίζειν βουλομένοις
καὶ ἀνδράσι καὶ γυναιξίν, ἀρχή τις Κανωβισμοῦ
καὶ τῆς ἐκεῖ λαμυρίας. ἀπὸ δὲ τῆς Ἐλευσῖνος
προελθοῦσι μικρὸν ἐν δεξιᾷ ἐστιν ἡ διῶρυξ ἀνά-

---

[1] For ἐντρέχειαν, Cobet conj. κακεντρέχειαν, citing 7. 3. 7.
[2] ὄντως CDFhnsx ; αὐτοῖς, Corais.

---

[1] i.e. the kind " devoted to sacred purposes." The superior
quality consisted of the middle and broadest (about 9½ inches)
strips of the plant ; but though originally called Hieratica,
it was later called Augusta in honour of Augustus (see
Encyclopædia Britannica, s. v. " Papyrus.")
[2] Dr. F. Zucker (Philologus 70, N.F. 24, 1911, pp. 79–105)
shows that the Romans established a government monopoly
of Aegyptian papyrus ; but his conclusion that under the
Ptolemies there was no such monopoly and that Strabo's
words, " some of those who wished to enhance the revenues,
etc.," mean that " a number of large proprietors misused their
power, and through limiting the cultivation to their own

being inferior, and the other superior, that is, the Hieratica.[1] And here, too, certain of those who wished to enhance the revenues adopted the shrewd practice of the Judaeans, which the latter had invented in the case of the palm tree (particularly the caryotic palm) and the balsam tree; for they do not allow the byblus to grow in many places, and because of the scarcity they set a higher price on it and thus increase the revenues, though they injure the common use of the plant.[2]

16. On the right of the Canobic Gate, as one goes out, one comes to the canal which is connected with the lake and leads to Canobus;[3] and it is by this canal that one sails, not only to Schedia, that is, to the great river, but also to Canobus, though first to Eleusis. Eleusis is a settlement near both Alexandria and Nicopolis, is situated on the Canobic canal itself, and has lodging-places and commanding views for those who wish to engage in revelry, both men and women, and is a beginning, as it were, of the "Canobic" life[4] and the shamelessness there current. On proceeding a slight distance from Eleusis, and on the right, one

advantage and to the injury of the public produced a rise in the price of papyrus," is vigorously opposed by Professor J. P. Mahaffy (*Hermathena*, 16, 1911, pp. 237–41), who rightly understands Strabo to refer to "certain chancellors of the exchequer (διοικηταί) who had to meet a sudden demand by raising money as best they could." However, in a later article (*Philologus* 74, N. F. 28, pp. 184–85) Zucker retracts his former interpretation of the passage, accepting Mahaffy's. See also Wilcken, *Papyruskunde, Grundzüge* I, 1, pp. 255–56.

[3] *i.e.* "connected" indirectly, by a short tributary southwest of the city.

[4] *i.e.* the luxurious life at Canobus, which was proverbial.

γουσα ἐπὶ τὴν Σχεδίαν. διέχει δὲ τετράσχοινον
τῆς Ἀλεξανδρείας ἡ Σχεδία, κατοικία πόλεως,
ἐν ᾗ τὸ ναύσταθμον τῶν θαλαμηγῶν πλοίων, ἐφ᾽
οἷς οἱ ἡγεμόνες εἰς τὴν ἄνω χώραν ἀναπλέουσιν·
ἐνταῦθα δὲ καὶ τὸ τελώνιον τῶν ἄνωθεν καταγομένων καὶ ἀναγομένων· οὗ χάριν καὶ σχεδία
ἔζευκται ἐπὶ τῷ ποταμῷ, ἀφ᾽ ἧς καὶ τοὔνομα τῷ
τόπῳ. μετὰ δὲ τὴν διώρυγα τὴν ἐπὶ Σχεδίαν
ἄγουσαν ὁ ἑξῆς ἐπὶ τὸν Κάνωβον πλοῦς ἐστι
παράλληλος τῇ παραλίᾳ τῇ ἀπὸ Φάρου μέχρι
τοῦ Κανωβικοῦ στόματος· στενὴ γάρ τις ταινία
μεταξὺ διήκει τοῦ τε πελάγους καὶ τῆς διώρυγος,
ἐν ᾗ ἐστιν ἥ τε μικρὰ Ταπόσειρις μετὰ τὴν Νικό-
πολιν καὶ τὸ Ζεφύριον, ἄκρα ναΐσκον ἔχουσα
Ἀρσινόης Ἀφροδίτης· τὸ δὲ παλαιὸν καὶ Θῶνίν
τινα πόλιν ἐνταῦθά φασιν, ἐπώνυμον τοῦ
βασιλέως τοῦ δεξαμένου Μενέλαόν τε καὶ Ἑλένην
ξενίᾳ. περὶ οὖν τῶν τῆς Ἑλένης φαρμάκων
C 801 φησὶν οὕτως ὁ ποιητής·

ἐσθλά, τά οἱ Πολύδαμνα πόρεν Θῶνος παρά-
κοιτις.

17. Κάνωβος δ᾽ ἐστὶ πόλις ἐν εἴκοσι καὶ ἑκατὸν
σταδίοις ἀπὸ Ἀλεξανδρείας πεζῇ ἰοῦσιν, ἐπώνυμος
Κανώβου τοῦ Μενελάου κυβερνήτου, ἀποθανόντος
αὐτόθι, ἔχουσα τὸ τοῦ Σαράπιδος ἱερὸν πολλῇ
ἁγιστείᾳ τιμώμενον καὶ θεραπείας ἐκφέρον, ὥστε
καὶ τοὺς ἐλλογιμωτάτους ἄνδρας πιστεύειν καὶ

---

[1] See § 24 below.
[2] i.e. "raft" or "pontoon bridge."
[3] Thonis was situated at the Canobic mouth of the Nile,
and in early times was the emporium of Aegypt (Diodorus

comes to the canal which leads up to Schedia. Schedia is four schoeni [1] distant from Alexandria; it is a settlement of the city, and contains the station of the cabin-boats on which the praefects sail to Upper Aegypt. And at Schedia is also the station for paying duty on the goods brought down from above it and brought up from below it; and for this purpose, also, a schedia [2] has been laid across the river, from which the place has its name. After the canal which leads to Schedia, one's next voyage, to Canobus, is parallel to that part of the coast-line which extends from Pharos to the Canobic mouth; for a narrow ribbon-like strip of land extends between the sea and the canal, and on this, after Nicopolis, lies the Little Taposeiris, as also the Zephyrium, a promontory which contains a shrine of Aphroditê Arsinoê. In ancient times, it is said, there was also a city called Thonis here,[3] which was named after the king who received Menelaüs and Helen with hospitality. At any rate, the poet speaks of Helen's drugs as follows: "goodly drugs which Polydamna, the wife of Thon, had given her." [4]

17. Canobus is a city situated at a distance of one hundred and twenty stadia from Alexandria, if one goes on foot, and was named after Canobus, the pilot of Menelaüs, who died there. It contains the temple of Sarapis, which is honoured with great reverence and effects such cures that even the most reputable men believe in it and sleep in it—them-

Siculus 1. 19); and King Thon was the warden of the Canobic mouth in the time of the Trojan war (Herodotus 1. 113).
    [4] *Odyssey* 4. 228.

ἐγκοιμᾶσθαι αὐτοὺς ὑπὲρ ἑαυτῶν ἢ ἑτέρους·
συγγράφουσι δέ τινες καὶ τὰς θεραπείας, ἄλλοι
δὲ ἀρετὰς τῶν ἐνταῦθα λογίων.[1] ἀντὶ πάντων
δ᾽ ἐστίν ὁ τῶν πανηγυριστῶν ὄχλος τῶν ἐκ τῆς
Ἀλεξανδρείας κατιόντων τῇ διώρυγι· πᾶσα γὰρ
ἡμέρα καὶ πᾶσα νὺξ πληθύει τῶν μὲν[2] ἐν τοῖς
πλοιαρίοις καταυλουμένων καὶ κατορχουμένων
ἀνέδην[3] μετὰ τῆς ἐσχάτης ἀκολασίας, καὶ ἀνδρῶν
καὶ γυναικῶν, τῶν δ᾽ ἐν αὐτῷ τῷ Κανώβῳ καταγωγὰς ἐχόντων, ἐπικειμένας τῇ διώρυγι εὐφυεῖς
πρὸς τὴν τοιαύτην ἄνεσιν καὶ εὐωχίαν.

18. Μετὰ δὲ τὸν Κάνωβόν ἐστι τὸ Ἡράκλειον[4]
Ἡρακλέους ἔχον ἱερόν· εἶτα τὸ Κανωβικὸν στόμα
καὶ ἡ ἀρχὴ τοῦ Δέλτα. τὰ δ᾽ ἐν δεξιᾷ τῆς
Κανωβικῆς διώρυγος ὁ Μενελαΐτης ἐστὶ νομὸς
ἀπὸ τοῦ ἀδελφοῦ τοῦ πρώτου Πτολεμαίου καλούμενος, οὐ μὰ Δία ἀπὸ[5] τοῦ ἥρωος, ὡς ἔνιοί φασιν,
ὧν καὶ Ἀρτεμίδωρος. μετὰ δὲ τὸ Κανωβικὸν
στόμα ἐστὶ τὸ Βολβίτινον, εἶτα τὸ Σεβεννυτικὸν,
καὶ τὸ Φατνιτικόν, τρίτον ὑπάρχον τῷ μεγέθει
παρὰ τὰ πρῶτα δύο, οἷς ὥρισται τὸ Δέλτα· καὶ
γὰρ οὐ[6] πόρρω τῆς κορυφῆς σχίζεται εἰς τὸ ἐντὸς
τοῦ Δέλτα. τῷ δὲ Φατνιτικῷ συνάπτει τὸ
Μενδήσιον, εἶτα τὸ Τανιτικὸν καὶ τελευταῖον τὸ
Πηλουσιακόν. ἔστι δὲ καὶ ἄλλα τούτων μεταξύ,
ὡς ἂν ψευδοστόματα, ἀσημότερα· ἔχει μὲν οὖν

---

[1] ἀρεταλογίων CDFh, ἀρετολογίων x, τερατολογίων i.
[2] μέν, Corais inserts.
[3] ἀνέδην h, and second hand in D ; ἀναίδην other MSS.
[4] τό, after Ἡράκλειον Ex omit.
[5] ἀπό EF, ὑπό other MSS.
[6] οὐ F, οὐδέ other MSS.

selves on their own behalf or others for them.[1]
Some writers go on to record the cures, and others
the virtues of the oracles there. But to balance
all this is the crowd of revellers who go down from
Alexandria by the canal to the public festivals; for
every day and every night is crowded with people
on the boats who play the flute and dance without
restraint and with extreme licentiousness, both men
and women, and also with the people of Canobus
itself, who have resorts situated close to the canal
and adapted to relaxation and merry-making of this
kind.

18. After Canobus one comes to the Heracleium,
which contains a temple of Heracles; and then to
the Canobic mouth and the beginning of the Delta.
The parts on the right of the Canobic canal are the
Menelaïte Nome, so called from the brother of the
first Ptolemy [2]—not, by heaven, from the hero, as
some writers say, among whom is also Artemidorus.
After the Canobic mouth one comes to the Bolbitine
mouth, and then to the Sebennytic, and to the
Phatnitic, which is third in size as compared with
the first two,[3] which form the boundaries of the
Delta; for not far from the vertex of the Delta the
Phatnitic splits, sending a branch into the interior
of the Delta. Lying close to the Phatnitic mouth
is the Mendesian; and then one comes to the
Tanitic, and, last of all, to the Pelusiac. There
are also others in among these, pseudo-mouths as
it were, which are rather insignificant. Their mouths

[1] Even Moses advocated this practice (16. 2. 35).
[2] On this Menelaüs see Diodorus Siculus (20. 21–53) and
Plutarch (*Demetrius* 15–17).
[3] The Canobic and Pelusiac.

εἰσαγωγὰς τὰ στόματα, ἀλλ' οὐκ εὐφυεῖς οὐδὲ μεγάλοις πλοίοις, ἀλλ' ὑπηρετικοῖς διὰ τὸ βραχέα εἶναι καὶ ἑλώδη. μάλιστα μέντοι τῷ Κανωβικῷ στόματι ἐχρῶντο ὡς ἐμπορίῳ, τῶν κατ' Ἀλεξάνδρειαν λιμένων ἀποκεκλεισμένων,[1] ὡς προείπομεν. Μετὰ δὲ τὸ Βολβίτινον στόμα ἐπὶ πλέον ἔκκειται ταπεινὴ καὶ ἀμμώδης ἄκρα· καλεῖται δὲ Ἄγνου κέρας· εἶθ' ἡ Περσέως σκοπὴ καὶ τὸ Μιλησίων τεῖχος· πλεύσαντες γὰρ ἐπὶ Ψαμμιτίχου τριάκοντα ναυσὶ Μιλήσιοι (κατὰ Κυαξάρη δ' οὗτος ἦν τὸν Μῆδον) κατέσχον εἰς τὸ στόμα τὸ Βολβίτινον, εἶτ' ἐκβάντες ἐτείχισαν τὸ λεχθὲν κτίσμα· χρόνῳ δ' ἀναπλεύσαντες εἰς τὸν Σαϊτικὸν νομὸν καταναυμαχήσαντες Ἰνάρων πόλιν
C 802 ἔκτισαν Ναύκρατιν οὐ πολὺ τῆς Σχεδίας ὕπερθεν. μετὰ δὲ τὸ τῶν Μιλησίων τεῖχος ἐπὶ τὸ Σεβεννυτικὸν προϊόντι[2] στόμα λίμναι εἰσίν, ὦν ἡ ἑτέρα Βουτικὴ καλεῖται ἀπὸ Βούτου πόλεως, καὶ ἡ Σεβεννυτικὴ δὲ πόλις καὶ ἡ Σάϊς, μητρόπολις τῆς κάτω χώρας, ἐν ᾗ τιμῶσι τὴν Ἀθηνᾶν· ἐν δὲ τῷ ἱερῷ αὐτῆς ἡ θήκη κεῖται τοῦ Ψαμμιτίχου. περὶ δὲ τὴν Βοῦτον καὶ Ἑρμοῦ πόλις ἐν νήσῳ κειμένη· ἐν δὲ τῇ Βούτῳ Λητοῦς ἐστι μαντεῖον.

19. Ἐν δὲ τῇ μεσογείῳ τῇ ὑπὲρ τοῦ Σεβεννυτικοῦ καὶ Φατνιτικοῦ στόματος Ξόις ἐστὶ καὶ νῆσος καὶ πόλις ἐν τῷ Σεβεννυτικῷ νομῷ. ἔστι

---

[1] ἀποκεκλειμένων D, ἀποκεκλιμένων other MSS.
[2] προϊόντι E, προσιόντι other MSS.

---

[1] i.e. to foreign imports (§ 6 above).
[2] Meaning "Willow-Horn," apparently.

indeed afford entrance to boats, but are adapted, not to large boats, but to tenders only, because the mouths are shallow and marshy. It is chiefly, however, the Canobic mouth that they used as an emporium, since the harbours at Alexandria were kept closed,[1] as I have said before. After the Bolbitine mouth one comes to a low and sandy promontory which projects rather far into the sea; it is called Agnu-Ceras.[2] And then to the Watch-tower of Perseus[3] and the Wall of the Milesians; for in the time of Psammitichus (who lived in the time of Cyaxares the Mede) the Milesians, with thirty ships, put in at the Bolbitine mouth, and then, disembarking, fortified with a wall the above-mentioned settlement; but in time they sailed up into the Saïtic Nome, defeated the city Inaros in a naval fight, and founded Naucratis, not far above Schedia. After the Wall of the Milesians, as one proceeds towards the Sebennytic mouth, one comes to two lakes, one of which, Buticê, has its name from the city Butus, and also to the Sebennytic city, and to Saïs, the metropolis of the lower country, in which Athena is worshipped; and in her temple lies the tomb of Psammitichus. In the neighbourhood of Butus is also an Hermupolis,[4] which is situated on an island; and in Butus there is an oracle of Leto.[5]

19. In the interior above the Sebennytic and Phatnitic mouths lies Xoïs, both an island and a city, in the Sebennytic Nome. Here, also, are an

---

[3] Herodotus (2. 15) appears to place the watch-tower at the Canobic mouth.

[4] "City of Hermes."

[5] On Leto's shrine and oracle in Butus, see Herodotus 2. 155.

δὲ καὶ Ἑρμοῦ πόλις καὶ Λύκου πόλις καὶ Μένδης,
ὅπου τὸν Πᾶνα τιμῶσι καὶ τῶν ζῴων τράγον·
ὡς δὲ Πίνδαρός φησιν, οἱ τράγοι ἐνταῦθα γυναιξὶ
μίγνυνται·

> Μένδητα παρὰ κρημνὸν θαλάσσης,
> ἔσχατον Νείλου κέρας, αἰγιβάται
> ὅθι τράγοι γυναιξὶ μίσγονται.[1]

πλησίον δὲ Μένδητος καὶ Διὸς πόλις καὶ αἱ περὶ
αὐτὴν λίμναι καὶ Λεοντόπολις· εἶτ᾽ ἀπωτέρω ἡ
Βούσιρις πόλις ἐν τῷ Βουσιρίτῃ νομῷ καὶ Κυνὸς
πόλις. φησὶ δ᾽ Ἐρατοσθένης κοινὸν μὲν εἶναι
τοῖς βαρβάροις πᾶσιν ἔθος τὴν ξενηλασίαν, τοὺς
δ᾽ Αἰγυπτίους ἐλέγχεσθαι διὰ τῶν περὶ τὸν
Βούσιριν μεμυθευμένων ἐν τῷ Βουσιρίτῃ νομῷ,
διαβάλλειν τὴν ἀξενίαν βουλομένων τοῦ τόπου
τούτου τῶν ὕστερον, οὐ βασιλέως, μὰ Δία, οὐδὲ
τυράννου γενομένου τινὸς Βουσίριδος· προσεπι-
φημισθῆναι δὲ καὶ τὸ

> Αἴγυπτόνδ᾽ ἰέναι δολιχὴν ὁδὸν ἀργαλέην τε,

προσλαμβάνοντος πρὸς τοῦτο πάμπολυ καὶ τοῦ
ἀλιμένου καὶ τοῦ μηδὲ τὸν ὄντα λιμένα ἀνεῖσθαι
τὸν πρὸς τῇ Φάρῳ, φρουρεῖσθαι δ᾽ ὑπὸ βουκόλων
λῃστῶν ἐπιτιθεμένων τοῖς προσορμιζομένοις·
Καρχηδονίους δὲ καταποντοῦν, εἴ τις τῶν ξένων
εἰς Σαρδὼ παραπλεύσειεν ἢ ἐπὶ Στήλας· διὰ δὲ

[1] The words Μένδητα . . . μίσγονται are not found in EF.
Kramer and later editors reject them.

---

[1] "City of Lycus."   [2] Frag. 201 (215), Schroeder.
[3] So Herodotus (2. 46), who also says that "In the
Aegyptian language both the he-goat and Pan are called
'Mendes.'"

Hermupolis and a Lycupolis,[1] and Mendes, at which place they worship Pan and, among animals, a he-goat; and, as Pindar[2] says, the he-goats have intercourse with women there:[3] "Mendes, along the crag of the sea, farthermost horn of the Nile, where the goat-mounting he-goats have intercourse with women." Near Mendes lie also a Diospolis[4] and the lakes in its neighbourhood and Leontopolis;[5] and then, at a greater distance, the city Busiris in the Busirite Nome, and Cynospolis.[6] According to Eratosthenes, the expulsion of foreigners is a custom common to all barbarians, and yet the Aegyptians are condemned for this fault because of the myths which have been circulated about Busiris in connection with the Busirite Nome,[7] since the later writers wish falsely to malign the inhospitality of this place, although, by heavens, no king or tyrant named Busiris ever existed; and, he says, the poet's words are also constantly cited—"to go to Aegypt, long and painful journey"—the want of harbours contributing very much to this opinion, as also the fact that even the harbour which Aegypt did have, the one at Pharos, gave no access, but was guarded by shepherds who were pirates and who attacked those who tried to bring ships to anchor there; and the Carthaginians likewise, he adds, used to drown in the sea any foreigners who sailed past their country to Sardo[8] or to the Pillars, and

---

[4] "City of Zeus."   [5] "Lion City."

[6] "Dog's City."

[7] The mythical king Busiris sacrificed all foreigners who entered Aegypt, but at last was slain by Heracles (Apollodorus 2. 5. 11).

[8] Sardinia.

ταῦτ᾽ ἀπιστεῖσθαι τὰ πολλὰ τῶν ἑσπερίων· καὶ τοὺς Πέρσας δὲ κακῶς ἡγεῖσθαι τοῖς πρέσβεσι τὰς ὁδοὺς κύκλῳ καὶ διὰ δυσκόλων.

20. Συνάπτει δὲ καὶ ὁ Ἀθριβίτης νομὸς καὶ Ἀθριβις πόλις καὶ ἔτι ὁ Προσωπίτης νομός, ἐν ᾧ Ἀφροδίτης πόλις. ὑπὲρ δὲ τὸ Μενδήσιον στόμα καὶ τὸ Τανιτικὸν λίμνη μεγάλη καὶ ὁ Μενδήσιός ἐστι νομὸς καὶ ὁ Λεοντοπολίτης καὶ πόλις Ἀφροδίτης καὶ ὁ Φαρβητίτης νομός· εἶτα τὸ Τανιτικὸν στόμα, ὅ τινες Σαϊτικὸν λέγουσι, καὶ ὁ Τανίτης νομὸς καὶ πόλις ἐν αὐτῷ μεγάλη Τάνις.

21. Μεταξὺ δὲ τοῦ Τανιτικοῦ καὶ τοῦ Πηλουσιακοῦ λίμναι καὶ ἕλη μεγάλα καὶ συνεχῆ κώμας πολλὰς ἔχοντα· καὶ αὐτὸ δὲ τὸ Πηλούσιον κύκλῳ περικείμενα ἔχει ἕλη, ἅ τινες Βάραθρα καλοῦσι, καὶ τέλματα· ᾤκισται δ᾽ ἀπὸ θαλάττης ἐν πλείοσιν ἢ εἴκοσι σταδίοις, τὸν δὲ κύκλον ἔχει τοῦ τείχους σταδίων εἴκοσιν· ὠνόμασται δ᾽ ἀπὸ τοῦ πηλοῦ καὶ τῶν τελμάτων. ταύτῃ δὲ καὶ δυσείσβολός ἐστιν ἡ Αἴγυπτος ἐκ τῶν ἑωθινῶν τόπων τῶν κατὰ Φοινίκην καὶ τὴν Ἰουδαίαν, καὶ ἐκ τῆς Ἀραβίας δὲ τῆς Ναβαταίων, ἥπερ ἐστὶ προσεχής· διὰ τούτων ἐπὶ τὴν Αἴγυπτον ἡ ὁδός. ἡ δὲ μεταξὺ τοῦ Νείλου καὶ τοῦ Ἀραβίου κόλπου Ἀραβία μέν ἐστι, καὶ ἐπί γε τῶν ἄκρων αὐτῆς ἵδρυται τὸ Πηλούσιον, ἀλλ᾽ ἔρημος ἅπασά ἐστι καὶ ἄβατος στρατοπέδῳ. ὁ δὲ μεταξὺ ἰσθμὸς Πηλουσίου καὶ τοῦ μυχοῦ τοῦ καθ᾽ Ἡρώων πόλιν χιλίων[1] μέν ἐστι σταδίων, ὡς δὲ Ποσειδωνιός

C 803

---

[1] χιλίων (as in 1. 2. 29 and Herodotus 2. 158, 4 11), Epitome and editors, for ἐννακοσίωι.

it is for this reason that most of the stories told
about the west are disbelieved; and also the
Persians, he says, would treacherously guide the
ambassadors over roundabout roads and through
difficult regions.

20. Bordering on this Nome is the Athribite Nome
and the city Athribis, and also the Prosopite Nome,
in which is a City of Aphroditê. Above the Mendesian and Tanitic mouths lie a large lake and the
Mendesian and Leontopolite Nomes and a City of
Aphroditê and the Pharbetite Nome; and then one
comes to the Tanitic mouth, which some call Saïtic,
and to the Tanite Nome, and to Tanis, a large city
therein.

21. Between the Tanitic and Pelusiac mouths lie
lakes, and large and continuous marshes which contain many villages. Pelusium itself also has marshes
lying all round it, which by some are called Barathra,[1]
and muddy ponds; its settlement lies at a distance of
more than twenty stadia from the sea, the wall has
a circuit of twenty stadia, and it has its name from
the *pelos*[2] and the muddy ponds. Here, too, Aegypt
is difficult to enter, I mean from the eastern regions
about Phoenicia and Judaea, and from the Arabia of
the Nabataeans, which is next to Aegypt; these are
the regions which the road to Aegypt traverses. The
country between the Nile and the Arabian Gulf is
Arabia, and at its extremity is situated Pelusium;
but the whole of it is desert, and impassable for an
army. The isthmus between Pelusium and the recess
of the gulf at Heroönpolis[3] is one thousand stadia,
but, according to Poseidonius, less than one thousand

---

[1] "Pits."   [2] *i.e.* "mud."
[3] "City of Heroes."

φησιν, ἐλαττόνων ἢ χιλίων καὶ πεντακοσίων·
πρὸς δὲ τῷ ἄνυδρος εἶναι καὶ ἀμμώδης ἑρπετῶν
πλῆθος ἔχει τῶν ἀμμοδυτῶν.

22. Ἀπὸ δὲ Σχεδίας ἀναπλέουσιν ἐπὶ Μέμφιν
ἐν δεξιᾷ μέν εἰσι πάμπολλαι κῶμαι μέχρι τῆς
Μαρείας¹ λίμνης, ὧν ἐστι καὶ ἡ Χαβρίου κώμη
καλουμένη· ἐπὶ δὲ τῷ ποταμῷ Ἑρμοῦ πόλις ἐστίν·
εἶτα Γυναικῶν πόλις καὶ νομὸς Γυναικοπολίτης·
ἐφεξῆς δὲ Μώμεμφις καὶ Μωμεμφίτης νομός·
μεταξὺ δὲ διώρυγες πλείους εἰς τὴν Μαρεῶτιν.
οἱ δὲ Μωμεμφῖται τὴν Ἀφροδίτην τιμῶσι, καὶ
τρέφεται θήλεια βοῦς ἱερά, καθάπερ ἐν Μέμφει
ὁ Ἆπις, ἐν Ἡλίου δὲ πόλει ὁ Μνεῦις· οὗτοι μὲν
οὖν θεοὶ νομίζονται, οἱ δὲ παρὰ τοῖς ἄλλοις (παρὰ
πολλοῖς γὰρ δὴ ἔν τε τῷ Δέλτα καὶ ἔξω αὐτοῦ
τοῖς μὲν ἄρρην, τοῖς δὲ θήλεια τρέφεται), οὗτοι δὲ
θεοὶ μὲν οὐ νομίζονται, ἱεροὶ δέ.

23. Ὑπὲρ δὲ Μωμέμφεώς εἰσι δύο νιτρίαι
πλεῖστον νίτρον ἔχουσαι καὶ νομὸς Νιτριώ-
της. τιμᾶται δ' ἐνταῦθα ὁ Σάραπις καὶ παρὰ
μόνοις τούτοις θύεται ἐν Αἰγύπτῳ πρόβατον·
πλησίον δὲ καὶ ἐνταῦθα πόλις Μενέλαος, ἐν
ἀριστερᾷ δὲ ἐν τῷ Δέλτα ἐπὶ μὲν τῷ ποταμῷ
Ναύκρατις, ἀπὸ δὲ τοῦ ποταμοῦ δίσχοινον διέχουσα ἡ Σάϊς· καὶ μικρὸν ταύτης ὕπερθε τὸ τοῦ
Ὀσίριδος ἄσυλον, ἐν ᾧ κεῖσθαι τὸν Ὄσιρίν
φασιν. ἀμφισβητοῦσι δὲ τούτου πολλοί, καὶ
μάλιστα οἱ τὰς Φιλὰς οἰκοῦντες τὰς ὑπὲρ Συήνης

¹ Μαρείας E, Σαμαρείας Dh, Σαμαρίας CF, Μαρίας moswxz.

---

¹ "City of Women."
² "City of the Sun."

five hundred; and in addition to its being waterless
and sandy, it contains a multitude of reptiles, the
sand-burrowers.

22. From Schedia, as one sails towards Memphis,
there are, on the right, a very large number of
villages, extending as far as Lake Mareia, among
which is the Village of Chabrias, as it is called;
and, on the river, one comes to an Hermupolis, and
then to Gynaeconpolis[1] and the Gynaeconpolite
Nome, and, next in order, to Momemphis and the
Momemphite Nome; but in the interval there are
several canals which empty into Lake Mareotis. The
Momemphitae honour Aphroditê; and a sacred cow
is kept there, as is Apis in Memphis and Mneuïs
in Heliupolis.[2] Now these animals are regarded as
gods, but those in the other places (for in many
places, indeed, both in the Delta and outside of it,
either a bull or cow is kept)—those others, I say,
are not regarded as gods, though they are held
sacred.

23. Above Momemphis are two nitre-beds, which
contain very large quantities of nitre,[3] and the
Nitriote Nome. Here Sarapis is held in honour;
and they are the only people in Aegypt who sacrifice
a sheep. Near by, and in this Nome, is a city
Menelaüs; and on the left, in the Delta, lies
Naucratis, which is on the river, whereas Saïs lies
at a distance of two schoeni from the river. A little
above Saïs is the asylum of Osiris, in which the body
of Osiris is said to lie; but many lay claim to this,
and particularly the inhabitants of the Philae which

---

[3] The ancients meant by "nitre" native sodium carbonate,
not potassium nitrate (saltpetre), the present meaning. Pliny
(31. 6) mentions the various kinds and their uses.

καὶ τῆς Ἐλεφαντίνης. μυθεύουσι γὰρ δή, διότι
ἡ Ἶσις κατὰ πολλοὺς τόπους κατὰ γῆς θείη
σοροὺς τοῦ Ὀσίριδος (μία δὲ τούτων ἦν ἔχουσα
τὸν Ὄσιριν, ἀφανὴς πᾶσι), τοῦτο δὲ πράξειε
λαθεῖν βουλομένη τὸν Τυφῶνα, μὴ ἐπελθὼν
ἐκρίψειε τὸ σῶμα τῆς θήκης.

24. Ἀπὸ μὲν δὴ τῆς Ἀλεξανδρείας ἐπὶ τὴν
τοῦ Δέλτα κορυφὴν αὕτη ἡ περιήγησις, φησὶ δ᾽ ὁ
Ἀρτεμίδωρος σχοίνων ὀκτὼ καὶ εἴκοσι τὸν ἀνά-
C 804 πλουν, τοῦτο δ᾽ εἶναι σταδίους ὀκτακοσίους
τετταράκοντα, λογιζόμενος τριακονταστάδιον τὴν
σχοῖνον· ἡμῖν μέντοι πλέουσιν ἄλλοτ᾽ ἄλλῳ
μέτρῳ χρώμενοι τῶν σχοίνων ἀπεδίδοσαν τὰ
διαστήματα, ὥστε καὶ τετταράκοντα σταδίους καὶ
ἔτι μείζους κατὰ τόπους ὁμολογεῖσθαι παρ᾽
αὐτῶν. καὶ διότι παρὰ τοῖς Αἰγυπτίοις ἄστατόν
ἐστι τὸ τῆς σχοίνου μέτρον, αὐτὸς ὁ Ἀρτεμίδωρος ἐν τοῖς ἑξῆς δηλοῖ. ἀπὸ μὲν γὰρ Μέμφεως
μέχρι Θηβαΐδος τὴν σχοῖνον ἑκάστην φησὶν εἶναι
σταδίων ἑκατὸν εἴκοσιν, ἀπὸ δὲ τῆς Θηβαΐδος
μέχρι Συήνης ἑξήκοντα, ἀπὸ δὲ Πηλουσίου πρὸς
τὴν αὐτὴν ἀναπλέουσι κορυφὴν σχοίνους μὲν
πέντε καὶ εἴκοσί φησι, σταδίους δὲ ἑπτακοσίους
πεντήκοντα, τῷ αὐτῷ μέτρῳ χρησάμενος. πρώτην
δ᾽ ἐκ τοῦ Πηλουσίου προελθοῦσιν εἶναι διώρυγα
τὴν πληροῦσαν τὰς κατὰ τὰ ἔλη καλουμένας
λίμνας, αἱ δύο μέν εἰσιν, ἐν ἀριστερᾷ δὲ κεῖνται
τοῦ μεγάλου ποταμοῦ ὑπὲρ τὸ Πηλούσιον ἐν τῇ
Ἀραβίᾳ· καὶ ἄλλας δὲ λέγει λίμνας καὶ διώρυγας

---

[1] So Diodorus Siculus (1. 22. 3).

is situated above Syenê and Elephantinê; [1] for they tell the mythical story, namely, that Isis [2] placed coffins of Osiris beneath the earth in several places (but only one of them, and that unknown to all, contained the body of Osiris), and that she did this because she wished to hide the body from Typhon, [3] fearing that he might find it and cast it out of its tomb.

24. Now this is the full description of the country from Alexandria to the vertex of the Delta; and, according to Artemidorus, the voyage up the river is twenty-eight schoeni, that is, eight hundred and forty stadia, reckoning the schoenus at thirty stadia. When I made the voyage, however, they used different measures at different times when they gave the distances, so that even forty stadia, or still more, was the accepted measure of the schoenus, according to the place. That the measure of the schoenus among the Aegyptians is unstable is made clear by Artemidorus himself in his next statement; for from Memphis to Thebaïs each schoenus, he says, is one hundred and twenty stadia, and from Thebaïs to Syenê sixty, and, as one sails up from Pelusium to the same vertex of the Delta, the distance, he says, is twenty-five schoeni, that is, seven hundred and fifty stadia, using the same measure. The first canal, as one proceeds from Pelusium, he says, is the one which fills the Marsh-lakes, as they are called, which are two in number and lie on the left of the great river above Pelusium in Arabia; and he also speaks of

[2] This goddess was both sister and wife of Osiris.
[3] Typhon came to be identified with the Aegyptian god " Set " (brother of Osiris and Isis), who murdered Osiris.

ἐν τοῖς αὐτοῖς μέρεσιν ἔξω τοῦ Δέλτα. ἔστι δὲ καὶ νομὸς Σεθρωίτης παρὰ τὴν ἑτέραν λίμνην· ἕνα δὲ τῶν δέκα τῶν ἐν τῷ Δέλτα διαριθμεῖται καὶ τοῦτον· εἰς δὲ τὰς αὐτὰς[1] λίμνας συμβάλλουσι καὶ ἄλλαι δύο διώρυγες.

25. Ἄλλη δ' ἐστὶν ἐκδιδοῦσα εἰς τὴν Ἐρυθρὰν καὶ τὸν Ἀράβιον κόλπον κατὰ[2] πόλιν Ἀρσινόην, ἣν ἔνιοι Κλεοπατρίδα καλοῦσι. διαρρεῖ δὲ καὶ διὰ τῶν πικρῶν καλουμένων λιμνῶν, αἳ πρότερον μὲν ἦσαν πικραί, τμηθείσης δὲ τῆς διώρυγος τῆς λεχθείσης μετεβάλοντο[3] τῇ κράσει τοῦ ποταμοῦ, καὶ νῦν εἰσιν εὔοψοι, μεσταὶ δὲ καὶ τῶν λιμναίων ὀρνέων. ἐτμήθη δὲ[4] ἡ διῶρυξ κατ' ἀρχὰς μὲν ὑπὸ Σεσώστριος πρὸ τῶν Τρωικῶν· οἱ δὲ ὑπὸ τοῦ Ψαμμιτίχου παιδός, ἀρξαμένου μόνον, εἶτ' ἐκλιπόντος τὸν βίον· ὕστερον δὲ ὑπὸ Δαρείου τοῦ πρώτου, διαδεξαμένου τὸ ἑξῆς ἔργον. καὶ οὗτος δὲ δόξῃ ψευδεῖ πεισθεὶς ἀφῆκε τὸ ἔργον περὶ συντέλειαν ἤδη· ἐπείσθη γὰρ μετεωροτέραν εἶναι τὴν Ἐρυθρὰν θάλατταν τῆς Αἰγύπτου καί, εἰ διακοπείη πᾶς ὁ μεταξὺ ἰσθμός, ἐπικλυσθήσεσθαι τῇ θαλάττῃ τὴν Αἴγυπτον· οἱ μέντοι Πτολεμαϊκοὶ βασιλεῖς διακόψαντες κλειστὸν ἐποίησαν τὸν εὔριπον, ὥστε, ὅτε βούλοιντο, ἐκπλεῖν ἀκωλύτως εἰς τὴν ἔξω θάλατταν καὶ εἰσπλεῖν πάλιν. εἴρηται

---

[1] τὰς αὐτάς Groskurd, for ταύτας τάς Ex, τοσαύτας other MSS. So Kramer and later editors.

[2] κατά, Brequigny, for καί; so the editors.

[3] μετεβαλοντο, x and the editors, for μετεβάλλοντο.

[4] Dhi insert καί before ἡ.

---

[1] The others are named in §§ 18–20 above. Pliny (5. 9) names still more.

other lakes and canals in the same regions outside the Delta. There is also the Sethroïte Nome by the second lake, although he counts this Nome too as one of the ten[1] in the Delta; and two other canals meet in the same lakes.

25. There is another canal which empties into the Red Sea and the Arabian Gulf near the city Arsinoê, a city which some call Cleopatris. It flows also through the Bitter Lakes, as they are called, which were indeed bitter in earlier times, but when the above-mentioned canal was cut they underwent a change because of the mixing with the river, and now are well supplied with fish and full also of aquatic birds. The canal was first cut by Sesostris before the Trojan War—though some say by the son of Psammitichus,[2] who only began the work and then died—and later by Dareius the First,[3] who succeeded to the next work done upon it. But he, too, having been persuaded by a false notion, abandoned the work when it was already near completion; for he was persuaded that the Red Sea was higher than Aegypt, and that if the intervening isthmus were cut all the way through, Aegypt would be inundated by the sea. The Ptolemaïc kings,[4] however, cut through it and made the strait a closed passage,[5] so that when they wished they could sail out without hindrance into the outer sea and sail in again. But I have

---

[2] *i.e.* by Necos (Diodorus Siculus 1. 33. 9), or Necho, who lost 120,000 men in the effort (Herodotus 2. 158).

[3] So Diodorus Siculus (**1.** 33. 9).

[4] "Ptolemy II" (Diodorus Siculus 1. 33. 11).

[5] "At the most advantageous place he built a cleverly contrived barrier" (Diodorus Siculus 1. 33. 11).

δὲ καὶ περὶ τῆς τῶν ὑδάτων ἐπιφανείας καὶ ἐν τοῖς πρώτοις ὑπομνήμασι.

26. Πλησίον δὲ τῆς Ἀρσινόης καὶ ἡ τῶν Ἡρώων ἐστὶ πόλις καὶ ἡ Κλεοπατρὶς ἐν τῷ μυχῷ τοῦ
C 805 Ἀραβίου κόλπου τῷ πρὸς Αἴγυπτον καὶ λιμένες καὶ κατοικίαι διώρυγές τε ¹ πλείους καὶ λίμναι πλησιά-ζουσαι τούτοις· ἐνταῦθα δ' ἐστὶ καὶ ὁ Φαγρωριο-πολίτης νομὸς καὶ πόλις Φαγρωριόπολις. ἡ δὲ ἀρχὴ τῆς διώρυγος τῆς ἐκδιδούσης εἰς τὴν Ἐρυθρὰν ἀπὸ κώμης ἄρχεται Φακούσσης, ᾗ συνεχής ἐστι καὶ ἡ Φίλωνος κώμη· πλάτος δ' ἔχει πηχῶν ἑκατὸν ἡ διῶρυξ, βάθος δ' ὅσον ἀρκεῖν μυριοφόρῳ νηΐ· οὗτοι δ' οἱ τόποι πλησιάζουσι τῇ κορυφῇ τοῦ Δέλτα.

27. Αὐτοῦ δὲ καὶ ἡ Βούβαστος πόλις καὶ ὁ Βουβαστίτης νομός· καὶ ὑπὲρ αὐτὸν ὁ Ἡλιο-πολίτης νομός. ἐνταῦθα δ' ἐστὶν ἡ τοῦ Ἡλίου πόλις ἐπὶ χώματος ἀξιολόγου κειμένη, τὸ ἱερὸν ἔχουσα τοῦ Ἡλίου καὶ τὸν βοῦν τὸν Μνεῦιν ἐν σηκῷ τινι τρεφόμενον, ὃς παρ' αὐτοῖς νενόμισται θεός, ὥσπερ καὶ ἐν Μέμφει ὁ Ἄπις. πρόκεινται δὲ τοῦ χώματος λίμναι, τὴν ἀνάχυσιν ἐκ τῆς πλησίον διώρυγος ἔχουσαι. νυνὶ μὲν οὖν ἐστι πανέρημος ἡ πόλις, τὸ ἱερὸν ἔχουσα τῷ Αἰγυπτίῳ τρόπῳ κατεσκευασμένον ἀρχαῖον, ἔχον πολλὰ τεκμήρια τῆς Καμβύσου μανίας καὶ ἱεροσυλίας, ὃς τὰ μὲν πυρί, τὰ δὲ σιδήρῳ διελωβᾶτο τῶν ἱερῶν, ἀκρωτηριάζων καὶ περικαίων, καθάπερ καὶ τοὺς ὀβελίσκους· ὧν δύο καὶ εἰς Ῥώμην ἐκο-μίσθησαν οἱ μὴ κεκακωμένοι τελέως, ἄλλοι δ' εἰσὶ κἀκεῖ καὶ ἐν Θήβαις, τῇ νῦν Διοσπόλει, οἱ μὲν ἑστῶτες ἀκμὴν πυρίβρωτοι, οἱ δὲ καὶ κείμενοι.

¹ τε, Corais, for δέ; so the later editors.

already discussed the levels of the bodies of water in my first commentaries.[1]

26. Near Arsinoê one comes also to Heroönpolis and Cleopatris, in the recess of the Arabian Gulf towards Aegypt, and to harbours and settlements, and near there, to several canals and lakes. Here, too, is the Phagroriopolite Nome and the city Phagroriopolis. The canal which empties into the Red Sea begins at Phacussa, a village, to which the Village of Philo is contiguous; the canal has a breadth of one hundred cubits and a depth sufficient for very large merchant-vessels; and these places are near the vertex of the Delta.

27. Here are both the city Bubastus and the Bubastite Nome; and above it is the Heliopolite Nome. In this Nome is Heliupolis, which is situated upon a noteworthy mound; it contains the temple of Helios, and the ox Mneuïs, which is kept in a kind of sanctuary and is regarded among the inhabitants as god, as is Apis in Memphis. In front of the mound are lakes, which receive the overflow from the neighbouring canal. The city is now entirely deserted; it contains the ancient temple constructed in the Aegyptian manner, which affords many evidences of the madness and sacrilege of Cambyses, who partly by fire and partly by iron sought to outrage the temples, mutilating them and burning them on every side, just as he did with the obelisks. Two of these, which were not completely spoiled, were brought to Rome, but others are either still there or at Thebes, the present Diospolis— some still standing, thoroughly eaten by the fire, and others lying on the ground.

[1] 1. 1. 20 and 1. 3. 8 ff.

28. Τῆς δὲ κατασκευῆς τῶν ἱερῶν ἡ διάθεσις τοιαύτη· κατὰ τὴν εἰσβολὴν τὴν εἰς τὸ τέμενος λιθόστρωτόν ἐστιν ἔδαφος, πλάτος μὲν ὅσον πλεθριαῖον ἢ καὶ ἔλαττον, μῆκος δὲ καὶ τριπλάσιον καὶ τετραπλάσιον, ἔστιν ὅπου καὶ μεῖζον· καλεῖται δὲ τοῦτο δρόμος, καθάπερ Καλλίμαχος εἴρηκεν·

ὁ δρομος ἱερὸς οὗτος Ἀνούβιδος.

διὰ δὲ τοῦ μήκους παντὸς ἑξῆς ἐφ’ ἑκάτερα τοῦ πλάτους σφίγγες ἵδρυνται λίθιναι, πήχει εἴκοσιν ἢ μικρῷ πλείους ἀπ’ ἀλλήλων διέχουσαι, ὥσθ’ ἕνα μὲν ἐκ δεξιῶν εἶναι στίχον τῶν σφιγγῶν, ἕνα δ’ ἐξ εὐωνύμων· μετὰ δὲ τὰς σφίγγας πρόπυλον μέγα, εἶτ’ ἄλλο προελθόντι πρόπυλον, εἶτ’ ἄλλο· οὐκ ἔστι δὲ διωρισμένος ἀριθμὸς οὔτε τῶν προπύλων οὔτε τῶν σφιγγῶν, ἄλλα δ’ ἐν ἄλλοις ἱεροῖς, ὥσπερ καὶ τὰ μήκη καὶ τὰ πλάτη τῶν δρόμων. μετὰ δὲ τὰ προπύλαια ὁ νεὼς πρόναον ἔχων μέγα καὶ ἀξιόλογον, τὸν δὲ σηκὸν σύμμετρον, ξόανον δ’ οὐδέν, ἢ οὐκ ἀνθρωπόμορφον, ἀλλὰ τῶν ἀλόγων ζῴων τινός· τοῦ δὲ προνάου παρ’ ἑκάτερον πρόκειται τὰ λεγόμενα[1] πτερά· ἔστι δὲ ταῦτα ἰσουψῆ τῷ νεῷ τείχη δύο, κατ’
C 806 ἀρχὰς μὲν ἀφεστῶτα ἀπ’ ἀλλήλων μικρὸν[2] πλέον ἢ τὸ πλάτος ἐστὶ τῆς κρηπῖδος τοῦ νεώ, ἔπειτ’ εἰς τὸ πρόσθεν προϊόντι κατ’ ἐπινευούσας[3] γραμ-

---

[1] Instead of λεγόμενα C reads μεγάλα. [2] μικρῷ Dz.
ἐπινευούσας, Corais and Groskurd emend to ἀπονενούσας.

---

[1] Strabo means the Aegyptian temples in general.
[2] A sketch of the plan may be found in Tozer's *Selections*, p. 356 ; but cp. the sketch of the pronaos in the Corais-Latronne edition.

28. The plan of the construction of the temples [1] is as follows: [2] at the entrance into the sacred precinct there is a floor paved with stones, with a breadth of about a plethrum, or less, and a length either three or four times as great, or in some cases more; and this is called the dromus,[3] as Callimachus states: "This is the dromus, sacred to Anubis." [4] Throughout its whole length are stone sphinxes placed in order on each of its two sides, at a distance from one another of twenty cubits or a little more, so that one row of the sphinxes is on the right and one row on the left. And after the sphinxes one comes to a large propylum,[5] and then, as one proceeds, another, and then another; but there is no prescribed number either of propyla or of sphinxes, and they are different in different temples, as are also the lengths and the breadths of the dromi. After the propylaea one comes to the naos,[6] which has a large and noteworthy pronaos,[7] and to a sanctuary of commensurate size, though it has no statue, or rather no statue of human form, but only of some irrational animal. On either side of the pronaos project the wings, as they are called. These are two walls equal in height to the naos, which are at first distant from one another a little more than the breadth of the foundation of the naos, and then, as one proceeds onward, follow

[3] Literally, "course" or "run."
[4] The Aegyptian Anpu, worshipped as "Lord of the Grave."
[5] Literally, "Front Gate"; but, like the Propylaea on the Acropolis at Athens, the propylum was a considerable building forming a gateway to the temple.
[6] *i.e.* the temple proper.
[7] *i.e.* front hall-room.

μὰς μέχρι πηχῶν πεντήκοντα ἢ ἑξήκοντα· ἀναγ-
λυφὰς δ' ἔχουσιν οἱ τοῖχοι οὗτοι μεγάλων εἰδώλων,
ὁμοίων τοῖς Τυρρηνικοῖς καὶ τοῖς ἀρχαίοις σφόδρα
τῶν παρὰ τοῖς Ἕλλησι δημιουργημάτων. ἔστι
δέ τις καὶ πολύστυλος οἶκος, καθάπερ ἐν Μέμφει,
βαρβαρικὴν ἔχων τὴν κατασκευήν· πλὴν γὰρ τοῦ
μεγάλων εἶναι καὶ πολλῶν καὶ πολυστίχων τῶν
στύλων ¹ οὐδὲν ἔχει χαρίεν οὐδὲ γραφικόν, ἀλλὰ
ματαιοπονίαν ἐμφαίνει μᾶλλον.

29. Ἐν δὲ τῇ Ἡλίου πόλει καὶ οἴκους εἴδομεν
μεγάλους, ἐν οἷς διέτριβον οἱ ἱερεῖς· μάλιστα γὰρ
δὴ ταύτην κατοικίαν ἱερέων γεγονέναι φασὶ τὸ
παλαιόν, φιλοσόφων ἀνδρῶν καὶ ἀστρονομικῶν·
ἐκλέλοιπε δὲ καὶ τοῦτο νυνὶ τὸ σύστημα καὶ ἡ
ἄσκησις. ἐκεῖ μὲν οὖν οὐδεὶς ἡμῖν ἐδείκνυτο τῆς
τοιαύτης ἀσκήσεως προεστώς, ἀλλ' οἱ ἱεροποιοὶ
μόνον καὶ ἐξηγηταὶ τοῖς ξένοις τῶν περὶ τὰ ἱερά.
παρηκολούθει δέ τις ἐξ Ἀλεξανδρείας ἀναπλέοντι
εἰς τὴν Αἴγυπτον Αἰλίῳ Γάλλῳ τῷ ἡγεμόνι
Χαιρήμων τοὔνομα, προσποιούμενος τοιαύτην τινὰ
ἐπιστήμην, γελώμενος δὲ τὸ πλέον ὡς ἀλαζὼν
καὶ ἰδιώτης. ἐκεῖ δ' οὖν ἐδείκνυντο οἵ τε τῶν
ἱερέων οἶκοι καὶ Πλάτωνος καὶ Εὐδόξου διατριβαί·
συνανέβη γὰρ δὴ τῷ Πλάτωνι ὁ Εὔδοξος δεῦρο
καὶ συνδιέτριψαν τοῖς ἱερεῦσιν ἐνταῦθα ἐκεῖνοι
τρισκαίδεκα ἔτη, ὡς εἴρηταί τισι· περιττοὺς γὰρ
ὄντας κατὰ τὴν ἐπιστήμην τῶν οὐρανίων, μυστι-

---

¹ *moz* change all these genitives to accusatives; so Corais.

---

¹ *i.e.* in the Etruscan tombs.
² Hardly Chaeremon the Alexandrian philosopher and
historian, as some think. Aelius Gallus made the voyage

converging lines as far as fifty or sixty cubits ; and
these walls have figures of large images cut in low
relief, like the Tyrrhenian [1] images and the very
old works of art among the Greeks. There is also
a kind of hall with numerous columns (as at
Memphis, for example), which is constructed in the
barbaric manner ; for, except for the fact that the
columns are large and numerous and form many
rows, the hall has nothing pleasing or picturesque,
but is rather a display of vain toil.

29. In Heliupolis I also saw large houses in which
the priests lived ; for it is said that this place in
particular was in ancient times a settlement of
priests who studied philosophy and astronomy ; but
both this organisation and its pursuits have now
disappeared.   At Heliupolis, in fact, no one was
pointed out to me as presiding over such pursuits,
but only those who performed the sacrifices and
explained to strangers what pertained to the sacred
rites.   When Aelius Gallus the praefect sailed up
into Aegypt, he was accompanied by a certain man
from Alexandria, Chaeremon [2] by name, who pretended to some knowledge of this kind, but was
generally ridiculed as a boaster and ignoramus.
However, at Heliupolis the houses of the priests and
schools of Plato and Eudoxus were pointed out to
us ; for Eudoxus went up to that place with Plato,
and they both passed thirteen years [3] with the priests,
as is stated by some writers ; for since these priests
excelled in their knowledge of the heavenly bodies,

about 25 B.C., but that Chaeremon was a tutor of Nero after
A.D. 49.

[3] The Epitome reads "three years," and Diogenes Laertius
(8. 87) "sixteen months."

κοὺς δὲ καὶ δυσμεταδότους, τῷ χρόνῳ καὶ ταῖς
θεραπείαις ἐξελιπάρησαν, ὥστε τινὰ τῶν θεωρη-
μάτων ἱστορῆσαι· τὰ πολλὰ δὲ ἀπεκρύψαντο οἱ
βάρβαροι. οὗτοι δὲ τὰ ἐπιτρέχοντα τῆς ἡμέρας
καὶ τῆς νυκτὸς μόρια ταῖς τριακοσίαις ἑξήκοντα
πέντε ἡμέραις εἰς τὴν ἐκπλήρωσιν τοῦ ἐνιαυσίου
χρόνου παρέδοσαν. ἀλλ᾽ ἠγνοεῖτο τέως ὁ ἐνιαυ-
τὸς παρὰ τοῖς Ἕλλησιν, ὡς καὶ ἄλλα πλείω,
ἕως οἱ νεώτεροι ἀστρολόγοι παρέλαβον παρὰ
τῶν μεθερμηνευσάντων εἰς τὸ Ἑλληνικὸν τὰ τῶν
ἱερέων ὑπομνήματα· καὶ ἔτι νῦν παραλαμβάν-
ουσι τὰ ἀπ᾽ ἐκείνων, ὁμοίως καὶ τὰ τῶν Χαλδαίων.

30. Ἐντεῦθεν δὴ[1] ὁ Νεῖλός ἐστιν ὁ ὑπὲρ τοῦ
Δέλτα· τούτου δὴ τὰ μὲν δεξιὰ καλοῦσι Λιβύην
ἀναπλέοντι, ὥσπερ καὶ τὰ περὶ τὴν Ἀλεξάνδρειαν καὶ τὴν Μαρεῶτιν, τὰ δ᾽ ἐν ἀριστερᾷ
Ἀραβίαν. ἡ μὲν οὖν Ἡλίου πόλις ἐν τῇ Ἀραβίᾳ
ἐστίν, ἐν δὲ τῇ Λιβύῃ Κερκέσουρα πόλις κατὰ
C 807 τὰς Εὐδόξου κειμένη σκοπάς· δείκνυται γὰρ
σκοπή τις πρὸ τῆς Ἡλίου πόλεως, καθάπερ καὶ
πρὸ τῆς Κνίδου, πρὸς ἣν ἐσημειοῦτο ἐκεῖνος τῶν
οὐρανίων τινὰς κινήσεις· ὁ δὲ νομὸς Λητοπολίτης
οὗτος. ἀναπλεύσαντι δ᾽ ἐστὶ Βαβυλών, φρούριον
ἐρυμνόν, ἀποστάντων ἐνταῦθα Βαβυλωνίων τινῶν,

---

[1] Instead of δή, Dh read δέ.

---

[1] As stated in § 46 (below), they divided the year into
twelve months of thirty days each, and at the end of the

albeit secretive and slow to impart it, Plato and
Eudoxus prevailed upon them in time and by
courting their favour to let them learn some of
the principles of their doctrines; but the barbarians
concealed most things. However, these men did
teach them the fractions of the day and the night
which, running over and above the three hundred
and sixty-five days, fill out the time of the true
year.[1] But at that time the true year was unknown
among the Greeks, as also many other things, until
the later astrologers learned them from the men
who had translated into Greek the records of the
priests; and even to this day they learn their
teachings, and likewise those of the Chaldaeans.

30. From Heliupolis, then, one comes to the Nile
above the Delta. Of this, the parts on the right, as
one sails up, are called Libya, as also the parts
round Alexandria and Lake Mareotis, whereas
those on the left are called Arabia. Now Heliupolis is in Arabia, but the city Cercesura, which
lies near the observatories of Eudoxus, is in Libya;
for a kind of watch-tower is to be seen in front of
Heliupolis, as also in front of Cnidus, with reference
to which Eudoxus would note down his observations
of certain movements of the heavenly bodies. Here
the Nome is the Letopolite. And, having sailed
farther up the river, one comes to Babylon, a stronghold, where some Babylonians had withdrawn in
revolt and then successfully negotiated for permission

twelve months added five days (so Herodotus 2. 4), and then
at the end of every fourth year added another day. Diodorus
Siculus (1. 50), however, puts it thus: "They add five and
one-fourth days to the twelve months and in this way complete
the annual period."

εἶτα διαπραξαμένων ἐνταῦθα κατοικίαν παρὰ τῶν βασιλέων· νυνὶ δ' ἐστὶ στρατόπεδον ἑνὸς τῶν τριῶν ταγμάτων τῶν φρουρούντων τὴν Αἴγυπτον. ῥάχις δ' ἐστὶν ἀπὸ τοῦ στρατοπέδου καὶ μέχρι Νείλου καθήκουσα, δι' ἧς ἀπὸ τοῦ ποταμοῦ τροχοὶ καὶ κοχλίαι τὸ ὕδωρ ἀνάγουσιν, ἀνδρῶν ἑκατὸν πεντήκοντα ἐργαζομένων δεσμίων· ἀφορῶνται δ' ἐνθένδε τηλαυγῶς αἱ πυραμίδες ἐν τῇ περαίᾳ ἐν Μέμφει καί εἰσι πλησίον.

31. Ἐγγὺς δὲ καὶ ἡ Μέμφις αὐτή, τὸ βασίλειον τῶν Αἰγυπτίων· ἔστι γὰρ ἀπὸ τοῦ Δέλτα τρίσχοινον εἰς αὐτήν. ἔχει δὲ ἱερά, τό τε τοῦ Ἄπιδος, ὅς ἐστιν ὁ αὐτὸς καὶ Ὄσιρις, ὅπου ὁ βοῦς ὁ Ἄπις ἐν σηκῷ τινι τρέφεται, θεός, ὡς ἔφην, νομιζόμενος, διάλευκος τὸ μέτωπον καὶ ἄλλα τινὰ μικρὰ τοῦ σώματος, τἆλλα δὲ μέλας· οἷς σημείοις ἀεὶ κρίνουσι τὸν ἐπιτήδειον εἰς τὴν διαδοχήν, ἀπογενομένου τοῦ τὴν τιμὴν ἔχοντος. ἔστι δ' αὐλὴ προκειμένη τοῦ σηκοῦ, ἐν ᾗ καὶ ἄλλος σηκὸς τῆς μητρὸς τοῦ βοός· εἰς ταύτην δὲ τὴν αὐλὴν ἐξαφιᾶσι τὸν Ἄπιν καθ' ὥραν τινά, καὶ μάλιστα πρὸς ἐπίδειξιν τοῖς ξένοις· ὁρῶσι μὲν γὰρ καὶ διὰ θυρίδος ἐν τῷ σηκῷ, βούλονται δὲ καὶ ἔξω· ἀποσκιρτήσαντα δ' ἐν αὐτῇ μικρὰ ἀναλαμβάνουσι πάλιν εἰς τὴν οἰκείαν στάσιν.

---

[1] Strabo's statement is too concise to be clear. He refers to certain Babylonian captives who, being unable to endure the hard work imposed upon them *in Aegypt*, revolted from the king, seized the stronghold along the river, and gained the concession in question after a successful war (Diodorus Siculus, 1. 56. 3).

[2] *i.e.* to Babylon.

[3] The pyramids of Gizeh, described by Herodotus (2. 124 ff.) and Pliny (36. 16).

from the kings to build a settlement;[1] but now it is an encampment of one of the three legions that guard Aegypt. There is a ridge extending from the encampment even as far as the Nile, on which the water is conducted up from the river[2] by wheels and screws; and one hundred and fifty prisoners are employed in the work; and from here one can clearly see the pyramids[3] on the far side of the river at Memphis, and they are near to it.[4]

31. Memphis itself, the royal residence of the Aegyptians, is also near Babylon; for the distance to it from the Delta is only three schoeni.[5] It contains temples, one of which is that of Apis, who is the same as Osiris; it is here that the bull Apis is kept in a kind of sanctuary, being regarded, as I have said, as god; his forehead and certain other small parts of his body are marked with white, but the other parts are black;[6] and it is by these marks that they always choose the bull suitable for the succession, when the one that holds the honour has died. In front of the sanctuary is situated a court, in which there is another sanctuary belonging to the bull's mother. Into this court they set Apis loose at a certain hour, particularly that he may be shown to foreigners; for although people can see him through the window in the sanctuary, they wish to see him outside also; but when he has finished a short bout of skipping in the court they take him back again to his familiar stall.

[4] According to Pliny (36. 16) the pyramids were seven and one-half miles (*i.e.* sixty stadia) from Memphis.

[5] On the "schoenus," see 17. 1. 24.

[6] "He is black, and has on his forehead a triangular white spot and on his back the likeness of an eagle" (Herodotus 3. 28). Pliny (8. 71) says, "a crescent-like white spot on the right side."

Τό τε δὴ τοῦ Ἄπιδός ἐστιν ἱερόν, παρακείμενον
τῷ Ἡφαιστείῳ, καὶ αὐτὸ τὸ Ἡφαίστειον πολυ-
τελῶς κατεσκευασμένον ναοῦ τε μεγέθει καὶ τοῖς
ἄλλοις. πρόκειται δ᾽ ἐν τῷ δρόμῳ καὶ μονόλιθος
κολοσσός· ἔθος δ᾽ ἐστὶν ἐν τῷ δρόμῳ τούτῳ
ταύρων ἀγῶνας συντελεῖσθαι πρὸς ἀλλήλους, οὓς
ἐπίτηδες τρέφουσί τινες, ὥσπερ οἱ ἱπποτρόφοι·
συμβάλλουσι γὰρ εἰς μάχην ἀφέντες, ὁ δὲ κρείτ-
των νομισθεὶς ἄθλου τυγχάνει. ἔστι δ᾽ ἐν Μέμφει
καὶ Ἀφροδίτης ἱερόν, θεᾶς Ἑλληνίδος νομιζομένης·
τινὲς δὲ Σελήνης[1] ἱερὸν εἶναί φασιν.

32. Ἔστι δὲ καὶ Σαράπιον ἐν ἀμμώδει τόπῳ
σφόδρα, ὥσθ᾽ ὑπ᾽ ἀνέμων θῖνας ἄμμων σωρεύεσ-
θαι, ὑφ᾽ ὧν αἱ σφίγγες αἱ μὲν καὶ μέχρι κεφαλῆς
ἑωρῶντο ὑφ᾽ ἡμῶν κατακεχωσμέναι, αἱ δ᾽ ἡμιφα-
νεῖς· ἐξ ὧν εἰκάζειν παρῆν τὸν κίνδυνον, εἰ τῷ
βαδίζοντι πρὸς τὸ ἱερὸν λαῖλαψ ἐπιπέσοι. πόλις
δ᾽ ἐστὶ μεγάλη τε καὶ εὔανδρος,[2] δευτέρα μετὰ
Ἀλεξάνδρειαν, μιγάδων ἀνδρῶν, καθάπερ καὶ τῶν
ἐκεῖ συνῳκισμένων. πρόκεινται δὲ καὶ λίμναι
τῆς πόλεως καὶ τῶν βασιλείων, ἃ νῦν μὲν κατέ-
C 808 σπασται καί ἐστιν ἔρημα, ἵδρυται δ᾽ ἐφ᾽ ὕψους
καθήκοντα μέχρι τοῦ κάτω τῆς πόλεως ἐδάφους·
συνάπτει δ᾽ ἄλσος αὐτῷ καὶ λίμνη.

33. Τετταράκοντα δ᾽ ἀπὸ τῆς πόλεως σταδίους

---

[1] For Σελήνης, Nolt conj. Ἑλένης, citing Herod. 2. 112.
[2] εὔδενδρος E.

---

[1] Diodorus Siculus refers to "images made of one stone,
both of himself (Sesostris) and of his wife, thirty cubits high,
and of his sons, twenty cubits, in the temple of Hephaestus
at Memphis."

There is here, then, not only the temple of Apis, which lies near the Hephaesteium, but also the Hephaesteium itself, which is a costly structure both in the size of its naos and in all other respects. In front, in the dromus, stands also a colossus made of one stone;[1] and it is the custom to hold bull-fights in this dromus, and certain men breed these bulls for the purpose, like horse-breeders; for the bulls are set loose and join in combat, and the one that is regarded as victor gets a prize. And at Memphis there is also a temple of Aphroditê, who is considered to be a Greek goddess,[2] though some say that it is a temple of Selenê.[3]

32. There is also a Sarapium at Memphis, in a place so very sandy that dunes of sand are heaped up by the winds; and by these some of the sphinxes which I saw were buried even to the head and others were only half-visible; from which one might guess the danger if a sand-storm should fall upon a man travelling on foot towards the temple. The city is both large and populous, ranks second after Alexandria, and consists of mixed races of people, like those who have settled together at Alexandria. There are lakes situated in front of the city and the palaces, which latter, though now in ruins and deserted, are situated on a height and extend down to the ground of the city below; and adjoining the city are a grove and a lake.

33. On proceeding forty stadia from the city, one

[2] Herodotus (2. 112) refers to the temple of the "Foreign Aphroditê" at Memphis and identifies her with Helen; but see Rawlinson (Vol. II, p. 157, footnote 9), who very plausibly identifies her with Astarte, the Phoenician and Syrian Aphroditê.

[3] Goddess of the Moon.

προελθόντι ὀρεινή τις ὀφρύς ἐστιν, ἐφ' ᾗ πολλαὶ
μέν εἰσι πυραμίδες, τάφοι τῶν βασιλέων, τρεῖς
δ' ἀξιόλογοι· τὰς δὲ δύο τούτων καὶ ἐν τοῖς ἑπτὰ
θεάμασι καταριθμοῦνται· εἰσὶ γὰρ σταδιαῖαι τὸ
ὕψος, τετράγωνοι τῷ σχήματι, τῆς πλευρᾶς
ἑκάστης μικρῷ μεῖζον τὸ ὕψος ἔχουσαι· μικρῷ
δὲ καὶ ἡ ἑτέρα τῆς ἑτέρας ἐστὶ μείζων· ἔχει δ'
ἐν ὕψει μέσως πως [1] τῶν πλευρῶν λίθον ἐξαιρέ-
σιμον· ἀρθέντος δὲ σύριγξ ἐστι σκολιὰ μέχρι τῆς

[1] Letronne conj. μιᾶς after πως; Groskurd, Meineke and
others so read.

---

[1] Cheops. [2] Khafra.

[3] *i.e.* "high up, approximately midway" (*horizontally*)
"between the sides" (the *two* sides of the triangle which
forms the northern face of the pyramid). This is the meaning of the Greek text as it stands; but all editors (from
Casaubon down), translators, and archæologists, so far as the
present translator knows, either emend the text or mis-
interpret it, or both (see critical note). Letronne (French
translation), who is followed by the later translators, insists
upon "moderately" as the meaning of μέσως πως (translated
above by "approximately midway between"), and errone-
ously quotes, as a similar use of μέσως πως, 11. 2. 18, where
there is no MS. authority for πως, and translates: "Elle
a sur ses côtés, et à une élévation médiocre, une pierre qui
peut s'ôter." The subsequent editors insert μιᾶς ("one")
before τῶν πλευρῶν ("the sides") ; and, following them, even
Sir W. M. Flinders Petrie in his monumental work (*The
Pyramids and Temples of Gizeh*, p. 168) translates: "The
Greater (Pyramid), a little way up one side, has a stone that
may be taken out." These interpretations accord with what
are known facts ; but so does the present interpretation,
which also brings out two additional facts of importance:
(1) It was hardly necessary for Strabo to state the obvious
fact that the stone door was "*moderately* high up one side"
of the pyramid (originally "about 55 feet vertically or 71
feet on the slope," according to a private letter from Petrie,

comes to a kind of mountain-brow; on it are
numerous pyramids, the tombs of kings, of which
three are noteworthy; and two of these are even
numbered among the Seven Wonders of the World,
for they are a stadium in height, are quadrangular
in shape, and their height is a little greater than the
length of each of the sides; and one[1] of them is
only a little larger than the other.[2] High up, approximately midway between the sides, it has a movable
stone,[3] and when this is raised up there is a sloping

dated Sept. 16, 1930), as compared with the height of the
vertex (nearly 500 feet), or that the one door was on *one*
side of the pyramid. What he means to say is that the door
was *literally* high up as compared with the convenient position
of an entrance close to the ground, knowing, as he did, that the
Aegyptians chose a high position for it in order to keep secret
the passage to the royal tombs; and, through his not unusual
conciseness in such cases, he leaves the fact to be inferred.
The wisdom of that secrecy is disclosed by the fact that
when the Arabs, ignorant of the doorway, wished to enter the
pyramid, they forced their way into it from a point near the
ground through 100 feet of solid masonry, and thus by chance
met the original sloping passage and discovered the original
doorway. Moreover, this "movable stone," which was either a
flap-door that worked on a stone pivot (Petrie *l.c.*) or a flat slab
that was easily tilted up (Borchardt, *Aegyptische Zeitschrift*,
XXXV. 87), must have fitted so nicely when closed that no
one unfamiliar with it could distinguish it. (2) "The sides"
here must refer to the north-west and north-east *edges* of the
pyramid, not to its *northern face*—much less *all four faces*—
just as "sides" in the preceding sentence must mean the
four sides of the base, not its plane surface. Hence, Strabo
means that the doorway was purposely placed to *one side of*
("actually 24 feet," again according to Petrie's letter), and
not *at*, a central point between the two edges above-
mentioned, which is the fact in the case—a most important
part of the ruse, as was later evidenced by the fact that the
Arabs began to force their way into the pyramid at the
centre (see the "Horizontal Section of the Great Pyramid"

θήκης. αὗται μὲν οὖν ἐγγὺς ἀλλήλων εἰσὶ [1] τῷ
αὐτῷ ἐπιπέδῳ· ἀπωτέρω δ᾽ ἐστὶν ἐν ὕψει μείζονι [2]
τῆς ὀρεινῆς ἡ τρίτη πολὺ ἐλάττων τῶν δυεῖν,
πολὺ δὲ μείζονος δαπάνης κατεσκευασμένη· ἀπὸ
γὰρ θεμελίων μέχρι μέσου σχεδόν τι μέλανος
λίθου ἐστίν, ἐξ οὗ καὶ τὰς θυίας κατασκευάζουσι,
κομίζοντες πόρρωθεν· ἀπὸ γὰρ τῶν τῆς Αἰθιοπίας
ὀρῶν, καὶ τῷ σκληρὸς εἶναι καὶ δυσκατέργαστος
πολυτελῆ τὴν πραγματείαν παρέσχε. λέγεται δὲ
τῆς ἑταίρας τάφος γεγονὼς ὑπὸ τῶν ἐραστῶν, ἣν
Σαπφὼ μέν, ἡ τῶν μελῶν ποιήτρια, καλεῖ Δωρίχαν,
ἐρωμένην τοῦ ἀδελφοῦ αὐτῆς Χαράξου γεγονυῖαν,
οἶνον κατάγοντος εἰς Ναύκρατιν Λέσβιον κατ᾽
ἐμπορίαν, ἄλλοι δ᾽ ὀνομάζουσι Ῥοδῶπιν·[3] μυθεύουσι δ᾽, ὅτι, λουομένης αὐτῆς, ἓν τῶν ὑποδη-
μάτων αὐτῆς ἁρπάσας ἀετὸς παρὰ τῆς θερα-
παίνης κομίσειεν εἰς Μέμφιν καί, τοῦ βασιλέως
δικαιοδοτοῦντος ὑπαιθρίου,[4] γενόμενος κατὰ κορυφὴν αὐτοῦ ῥίψειε τὸ ὑπόδημα εἰς τὸν κόλπον·

---

[1] ἐπί, before τῷ, Meineke inserts, following Kramer; ἐν,
Corais.
[2] μείζονι *moxz*, μείζων other MSS.
[3] Ῥοδῶπιν, Corais, for Ῥόδοπιν EF, Ῥοδόπην other MSS.
[4] ὑπαιθρίου, Kramer; ἐν ὑπαίθρῳ *x*, ὑπαίθριος other MSS.

---

in Richard A. Proctor's *The Great Pyramid*, opposite p. 138).
In short (1) μέσως πως cannot mean "moderately" in a
matter of measurement (if indeed it ever means the same as
μετρίως) and naturally goes with τῶν πλευρῶν, not ἐν ὕψει;
and in fact some interpreters utterly ignore the πως. (2)
The insertion of μιᾶς is not only unnecessary but eliminates
two important observations.

[1] This passage "sloped steeply down through masonry and
solid rock for 318 feet," passing through an unfinished vault

passage to the vault.[1] Now these pyramids are near
one another and on the same level; but farther on, at
a greater height of the hill, is the third, which is much
smaller than the two, though constructed at much
greater expense; for from the foundations almost to
the middle it is made of black stone, the stone from
which mortars are made, being brought from a great
distance, for it is brought from the mountains of
Aethiopia; and because of its being hard and difficult
to work into shape it rendered the undertaking very
expensive. It is called "Tomb of the Courtesan,"
having been built by her lovers—the courtesan
whom Sappho[2] the Melic poetess calls Doricha, the
beloved of Sappho's brother Charaxus, who was engaged in transporting Lesbian wine to Naucratis for
sale,[3] but others give her the name Rhodopis.[4] They
tell the fabulous story that, when she was bathing,
an eagle snatched one of her sandals from her maid
and carried it to Memphis; and while the king was
administering justice in the open air, the eagle,
when it arrived above his head, flung the sandal into

(subterranean chamber) "46 feet long, 27 feet wide, and 10.6
feet high," and "ended in a cul-de-sac," being "intended to
mislead possible riflers of the " royal "tomb " above (Knight,
l.c.). Petrie's translation of μέχρι τῆς θήκης ("to the very
foundations," instead of "to the vault ") is at least mis-
leading. In the very next sentence Strabo refers to the
"foundations " (θεμελίων). Since Strabo fails to mention the
vaults of the king and the queen high above, the natural
inference might be that he regarded the subterranean vault
as the actual royal tomb; and in that case one might assume
that the tombs were rifled, not by Augustus, but before his
time, perhaps by the Persians.

[2] *Frag.* 138 (Bergk) and *Lyra Graeca*, L.C.L., Vol. I, p.
207 (Edmunds).
[3] So Athenaeus, 13. 68.
[4] See Herodotus 2. 134–135.

ὁ δὲ καὶ τῷ ῥυθμῷ τοῦ ὑποδήματος καὶ τῷ
παραδόξῳ κινηθεὶς περιπέμψειεν εἰς τὴν χώραν
κατὰ ζήτησιν τῆς φορούσης ἀνθρώπου τοῦτο·
εὑρεθεῖσα δ' ἐν τῇ πόλει τῶν Ναυκρατιτῶν
ἀναχθείη καὶ γένοιτο γυνὴ τοῦ βασιλέως, τελευ-
τήσασα δὲ τοῦ λεχθέντος τύχοι τάφου.

34. Ἕν δέ τι τῶν ὁραθέντων ὑφ' ἡμῶν ἐν ταῖς
πυραμίσι παραδόξων οὐκ ἄξιον παραλιπεῖν. ἐκ
γὰρ τῆς λατύπης σωροί τινες πρὸ τῶν πυραμίδων
κεῖνται· ἐν τούτοις δ' εὑρίσκεται ψήγματα καὶ
τύπῳ καὶ μεγέθει φακοειδῆ· ἐνίοις δὲ καὶ ὡς ἂν
πτίσμα οἷον ἡμιλεπίστων ὑποτρέχει·[1] φασὶ δ'
ἀπολιθωθῆναι λείψανα τῆς τῶν ἐργαζομένων
τροφῆς· οὐκ ἀπέοικε[2] δέ· καὶ γὰρ οἴκοι παρ'
ἡμῖν λόφος ἐστὶν ἐν πεδίῳ παραμήκης, οὗτος δ'
ἐστὶ μεστὸς ψήφων φακοειδῶν λίθου πωρείας·[3] καὶ
αἱ θαλάττιαι δὲ καὶ αἱ ποτάμιαι ψῆφοι σχεδόν τι
τὴν αὐτὴν ἀπορίαν ὑπογράφουσιν· ἀλλ' αὗται μὲν
C 809 ἐν τῇ κινήσει τῇ διὰ τοῦ ῥεύματος εὑρεσιλογίαν
τινὰ ἔχουσιν, ἐκεῖ δ' ἀπορωτέρα ἡ σκέψις.
εἴρηται δ' ἐν ἄλλοις καὶ διότι περὶ τὸ μέταλλον
τῶν λίθων, ἐξ ὧν αἱ πυραμίδες γεγόνασιν, ἐν
ὄψει[4] ταῖς πυραμίσιν ὃν πέραν ἐν τῇ Ἀραβίᾳ,
Τρωικόν τι καλεῖται πετρῶδες ἱκανῶς ὄρος καὶ
σπήλαια ὑπ' αὐτῷ καὶ κώμη πλησίον καὶ τούτοις καὶ τῷ ποταμῷ, Τροία καλουμένη, κατοικία

---

[1] ἐπιτρέχει s, Corais following.
[2] For ἀπέοικε Letronne conj. ἐπέοικε.
[3] πωρείας, Meineke, for πορίας DEF, πωρίας other MSS.;
πωρίνου Siebenkees and Groskurd.
[4] ὄψει, Corais, for ὕψει; so the later editors.

his lap; and the king, stirred both by the beautiful shape of the sandal and by the strangeness of the occurrence, sent men in all directions into the country in quest of the woman who wore the sandal; and when she was found in the city of Naucratis, she was brought up to Memphis, became the wife of the king, and when she died was honoured with the above-mentioned tomb.

34. One of the marvellous things I saw at the pyramids should not be omitted: there are heaps of stone-chips lying in front of the pyramids; and among these are found chips that are like lentils both in form and size; and under some of the heaps lie winnowings, as it were, as of half-peeled grains. They say that what was left of the food of the workmen has petrified; and this is not improbable. Indeed, in my home-country,[1] in a plain, there is a long hill which is full of lentil-shaped pebbles of porous stone;[2] and the pebbles both of the seas and of the rivers present about the same puzzling question; but while these latter find an explanation in the motion caused by the current of water, the speculation in that other case is more puzzling. It has been stated elsewhere[3] that in the neighbourhood of the quarry of the stones from which the pyramids are built, which is in sight of the pyramids, on the far side of the river in Arabia, there is a very rocky mountain which is called "Trojan," and that there are caves at the foot of it, and a village near both these and the river which is called Troy, being an ancient settle-

---

[1] Strabo was born at Amaseia in Pontus (*Introduction,* p. xiv).

[2] *i.e.* "tufa."

[3] Not in Strabo's *Geography*; perhaps in his *History* (see Vol. I, p. 47, note 1).

παλαιὰ τῶν Μενελάῳ συγκατακολουθησάντων
αἰχμαλώτων Τρώων, καταμεινάντων δ' αὐτόθι.

35. Μετὰ δὲ Μέμφιν Ἄκανθος πόλις ὁμοίως
ἐν τῇ Λιβύῃ καὶ τὸ τοῦ Ὀσίριδος ἱερὸν καὶ τὸ τῆς
ἀκάνθης ἄλσος τῆς Θηβαϊκῆς, ἐξ ἧς τὸ κόμμι.
εἶθ' ὁ Ἀφροδιτοπολίτης νομὸς καὶ ἡ ὁμώνυμος
πόλις ἐν τῇ Ἀραβίᾳ, ἐν ᾗ λευκὴ βοῦς ἱερὰ
τρέφεται. εἶθ' ὁ Ἡρακλεώτης νομὸς ἐν νήσῳ
μεγάλῃ, καθ' ἣν ἡ διῶρύξ ἐστιν ἐν δεξιᾷ εἰς τὴν
Λιβύην ἐπὶ τὸν Ἀρσινοΐτην νομόν, ὥστε καὶ
δίστομον εἶναι τὴν διώρυγα, μεταξὺ μέρους τινὸς
τῆς νήσου παρεμπίπτοντος. ἔστι δ' ὁ νομὸς
οὗτος ἀξιολογώτατος τῶν ἁπάντων κατά τε τὴν
ὄψιν καὶ τὴν ἀρετὴν καὶ τὴν κατασκευήν· ἐλαιό-
φυτός τε γὰρ μόνος ἐστὶ μεγάλοις καὶ τελείοις δένδρεσι καὶ καλλικάρποις, εἰ δὲ συγκομίζοι καλῶς
τις, καὶ εὐέλαιος· ὀλιγωροῦντες δὲ τούτου πολὺ
μὲν ποιοῦσιν ἔλαιον, μοχθηρὸν δὲ κατὰ τὴν ὀδμήν
(ἡ δ' ἄλλη Αἴγυπτος ἀνέλαιός ἐστι πλὴν τῶν
κατ' Ἀλεξάνδρειαν κήπων, οἳ μέχρι τοῦ ἐλαίαν
χορηγεῖν ἱκανοί εἰσιν, ἔλαιον δ' οὐχ ὑπουργοῦσιν)·
οἶνόν τε οὐκ ὀλίγον ἐκφέρει σῖτόν τε καὶ ὄσπρια
καὶ τὰ ἄλλα σπέρματα πάμπολλα. θαυμαστὴν
δὲ καὶ τὴν λίμνην ἔχει τὴν Μοίριδος [1] καλουμένην,
πελαγίαν τῷ μεγέθει καὶ τῇ χρόᾳ θαλαττοειδῆ·
καὶ τοὺς αἰγιαλοὺς δέ ἐστιν ὁρᾶν ἐοικότας τοῖς
θαλαττίοις· ὡς ὑπονοεῖν τὰ αὐτὰ περὶ τῶν κατὰ

1 Μοίριδος Ew, Μούριδος other MSS.

---

1 So Diodorus Siculus 1. 56. 4. 2 i.e. Mimosa Nilotica.
3 i.e. gum arabic. 4 See § 37 below.

ment of the captive Trojans who accompanied
Meneläus but stayed there.[1]

35. After Memphis one comes to a city Acanthus,
likewise situated in Libya, and to the temple of Osiris
and the grove of the Thebaïc acantha,[2] from which the
gum [3] is obtained. Then to the Aphroditopolite Nome,
and to the city of like name in Arabia, where is
kept a white cow which is sacred. Then to the
Heracleote Nome, on a large island, where, on the
right, is the canal which leads into Libya to the Arsinoïte Nome, so that the canal has two mouths, a part
of the island intervening between the two.[4] This
Nome is the most noteworthy of all in respect to its
appearance, its fertility, and its material development,
for it alone is planted with olive trees that are large
and full-grown and bear fine fruit, and it would also
produce good olive oil if the olives were carefully
gathered.[5] But since they neglect this matter,
although they make much oil, it has a bad smell (the
rest of Aegypt has no olive trees, except the gardens
near Alexandria, which are sufficient for supplying
olives, but furnish no oil). And it produces wine in no
small quantity, as well as grain, pulse, and the other
seed-plants in very great varieties. It also contains
the wonderful lake called the Lake of Moeris, which
is an open sea in size and like a sea in colour; and its
shores, also, resemble those of a sea, so that one may
make the same supposition about this region as about

---

[5] In some countries, and generally in Asia, "the olives are
beaten down by poles or by shaking the boughs, or even
allowed to drop naturally, often lying on the ground until the
convenience of the owner admits of their removal; much of
the inferior oil owes its bad quality to the carelessness of the
proprietor of the trees" (*Encyc. Brit.* s.v. "Olive").

97

Ἄμμωνα τόπων καὶ τούτων (καὶ γὰρ οὐδὲ πάμπολυ ἀφεστᾶσιν ἀλλήλων καὶ τοῦ Παραιτονίου),
μὴ ὥσπερ τὸ ἱερὸν ἐκεῖνο εἰκάζειν ἔστι πρότερον
ἐπὶ τῇ θαλάττῃ ἱδρῦσθαι διὰ τὸ πλῆθος τῶν
τεκμηρίων, καὶ ταῦθ' ὁμοίως τὰ χωρία πρότερον
ἐπὶ τῇ θαλάττῃ ὑπῆρχεν. ἡ δὲ κάτω Αἴγυπτος
καὶ τὰ μέχρι τῆς λίμνης τῆς Σιρβωνίτιδος πέλαγος
ἦν, σύρρουν τυχὸν ἴσως τῇ Ἐρυθρᾷ τῇ κατὰ
Ἡρώων πόλιν καὶ τὸν Αἰλανίτην[1] μυχόν.

36. Εἴρηται δὲ περὶ τούτων διὰ πλειόνων ἐν
τῷ πρώτῳ ὑπομνήματι τῆς γεωγραφίας, καὶ νῦν
δ' ἐπὶ τοσοῦτον ὑπομνηστέον τὸ[2] τῆς φύσεως ἅμα
καὶ τὸ τῆς προνοίας ἔργον εἰς ἓν συμφέροντας·
τὸ μὲν τῆς φύσεως, ὅτι τῶν πάντων ὑφ'[3] ἓν
συννευόντων τὸ τοῦ ὅλου μέσον καὶ σφαιρουμένων[4] περὶ τοῦτο, τὸ μὲν πυκνότατον καὶ μεσαί-
τατόν ἐστιν ἡ γῆ, τὸ δ' ἧττον τοιοῦτον καὶ
ἐφεξῆς τὸ ὕδωρ, ἑκάτερον δὲ σφαῖρα, ἡ μὲν
στερεά, ἡ δὲ κοίλη, ἐντὸς ἔχουσα τὴν γῆν· τὸ δὲ
τῆς προνοίας, ὅτι βεβούληται, καὶ αὐτὴ ποι-
κίλτριά τις οὖσα καὶ μυρίων ἔργων δημιουργός,
ἐν τοῖς πρώτοις ζῷα γεννᾶν, ὡς πολὺ διαφέροντα
τῶν ἄλλων, καὶ τούτων τὰ κράτιστα θεούς τε καὶ
ἀνθρώπους, ὧν ἕνεκεν καὶ τὰ ἄλλα συνέστηκε.
τοῖς μὲν οὖν θεοῖς ἀπέδειξε τὸν οὐρανόν, τοῖς δ'
ἀνθρώποις τὴν γῆν, τὰ ἄκρα τῶν τοῦ κόσμου
μερῶν· ἄκρα δὲ τῆς σφαίρας τὸ μέσον καὶ τὸ

C 810

---

[1] Ἐλανίτην D.   [2] τό, Corais inserts.
[3] εἰς ἓν Dhi.
[4] σφαιρουμένων, Corais, for σφαιρούμενον.

---

that of Ammon (in fact, Ammon and the Heracleote Nome are not very far distant from one another or from Paraetonium), that, just as from the numerous evidences one may surmise that that temple was in earlier times situated on the sea, so likewise these districts were in earlier times on the sea. And Lower Aegypt and the parts extending as far as Lake Sirbonis were sea—this sea being confluent, perhaps, with the Red Sea in the neighbourhood of Heröonpolis and the Aelanites[1] Gulf.

36. I have already discussed this subject at greater length in the First Commentary of my *Geography*,[2] but now also I must comment briefly on the work of Nature and at the same time upon that of Providence, since they contribute to one result.[3] The work of Nature is this, that all things converge to one thing, the centre of the whole, and form a sphere around this; and the densest and most central thing is the earth, and the thing that is less so and next in order after it is the water; and that each of the two is a sphere, the former solid, the latter hollow, having the earth inside of it. And the work of Providence is this, that being likewise a broiderer, as it were, and artificer of countless works, it has willed, among its first works, to beget living beings, as being much superior to everything else, and among these the most excellent beings, both gods and men, on whose account everything else has been formed. Now to the gods Providence assigned the heavens and to men the earth, which are the extremities of the two parts of the universe; and the two extremities of the sphere are the central part and the outermost

[3] The reader will remember that Strabo was a Stoic philosopher (1. 2. 3, 34).

ἐξωτάτω. ἀλλ' ἐπειδὴ τῇ γῇ περίκειται τὸ ὕδωρ,
οὐκ ἔστι δ' ἔνυδρον ζῷον ὁ ἄνθρωπος, ἀλλὰ χερ-
σαῖον καὶ ἐναέριον καὶ πολλοῦ κοινωνικὸν φωτός,
ἐποίησεν ἐξοχὰς ἐν τῇ γῇ πολλὰς[1] καὶ εἰσοχάς,
ὥστ' ἐν αἷς μὲν ἀπολαμβάνεσθαι τὸ σύμπαν ἢ καὶ
τὸ πλέον ὕδωρ ἀποκρύπτον τὴν ὑπ' αὐτῷ γῆν, ἐν
αἷς δ' ἐξέχειν τὴν γῆν ἀποκρύπτουσαν ὑφ' ἑαυτῇ
τὸ ὕδωρ, πλὴν ὅσον χρήσιμον τῷ ἀνθρωπείῳ
γένει καὶ τοῖς περὶ αὐτὸ ζῴοις καὶ φυτοῖς. ἐπεὶ
δ' ἐν κινήσει συνεχεῖ τὰ σύμπαντα καὶ μετα-
βολαῖς μεγάλαις (οὐ γὰρ οἷόν τε ἄλλως τὰ
τοιαῦτα καὶ τοσαῦτα καὶ τηλικαῦτα ἐν τῷ κόσμῳ
διοκεῖσθαι), ὑποληπτέον, μήτε τὴν γῆν ἀεὶ συμ-
μένειν οὕτως, ὥστ' ἀεὶ τηλικαύτην εἶναι μηδὲν
προστιθεῖσαν ἑαυτῇ μηδ' ἀφαιροῦσαν, μήτε τὸ
ὕδωρ, μήτε τὴν ἕδραν ἔχειν τὴν αὐτὴν ἑκάτερον,
καὶ ταῦτα εἰς ἄλληλα φυσικωτάτης οὔσης καὶ
ἐγγυτάτω τῆς μεταπτώσεως· ἀλλὰ καὶ τῆς γῆς
πολλὴν εἰς ὕδωρ μεταβάλλειν, καὶ τῶν ὑδάτων
πολλὰ χερσοῦσθαι τὸν αὐτὸν τρόπον, ὅνπερ καὶ ἐν
τῇ γῇ, καθ' ἣν αὐτήν[2] τοσαῦται διαφοραί· ἡ
μὲν γὰρ εὔθρυπτος, ἡ δὲ στερεὰ καὶ πετρώδης καὶ
σιδηρῖτις καὶ οὕτως ἐπὶ τῶν ἄλλων. ὁμοίως
δὲ καὶ ἐπὶ τῆς ὑγρᾶς οὐσίας· ἡ μὲν ἁλμυρίς, ἡ
δὲ γλυκεῖα καὶ πότιμος, ἡ δὲ φαρμακώδης καὶ
σωτήριος καὶ ὀλέθριος καὶ ψυχρὰ καὶ θερμή. τί
οὖν θαυμαστόν, εἴ τινα μέρη τῆς γῆς, ἃ νῦν
οἰκεῖται, θαλάττῃ πρότερον κατείχετο, τὰ δὲ νῦν

---

[1] πολλάς, Tzschucke, for πολλοῖς.
[2] καθ' ἣν αὐτήν, Groskurd, for καθ' ἑαυτήν.

part.[1] But since water surrounds the earth, and man is not an aquatic animal, but a land animal that needs air and requires much light, Providence has made numerous elevations and hollows on the earth, so that the whole, or the most, of the water is received in the hollows, hiding the earth beneath it, and the earth projects in the elevations, hiding the water beneath itself, except so much of the latter as is useful for the human race, as also for the animals and plants round it. But since all things are continually in motion and undergo great changes (for it is not possible otherwise for things of this kind and number and size in the universe to be regulated), we must take it for granted, first, that the earth is not always so constant that it is always of this or that size, adding nothing to itself nor subtracting anything, and, secondly, that the water is not, and, thirdly, that neither of the two keeps the same fixed place, especially since the reciprocal change of one into the other is most natural and very near at hand; and also that much of the earth changes into water, and many of the waters become dry land in the same manner as on the earth, where also so many variations take place; for one kind of earth crumbles easily and others are solid, or rocky, or contain iron ore, and so with the rest. And the case is the same with the properties of liquids: one water is salty, another sweet and potable, and others contain drugs, salutary or deadly, or are hot or cold. Why, then, is it marvellous if some parts of the earth which are at present inhabited were covered with sea in earlier times, and

[1] Heaven is the outermost periphery, in which is situated everything that is divine (Poseidonius, quoted by Diogenes Laërtius, 7. 138).

πελάγη πρότερον ᾠκεῖτο; καθάπερ καὶ πηγὰς
τὰς[1] πρότερον ἐκλιπεῖν συνέβη, τὰς δ' ἀνεῖσθαι,
καὶ ποταμοὺς καὶ λίμνας, οὕτω δὲ καὶ ὄρη καὶ
πεδία εἰς ἄλληλα μεταπίπτειν· περὶ ὧν καὶ
πρότερον εἰρήκαμεν πολλά, καὶ νῦν εἰρήσθω.

37. Ἡ δ' οὖν Μοίριδος[2] λίμνη διὰ τὸ μέγεθος
καὶ τὸ βάθος ἱκανή ἐστι κατὰ[3] τὰς ἀναβάσεις
τὴν πλημμυρίδα φέρειν καὶ μὴ ὑπερπολάζειν εἰς
τὰ οἰκούμενα καὶ πεφυτευμένα, εἶτα ἐν τῇ ἀπο-
C 811 βάσει τὸ πλεονάζον ἀποδοῦσα τῇ αὐτῇ διώρυγι
κατὰ θάτερον τῶν στομάτων ἔχειν ὑπολειπόμενον
τὸ χρήσιμον πρὸς τὰς ἐποχετείας καὶ αὐτὴ καὶ
ἡ διῶρυξ. ταῦτα μὲν φυσικά, ἐπίκειται δὲ τοῖς
στόμασιν ἀμφοτέροις τῆς διώρυγος κλεῖθρα, οἷς
ταμιεύουσιν οἱ ἀρχιτέκτονες τό τε εἰσρέον ὕδωρ
καὶ τὸ ἐκρέον. πρὸς δὲ τούτοις ἡ τοῦ λαβυρίνθου
κατασκευὴ πάρισον ταῖς πυραμίσιν ἐστὶν ἔργον
καὶ ὁ παρακείμενος τάφος τοῦ κατασκευάσαντος
βασιλέως τὸν λαβύρινθον. ἔστι δὲ κατὰ[4] τὸν
πρῶτον εἴσπλουν τὸν εἰς τὴν διώρυγα προελθόντι
ὅσον τριάκοντα ἢ τετταράκοντα σταδίους ἐπί-
πεδόν τι τραπεζῶδες χωρίον, ἔχον κώμην τε καὶ
βασίλειον μέγα ἐκ πολλῶν βασιλείων,[5] ὅσοι πρότερον ἦσαν νομοί· τοσαῦται γάρ εἰσιν αὐλαὶ
περίστυλοι, συνεχεῖς ἀλλήλαις, ἐφ' ἕνα στίχον
πᾶσαι καὶ ἐφ' ἑνὸς τοίχου, ὡς ἂν τείχους μακροῦ[6]
προκειμένας ἔχοντος[7] τὰς αὐλάς· αἱ δ' εἰς αὐτὰς

---

[1] καὶ τὰς πηγάς Dh.   [2] Μούριδος Dhimowuz.
[3] All MSS. except E read τε after κατά.
[4] δὲ κατά E, δὲ τὸ κατά DFh, δὲ τῷ κατά other MSS.
[5] βασιλείων, Corais, for βασιλέων.
[6] μακροῦ, Corais, for μικροῦ.
[7] ἔχοντος, Corais, for ἔχοντες.

if what are now seas were inhabited in earlier times? Just as fountains of earlier times have given out and others have sprung forth, and rivers and lakes, so also mountains and plains have changed one into another. But I have discussed this subject at length before,[1] and now let this suffice.

37. Be this as it may, the Lake of Moeris,[2] on account of its size and its depth, is sufficient to bear the flood-tides at the risings of the Nile and not overflow into the inhabited and planted parts, and then, in the retirement of the river, to return the excess water to the river by the same canal at each of its two mouths[3] and, both itself and the canal, to keep back an amount remaining that will be useful for irrigation. While these conditions are the work of nature, yet locks have been placed at both mouths of the canal, by which the engineers[4] regulate both the inflow and the outflow of the water. In addition to the things mentioned, this Nome has the Labyrinth, which is a work comparable to the pyramids, and, near it, the tomb of the king who built the Labyrinth.[5] Near the first entrance to the canal, and on proceeding thence about thirty or forty stadia, one comes to a flat, trapezium-shaped place, which has a village, and also a great palace composed of many palaces—as many in number as there were Nomes in earlier times;[6] for this is the number of courts, surrounded by colonnades, continuous with one another, all in a single row and along one wall, the structure being as it were a long wall with the courts in front of it; and the

---

[1] 1. 3. 4, 12–15.   [2] On this lake, cp. Herodotus 2. 149.
[3] Cp. § 35 above.   [4] Literally, "architects."
[5] On this Labyrinth, cp. Herodotus 2. 148, Diodorus Siculus 1. 66. 3, and Pliny 36. 19.
[6] See 17. 1. 3.

ὁδοὶ καταντικρὺ τοῦ τείχους εἰσί. πρόκεινται δὲ
τῶν εἰσόδων κρυπταί τινες μακραὶ καὶ πολλαί,
δι' ἀλλήλων ἔχουσαι σκολιὰς τὰς ὁδούς, ὥστε
χωρὶς ἡγεμόνος μηδενὶ τῶν ξένων εἶναι δυνατὴν
τὴν εἰς ἑκάστην αὐλὴν πάροδόν τε καὶ ἔξοδον.
τὸ δὲ θαυμαστόν, ὅτι αἱ στέγαι τῶν οἴκων ἑκάστου
μονόλιθοι,[1] καὶ τῶν κρυπτῶν τὰ πλάτη μονολίθοις
ὡσαύτως ἐστέγασται πλαξίν, ὑπερβαλλούσαις τὸ
μέγεθος, ξύλων οὐδαμοῦ καταμεμιγμένων οὐδ'
ἄλλης ὕλης οὐδεμιᾶς. ἀναβάντα τε[2] ἐπὶ τὸ στέγος,
οὐ μεγάλῳ[3] ὕψει, ἅτε μονοστέγῳ, ἔστιν ἰδεῖν
πεδίον λίθινον ἐκ τηλικούτων λίθων, ἐντεῦθεν δὲ
πάλιν εἰς τὰς αὐλὰς ἐκπίπτοντα[4] ἑξῆς ὁρᾶν
κειμένας ὑπὸ μονολίθων κιόνων ὑπηρεισμένας
ἑπτὰ καὶ εἴκοσι· καὶ οἱ τοῖχοι δὲ οὐκ ἐξ ἐλαττόνων τῷ μεγέθει λίθων σύγκεινται. ἐπὶ τέλει
δὲ τῆς οἰκοδομίας ταύτης πλέον ἢ στάδιον ἐπεχούσης[5] ὁ τάφος ἐστί, πυραμὶς τετράγωνος,
ἑκάστην τετράπλεθρόν πως ἔχουσα τὴν πλευρὰν
καὶ τὸ ἴσον ὕψος· Ἰμάνδης[6] δ' ὄνομα ὁ ταφείς.
πεποιῆσθαι δέ φασι τὰς αὐλὰς τοσαύτας, ὅτι
τοὺς νομοὺς ἔθος ἦν ἐκεῖσε συνέρχεσθαι πάντας
ἀριστίνδην[7] μετὰ τῶν οἰκείων ἱερέων καὶ ἱερειῶν,
θυσίας τε καὶ θεοδοσίας καὶ δικαιοδοσίας[8] περὶ

[1] μονόλιθοι D, μονολίθου F, μονολίθῳ other MSS.
[2] All MSS. except E read ἐστι after τε.
[3] Müller-Dübner, following conj. of Meineke, emend μέγα
τῷ to μεγάλῳ. One would expect ἐν before the οὐ.
[4] For ἐκπίπτοντα, Letronne conj. ἐκκύπτοντα, Kramer
εἰσβλέποντα.
[5] ἐπεχούσης, Corais, for ἀπεχούσης.
[6] Ἰμάνδης, Meineke and Müller-Dübner, for Ἰσμάνδης MSS.,
Μαίνδης Epit. (cp. Ἰσμάνδης § 42 below).

roads leading into them are exactly opposite the wall.
In front of the entrances are crypts, as it were, which
are long and numerous and have winding passages
communicating with one another, so that no stranger
can find his way either into any court or out of it
without a guide. But the marvellous thing is that
the roof of each of the chambers consists of a single
stone, and that the breadths of the crypts are likewise
roofed with single slabs of surpassing size, with no
intermixture anywhere of timber or of any other
material. And, on ascending to the roof, which is at
no great height, inasmuch as the Labyrinth has only
one story, one can see a plain of stone, consisting of
stones of that great size ; and thence, descending out
into the courts again, one can see that they lie in a
row and are each supported by twenty-seven monolithic pillars ; and their walls, also, are composed of
stones that are no smaller in size. At the end of
this building, which occupies more than a stadium, is
the tomb, a quadrangular pyramid, which has sides
about four plethra in width and a height equal thereto.
Imandes [1] is the name of the man buried there. It
is said that this number of courts was built because it
was the custom for all the Nomes to assemble there
in accordance with their rank, together with their
own priests and priestesses, for the sake of sacrifice
and of offering gifts to the gods and of administering

[1] Perhaps an error for "Mandes." The name is spelled
Ismandes in §42 below. Diodorus says "Mendes, whom
some give the name Marrus." The real builder was Maindes,
or Amon-em-hat III, of the twelfth dynasty (Sayce, *The Egypt
of the Hebrews*, p. 281).

[7] ἀριστίνδην, Tyrwhitt, for ἄριστον δ᾽ ἦν.
[8] καὶ δικαιοδοσίας, suspected by Corais and Müller-Dübner.

τῶν μεγίστων χάριν. κατήγετο δὲ τῶν νομῶν
ἔκαστος εἰς τὴν ἀποδειχθεῖσαν αὐλὴν αὐτῷ.

38. Παραπλεύσαντι δὲ ταῦτα ἐφ' ἑκατὸν σταδίους πόλις ἐστὶν Ἀρσινόη, Κροκοδείλων δὲ πόλις
ἐκαλεῖτο πρότερον· σφόδρα γὰρ ἐν τῷ νομῷ τούτῳ
τιμῶσι τὸν κροκόδειλον, καί ἐστιν ἱερὸς παρ'
αὐτοῖς ἐν λίμνῃ καθ' αὑτὸν τρεφόμενος, χειροήθης
τοῖς ἱερεῦσι. καλεῖται δὲ Σοῦχος· τρέφεται δὲ
σιτίοις καὶ κρέασι καὶ οἴνῳ, προσφερόντων ἀεὶ τῶν
C 812 ξένων τῶν ἐπὶ τὴν θέαν ἀφικνουμένων. ὁ γοῦν ἡμέ-
τερος ξένος, ἀνὴρ τῶν ἐντίμων, αὐτόθι μυσταγωγῶν
ἡμᾶς, συνῆλθεν ἐπὶ τὴν λίμνην, κομίζων ἀπὸ τοῦ
δείπνου πλακουντάριόν[1] τι καὶ κρέας ὀπτὸν καὶ
προχοΐδιόν τι μελικράτου. εὕρομεν δὲ ἐπὶ τῷ
χείλει κείμενον τὸ θηρίον· προσιόντες δὲ οἱ ἱερεῖς,
οἱ μὲν διέστησαν αὐτοῦ τὸ στόμα, ὁ δὲ ἐνέθηκε
τὸ πέμμα, καὶ πάλιν τὸ κρέας, εἶτα τὸ μελίκρατον
κατήρασε. καθαλόμενος δὲ εἰς τὴν λίμνην διῆξεν
εἰς τὸ πέραν· ἐπελθόντος δὲ καὶ ἄλλου τῶν ξένων,
κομίζοντος ὁμοίως ἀπαρχήν,[2] λαβόντες περιῆλθον
δρόμῳ καὶ καταλαβόντες προσήνεγκαν ὁμοίως τὰ
προσενεχθέντα.

39. Μετὰ δὲ τὸν Ἀρσινοΐτην καὶ[3] τὸν Ἡρακ-
λεωτικὸν νομὸν Ἡρακλέους πόλις, ἐν ᾗ ὁ ἰχνεύμων
τιμᾶται ὑπεναντίως τοῖς Ἀρσινοΐταις· οἱ μὲν γὰρ
τοὺς κροκοδείλους τιμῶσι, καὶ διὰ τοῦτο ἥ τε

---

[1] πλακούντιον E. [2] ἀπαρχάς E.
[3] καί, Letronne emends to κατά, Groskurd to καὶ κατά.

---

[1] For proposed restorations of the Labyrinth, see the
Latronne Edition, and Petrie (*The Labyrinth, Gerzeh, and*

justice in matters of the greatest importance. And each of the Nomes was conducted to the court appointed to it.[1]

38. Sailing along shore for a distance of one hundred stadia, one comes to the city Arsinoê, which in earlier times was called Crocodeilonpolis; for the people in this Nome hold in very great honour the crocodile, and there is a sacred one there which is kept and fed by itself in a lake, and is tame to the priests. It is called Suchus; and it is fed on grain and pieces of meat and on wine, which are always being fed to it by the foreigners who go to see it. At any rate, our host, one of the officials, who was introducing us into the mysteries there, went with us to the lake, carrying from the dinner a kind of cooky and some roasted meat and a pitcher of wine mixed with honey. We found the animal lying on the edge of the lake; and when the priests went up to it, some of them opened its mouth and another put in the cake, and again the meat, and then poured down the honey mixture. The animal then leaped into the lake and rushed across to the far side; but when another foreigner arrived, likewise carrying an offering of first-fruits, the priests took it, went around the lake in a run, took hold of the animal, and in the same manner fed it what had been brought.

39. After the Arsinoïte and Heracleotic Nomes, one comes to a City of Heracles, where the people hold in honour the ichneumon, the very opposite of the practice of the Arsinoïtae; for whereas the latter hold the crocodile in honour—and on this account

Mazghuneh, p. 28), and Myres (*Annals of Archaeology and Anthropology*, III, 134).

STRABO

διῶρυξ αὐτῶν ἐστι μεστὴ τῶν κροκοδείλων καὶ
ἡ τοῦ Μοίριδος¹ λίμνη· σέβονται γὰρ καὶ ἀπέ-
χονται αὐτῶν· οἱ δὲ τοὺς ἰχνεύμονας τοὺς ὀλεθριω-
τάτους τοῖς κροκοδείλοις, καθάπερ καὶ ταῖς
ἀσπίσι· καὶ γὰρ τὰ ὠὰ διαφθείρουσιν αὐτῶν καὶ
αὐτὰ τὰ θηρία, τῷ πηλῷ θωρακισθέντες· κυλισ-
θέντες γὰρ ἐν αὐτῷ ξηραίνονται πρὸς τὸν ἥλιον,
εἶτα τὰς ἀσπίδας μὲν ἢ τῆς κεφαλῆς ἢ τῆς οὐρᾶς
λαβόμενοι κατασπῶσιν εἰς τὸν ποταμὸν καὶ δια-
φθείρουσι· τοὺς δὲ κροκοδείλους ἐνεδρεύσαντες,
ἡνίκ' ἂν ἡλιάζωνται κεχηνότες, ἐμπίπτουσιν εἰς τὰ
χάσματα καὶ διαφαγόντες τὰ σπλάγχνα καὶ τὰς
γαστέρας ἐκδύνουσιν ἐκ νεκρῶν τῶν σωμάτων.

40. Ἑξῆς δ' ἐστὶν ὁ Κυνοπολίτης νομὸς καὶ
Κυνῶν πόλις, ἐν ᾗ ὁ Ἄνουβις τιμᾶται καὶ τοῖς
κυσὶ τιμὴ καὶ σίτισις τέτακταί τις ἱερά. ἐν δὲ
τῇ περαίᾳ Ὀξύρυγχος πόλις καὶ νομὸς ὁμώνυμος.
τιμῶσι δὲ τὸν ὀξύρυγχον καὶ ἔστιν αὐτοῖς ἱερὸν
Ὀξυρύγχου, καίτοι καὶ τῶν ἄλλων Αἰγυπτίων
κοινῇ τιμώντων τὸν ὀξύρυγχον. τινὰ μὲν γὰρ
τῶν ζῴων ἅπαντες κοινῇ τιμῶσιν Αἰγύπτιοι,
καθάπερ τῶν μὲν πεζῶν τρία, βοῦν, κύνα,
αἴλουρον, τῶν δὲ πτηνῶν δύο, ἱέρακα καὶ ἶβιν,
τῶν δ' ἐνύδρων δύο, λεπιδωτὸν ἰχθὺν καὶ
ὀξύρυγχον· ἄλλα δ' ἔστιν, ἃ τιμῶσι καθ' ἑαυτοὺς
ἕκαστοι, καθάπερ Σαῖται πρόβατον καὶ Θηβαῖται,
λάτον δὲ τῶν ἐν τῷ Νείλῳ τινὰ ἰχθὺν Λατοπο-

Μοίριδος, Xylander, for Μούριδος.

So in § 44 below.
² "City of Dogs."

108

both their canal and the Lake of Moeris are full of
crocodiles, for the people revere them and abstain
from harming them [1]—the former hold in honour the
ichneumons, which are the deadliest enemies of the
crocodile, as also of the asp; for they destroy, not
only the eggs of the asps, but also the asps themselves,
having armed themselves with a breastplate of mud;
for they first roll themselves in mud, make it dry in
the sun, and then, seizing the asps by either the
head or the tail, drag them down into the river and
kill them; and as for the crocodiles, the ichneumons
lie in wait for them, and when the crocodiles are
basking in the sun with their mouths open the ichneumons throw themselves into their open jaws, eat
through their entrails and bellies, and emerge from
their dead bodies.

40. One comes next to the Cynopolite Nome,
and to Cynonpolis,[2] where Anubis is held in honour
and where a form of worship and sacred feeding has
been organised for all dogs. On the far side of the
river lie the city Oxyrynchus and a Nome bearing the
same name. They hold in honour the oxyrynchus [3]
and have a temple sacred to Oxyrynchus, though
the other Aegyptians in common also hold in honour
the oxyrynchus. In fact, certain animals are worshipped by all Aegyptians in common, as, for example,
three land animals, bull and dog and cat, and two
birds, hawk and ibis, and two aquatics, scale-fish and
oxyrynchus, but there are other animals which are
honoured by separate groups independently of the
rest, as, for example, a sheep by the Saïtae and also
by the Thebans; a *latus*, a fish of the Nile, by

---

[3] *i.e.* "sharp-snouted" (fish). A species of fish like our
pike.

λῖται, λύκον τε Λυκοπολῖται, κυνοκέφαλον δὲ
Ἑρμοπολῖται, κῆβον δὲ Βαβυλώνιοι οἱ κατὰ
Μέμφιν· ἔστι δ' ὁ κῆβος τὸ μὲν πρόσωπον
ἐοικὼς σατύρῳ, τἆλλα δὲ κυνὸς καὶ ἄρκτου
μεταξύ, γεννᾶται δ' ἐν Αἰθιοπίᾳ· ἀετὸν δὲ
C 813 Θηβαῖοι, λέοντα δὲ Λεοντοπολῖται, αἶγα δὲ καὶ
τράγον Μενδήσιοι, μυγαλῆν δὲ Ἀθριβῖται, ἄλλοι
δ' ἄλλο τι· τὰς δ' αἰτίας οὐχ ὁμολογουμένας
λέγουσιν.

41. Ἑξῆς δ' ἐστὶν Ἑρμοπολιτικὴ φυλακή,
τελώνιόν τι τῶν ἐκ τῆς Θηβαΐδος καταφερο-
μένων· ἐντεῦθεν ἀρχὴ τῶν ἑξηκονταστάδιων
σχοίνων, ἕως Συήνης καὶ Ἐλεφαντίνης· εἶτα ἡ
Θηβαϊκὴ φυλακὴ καὶ διῶρυξ φέρουσα ἐπὶ Τάνιν·
εἶτα Λύκων πόλις καὶ Ἀφροδίτης καὶ Πανῶν
πόλις, λινουργῶν καὶ λιθουργῶν κατοικία
παλαιά.

42. Ἔπειτα Πτολεμαϊκὴ πόλις, μεγίστη τῶν
ἐν τῇ Θηβαΐδι καὶ οὐκ ἐλάττων Μέμφεως, ἔχουσα
καὶ σύστημα πολιτικὸν ἐν τῷ Ἑλληνικῷ τρόπῳ.
ὑπὲρ δὲ ταύτης ἡ Ἄβυδος, ἐν ᾗ τὸ Μεμνόνιον,
βασίλειον θαυμαστῶς κατεσκευασμένον ὁλόλιθον [1]
τῇ αὐτῇ κατασκευῇ, ᾗπερ τὸν λαβύρινθον ἔφαμεν,
οὐ πολλαπλοῦν δέ· καὶ κρήνη ἐν βάθει κειμένη,
ὥστε καταβαίνειν εἰς αὐτὴν διὰ κατακαμφθεισῶν [2]
ψαλίδων μονολίθων ὑπερβαλλουσῶν τῷ μεγέθει

---

[1] ὁλόλιθον, omitted by E.
[2] κατακαμφθεισῶν (see Diodorus Siculus 2. 9), Corais, for
κατακαμφθέντων. For conjectures, see Kramer.

---

[1] i.e. the Aegyptian jackal (Canis lupaster).
[2] i.e. the dog-faced baboon (Simia hamadryas).
[3] See 16. 4. 16 and footnote.

the Latopolitae; a *lycus*[1] by the Lycopolitae; a
cynocephalus[2] by the Hermopolitae; a *cebus*[3] by
the Babylonians who live near Memphis (the *cebus*
has a face like a satyr, is between a dog and a bear
in other respects, and is bred in Aethiopia); an eagle
by the Thebans; a lion by the Leontopolitae; a
female and male goat by the Mendesians; a shrew-
mouse[4] by the Athribitae, and other animals by
other peoples; but the reasons which they give for
such worship are not in agreement.

41. One comes next to the Hermopolitic garrison,
a kind of toll-station for goods brought down from
the Thebaïs; here begins the reckoning of schoeni
at sixty stadia,[5] extending as far as Syenê and
Elephantinê; and then to the Thebaïc garrison and
the canal that leads to Tanis; and then to Lycopolis
and to Aphroditopolis and to Panopolis, an old
settlement of linen-workers and stone-workers.

42. Then one comes to the city of Ptolemaïs,
which is the largest of the cities in the Thebaïs, is
no smaller than Memphis, and has also a form of
government modelled on that of the Greeks. Above
this city lies Abydus, where is the Memnonium, a
royal building, which is a remarkable structure built
of solid stone, and of the same workmanship as that
which I ascribed to the Labyrinth, though not
multiplex; and also a fountain[6] which lies at a great
depth, so that one descends to it down vaulted
galleries made of monoliths of surpassing size and

[4] *Mus araneus.*
[5] See § 24 above, and 11. 11. 5.
[6] Known as "Strabo's Well." See Petrie, *The Osireion at Abydos*, p. 2; and Naville, *The Tomb of Osiris, London Times,* March 6 and 17, 1914.

καὶ τῇ κατασκευῇ. ἔστι δὲ διῶρυξ ἄγουσα ἐπὶ τὸν τόπον ἀπὸ τοῦ μεγάλου ποταμοῦ. περὶ δὲ τὴν διώρυγα ἀκανθῶν Αἰγυπτίων ἄλσος ἐστὶν ἱερὸν τοῦ Ἀπόλλωνος. ἔοικε δὲ ὑπάρξαι ποτὲ ἡ Ἄβυδος πόλις μεγάλη, δευτερεύουσα μετὰ τὰς Θήβας, νυνὶ δ' ἐστὶ κατοικία μικρά· εἰ δ', ὥς φασιν, ὁ Μέμνων ὑπὸ τῶν Αἰγυπτίων Ἰσμάνδης[1] λέγεται, καὶ ὁ λαβύρινθος Μεμνόνιον ἂν εἴη καὶ τοῦ αὐτοῦ ἔργον, οὗπερ καὶ τὰ ἐν Ἀβύδῳ καὶ τὰ ἐν Θήβαις· καὶ γὰρ ἐκεῖ λέγεταί τινα Μεμνόνια. κατὰ δὲ τὴν Ἄβυδόν ἐστιν ἡ πρώτη αὔασις ἐκ τῶν λεχθεισῶν τριῶν ἐν τῇ Λιβύῃ, διέχουσα ὁδὸν ἡμερῶν ἑπτὰ ἐνθένδε δι' ἐρημίας, εὔυδρός τε κατοικία καὶ εὔοινος καὶ τοῖς ἄλλοις ἱκανή· δευτέρα δ' ἡ κατὰ τὴν Μοίριδος[2] λίμνην· τρίτη δὲ ἡ κατὰ τὸ μαντεῖον τὸ ἐν Ἄμμωνι· καὶ αὗται δὲ κατοικίαι εἰσὶν ἀξιόλογοι.

43. Πολλὰ δ' εἰρηκότες περὶ τοῦ Ἄμμωνος τοσοῦτον εἰπεῖν βουλόμεθα, ὅτι τοῖς ἀρχαίοις μᾶλλον ἦν ἐν τιμῇ καὶ ἡ μαντικὴ καθόλου καὶ τὰ χρηστήρια, νυνὶ δ' ὀλιγωρία κατέχει πολλή, τῶν Ῥωμαίων ἀρκουμένων τοῖς Σιβύλλης χρησμοῖς καὶ τοῖς Τυρρηνικοῖς θεοπροπίοις διά τε σπλάγχνων καὶ ὀρνιθείας καὶ διοσημῶν.[3] διόπερ καὶ τὸ ἐν Ἄμμωνι σχεδόν τι ἐκλέλειπται χρηστήριον, πρότερον δὲ ἐτετίμητο. δηλοῦσι δὲ μάλιστα τοῦτο οἱ τὰς Ἀλεξάνδρου πράξεις ἀναγράψαντες,

---

[1] Σμάνδης F, Ἰμάνδης xz, Μάνδης w (cp. Ἰμάνδης 17. 1. 37).
[2] Μοίριδος E, Μούριδος other MSS.
[3] διοσημιῶν, Corais, for διασημειῶν.

---

[1] Spelled "Imandes" in § 37 above (see footnote there).

workmanship. There is a canal leading to the place from the great river; and in the neighbourhood of the canal is a grove of Aegyptian *acantha*, sacred to Apollo. Abydus appears once to have been a great city, second only to Thebes, but it is now only a small settlement. But if, as they say, Memnon is called Ismandes[1] by the Aegyptians, the Labyrinth might also be a Memnonium and a work of the same man who built both the Memnonia in Abydus and those in Thebes; for it is said that there are also some Memnonia in Thebes. Opposite Abydus is the first of the above-mentioned three oases in Libya; it is a seven days' journey distant from Abydus through a desert; and it is a settlement which abounds in water and in wine, and is sufficiently supplied with other things. The second oasis is that in the neighbourhood of the Lake of Moeris; and the third is that in the neighbourhood of the oracle in Ammon; and these, also, are noteworthy settlements.

43. Now that I have already said much about Ammon,[2] I wish to add only this: Among the ancients both divination in general and oracles were held in greater honour, but now great neglect of them prevails, since the Romans are satisfied with the oracles of Sibylla, and with the Tyrrhenian prophecies obtained by means of the entrails of animals, flight of birds, and omens from the sky; and on this account, also, the oracle at Ammon has been almost abandoned, though it was held in honour in earlier times; and this fact is most clearly shown by those who have recorded the deeds of Alexander, since,

---

[2] See references in *Index*.

προστιθέντες μὲν πολὺ καὶ τὸ τῆς κολακείας
εἶδος, ἐμφαίνοντες δέ τι[1] καὶ πίστεως ἄξιον. ὁ
C 814 γοῦν Καλλισθένης φησὶ τὸν Ἀλέξανδρον φιλο-
δοξῆσαι μάλιστα ἀνελθεῖν ἐπὶ τὸ χρηστήριον,
ἐπειδὴ καὶ Περσέα ἤκουσε[2] πρότερον ἀναβῆναι
καὶ Ἡρακλέα· ὁρμήσαντα δ' ἐκ Παραιτονίου,
καίπερ νότων ἐπιπεσόντων, βιάσασθαι· πλανώ-
μενον δ' ὑπὸ τοῦ κονιορτοῦ σωθῆναι, γενομένων
ὄμβρων καὶ δυεῖν κοράκων ἡγησαμένων τὴν ὁδόν,
ἤδη τούτων κολακευτικῶς λεγομένων· τοιαῦτα δὲ
καὶ τὰ ἑξῆς· μόνῳ γὰρ δὴ τῷ βασιλεῖ τὸν ἱερέα
ἐπιτρέψαι παρελθεῖν εἰς τὸν νεὼ μετὰ τῆς συνή-
θους στολῆς, τοὺς δ' ἄλλους μετενδῦναι τὴν
ἐσθῆτα, ἔξωθέν τε τῆς θεμιστείας ἀκροάσασθαι
πάντας πλὴν Ἀλεξάνδρου, τοῦτον δ' ἔνδοθεν
εἶναι δὲ[3] οὐχ ὥσπερ ἐν Δελφοῖς καὶ Βραγχίδαις
τὰς ἀποθεσπίσεις διὰ λόγων, ἀλλὰ νεύμασι καὶ
συμβόλοις τὸ πλέον, ὡς καὶ παρ' Ὁμήρῳ,

ἦ καὶ κυανέῃσιν ἐπ' ὀφρύσι νεῦσε Κρονίων,

τοῦ προφήτου τὸν Δία ὑποκριναμένου· τοῦτο
μέντοι ῥητῶς εἰπεῖν τὸν ἄνθρωπον πρὸς τὸν
βασιλέα, ὅτι εἴη Διὸς υἱός. προστραγῳδεῖ δὲ
τούτοις ὁ Καλλισθένης, ὅτι τοῦ Ἀπόλλωνος τὸ
ἐν Βραγχίδαις μαντεῖον ἐκλελοιπότος, ἐξ ὅτου
τὸ ἱερὸν ὑπὸ τῶν Βραγχιδῶν σεσύλητο ἐπὶ Ξέρξου
περσισάντων, ἐκλελοιπυίας δὲ καὶ τῆς κρήνης,
τότε ἥ τε κρήνη ἀνάσχοι καὶ μαντεῖα πολλὰ οἱ

---

[1] δέ τι, the editors, for δ' ἔτι x, δ' ὅτι other MSS.
[2] ἤκουε DF.   [3] δέ, Meineke inserts.

---

[1] Cp. 2. 1. 5, 11. 6. 4, 15. 1. 21, 28.

although they add numerous forms of mere flattery,[1] yet they do indicate some things that are worthy of belief. At any rate, Callisthenes says that Alexander conceived a very great ambition to go inland to the oracle, since he had heard that Perseus, as also Heracles, had done so in earlier times ; and that he started from Paraetonium, although the south winds had set in, and forced his way ; and that when he lost his way because of the thick dust, he was saved by rainfalls and by the guidance of two crows. But this last assertion is flattery and so are the next : that the priest permitted the king alone to pass into the temple in his usual dress, but the rest changed their clothes ; that all heard the oracles from outside except Alexander, but he inside ; that the oracular responses were not, as at Delphi and among the Branchidae,[2] given in words, but mostly by nods and tokens, as in Homer,[3] "Cronion spoke and nodded assent with his dark brows"—the prophet having assumed the rôle of Zeus ; that, however, the fellow expressly told the king that he, Alexander, was son of Zeus. And to this statement Callisthenes dramatically adds that,[4] although the oracle of Apollo among the Branchidae had ceased to speak from the time the temple had been robbed by the Branchidae, who sided with the Persians in the time of Xerxes,[5] and although the spring also had ceased to flow, yet at Alexander's arrival the spring began to flow again and that many oracles were carried by the Milesian

---

[2] *i.e.* at Didyma, near Miletus (14. 1. 5).
[3] *Iliad* 1. 528.
[4] Literally, "although Apollo had deserted the oracle among the Branchidae."
[5] 11. 11. 4.

Μιλησιων πρέσβεις κομίσαιεν[1] εἰς Μέμφιν περὶ
τῆς ἐκ Διὸς γενέσεως τοῦ Ἀλεξάνδρου καὶ τῆς
ἐσομένης περὶ Ἄρβηλα νίκης καὶ τοῦ Δαρείου
θανάτου καὶ τῶν ἐν Λακεδαίμονι νεωτερισμῶν.
περὶ δὲ τῆς εὐγενείας[2] καὶ τὴν Ἐρυθραίαν Ἀθη-
ναΐδα φησὶν ἀνειπεῖν· καὶ γὰρ ταύτην ὁμοίαν
γενέσθαι τῇ παλαιᾷ Σιβύλλῃ τῇ Ἐρυθραίᾳ. τὰ
μὲν δὴ τῶν συγγραφέων τοιαῦτα.

44. Ἐν δὲ τῇ Ἀβύδῳ τιμῶσι τὸν Ὄσιριν· ἐν
δὲ τῷ ἱερῷ τοῦ Ὀσίριδος οὐκ ἔξεστιν οὔτε ᾠδὸν
οὔτε αὐλητὴν οὔτε ψάλτην ἀπάρχεσθαι τῷ θεῷ,
καθάπερ τοῖς ἄλλοις θεοῖς ἔθος. μετὰ δὲ τὴν
Ἄβυδον Διὸς πόλις ἡ μικρά, εἶτα Τέντυρα πόλις·
ἐνταῦθα δὲ διαφερόντως παρὰ τοὺς ἄλλους
Αἰγυπτίους ὁ κροκόδειλος ἠτίμωται καὶ ἔχθιστος
τῶν ἁπάντων θηρίων νενόμισται. οἱ μὲν γὰρ
ἄλλοι, καίπερ εἰδότες τὴν κακίαν τοῦ ζῴου, καὶ
ὡς ὀλέθριον τῷ ἀνθρωπίνῳ γένει, σέβονται ὅμως
καὶ ἀπέχονται· οὗτοι δὲ πάντα τρόπον ἀν-
ιχνεύουσι καὶ ἐκφθείρουσιν[3] αὐτούς. ἔνιοι δ᾽
ὥσπερ τοὺς Ψύλλους φασὶ τοὺς πρὸς τῇ Κυρηναίᾳ
φυσικήν τινα ἀντιπάθειαν ἔχειν πρὸς τὰ ἑρπετά,
οὕτω καὶ τοὺς Τεντυρίτας πρὸς τοὺς κροκοδείλους,
ὥστε μηδὲν ὑπ᾽ αὐτῶν πάσχειν, ἀλλὰ καὶ κο-
λυμβᾶν ἀδεῶς καὶ διαπερᾶν, μηδενὸς ἄλλου θαρ-
ροῦντος. εἴς τε τὴν Ῥώμην κομισθεῖσι τοῖς
C 815 κροκοδείλοις ἐπιδείξεως χάριν συνηκολούθουν οἱ
Τεντυρῖται· γενομένης τε δεξαμενῆς καὶ πήγματός
τινος ὑπὲρ μιᾶς τῶν πλευρῶν, ὥστε τοῖς θηρίοις

---

[1] κομίσαιεν, Casaubon, for κομισθέντες.
[2] Meineke conj. διογενείας or θεογενείας.
[3] ἐκφθείρουσιν DF, διαφθείρουσιν other MSS.

ambassadors to Memphis concerning Alexander's descent from Zeus, his future victory in the neighbourhood of Arbela, the death of Dareius, and the revolutionary attempts in Lacedaemon. And he says that the Erythraean Athenaïs [1] also gave out an utterance concerning Alexander's high descent; for, he adds, this woman was like the ancient Erythraean Sibylla. Such, then, are the accounts of the historians.

44. At Abydus they hold in honour Osiris; and in the temple of Osiris [2] neither singer nor flute-player nor harp-player is permitted to begin the rites in honour of the god, as is the custom in the case of the other gods. After Abydus one comes to the Little Diospolis, and to the city Tentyra, where the people, as compared with the other Aegyptians, hold in particular dishonour the crocodile and deem it the most hateful of all animals. For although the others know the malice of the animal and how destructive it is to the human race, still they revere it and abstain from harming it,[3] whereas the Tentyritae track them and destroy them in every way. Some say that, just as there is a kind of natural antipathy between the Psylli [4] near Cyrenaea and reptiles, so there is between the Tentyritae and crocodiles, so that they suffer no injury from them, but even dive in the river without fear and cross over, though no others are bold enough to do so. When the crocodiles were brought to Rome for exhibition, they were attended by the Tentyritae; and when a reservoir and a kind of stage above one of the sides had been made for them, so that they could go out of the

---

[1] 14. 1. 34.
[2] On this temple, see Petrie, *The Osireion at Abydos.*
[3] So in § 39 above.   [4] Cp. 13. 1. 14.

ἐκβᾶσι τοῦ ὕδατος ἡλιαστήριον εἶναι, ἐκεῖνοι
ἦσαν οἱ τοτὲ μὲν ἐξέλκοντες δικτύῳ πρὸς τὸ
ἡλιαστήριον, ὡς καὶ ὑπὸ τῶν θεατῶν ὁραθῆναι,
ἐμβαίνοντες ἅμα εἰς τὸ ὕδωρ, τοτὲ δὲ πάλιν εἰς
τὴν δεξαμενὴν κατασπῶντες. τιμῶσι δὲ Ἀφρο-
δίτην· ὄπισθεν δὲ τοῦ νεὼ τῆς Ἀφροδίτης Ἴσιδός
ἐστιν ἱερόν· εἶτα τὰ Τυφώνια καλούμενα καὶ ἡ
εἰς Κοπτὸν διῶρυξ, πόλιν κοινὴν Αἰγυπτίων τε
καὶ Ἀράβων.

45. Ἐντεῦθέν ἐστιν ἰσθμὸς εἰς τὴν Ἐρυθρὰν
κατὰ πόλιν Βερενίκην, ἀλίμενον μέν, τῇ δ' εὐκαιρίᾳ
τοῦ ἰσθμοῦ καταγωγὰς ἐπιτηδείους ἔχουσαν.
λέγεται δ' ὁ Φιλάδελφος πρῶτος στρατοπέδῳ
τεμεῖν τὴν ὁδὸν ταύτην, ἄνυδρον οὖσαν, καὶ
κατασκευάσαι σταθμούς, ὥσπερ τοῖς ἐμπορίοις[1]
ὁδεύμασι καὶ διὰ τῶν καμήλων, τοῦτο δὲ πρᾶξαι
διὰ τὸ τὴν Ἐρυθρὰν δύσπλουν εἶναι, καὶ μάλιστα
τοῖς ἐκ τοῦ μυχοῦ πλοϊζομένοις. ἐφάνη δὴ τῇ
πείρᾳ πολὺ τὸ χρήσιμον, καὶ νῦν ὁ Ἰνδικὸς φόρτος[2] ἅπας καὶ ὁ Ἀράβιος καὶ τοῦ Αἰθιοπικοῦ
ὁ τῷ Ἀραβίῳ κόλπῳ κατακομιζόμενος εἰς Κοπτὸν
φέρεται, καὶ τοῦτ' ἔστιν ἐμπόριον τῶν τοιούτων
φορτίων. οὐκ ἄπωθεν δὲ τῆς Βερενίκης ἐστὶ
Μυὸς ὅρμος, πόλις ἔχουσα τὸ ναύσταθμον τῶν
πλοϊζομένων, καὶ τῆς Κοπτοῦ οὐ πολὺ ἀφέστηκεν
ἡ καλουμένη Ἀπόλλωνος πόλις, ὥστε καὶ αἱ
διορίζουσαι τὸν ἰσθμὸν δύο πόλεις ἑκατέρωθεν

---

[1] Arrian (*Indica* 41) likewise uses ἐμπορίοις as an adjective,
instead of ἐμπορικοῖς. It is so used nowhere else in Strabo
apparently ; but the clause appears to be a direct quotation
from one of Arrian's sources. Kramer and Meineke reject
it as a gloss ; Groskurd and C. Müller emend it drastically
(see Kramer).   [2] φόρτος z, φόρος other MSS.

water and have a basking-place in the sun, these men at one time, stepping into the water all together, would drag them in a net to the basking-place, so that they could be seen by the spectators, and at another would pull them down again into the reservoir. They worship Aphrodite; and back of her shrine is a temple of Isis. And then one comes to the Typhonia, as they are called, and to the canal that leads to Coptus, a city common to the Aegyptians and the Arabians.

45. Thence one crosses an isthmus, which extends to the Red Sea, near a city Berenicê. The city has no harbour, but on account of the favourable lay of the isthmus has convenient landing-places. It is said that Philadelphus was the first person, by means of an army, to cut this road, which is without water, and to build stations, as though for the travels of merchants on camels, and that he did this because the Red Sea was hard to navigate, particularly for those who set sail from its innermost recess. So the utility of his plan was shown by experience to be great, and now all the Indian merchandise, as well as the Arabian and such of the Aethiopian as is brought down by the Arabian Gulf, is carried to Coptus, which is the emporium for such cargoes. Not far from Berenicê lies Myus Hormus,[1] a city containing the naval station for sailors; and not far distant from Coptus lies Apollonospolis,[2] as it is called, so that on either side there are two cities which form the boundaries of

---

[1] But the well-known Berenicê (now Suakim) was about as far from Myus Hormus (now Kosseir) as from Coptus (now Kench); see footnote 2, next page.

[2] "City of Apollo."

εἰσιν. ἀλλὰ νῦν ἡ Κοπτὸς καὶ ὁ Μυὸς ὅρμος
εὐδοκιμεῖ, καὶ χρῶνται τοῖς τόποις τούτοις. πρότερον μὲν οὖν ἐνυκτοπόρουν πρὸς τὰ ἄστρα βλέ-
ποντες οἱ καμηλέμποροι καὶ καθάπερ[1] οἱ πλέοντες
ὥδευον κομίζοντες καὶ ὕδωρ, νυνὶ δὲ καὶ ὑδρεῖα
κατεσκευάκασιν, ὀρύξαντες πολὺ βάθος, καὶ ἐκ
τῶν οὐρανίων, καίπερ ὄντων σπανίων, ὅμως δεξα-
μενὰς πεποίηνται. ἡ δ᾽ ὁδός ἐστιν ἐξ ἢ ἑπτὰ
ἡμερῶν. ἐπὶ δὲ τῷ ἰσθμῷ τούτῳ καὶ τὰ τῆς
σμαράγδου μέταλλά ἐστι, τῶν Ἀράβων ὀρυτ-
τόντων βαθεῖς τινας ὑπονόμους, καὶ ἄλλων λίθων
πολυτελῶν.

46. Μετὰ δὲ τὴν Ἀπόλλωνος πόλιν οἱ Θῆβαι
(καλεῖται δὲ νῦν Διὸς πόλις),

αἵθ᾽ ἑκατόμπυλοί εἰσι, διηκόσιοι δ᾽ ἀν᾽ ἑκάστην
ἀνέρες ἐξοιχνεῦσι σὺν ἵπποισιν καὶ ὄχεσφιν.

Ὅμηρος μὲν οὕτω· λέγει δὲ καὶ τὸν πλοῦτον·

οὐδ᾽ ὅσα Θήβας

C 816   Αἰγυπτίας, ὅθι πλεῖστα δόμοις ἐνὶ κτήματα
κεῖται.

καὶ ἄλλοι δὲ τοιαῦτα λέγουσι, μητρόπολιν τιθέντες
τῆς Αἰγύπτου ταύτην· καὶ νῦν δ᾽ ἴχνη δείκνυται

---

[1] καὶ καθάπερ, omitted by F, καί by Dh.

---

[1] Cp. 2. 5. 12.
[2] Pliny (6. 26), who speaks only of the route from Coptus
to Berenicê, says that the distance was 257 Roman miles
and required twelve days, and that one of the watering-
places, Old Hydreuma ("Watering-place"), near Berenicê,
could accommodate 2000 persons. Strabo seems to be confused on the subject, since (1) there were two distinct routes;

the isthmus. But now it is Coptus and Myus Hormus [1] that have high repute; and people frequent these places. Now in earlier times the camel-merchants travelled only by night, looking to the stars for guidance, and, like the mariners, also carried water with them when they travelled; but now they have constructed watering-places, having dug down to a great depth, and, although rain-water is scarce, still they have made cisterns for it. The journey takes six or seven days. [2] On this isthmus are also the mines of smaragdus, [3] where the Arabians dig deep tunnels, I might call them, and of other precious stones.

46. After Apollonospolis one comes to Thebes [4] (now called Diospolis [5]), "Thebes of the hundred gates, whence sally forth two hundred men through each with horses and chariots." [6] So Homer; and he speaks also of its wealth, "even all the revenue of Aegyptian Thebes, where lies in treasure-houses the greatest wealth." And others also say things of this kind, making this city the metropolis of Aegypt. Even now traces of its magnitude are

(2) Myus Hormus and the well-known Berenicê were far apart (see footnote above); (3) the journey from Coptus to the latter required about twice as much time as that to the former (cp. Mahaffy, *The Empire of the Ptolemies*, pp. 135, 184, 395, 482), and (4) if Strabo was not thinking of a Berenicê *near* Myus Hormus, his "isthmus" has a very odd shape (see *Map* at end of volume).

[3] Pliny (37. 17) says that there are no fewer than twelve different kinds of smaragdus, and ranks the Aegyptian as third. The Aegyptian appears to have been a genuine emerald. For an account of the mines, see *Encyc. Brit.* s.v. "Emerald."

[4] Luxor.   [5] "City of Zeus."
[6] *Iliad* 9. 383.

τοῦ μεγέθους αὐτῆς ἐπὶ ὀγδοήκοντα σταδίους τὸ
μῆκος. ἔστι δ᾽ ἱερὰ¹ πλείω, καὶ τούτων δὲ τὰ
πολλὰ ἠκρωτηρίασε Καμβύσης. νυνὶ δὲ κωμηδὸν
συνοικεῖται, μέρος μέν² τι ἐν τῇ Ἀραβίᾳ, ἐν
ᾗπερ ἡ πόλις, μέρος δέ τι³ καὶ ἐν τῇ περαίᾳ,
ὅπου τὸ Μεμνόνιον. ἐνταῦθα δὲ δυεῖν κολοσσῶν
ὄντων μονολίθων ἀλλήλων πλησίον, ὁ μὲν σώζεται,
τοῦ δ᾽ ἑτέρου τὰ ἄνω μέρη τὰ ἀπὸ τῆς καθέδρας
πέπτωκε σεισμοῦ γενηθέντος, ὥς φασι. πεπί-
στευται δ᾽, ὅτι ἅπαξ καθ᾽ ἡμέραν ἑκάστην ψόφος,
ὡς ἂν πληγῆς οὐ μεγάλης, ἀποτελεῖται ἀπὸ τοῦ
μένοντος ἐν τῷ θρόνῳ καὶ τῇ βάσει μέρους· κἀγὼ
δὲ παρὼν ἐπὶ τῶν τόπων μετὰ Γάλλου Αἰλίου
καὶ τοῦ πλήθους τῶν συνόντων αὐτῷ φίλων τε
καὶ στρατιωτῶν περὶ ὥραν πρώτην ἤκουσα τοῦ
ψόφου, εἴτε δὲ ἀπὸ τῆς βάσεως εἴτε ἀπὸ τοῦ
κολοσσοῦ εἴτ᾽ ἐπίτηδες τῶν κύκλῳ καὶ περὶ τὴν
βάσιν ἱδρυμένων τινὸς ποιήσαντος τὸν ψόφον, οὐκ
ἔχω διισχυρίσασθαι. διὰ γὰρ τὸ ἄδηλον τῆς
αἰτίας πᾶν μᾶλλον ἐπέρχεται πιστεύειν ἢ τὸ
ἐκ τῶν λίθων οὕτω τεταγμένων ἐκπέμπεσθαι τὸν
ἦχον. ὑπὲρ δὲ τοῦ Μεμνονίου θῆκαι βασιλέων
ἐν σπηλαίοις λατομηταὶ περὶ τετταράκοντα, θαυμαστῶς κατεσκευασμέναι καὶ⁴ θέας ἄξιαι. ἐν δὲ
ταῖς θήκαις⁵ ἐπί τινων ὀβελίσκων ἀναγραφαὶ

---

¹ Kramer inserts τά after ἱερά; and so the later editors.
² μέν, Corais, for δέ.
³ μέρος δέ τι, Corais, for μέρος δὲ καί E, μέρος δ᾽ ἐστί other
MSS. ; and so the later editors.
⁴ Omitted by MSS. except EF.
⁵ Meineke, following conjecture of Zoega (De Usu Obelisc.
p. 169), which is approved by Kramer and Forbiger, emends
θήκαις to Θήβαις.

pointed out, extending as they do for a distance
of eighty stadia in length;[1] and there are several
temples, but most of these, too, were mutilated by
Cambyses;[2] and now it is only a collection of
villages, a part of it being in Arabia, where was
the city, and a part on the far side of the river,
where was the Memnonium. Here are two colossi,
which are near one another and are each made of a
single stone; one of them is preserved, but the
upper parts of the other, from the seat up, fell
when an earthquake took place, so it is said. It
is believed that once each day a noise, as of a slight
blow, emanates from the part of the latter that
remains on the throne and its base; and I too,
when I was present at the places with Aelius Gallus
and his crowd of associates, both friends and soldiers,
heard the noise at about the first hour,[3] but whether
it came from the base or from the colossus, or
whether the noise was made on purpose by one
of the men who were standing all round and near
to the base, I am unable positively to assert; for on
account of the uncertainty of the cause I am induced
to believe anything rather than that the sound issued
from stones thus fixed. Above the Memnonium, in
caves, are tombs of kings, which are stone-hewn,
are about forty in number, are marvellously constructed, and are a spectacle worth seeing. And
among the tombs,[4] on some obelisks,[5] are inscriptions

[1] Diodorus (1. 45) puts the circuit of the city at 140 stadia.
[2] See § 27 above and 10. 3. 21.
[3] *i.e.* as reckoned from sunrise.
[4] Perhaps an error for " And at Thebes " (see critical note).
[5] One of these obelisks, which were erected by Rameses II,
now stands in the "Place de la Concorde" at Paris, a gift to
Louis XIV from Mehemet Ali.

δηλοῦσαι τὸν πλοῦτον τῶν τότε βασιλέων καὶ
τὴν ἐπικράτειαν, ὡς μέχρι Σκυθῶν καὶ Βακτρίων
καὶ Ἰνδῶν καὶ τῆς νῦν Ἰωνίας διατείνασαν, καὶ
φόρων πλῆθος καὶ στρατιᾶς περὶ ἑκατὸν μυριάδας.
λέγονται δὲ καὶ ἀστρονόμοι καὶ φιλόσοφοι μάλιστα οἱ ἐνταῦθα ἱερεῖς· τούτων δ᾽ ἐστὶ καὶ τὸ
τὰς ἡμέρας μὴ κατὰ σελήνην ἄγειν, ἀλλὰ κατὰ
ἥλιον, τοῖς τριακοιθημέροις δώδεκα μησὶν ἐπα-
γόντων πέντε ἡμέρας κατ᾽ ἐνιαυτὸν ἕκαστον· εἰς
δὲ τὴν ἐκπλήρωσιν τοῦ ὅλου ἐνιαυτοῦ, ἐπιτρέχοντος
μορίου τινὸς τῆς ἡμέρας, περίοδόν τινα συντιθέασιν
ἐξ ὅλων ἡμερῶν καὶ ὅλων ἐνιαυτῶν τοσούτων, ὅσα
μόρια τὰ ἐπιτρέχοντα συνελθόντα ποιεῖ ἡμέραν.
ἀνατιθέασι δὲ τῷ Ἑρμῇ πᾶσαν τὴν τοιαύτην[1]
μάλιστα[2] σοφίαν· τῷ δὲ Διί, ὃν μάλιστα τιμῶσιν,
εὐειδεστάτη καὶ γένους λαμπροτάτου παρθένος
ἱερᾶται, ἃς καλοῦσιν οἱ Ἕλληνες παλλάδας·[3]
αὕτη δὲ καὶ παλλακεύει καὶ σύνεστιν οἷς βούλεται,
μέχρις ἂν ἡ φυσικὴ γένηται κάθαρσις τοῦ σώματος·
μετὰ δὲ τὴν κάθαρσιν δίδοται πρὸς ἄνδρα·[4] πρὶν
δὲ δοθῆναι, πένθος αὐτῆς ἄγεται μετὰ τὸν τῆς
παλλακείας καιρόν.

C 817   47. Μετὰ δὲ Θήβας Ἑρμωνθὶς πόλις, ἐν ᾗ ὅ

---

[1] τοσαύτην C m o x z.

[2] μάλιστα, after τοιαύτην, is omitted by the editors before
Kramer.

[3] For παλλάδας Xylander conj. παλλακίδας (see Thesaurus,
s.v. παλλακή).

[4] ἄνδρα o z and the editors, ἄνδρας other MSS.

---

[1] i.e. each true " whole day " is $1\frac{1}{1460}$ days, and each true
" whole year " is $365\frac{365}{1460}$, or $365\frac{1}{4}$ days.   Hence they formed

which show the wealth of the kings at that time, and also their dominion, as having extended as far as the Scythians and the Bactrians and the Indians and the present Ionia, and the amount of tributes they received, and the size of army they had, about one million men. The priests there are said to have been, for the most part, astronomers and philosophers; and it is due to these priests also that people reckon the days, not by the moon, but by the sun, adding to the twelve months of thirty days each five days each year; and, for the filling out of the whole year, since a fraction of the day runs over and above, they form a period of time from enough whole days, or whole years, to make the fractions that run over and above, when added together, amount to a day.[1] They attribute to Hermes all wisdom of this particular kind; but to Zeus, whom they hold highest in honour, they dedicate a maiden of greatest beauty and most illustrious family (such maidens are called "pallades"[2] by the Greeks); and she prostitutes herself, and cohabits with whatever men she wishes until the natural cleansing of her body takes place;[3] and after her cleansing she is given in marriage to a man; but before she is married, after the time of her prostitution, a rite of mourning is celebrated for her.

47. After Thebes, one comes to a city Hermonthis,

a period out of enough of these supernumerary fractions, when added together, to make one day; *i.e.* they intercalated a day every fourth year; a practice which later passed into the Julian Calendar. Cp. § 29 (above) and footnote.

[2] *i.e.* "virgin-priestesses," if the text is correct (see critical note). Diodorus Siculus (1. 47. 1) calls these maidens "pallacides (*i.e.* concubines) of Zeus."

[3] *i.e.* until "menstruation."

τε Ἀπόλλων τιμᾶται καὶ ὁ Ζεύς· τρέφεται δὲ
καὶ ἐνταῦθα βοῦς· ἔπειτα Κροκοδείλων πόλις,
τιμῶσα τὸ θηρίον· εἶτα Ἀφροδίτης πόλις καὶ
μετὰ ταῦτα Λατόπολις, τιμῶσα Ἀθηνᾶν καὶ τὸν
λάτον· εἶτα Εἰλειθυίας πόλις καὶ ἱερόν· ἐν δὲ
τῇ περαίᾳ Ἱεράκων πόλις, τὸν ἱέρακα τιμῶσα·
εἶτ' Ἀπόλλωνος πόλις, καὶ αὕτη πολεμοῦσα τοῖς
κροκοδείλοις.

48. Ἡ δὲ Συήνη καὶ ἡ Ἐλεφαντίνη, ἡ μὲν ἐπὶ
τῶν ὅρων τῆς Αἰθιοπίας καὶ τῆς Αἰγύπτου πόλις,
ἡ δ' ἐν τῷ Νείλῳ προκειμένη τῆς Συήνης νῆσος
ἐν ἡμισταδίῳ καὶ ἐν ταύτῃ πόλις ἔχουσα ἱερὸν
Κνούφιδος καὶ νειλομέτριον, καθάπερ Μέμφις.
ἔστι δὲ τὸ νειλομέτριον συννόμῳ λίθῳ[1] κατεσκευασμένον ἐπὶ τῇ ὄχθῃ τοῦ Νείλου φρέαρ, ἐν ᾧ τὰς
ἀναβάσεις τοῦ Νείλου[2] σημειοῦνται τὰς μεγίστας
τε καὶ ἐλαχίστας καὶ τὰς μέσας· συναναβαίνει
γὰρ καὶ συνταπεινοῦται τῷ ποταμῷ τὸ ἐν τῷ
φρέατι ὕδωρ. εἰσὶν οὖν ἐν τῷ τοίχῳ τοῦ φρέατος
παραγραφαί, μέτρα τῶν τελείων καὶ τῶν ἄλλων
ἀναβάσεων. ἐπισκοποῦντες οὖν ταύτας διαση-
μαίνουσι τοῖς ἄλλοις, ὅπως εἰδεῖεν· πρὸ πολλοῦ
γὰρ ἴσασιν ἐκ τῶν τοιούτων σημείων καὶ τῶν
ἡμερῶν[3] τὴν ἐσομένην ἀνάβασιν καὶ προδηλοῦσι.
τοῦτο δὲ καὶ τοῖς γεωργοῖς χρήσιμον τῆς τῶν

---

[1] συννόμῳ λίθῳ, Casaubon, for σὺν μονολίθῳ; so the later editors.

[2] E reads μονολίθου instead of Νείλου.

[3] For καὶ τῶν ἡμερῶν Casaubon conj. καὶ τεκμηρίων ("evidences"); Corais writes καὶ μέτρων ("measures"), Kramer approving.

---

[1] See § 40 above.

where both Apollo and Zeus are worshipped; and there, too, a bull is kept. And then to a City of Crocodiles, which holds in honour that animal. And then to a City of Aphroditê, and, after this, to Latopolis, which holds in honour Athena and the *latus*;[1] and then to a City of Eileithuia[2] and a temple; and on the far side of the river lies a City of Hawks, which holds the hawk in honour;[3] and then to Apollonospolis, which also carries on war against the crocodiles.

48. As for Syenê[4] and Elephantinê, the former is a city on the borders of Aethiopia and Aegypt, and the latter is an island in the Nile, being situated in front of Syenê at a distance of half a stadium, and a city therein which has a temple of Cnuphis and, like Memphis, a nilometer. The nilometer is a well on the bank of the Nile constructed with close-fitting stones,[5] in which are marks showing the greatest, least, and mean rises of the Nile; for the water in the well rises and lowers with the river. Accordingly, there are marks on the wall of the well, measures of the complete rises and of the others. So when watchers inspect these, they give out word to the rest of the people, so that they may know; for long beforehand they know from such signs and the days[6] what the future rise will be, and reveal it beforehand. This is useful, not only to the farmers with regard to the

[2] The goddess of childbirth.
[3] The hawk ("hierax"; see § 49 below) was sacred to Apollo, as was the eagle to Zeus (Aristophanes, *Birds*, 516).
[4] Assuan.
[5] Cp. the structure of the sewers at Rome (5. 3. 8).
[6] *i.e.* apparently, from the times of the observations as compared with the readings of the meter (but see critical note).

ὑδάτων ταμιείας χάριν καὶ παραχωμάτων καὶ
διωρύγων καὶ ἄλλων τοιούτων, καὶ τοῖς ἡγεμόσι
τῶν προσόδων χάριν· αἱ γὰρ μείζους ἀναβάσεις
μείζους καὶ τὰς προσόδους ὑπαγορεύουσιν. ἐν δὲ
τῇ Συήνῃ καὶ τὸ φρέαρ ἐστὶ τὸ διασημαῖνον τὰς
θερινὰς τροπάς,[1] διότι τῷ τροπικῷ κύκλῳ ὑπό-
κεινται οἱ τόποι οὗτοι καὶ ποιοῦσιν ἀσκίους τοὺς
γνώμονας κατὰ μεσημβρίαν·[2] ἀπὸ γὰρ τῶν
ἡμετέρων τόπων, λέγω δὲ τῶν Ἑλλαδικῶν, προϊοῦ-
σιν ἐπὶ τὴν μεσημβρίαν ἐνταῦθα πρῶτον ὁ ἥλιος
κατὰ κορυφὴν ἡμῖν γίνεται καὶ ποιεῖ τοὺς γνώμονας ἀσκίους κατὰ μεσημβρίαν· ἀνάγκη δέ,
κατὰ κορυφὴν ἡμῖν γινομένου, καὶ εἰς τὰ φρέατα
βάλλειν μέχρι τοῦ ὕδατος τὰς αὐγάς, κἂν βαθύ-
τατα ᾖ· κατὰ κάθετον γὰρ ἡμεῖς τε ἕσταμεν καὶ
τὰ ὀρύγματα τῶν φρεάτων κατεσκεύασται. εἰσὶ
δ' ἐνταῦθα τρεῖς σπεῖραι Ῥωμαίων ἱδρυμέναι
φρουρᾶς χάριν.

49. Μικρὸν δ' ὑπὲρ τῆς Ἐλεφαντίνης ἐστὶν ὁ
μικρὸς καταράκτης,[3] ἐφ' ᾧ καὶ θέαν τινὰ οἱ
σκαφῖται τοῖς ἡγεμόσιν ἐπιδείκνυνται· ὁ μὲν γὰρ
καταράκτης ἐστὶ κατὰ μέσον τὸν ποταμόν, πετρώδης τις ὀφρύς, ἐπίπεδος μὲν ἄνωθεν, ὥστε
δέχεσθαι τὸν ποταμόν, τελευτῶσα δ' εἰς κρημνόν,
καθ' οὗ καταρρήγνυται τὸ ὕδωρ, ἑκατέρωθεν δὲ
πρὸς τῇ γῇ ῥεῖθρον, ὃ μάλιστα καὶ ἀνάπλουν
C 818 ἔχει· ἀναπλεύσαντες οὖν ταύτῃ καταρρέουσιν ἐπὶ
τὸν καταράκτην καὶ ὠθοῦνται μετὰ τῆς σκάφης

---

[1] καί, before διότι, the editors omit.

[2] The words καὶ ποιοῦσιν . . . μεσημβρίαν are rejected by
Kramer and Meineke.

[3] καταράκτης DE, καταρράκτης other MSS.; and so in the
succeeding uses of the word.

water-distribution, embankments, canals, and other
things of this kind, but also to the praefects, with
regard to the revenues; for the greater rises indicate that the revenues also will be greater.   But
in Syenê [1] is also the well that marks the summer
tropic, for the reason that this region lies under the
tropic circle and causes the gnomons to cast no
shadow at midday; for if from our region, I mean
that of Greece, we proceed towards the south, it is
at Syenê that the sun first gets over our heads and
causes the gnomons to cast no shadow at midday;
and necessarily, when the sun gets over our heads,
it also casts its rays into wells as far as the water,
even if they are very deep; for we ourselves stand
perpendicular to the earth and wells are dug perpendicular to the surface.   And here are stationed
three cohorts as a guard.

49. A little above Elephantinê is the little cataract,
on which the boatmen exhibit a kind of spectacle
for the praefects; [2] for the cataract is at the middle
of the river, and is a brow of rock, as it were, which
is flat on top, so that it receives the river, but ends
in a precipice, down which the water dashes; whereas
on either side towards the land there is a stream
which generally can even be navigated up-stream.
Accordingly, the boatmen, having first sailed up-
stream here, drift down to the cataract, are thrust
along with the boat over the precipice, and escape

---

[1] So Pliny (2. 75) and Arrian (*Indica*, 25. 7); but in
reality Syenê was slightly to the north of the tropic, its
latitude being 24° 1'. The obliquity of the ecliptic in
Eratosthenes' time was about 23° 44', in Strabo's time about
23° 42', and to-day is about 23° 27'.

[2] *e.g.* Aelius Gallus, whom Strabo accompanied.

ἐπὶ τὸν κρημνὸν καὶ σώζονται σὺν αὐτῇ[1] ἀπαθεῖς. τοῦ δὲ καταράκτου μικρὸν ἐπάνω τὰς Φιλὰς εἶναι συμβαίνει, κοινὴν κατοικίαν Αἰθιόπων τε καὶ Αἰγυπτίων, κατεσκευασμένην ὥσπερ καὶ τὴν Ἐλεφαντίνην καὶ τὸ μέγεθος ἴσην, ἱερὰ ἔχουσαν Αἰγύπτια· ὅπου καὶ ὄρνεον τιμᾶται, ὃ καλοῦσι μὲν ἱέρακα, οὐδὲν δὲ ὅμοιον ἔμοιγε ἐφαίνετο ἔχειν τοῖς παρ' ἡμῖν καὶ ἐν Αἰγύπτῳ ἱέραξιν, ἀλλὰ καὶ τῷ μεγέθει μεῖζον ἦν καὶ τῇ ποικιλίᾳ πολὺ ἐξηλλαγμένον. Αἰθιοπικὸν δ' ἔφασαν εἶναι, κἀκεῖθεν κομίζεσθαι, ὅταν ἐκλίπῃ, καὶ πρότερον.[2] καὶ δὴ καὶ τότε ἐδείχθη ἡμῖν πρὸς ἐκλείψει ὂν διὰ νόσον.

50. Ἤλθομεν δ' εἰς Φιλὰς ἐκ Συήνης ἀπήνῃ δι' ὁμαλοῦ σφόδρα πεδίου σταδίους ὁμοῦ τι ἑκατόν.[3] παρ' ὅλην δὲ τὴν ὁδὸν ἦν ἰδεῖν ἑκατέρωθεν πολλαχοῦ, ὥσπερ ἑρμαῖα, πέτρον ἠλίβατον στρογγύλον, λεῖον ἱκανῶς, ἐγγὺς σφαιροειδοῦς, τοῦ μέλανος καὶ σκληροῦ λίθου, ἐξ οὗ αἱ θυῖαι γίνονται, ἐπὶ πέτρῳ κείμενον μείζονι καὶ ἐπ' ἐκείνῳ πάλιν ἄλλον· ἔστι δ' ὅτε αὐτοὶ καθ' αὑτοὺς ἔκειντο οἱ πέτροι· ἦν δ' ὁ μὲν μέγιστος τὴν διάμετρον ποδῶν οὐκ ἐλαττόνων ἢ δώδεκα, ἅπαντες δὲ μείζους ἢ ἡμίσεις τούτων. διέβημεν δὲ εἰς τὴν νῆσον ἐπὶ πάκτωνος· ὁ δὲ πάκτων διὰ σκυταλίδων πεπηγός ἐστι σκάφιον, ὥστ' ἐοικέναι

---

[1] αὐτῇ E, αὐταῖς other MSS.
[2] καὶ πρότερον is omitted by F.
[3] For ἑκατόν (ρ') Groskurd reads πεντήκοντα (ν').

---

[1] Probably an error for "fifty," as Groskurd suggests (see critical note).

unharmed, boat and all. A little above the cataract lies Philae, a common settlement of Aethiopians and Aegyptians, which is built like Elephantinê and is equal to it in size; and it has Aegyptian temples. Here, also, a bird is held in honour, which they call a hawk, though to me it appeared to be in no respect like the hawks in our country and in Aegypt, but was both greater in size and far different in the varied colouring of its plumage. They said that it was an Aethiopian bird, and that another was brought from Aethiopia whenever the one at hand died, or before. And in fact the bird shown to us at the time mentioned was nearly dead because of disease.

50. We went to Philae from Syenê by wagon through an exceedingly level plain—a distance all told of about one hundred [1] stadia. Along the whole road on either side one could see in many places a stone like our Hermae; [2] it was huge, round, quite smooth, nearly sphere-shaped, and consisted of the black, hard stone from which mortars are made—a smaller stone lying on a larger, and on that stone again another. [3] Sometimes, however, it was only a single stone; and the largest was in diameter no less than twelve feet, though one and all were larger than half this measure. We crossed to the island on a *pacton*. The *pacton* is a small boat constructed of withes, so that it resembles woven-work;

[2] *i.e.* quadrangular pillars surmounted by a head or bust of Hermes, which were used as sign-posts or boundary-marks.

[3] Pocock (*Travels in Egypt*, in *Pinkerton's Voyages and Travels*, Vol. XV, p. 265), who saw some of these stones, says that they were rocks of red granite which had turned blackish on the outside; "a rock standing up like a pillar, and a large rock on it, hieroglyphics being cut on some of them."

διαπλοκίνῳ· ἑστῶτες δ' ἐν ὕδατι ἢ καὶ σανιδίοις
τισὶ προσκαθήμενοι ῥᾳδίως ἐπεραιώθημεν, δεδιότες[1] μάτην·[2] ἀκίνδυνα γάρ ἐστιν, ἂν μή τις
ὑπέργομον ποιήσῃ τὸ πορθμεῖον.

51. Καθ' ὅλην δὲ τὴν Αἴγυπτον τοῦ φοίνικος
ἀγεννοῦς ὄντος καὶ ἐκφέροντος καρπὸν οὐκ
εὔβρωτον ἐν τοῖς περὶ τὸ Δέλτα τόποις καὶ περὶ
τὴν Ἀλεξάνδρειαν, ὁ ἐν τῇ Θηβαΐδι φοῖνιξ
ἄριστος τῶν ἄλλων φύεται. θαυμάζειν οὖν
ἄξιον, πῶς ταὐτὸ κλίμα οἰκοῦντες τῇ Ἰουδαίᾳ
καὶ ὅμοροι οἱ περὶ τὸ Δέλτα καὶ τὴν Ἀλεξάνδρειαν, τοσοῦτον διαλλάττουσιν, ἐκείνης πρὸς
ἄλλῳ φοίνικι καὶ τὸν καρυωτὸν γεννώσης, οὐ
πολὺ κρείττονα τοῦ Βαβυλωνίου. διττὸς δ'
ἐστὶν ὅ τε ἐν τῇ Θηβαΐδι καὶ ὁ ἐν τῇ Ἰουδαίᾳ,
ὅ τε ἄλλος καὶ ὁ καρυωτός, σκληρότερος δ' ὁ
Θηβαϊκός, ἀλλὰ τῇ γεύσει εὐστομώτερος. ἔστι
δὲ καὶ νῆσος ἡ μάλιστα ἐκφέρουσα τὸν ἄριστον,
μεγίστην τελοῦσα πρόσοδον τοῖς ἡγεμόσι·
βασιλικὴ γὰρ ἦν, ἰδιώτῃ δ' οὐ μετῆν, καὶ νῦν
τῶν ἡγεμόνων ἐστί.

52. Πολλὰ δ' Ἡρόδοτός τε καὶ ἄλλοι φλυαροῦ-
σιν, ὥσπερ μέλος ἢ ῥυθμὸν ἢ ἥδυσμά τι τῷ
C 819 λόγῳ τὴν τερατείαν προσφέροντες· οἷον καὶ τὸ
φάσκειν περὶ τὰς νήσους τὰς πρὸς τῇ Συήνῃ
καὶ τῇ Ἐλεφαντίνῃ, πλείους δ' εἰσί, τὰς πηγὰς
τοῦ Νείλου εἶναι, καὶ βάθος ἄβυσσον ἔχειν τὸν
πόρον κατὰ τοῦτον τὸν τόπον. νήσους δ' ὁ Νεῖλος
κατεσπαρμένας ἔχει παμπόλλας, τὰς μὲν καλυπ-
τομένας ὅλας ἐν ταῖς ἀναβάσεσι, τὰς δ' ἐκ

---

[1] *moz* read οὐ before δεδιότες.
[2] μάτην EF, omitted by other MSS.

and though standing in water or seated on small boards, we crossed easily, being afraid without cause, for there is no danger unless the ferry-boat is over-laden.

51. Throughout the whole of Aegypt the palm tree is not of a good species; and in the region of the Delta and Alexandria it produces fruit that is not good to eat; but the palm tree in the Thebaïs is better than any of the rest. Now it is a thing worth marvelling at, that a country which is in the same latitude as Judaea and borders on it, I mean the country round the Delta and Alexandria, differs so much, since Judaea, in addition to another palm, produces also the caryotic, which is somewhat better than the Babylonian. There are two kinds in the Thebaïs as well as in Judaea, both the caryotic and the other; and the Thebaïc date is harder, but more agreeable to the taste. There is also an island which is particularly productive of the best date, yielding a very large revenue for the praefects; for it used to be a royal possession, and no private individual shared in it, but it now belongs to the praefects.

52. Both Herodotus[1] and others talk much non-sense, adding to their account marvellous tales, to give it, as it were, a kind of tune or rhythm or relish; as, for example, the assertion that the sources of the Nile are in the neighbourhood of the islands near Syenê and Elephantinê (of which there are several), and that at this place its channel has a bottomless depth. The Nile has very many islands scattered along its course, of which some are wholly covered at its risings and others only partly; but

[1] 2. 28.

μέρους, ἐποχετεύεται δὲ τοῖς κοχλίαις τὰ λίαν ἔξαλα.

53. Ἦν μὲν οὖν ἡ Αἴγυπτος εἰρηνικὴ τὸ πλέον ἐξ ἀρχῆς διὰ τὸ αὔταρκες τῆς χώρας καὶ τὸ δυσείσβολον τοῖς ἔξωθεν, ἀπὸ μὲν τῶν ἄρκτων ἀλιμένῳ παραλίᾳ καὶ πελάγει τῷ Αἰγυπτίῳ φρουρουμένη, ἀπὸ δὲ τῆς ἕω καὶ τῆς ἑσπέρας ἐρήμοις ὄρεσι, τοῖς τε Λιβυκοῖς καὶ τοῖς Ἀραβίοις, ὥσπερ ἔφαμεν· λοιπὰ δὲ τὰ πρὸς νότον Τρωγλοδύται καὶ Βλέμμυες καὶ Νοῦβαι καὶ Μεγάβαροι οἱ ὑπὲρ Συήνης Αἰθίοπες· εἰσὶ δ᾽ οὗτοι νομάδες καὶ οὐ πολλοὶ οὐδὲ μάχιμοι, δοκοῦντες δὲ τοῖς πάλαι διὰ τὸ ληστρικῶς ἀφυλάκτοις ἐπιτίθεσθαι πολλάκις· οἱ δὲ πρὸς μεσημβρίαν καὶ Μερόην ἀνήκοντες Αἰθίοπες, οὐδ᾽ οὗτοι πολλοὶ οὔτε ἐν συστροφῇ, ἅτε ποταμίαν μακρὰν στενὴν καὶ σκολιὰν οἰκοῦντες, οἵαν προείπομεν· οὐδὲ παρεσκευασμένοι καλῶς οὔτε πρὸς πόλεμον οὔτε πρὸς τὸν ἄλλον βίον. καὶ νῦν δὲ διάκειται παραπλησίως ἡ χώρα πᾶσα· σημεῖον δέ· τρισὶ γοῦν σπείραις, οὐδὲ ταύταις ἐντελέσιν, ἱκανῶς ὑπὸ τῶν Ῥωμαίων ἡ χώρα φρουρεῖται· τολμήσασι δὲ τοῖς Αἰθίοψιν ἐπιθέσθαι κινδυνεῦσαι τῇ χώρᾳ συνέπεσε τῇ σφετέρᾳ. καὶ αἱ λοιπαὶ δὲ δυνάμεις αἱ ἐν Αἰγύπτῳ οὔτε τοσαῦταί τινές εἰσιν οὔτε ἀθρόαις ἐχρήσαντο οὐδ᾽ ἅπαξ Ῥωμαῖοι· οὐ γάρ εἰσιν οὔτ᾽ αὐτοὶ Αἰγύπτιοι πολεμισταί, καίπερ ὄντες παμπληθεῖς, οὔτε τὰ πέριξ ἔθνη. Γάλλος μέν γε Κορνήλιος, ὁ πρῶτος κατασταθεὶς ἔπαρχος

---

[1] Cp. § 30 above.   [2] Cp. § 4 above.
[3] See §§ 3 and 4 above.

the exceedingly high parts of the latter are irrigated by means of screws.[1]

53. Now Aegypt was generally inclined to peace from the outset, because of the self-sufficiency of the country and of the difficulty of invasion by outsiders, being protected on the north by a harbourless coast and by the Aegyptian Sea, and on the east and west by the desert mountains of Libya and Arabia, as I have said;[2] and the remaining parts, those towards the south, are inhabited by Troglodytes, Blemmyes, Nubae, and Megabari, those Aethiopians who live above Syenê. These are nomads, and not numerous, or warlike either, though they were thought to be so by the ancients, because often, like brigands, they would attack defenceless persons. As for those Aethiopians who extend towards the south and Meroê, they are not numerous either, nor do they collect in one mass, inasmuch as they inhabit a long, narrow, and winding stretch of river-land, such as I have described before;[3] neither are they well equipped either for warfare or for any other kind of life. And now, too, the whole of the country is similarly disposed to peace. And the following is a sign of the fact: the country is sufficiently guarded by the Romans with only three cohorts, and even these are not complete; and when the Aethiopians dared to make an attack upon them, they imperilled their own country. The remaining Roman forces in Aegypt are hardly as large as these, nor have the Romans used them collectively even once; for neither are the Aegyptians themselves warriors, although they are very numerous, nor are the surrounding tribes. Cornelius Gallus, the first man appointed praefect of the country by Caesar, attacked

τῆς χώρας ὑπὸ Καίσαρος, τήν τε Ἡρώων πόλιν
ἀποστᾶσαν ἐπελθὼν δι᾿ ὀλίγων εἷλε, στάσιν τε
γενηθεῖσαν ἐν τῇ Θηβαΐδι διὰ τοὺς φόρους ἐν
βραχεῖ κατέλυσε. Πετρώνιός τε ὕστερον τοῦ
Ἀλεξανδρέων πλήθους τοσούτων μυριάδων
ὁρμήσαντος ἐπ᾿ αὐτὸν μετὰ λίθων βολῆς, αὐτοῖς
τοῖς περὶ ἑαυτὸν στρατιώταις ἀντέσχε, καὶ
διαφθείρας τινὰς αὐτῶν τοὺς λοιποὺς ἔπαυσε.
Γάλλος τε Αἴλιος μέρει τῆς ἐν Αἰγύπτῳ φρουρᾶς
εἰς τὴν Ἀραβίαν ἐμβαλὼν εἴρηται, τίνα τρόπον
ἐξήλεγξε τοὺς ἀνθρώπους ἀπολέμους ὄντας· εἰ δὴ
μὴ ὁ Συλλαῖος αὐτὸν προυδίδου, κἂν κατεστρέ-
ψατο τὴν Εὐδαίμονα πᾶσαν.

C 820   54. Ἐπειδὴ δὲ οἱ Αἰθίοπες, καταφρονήσαντες
τῷ μέρος τι τῆς ἐν Αἰγύπτῳ δυνάμεως ἀπεσπάσθαι
μετὰ Γάλλου Αἰλίου πολεμοῦντος πρὸς τοὺς
Ἄραβας, ἐπῆλθον[1] τῇ Θηβαΐδι καὶ τῇ φρουρᾷ
τῶν τριῶν σπειρῶν τῶν κατὰ Συήνην καὶ ἑλόντες
ἔφθασαν τήν τε Συήνην καὶ τὴν Ἐλεφαντίνην
καὶ Φιλὰς ἐξ ἐφόδου διὰ τὸ αἰφνίδιον καὶ
ἐξηνδραποδίσαντο, ἀνέσπασαν δὲ καὶ τοὺς
Καίσαρος ἀνδριάντας· ἐπελθὼν δὲ ἐλάττοσιν ἢ
μυρίοις πεζοῖς Πετρώνιος, ἱππεῦσι δὲ ὀκτακο-
σίοις πρὸς ἄνδρας τρισμυρίους, πρῶτον μὲν
ἠνάγκασεν ἀναφυγεῖν αὐτοὺς εἰς Ψέλχιν, πόλιν
Αἰθιοπικήν, καὶ πρεσβεύεται τά τε ληφθέντα
ἀπαιτῶν καὶ τὰς αἰτίας, δι᾿ ἃς ἦρξαν πολέμου·
λεγόντων δ᾿, ὡς ἀδικοῖντο ὑπὸ τῶν νομάρχων,[2]
ἀλλ᾿ οὐκ ἔφη τούτους ἡγεμόνας εἶναι τῆς χώρας,
ἀλλὰ Καίσαρα· αἰτησαμένων δ᾿ ἡμέρας τρεῖς εἰς

---

[1] ἐπῆλθον, Corais, for ἐπελθόντες.

Heroönpolis, which had revolted, and took it with
only a few soldiers, and in only a short time broke
up a sedition which had taken place in the Thebaïs
on account of the tributes. And at a later time
Petronius, when all that countless multitude of
Alexandrians rushed to attack him with a throwing
of stones, held out against them with merely his
own body-guard, and after killing some of them put
a stop to the rest. And I have already stated [1] how
Aelius Gallus, when he invaded Arabia with a part
of the guard stationed in Aegypt, discovered that
the people were unwarlike; indeed, if Syllaeus had
not betrayed him, he would even have subdued the
whole of Arabia Felix.

54. But the Aethiopians, emboldened by the fact
that a part of the Roman force in Aegypt had been
drawn away with Aelius Gallus when he was carrying
on war against the Arabians, attacked the Thebaïs
and the garrison of the three cohorts at Syenê, and by
an unexpected onset took Syenê and Elephantinê
and Philae, and enslaved the inhabitants, and also
pulled down the statues of Caesar. But Petronius,
setting out with less than ten thousand infantry and
eight hundred cavalry against thirty thousand men,
first forced them to flee back to Pselchis, an
Aethiopian city, and sent ambassadors to demand
what they had taken, as also to ask the reasons why
they had begun war; and when they said that they
had been wronged by the Nomarchs,[2] he replied that
these were not rulers of the country, but Caesar;
and when they had requested three days for delibera-

---

[1] 16. 4. 23.   [2] " Nome-rulers."

[2] νομάρχων s, μονάρχων other MSS.

STRABO

βουλὴν καὶ μηδέν, ὧν ἐχρῆν, ποιούντων, προσβαλὼν ἠνάγκασε προελθεῖν εἰς μάχην, ταχὺ δὲ
τροπὴν ἐποίησε, συντεταγμένων τε κακῶς καὶ
ὡπλισμένων· μεγάλους γὰρ εἶχον θυρεούς, καὶ
τούτους ὠμοβοΐνους, ἀμυντήρια δὲ πελέκεις, οἱ δὲ
κοντούς, οἱ δὲ καὶ ξίφη. τινὲς μὲν οὖν εἰς τὴν πόλιν
συνηλάθησαν, οἱ δ᾽ εἰς τὴν ἐρημίαν ἔφυγον, τινὰς
δὲ νῆσος πλησίον ὑπεδέξατο ἐμβάντας¹ εἰς τὸν
πόρον, οὐ γὰρ πολλοὶ ἦσαν ἐνταῦθα οἱ κροκό-
δειλοι διὰ τὸν ῥοῦν. τούτων δ᾽ ἦσαν καὶ οἱ τῆς
βασιλίσσης στρατηγοὶ τῆς Κανδάκης, ἣ καθ᾽
ἡμᾶς ἦρξε τῶν Αἰθιόπων, ἀνδρική τις γυνὴ
πεπηρωμένη τὸν ἕτερον τῶν ὀφθαλμῶν· τούτους
τε δὴ ζωγρίᾳ λαμβάνει ἅπαντας, ἐπιπλεύσας
σχεδίαις τε καὶ ναυσί, καὶ καταπέμπει παρα-
χρῆμα εἰς Ἀλεξάνδρειαν, ἐπελθών τε τὴν Ψέλχιν
αἱρεῖ· προσαριθμουμένου δὲ τοῖς ἑαλωκόσι τοῦ
πλήθους τῶν πεσόντων ἐν τῇ μάχῃ, τοὺς σωθέν-
τας ὀλίγους παντάπασι γενέσθαι συνέβη. ἐκ δὲ
Ψέλχιος ἧκεν εἰς Πρῆμνιν, ἐρυμνὴν πόλιν, διελθὼν
τοὺς θῖνας, ἐν οἷς ὁ Καμβύσου κατεχώσθη
στρατὸς ἐμπεσόντος ἀνέμου. προσβαλὼν δὲ ἐξ
ἐφόδου τὸ φρούριον αἱρεῖ, καὶ μετὰ ταῦτα
ὥρμησεν ἐπὶ Ναπάτων· τοῦτο δ᾽ ἦν τὸ βασίλειον
τῆς Κανδάκης, καὶ ἦν ἐνταῦθα υἱὸς αὐτῆς. καὶ
αὐτὴ δ᾽ ἔν τινι πλησίον ἵδρυτο χωρίῳ. πρεσ-
βευσαμένης δὲ περὶ φιλίας καὶ ἀποδούσης τοὺς
ἐκ Συήνης αἰχμαλώτους καὶ τοὺς ἀνδριάντας,
ἐπελθὼν λαμβάνει καὶ τὰ Νάπατα, φυγόντος
τοῦ παιδός, καὶ κατασκάπτει· ἐξανδραποδισά-

¹ For ἐμβάντας, Jones conj. ἐμβαλόντας.

138

tion, but did nothing they should have done, he made an attack and forced them to come forth to battle; and he quickly turned them to flight, since they were badly marshalled and badly armed; for they had large oblong shields, and those too made of raw ox-hide, and as weapons some had only axes, others pikes, and others swords. Now some were driven together into the city, others fled into the desert, and others found refuge on a neighbouring island, having waded[1] into the channel, for on account of the current the crocodiles were not numerous there. Among these fugitives were the generals of Queen Candacê, who was ruler of the Aethiopians in my time—a masculine sort of woman, and blind in one eye. These, one and all, he captured alive, having sailed after them in both rafts and ships, and he sent them forthwith down to Alexandria; and he also attacked Pselchis and captured it; and if the multitude of those who fell in the battle be added to the number of the captives, those who escaped must have been altogether few in number. From Pselchis he went to Premnis, a fortified city, after passing through the sand-dunes, where the army of Cambyses was overwhelmed when a wind-storm struck them; and having made an attack, he took the fortress at the first onset. After this he set out for Napata. This was the royal residence of Candacê; and her son was there, and she herself was residing at a place near by. But though she sent ambassadors to treat for friendship and offered to give back the captives and the statues brought from Syenê, Petronius attacked and captured Napata too, from which her son had fled, and rased it to the

[1] See critical note.

μενος δ' ἀναστρέφει πάλιν εἰς τοὐπίσω μετὰ τῶν
λαφύρων, δύσοδα κρίνας τὰ προσωτέρω. τὴν δὲ
Πρῆμνιν τειχίσας βέλτιον, φρουρὰν ἐμβαλὼν καὶ
τροφὴν δυεῖν ἐνιαυτῶν τετρακοσίοις ἀνδράσιν,
ἀπῆρεν εἰς Ἀλεξάνδρειαν. καὶ τῶν αἰχμαλώτων
C 821 τοὺς μὲν ἐλαφυροπώλησε, χιλίους δὲ Καίσαρι
ἔπεμψε νεωστὶ ἐκ Καντάβρων ἥκοντι, τοὺς δὲ
νόσοι διεχρήσαντο. ἐν τούτῳ μυριάσι Κανδάκη
πολλαῖς ἐπὶ τὴν φρουρὰν ἐπῆλθε· Πετρώνιος δ'
ἐξεβοήθησε καὶ φθάνει προσελθὼν[1] εἰς τὸ φρούριον, καὶ πλείοσι παρασκευαῖς ἐξασφαλισάμενος
τὸν τόπον, πρεσβευσαμένων, ἐκέλευσεν ὡς Καίσαρα πρεσβεύεσθαι· οὐκ εἰδέναι δὲ φασκόντων,
ὅστις εἴη Καῖσαρ καὶ ὅπη βαδιστέον εἴη παρ'
αὐτόν, ἔδωκε τοὺς παραπέμψοντας· καὶ ἦκον εἰς
Σάμον, ἐνταῦθα τοῦ Καίσαρος ὄντος καὶ μέλλοντος
εἰς Συρίαν ἐντεῦθεν προϊέναι, Τιβέριον εἰς Ἀρ-
μενίαν στέλλοντος. πάντων δὲ τυχόντων, ὧν
ἐδέοντο, ἀφῆκεν αὐτοῖς καὶ τοὺς φόρους, οὓς
ἐπέστησε.

II

1. Πολλὰ δ' εἴρηται περὶ τῶν Αἰθιοπικῶν ἐν
τοῖς πρότερον, ὥστε συμπεριωδευμένα ἂν εἴη τῇ
Αἰγύπτῳ καὶ τὰ τούτων. ὡς δ' εἰπεῖν, τὰ ἄκρα
τῆς οἰκουμένης τὰ παρακείμενα τῇ δυσκράτῳ καὶ
ἀοικήτῳ διὰ καῦμα ἢ ψῦχος ἀνάγκη ἀποτεύγματα
εἶναι τῆς εὐκράτου καὶ ἐλαττώματα· ταῦτα δ'

---

[1] προσελθών F and first hand in D, προσεισελθών C, προεισ-
ελθών other MSS.

ground; and having enslaved its inhabitants, he turned back again with the booty, having decided that the regions farther on would be hard to traverse. But he fortified Premnis better, threw in a garrison and food for four hundred men for two years, and set out for Alexandria. As for the captives, he sold some of them as booty, and sent one thousand to Caesar, who had recently returned from Cantabria; and the others died of diseases. Meantime Candacê marched against the garrison with many thousands of men, but Petronius set out to its assistance and arrived at the fortress first; and when he had made the place thoroughly secure by sundry devices, ambassadors came, but he bade them go to Caesar; and when they asserted that they did not know who Caesar was or where they should have to go to find him, he gave them escorts; and they went to Samos, since Caesar was there and intended to proceed to Syria from there, after despatching Tiberius to Armenia. And when the ambassadors had obtained everything they pled for, he even remitted the tributes which he had imposed.

II

1. In the earlier parts of my work I have already said many things about the Aethiopian[1] tribes, so that the description of their country may be said to be included with that of Aegypt. In general, the extremities of the inhabited world, which lie alongside the part of the earth that is not temperate and habitable, because of heat or cold, must needs be defective and inferior to the temperate part;

---

[1] See *Index*, s.v. "Aethiopians."

ἐκ τῶν βίων δῆλα καὶ τῆς πρὸς τὰς χρείας τὰς
ἀνθρωπικὰς ἀπορίας. κακόβιοί τε δὴ καὶ γυμνῆτές εἰσι τὰ πολλὰ καὶ νομάδες· τά τε βοσκήματα
αὐτοῖς ἐστι μικρά, πρόβατα καὶ αἶγες καὶ βόες·
καὶ κύνες μικροί, τραχεῖς[1] δὲ καὶ μάχιμοι.
τάχα δὲ καὶ τοὺς Πυγμαίους ἀπὸ τῆς τούτων
μικροφυΐας ὑπενόησαν καὶ ἀνέπλασαν· ἑωρακὼς
μὲν γὰρ οὐδεὶς ἐξηγεῖται τῶν πίστεως ἀξίων
ἀνδρῶν.

2. Ζῶσί τ' ἀπὸ κέγχρου καὶ κριθῆς, ἀφ' ὧν καὶ
ποτὸν αὐτοῖς ἐστιν ἀντ' ἐλαίου δὲ[2] βούτυρον καὶ
στέαρ· οὐδ' ἀκρόδρυα ἔχουσι πλὴν φοινίκων
ὀλίγων ἐν κήποις βασιλικοῖς· ἔνιοι δὲ καὶ πόαν
σιτοῦνται καὶ κλῶνας ἁπαλοὺς καὶ λωτὸν καὶ
καλάμου ῥίζαν· κρέασι δὲ χρῶνται καὶ αἵματι
καὶ γάλακτι καὶ τυρῷ. σέβονται δ' ὡς θεοὺς
τοὺς βασιλέας, κατακλείστους ὄντας καὶ οἰκουροὺς
τὸ πλέον. ἔστι δὲ τὸ μέγιστον αὐτοῖς βασίλειον ἡ Μερόη, πόλις ὁμώνυμος τῇ νήσῳ. τὴν
δὲ νῆσον θυρεοειδῆ φασι τὸ σχῆμα, τό τε μέγεθος
τάχα πρὸς ὑπερβολὴν εἴρηται μῆκος μὲν ὅσον
τρισχιλίων σταδίων, εὖρος δὲ χιλίων. ἔχει δ' ἡ
νῆσος[3] συχνὰ καὶ ὄρη καὶ δάση μεγάλα· οἰκοῦσι
δ' οἱ μὲν νομάδες, οἱ δὲ θηρευτικοί, οἱ δὲ γεωργοί·
ἔστι δὲ καὶ χαλκωρυχεῖα καὶ σιδηρουργεῖα καὶ
χρυσεῖα καὶ λίθων γένη πολυτελῶν· περιέχεται δ'
ἀπὸ μὲν τῆς Λιβύης θισὶ μεγάλοις, ἀπὸ δὲ τῆς
Ἀραβίας κρημνοῖς συνεχέσιν, ἄνωθεν δ' ἐκ νότου

---

[1] ταχεῖς Eo, perhaps rightly.
[2] The MSS. read ποτὸν ποιοῦσιν αὐτοῖς ἐστιν· ἔλαιον δὲ κτλ.,
except that x omits ἐστιν. Corais reads ποτὸν αὐτοῖς ἐστιν·
ἀντὶ δὲ ἐλαίου κτλ.; but Jones reads as above, copying the
phrase ἀντ' ἐλαίου δέ from 3. 3. 7.

and this is clear from the modes of life of the inhabitants and from their lack of human necessities. They indeed live a hard life, go almost naked, and are nomads; and their domestic animals—sheep, goats, and cattle—are small; and their dogs are small though rough[1] and pugnacious. And perhaps it is from the natural smallness of the people that men have conceived of Pygmies and fabricated them; for no man worthy of belief professes to have seen them.

2. The Aethiopians live on millet and barley, from which they also make a drink; but instead of olive-oil they have butter and tallow. Neither do they have fruit trees, except a few date-palms in the royal gardens. But some use grass as food, as also tender twigs, lotus, and reed-roots; and they use meats, blood, milk, and cheese. They reverence as gods their kings, who generally stay shut up at home. Their greatest royal seat is Meroê, a city bearing the same name as the island. The island is said to be like an oblong shield in shape. Its size has perhaps been exaggerated: about three thousand stadia in length and one thousand in breadth. The island has both numerous mountains and large thickets; it is inhabited partly by nomads, partly by hunters, and partly by farmers; and it has mines of copper, iron, gold, and different kinds[2] of precious stones. It is bounded on the Libyan side by large sand-dunes, and on the Arabian side by continuous

---

[1] Possibly an error for "swift" (see critical note).
[2] Diodorus Siculus (1. 33) says "*all kinds* of precious stones."

---

[3] ἡ νῆσος is omitted by all MSS. except F; E reads ἡ Μερόη.

ταῖς συμβολαῖς τῶν ποταμῶν, τοῦ τε Ἀσταβόρα[1]
C 822 καὶ τοῦ Ἀστάποδος καὶ τοῦ Ἀστασόβα· πρὸς
ἄρκτον δ' ἡ ἐφεξῆς ῥύσις τοῦ Νείλου καὶ μέχρι
Αἰγύπτου κατὰ τὴν λεχθεῖσαν πρότερον σκολιό-
τητα τοῦ ποταμοῦ. ἐν δὲ ταῖς πόλεσιν αἱ οἰκήσεις
ἐκ φοινικίνων σχιζῶν διαπλεκομένων[2] ἢ πλίνθων.
ὀρυκτοὶ δὲ ἅλες, καθάπερ ἐν τοῖς Ἄραψι· πλεο-
νάζει δὲ τῶν φυτῶν ὅ τε φοίνιξ καὶ ἡ περσέα
καὶ ὁ ἔβενος καὶ ἡ κερατία·[3] θήρα δὲ καὶ ἐλεφάντων ἐστὶ καὶ λεόντων καὶ παρδάλεων· εἰσὶ δὲ καὶ
δράκοντες οἱ ἐλεφαντομάχοι καὶ ἄλλα θηρία
πλείω· καταφεύγει γὰρ ἀπὸ τῶν ἐμπυρωτέρων
καὶ αὐχμηροτέρων ἐπὶ τὰ ὑδρηλὰ καὶ ἑλώδη.

3. Ὑπέρκειται δὲ τῆς Μερόης ἡ Ψεβώ, λίμνη
μεγάλη νῆσον ἔχουσα οἰκουμένην ἱκανῶς. συμβαίνει δὲ τοῦ Νείλου τὴν μὲν δυσμικὴν παραπο-
ταμίαν ἐχόντων τῶν Λιβύων, τὴν δὲ πέραν
Αἰθιόπων, παρὰ μέρος αὐτῶν τὴν ἐπικράτειαν εἶναι
τῶν νήσων καὶ τῆς ποταμίας, ἐξελαυνομένων τῶν
ἑτέρων καὶ παραχωρούντων τοῖς κρείττοσι γενο-
μένοις. χρῶνται δὲ καὶ τόξοις Αἰθίοπες τετρα-
πήχεσι ξυλίνοις πεπυρακτωμένοις·[4] ὁπλίζουσι
δὲ καὶ τὰς γυναῖκας, ὧν αἱ πλείους κεκρίκωνται
τὸ χεῖλος τοῦ στόματος χαλκῷ κρίκῳ· κωδιοφόροι
δ' εἰσίν, ἐρέαν οὐκ ἔχοντες, τῶν προβάτων
αἰγοτριχούντων· οἱ δὲ γυμνῆτές εἰσιν, οἳ καὶ[5]

---

[1] Ἀσταβόρα F, Ἀσταβάρα other MSS.

[2] διαπλεκομένων, Groskurd, for διαπλεκόμεναι, after which *moz* read καὶ τοίχων ἐκ πλίνθων, other MSS. τοίχων ἢ πλίνθων. Jones, following Kramer and C. Müller, ejects τοίχων.

[3] καὶ ἡ κερατία *moxz*, καὶ κεράτια other MSS.

[4] On a conjectural omission here, see C. Müller, *Ind. Var. Lect.* p. 1042.

precipices, and above, on the south, by the confluences
of the three rivers—the Astaboras, and the Astapus
and the Astasobas [1]—and on the north by the next
course of the Nile, which extends to Aegypt along
the aforesaid windings of the river. In the cities
the dwellings are made of split pieces of palm-wood
woven together, or of brick. And they have quarried
salt, as do the Arabians. And, among the plants,
the palm, the *persea*,[2] the ebony, and the *ceratia*[3]
are found in abundance. And they have, not only
elephants to hunt, but also lions and leopards. They
also have serpents, the elephant-fighters, as also
many other wild animals; for the animals flee for
refuge from the hotter and more arid regions to
those that are watery and marshy.

3. Above Meroê lies Psebo, a large lake containing
an island that is rather well settled. And since the
Libyans hold the land on the western side of the
Nile and the Aethiopians that on the opposite side,
it comes to pass that they take turns in dominating
the islands and the river-land, one of the two being
driven out and yielding place to those who have
proved stronger. The Aethiopians also use bows,
which are four cubits long, are made of wood, and
are hardened by fire; and they arm the women also,
most of whom have a copper ring through the lip; and
they wear sheep-skins, since they have no wool,
their sheep having hair like that of goats; and some
go naked, or wear round their loins small sheep-

[1] Cp. 17. 1. 2.
[2] This tree is carefully described by Pliny (*N. H.*, 13. 17).
[3] The *carob* or *locust-tree*.

---

[5] οἱ καί EF*h*, ἢ καί other MSS., perhaps rightly.

περιέζωνται μικρὰ κώδια ἢ τρίχινα πλέγματα
εὐυφῆ. θεὸν δὲ νομίζουσι τὸν μὲν ἀθάνατον, τοῦτον δ' εἶναι τὸν αἴτιον τῶν πάντων, τὸν δὲ
θνητόν, ἀνώνυμόν τινα καὶ οὐ σαφῆ. ὡς δ' ἐπὶ
τὸ πολὺ τοὺς εὐεργέτας καὶ βασιλικοὺς θεοὺς
νομίζουσι, καὶ τούτων τοὺς μὲν βασιλέας κοινοὺς
ἁπάντων σωτῆρας καὶ φύλακας, τοὺς δ' ἰδιώτας
ἰδίως τοῖς εὖ παθοῦσιν ὑπ' αὐτῶν. τῶν δὲ πρὸς
τῇ διακεκαυμένῃ τινὲς καὶ ἄθεοι νομίζονται, οὕς
γε καὶ τὸν ἥλιόν φασιν ἐχθαίρειν καὶ κακῶς
λέγειν, ἐπειδὰν προσίδωσιν ἀνίσχοντα, ὡς καίοντα
καὶ πολεμοῦντα αὐτοῖς, καταφεύγειν τε εἰς τὰ
ἕλη. οἱ δ' ἐν Μερόῃ καὶ Ἡρακλέα καὶ Πᾶνα καὶ
Ἶσιν σέβονται πρὸς ἄλλῳ τινὶ βαρβαρικῷ θεῷ.
τοὺς δὲ νεκροὺς οἱ μὲν εἰς τὸν ποταμὸν ἐκρίπτου-
σιν, οἱ δ' οἴκοι κατέχουσι περιχέαντες ὕαλον·
τινὲς δὲ ἐν κεραμίαις σοροῖς κατορύττουσι κύκλῳ
τῶν ἱερῶν, ὅρκον τε τὸν ὑπὲρ αὐτῶν ἀπαιτοῦσι
καὶ πάντων ἁγιστεύουσι μάλιστα. βασιλέας τε
καθιστᾶσι τοὺς κάλλει διαφέροντας ἢ ἀρετῇ
κτηνοτροφίας ἢ ἀνδρείᾳ ἢ πλούτῳ. ἐν δὲ τῇ
Μερόῃ κυριωτάτην τάξιν ἐπεῖχον οἱ ἱερεῖς τὸ
παλαιόν, οἵ γε καὶ τῷ βασιλεῖ προσέταττον ἔσθ'
ὅτε ἀποθνήσκειν πέμψαντες ἄγγελον καὶ κα-
C 823 θίστασαν ἀντ' αὐτοῦ ἕτερον· ὕστερον δὲ κατέλυσέ
τις τῶν βασιλέων τὸ ἔθος, ἐπιὼν μεθ' ὅπλων ἐπὶ
τὸ ἱερόν, ὅπου ὁ χρυσοῦς νεώς ἐστι, καὶ τοὺς
ἱερέας ἀποσφάξας πάντας. ἔστι δὲ καὶ τοῦτο

---

[1] Diodorus Siculus (3. 39) names Zeus in connection with
the three others.

[2] See 17. 1. 8 and footnote on " glass."

skins or girdles of well-woven hair. They regard as
god the immortal being, whom they consider the
cause of all things, and also the mortal being, who
is without name and not to be identified. But in
general they regard their benefactors and royal per-
sonages as gods : of these the kings as the common
saviours and guardians of all, and special individuals
as in a special sense gods to those who have
received benefactions from them. Among those
who live near the torrid zone, some are considered
atheists, since it is said that they hate even the sun,
and revile it when they behold it rising, on the
ground that it burns them and carries on war with
them, and flee for refuge from it into the marshes.
The inhabitants of Meroê worship Heracles, Pan,
and Isis, in addition to some other, barbaric, god.[1]
As for the dead, some cast them into the river,
others enclose them in glass [2] and keep them at
home ; but some bury them around the temples in
coffins made of clay ; and they exact fulfilment of
oaths sworn over the dead,[3] and consider them the
most sacred of all things. They appoint as kings
those who excel in beauty, or in superiority in cattle-
breeding, or in courage, or in wealth. In Meroê
the highest rank was in ancient times held by the
priests, who indeed would give orders even to
the king, sometimes ordering him through a mes-
senger to die, and would appoint another in his
stead ; but later one of the kings broke up the
custom by marching with armed men against the
temple where the golden shrine is and slaughtering
all the priests. The following is also an Aethiopian

[3] *i.e.* they make the oath binding by invoking the dead as
witnesses.

ἔθος Αἰθιοπικόν· ὃς γὰρ ἂν τῶν βασιλέων
πηρωθῇ μέρος τι τοῦ σώματος ὁπωσοῦν τὸ αὐτὸ
πάσχουσιν οἱ συνόντες αὐτῷ μάλιστα, οἱ δ' αὐτοὶ
καὶ συναποθνήσκουσιν· ἐκ δὲ τούτου φυλακὴ τοῦ
βασιλέως ἐστὶ πλείστη παρ' αὐτῶν. περὶ μὲν
Αἰθιόπων ἀρκέσει ταῦτα.

4. Τοῖς δ' Αἰγυπτιακοῖς καὶ ταῦτα προσθετέον
ὅσα ἰδιάζοντα, οἷον ὁ Αἰγύπτιος λεγόμενος κύαμος
ἐξ οὗ τὸ κιβώριον, καὶ ἡ βύβλος· ἐνταῦθα γὰρ
καὶ παρ' Ἰνδοῖς μόνον· ἡ δὲ περσέα ἐνταῦθα μόνον
καὶ παρ' Αἰθίοψι, δένδρον μέγα, καρπὸν ἔχον
γλυκὺν καὶ μέγαν, καὶ ἡ συκάμινος ἡ ἐκφέρουσα
τὸν λεγόμενον καρπὸν συκόμορον· σύκῳ γὰρ
ἔοικεν, ἄτιμον δ' ἐστὶ κατὰ τὴν γεῦσιν· γίνεται
δὲ καὶ τὸ κόρσιον καὶ ὅμοιόν τι[1] πεπέρει[2] τρά-
γημα, μικρῷ αὐτοῦ μεῖζον. ἰχθύες δ' ἐν τῷ
Νείλῳ πολλοὶ μὲν καὶ ἄλλοι χαρακτῆρα ἔχοντες
ἴδιον καὶ ἐπιχώριον, γνωριμώτατοι δὲ ὅ τε
ὀξύρυγχος καὶ ὁ λεπιδωτὸς καὶ λάτος καὶ ἀλάβης
καὶ κορακῖνος καὶ χοῖρος καὶ φαγρώριος, ὃν καὶ
φάγρον καλοῦσιν, ἔτι σίλουρος, κιθαρός, θρίσσα,
κεστρεύς, λύχνος, φῦσα, βοῦς· ὀστρακίων δὲ
κοχλίαι[3] μεγάλοι, φωνὴν ὀλολυγόσιν ὁμοίαν
φθεγγόμενοι· ζῷα δ'[4] ἐπιχώρια καὶ ὁ ἰχνεύμων
καὶ ἡ ἀσπὶς ἡ Αἰγυπτία, ἴδιόν τι[5] ἔχουσα παρὰ
τὰς ἐν ἄλλοις· διττὴ δ' ἐστίν, ἡ μὲν σπιθαμιαία,
ἥπερ καὶ ὀξυθανατωτέρα, ἡ δ' ἐγγὺς ὀργυιᾶς, ὡς

----

[1] τό F, τῇ CDhi, τῷ other MSS.
[2] πεπέρει CE, πέπερι other MSS.
[3] The text follows Corais. E reads ὀστράκων δὲ λύχνος,
φῦσα, βοῦς, κοχλίαι; other MSS. ὀστρακίων δίλυχνος. φύσα (F
φύσσα), βοῦς, κοχλίαι.
[4] δ', Corais inserts.

custom : whenever any one of the kings is maimed
in any part of his body in any way whatever, his
closest associates suffer the same thing, and they
even die with him ; and hence these men guard the
king most carefully. This will suffice on the subject
of the Aethiopians.

4. But to my account of things Aegyptian I must
add an enumeration of the things that are peculiar
to that country, as, for example, the Aegyptian
cyamus,[1] as it is called, from which *ciborium* is
derived, and the *byblus*, for the *byblus* is found only
here and among the Indians ; and the *persea*[2] is
found only here and among the Aethiopians—a large
tree with large, sweet fruit ; and the *sycaminus* that
produces the fruit called *sycomorus*, for it resembles
a *sycum*,[3] though it is not prized for its taste ; and
the *corsium* is also found here—a relish somewhat
like pepper, but slightly larger. As for fish in the
Nile, they are indeed many in number and different in
kind, with a special indigenous character, but the best
known are the *oxyrynchus* and the *lepidotus, latus,
alabes, coracinus, choerus,* and *phagrorius,* also called
phagrus, and, besides, the *silurus, citharus, thrissa,
cestreus, lychnus, physa,* and *bos* ; and, among shell-
creatures, there are large *conchliae* which emit a
sound like a croak. As for indigenous animals,
Aegypt has also the ichneumon and the Aegyptian
asp, which latter has a peculiarity as compared with
the asp of other countries ; but it is of two kinds,
one only a span long, which causes a quicker death,
and the other nearly a fathom, as is stated by

[1] See 17. 1. 15.   [2] See § 2 above.
[3] *i.e.* "fig."

---

[5] Ἴδιόν τι E, Ἴδιον δέ τι other MSS.

καὶ Νίκανδρος ὁ τὰ Θηριακὰ γράψας εἴρηκε.
καὶ τῶν ὀρνέων ἶβις καὶ ἱέραξ ὁ Αἰγύπτιος,
ἥμερος παρὰ[1] τοὺς ἄλλοθι, ὡς καὶ ἡ αἴλουρος·
καὶ ὁ[2] νυκτικόραξ ἰδιότροπος ἐνθάδε· παρ᾽ ἡμῖν
μὲν γὰρ ἀετοῦ μέγεθος ἴσχει καὶ φθέγγεται βαρύ,
ἐν Αἰγύπτῳ δὲ κολοιοῦ μέγεθος καὶ φθογγὴ
διάφορος. ἡμερώτατον δ᾽ ἡ ἶβις, πελαργώδης
μὲν κατὰ σχῆμα καὶ μέγεθος, διττὴ δὲ τὴν χρόαν,
ἡ μὲν πελαργώδης, ἡ δὲ ὅλη μέλαινα. μεστὴ δ᾽
αὐτῶν ἅπασα τρίοδος ἐν Ἀλεξανδρείᾳ, πῆ μὲν
χρησίμως, πῆ δ᾽ οὐ χρησίμως· χρησίμως μέν,
ὅτι πᾶν[3] θηρίον ἐκλέγει καὶ τὰ ἐν τοῖς κρεω-
πωλίοις καὶ τοῖς ὀψοπωλίοις[4] ἀποκαθάρματα·
δυσχρήστως δέ, ὅτι παμφάγον καὶ ἀκάθαρτον καὶ
δυσκόλως ἀπειργόμενον ἀπὸ τῶν καθαρίων καὶ
τῶν ἀλλοτρίων μολυσμοῦ παντός.

5. Ἀληθὲς δὲ καὶ τὸ[5] Ἡροδότου καί ἐστιν
Αἰγυπτιακὸν τὸ τὸν μὲν πηλὸν ταῖς χερσὶ φυρᾶν,
τὸ δὲ στέαρ[6] τὸ εἰς τὴν ἀρτοποιίαν τοῖς ποσί.
C 824 καὶ οἱ κάκεις[7] δὲ ἴδιόν τι ἄρτου γένος, στατικὸν
κοιλίας, καὶ τὸ κίκι καρπός τις σπειρόμενος ἐν
ἀρούραις, ἐξ οὗ ἔλαιον ἀποθλίβεται εἰς μὲν
λύχνον τοῖς ἀπὸ τῆς χώρας σχεδόν τι πᾶσιν, εἰς
ἄλειμμα δὲ τοῖς πενεστέροις καὶ ἐργατικωτέροις

---

[1] ἥμερος παρά E, ἥμερος γὰρ παρά other MSS.
[2] ὁ Cz, ἡ other MSS.
[3] After πᾶν, Jones conj. that πήμονα has fallen out of the text.
[4] ὀψοπωλίοις Casaubon, ὀψοπώλαις E, ὀψοπώλεσιν other MSS.
[5] τοῦ CEFh.
[6] στέας DF, σταῖς second hand Dh, as in Herodotus 2. 36.
[7] οἱ κάκης E, κυλλάστεις conj. Dindorf in Thesaurus, s.v.

---

[1] Theriaca 168.
[2] A poem on poisonous animals, as the name implies.

Nicander,[1] who wrote the *Theriaca*.[2] Among the
birds are found the ibis and the Aegyptian *hierax*,
which latter is tame, like the cat, as compared with
those elsewhere; and also the *nycticorax*[3] is here of
a peculiar species, for in our country it has the size
of an eagle and a harsh caw, but in Aegypt the size
of a jackdaw and a different caw. The ibis, however,
is the tamest bird; it is like a stork in shape and
size, but it is of two kinds in colour, one kind like
the stork and the other black all over.[4] Every
cross-road in Alexandria is full of them; and though
they are useful in one way, they are not useful in
another. The bird is useful because it singles out
every[5] animal[6] and the refuse in the meat-shops and
bakeries, but not useful because it eats everything,
is unclean, and can only with difficulty be kept away
from things that are clean and do not admit of any
defilement.

5. The statement of Herodotus[7] is also true, that
it is an Aegyptian custom to knead mud with their
hands, but suet for bread-making with their feet.
Further, *kakeis* is a peculiar kind of bread which
checks the bowels; and *kiki* is a kind of fruit sown
in the fields, from which oil is pressed, which is used
not only in lamps by almost all the people in the
country, but also for anointing the body by the
poorer classes and those who do the heavier labour,

[3] *i.e.* "night-crow."
[4] The former is the White or Sacred Ibis; it regularly
visits Aegypt at the time of the inundation, coming from
Nubia.
[5] The translator conjectures that "baneful" has fallen out
of the text after "every" (see critical note).
[6] *e.g.* serpents (Josephus 2. 10), scorpions (Aelian 10. 29),
locusts and caterpillars (Diodorus Siculus 1. 87).
[7] 2. 36.

καὶ ἀνδράσι καὶ γυναιξί. καὶ τὰ κοΐκινα [1] δὲ
πλέγματα Αἰγυπτιακά ἐστι, φυτοῦ τινος, ὅμοια
τοῖς σχοινίνοις ἢ φοινικίνοις. τὸ δὲ ζύθος [2] ἰδίως
μὲν σκευάζεται παρ᾽ ἐκείνοις, κοινὸν δ᾽ ἐστὶ
πολλοῖς, καὶ παρ᾽ ἑκάστοις δὲ αἱ σκευασίαι
διάφοροι. καὶ τοῦτο δὲ τῶν μάλιστα ζηλουμένων
παρ᾽ αὐτοῖς τὸ πάντα τρέφειν τὰ γεννώμενα
παιδία καὶ τὸ περιτέμνειν καὶ τὰ θήλεα ἐκτέμνειν,
ὅπερ καὶ τοῖς Ἰουδαίοις νόμιμον· καὶ οὗτοι δ᾽ εἰσὶν
Αἰγύπτιοι τὸ ἀνέκαθεν, καθάπερ εἰρήκαμεν ἐν τῷ
περὶ ἐκείνων λόγῳ. φησὶ δ᾽ Ἀριστόβουλος, ἐκ
τῆς θαλάττης μηδὲν ἀνατρέχειν ὄψον εἰς τὸν
Νεῖλον πλὴν κεστρέως καὶ θρίσσης καὶ δελφῖνος
διὰ τοὺς κροκοδείλους· τοὺς μὲν δελφῖνας διὰ τὸ
κρείττους εἶναι, τοὺς δὲ κεστρέας τῷ παρα-
πέμπεσθαι ὑπὸ τῶν χοίρων παρὰ γῆν κατά τινα
οἰκείωσιν φυσικήν· τῶν δὲ χοίρων ἀπέχεσθαι
τοὺς κροκοδείλους, στρογγύλων ὄντων καὶ ἐχόντων
ἀκάνθας ἐπὶ τῇ κεφαλῇ φερούσας κίνδυνον τοῖς
θηρίοις· ἀναθεῖν μὲν οὖν ἔαρος τοὺς κεστρέας
γόνον ἔχοντας, μικρὸν δὲ πρὸ δύσεως Πλειάδος
καταβαίνειν τεξομένους ἀθρόους, ὅτε καὶ ἡ ἅλωσις
αὐτῶν γίνεται περιπιπτόντων τοῖς φράγμασιν
ἀθρόων.[3] τοιαύτην δέ τινα εἰκάζειν ἔστι καὶ
περὶ τῆς θρίσσης αἰτίαν. ταῦτα καὶ περὶ
Αἰγύπτου.

---

[1] κοΐκινα (textures "made of the coïx-palm"), Casaubon
and Meineke, for κόκκινα; but Kramer prefers κούκινα ("made
from the coco-palm").
[2] ζύθος Ew, ζύγος other MSS.
[3] ἀθρόων Dh, ἀθρόον other MSS.

both men and women; and further, the *koïkina*[1] are Aegyptian textures made of some plant, and are like those made of rush or the date-palm. And beer is prepared in a peculiar way among the Aegyptians; it is a drink common to many peoples, but the ways of preparing it in the different countries are different. One of the customs most zealously observed among the Aegyptians is this, that they rear every child that is born, and circumcise the males, and excise the females,[2] as is also customary among the Jews, who are also Aegyptians in origin, as I have already stated in my account of them.[3] Aristobulus says that on account of the crocodiles no fish swim up into the Nile from the sea except the *cestreus* and the *thrissa* and the dolphin—the dolphin, because it is stronger than the crocodile, and the *cestreus*, because it is escorted by the *choeri*[4] along the bank, in accordance with some natural affinity; and that the crocodiles keep away from the *choeri*, since the latter are round and have spines on the head which offer danger to the beasts. Now the *cestreus*, he says, runs up the river in spring when it is carrying its spawn, but for the purpose of spawning comes down in schools before the setting of the Pleiad, at which time they are captured, being caught in schools by the fenced enclosures. And some such cause might be conjectured also in the case of the *thrissa*. So much for Aegypt.

[1] See critical note.

[2] *i.e.* remove portions of the *nymphae*, and sometimes of the *clitoris*, of the females. The operation is harmless, and analogous to that of circumcision.

[3] 16. 2. 34.

[4] *i.e.* "pig" fish (see Athenaeus 6).

III

Περὶ δὲ Λιβύης ἐφεξῆς λέγωμεν, ὅπερ λείπεται μέρος τῆς συμπάσης γεωγραφίας.[1] εἴρηται μὲν οὖν καὶ πρότερον πολλὰ καὶ περὶ αὐτῆς, ἀλλὰ καὶ νῦν ὅσα καίρια προσυπομνηστέον, προστιθέντας[2] καὶ τὰ μὴ λεχθέντα πρότερον. οἱ μὲν οὖν πρὸς τὰς ἠπείρους τὴν οἰκουμένην διελόντες ἀνίσως διεῖλον, ἐμφαίνει γὰρ τὸ τριχῇ τὸ εἰς τρία ἴσα, τοσοῦτο δ᾽ ἀπολείπεται τοῦ τρίτον εἶναι μέρος τῆς οἰκουμένης ἡ Λιβύη, ὥστε καὶ συντεθεῖσα μετὰ τῆς Εὐρώπης οὐκ ἂν ἐξισάζειν δόξειε τῇ Ἀσίᾳ. τάχα δὲ καὶ τῆς Εὐρώπης ἐλάττων ἐστί, κατὰ δὲ τὴν δύναμιν καὶ πολλῷ τινι, ἔρημος γάρ ἐστιν ἡ πολλὴ τῆς μεσογαίας καὶ τῆς παρωκεανίτιδος, κατοικίαις δὲ κατάστικτός ἐστι μικραῖς, καὶ σποράσι καὶ νομαδικαῖς ταῖς πλείσταις· πρὸς δὲ τῇ ἐρημίᾳ καὶ τὸ θηριοτρόφον ἐξελαύνει καὶ ἐκ τῆς δυναμένης C 825 οἰκεῖσθαι· πολὺ δὲ καὶ τῆς διακεκαυμένης ἐπιλαμβάνει ζώνης. ἡ μέντοι καθ᾽ ἡμᾶς εὐδαιμόνως οἰκεῖται πᾶσα παραλία ἡ μεταξὺ Νείλου καὶ Στηλῶν, καὶ μάλιστα ἡ ὑπὸ Καρχηδονίοις γενομένη· ἄνυδραι δέ τινες κἀνταῦθα παρεμπίπτουσιν, οἷαι περί τε τὰς Σύρτεις καὶ τοὺς Μαρμαρίδας καὶ τὸν Καταβαθμόν.

Ἔστι δὲ ὀρθογωνίου τριγώνου τὸ σχῆμα, ὡς ἄν τις ἐν ἐπιπέδῳ νοήσειε, βάσιν μὲν ἔχον τὴν καθ᾽ ἡμᾶς παραλίαν τὴν ἀπὸ τῆς Αἰγύπτου καὶ

---

[1] γεωμετρίας CDEF.
[2] προστιθέντας F, προσθέντας other MSS.

III

1. Next let me describe Libya, which is the only part left for the completion of my Geography as a whole. Now I have said much about this country before,[1] but I must now comment also on other matters in so far as they may be timely, adding what has not been said before. Now the writers who have divided the inhabited world according to continents have divided it unequally, for the threefold division indicates a division into three equal parts; but Libya lacks so much of being a third part of the inhabited world that even if it were combined with Europe it would seem not to be equal to Asia. Perhaps it is even smaller than Europe; and in power it is much inferior, for the greater part of the interior and of its ocean-coast is desert, and it is dotted with settlements that are small, scattered, and mostly nomadic; and in addition to its deserts, its being a nursery of wild beasts drives out people even from land that could be inhabited; and it overlaps a considerable part of the torrid zone. However, the whole of the coast opposite to us, I mean that between the Nile and the Pillars, and particularly the part which was subject to the Carthaginians, is settled and prosperous; but here too some parts here and there are destitute of water, as, for example, in the regions about the Syrtes, the Marmaridae,[2] and Catabathmus.

Libya has the shape of a right-angled triangle, conceived of as drawn on a plane surface, having as base the coast opposite us, from Aegypt and the

----

[2] See § 23 following.

Νείλου μέχρι Μαυρουσίας καὶ Στηλῶν, πρὸς
ὀρθὰς δὲ ταύτῃ πλευράν, ἣν ὁ Νεῖλος ποιεῖ μέχρι
Αἰθιοπίας, προσεκβαλλόντων ἡμῶν ἕως Ὠκεανοῦ,
τὴν δ' ὑποτείνουσαν τῇ ὀρθῇ τὴν παρωκεανῖτιν
ἅπασαν τὴν μεταξὺ Αἰθιόπων καὶ Μαυρουσίων.
τὸ μὲν οὖν κατ' αὐτὴν τὴν κορυφὴν τοῦ λεχθέντος
σχήματος, ἤδη πως ὑποπῖπτον τῇ διακεκαυμένῃ,
λέγομεν ἐξ εἰκασμοῦ διὰ τὸ ἀπρόσιτον, ὥστ' οὐδὲ
τὸ μέγιστον πλάτος τῆς χώρας ἔχοιμεν ἂν λέγειν·
τὸ μέντοι τοσοῦτον ἐν τοῖς πρόσθεν λόγοις
ἔφαμεν, ὅτι ἐξ Ἀλεξανδρείας εἰς Μερόην τὸ
βασίλειον τῶν Αἰθιόπων πρὸς νότον ἰόντι στάδιοί
εἰσι περὶ μυρίους, ἐκεῖθεν δ' ἐπ' εὐθείας ἐπὶ τοὺς
ὅρους τῆς διακεκαυμένης καὶ τῆς οἰκουμένης ἄλλοι
τρισχίλιοι.   τὸ γοῦν αὐτὸ θετέον τὸ μέγιστον
πλάτος τῆς Λιβύης, μυρίους καὶ τρισχιλίους ἢ
τετρακισχιλίους στάδιους, μῆκος δὲ μικρῷ ἔλαττον
ἢ διπλάσιον. τὰ καθ' ὅλου μὲν ταῦτα περὶ
Λιβύης· τὰ καθ' ἕκαστα δὲ λεκτέον, ἀρξαμένοις
ἀπὸ τῶν ἑσπερίων μερῶν καὶ τῶν ἐπιφανεστέρων.

2. Οἰκοῦσι δ' ἐνταῦθα Μαυρούσιοι μὲν ὑπὸ
τῶν Ἑλλήνων λεγόμενοι, Μαῦροι δ' ὑπὸ τῶν
Ῥωμαίων καὶ τῶν ἐπιχωρίων,[1] Λιβυκὸν ἔθνος
μέγα καὶ εὔδαιμον, ἀντίπορθμον τῇ Ἰβηρίᾳ.
κατὰ τοῦτο δὲ καὶ ὁ κατὰ τὰς Στήλας τὰς
Ἡρακλείους πορθμός ἐστι, περὶ οὗ πολλὰ εἴρηται.
ἔξω δὲ προελθόντι τοῦ κατὰ τὰς Στήλας πορθμοῦ,
τὴν Λιβύην ἐν ἀριστερᾷ ἔχοντι ὄρος ἐστίν, ὅπερ
οἱ μὲν Ἕλληνες Ἄτλαντα καλοῦσιν, οἱ βάρβαροι
δὲ Δύριν. ἐντεῦθεν δὲ πρόπους ἔκκειταί τις

[1] Μαῦροι . . . ἐπιχωρίων, Kramer transfers from a position
after εὔδαιμον.

Nile to Maurusia and the Pillars, and as the side perpendicular to this that which is formed by the Nile as far as Aethiopia and by me produced to the ocean, and as the side subtending the right angle the whole of the coast between the Aethiopians and the Maurusians. Now as for the part at the very vertex of the above-mentioned figure, which begins approximately with the torrid zone, I speak only from conjecture, because it is inaccessible, so that I cannot tell even its maximum breadth, although in a previous part of my work [1] I have said thus much, that, as one goes southward from Alexandria to Meroê, the royal seat of the Aethiopians, the distance is about ten thousand stadia, and from there in a straight line to the boundaries between the torrid zone and the inhabited world three thousand more. At any rate, the same should be put down as the maximum breadth of Libya, I mean thirteen or fourteen thousand stadia, and a little less than double that sum as the length. This, then, is my account of Libya as a whole, but I must describe it in detail, beginning with its western, or more famous, parts.

2. Here dwell a people whom the Greeks call Maurusians, and the Romans and the natives Mauri— a large and prosperous Libyan tribe, who live on the side of the strait opposite Iberia. Here also is the strait which is at the Pillars of Heracles, concerning which I have often spoken. On proceeding outside the strait at the Pillars, with Libya on the left, one comes to a mountain which the Greeks call Atlas and the barbarians Dyris. From this mountain pro-

---

[1] 1. 4. 2.

ὕστατος πρὸς δύσιν τῆς Μαυρουσίας αἱ Κώτεις
λεγόμεναι· πλησίον δὲ καὶ πολίχνιον μικρὸν
ὑπὲρ τῆς θαλάττης, ὅπερ Τίγγα[1] καλοῦσιν οἱ
βάρβαροι, Λύγγα[2] δ' ὁ Ἀρτεμίδωρος προση-
γόρευκε, Ἐρατοσθένης δὲ Λίξον· κεῖται δ' ἀντίπορθμον τοῖς Γαδείροις ἐν διάρματι σταδίων
ὀκτακοσίων, ὅσον ἑκάτερα διέχει τοῦ κατὰ τὰς
Στήλας πορθμοῦ· πρὸς νότον δὲ τῇ Λίξῳ καὶ
ταῖς Κώτεσι παράκειται κόλπος Ἐμπορικὸς
C 826 καλούμενος, ἔχων Φοινικικὰς ἐμπορικὰς κατοικίας.
ἔστι μὲν οὖν πᾶσα ἡ συνεχὴς τῷ κόλπῳ τούτῳ
παραλία κολπώδης, ὑπεξαιρουμένῳ δὲ τοὺς κόλπους καὶ τὰς ἐξοχὰς κατὰ τὸ σχῆμα τὸ τριγω-
νοειδές, ὃ ὑπέγραψα, νοείσθω μᾶλλον ἐπὶ τὴν
μεσημβρίαν ἅμα καὶ τὴν ἕω λαμβάνουσα τὴν
αὔξησιν ἡ ἤπειρος. τὸ δ' ὄρος διὰ μέσης ἐκτεινό-
μενον τῆς Μαυρουσίας τὸ ἀπὸ τῶν Κώτεων μέχρι
καὶ Σύρτεων οἰκεῖται καὶ αὐτὸ καὶ ἄλλα παράλ-
ληλα αὐτῇ κατ' ἀρχὰς μὲν ὑπὸ τῶν Μαυρουσίων,
ἐν βάθει δὲ τῆς χώρας ὑπὸ τοῦ μεγίστου τῶν
Λιβυκῶν ἐθνῶν, οἳ Γαίτουλοι λέγονται.

3. Πλεῖστα δὲ πλάσματα τῇ Λιβυκῇ παραλίᾳ
τῇ ἐκτὸς προσεψεύσαντο οἱ συγγραφεῖς, ἀρξάμενοι
ἀπὸ τοῦ Ὀφέλα[3] περίπλου· περὶ ὧν ἐμνήσθημέν
που καὶ πρότερον, καὶ νῦν δὲ λέγομεν, συγγνώμην
αἰτούμενοι τῆς τερατολογίας, ἐάν που βιασθῶμεν

---

[1] Τρίγκα E.   [2] Λύγκα E.
[3] Ὀφρύα Ald.; Tyrwhitt conj. Ἀπέλλα.

---

[1] The same as Tingis (3. 1. 8).
[2] Strabo is confusing Tingis (now Tangiers) with Lynx or
Lixus (now El Araisch or Larasch) ; see § 8 following.
[3] Cadiz.   [4] *i.e.* "Mercantile."

jects a farthermost spur, as it were, towards the west of Maurusia—the Coteis, as it is called; and near by is a small town above the sea which the barbarians call Tinx,[1] though Artemidorus has given it the name Lynx and Eratosthenes Lixus.[2] It is situated across the strait opposite Gadeira[3] at a distance of eight hundred stadia, which is about the distance of each of the two places from the strait at the Pillars. To the south of Lixus and the Coteis lies a gulf called the Emporicus[4] Gulf, which contains settlements of Phoenician merchants. Now the whole of the coast continuous with this gulf is indented by gulfs, but one should exclude from consideration the gulfs and the projections of land, in accordance with the triangular figure which I have suggested, and conceive rather of the continent as increasing in extent in the direction of the south and east.[5] The mountain,[6] which extends through the middle of Maurusia from the Coteis to the Syrtes, is inhabited, both itself and other mountains that run parallel with Maurusia, at first by the Maurusians but deep in the interior by the largest of the Libyan tribes, who are called Gaetulians.

3. The historians, beginning with *The Circumnavigation of Ophelas*,[7] have added numerous other fabrications in regard to the outside coast of Libya; and these I have already mentioned somewhere before,[8] but I am again speaking of them, asking pardon for introducing marvellous stories, if per-

[5] *i.e.* this side forms the hypotenuse and runs in a south-easterly direction.

[6] Atlas.

[7] Ophelas of Cyrenê (Diodorus Siculus 18. 21, 20. 40–42, and Plutarch, *Demetrius* 14); see critical note.

[8] 1. 1. 5, and 3. 2. 13.

ἐκπεσεῖν εἴς τι τοιοῦτο, φεύγοντες τὸ πάντα σιγῇ
παραπέμπειν καὶ τρόπον τινὰ πηροῦν[1] τὴν
ἱστορίαν. φασὶ δ' οὖν τὸν Ἐμπορικὸν κόλπον
ἄντρον ἔχειν εἴσω δεχόμενον τὴν θάλατταν ἐν
ταῖς πλημμυρίσι μέχρι καὶ ἑπτὰ σταδίων, προκείμενον δὲ τούτου ταπεινὸν καὶ ὁμαλὸν χωρίον,
ἔχον Ἡρακλέους βωμόν, ὃν οὐκ ἐπικλύζεσθαί
φασιν ὑπὸ τῆς πλημμυρίδος· ἐν δὲ δή τι τῶν
πλασμάτων νομίζω τοῦτο. ἐγγὺς δὲ τούτῳ τὸ ἐν
τοῖς ἑξῆς κόλποις κατοικίας λέγεσθαι παλαιὰς
Τυρίων, ἃς ἐρήμους εἶναι νῦν, οὐκ ἐλαττόνων ἢ
τριακοσίων πόλεων, ἃς οἱ Φαρούσιοι καὶ οἱ
Νιγρῖται[2] ἐξεπόρθησαν· διέχειν δὲ τούτους τῆς
Λυγγὸς φασιν ἡμερῶν τριάκοντα ὁδόν.

4. Τὸ μέντοι τὴν Μαυρουσίαν εὐδαίμονα εἶναι[3]
χώραν πλὴν ὀλίγης ἐρήμου καὶ ποταμοῖς τε καὶ
λίμναις κεχορηγῆσθαι παρὰ πάντων ὁμολογεῖται.
μεγαλόδενδρός τε καὶ πολύδενδρος ὑπερβαλλόντως
ἐστὶ καὶ πάμφορος· τὰς γοῦν μονοξύλους τρα-
πέζας ποικιλωτάτας καὶ μεγίστας ἐκείνη τοῖς
Ῥωμαίοις χορηγεῖ. τοὺς δὲ ποταμοὺς ἔχειν φασὶ
καὶ κροκοδείλους καὶ ἄλλα γένη ζώων ἐμφερῆ
τοῖς ἐν τῷ Νείλῳ· τινὲς δὲ καὶ τὰς τοῦ Νείλου
πηγὰς πλησιάζειν οἴονται τοῖς ἄκροις τῆς Μαυρουσίας. ἐν ποταμῷ δέ τινι γεννᾶσθαι βδέλλας
ἑπταπήχεις, κατατετρημένα ἐχούσας τὰ βραγχία,
δι' ὧν ἀναπνέουσι. καὶ ταῦτα δὲ λέγουσι περὶ
τῆς χώρας, ὅτι ἄμπελος φύεται δυσὶν ἀνδράσι τὸ
πάχος δυσπερίληπτος, βότρυν πηχυαῖόν πως

[1] πηροῦν E, πληροῦν other MSS.
[2] Νιγρῖται Eh, Νηγρῖται D, Νιγρῆται other MSS.
[3] ἔχειν E.

chance I shall be forced to digress into a thing of that sort, since I am unwilling wholly to pass them over in silence and in a way to cripple my history. Now they say that the Emporicus Gulf has a cave which at the full tides admits the sea inside it for a distance of even seven stadia, and that in front of this gulf there is a low, level place containing an altar of Heracles, which, they say, is never inundated by the tide—and it is this that I regard as one of their fabrications. And nearly as bad as this is the statement that on the gulfs which come next after the Emporicus Gulf there were ancient settlements of Tyrians, now deserted—no fewer than three hundred cities, which were destroyed by the Pharusians and the Nigritae; and these people, they say, are at a distance of a thirty days' journey from Lynx.

4. However, it is agreed by all that Maurusia is a fertile country, except a small desert part, and is supplied with both lakes and rivers. It is surpassing in the size and in the number of its trees, and is also productive of everything; at any rate, this is the country which supplies the Romans with the tables that are made of one single piece of wood, very large and most variegated. The rivers are said to contain crocodiles, as also other kinds of animals similar to those in the Nile. Some think that even the sources of the Nile are near the extremities of Maurusia. And they say that in a certain river are found leeches[1] seven cubits long, with gills pierced through with holes, through which they breathe. They also say of this country that it produces a vine so thick that it can hardly be encircled by the arms of two men, and that it yields clusters of

---

[1] They meant leech-*fish*, *i.e.* lampreys.

ἀποδιδοῦσα· βοτάνη τε ὑψηλὴ πᾶσα καὶ λάχα-
νον, οἷον¹ ἄρον² καὶ δρακόντιον, οἱ δὲ τῶν
σταφυλίνων καυλοὶ καὶ ἱππομαράθου καὶ σκο-
λύμων δωδεκαπήχεις, τὸ δὲ πάχος παλαιστῶν
C 827 τεττάρων· καὶ δρακόντων δὲ καὶ ἐλεφάντων καὶ
δορκάδων καὶ βουβάλων καὶ τῶν παραπλησίων
ζῴων, λεόντων τε καὶ παρδάλεων, παντοδαπὴ
τροφὸς ἡ χώρα ἐστί. φέρει δὲ καὶ γαλᾶς αἰλού-
ροις ἴσας καὶ ὁμοίας, πλὴν ὅτι τὰ ῥύγχη προ-
πέπτωκε μᾶλλον, πιθήκων τε πάμπολυ πλῆθος,
περὶ ὧν καὶ Ποσειδώνιος εἴρηκεν, ὅτι πλέων ἐκ
Γαδείρων εἰς τὴν Ἰταλίαν προσενεχθείη τῇ
Λιβυκῇ παραλίᾳ καὶ ἴδοι τῶν θηρίων μεστόν
τινα τούτων ἀλιτενῆ δρυμόν, τῶν μὲν ἐπὶ τοῖς
δένδρεσι, τῶν δ' ἐπὶ γῆς, ἐχόντων ἐνίων καὶ
σκύμνους καὶ ἐπεχόντων μαστόν· γελᾶν οὖν
ὁρῶν βαρυμάστους, ἐνίους δὲ φαλακρούς, τοὺς δὲ
κηλήτας καὶ ἄλλα τοιαῦτα ἐπιφαίνοντας σίνη.

5. Ὑπὲρ ταύτης δ' ἐστὶν ἐπὶ τῇ ἔξω θαλάττῃ ἡ
τῶν ἑσπερίων καλουμένων Αἰθιόπων χώρα, κακῶς
οἰκουμένη τὸ πλέον. ἐνταῦθα δὲ καὶ καμηλο-
παρδάλεις φησὶν Ἰφικράτης³ γεννᾶσθαι καὶ
ἐλέφαντας καὶ τοὺς καλουμένους ῥίζεις, οἳ ταυ-
ροειδεῖς μέν εἰσι τὴν μορφήν, κατὰ δὲ τὴν δίαιταν
καὶ τὸ μέγεθος καὶ τὴν ἀλκὴν τὴν πρὸς μάχην

---

¹ οἷον, Jones inserts (Groskurd οἷον τό).
² ἄρον, Corais, for νεαρόν.   ³ Ὑψικράτης, Corais.

---

¹ They meant in *length*, apparently, and not in *circumference* (cp. 2. 1. 14 and 11. 10. 1).
² Apparently *Arum maculatum* (cuckoo-pint) and *Dracun-
culus* (cp. Pliny 24. 91–92 and Theophrastus 1. 6. 6, 7. 12. 2).
³ A kind of carrot or parsnip.

about one cubit ;[1] and that every herb grows high, and every vegetable, as, for example, *arum* and *dracontium* ;[2] and the stalks of the *staphylini*[3] and the *hippomarathi*[4] and the *scolymi*[5] grow twelve cubits high and four palms thick. And for serpents, also, and elephants and gazelles and *bubali*[6] and similar animals, as also for lions and leopards, the country is a nurse in every way. It also produces ferrets[7] equal in size to cats, and like them, except that their noses project further ; and also a very great number of apes, concerning which Poseidonius states that, when he was sailing from Gadeira to Italy, he was carried close to the Libyan coast and saw on a low-lying shore a forest full of these animals, some in the trees and others on the ground, and some having young and suckling them ; that he fell to laughing, however, when he saw some with heavy udders, some with bald heads, and others ruptured or displaying other disabilities of that kind.

5. Above Maurusia, on the outside sea, lies the country of the western Aethiopians, as they are called, a country for the most part poorly settled. Here too, according to Iphicrates,[8] are found camelopards, elephants, and the *rhizeis*,[9] as they are called, which are like bulls in their form, but like elephants in their manner of living and their

---

[4] *i.e.* horse-fennel.   [5] An edible kind of thistle.

[6] Apparently the antelope *bubalis*.

[7] Cp. 3. 2. 6.

[8] Possibly a copyist's error for "Hypicrates" (see Vol. III, p. 245, note 2).

[9] *i.e.* animals with noses "like roots" ; perhaps the writer quoted meant the rhinoceros, but elsewhere (16. 4. 15) Strabo himself uses the word "rhinoceros."

ἐλέφασιν ἐοίκασι· δράκοντάς τε λέγει μεγάλους,
ὥστε[1] καὶ πόαν ἐπιπεφυκέναι· τοὺς δὲ λέοντας
τοῖς πώλοις τῶν ἐλεφάντων ἐπιτίθεσθαι, αἱμά-
ξαντας δὲ φεύγειν, ἐπιουσῶν τῶν μητέρων· τὰς
δ', ἐπειδὰν ἴδωσιν ἡμαγμένους, κτείνειν· ἐπανιόντας
δὲ τοὺς λέοντας ἐπὶ τὰ πτώματα νεκροφαγεῖν.
Βόγον δέ, τὸν βασιλέα τῶν Μαυρουσίων, ἀναβάντα ἐπὶ τοὺς ἑσπερίους Αἰθίοπας, καταπέμψαι
τῇ γυναικὶ δῶρα καλάμους τοῖς Ἰνδικοῖς ὁμοίους,
ὧν ἕκαστον γόνυ χοίνικας χωρεῖν[2] ὀκτώ· καὶ
ἀσπαράγων δ' ἐμφερῆ μεγέθη.

6. Εἰς δὲ τὴν ἐντὸς θάλατταν πλέουσιν ἀπὸ
Λυγγὸς πόλις ἐστὶ Ζῆλις καὶ Τίγξ,[3] εἶτα τῶν
Ἑπτὰ ἀδελφῶν μνήματα καὶ τὸ ὑπερκείμενον
ὄρος ὄνομα Ἀβίλη,[4] πολύθηρον καὶ μεγαλόδενδρον.
τοῦ δὲ κατὰ τὰς Στήλας πορθμοῦ τὸ μὲν μῆκος
λέγεται σταδίων ἑκατὸν εἴκοσι, τὸ δ' ἐλάχιστον
πλάτος κατὰ τὸν Ἐλέφαντα ἑξήκοντα. εἰσπλεύσαντι δ' ἑξῆς πόλεις τε καὶ ποταμοὶ πλείους
μέχρι Μολοχὰθ ποταμοῦ, ὃς ὁρίζει τὴν Μαυρουσίων καὶ τὴν Μασαισυλίων[5] γῆν. κεῖται[6]
δὲ καὶ ἄκρα μεγάλη πλησίον τοῦ ποταμοῦ καὶ
Μεταγώνιον, τόπος ἄνυδρος καὶ λυπρός, σχεδὸν
δέ τι καὶ τὸ ὄρος τὸ ἀπὸ τῶν Κώτεων[7] μέχρι
δεῦρο παρατείνει· μῆκος δὲ τὸ ἀπὸ τῶν Κώτεων
ἐπὶ τοὺς ὄρους τοὺς τῶν Μασαισυλίων[8] στάδιοι

---

[1] οἷς γε, Corais.　　[2] χωροῦν Εοxz.
[3] Τίγξ, the editors, for Τίγα.
[4] Ἀβίλη οz, Ἀβύλη Dhi.
[5] Μασαισυλίων Eh, Μασαισυλίων F, Μασσαισυλίων other MSS.
[6] κεῖται, Kramer, for καλεῖται.
[7] Κώτεων E, Κωταίων other MSS.

size and their courage in fighting. And he speaks
of serpents so large that even grass grows upon
their backs; and says that the lions attack the young
of the elephants, but, after they have drawn blood,
flee when the mothers approach, and that the
mothers, when they see their young stained with
blood, kill them, and that the lions return to the
victims and eat them. And he says that Bogus,
the king of the Maurusians, when he went up
against the western Aethiopians, sent down to his
wife as gifts reeds like those of India, of which each
joint held eight choenices,[1] and also asparagus of
similar size.

6. As one sails into the inner sea from Lynx, one
comes to the city Zelis and to Tinx; and then to
the Monuments of the Seven Brothers[2] and to the
mountain that lies above them, Abilê by name,
which abounds in wild animals and large trees.
The length of the strait at the Pillars is said to
be one hundred and twenty stadia, and the minimum
breadth, measured at Elephas, sixty. On sailing into
the sea, one comes next to several cities and rivers—
to the Molochath[3] River, which forms the boundary
between the lands of the Maurusians and the Masaesylians. Near the river lies a large promontory, and
also Metagonium, a waterless and barren place; and
I might almost say that the mountain which begins
at the Coteis extends as far as this; and its length
from the Coteis to the boundaries of the Masaesylians

---

[1] About a gallon and a half.
[2] The seven "Monuments" or mountain-peaks.
[3] Now the Mulujah.

---

[8] Μασαισυλίων, Kramer, for Μασαισύλων F, Μασσαισυλίωτ
other MSS.

πεντακισχίλιοι. ἔστι δὲ τὸ Μεταγώνιον κατὰ
νέαν που Καρχηδόνα ἐν τῇ περαίᾳ· Τιμοσθένης
δ' οὐκ εὖ κατὰ Μασσαλίαν φησίν. ἔστι δ' ἐκ
C 828 Καρχηδόνος νέας δίαρμα εἰς Μεταγώνιον στάδιοι
τρισχίλιοι, παράπλους δὲ εἰς Μασσαλίαν ὑπὲρ
ἑξακισχιλίων.

7. Οὕτω δ' εὐδαίμονα χώραν οἰκοῦντες τὴν
πλείστην οἱ Μαυρούσιοι διατελοῦσιν, ὅμως καὶ
μέχρι δεῦρο τοῦ χρόνου νομαδικῶς ζῶντες οἱ
πολλοί. καλλωπίζονται δ' ὅμως κόμης ἐμπλοκῇ
καὶ πώγωνι καὶ χρυσοφορίᾳ σμήξει τε ὀδόντων
καὶ ὀνυχισμῷ· σπάνιόν τε ἂν ἴδοις ἁπτομένους
ἀλλήλων ἐν τοῖς περιπάτοις τοῦ παραμένειν
αὐτοῖς ἄθικτον τὸν κόσμον τῶν τριχῶν. μάχονται
δ' ἱππόται τὸ πλέον ἀπὸ ἄκοντος, σχοινοχαλίνοις
χρώμενοι τοῖς ἵπποις καὶ γυμνοῖς, ἔχουσι δὲ καὶ
μαχαίρας· οἱ δὲ πεζοὶ τὰς τῶν ἐλεφάντων δορὰς
ὡς ἀσπίδας προβάλλονται· τὰς δὲ τῶν λεόντων
καὶ παρδάλεων καὶ ἄρκτων ἀμπέχονται καὶ
ἐγκοιμῶνται. σχεδὸν δέ τι καὶ οὗτοι καὶ οἱ
ἐφεξῆς Μασαισύλιοι[1] καὶ κοινῶς Λίβυες κατὰ
τὸ πλέον ὁμοιόσκευοί εἰσι καὶ τὰ ἄλλα ἐμφερεῖς,
μικροῖς ἵπποις χρώμενοι, ὀξέσι δὲ καὶ εὐπειθέσιν,
ὥστ' ἀπὸ ῥαβδίου οἰακίζεσθαι. περιτραχήλια δὲ
ξύλινα ἢ τρίχινα, ἀφ' ὧν ὁ ῥυτὴρ ἀπήρτηται·
ἔνιοι δὲ καὶ χωρὶς ὁλκῆς ἕπονται ὡς κύνες.
πέλτη μικρὰ βυρσίνη, πλατύλογχα μικρά, ἄζω-
στοι πλατύσημοι χιτῶνες, ἐπιπόρπημα, ὡς ἔφην,
δορὰ καὶ προθωράκιον. Φαρούσιοι[2] δὲ καὶ

---

[1] Μασαισύλιοι E, Μασαίσυλοι F, Μασσάσυλοι D, Μασσαίσυλοι
other MSS.
[2] Φαυρούσιοι E, Φαροούσιοι C

is five thousand stadia. Metagonium is about opposite
New Carthage,[1] on the other side of the sea, but
Timosthenes wrongly says that it is opposite Mas-
salia.[2] The passage across from New Carthage to
Metagonium is three thousand stadia, and the
coasting-voyage to Massalia is over six thousand.

7. Although the most of the country inhabited
by the Maurusians is so fertile, yet even to this
time most of the people persist in living a nomadic
life. But nevertheless they beautify their appearance by braiding their hair, growing beards, wearing
golden ornaments, and also by cleaning their teeth
and paring their nails. And only rarely can you
see them touch one another in walking, for fear
that the adornment of their hair may not remain
intact. Their horsemen fight mostly with a javelin,
using bridles made of rush, and riding bareback;
but they also carry daggers. The foot-soldiers hold
before them as shields the skins of elephants, and
clothe themselves with the skins of lions, leopards,
and bears, and sleep in them. I might almost say
that these people, and the Masaesylians, who live
next after them, and the Libyans in general, dress
alike and are similar in all other respects, using
horses that are small but swift, and so ready to
obey that they are governed with a small rod. The
horses wear collars made of wood[3] or of hair, to
which the rein is fastened, though some follow even
without being led, like dogs. These people have
small shields made of raw-hide, small spears with
broad heads, wear ungirded tunics with wide borders,
and, as I have said, use skins as mantles and shields.

---

[1] Now Cartagena.   [2] Now Marseilles.
[3] *i.e.* of tree-wool.

Νίγρητες [1] οἱ ὑπὲρ τούτων οἰκοῦντες πρὸς τοῖς
ἑσπερίοις Αἰθίοψι καὶ τοξεύουσι, καθάπερ καὶ
οἱ Αἰθίοπες· χρῶνται δὲ καὶ δρεπανηφόροις
ἅρμασι. μίσγονται δὲ καὶ τοῖς Μαυρουσίοις οἱ
Φαρούσιοι διὰ τῆς ἐρήμου σπανίως, ὑπὸ ταῖς
κοιλίαις τῶν ἵππων ὑπαρτῶντες τοὺς ἀσκοὺς τοῦ
ὕδατος· ἔστι δ' ὅτε καὶ εἰς Κίρταν ἀφικνοῦνται
διά τινων τόπων ἑλωδῶν καὶ λιμνῶν. τινὰς δ'
αὐτῶν καὶ Τρωγλοδυτικῶς οἰκεῖν φασιν ὀρύτ-
τοντας τὴν γῆν. λέγεται δὲ κἀνταῦθα τοὺς
θερινοὺς ὄμβρους ἐπιπολάζειν, χειμῶνος δὲ εἶναι
ἀνυδρίαν· ἐνίους δὲ τῶν ταύτῃ βαρβάρων καὶ
ὄφεων καὶ ἰχθύων δοραῖς ἀμπεχόναις τε καὶ
στρώμασι χρῆσθαι. τοὺς δὲ Μαυρουσίους [2] ἔνιοί
φασιν Ἰνδοὺς εἶναι τοὺς συγκατελθόντας Ἡρακλεῖ
δεῦρο. μικρὸν μὲν οὖν πρὸ ἡμῶν οἱ περὶ Βόγον [3]
βασιλεῖς καὶ Βόκχον κατεῖχον αὐτήν, φίλοι
Ῥωμαίων ὄντες· ἐκλιπόντων δὲ τούτων, Ἰούβας
παρέλαβε τὴν ἀρχήν, δόντος τοῦ Σεβαστοῦ Καίσαρος καὶ ταύτην αὐτῷ τὴν ἀρχὴν πρὸς τῇ
πατρῴᾳ· υἱὸς δ' ἦν Ἰούβα τοῦ πρὸς Καίσαρα
τὸν θεὸν πολεμήσαντος μετὰ Σκιπίωνος. Ἰούβας
μὲν οὖν νεωστὶ ἐτελεύτα τὸν βίον, διαδέδεκται δὲ
τὴν ἀρχὴν υἱὸς Πτολεμαῖος, γεγονὼς ἐξ Ἀντωνίου
θυγατρὸς καὶ Κλεοπάτρας.

C 829   8. Ἀρτεμίδωρος δ' Ἐρατοσθένει μὲν ἀντιλέγει,
διότι Λίξον [4] τινά φησι πόλιν περὶ τὰ ἄκρα τῆς

---

[1] Νίγρητες DF*h*.
[2] For Μαυρουσίους, Meineke writes Φαρουσίους.
[3] Βόγον, Casaubon, for Βόκχο· *h*, Βόγκον *i*, Βόγχοι other
MSS.
[4] Λίξον Fs, Λίζον other MSS.

The Pharusians and Nigretes [1] who live above these people near the western Aethiopians also use bows, like the Aethiopians; and they also use scythe-bearing chariots. The Pharusians mingle only rarely even with the Maurusians when passing through the desert, since they carry skins of water fastened beneath the bellies of their horses. Sometimes, however, they come even to Cirta, passing through certain marshy regions and over lakes. Some of them are said to live like Troglodytes, digging homes in the earth. And it is said that here too the summer rains are prevalent, but that in winter there is a drought, and that some of the barbarians in this part of the world use also the skins of snakes and fish both as wraps and as bed-covers. And the Maurusians [2] are said by some to be the Indians who came thither with Heracles. Now a little before my time the kings of the house of Bogus and of Bocchus, who were friends of the Romans, possessed the country, but when these died Juba succeeded to the throne, Augustus Caesar having given him this in addition to his father's empire. He was the son of the Juba who with Scipio waged war against the deified Caesar. Now Juba died lately,[3] but his son Ptolemy, whose mother was the daughter of Antony and Cleopatra, has succeeded to the throne.

8. Artemidorus disputes the view of Eratosthenes because the latter calls a certain city in the neigh-

----

[1] Apparently a copyist's error for "Nigritae" (the spelling in 2. 5. 33, 16. 4. 37 and 17. 3. 3).

[2] Apparently an error for "Pharusians" (see Sallust, *Jugurtha*, 18, Pomponius Mela, 3. 10, Pliny, 5. 8, and critical note).

[3] About A.D. 19.

Μαυρουσίας τὰ ἑσπέρια ἀντὶ Λυγγός· Φοινικικὰς
δὲ πόλεις κατεσκαμμένας [1] παμπόλλας τινάς, ὧν
οὐδὲν ἰδεῖν ἐστιν ἴχνος· ἐν δὲ τοῖς ἑσπερίοις
Αἰθίοψι, τοὺς ἀέρας πλατεῖς φήσας,[2] ταῖς τε
ὀρθριναῖς ὥραις καὶ ταῖς δειλιναῖς παχεῖς καὶ
ἀχλυώδεις εἶναι τοὺς ἀέρας· πῶς γὰρ ἐν αὐχμώ-
δεσι καὶ καυματηροῖς τόποις ταῦτ' εἶναι ; αὐτὸς
δὲ τούτων πολὺ χείρω λέγει περὶ τοὺς αὐτοὺς
τόπους· μετανάστας γάρ τινας ἱστορεῖ Λωτο-
φάγους, οἳ τὴν ἄνυδρον νέμοιντο, σιτοῖντο δὲ
λωτόν, πόαν τινὰ καὶ ῥίζαν, ἀφ' ἧς οὐδὲν δέοιντο
ποτοῦ· παρήκειν δ' αὐτοὺς μέχρι τῶν ὑπὲρ
Κυρήνης τόπων· τοὺς δ' ἐκεῖ καὶ γαλακτοποτεῖν
καὶ κρεωφαγεῖν, καίπερ ταὐτοκλινεῖς ὄντας. καὶ
Γαβίνιος [3] δὲ ὁ τῶν Ῥωμαίων συγγραφεὺς [4] οὐκ
ἀπέχεται τῆς τερατολογίας τῆς περὶ τὴν Μαυ-
ρουσίαν· πρὸς γὰρ τῇ Λυγγὶ [5] Ἀνταίου μνῆμα
ἱστορεῖ καὶ σκελετὸν πηχῶν ἑξήκοντα, ὃν Σερ-
τώριον γυμνῶσαι καὶ πάλιν ἐπιβαλεῖν γῆν. καὶ
τὰ περὶ τῶν ἐλεφάντων μυθώδη· φησὶ γὰρ τἆλλα
μὲν θηρία φεύγειν τὸ πῦρ, τοὺς δ' ἐλέφαντας
πολεμεῖν καὶ ἀμύνεσθαι, διότι τὴν ὕλην φθείρει·
πρὸς δὲ τοὺς ἀνθρώπους διαμάχεσθαι, κατα-
σκόπους προπέμποντας, καί, ὅταν ἴδωσιν ἐκείνους
φεύγοντας,[6] φεύγειν καὶ αὐτούς, ἐπειδὰν δὲ [7]

---

[1] κατεσπασμένας F, κατεσκευασμένας mox.
[2] τοὺς ἀέρας πλατεῖς φήσας, Corais and others bracket,
Meineke ejects.
[3] Τανύσιος F, Τανίσιος w.
[4] συγγραφέων MSS.
[5] Λιγγί Dmoxz.
[6] φεύγοντας, Corais inserts.

bourhood of western extremities of Maurusia " Lixus "
instead of Lynx ; and because he calls " Phoenician "
a very great number of rased cities of which no trace
is to be seen ;[1] and because, after calling the air among
the western Aethiopians " salty," [2] he says that the
air is thick and misty in the hours both of early morning
and of evening.   For, argues Artemidorus, how can
these things be in a region that is arid and torrid ?
But he himself gives a much worse account of the
same region, for he tells a story of certain migrants,
Lotophagi,[3] who roam the waterless country and feed
on lotus, a kind of plant and root, from eating which
they have no need of drink ; and that they extend as
far as the region above Cyrenê; but that those in
that region also drink milk and eat meat, although
they are in the same latitude.   And Gabinius also,
the Roman historian, does not abstain from telling
marvellous stories of Maurusia ; for example, he tells
a story of a tomb of Antaeus near Lynx, and a skeleton
sixty feet in length, which, he says, Sertorius exposed
to view, and then covered again with earth.[4]   And he
tells fabulous stories about the elephants ; for example,
he says that whereas the other animals flee from fire,
the elephants carry on war with it and defend themselves against it, because it destroys the timber, and
that they engage in battle with human beings, sending out scouts before them, and that when they
see them fleeing, they flee too, and that when they

[1] See § 3 (above).
[2] The usual meaning of the Greek adjective is "broad"
or "flat"; but Eratosthenes must have used it in the sense of
"salty."
[3] Lotus-eaters.   [4] So Plutarch (*Sertorius* 9).

---

[7] δέ, omitted by MSS. except E*i*.

τραύματα λάβωσιν, ἱκετηρίαν [1] προτείνειν κλάδους
ἢ βοτάνην ἢ κόνιν.

9. Μετὰ δὲ τὴν τῶν Μαυρουσίων γῆν ἡ τῶν
Μασαισυλίων [2] ἐστίν, ἀπὸ τοῦ Μολοχὰθ ποταμοῦ
τὴν ἀρχὴν λαμβάνουσα, τελευτῶσα δὲ ἐπὶ τὴν
ἄκραν, ἣ καλεῖται Τρητόν, [3] ὅριον τῆς τε Μασαισυλίων [4] καὶ τῆς Μασυλιέων [5] γῆς. στάδιοι δ'
εἰσὶν ἀπὸ τοῦ Μεταγωνίου μέχρι τοῦ Τρητοῦ ἑξα-
κισχίλιοι· οἱ δ' ἐλάττους φασίν. ἔχει δ' ἡ παραλία
πόλεις τε πλείους καὶ ποταμοὺς καὶ χώραν εὐφυῆ,
τῶν δ' ἐν ὀνόματι ἀρκεῖ μνησθῆναι. ἔστι δὲ
πόλις Σίγα ἐν χιλίοις σταδίοις ἀπὸ τῶν λεχθέν-
των ὅρων, καὶ βασίλειον Σόφακος· [6] κατέσπασται
δὲ νῦν· τὴν δὲ χώραν μετὰ Σόφακα [7] κατέσχε
Μασανάσσης, [8] εἶτα Μικίψας, εἶτα καὶ οἱ ἐκεῖνον
διαδεξάμενοι, καθ' ἡμᾶς δὲ Ἰούβας ὁ πατὴρ τοῦ
νεωστὶ τελευτήσαντος Ἰούβα· κατέσπασται δὲ
καὶ Ζάμα τὸ τούτου βασίλειον ὑπὸ Ῥωμαίων·
μετὰ δὲ τὴν Σίγαν [9] Θεῶν λιμὴν ἐν ἑξακοσίοις
σταδίοις· εἶτ' ἄλλοι ἄσημοι τόποι. τὰ μὲν οὖν
ἐν βάθει τῆς χώρας ὀρεινὰ καὶ ἔρημα [10] (ἔσθ' ὅτε
παρέσπαρται, ἃ κατέχουσιν οἱ Γαίτουλοι [11]) μέχρι
καὶ Σύρτεων, τὰ δ' ἐκεῖ πρὸς θαλάττῃ καὶ πεδία

[1] ἱκετηρίαν, Corais, for ἱκητήριον.
[2] Μασαισυλίων EF, Μασσαισυλίων other MSS.
[3] Τρητόν, inserted by the later editors from conj. of
Casaubon.
[4] Μασαισυλίων F, Μασσαισυλίων z, Μασσαισύλων other MSS.
[5] Μασυλιέων, Kramer, for Μασυλίβων ; Μασσυλιαίων, Corais.
[6] Συόφακος C, Συοφάκας DF*hrxz*, Σύφακος editors before
Kramer.
[7] Σόφακα (but *o* above ω) C, Σοφάκα D*h*, Συοφάκαν *xz*.
[8] Μασανάσσης C*i*, Μασανίσσης editors before Kramer.
[9] Σίγαν, Corais, for Σίγα.

receive wounds, as suppliants they hold out branches
of a tree or an herb or dust.

9. After the land of the Maurusians, one comes to
that of the Masaesylians, which takes its beginning at
the Molochath River and ends at the promontory
which is called Tretum, the boundary between the
lands of the Masaesylians and the Masylians. The
distance from Metagonium to Tretum is six thousand
stadia, though some say less. The coast has several
cities and rivers and a goodly territory, but it is
sufficient to mention only those of renown. At a
distance of one thousand stadia from the above-
mentioned boundaries is Siga, which was the royal
residence of Sophax, though it is now in ruins. After
Sophax the country was possessed by Masanasses, and
then by Micipsas, and then by his successors, and in
my time by Juba, the father of the Juba who
recently died. Zama, his royal residence, has also
been laid in ruins by the Romans. After Siga, and
at a distance of six hundred stadia, one comes to
Theon Limen ;[1] and then to the other, insignificant,
places. Now the parts deep in the interior[2] are indeed mountainous and desert (sometimes they are
interspersed with habitations and these parts are held
by the Gaetulians[3]), even as far as the Syrtes, but the

---

[1] "Gods' Harbour."

[2] See 17. 3. 2 (end).

[3] The text of the passage in parentheses is doubtful (see
critical note).

---

[10] After ἔρημα Groskurd inserts τινὰ δὲ καὶ οἰκήσιμα ;
Meineke indicates a lacuna there ; Corais conj. ὅπη for
πότε.

[11] Γετοῦλοι E, Γέτουλοι other MSS.

εὐδαίμονά ἐστι καὶ πόλεις πολλαὶ καὶ ποταμοὶ καὶ λίμναι.

C 830   10. Ποσειδώνιος δ᾽ οὐκ οἶδ᾽ εἰ ἀληθεύει,[1] φήσας ὀλίγοις καὶ μικροῖς διαρρεῖσθαι ποταμοῖς τὴν Λιβύην· αὐτοὺς γάρ, οὓς ᾽Αρτεμίδωρος εἴρηκε, τοὺς μεταξὺ τῆς Λυγγὸς καὶ Καρχηδόνος καὶ πολλοὺς εὕρηκε[2] καὶ μεγάλους. ἐν δὲ τῇ μεσογαίᾳ ταῦτ᾽ ἀληθέστερον εἰπεῖν· εὕρηκε δὲ τούτου τὴν αἰτίαν αὐτός, μὴ γὰρ κατομβρεῖσθαι τοῖς ἀρκτικοῖς μέρεσι, καθάπερ οὐδὲ τὴν Αἰθιοπίαν φασί· διὸ πολλάκις λοιμικὰ ἐμπίπτειν ὑπὸ αὐχμῶν καὶ τὰς λίμνας τελμάτων πίμπλασθαι καὶ τὴν ἀκρίδα ἐπιπολάζειν. ἔτι φησὶ τὰ μὲν ἀνατολικὰ ὑγρὰ εἶναι, τὸν γὰρ ἥλιον ἀνίσχοντα ταχὺ παραλλάττειν, τὰ δ᾽ ἑσπέρια ξηρά, ἐκεῖ γὰρ καταστρέφειν. ὑγρὰ γὰρ καὶ ξηρά, τὰ μὲν παρ᾽ ὑδάτων ἀφθονίαν ἢ σπάνιν λέγεται, τὰ δὲ παρὰ τὴν τῶν ἡλίων· βούλεται δὲ λέγειν τὰ παρὰ τοὺς ἡλίους· ταῦτα δὲ πάντες ἀρκτικοῖς καὶ μεσημβρινοῖς κλίμασιν ἀφορίζουσι· καὶ μὴν ἀνατολικά τε καὶ δυσμικά, τὰ μὲν πρὸς τὰς οἰκήσεις λεγόμενα, καθ᾽ ἑκάστην τὴν οἴκησιν καὶ τὴν μετάπτωσιν τῶν ὁριζόντων ἄλλα ἐστίν, ὥστ᾽ οὐδ᾽ ἔνεστι[3] καθολικῶς εἰπεῖν ἐπὶ τῶν ἀπεριλήπτων τὸ πλῆθος, ὅτι τὰ μὲν ἀνατολικὰ ὑγρά, τὰ δὲ δυσμικὰ ξηρά. ὡς δὲ λέγεται πρὸς τὴν οἰκουμένην ὅλην καὶ τὰς

---

[1] ἀληθεύει E, ἀληθής uz, ἀληθῇ other MSS.
[2] τοὺς μεταξὺ . . . εἴρηκε, omitted by MSS. except EF.
[3] οὐδ᾽ ἔνεστι, Corais, for οὐδέν ἐστι.

---

[1] The text is corrupt. Strabo probably wrote merely this: "for Artemidorus calls them many and large" (see critical note).

parts there near the sea consist of fertile plains, many cities, rivers, and lakes.

10. I do not know whether Poseidonius tells the truth when he says that Libya is intersected by rivers "only few and small"; for merely the rivers mentioned by Artemidorus, those between Lynx and Carthage, are by him called "both many and large."[1] This statement can be made more truthfully in regard to the interior of the country; and he himself[2] states the cause of this, saying that "no rain falls in the northern parts," as is also said to be the case in Aethiopia, and therefore pestilences often ensue because of droughts, and the lakes are filled with mud, and the locust is prevalent. And he further says that "the eastern regions are moist, for the sun passes quickly when it is rising, whereas the western regions are arid, for there it turns back."[3] For regions are called moist and arid, partly in proportion to abundance or scarcity of waters, and partly in proportion to that of the sun's rays; but Poseidonius means to speak only of the effects of the sun's rays; and these effects are by all writers defined by latitude, north or south; and indeed both the eastern and western regions, when spoken of with reference to the habitations of man, vary according to each several habitation and the change in their horizons, so that it is also impossible to make a general assertion in regard to places whose number passes all comprehension that the eastern are moist and the western arid; but since such statements are made with reference to the in-

[2] Poseidonius.
[3] Thus slowing down in making the turn back, as Strabo interprets it.

ἐσχατιὰς τὰς τοιαύτας, οἷα καὶ ἡ Ἰνδικὴ καὶ ἡ
Ἰβηρία, λέγοι ἄν, εἰ ἄρα,[1] τὴν τοιαύτην ἀπόφα-
σιν. τίς οὖν ἡ πιθανότης τῆς αἰτιολογίας; ἐν
γὰρ περιφορᾷ συνεχεῖ τε καὶ ἀδιαλείπτῳ τοῦ
ἡλίου τίς ἂν εἴη καταστροφή; τό τε τάχος τῆς
παραλλαγῆς[2] πανταχοῦ ἴσον. ἄλλως τε παρὰ
τὴν ἐνάργειάν[3] ἐστι, τὰ ἔσχατα τῆς Ἰβηρίας ἢ
τῆς Μαυρουσίας τὰ πρὸς δύσιν ξηρὰ λέγειν
ἁπάντων μάλιστα· καὶ γὰρ τὸ περιέχον εὔκρατον
ἔχει[4] καὶ πλείστων ὑδάτων εὐπορεῖ. εἰ δὲ τὸ
καταστρέφειν τοιοῦτον εἴληπται, ὅτι ἐνταῦθα τὰ
ὕστατα τῆς οἰκουμένης ὑπὲρ γῆς γίνεται, τί
τοῦτο συντείνει πρὸς ξηρασίαν; καὶ γὰρ ἐνταῦθα
καὶ ἐν τοῖς ἄλλοις τόποις τῆς οἰκουμένης τοῖς
ταὐτοκλινέσι, τὸν ἴσον διαλιπὼν χρόνον τὸν τῆς
νυκτός, ἐπάνεισι πάλιν καὶ θερμαίνει[5] τὴν
γῆν.

11. Ἔστι δέ που αὐτόθι καὶ ἀσφάλτου πηγὴ
καὶ χαλκωρυχεῖα· καὶ σκορπίων δὲ καὶ πτηνῶν[6]
καὶ ἀπτέρων λέγεται πλῆθος, μεγέθει δὲ[7] ἑπτασ-
πονδύλων, ὁμοίως δὲ καὶ φαλάγγια καὶ μεγέθει
καὶ πλήθει διαφέροντα· σαύρας δὲ διπήχεις
φασίν. ἐν μὲν οὖν τῇ παρορείῳ λίθους εὑρίσκεσ-
θαί φασι τοὺς λυχνίτας καὶ καρχηδονίους λεγο-

---

[1] εἰ, moz omit ; ἄρα, x omits ; the editors before Kramer
read κατά γε instead of εἰ ἄρα.
[2] καταστροφῆς F.   [3] ἐνέργειαν F.
[4] ἔχει, Letronne, for ἔχειν.
[5] διαθερμαίνει E.
[6] E inserts τε after πτηνῶν.
[7] After δέ, Letronne, citing 15. 1. 37 (σκορπίους . . .
ὑπερβάλλοντας μεγέθεσι) and Lucian De Dipsad. 3, inserts
ὑπερβαλλόντων καί.

habited world as a whole and to such extremities of it as India and Iberia, perhaps he could make such a statement. What plausibility, however, can there be in his explanation of the cause? For in the revolution of the sun, which is continuous and unintermitting, what "turning back" could there be? And further, the speed of the sun's transit is everywhere equal. Besides, it is contrary to the evidence [1] to call the extremities of Iberia or Maurusia, I mean the extremities on the west, the most arid places in the world, for they not only have a temperate atmosphere but also are well supplied with numerous waters. But if the "turning back" of the sun is interpreted in this way, that there it is last above the inhabited world, wherein does this contribute to aridity? For there, as well as in the other places of the inhabited world that are in the same latitude, the sun leaves an equal interval of night, and comes back again and warms the earth.

11. Somewhere here [2] there are also copper mines and a spring of asphalt; and writers speak also of a multitude of scorpions, both winged and wingless, which in size are heptaspondylic,[3] and likewise of tarantulas [4] which are exceptional both in size and in number; and lizards which are said to be two cubits long. Now on the mountain-side [5] are said to be found the "Lychnite" [6] and Carthaginian

[1] One MS. reads "actuality" instead of "evidence" (see critical note).
[2] *i.e.* in Masaesylia.
[3] *i.e.* they have "seven vertebrae" (the *Pandinus heros*); see critical note, and cp. 15. 1. 37.
[4] Cp. 16. 4. 12.
[5] Cp. § 19 following.
[6] *i.e.* "Luminous" stones; apparently a tourmaline.

μένους· ἐν δὲ τοῖς πεδίοις ὀστρακίων καὶ χηρα-
μύδων[1] πλῆθος, οἷον ἐν τοῖς περὶ τοῦ Ἄμμωνος
C 831 λόγοις εἰρήκαμεν· καὶ δένδρον δέ ἐστι μελίλωτον
καλούμενον, ἐξ οὗ σκευάζουσιν οἶνον. τινὲς δ'
αὐτῶν καὶ δίκαρπον ἔχουσι τὴν γῆν, καὶ δύο
θεριστικὰ καρποῦνται, τὰ μὲν θερινά, τὰ δ'
ἐαρινά· ἔστι δὲ ἡ καλάμη πεντάπηχυς τὸ ὕψος,
πάχος δὲ τοῦ μικροῦ δακτύλου, τὸν δὲ καρπὸν
διακοσιοκαιτετταρακοντάχουν ἀποδίδωσι. τοῦ δὲ
ἔαρος οὐδὲ σπείρουσιν, ἀλλὰ παλιούροις συνδεδε-
μέναις ἐπικαταψήσαντες τὴν χώραν τῷ ἐκπεσόντι
στάχυϊ κατὰ τὸν θερισμὸν ἀρκοῦνται· τελεσι-
καρπεῖ γὰρ τὸν θερινὸν καρπόν. διὰ δὲ τὸ
πλῆθος τῶν θηρίων κνημῖδας ἔχοντες ἐργάζονται
καὶ τἆλλα δὲ μέρη διφθεροῦνται· καθεύδοντες δὲ
περιχρίουσι τοὺς κλινόποδας σκορόδοις τῶν
σκορπίων χάριν καὶ παλιούροις περιδοῦσιν.

12. Ἦν δ' ἐν[2] τῇ παραλίᾳ ταύτῃ πόλις Ἰὼλ
ὄνομα, ἣν ἐπικτίσας Ἰούβας ὁ τοῦ Πτολεμαίου
πατὴρ μετωνόμασε Καισάρειαν, ἔχουσαν καὶ
λιμένα καὶ πρὸ τοῦ λιμένος νησίον. μεταξὺ δὲ
τῆς Καισαρείας καὶ τοῦ Τρητοῦ μέγας ἐστὶ λιμήν,
ὃν Σάλδαν καλοῦσι· τοῦτο δ' ἐστὶν ὅριον τῆς
ὑπὸ τῷ Ἰούβᾳ[3] καὶ τῆς ὑπὸ τοῖς Ῥωμαίοις·
πολυτρόπως γὰρ οἱ μερισμοὶ γεγένηνται τῆς
χώρας, ἅτε τῶν νεμομένων αὐτὴν πλειόνων

---

[1] χημίδων E, χηραμίδων Dx.
[2] δ' ἐν, Casaubon, for δέ.   [3] Ἰόβα E.

---

[1] A carbunculus (see Pliny, 37. 25 and 30).
[2] 1. 3. 4.
[3] i.e. "honey-lotus." Strabo calls the melilotus a "tree,"

stones,[1] as they are called, and, in the plains, oyster-
shells and mussel-shells in great quantities, like
those mentioned by me in my description of
Ammon.[2]   And there is also a tree called melilotus,[3]
from which they prepare a wine.   And some of the
people have land that produces two crops of grain,
reaping two harvests, one in spring and the other
in summer; and the stalk is five cubits in height,
has the thickness of the little finger, and yields a
crop 240-fold.   In the spring they do not even sow
seed, but harrow the ground lightly with bundles of
paliuri,[4] and are satisfied with the seed-grain that
has fallen out of the ear at the time of the harvest;
for this produces a perfect summer crop.   On
account of the number of wild animals [5] they work
with leggings on and also clothe the rest of their
bodies with skins.   And when they lie down to
sleep, they smear the feet of their beds with garlic
and tie a bunch of paliuri around them, on account
of the scorpions.

12. On this coast was a city named Iol, which
Juba, the father of Ptolemy, rebuilt, changing its
name to Caesareia; it has a harbour, and also, in
front of the harbour, a small island.   Between
Caesareia and Tretum is a large harbour called
Salda, which is now a boundary between the
territories subject to Juba and the Romans; for the
divisions of the country have been made in various
ways, inasmuch as its occupants have been several

both here and in § 17 following, but other writers (e.g.
Theophrastus, 9. 40, 49) apply the name to a kind of
clover.
  [4] A kind of thorny shrub (*Rhamnus paliurus*).
  [5] *i.e.* reptiles in particular, apparently.

γενομένων καὶ τῶν Ῥωμαίων ἄλλοτ' ἄλλως
τούτων τοῖς μὲν φίλοις χρωμένων, τοῖς δὲ καὶ
πολεμίοις· ὥστε καὶ ἀφαιρεῖσθαι καὶ χαρίζεσθαι
συνέβαινεν ἄλλοις ἄλλα καὶ οὐ τὸν αὐτὸν τρόπον.
ἦν δὲ ἡ μὲν πρὸς τῇ Μαυρουσίᾳ προσοδικωτέρα τε
καὶ δυναμικωτέρα, ἡ δὲ πρὸς τῇ Καρχηδονίᾳ καὶ
τῇ Μασυλιέων [1] ἀνθηροτέρα τε καὶ κατεσκευασμένη βέλτιον, καίπερ κεκακωμένη διὰ τὰ Καρχη-
δόνια τὸ πρῶτον, ἔπειτα διὰ τὸν πρὸς Ἰουγούρθαν
πόλεμον· ἐκεῖνος γὰρ Ἀδάρβαλα ἐκπολιορκήσας
ἐν Ἰτύκῃ καὶ ἀνελών, φίλον ὄντα Ῥωμαίων,
ἐνέπλησε τὴν χώραν πολέμου· εἶτ' ἄλλοι ἐπ'
ἄλλοις συνέστησαν πόλεμοι, τελευταῖος δὲ ὁ πρὸς
Σκιπίωνα Καίσαρι τῷ θεῷ συστάς, ἐν ᾧ καὶ
Ἰούβας ἀπέθανε· συνηφανίσθησαν δὲ τοῖς ἡγεμόσι
καὶ αἱ πόλεις, Τισιαοῦς τε καὶ Οὐάγα [2] καὶ Θάλα,
ἔτι δὲ καὶ Κάψα, τὸ γαζοφυλάκιον τοῦ Ἰου-
γούρθα, καὶ Ζάμα καὶ Ζίγχα [3] καὶ πρὸς αἷς
κατεπολέμησε Καῖσαρ Σκιπίωνα ὁ θεός, πρὸς
Ῥουσπίνῳ [4] μὲν πρῶτον νικῶν, εἶτα πρὸς Οὐζίτοις,
εἶτα πρὸς Θάψῳ καὶ τῇ πλησίον λίμνῃ, καὶ ταῖς
ἄλλαις· πλησίον δὲ καὶ Ζέλλα καὶ Ἀχόλλα,
ἐλεύθεραι πόλεις. εἷλε δ' ἐξ ἐφόδου Καῖσαρ τὴν
Κέρκινναν [5] νῆσον καὶ Θέναν, πολίχνην ἐπιθαλατ-
τιδίαν. τούτων πασῶν αἱ μὲν τελέως ἠφανίσ-
θησαν, αἱ δ' ἡμίσπαστοι κατελείφθησαν· Φαρὰν
δ' οἱ Σκιπίωνος ἱππεῖς ἐνέπρησαν.

---

[1] Μασσαιλίων moz, Μασσαισυλίων x, Μασσυλιαίων other MSS.
[2] Οὐάγα, Letronne, Kramer, and Meineke, for Οὔατα; C.
Müller conj. Οὔβατα.
[3] Ζίγχα, Xylander, for Ζάκμα.
[4] Ῥουσπίνῳ, Corais, for Ῥουσπῖνον.

in number and the Romans have dealt with them
in different ways at different times, treating some
as friends and others as enemies, the result being
that different parts were taken away from, or
presented to, different peoples, but not in the same
way. The country towards Maurusia not only produced more revenue but was also more powerful,
whereas that towards Carthage and the Masylians
was both more flourishing and better built up,
although it had been put in a bad plight, first,
on account of the Carthaginian Wars, and then on
account of the war against Jugurtha; for he took
by siege Adarbal, a friend of the Romans, at Itycê [1]
and slew him, and thus filled all Libya with war;
and then wars on wars broke out, and, last of all,
the war that broke out between the deified Caesar
and Scipio, in which even Juba was killed; and
with the leaders the cities were wiped out too, I
mean Tisiäus, Vaga, and Thala, as also Capsa, the
treasure-hold of Jugurtha, and Zama, and Zincha,
and those cities near which the deified Caesar
defeated Scipio, first winning a victory over him
near Ruspinum, and then near Uzita, and then
near Thapsus and the lake near by, and the other
cities. And near by also are Zella and Acholla,
free cities. And Caesar captured at the first onset
the island Cercinna, and Thena, a town on the
coast. Of all these, some were utterly wiped out
and the others left half-destroyed; but Phara was
burned by Scipio's cavalry.

---

[1] *i.e.* "Utica." But Sallust (*Jug.* 25–26) says "Cirta."

[5] Κέρκιυναυ, Casaubon inserts.

C 832 13. Μετὰ δ᾿ οὖν Τρητὸν ἡ Μασυλιέων [1] ἐστὶ καὶ ἡ Καρχηδονίων παραπλησία χώρα. Κίρτα τέ ἐστιν ἐν μεσογαίᾳ, τὸ Μασανάσσου [2] καὶ τῶν ἑξῆς διαδόχων βασίλειοι, πόλις εὐερκεστάτη καὶ κατεσκευασμένη καλῶς τοῖς πᾶσι, καὶ μάλιστα ὑπὸ Μικίψα, ὅστις καὶ Ἕλληνας συνῴκισεν ἐν αὐτῇ καὶ τοσαύτην ἐποίησεν, ὥστ᾿ ἐκπέμπειν μυρίους ἱππέας, διπλασίους δὲ πεζούς. ἥ τε δὴ Κίρτα ἐνταῦθα καὶ οἱ δύο Ἱππῶνες, ὁ μὲν πλησίον Ἰτύκης, ὁ δὲ ἀπωτέρω πρὸς τῷ [3] Τρητῷ μᾶλλον, ἄμφω βασίλεια. ἡ δὲ Ἰτύκη δευτέρα μετὰ Καρχηδόνα τῷ μεγέθει καὶ τῷ ἀξιώματι· καταλυθείσης δὲ Καρχηδόνος, ἐκείνη ἦν ὡς ἂν μητρόπολις τοῖς Ῥωμαίοις καὶ ὁρμητήριον πρὸς τὰς ἐν Λιβύῃ πράξεις. ἵδρυται δ᾿ ἐν τῷ αὐτῷ κόλπῳ τῷ Καρχηδονιακῷ, πρὸς θατέρῳ τῶν ἀκρωτηρίων τῶν ποιούντων τὸν κόλπον, ὧν τὸ μὲν πρὸς τῇ Ἰτύκῃ καλοῦσιν Ἀπολλώνιον, θάτερον δ᾿ Ἑρμαίαν· καί εἰσιν ἐν ἐπόψει [4] ἀλλήλαις αἱ πόλεις. ῥεῖ δὲ τῆς Ἰτύκης πλησίον ὁ Βαγράδας [5] ποταμός. εἰσὶ δ᾿ ἀπὸ Τρητοῦ μέχρι Καρχηδόνος στάδιοι δισχίλιοι πεντακόσιοι. οὔτε [6] τοῦθ᾿ ὁμολογεῖται δὲ τὸ διάστημα οὔτε τὸ μέχρι Σύρτεων.

14. Καὶ Καρχηδὼν δὲ ἐπὶ χερρονήσου τινὸς ἵδρυται, περιγραφούσης κύκλον τριακοσίων ἑξήκοντα σταδίων ἔχοντα τεῖχος, οὗ τὸ ἑξηκοντα-στάδιον μῆκος [7] αὐτὸς ὁ αὐχὴν ἐπέχει, καθῆκον [8]

[1] Μασυλιέων E, Μασσαισυλίων x, Μασυλιαίων z, Μασσυλιαιων other MSS.
[2] Μασανάσσου, Kramer, for Μασσανάσσου iwx, Μασανάσου morz, Σανάσσου O, Μασανίσσου other MSS.

13. Now after Tretum one comes to the land of the Masylians, and to the land of the Carthaginians, which is similar thereto. Cirta, the royal residence of Masanasses and his successors, is in the interior; it is very strongly fortified and has been beautifully built up in every way, particularly by Micipsas, who not only settled a colony of Greeks in it, but also made it so great that it could send forth ten thousand cavalry and twice as many infantry. Cirta, then, is here, and so are the two Hippos, one near Itycê and the other farther away, rather towards Tretum; and both are royal residences. Itycê was second only to Carthage in size and importance, and when Carthage was destroyed, that city served the Romans as a metropolis, and as a base of operations for their activities in Libya. It is situated in the same gulf as Carthage, near one of the two promontories which form the gulf, of which the one near Itycê is called Apollonium and the other Hermaea; and the two cities are in sight of one another. Near Itycê flows the Bagradas River. The distance from Tretum to Carthage is two thousand five hundred stadia. But neither this distance nor that to the Syrtes is generally agreed upon.

14. Carthage, also, is situated on a kind of peninsula, which comprises a circuit of three hundred and sixty stadia; and this circuit has a wall; and sixty stadia of the length of this circuit are occupied by the neck itself, which extend from sea to

---

³ τῷ, Corais, for τῇ.   ⁴ ἐν ὄψει E.
⁵ Βαγράδας E, Μαγάδρας hi, Βαγάδρας other MSS.
⁶ οὔτε, Corais, for οὐδέ.
⁷ τεῖχος Dhi.
⁸ καθῆκον, Groskurd, for καθήκων.

ἀπὸ θαλάττης ἐπὶ θάλατταν, ὅπου τοῖς Καρχηδονίοις ἦσαν αἱ τῶν ἐλεφάντων στάσεις, καὶ τόπος
εὐρυχωρής. κατὰ μέσην δὲ τὴν πόλιν ἡ ἀκρό-
πολις, ἣν ἐκάλουν Βύρσαν, ὀφρὺς ἱκανῶς ὀρθία,
κύκλῳ περιοικουμένη, κατὰ δὲ τὴν κορυφὴν
ἔχουσα Ἀσκληπιεῖον, ὅπερ κατὰ τὴν ἅλωσιν ἡ
γυνὴ τοῦ Ἀσδρούβα συνέπρησεν αὐτῇ.[1] ὑπό-
κεινται δὲ τῇ ἀκροπόλει οἵ τε λιμένες καὶ ὁ Κώθων,
νησίον περιφερὲς εὐρίπῳ περιεχόμενον, ἔχοντι[2]
νεωσοίκους ἑκατέρωθεν κύκλῳ.

15. Κτίσμα δ᾽ ἐστὶ Διδοῦς ἀγαγούσης ἐκ Τύρου
λαόν· οὕτω δ᾽ εὐτυχὴς ἡ ἀποικία τοῖς Φοίνιξιν
ὑπῆρξε καὶ αὕτη καὶ ἡ μέχρι τῆς Ἰβηρίας τῆς
τε ἄλλης καὶ τῆς ἔξω Στηλῶν, ὥστε τῆς Εὐρώπης
ἔτι νῦν τὴν ἀρίστην νέμονται Φοίνικες κατὰ τὴν
ἤπειρον καὶ τὰς προσεχεῖς νήσους, τήν τε Λιβύην
κατεκτήσαντο πᾶσαν, ὅσην[3] μὴ νομαδικῶς οἶόν
τ᾽ ἦν οἰκεῖν. ἀφ᾽ ἧς δυνάμεως πόλιν τε ἀντί-
παλον τῇ Ῥώμῃ κατεσκευάσαντο καὶ τρεῖς ἐπολέ-
μησαν μεγάλους πρὸς αὐτοὺς πολέμους. γένοιτο
δ᾽ ἂν εὔδηλος ἡ δύναμις αὐτῶν ἐκ τοῦ ὑστάτου
πολέμου, ἐν ᾧ κατελύθησαν ὑπὸ Σκιπίωνος τοῦ
Αἰμιλιανοῦ, καὶ ἡ πόλις ἄρδην ἠφανίσθη. ὅτε
C 833 γὰρ ἤρξαντο πολεμεῖν τοῦτον τὸν πόλεμον,[4]
πόλεις μὲν εἶχον τριακοσίας ἐν τῇ Λιβύῃ, ἀνθρώπων δ᾽ ἐν τῇ πόλει μυριάδας ἑβδομήκοντα·
πολιορκούμενοι δὲ καὶ ἀναγκασθέντες τραπέσθαι
πρὸς ἔνδοσιν, πανοπλιῶν μὲν ἔδοσαν μυριάδας

---

[1] αὐτῇ, Corais, for αὐτῆ.
[2] ἔχοντι, Corais, for ἔχον τε.
[3] ὅσην E, ὅσον other MSS.
[4] πόλεμον EF, τρόπον other MSS.

sea; and this, a spacious place, is where the Carthaginians had their elephant-stalls. Near the middle of the city was the acropolis, which they called Byrsa;[1] it was a fairly steep height and inhabited on all sides, and at the top it had a temple ot Asclepius, which, at the time of the capture of the city, the wife of Asdrubal burnt along with herself. Below the acropolis lie the harbours, as also Cothon, a circular isle surrounded by a strait, which latter has ship-houses all round on either side.[2]

15. Carthage was founded by Dido, who brought a host of people from Tyre. The colonisation proved to be so fortunate an enterprise for the Phoenicians, both this at Carthage and that which extended as far as Iberia—I mean the part of Iberia outside the Pillars as well as the rest of it —that even to this day the best part of continental Europe and also the adjacent islands are occupied by Phoenicians; and they also gained possession of all that part of Libya which men can live in without living a nomadic life. From this dominion they not only raised their city to be a rival of Rome, but also waged three great wars against the Romans. Their power might become clearly evident from the last war, in which they were defeated by Scipio Aemilianus and their city was utterly wiped out. For when they began to wage this war they had three hundred cities in Libya and seven hundred thousand people in their city; and when they were being besieged and were forced to resort to surrender, they gave up two hundred thousand full

[1] "Hide."
[2] *i.e.* both on the island and on the mainland.

εἴκοσι, καταπελτικὰ δὲ ὄργανα τρισχίλια,[1] ὡς
οὐ πολεμηθησόμενοι· κριθέντος δὲ πάλιν τοῦ
ἀναπολεμεῖν, ἐξαίφνης ὁπλοποιίαν συνεστήσαντο,
καὶ ἑκάστης ἡμέρας ἀνεφέροντο θυρεοὶ μὲν ἑκατὸν
καὶ τετταράκοντα πεπηγότες, μάχαιραι δὲ τρια-
κόσιαι καὶ λόγχαι πεντακόσιαι, χίλια δὲ βέλη
καταπελτικά, τρίχα δὲ τοῖς καταπέλταις αἱ θερά-
παιναι παρεῖχον. ἔτι τοίνυν ναῦς ἔχοντες δώδεκα
ἐξ ἐτῶν πεντήκοντα κατὰ τὰς ἐν τῷ δευτέρῳ
πολέμῳ συνθήκας, τότε, καίπερ ἤδη συμπεφευ-
γότες εἰς τὴν Βύρσαν, ἐν διμήνῳ κατεσκευάσαντο
ναῦς ἑκατὸν εἴκοσι καταφράκτους, καὶ τοῦ στόματος τοῦ Κώθωνος φρουρουμένου, διώρυξαν ἄλλο
στόμα, καὶ προῆλθεν αἰφνιδίως ὁ στόλος· ὕλη
γὰρ ἦν ἀποκειμένη παλαιὰ καὶ τεχνιτῶν πλῆθος
προσεδρεῦον καὶ σιταρχούμενον[2] δημοσίᾳ. τοιαύτη
δ' οὖσα Καρχηδὼν ὅμως ἑάλω καὶ κατεσκάφη.
τὴν δὲ χώραν, τὴν μὲν ἐπαρχίαν ἀπέδειξαν
Ῥωμαῖοι, τὴν ὑπὸ τοῖς Καρχηδονίοις, τῆς δὲ
Μασανάσσην ἀπέδειξαν κύριον καὶ τοὺς ἀπογό-
νους τοὺς περὶ Μικίψαν. μάλιστα γὰρ ἐσπου-
δάσθη παρὰ τοῖς Ῥωμαίοις ὁ Μασανάσσης δι'
ἀρετὴν καὶ φιλίαν· καὶ γὰρ δὴ καὶ οὗτός ἐστιν ὁ
τοὺς Νομάδας πολιτικοὺς κατασκευάσας καὶ
γεωργούς, ἔτι δ' ἀντὶ τοῦ λῃστεύειν διδάξας
στρατεύειν. ἴδιον γάρ τι τοῖς ἀνθρώποις συνέβη

---

[1] For τρισχίλια Letronne (citing Polybius 36. 4 and Appian
80) conj. δισχίλια.
[2] σιταρκούμενον xz.

---

suits of armour and three thousand [1] catapults, on
the assumption that they would not be engaged in
war again; but when they resolved to renew the war,
they suddenly organised the manufacture of arms,
and each day produced one hundred and forty
finished shields, three hundred swords, five hundred
spears, and one thousand missiles for the catapults;
and the women-servants furnished hair for the
catapults. Furthermore, although from fifty years
back they had possessed only twelve ships, in
accordance with the treaty made at the second war,
they then, although they had already fled together
for refuge into the Byrsa, built one hundred and
twenty decked ships in two months; and since the
mouth of Cothon was being guarded, they dug
another mouth through and their fleet sallied forth
unexpectedly; for old timber had been stored away
in readiness, and a large number of skilled workmen,
maintained at public expense, had been lying in
wait for this occasion. But though Carthage was so
resourceful, still it was captured and rased to the
ground. As for the country, the Romans proclaimed
one part of it a Province, I mean the part which
had been subject to the Carthaginians, and appointed as sovereign of the other part Masanasses, as
also his descendants, the house of Micipsas; [2] for
Masanasses was held in very high respect among the
Romans because of his valour and friendship; and
indeed it was he who transformed the Nomads into
citizens and farmers, and taught them to be soldiers
instead of brigands. For a peculiar thing had hap-

---

[2] *i.e.* the three sons: Micipsas king, Golossa head of the
department of war, and Mastanaba head of the department of
justice (Appian, § 106).

τούτοις· χώραν γὰρ οἰκοῦντες εὐδαίμονα, πλὴν
τοῦ θηρίοις πλεονάζειν, ἐάσαντες ἐκφθείρειν[1]
ταῦτα καὶ τὴν γῆν ἐργάζεσθαι μετὰ ἀδείας ἐπ'
ἀλλήλοις ἐτρέποντο, τὴν δὲ γῆν τοῖς θηρίοις
ἀφεῖσαν. οὕτω δ' αὐτοῖς συνέβαινε πλάνητα καὶ
μετανάστην βίον ζῆν, μηδὲν ἧττον τῶν ὑπὸ
ἀπορίας καὶ λυπρότητος τόπων ἢ ἀέρων εἰς
τοῦτο περισταμένων τῶν βίων, ὥστε καὶ ἴδιον
τοῦθ' εὑρίσκεσθαι τοὔνομα τοὺς Μασαισυλίους,
καλοῦνται γὰρ Νομάδες, ἀνάγκη δὲ τοὺς τοιούτους
εὐτελεῖς εἶναι τοῖς βίοις καὶ τὸ πλέον ῥιζοφάγους
ἢ κρεωφάγους, γάλακτι δὲ καὶ τυρῷ τρεφομένους.
ἠρημωμένης δ' οὖν ἐπὶ πολὺν χρόνον τῆς Καρχηδόνος, καὶ σχεδόν τι τὸν αὐτὸν χρόνον, ὅνπερ καὶ
Κόρινθος, ἀνελήφθη πάλιν περὶ τοὺς αὐτούς πως
χρόνους ὑπὸ Καίσαρος τοῦ θεοῦ, πέμψαντος
ἐποίκους Ῥωμαίων τοὺς προαιρουμένους καὶ τῶν
στρατιωτῶν τινας· καὶ νῦν εἴ τις ἄλλη καλῶς
οἰκεῖται τῶν ἐν Λιβύῃ πόλεων.

C 834   16. [2] Κατὰ μέσον δὲ τὸ στόμα τοῦ Καρχηδονίου
κόλπου νῆσός ἐστι Κόρσουρα. ἀντίπορθμος δ'
ἐστὶν ἡ Σικελία τοῖς τόποις τούτοις ἡ κατὰ
Λιλύβαιον, ὅσον ἐν διαστήματι χιλίων καὶ
πεντακοσίων σταδίων· τοσοῦτον γάρ φασι[3]
τὸ ἐκ Λιλυβαίου μέχρι Καρχηδόνος. οὐ πολὺ
δὲ τῆς Κορσούρας διέχουσιν οὐδὲ τῆς Σικελίας

---

[1] ἐκφθείρειν (as in 17. 1. 44), Jones, for ἐκφέρειν.
[2] Meineke ejects Κατὰ μέσον . . . Αἰγίμουρος from the text,
following conj. of Kramer.   [3] φασι F, φησι other MSS.

---

[1] "Nomades" ("Nomads") is the Greek name corres-
ponding to the Latin "Numidae" ("Numidians").

pened in the case of these people, that is, although they lived in a country blest by nature, except for the fact that it abounded in wild animals, they would forbear to destroy these and thus work the land in security, and would turn against one another, abandoning the land to the wild animals. In this way it came to pass that they kept leading a wandering and migratory life, no less so than peoples who are driven by poverty and by wretched soil or climate to resort to this kind of life ; so that the Masaesylians have obtained this as their special designation, for they are called Nomades.[1] Such people of necessity must lead a frugal life, being more often root-eaters than meat-eaters, and using milk and cheese for food. Be that as it may, Carthage for a long time remained desolate, about the same length of time as Corinth,[2] but it was restored again at about the same time as Corinth by the deified Caesar, who sent thither as colonists such Romans as preferred to go there and some soldiers ; and now it is as prosperous a city as any other in Libya.

16. Opposite[3] the middle of the mouth of the Carthaginian Gulf is Corsura,[4] an island. Across the arm of the sea, opposite this region, is that part of Sicily wherein lies Lilybaeum, at a distance of about one thousand five hundred stadia ; for the distance from Lilybaeum to Carthage is said to be as great as this. Not far distant from Corsura,

[2] Corinth was destroyed by L. Mummius in 146 B.C., but was restored by Julius Caesar and Augustus.

[3] This passage, "Opposite . . . other islands," is ejected from the text by Meineke (see critical note).

[4] "Corsura," unless it is here confused in some way with Cossura (Pantellaria), is otherwise unknown.

ἄλλαι τε νῆσοι καὶ Αἰγίμουρος.[1] διάπλους
δ' ἐστὶν ἐκ Καρχηδόνος ἑξήκοντα σταδίων
εἰς τὴν προσεχῆ περαίαν, ὅθεν εἰς Νέφεριν ἀνάβασις σταδίων ἑκατὸν εἴκοσι, πόλιν[2] ἐρυμνὴν
ἐπὶ πέτρας ᾠκισμένην. ἐν αὐτῷ δὲ τῷ κόλπῳ,
ἐν ᾧπερ καὶ ἡ Καρχηδών, Τύνις ἐστὶ πόλις καὶ
θερμὰ καὶ λατομίαι τινές· εἶθ' ἡ Ἑρμαία ἄκρα
τραχεῖα, καὶ ἐπ' αὐτῇ[3] πόλις ὁμώνυμος· εἶτα
Νεάπολις· εἶτ' ἄκρα Ταφῖτις, καὶ ἐπ' αὐτῇ λόφος
Ἀσπὶς καλούμενος ἀπὸ τῆς ὁμοιότητος, ὅνπερ
συνῴκισεν ὁ τῆς Σικελίας τύραννος Ἀγαθοκλῆς,
καθ' ὃν καιρὸν ἐπέπλευσε τοῖς Καρχηδονίοις.
συγκατεσπάσθησαν δὲ τῇ Καρχηδονίᾳ ὑπὸ
Ῥωμαίων αἱ πόλεις αὗται. ἀπὸ δὲ τῆς Ταφί-
τιδος ἐν τετρακοσίοις σταδίοις νῆσός ἐστι Κόσ-
σουρος[4] κατὰ Σελινοῦντα τῆς Σικελίας ποταμόν,
καὶ πόλιν ἔχουσα ὁμώνυμον, ἑκατὸν καὶ πεντήκοντα σταδίων οὖσα[5] τὴν περίμετρον, διέχουσα
τῆς Σικελίας περὶ ἑξακοσίους σταδίους· ἔστι δὲ
καὶ Μελίτη νῆσος ἐν πεντακοσίοις σταδίοις ἀπὸ
τῆς Κοσσούρου.[6] εἶτα Ἀδρύμης[7] πόλις, ἐν ᾗ καὶ
νεώρια ἦν· εἶθ' αἱ Ταριχεῖαι λεγόμεναι, νησία
πολλὰ καὶ πυκνά· εἶτα Θάψος πόλις, καὶ μετὰ
ταύτην νῆσος πελαγία Λοπαδοῦσσα· εἶτα ἄκρα

---

[1] Αἰγίμορος F.   [2] δ', after πόλιν, Corais omits.
[3] αὐτῆς E, αὐτήν other MSS.   [4] Κόρσουρα moz.
[5] οὖσαν MSS.   [6] Κοσσούρας moz.
[7] Ἀδρυμής F, Ἀδρύμις hix, Ἄδρυμις E, Ἀδρύμη moz.

---

[1] Al Djamur.
[2] i.e. apparently the eastern side of the Carthaginian
Gulf.
[3] Tunis, or Tunes, was situated to the south of Carthage
and at the head of a vast marshy lagoon.

nor yet from Sicily, are Aegimuros[1] and other
islands. The voyage from Carthage across to the
nearest point of the opposite mainland[2] is sixty
stadia, from which the journey inland to Nepheris is
one hundred and twenty stadia—a city fortified by
nature and built upon a rock. But on the same
gulf as that on which Carthage is situated lies a city
Tynis,[3] as also hot springs and stone-quarries; and
then one comes to the rugged promontory Hermaea,
and to a city on it bearing the same name; and
then to Neapolis; and then to a promontory Taphitis,
and to a hill on it, which, from the resemblance, is
called Aspis;[4] this is the hill that Agathocles, the
tyrant of Sicily, colonised at the time when he
sailed against the Carthaginians. But these cities
were demolished by the Romans at the same time
as Carthage. At a distance of four hundred stadia
from Taphitis lies an island Cossurus,[5] opposite the
Selinus River in Sicily, and a city bearing the same
name, which is one hundred and fifty stadia in
circuit and is about six hundred stadia distant from
Sicily; and there is also an island Melitê[6] at a
distance of five hundred stadia from the island
Cossurus.[7] Then one comes to a city Adrymes,[8] at
which there was also a naval arsenal; and then to
the Taricheiae, as they are called, which are
numerous small islands lying close together; and
then to a city Thapsus; and after this to Lopadussa,
an island in the open sea; and then to a promontory

---

[4] *i.e.* "Shield."
[5] The same, apparently, as Cossura (cp. 2. 5. 19 and
6. 2. 11).
[6] Malta.   [7] See preceding footnote.
[8] Also called Adrumetum.

Ἄμμωνος Βαλίθωνος, πρὸς ἧ θυννοσκοπεῖον· [1]
εἶτα Θένα[2] πόλις παρὰ τὴν ἀρχὴν κειμένη τῆς
μικρᾶς Σύρτεως. πολλαὶ δ' εἰσὶ καὶ ἄλλαι
μεταξὺ πολίχναι οὐκ ἄξιαι μνήμης. παράκειται
δὲ τῇ ἀρχῇ τῆς Σύρτεως νῆσος παραμήκης, ἡ
Κέρκιννα,[3] εὐμεγέθης, ἔχουσα ὁμώνυμον πόλιν,
καὶ ἄλλη ἐλάττων Κερκιννῖτις.[4]

17. Συνεχὴς δ' ἐστὶν ἡ μικρὰ Σύρτις, ἣν καὶ
Λωτοφαγῖτιν Σύρτιν λέγουσιν. ἔστι δ' ὁ μὲν
κύκλος τοῦ κόλπου τούτου σταδίων χιλίων
ἑξακοσίων, τὸ δὲ πλάτος τοῦ στόματος ἑξακοσίων·
καθ' ἑκατέραν δὲ[5] τὴν ἄκραν τὴν ποιοῦσαν τὸ
στόμα προσεχεῖς εἰσι τῇ ἠπείρῳ νῆσοι, ἥ τε
λεχθεῖσα Κέρκιννα καὶ ἡ Μῆνιγξ, πάρισοι τοῖς
μεγέθεσι. τὴν δὲ Μήνιγγα νομίζουσιν εἶναι τὴν
τῶν Λωτοφάγων γῆν τὴν ὑφ' Ὁμήρου λεγομένην,
καὶ δείκνυταί τινα σύμβολα, καὶ βωμὸς Ὀδυσ-
σέως καὶ αὐτὸς ὁ καρπός· πολὺ γάρ ἐστι τὸ
δένδρον ἐν αὐτῇ τὸ καλούμενον λωτόν, ἔχον
ἥδιστον καρπόν. πλείους δ' εἰσὶν ἐν αὐτῇ πολίχναι,
C 835 μία δ' ὁμώνυμος τῇ νήσῳ. καὶ ἐν αὐτῇ δὲ τῇ Σύρτει
πολίχναι τινές εἰσι. κατὰ δὲ τὸν μυχόν ἐστι
παμμέγεθες ἐμπόριον, ποταμὸν ἔχον ἐμβάλλοντα
εἰς τὸν κόλπον· διατείνει δὲ μέχρι δεῦρο τὰ τῶν
ἀμπώτεων πάθη καὶ τῶν πλημμυρίδων, καθ' ὃν
καιρὸν ἐπὶ τὴν θήραν τῶν ἰχθύων ἐπιπηδῶσιν οἱ
πρόσχωροι κατὰ σπουδὴν θέοντες.

18. Μετὰ δὲ τὴν Σύρτιν Ζουχίς ἐστι λίμνη

---

[1] ᾗ θυννοσκοπεῖον, conj. Kramer, for θυννοσκοπίαν ; E reads
ἐν ᾗ θυννοσκοπίᾳ.
[2] Θένα, Corais, for Θαίνα.   [3] Κέρκινα F.
[4] Κερκινῖτις F, Κερκινῆτις i.

of Ammon Balithon, near which is a place for watching for the tunny-fish;[1] and then to a city Thena, which lies near the beginning of the Little Syrtis. In the interval lie numerous small towns not worth mentioning. Near the beginning of the Syrtis lies a long island, Cercinna, which is rather large and contains a city of the same name; and there is another smaller island, Cercinnitis.

17. Continuous with these is the Little Syrtis, which is also called the Syrtis of the Lotus-eaters. The circuit of this gulf is one thousand six hundred stadia, and the breadth of the mouth six hundred; and at each of the two promontories which form its mouth are islands close to the mainland—the Cercinna above-mentioned and Meninx, which are about equal in size. Meninx is regarded as the land of the Lotus-eaters mentioned by Homer; and certain tokens of this are pointed out—both an altar of Odysseus and the fruit itself; for the tree which is called the lotus abounds in the island, and its fruit is delightful. There are several towns on Meninx, and one of them bears the same name as the island. On the coast of the Syrtis itself are several small towns. In the recess of the gulf is a very large emporium, which has a river that empties into the gulf; and the effects of the flow and ebb of the tides extend thus far, at which times the neighbouring inhabitants rush forth on the run to catch the fish.

18. After the Syrtis, one comes to Zuchis, a lake

----

[1] Cp. 5. 2. 6, 8.

[6] δέ, omitted by MSS. except *i*.

σταδίων τετρακοσίων στενὸν ἔχουσα εἴσπλουν
καὶ παρ' αὐτὴν πόλις ὁμώνυμος πορφυροβαφεῖα
ἔχουσα καὶ ταριχείας παντοδαπάς· εἶτ' ἄλλη
λίμνη πολὺ ἐλάττων· καὶ μετὰ ταύτην Ἀβρό-
τονον πόλις καὶ ἄλλαι τινές, συνεχῶς δὲ Νεάπολις,
ἣν καὶ Λέπτιν καλοῦσιν· ἐντεῦθεν δ' ἐστὶ δίαρμα
τὸ ἐπὶ Λοκρῶν τῶν Ἐπιζεφυρίων τρισχίλιοι
ἑξακόσιοι στάδιοι. ἑξῆς δ' ἐστὶ ποταμός· καὶ
μετὰ ταῦτα διατείχισμά τι, ὃ ἐποίησαν Καρχηδόνιοι, γεφυροῦντες βάραθρά[1] τινα εἰς τὴν χώραν
ἀνέχοντα· εἰσὶ δὲ καὶ ἀλίμενοί τινες ἐνταῦθα
τόποι, τῆς ἄλλης παραλίας ἐχούσης λιμένας.
εἶτ' ἄκρα ὑψηλὴ καὶ ὑλώδης, ἀρχὴ τῆς μεγάλης
Σύρτεως, καλοῦσι δὲ Κεφαλάς· εἰς ταύτην δὲ τὴν
ἄκραν ἐκ Καρχηδόνος στάδιοί εἰσι μικρῷ πλείους
τῶν πεντακισχιλίων.

19. Ὑπέρκειται δὲ τῆς ἀπὸ Καρχηδόνος παραλίας μέχρι Κεφαλῶν καὶ μέχρι τῆς Μασαισυλίων[2]
ἡ τῶν Λιβοφοινίκων γῆ μέχρι τῆς τῶν Γαιτούλων[3]
ὀρεινῆς, ἤδη Λιβυκῆς οὔσης. ἡ δ' ὑπὲρ τῶν
Γαιτούλων ἐστὶν ἡ τῶν Γαραμάντων γῆ παράλληλος ἐκείνῃ, ὅθεν οἱ Καρχηδόνιοι κομίζονται
λίθοι. τοὺς δὲ Γαράμαντας ἀπὸ τῶν Αἰθιόπων
τῶν[4] παρωκεανιτῶν ἀφεστάναι φασὶν ἡμερῶν
ἐννέα ἢ καὶ δέκα ὁδόν, τοῦ δὲ Ἄμμωνος καὶ
πεντεκαίδεκα. μεταξὺ δὲ τῆς Γαιτούλων καὶ

---

[1] βάθρα Dhi.

[2] Μασαισυλίων, Kramer, for Μασσαισυλείων F, Μασσαισυλίων
other MSS.

[3] Γαιτούλων, Xylander, for Γετούλων.

[4] καί, before τῶν, Meineke omits.

---

[1] The Cinifo.

with a circuit of four hundred stadia; it has a narrow entrance, and near it is a city bearing the same name which contains dye-factories and all kinds of fish-salting establishments; and then to another lake, which is much smaller; and after this to a city Abrotonum and to several others; and contiguous to these is Neapolis, which is also called Leptis; and from here the passage across to the Epizephyrian Locrians is three thousand six hundred stadia. Next in order one comes to a river;[1] and afterwards to a kind of cross-wall which the Carthaginians built, wishing to bridge over some gorges which extend up into the interior. There are also some harbourless regions here, although the rest of the coast has harbours. Then one comes to a lofty, wooded promontory, which forms the beginning of the Great Syrtis and is called Cephalae;[2] and the distance to this promontory from Carthage is a little more than five thousand stadia.

19. Above the coast-line which extends from Carthage to Cephalae and to the land of Masaesylians lies the land of the Libo-Phoenicians, which extends to the mountainous country of the Gaetulians, where Libya[3] begins. The land above the Gaetulians is that of the Garamantes, which lies parallel to the former and is the land whence the Carthaginian stones are brought.[4] The Garamantes are said to be distant from the Aethiopians who live on the ocean a nine or ten days' journey, and from Ammon fifteen. Between the Gaetulians and our seaboard[5] there

---

[2] "Heads."
[3] *i.e.* the true Libya, as distinguished from Libo-Phoenicia.
[4] See 17. 3. 11.
[5] *i.e.* the Mediterranean seaboard.

τῆς ἡμετέρας παραλίας πολλὰ μὲν πεδία, πολλὰ δὲ ὄρη καὶ λίμναι μεγάλαι καὶ ποταμοί, ὧν τινες καὶ καταδύντες ὑπὸ γῆς ἀφανεῖς γίνονται. λιτοὶ δὲ σφόδρα τοῖς βίοις εἰσὶ καὶ τῷ κόσμῳ, πολυγύναικες δὲ καὶ πολύπαιδες, τἆλλα δὲ ἐμφερεῖς τοῖς νομάσι τῶν Ἀράβων· καὶ ἵπποι δὲ καὶ βόες μακροτραχηλότεροι[1] τῶν παρ' ἄλλοις. ἱπποφόρβια δ' ἐστὶν ἐσπουδασμένα διαφερόντως τοῖς βασιλεῦσιν, ὥστε καὶ ἀριθμὸν ἐξετάζεσθαι πώλων κατ' ἔτος εἰς μυριάδας δέκα. τὰ δὲ πρόβατα γάλακτι καὶ κρέασιν ἐκτρέφεται, καὶ μάλιστα πρὸς τοῖς Αἰθίοψι. τοιαῦτα μὲν τὰ ἐν τῇ μεσογαίᾳ.

20. Ἡ δὲ μεγάλη Σύρτις τὸν μὲν κύκλον ἔχει σταδίων τρισχιλίων[2] ἐννακοσίων τριάκοντά που, τὴν δ' ἐπὶ τὸν μυχὸν διάμετρον χιλίων πεντακοσίων, τοσοῦτον δέ που καὶ τὸ τοῦ στόματος πλάτος. ἡ χαλεπότης δὲ καὶ ταύτης τῆς Σύρτεως καὶ τῆς
C 836 μικρᾶς, ὅτι πολλαχοῦ τεναγώδης ἐστὶν ὁ βυθὸς καὶ κατὰ τὰς ἀμπώτεις καὶ τὰς πλημμυρίδας συμβαίνει τισὶν ἐμπίπτειν εἰς τὰ βράχη καὶ καθίζειν, σπάνιον δ' εἶναι τὸ σωζόμενον σκάφος. διόπερ πόρρωθεν τὸν παράπλουν ποιοῦνται, φυλαττόμενοι, μὴ ἐμπέσοιεν εἰς τοὺς κόλπους ὑπ' ἀνέμων ἀφύλακτοι ληφθέντες· τὸ μέντοι παρακίνδυνον τῶν ἀνθρώπων ἁπάντων διαπειρᾶσθαι ποιεῖ, καὶ μάλιστα τῶν παρὰ γῆν περίπλων· εἰσπλέοντι δὴ τὴν μεγάλην Σύρτιν ἐν δεξιᾷ μετὰ τὰς Κεφαλάς ἐστι λίμνη τριακοσίων που σταδίων τὸ μῆκος, ἑβδομήκοντα δὲ τὸ πλάτος, ἐκδιδοῦσα εἰς τὸν κόλπον,

---

[1] μακροτράχηλοι E, μακροτραχηλότεροι CDhz.
[2] τρισχιλίων (͵γ), Kramer inserts.

are not only many plains, but also many mountains, large lakes, and rivers, some of which sink beneath the earth and become invisible. The inhabitants are very simple in their modes of life and in their dress; but the men have many wives and many children, and in other respects are like the nomadic Arabians; and both horses and cattle have longer necks than those of other countries. Horse-breeding is followed with such exceptional interest by the kings that the number of colts every year amounts to one hundred thousand. The sheep are brought up on milk and meats, particularly in the regions near Aethiopia. Such is my account of the interior.

20. The Great Syrtis has a circuit of about three thousand and nine hundred and thirty stadia, and a diameter, to the inmost recess, of one thousand five hundred stadia, and also a breadth at the mouth of about one thousand five hundred. The difficulty with both this Syrtis and the Little Syrtis is that in many places their deep waters contain shallows, and the result is, at the ebb and the flow of the tides, that sailors sometimes fall into the shallows and stick there, and that the safe escape of a boat is rare. On this account sailors keep at a distance when voyaging along the coast, taking precautions not to be caught off their guard and driven by winds into these gulfs. However, the disposition of man to take risks causes him to try anything in the world, and particularly voyages along coasts. Now as one sails into the Great Syrtis, on the right, after Cephalae is passed, one comes to a lake about three hundred stadia in length and seventy in breadth, which empties into the gulf and contains both small islands

ἔχουσα καὶ νησία καὶ ὕφορμον πρὸ τοῦ στόματος.
μετὰ δὲ τὴν λίμνην τόπος ἐστὶν Ἀσπὶς καὶ λιμὴν
κάλλιστος τῶν ἐν τῇ Σύρτει. συνεχὴς δὲ ὁ
Εὐφράντας πύργος ἐστίν, ὅριον τῆς πρότερον
Καρχηδονίας γῆς καὶ τῆς Κυρηναίας τῆς ὑπὸ
Πτολεμαίῳ· εἶτ᾽ ἄλλος τόπος, Χάραξ καλούμενος, ᾧ ἐμπορίῳ ἐχρῶντο Καρχηδόνιοι κομίζοντες
οἶνον, ἀντιφορτιζόμενοι δὲ ὀπὸν καὶ σίλφιον παρὰ
τῶν ἐκ Κυρήνης λάθρα παρακομιζόντων· εἶθ᾽ οἱ
Φιλαίνων βωμοί· καὶ μετὰ τούτους Αὐτόμαλα,
φρούριον φυλακὴν ἔχον, ἱδρυμένον κατὰ τὸν
μυχὸν τοῦ κόλπου παντός. ἔστι δ᾽ ὁ διὰ τοῦ
μυχοῦ τούτου παράλληλος, τοῦ μὲν δι᾽ Ἀλεξανδρείας μικρῷ νοτιώτερος, χιλίοις σταδίοις, τοῦ δὲ
διὰ Καρχηδόνος ἐλάττοσιν ἢ δισχιλίοις· συμπίπτοι[1] δ᾽ ἂν τῇ μὲν καθ᾽ Ἡρώων πόλιν τὴν ἐν τῷ
μυχῷ τοῦ Ἀραβίου κόλπου, τῇ δὲ κατὰ τὴν
μεσόγαιαν τῶν Μασαισυλίων[2] καὶ τῶν Μαυρουσίων.[3] τὸ λειπόμενον ἤδη τῆς παραλίας ἐστὶν
εἰς πόλιν Βερενίκην στάδιοι χίλιοι[4] πεντακόσιοι.
ὑπέρκεινται δὲ τοῦ μήκους τοῦδε[5] παρήκοντες καὶ
μέχρι τῶν Φιλαίνων βωμῶν οἱ προσαγορευόμενοι
Νασαμῶνες, Λιβυκὸν ἔθνος· ἔχει δὲ τὸ μεταξὺ
διάστημα καὶ λιμένας οὐ πολλοὺς ὑδρεῖά τε
σπάνια. ἔστι δὲ ἄκρα λεγομένη Ψευδοπενιάς,[6]
ἐφ᾽ ἧς ἡ Βερενίκη τὴν θέσιν ἔχει παρὰ λίμνην
τινὰ Τριτωνιάδα, ἐν ᾗ μάλιστα νησίον ἐστὶ καὶ

[1] συμπίπτοι, Jones, for πίπτοι.   [2] Μασαισύλων MSS.
[3] ὅπου, before τὸ λειπόμενον, Kramer ejects.
[4] χίλιοι, Letronne, for ἐννακισχίλιοι.
[5] πλάτους, after τοῦδε, the editors omit.
[6] Ψευδοπελίας E.

and a mooring place in front of its mouth. After
the harbour one comes to a place called Aspis,[1] and
to the finest harbour in the Syrtis. Continuous with
this is the Euphrantas Tower, the boundary between
the former country of the Carthaginians and the
Cyrenaean country as it was under Ptolemy;[2]
and then one comes to another place, called Charax,
which the Carthaginians used as an emporium, taking
wine thither and in exchange receiving loads of
silphium-juice and silphium from merchants who
brought them clandestinely from Cyrenê; and then
to the Altars of the Philaeni; and after these to
Automala, a stronghold which has a garrison and is
situated at the inmost recess of the whole gulf.
The parallel of latitude through this gulf is a little
more to the south than that through Alexandria,
one thousand stadia, and than that through Carthage,
less than two thousand stadia; but it would coincide
with the parallel which passes through the Heroönpolis situated on the recess of the Arabian Gulf
and through the interior of the countries of the
Masaesylians and the Maurusians. The remainder
of the coast from here on to the city Berenicê is one
thousand five hundred stadia in length. Lying
inland above this stretch of coast, and extending
even as far as the Altars of the Philaeni, is the
country of the Nasamones, as they are called, a
Libyan tribe. In the intervening distance there
are only a few harbours; and the watering-places
are scarce. There is, however, a promontory called
Pseudo-penias, on which Berenicê is situated, near a
certain lake, Tritonias, in which the principal things

---

[1] *i.e.* "Shield."   [2] See 17. 1. 5.

STRABO

ἱερὸν τῆς Ἀφροδίτης ἐν αὐτῷ. ἔστι δὲ καὶ λιμὴν [1] Ἑσπερίδων, καὶ ποταμὸς ἐμβάλλει Λάθων. ἐνδοτέρω δὲ τῆς Βερενίκης ἐστὶ τὸ μικρὸν ἀκρωτήριον λεγόμενον Βόρειον, ὃ ποιεῖ τὸ στόμα τῆς Σύρτεως πρὸς τὰς Κεφαλάς. κεῖται δὲ ἡ Βερενίκη κατὰ τὰ ἄκρα τῆς Πελοποννήσου, κατὰ τὸν καλούμενον Ἰχθύν· καὶ ἔτι κατὰ τὴν Ζάκυνθον, ἐν διάρματι σταδίων τρισχιλίων ἑξακοσίων. ἐκ ταύτης τῆς πόλεως τριακοσταῖος πεζῇ περιώδευσε τὴν Σύρτιν Μάρκος Κάτων, κατάγων στρατιὰν πλειόνων ἢ μυρίων ἀνδρῶν, εἰς μέρη διελὼν τῶν ὑδρείων χάριν· ὥδευσε δὲ πεζὸς ἐν ἄμμῳ βαθείᾳ καὶ καύμασι. μετὰ δὲ Βερενίκην πόλις ἐστὶ Ταύχειρα,[2] ἣν καὶ Ἀρσινόην καλοῦσιν·

C 837 εἶθ' ἡ Βάρκη πρότερον, νῦν δὲ Πτολεμαΐς· εἶτα Φυκοῦς ἄκρα, ταπεινὴ μέν, πλεῖστον δ' ἐκκειμένη [3] πρὸς ἄρκτον παρὰ τὴν ἄλλην Λιβυκὴν παραλίαν· κεῖται δὲ κατὰ Ταίναρον τῆς Λακωνικῆς ἐν διάρματι δισχιλίων ὀκτακοσίων σταδίων· ἔστι δὲ καὶ πολίχνιον ὁμώνυμον τῇ ἄκρᾳ. οὐ πολὺ δὲ τοῦ Φυκοῦντος ἀπέχει τὸ τῶν Κυρηναίων ἐπίνειον ἡ Ἀπολλωνία,[4] ὅσον ἑκατὸν καὶ ἑβδομήκοντα σταδίοις, τῆς δὲ Βερενίκης χιλίοις, τῆς δὲ Κυρήνης ὀγδοήκοντα, πόλεως μεγάλης ἐν τραπεζοειδεῖ πεδίῳ κειμένης, ὡς ἐκ τοῦ πελάγους ἑωρῶμεν αὐτήν.

---

[1] For λίμην, Dodwell conj. λίμνη, and Kramer and Meineke so write (but see Kramer's note).
[2] Ταύχειρα E, Τάρχειρα CDF*hisw*, Τεύχειρα other MSS.
[3] δ' ἐκκειμένη, Casaubon, for δὲ κειμένη.
[4] Ἀπολλωνία (as in § 21 following), Meineke, for Ἀπολλωνιάς.

are an isle and on it a temple of Aphroditê. In this region are also the Harbour [1] of the Hesperides and the river Lathon which empties into it. Farther inside [2] than Berenicê lies the small promontory called Boreium, which with Cephalae forms the mouth of the Syrtis. Berenicê lies opposite the promontories of the Peloponnesus, opposite Ichthys, as it is called, and also opposite Zacynthos, the distance across being three thousand six hundred [3] stadia. Setting out from this city Marcus Cato travelled round the Syrtis by land in thirty days, [4] leading an army of more than ten thousand men, having separated them into divisions on account of the scarcity of watering-places; and he travelled on foot in deep sand and scorching heat. After Berenicê one comes to a city Taucheira, which is also called Arsinoê; and then to a city formerly called Barcê, but now Ptolemaïs; and then to a promontory Phycus, which is low-lying and projects farthest towards the north as compared with the rest of the Libyan coast; it lies opposite Taenarum in Laconia, the distance across being two thousand and eight hundred stadia; and there is also a small town which bears the same name as the promontory. Not far distant from Phycus is the naval station of the Cyrenaeans, Apollonia, about one hundred and seventy stadia from Phycus, one thousand from Berenicê, and eighty from Cyrenê, a large city situated in a trapezium-shaped plain, as it looked to me from the sea.

[1] Some would emend "Harbour" to "Lake" (see critical note).

[2] *i.e.* inside the Syrtis, towards the south (see Map XV, end of vol.).

[3] Cp. 10. 2. 18.

[4] In 47 B.C., on his march to join Metellus Scipio.

21. Ἔστι δὲ Θηραίων κτίσμα, Λακωνικῆς νήσου, ἣν καὶ Καλλίστην ὠνόμαζον τὸ παλαίον, ὥς φησι καὶ Καλλίμαχος·

Καλλίστη τὸ πάροιθε, τὸ δ' ὕστερον οὔνομα
    Θήρη,
μήτηρ εὐίππου πατρίδος ἡμετέρης.

κεῖται δὲ τὸ τῶν Κυρηναίων ἐπίνειον κατὰ τὸ ἑσπέριον τῆς Κρήτης ἄκρον, τὸ τοῦ Κριοῦ μέτωπον, ἐν διάρματι δισχιλίων¹ σταδίων· ὁ πλοῦς Λευκονότῳ. λέγεται δὲ ἡ Κυρήνη κτίσμα Βάττου· πρόγονον δὲ τούτον ἑαυτοῦ φάσκει Καλλίμαχος· ηὐξήθη δὲ διὰ τὴν ἀρετὴν τῆς χώρας· καὶ γὰρ ἱπποτρόφος ἐστὶν ἀρίστη καὶ καλλίκαρπος, καὶ πολλοὺς ἄνδρας ἀξιολόγους ἔσχε καὶ δυναμένους ἐλευθερίας ἀξιολόγως προΐστασθαι καὶ πρὸς τοὺς ὑπερκειμένους βαρβάρους ἰσχυρῶς ἀντέχειν. τὸ μὲν οὖν παλαιὸν αὐτόνομος ἦν ἡ πόλις· εἶτα οἱ τὴν Αἴγυπτον κατασχόντες Μακεδόνες αὐξηθέντες ἐπέθεντο αὐτοῖς, ἀρξάντων τῶν περὶ Θίβρωνα τῶν ἀνελόντων τὸν Ἅρπαλον· βασιλευθέντες δὲ χρόνους τινὰς εἰς τὴν Ῥωμαίων ἐξουσίαν ἦλθον, καὶ νῦν ἐστιν ἐπαρχία τῇ Κρήτῃ συνεζευγμένη. τῆς δὲ Κυρήνης ἐστὶ περιπόλια ἥ τε Ἀπολλωνία καὶ ἡ Βάρκη καὶ ἡ Ταύχειρα² καὶ Βερενίκη καὶ τὰ ἄλλα πολίχνια τὰ πλησίον.

22. Ὁμορεῖ δὲ τῇ Κυρηναίᾳ ἡ τὸ σίλφιον φέρουσα καὶ τὸν ὀπὸν τὸν Κυρηναῖον, ὃν ἐκφέρει τὸ σίλφιον ὄπισθεν. ἐγγὺς δ' ἦλθε τοῦ ἐκλιπεῖν, ἐπελθόντων τῶν βαρβάρων κατὰ ἔχθραν τινὰ καὶ

---

¹ δισχιλίων (˒β) Casaubon, for χιλίων (˒α).
² Ταύχειρα (ευ above αυ) E, Τεύχειρα moz.

21. Cyrenê was founded by colonists from Thera, a Laconian island, which in ancient times was called Callistê, as Callimachus says: " Callistê was its first name, but its later name was Thera, mother of my fatherland, famed for its good horses." The naval station of the Cyrenaeans lies opposite the western promontory of Crete, Criume-topon, the distance across being two thousand stadia. The voyage is made with Leuconotus.[1] Cyrenê is said to have been founded by Battus;[2] and Calli-machus asserts that Battus was his ancestor. Cyrenê grew strong because of the fertility of its territory, for it is excellent for the breeding of horses and produces beautiful fruit, and it had many men who were noteworthy and who were able to defend its liberty in a noteworthy manner and to resist strongly the barbarians who lived above them. Now in ancient times the city was independent; and then the Macedonians, who had taken possession of Aegypt, grew in power and attacked the Cyrenaeans, under the leadership of Thibron and his associates, who had slain Harpalus; and having been ruled by kings for some time the city came under the power of the Romans and is now joined with Crete into one Province. But Apollonia, Barcê, Taucheira, Berenicê, and the other towns near by, are depen-dencies of Cyrenê.

22. Bordering on Cyrenaea is the country which produces silphium and the Cyrenaean juice, which latter is produced by the silphium through the extraction of its juice. But it came near giving out when the barbarians invaded the country be-

---

[1] A south wind (see 1. 2. 21).
[2] About 631 B.C.

φθειράντων¹ τὰς ῥίζας τοῦ φυτοῦ. εἰσὶ δὲ
νομάδες. ἄνδρες δ' ἐγένοντο γνώριμοι Κυρηναῖοι
Ἀρίστιππός τε ὁ Σωκρατικός, ὅστις καὶ τὴν
Κυρηναϊκὴν κατεβάλετο φιλοσοφίαν, καὶ θυγάτηρ,
Ἀρήτη τοὔνομα, ἥπερ διεδέξατο τὴν σχολήν, καὶ
ὁ ταύτην πάλιν διαδεξάμενος υἱὸς Ἀρίστιππος,
ὁ κληθεὶς Μητροδίδακτος, καὶ Ἀννίκερις, ὁ δοκῶν
ἐπανορθῶσαι τὴν Κυρηναϊκὴν αἵρεσιν καὶ παρα-
γαγεῖν ἀντ' αὐτῆς τὴν Ἀννικερίαν. Κυρηναῖος δ'
C 838 ἐστὶ καὶ Καλλίμαχος καὶ Ἐρατοσθένης, ἀμφότεροι
τετιμημένοι παρὰ τοῖς Αἰγυπτίων βασιλεῦσιν,
ὁ μὲν ποιητὴς ἅμα καὶ περὶ γραμματικὴν ἐσπου-
δακώς, ὁ δὲ καὶ ταῦτα καὶ περὶ φιλοσοφίαν καὶ τὰ
μαθήματα, εἴ τις ἄλλος, διαφέρων. ἀλλὰ μὴν
καὶ Καρνεάδης (οὗτος δὲ τῶν ἐξ Ἀκαδημίας
ἄριστος φιλοσόφων ὁμολογεῖται) καὶ ὁ Κρόνος
δὲ Ἀπολλώνιος ἐκεῖθέν ἐστιν, ὁ τοῦ διαλεκτικοῦ
Διοδώρου διδάσκαλος, τοῦ καὶ αὐτοῦ Κρόνου
προσαγορευθέντος, μετενεγκάντων τινῶν τὸ τοῦ
διδασκάλου ἐπίθετον ἐπὶ τὸν μαθητήν. μετὰ δὲ
τὴν Ἀπολλωνίαν ἐστὶν ἡ λοιπὴ τῶν Κυρηναίων
παραλία μέχρι Καταβαθμοῦ σταδίων δισχιλίων
διακοσίων, οὐ πάνυ εὐπαράπλους· καὶ γὰρ
λιμένες ὀλίγοι καὶ ὕφορμοι καὶ κατοικίαι καὶ
ὑδρεῖα. τῶν δὲ μάλιστα ὀνομαζομένων κατὰ τὸν
παράπλουν τόπων τό τε Ναύσταθμόν ἐστι καὶ
τὸ Ζεφύριον πρόσορμον ἔχον καὶ ἄλλο Ζεφύριον
καὶ ἄκρα Χερρόνησος λιμένα ἔχουσα· κεῖται δὲ

¹ φθειρόντων E.

cause of some grudge and destroyed the roots of the plant. The inhabitants are nomads. The Cyrenaeans who became famous were Aristippus the Socratic philosopher, who also laid the foundations of the Cyrenaïc philosophy; and his daughter, Aretê by name, who succeeded him as head of the school; and again her son Aristippus, Aretê's successor, who was called Mêtrodidactus;[1] and Anniceris, who is reputed to have revised the doctrines of the Cyrenaïc sect and to have introduced in place of it those of the Annicerian sect. Callimachus, also, was a Cyrenaean, and Eratosthenes, both of whom were held in honour by the Aegyptian kings, the former being a poet and at the same time a zealous student of letters, and the latter being superior, not only in these respects, but also in philosophy, and in mathematics, if ever a man was. Furthermore, Carneades, who by common agreement was the best of the Academic philosophers, and also Apollonius Cronus, were from Cyrenê, the latter being the teacher of Diodorus the Dialectician, who also was given the appellation "Cronus," certain persons having transferred the epithet of the teacher to the pupil. After Apollonia one comes to the remainder of the coast of the Cyrenaeans, which extends as far as Catabathmus, a distance of two thousand two hundred stadia; the coasting-voyage is not at all easy, for there are but few harbours, mooring-places, settlements, and watering-places. Among the places along the coast that are best known are Naustathmus and Zephyrium, which has anchorage, and a second Zephyrium, and a promontory Cherronesus, which has a harbour. This

---

[1] *i.e.* "Mother-taught."

κατὰ Κύκλον[1] τῆς Κρήτης ἐν διάρματι χιλίων
καὶ πεντακοσίων σταδίων νότῳ· εἶτα Ἡράκλειόν τι
ἱερὸν καὶ ὑπὲρ αὐτοῦ κώμη Παλίουρος· εἶτα λιμὴν
Μενέλαος καὶ Ἀρδανίς,[2] ἄκρα ταπεινὴ ὕφορμον
ἔχουσα· εἶτα μέγας λιμήν, καθ᾿ ὃν ἡ ἐν τῇ Κρήτῃ
Χερρόνησος ἵδρυται, δισχιλίων[3] που σταδίων
διάρμα ἀπολείπουσα μεταξύ· ὅλη γὰρ σχεδόν τι
τῇ παραλίᾳ ταύτῃ ἀντίκειται παράλληλος ἡ
Κρήτη στενὴ καὶ μακρά. μετὰ δὲ τὸν μέγαν λιμένα
ἄλλος λιμὴν Πλῦνος, καὶ ὑπὲρ αὐτὸν Τετρα-
πυργία·[4] καλεῖται δὲ ὁ τόπος Κατάβαθμος·
μέχρι δεῦρο ἡ Κυρηναία. τὸ δὲ λοιπὸν ἤδη
μέχρι Παραιτονίου, κἀκεῖθεν εἰς Ἀλεξάνδρειαν,
εἴρηται ἡμῖν ἐν τοῖς Αἰγυπτιακοῖς.

23. Τὴν δ᾿ ὑπερκειμένην ἐν βάθει χώραν τῆς
Σύρτεως καὶ τῆς Κυρηναίας κατέχουσιν οἱ Λίβυες,
παράλυπρον καὶ αὐχμηράν· πρῶτοι μὲν οἱ Νασαμῶνες, ἔπειτα Ψύλλοι καί τινες Γαίτουλοι,[5]
ἔπειτα Γαράμαντες· πρὸς ἕω δ᾿ ἔτι μᾶλλον οἱ
Μαρμαρίδαι,[6] προσχωροῦντες ἐπὶ πλέον τῇ Κυρηναίᾳ καὶ παρατείνοντες μέχρι Ἄμμωνος. τεταρ-
ταίους μὲν οὖν φασιν ἀπὸ τοῦ μυχοῦ τῆς μεγάλης
Σύρτεως τοῦ κατ᾿ Αὐτόμαλά πως[7] βαδίζοντας ὡς

---

[1] For Κύκλον, Corais (citing 8. 5. 1) writes Κώρυκον ; but
Kramer rightly objects, proposing Μάταλον instead.

[2] Ἀρδανίς, Meineke, following Kramer, for Ἀρδανίξις.

[3] δισχιλίων, Letronne and most later editors, for τρισχιλίων.

[4] The words καλεῖται . . . Κυρηναία are rightly transposed
from a position after Ἀλεξανδρείαν by Kramer, who also
omits ἢ καί before εἴρηται.

[5] Γέτουλοι MSS.

[6] Μαρμαρίδαι E, Μαρμαρῖται other MSS.

promontory lies opposite Cyclus [1] in Crete; and the
distance across is one thousand five hundred stadia
if one has a south-west wind; and then one comes
to a kind of temple of Heracles, and, above it, to
a village called Paliurus; and then one comes to a
harbour, Menelaüs, and to Ardanis, which is a low-
lying promontory with a mooring-place; and then to
a large harbour, opposite which lies the Cherronesus
in Crete, the interval between the two places being
about two [2] thousand stadia; indeed, I might almost
say that Crete as a whole, being narrow and long,
lies opposite, and parallel, to this coast. After the
large harbour one comes to another harbour, which
is called Plynus, and above it lies Tetrapyrgia; [3] but
the place is called Catabathmus; and Cyrenaea extends thus far. The remaining part of the coast,
extending to Paraetonium and thence to Alexandria,
I have already mentioned in my account of Egypt.

23. The country lying deep in the interior above
the Syrtis and Cyrenaea, a barren and arid region,
is occupied by the Libyans: first by the Nasamones,
and then by the Psyllians and certain Gaetulians,
and then by the Garamantes, and, still more towards
the east, by the Marmaridae, who border to a
greater extent on Cyrenaea and extend as far as
Ammon. Now it is said that persons going on foot
from the recess of the Great Syrtis, from about the
neighbourhood of Automala, approximately in the

[1] "Cyclus" is doubtful (see critical note).
[2] The MSS. read "three" (see critical note).
[3] *i.e.* "Four Towers."

---

[7] τοῦ κατ' Αὐτόμαλά πως, Kramer, for τοὺς κατ' αὐτὸ
μαλακῶς.

ἐπὶ χειμερινὰς ἀνατολὰς εἰς Αὔγιλα[1] ἀφικνεῖσθαι.
ἔστι δὲ ὁ τόπος οὗτος ἐμφερὴς τῷ Ἄμμωνι,
φοινικοτρόφος τε καὶ εὔυδρος· ὑπέρκειται δὲ τῆς
Κυρηναίας[2] πρὸς μεσημβρίαν· μέχρι μὲν σταδίων
ἑκατὸν καὶ δενδροφόρος ἐστὶν ἡ γῆ· μέχρι δ᾽
ἄλλων ἑκατὸν σπείρεται μόνον, οὐκ ὀρυζοτροφεῖ[3]
δ᾽ ἡ γῆ διὰ τὸν αὐχμόν. ὑπὲρ δὲ τούτων ἡ τὸ
σίλφιον φέρουσά[4] ἐστιν· εἶθ᾽ ἡ ἀοίκητος καὶ ἡ
C 839 τῶν Γαραμάντων. ἔστι δ᾽ ἡ τὸ σίλφιον φέρουσα
στενὴ καὶ παραμήκης καὶ παράξηρος, μῆκος μὲν
ὡς ἐπὶ τὰς ἀνατολὰς ἰόντι ὅσον σταδίων χιλίων,
πλάτος δὲ τριακοσίων ἢ μικρῷ πλειόνων τό γε
γνώριμον· εἰκάζειν μὲν γὰρ ἅπασαν πάρεστι
διηνεκῶς τὴν ἐπὶ τοῦ αὐτοῦ παραλλήλου κειμένην
τοιαύτην εἶναι κατά τε τοὺς ἀέρας καὶ τὴν τοῦ
φυτοῦ φοράν, ἐπεὶ δ᾽ ἐμπίπτουσιν ἐρημίαι πλείους,
οὐ[5] τοὺς πάντας τόπους ἴσμεν. παραπλησίως δ᾽
ἀγνοεῖται καὶ τὰ ὑπὲρ τοῦ Ἄμμωνος καὶ τῶν
αὐάσεων μέχρι τῆς Αἰθιοπίας. οὐδ᾽ ἂν ἔχοιμεν
λέγειν τοὺς ὅρους οὔτε τῆς Αἰθιοπίας οὔτε τῆς
Λιβύης, ἀλλ᾽ οὐδὲ τῆς πρὸς Αἰγύπτῳ τρανῶς,
μή τι γε τῆς πρὸς τῷ ὠκεανῷ.

24. Τὰ μὲν οὖν μέρη τῆς καθ᾽ ἡμᾶς οἰκουμένης[6]
οὕτω διάκειται· ἐπεὶ δ᾽ οἱ Ῥωμαῖοι τὴν ἀρίστην

---

[1] εἰς Αὔγιλα, Kramer inserts.
[2] τῆς, after Κυρηναίας, Groskurd ejects.
[3] E reads οὐ ῥιζοτροφεῖ, other MSS. ὀρυζοτροφεῖ, before
which Corais and the later editors insert οὐκ.
[4] φέρουσα, omitted by all MSS. except i.
[5] οὐ, Hopper inserts.

direction of winter sunrise,[1] arrive at Augila on the fourth day. This region resembles Ammon, being productive of palm-trees and also well supplied with water. It lies above Cyrenaea to the south, and for a distance of one hundred stadia produces trees, but for another hundred the land is only sown, although, on account of its aridity, the land does not grow rice.[2] Above this region is the country which produces silphium; and then one comes to the uninhabited country and to that of the Garamantes. The country which produces silphium is narrow, long, and somewhat arid, extending in length, as one goes approximately towards the east, about one thousand stadia, and in breadth three hundred or a little more, at least that part which is known; for we may conjecture that all lands lying in unbroken succession on the same parallel of latitude are similar as regards both climate and plants, but since several deserts intervene, we do not know all these regions. Similarly, the regions above Ammon and the oases as far as Aethiopia are likewise unknown. Neither can we tell the boundaries either of Aethiopia or of Libya, nor yet accurately even those of the country next to Aegypt, much less of that which borders on the Ocean.

24. This, then, is the lay of the different parts of our inhabited world; but since the Romans occupy

---

[1] See Vol. I, p. 105.
[2] One major MS. reads "roots" instead of "rice" (see critical note).

---

[6] Τὰ μὲν οὖν μέρη τῆς καθ' ἡμᾶς οἰκουμένης (as in 2. 5. 34), Kramer, for τὰ μὲν οὖν μέρη τῆς οἰκουμένης (Dhz adding τά before μέρη).

αὐτῆς καὶ γνωριμωτάτην κατέχουσιν, ἅπαντας
ὑπερβεβλημένοι τοὺς πρότερον ἡγεμόνας, ὧν
μνήμην ἴσμεν, ἄξιον καὶ διὰ βραχέων καὶ τὰ
τούτων εἰπεῖν. ὅτι μὲν οὖν ἐκ μιᾶς ὁρμηθέντες
πόλεως τῆς Ῥώμης ἅπασαν τὴν Ἰταλίαν ἔσχον
διὰ τὸ πολεμεῖν καὶ πολιτικῶς ἄρχειν, εἴρηται,
καὶ διότι μετὰ τὴν Ἰταλίαν τὰ κύκλῳ προσεκτή-
σαντο, τῇ αὐτῇ ἀρετῇ χρώμενοι. τριῶν δὲ
ἠπείρων οὐσῶν, τὴν μὲν Εὐρώπην σχεδόν τι
πᾶσαν ἔχουσι, πλὴν τῆς[1] ἔξω τοῦ Ἴστρου καὶ
τῶν μεταξὺ τοῦ Ῥήνου καὶ τοῦ Τανάϊδος παρω-
κεανιτῶν· τῆς δὲ Λιβύης ἡ καθ' ἡμᾶς παραλία
πᾶσα ὑπ' αὐτοῖς ἐστιν, ἡ δὲ ἄλλη ἀοίκητός ἐστιν
ἢ λυπρῶς καὶ νομαδικῶς οἰκεῖται· ὁμοίως δὲ καὶ
τῆς Ἀσίας ἡ καθ' ἡμᾶς παραλία πᾶσα ὑποχείριός
ἐστιν, εἰ μή τις τὰ τῶν Ἀχαιῶν καὶ Ζυγῶν καὶ
Ἡνιόχων ἐν λόγῳ τίθεται, ληστρικῶς καὶ νομαδικῶς ζώντων ἐν στενοῖς καὶ λυπροῖς χωρίοις·
τῆς δὲ μεσογαίας καὶ τῆς ἐν βάθει τὴν μὲν
ἔχουσιν αὐτοί, τὴν δὲ Παρθναῖοι καὶ οἱ[2] ὑπὲρ
τούτων βάρβαροι, πρός τε ταῖς ἀνατολαῖς καὶ
ταῖς ἄρκτοις Ἰνδοὶ καὶ Βάκτριοι καὶ Σκύθαι,
εἶτ' Ἄραβες καὶ Αἰθίοπες· προστίθεται δὲ ἀεί
τι παρ' ἐκείνων αὐτοῖς. ταύτης δὲ τῆς συμπάσης
χώρας τῆς ὑπὸ Ῥωμαίοις ἡ μὲν βασιλεύεται, ἡν[3]
δ' ἔχουσιν αὐτοὶ καλέσαντες ἐπαρχίαν, καὶ πέμ-
πουσιν ἡγεμόνας καὶ φορολόγους. εἰσὶ δέ τινες

---

[1] τῶν E.   [2] οἱ, omitted by all MSS. except E.
   [3] ἥν, Corais, for ἡ.

---

[1] 6. 4. 2.   [2] Danube.   [3] Rhine.
[4] Don.   [5] See 11. 2. 12.   [6] i.e. on the south.

the best and the best known portions of it, having surpassed all former rulers of whom we have record, it is worth while, even though briefly, to add the following account of them. Now I have already stated [1] that, setting out with only one city, Rome, the Romans acquired the whole of Italy through warfare and statesmanlike rulership, and that, after Italy, by exercising the same superior qualities, they also acquired the regions round about Italy. And of the continents, being three in number, they hold almost the whole of Europe, except that part of it which lies outside the Ister [2] River and the parts along the ocean which lie between the Rhenus [3] and the Tanaïs [4] Rivers. Of Libya, the whole of the coast on Our Sea is subject to them; and the rest of the country is uninhabited or else inhabited only in a wretched or nomadic fashion. In like manner, of Asia also, the whole of the coast on Our Sea is subject to them, unless one takes into account the regions of the Achaei and the Zygi and the Heniochi,[5] who live a piratical and nomadic life in narrow and sterile districts; and of the interior and the country deep inland, one part is held by the Romans themselves and another by the Parthians and the barbarians beyond them; and on the east and north live Indians and Bactrians and Scythians, and then [6] Arabians and Aethiopians; but some further portion is constantly being taken from these peoples and added to the possessions of the Romans. Of this whole country that is subject to the Romans, some parts are indeed ruled by kings, but the Romans retain others themselves, calling them Provinces, and send to them praefects and collectors of tribute. But there are also some free cities,

καὶ ἐλεύθεραι πόλεις, αἱ μὲν ἐξ ἀρχῆς κατὰ φιλίαν
προσελθοῦσαι, τὰς δ' ἠλευθέρωσαν αὐτοὶ κατὰ
τιμήν. εἰσὶ δὲ καὶ δυνάσται τινὲς καὶ φύλαρχοι
καὶ ἱερεῖς ὑπ' αὐτοῖς. οὗτοι μὲν δὴ ζῶσι κατά
τινας πατρίους νόμους.

C 840   25. Αἱ δ' ἐπαρχίαι διῄρηνται ἄλλοτε μὲν ἄλλως,
ἐν δὲ τῷ παρόντι, ὡς Καῖσαρ ὁ Σεβαστὸς διέ-
ταξεν· ἐπειδὴ γὰρ ἡ πατρὶς ἐπέτρεψεν αὐτῷ τὴν
προστασίαν τῆς ἡγεμονίας καὶ πολέμου καὶ
εἰρήνης κατέστη κύριος διὰ βίου, δίχα διεῖλε
πᾶσαν τὴν χώραν καὶ τὴν μὲν ἀπέδειξεν ἑαυτῷ,
τὴν δὲ τῷ δήμῳ· ἑαυτῷ μέν, ὅση στρατιωτικῆς
φρουρᾶς ἔχει χρείαν (αὕτη δ' ἐστὶν ἡ βάρβαρος
καὶ πλησιόχωρος τοῖς μήπω κεχειρωμένοις ἔθνεσιν
ἢ λυπρὰ καὶ δυσγεώργητος, ὥσθ' ὑπὸ ἀπορίας
τῶν ἄλλων, ἐρυμάτων δ' εὐπορίας ἀφηνιάζειν καὶ
ἀπειθεῖν), τῷ δήμῳ δὲ τὴν ἄλλην, ὅση[1] εἰρηνικὴ
καὶ χωρὶς ὅπλων ἄρχεσθαι ῥᾳδία· ἑκατέραν δὲ
τὴν μερίδα εἰς ἐπαρχίας διένειμε πλείους, ὧν αἱ
μὲν καλοῦνται Καίσαρος, αἱ δὲ τοῦ δήμου. καὶ
εἰς μὲν τὰς Καίσαρος ἡγεμόνας[2] καὶ διοικητὰς
Καῖσαρ πέμπει, διαιρῶν ἄλλοτε ἄλλως τὰς χώρας
καὶ πρὸς τοὺς καιροὺς πολιτευόμενος, εἰς δὲ τὰς
δημοσίας ὁ δῆμος στρατηγοὺς ἢ ὑπάτους. καὶ
αὗται δ' εἰς μερισμοὺς ἄγονται διαφόρους, ἐπειδὰν

[1] ὅση F, ὅσην ἦν other MSS.
[2] ἡγεμόνας, Casaubon, for ἡγεμονείας F, ἡγεμονίας other
MSS.

---

[1] i.e. "tribal chiefs."   [2] In Latin principatus.
[3] During office called "propraetors."

of which some came over to the Romans at the outset as friends, whereas others were set free by the Romans themselves as a mark of honour. There are also some potentates and phylarchs [1] and priests subject to them. Now these live in accordance with certain ancestral laws.

25. But the Provinces have been divided in different ways at different times, though at the present time they are as Augustus Caesar arranged them; for when his native land committed to him the foremost place [2] of authority and he became established as lord for life of war and peace, he divided the whole of his empire into two parts, and assigned one portion to himself and the other to the Roman people; to himself, all parts that had need of a military guard (that is, the part that was barbarian and in the neighbourhood of tribes not yet subdued, or lands that were sterile and difficult to bring under cultivation, so that, being unprovided with everything else, but well provided with strongholds, they would try to throw off the bridle and refuse obedience), and to the Roman people all the rest, in so far as it was peaceable and easy to rule without arms; and he divided each of the two portions into several Provinces, of which some are called " Provinces of Caesar " and the others " Provinces of the People." And to the " Provinces of Caesar " Caesar sends legati [3] and procurators, dividing the countries in different ways at different times and administering them as the occasion requires, whereas to the " Provinces of the People " the people send praetors or proconsuls, and these Provinces also are brought under different divisions whenever expediency requires. But at the outset

κελεύῃ τὸ συμφέρον. ἀλλ' ἐν ἀρχαῖς γε[1] διέθηκε ποιήσας ὑπατικὰς μὲν δύο, Λιβύην τε, ὅση ὑπὸ Ῥωμαίοις ἔξω τῆς ὑπὸ Ἰούβᾳ μὲν πρότερον, νῦν δὲ Πτολεμαίῳ τῷ ἐκείνου παιδί, καὶ Ἀσίαν τὴν ἐντὸς Ἅλυος καὶ τοῦ Ταύρου πλὴν Γαλατῶν καὶ τῶν ὑπὸ Ἀμύντα γενομένων ἐθνῶν, ἔτι δὲ Βιθυνίας καὶ τῆς Προποντίδος· δέκα δὲ στρατηγικάς,[2] κατὰ μὲν τὴν Εὐρώπην καὶ τὰς πρὸς αὐτῇ νήσους τήν τε ἐκτὸς Ἰβηρίαν λεγομένην, ὅση περὶ τὸν Βαῖτιν ποταμὸν καὶ τὸν Ἄναν[3] καὶ τῆς Κελτικῆς τὴν Ναρβωνῖτιν, τρίτην δὲ Σαρδὼ μετὰ Κύρνου, καὶ Σικελίαν τετάρτην, πέμπτην δὲ καὶ ἕκτην τῆς Ἰλλυρίδος τὴν πρὸς τῇ Ἠπείρῳ καὶ Μακεδονίαν, ἑβδόμην δ' Ἀχαΐαν μέχρι Θετταλίας καὶ Αἰτωλῶν καὶ Ἀκαρνάνων καί τινων Ἠπειρωτικῶν ἐθνῶν, ὅσα τῇ Μακεδονίᾳ προσώριστο, ὀγδόην δὲ Κρήτην μετὰ τῆς Κυρηναίας, ἐννάτην δὲ Κύπρον, δεκάτην δὲ Βιθυνίαν μετὰ τῆς Προποντίδος καὶ τοῦ Πόντου τινῶν μερῶν. τὰς δὲ ἄλλας ἐπαρχίας ἔχει Καῖσαρ, ὧν εἰς ἃς μὲν πέμπει τοὺς ἐπιμελησομένους ὑπατικοὺς ἄνδρας, εἰς ἃς δὲ στρατηγικούς, εἰς ἃς δὲ καὶ ἱππικούς. καὶ βασιλεῖς δὲ καὶ δυνάσται καὶ δεκαρχίαι τῆς ἐκείνου μερίδος καὶ εἰσὶ καὶ ὑπῆρξαν ἀεί.

[1] γε, Corais, for τε.
[2] στρατηγικάς, Corais, for στρατηγίας.
[3] καὶ τὸν Ἄναν, editors before Kramer, for καὶ τὸν Ἄτακα (Ἄτακα MSS.), which is suspected by later editors and ejected by Meineke.

Caesar organised the Provinces of the People by creating, first, two consular provinces; I mean (1) Libya, in so far as it was subject to the Romans, except the part which was formerly subject to Juba and is now subject to Ptolemy his son, and (2) the part of Asia that lies this side the Halys River and the Taurus, except the countries of the Galatians and of the tribes which had been subject to Amyntas, and also of Bithynia and the Propontis; and, secondly, ten praetorial provinces, first, in Europe and the islands near it, I mean (1) Iberia Ulterior, as it is called, in the neighbourhood of the Baetis and Anas[1] Rivers, (2) Narbonitis in Celtica, (3) Sardo[2] together with Cyrnus,[3] (4) Sicily, (5 and 6) Macedonia and, in Illyria, the country next to Epeirus, (7) Achaea as far as Thessaly and Aetolia and Acarnania and certain Epeirotic tribes which border on Macedonia, (8) Crete along with Cyrenaea, (9) Cypros, and (10) Bithynia along with the Propontis and certain parts of the Pontus. But the rest of the Provinces are held by Caesar; and to some of these he sends as curators men of consular rank, to others men of praetorian rank, and to others men of the rank of knights. Kings, also, and potentates and decarchies are now, and always have been, in Caesar's portion.

---

[1] "Anas" is a correction for "Atax," the Atax being the present Aude in France.
[2] Sardinia. [3] Corsica.

INDEX OF NAMES, PLACES, AND SUBJECTS

[The translator has tried to make this *Index* virtually complete. The references are to volume and page.]

A

AARASSUS, a city in Pisidia, **5**. 481

Aba in Phocis, whence Thracian colonists set out for Euboea, **5**. 5

Aba, daughter of Xenophanes and queen of Cilicia, **6**. 343

Abae, the oracle of, in Phocis, **4**. 369

"Abantes," Homer's name for the Euboeans, **5**. 5

"Abantis," a former name of Euboea, **5**. 5

Abaris, "Hyperborian" priest and prophet of Apollo, healer, traveller, and deliverer from plagues; held in high esteem by the Greeks, **3**. 201

Abas the hero, brought a colony to the plain of the Thessalians and named the plain "Pelasgian Argos," **4**. 403; early king of Abantis (Euboea), **5**. 5

Abdera in Iberia, founded by the Phoenicians, **2**. 81

Abdera (Balastra) in Thrace, scene of the myths about Abderus, and ruled over by Diomedes, **3**. 365; named after Abderus, **3**. 367; temple of Jason at, built by Parmenion, **5**. 333; "beautiful colony of the Teïans," **6**. 239

Abderus of Abdera in Thrace; the myths about, **3**. 365; devoured by the horses of Diomedes, **3**. 367

Abeacus, king of the Siraces in the time of King Pharnaces, once sent forth 20,000 cavalry, **5**. 243

Abella (Avella Vecchia), in Campania, **2**. 461

Abii ("Resourceless men"), the Homeric, "men most just," are wagon-dwelling Scythians and Sarmatians, **3**. 179, 181, 189, 195, 205, 209, 245 ("just and resourceless"), **5**. 419

Abilê (or Abilyx, *q.v.*), Mt., in Maurusia, at the Strait of Gibraltar, abounds in wild animals and trees, **8**. 165

Abilyx (Ape) Mountain, in Libya, by some regarded as one of the Pillars of Heracles, **2**. 135

Abisarus, a king in India, **7**. 49

Abonuteichus in Paphlagonia, **5**. 387

Aboracê, in the Syndic territory, near the Cimmerian Bosporus, **5**. 199

Aborras River, the, in Mesopotamia, **7**. 233

Abrettenê, in Mysia in Asia, **5**. 499

Abrotonum, a city on coast of Libya, **8**. 195

Abus, Mt., in Asia, whence flow the Euphrates and the Araxes, **5**. 321; a part of the Taurus, **5**. 335

Abydon (the Homeric Amydon), on the Axius River in Macedonia, **3**. 341, 343, 345, 347

Abydus, **6**. 5; 30 stadia from Sestus, **3**. 379; by Scylax called a boundary of Troy, **6**. 9, 19, 21; the voyage to, from Byzantium, **6**. 13; the parts round, colonised by the Thracians after the Trojan War, **6**. 23; mentioned by Homer, **6**. 37; history and geographical position of, **6**. 41; length of pontoon-bridge at, **6**. 43; after the Trojan War the

217

INDEX OF NAMES, PLACES, AND SUBJECTS

home of Thracians, and then of Milesians, and later burned by Dareius, **6.** 43; distance from, to the Aesepus River, **6.** 45; 70 stadia from Dardanus, **6.** 59; colonised by Milesians, **6.** 207

Abydus near the Nile, where are the Memnonium, of the same workmanship as the Labyrinth, and a marvellous fountain ("Strabo's Well"), **8.** 111; now only a small settlement, **8.** 113; Osiris worshipped at, **8.** 117

Acacesium, in Arcadia, falsified by some writers, according to Callimachus, **3.** 193

Academia, the, at Athens, **4.** 265

Academic, philosophers, the; Carneades the best of, **8.** 205

Acalandrus (Salandra) River, the, in southern Italy, **3.** 117

Acamas the Athenian, founded Soli in Cypros, **6.** 381

Acamas, Cape, in Cypros, **6.** 375, 381, 383

Acantha, the Thebaïc (*Mimosa Nilotica*), from which gum arabic is obtained, **8.** 97; the Aegyptian, a grove of, near Abydus, sacred to Apollo, **8.** 113

Acanthus (Hierisos), on the isthmus of Athos, founded by the Andrians, **3.** 353; on the Singitic Gulf near the canal of Xerxes, **3.** 355

Acanthus, in Libya, above Memphis, **8.** 97

Acarnan, son of Alcmaeon; Acarnania named after, **5.** 73

Acarnania, borders on the Ambracian Gulf, **3.** 301; acquired by Diomedes, **3.** 305; bounded by the Acheloüs River, **4.** 17; deserted lands of, well adapted to horse-raising, **4.** 229; borders on Thessaly, **4.** 395; description of, **5.** 23–31; Leucas once a peninsula of, **5.** 31; once ruled by Icarius, father of Penelopê, and his sons, **5.** 35, 69; various places in, **5.** 61, 63; acquired by Laertes and the Cephallenians, **5.** 67; took part in the Trojan war, but was not so-named at that time, **5.** 69, though Ephorus says it did not take part in it, **5.** 71; obtained autonomy from the Romans, **5.** 73;

the Curetes withdrew to, from Aetolia, **5.** 77; now included within a Roman Province, **8.** 215

Acarnanians, the, a Greek people, **4.** 5; joined the Aetolians in war, **4.** 389; disputed the possession of Paracheloïtis with the Aetolians, **5.** 57; now reduced to impotence, **5.** 65; so named, according to Archamachus, because they kept their heads "unshorn," **5.** 185.

Acarnanians, The Polity of the, by Aristotle, **3.** 289

Acathartus Gulf, the, in the Arabian Gulf, **7.** 317

Acê in Phoenicia (see Ptolemaïs), **7.** 271

Acerrae (see Acherrae)

Acesines River, the, in India, **7.** 27, 35, 47, 49, 51

Achaea in Asia, settled by the Achaeans in Jason's crew, **5.** 203; welcomed Mithridates Eupator, **5.** 205; coast of, **5.** 207; life and country of, **8.** 2

Achaea in the Peloponnesus (also referred to as "Ionia"), occupied by the Achaeans from Laconia, **4.** 133; subject to Agamemnon, **4.** 167; colonised by Tisamenus after the return of the Heracleidae, **4.** 235

Achaea in Thessaly, by some called the same as Phthia, **4.** 403

Achaeae, the; abrupt cliffs in Triphylia, **4.** 63

"Achaean Argos," Laconia called by Homer, **4.** 137, and the whole Peloponnesus called, **4.** 155

Achaean League, the, joined by the Argives, **4.** 185; voluntarily gave Aratus of Sicyon the supreme authority; and places belonging to, **4.** 207; famous for its constitution, arbitrator for the Thebans, and dissolved by the Macedonians, **4.** 211; organisation, administration, and members of, and the time of its reaching the height of its power, and the time of its dissolution, **4.** 217; dissolution of, compared with that of the Amphictyonic, **4.** 357

Achaeans, the; Homeric use of term, **1.** 129, **4.** 401, **5.** 495; migrations of, **1.** 227; in Asia, **1.** 495; cities of, in southern Italy, **3.** 41; sent Leucippus to colonise Metapontium, **3.** 55;

INDEX OF NAMES, PLACES, AND SUBJECTS

an Aeolic tribe, drove the Ionians out of the Peloponnesus, **4.** 7; country of, extends from Cape Araxus to Sicyonia, **4.** 15; once had charge of temple at Olympia, **4.** 103; in Laconia, emigrated to Peloponnesian Ionia (Achaea), **4.** 133, 137; in Thessaly, came with Pelops into the Peloponnesus and settled in Laconia, **4.** 135; came under the dominion of Rome, **4.** 185; drove the Athenian Ionians out of the Aegialus, **4.** 209, 219; long remained a powerful and independent people, both under kings and later under democracy, **4.** 211; after the submersion of Helicê divided its territory among the neighbours, **4.** 215; once surpassed even the Lacedaemonians, **4.** 217; the twelve places settled by, **4.** 219; in Pontus, are a colony of the Orchomenians, **4.** 341; all the Phthiotae in Thessaly, subjects of Achilles, so called, **4.** 401, 413; Naval Station of, at Troy, **6.** 61, 71, about 20 stadia from the present Ilium, if not to be identified with the Harbour of the Achaeans, only about 12 stadia from it, **6.** 73, where are the altars of the twelve gods, **6.** 159; the beach of, in Cypros, **6.** 377

Achaecarus, great diviner among the Bosporeni, **7.** 289

Achaeïum, the, where begins the part of the mainland that belongs to Tenedos, **6.** 63, 89, 91, 93

Achaemenidae, the, a tribe in Persis, **7.** 157

Achaeus, grandfather of Attalus I., **6.** 167

Achaeus, the son of Xuthus, after whom the Achaeans were named, **4.** 209

Achaïa, a city in Aria, **5.** 279

Acharaca in Asia, between Tralleis and Nysa, where is the Plutonium, and also the Charonium, at which remarkable cures occur, **6.** 259

Achardeüs River, the; rises in the Caucasus and empties into Lake Maeotis, **5.** 243

Acheloüs the river-god, defeated by Heracles, **5.** 57, 59

Acheloüs River (Aspropotamos), once

called "Thoas," the; by silting up sea joined isles to mainland, **1.** 221; joined by the Inachus, **3.** 79; empties into the sea, **3.** 309, 311; separates Aetolia from Acarnania, **4.** 17, **5.** 23, 25, 55; myths concerning god of, **5.** 57, 59

Acheloüs River (also called Peirus), in Elis, **4.** 43

Acheloüs River, the, in Phthiotis, flows near Lamia, **4.** 413

Acheron (Arconti?) River, the, in Italy, which flows past Pandosia in Bruttium, **3.** 17

Acheron (Phanariotikos) River, the, in Thesprotia, **3.** 17; flows past Pandosia and empties into Glycys Limen ("Sweet Harbour"), **3.** 299; flows from the Acherusian Lake, **3.** 301

Acheron River, the, in Triphylia, empties into the Alpheius; why so named, **4.** 53

Acherrae (Gela), in Campania, **2.** 461

Acherusian Lake (Lago di Fusaro), the, in Campania, **1.** 95, **2.** 439, 443; by some identified with Gulf Lucrinus and by Apollodorus with Gulf Avernus, **2.** 447

Acherusian Lake, the (a marsh near Kastri), whence flows the Acheron River in Thesprotia, **3.** 301 (in footnote 2, page 209, "Fusaro" is an error)

Achilleïum in Asia, a village on the Cimmerian Bosporus where the strait is narrowest, **3.** 241; has a temple of Achilles, **5.** 197

Achilleïum, the, in the Troad, fortified by the Mitylenaeans against Sigeium, **6.** 77; where is the monument of Achilles, **6.** 79, 91

Achilles, the shield of, bordered by Oceanus, **1.** 13; sacked Lesbos but spared Lemnos, **1.** 165; the island Leucê, off the mouth of the Borysthenes in the Euxine, sacred to, **3.** 221, 227; the Race Course of (Cape Tendra), **3.** 227, 229; grandfather of the Pyrrhus who ruled over the Molossians, **3.** 309; the subjects of, called Phthians, **3.** 385; promised seven cities on the Messenian and Asinaean Gulfs by Agamemnon, **4.** 109, one of these being Pedasus

219

INDEX OF NAMES, PLACES, AND SUBJECTS

(Methonê, now Modon), 4. 111, 115; promised to bring Patroclus back to his native city Opus in Locris, 4. 379; the domain of, in Thessaly, 4. 399–419; son-in-law of Lycomedes and father of Neoptolemus, 4. 427; "alone knew how to hurl the Pelian ashen spear," 5. 21; temple of, at Achilleium on the Cimmerian Bosporus, 5. 197; numerous cities in the Troad outside Ilium sacked by, and Brisëis taken captive by, at Lyrnessus, 6. 15; slew King Cycnus of Colonae, 6. 35; monument of, near Sigeium in the Troad, 6. 61; on the cowardice of Hector, 6. 71; pursued Aeneias to Lyrnessus, 6. 105, 107; laid waste Thebê and Lyrnessus, taking captive Chrysëis and Brisëis, 6. 121; Palisade of, at Astyra, 6. 129; slew Eëtion, 6. 149, and his seven sons, 6. 151

Acholla in Libya, a free city, 8. 181

Acidon River, the, in Triphylia, flows past Chaa and the tomb of Iardanus, 4. 65

Acila, Cape, in Arabia, opposite Cape Deirê, 7. 315

Acilisenê in Asia; followers of Armenus settled in, 5. 231, 333; the Euphrates borders on, 5. 297, 425; geographical position of, 5. 321; annexed to Armenia, 5. 325; has many temples of Anaïtis, 5. 341

Aciris (Agri) River, the, in Italy, 3. 49

Acisenê (Acilisenê?) in Armenia; Artaxias the king of, 5. 325

Acmon, one of the Idaean Dactyli, 5. 117

Aconite, the plant, grows in the territory of Heracleia Pontica, 5. 381

Aconites, the, a tribe in Sardinia, 2. 361

Acontius, Mt., in Phocis, extending 60 stadia to Parapotamii, and whither the Orchomenians emigrated, 4. 341

Acorns, eaten two-thirds of the year by Lusitanian mountaineers, 2. 75; the, in Persia, 7. 181

Acqui (see Aquae Statiellae)

Acra, a village on the Cimmerian Bosporus, 5. 197

Acraea, in Laconia, 4. 47

Acraephiae (or Acraephium, q.v.), a city on Lake Copaïs, 4. 321

Acraephium (or Acraephiae, q.v., now in ruins near Karditza) in Boeotia, on a height near Mt. Ptoüs and Lake Copaïs, 4. 329, and identified with the Homeric Arnê, which by some is said to have been swallowed up by Lake Copaïs, 4. 331

Acragantini, the Emporium of the, 20 Roman miles from the Heracleium, 3. 57

Acragas, still endures, 3. 81; the salt-lakes near, on which people float like wood, 3. 91

Acrathos, Cape, on the Strymonic Gulf, 3. 353

Acridophagi ("Locust-eaters"), the, in Aethiopia; manner of capture of locusts by, 7. 327

Acrisius, reputed to have been the first head of the Amphictyonic League, 4. 357

Acritas (Cape Gallo), the beginning of the Messenian Gulf, 4. 113

Acrocorinthus, the, one of the two strategic points in the Peloponnesus, according to Demetrius of Pharos, 4. 119, 121; taken by Aratus from Antigonus Gonatas, 4. 217; whence Strabo says he beheld Cleonae, 4. 187; description of, 4. 191–195; altitude of, 3½ stadia, 4. 191; has a small temple of Aphroditê and the spring Peirenê, 4. 193; wide view from summit of, 4. 195

Acrolissus, a fortress near Lissus in Illyria, 3. 265

Acrothoï, a city "near the crest of Athos," 3. 355, 357

Actê, the eastern coast of Argolis, colonised by Agaeus and Deïphontes after the return of the Heracleidae, 4. 235

Actê (or Acticê, i.e. Attica), takes a crescent-shaped bend towards Oropus, 4. 243

Actian Apollo (see Apollo, the Actian), the; temple of, near the Ambracian Gulf, 5. 25, 31

Actian Games, the, sacred to Actian Apollo, designated as "Olympian," celebrated in the suburbs of Nicopolis Actia, 3. 305

INDEX OF NAMES, PLACES, AND SUBJECTS

INDEX OF NAMES, PLACES, AND SUBJECTS

after the city Atria (Adria), **2.** 317; temple of Diomedes in very recess of, **2.** 319; visible, according to Polybius, from the Haemus Mountain, **3.** 251; term " Adriatic " originally applied only to inner part of, but now also to whole of, and derived from the name of a river, **3.** 267, 269 (see footnote on " a river ")

Adrumetum (see Adrymes)

Adrymes (Adrumetum), in Carthaginia, where is a naval arsenal, **8.** 191

Adula (Saint-Gothard), Mt., in the Alps, **2.** 227, 273, 313

Adultery; death the penalty for, in Arabia Felix, **7.** 365

Aea, on the Phasis River in Colchis; Jason's expedition to, **1.** 75, 167, 171

Aea, the spring, empties into the Axius River, **3.** 343, 347

Aeacidae, the; the kings of the Molossians belonged to family of, **3.** 297; ancestors of Alexander the Great, **6.** 57

Aeacus, son of Zeus and Aegina, king of Aegina, head of the house of the Aeacidae, and finally one of the judges in Hades, **3.** 297, **4.** 179

" Aeaea," home of Circê, invented by Homer, **1.** 75, 171

Aeaneium, a sacred precinct in Locris named after Aeanes who was slain by Patroclus, **4.** 381

Aeanes, slain involuntarily by Patroclus; a sacred precinct and spring in Locris named after, **4.** 381

Aeanis, a spring in Locris named after Aeanes who was slain by Patroclus, **4.** 381

Aeas River, the, in Greece, flows towards the west into Apollonia, **3.** 79

Aeci, the (see Aequi)

Aedepsus (Lipso), in Euboea; hot springs at, once ceased to flow because of earthquake, **1.** 223; lies opposite Cynus in Locris, and is 160 stadia distant from it, **4.** 379; seized by Ellops, **5.** 7

Aedile, the, at Nemausus, a Roman citizen, **2.** 203

Aedui, the, separated from the Sequani by the Arar River, **2.** 199; geographical position of, **2.** 225, 229

Aeëtes, ruler of Colchis, **1.** 167, 169, 171

Aega, the promontory; used to be the name of the whole of the mountain now called Canê or Canae, **6.** 133

Aegae in Asia, an Aeolian city, **6.** 159

Aegae, one of the twelve cities in which the Achaeans settled, has a temple of Poseidon, but inhabitants of were later transferred to Aegeira, **4.** 219; also called Aega, now uninhabited, and is owned by Aegium, **4.** 223

Aegae (Limni), in Euboea, has the same name as the city in Achaea, **4.** 219; whence, probably, the Aegaean Sea took its name, **4.** 221; on a high mountain, where is the temple of Aegaean Poseidon, lying 120 stadia from Anthedon, **4.** 297

Aegaeae in Cilicia, **6.** 355

Aegaean Sea, the; dimensions of, and islands in, **1.** 477, 481; washes Greece on two sides, **3.** 295, 297, 327, 353, 381; probably took its name from Aegae (Limni) in Euboea, **4.** 221; borders on Crete, **5.** 121; origin of name of, **6.** 133

Aegaleum (Malia), Mt., in Messenia; the Messenian Pylus at foot of, **4.** 109

Aegeira, one of the twelve cities in which the Achaeans settled, **4.** 219

Aegeirussa in Megara, **4.** 255

Aegesta in Sicily (Egesta or Segesta or Aegestaea, now near Calatafimi), founded by Aegestes the Trojan, **3.** 11, 57, 81; the hot springs at, **3.** 91; where Aeneias is said to have landed, **6.** 107; rivers near, named by Aeneias, **6.** 109

Aegestes the Trojan, founded Aegesta in Sicily, **3.** 11, 81

Aegeus, son of King Pandion, received from his father the shore-lands of Attica, **4.** 247, 249

Aegiali (or Aegialeia), earlier name of Sicyon, **4.** 207

Aegialians, the, inhabitants of the Peloponnesian Ionia (Achaea), **4.** 167

Aegialus, a village and shore in Paphlagonia, mentioned by Homer, **5.** 377, 387

Aegialus (or Aegialeia," Shore-land "), the, in the Peloponnesus, the Homeric, **4.** 185; joined the Achaean League, and was once called Ionia, **4.** 207, 209

INDEX OF NAMES, PLACES, AND SUBJECTS

INDEX OF NAMES, PLACES, AND SUBJECTS

INDEX OF NAMES, PLACES, AND SUBJECTS

Homeric " Enianians," **4.** 443, 447; long lived in the Dotian Plain, but were driven out by the Lapiths, **4.** 449; in Asia, **5.** 249, 335

" Aeniates," a Paphlagonian name used in Cappadocia, **5.** 415

Aenius River, the, in the Troad (error for Aesepus?), **6.** 89

Aenus (Nero, or Elatovouno), Mt., in Cephallenia, has a temple of Zeus Aenesius, **5.** 51

Aenus (called " Apsinthus," now Enos), near the Hebrus River and on the Melas Gulf; once called Poltyobria, **3.** 279; founded by Mitylenaeans and Cumaeans, and still earlier by the Alopeconnesians, **3.** 373; so named after the Aenius River and village near Ossa, **3.** 375

Aeolian cities in Asia, the; Aegae one of, **6.** 159

Aeolian colonisations, the, in Asia, preceded the Ionian by four generations, **6.** 7, 199

Aeolian colony, the, led by Penthilus, composed largely of Boeotians, **4.** 287

Aeolian fleet, the, despatched to Asia by the sons of Orestes, **4.** 283

Aeolians, the; migrations of, **1.** 227; use of the name to-day, **4.** 5, 7; took up their abode among the Aetolians, **4.** 367, and destroyed the Epeians under Aetolus, **4.** 367; some of, in the army of Penthilus, settled in Euboea, **5.** 13; destroyed Olenus in Aetolia, and moved Pylenê in Aetolia to higher ground, **5.** 29; compelled to migrate from Thessaly, and settled in Aetolia, **5.** 81, 83; once held the mastery, after the Trojan War, **5.** 463; in Asia, scattered throughout all Trojan country, **6.** 7; cities of, on the Adramyttene Gulf, **6.** 13; the country and cities of, **6.** 23, 97; stretch of coast subject to, in ancient times, **6.** 79; call a certain month " Pornopion " (" Locusts "), **6.** 127; seized the Old Smyrna, **6.** 203

Aeolic dialect, the; the same as the Doric, **4.** 5; spoken by the Eleians, **4.** 9

Aeolis in Asia, a part of the Ois-

Halys country, **1.** 497; Phocaea the end of, **6.** 5; extent of, **6.** 7; by Homer united with Troy into one country, **6.** 23

Aeolus, king of the winds and of the Liparaean Islands; an historical fact, **1.** 73, 85; Islands of, produced by volcanic eruption, **1.** 99, and volcanic disturbances in, **1.** 213; identified with Methonê, **4.** 117; "steward of the winds," and lived on Strongylê (Stromboli), **3.** 19, 99; father of Cercaphus and ancestor of Eurypylus, **4.** 435

Aeolus, the, of Euripides, on the kingdom of Salmoneus in Elis, **4.** 99

Aepeia, " beautiful," the Homeric, **4.** 109; now called Thuria, and situated on a lofty hill, **4.** 115; by some identified with Methonê, **4.** 117

" Aepy (" Steep ") well-built," the Homeric, **4.** 71, 73

Aepytus, son of Neleus, founded Prienê in Asia, **6.** 199

Aequi (Aeci), the, in Latium, **2.** 379; nearest neighbours of the Curites, **2.** 387, 415

Aequum Faliscum (see Faliscum, Aequum)

Aeria (Carpentras), **2.** 197

Aesarus River, the, in Italy, **3.** 41

Aeschines, the Athenian orator, ridiculed by Demosthenes, **5.** 109

Aeschines the orator, native of Miletus, contemporary of Strabo, remained in exile to the end because of his unrestrained speech, **6.** 207

Aeschylus the tragic poet; his *Prometheus Unbound* quoted on the Aethiopians, **1.** 123; his mythical epithets of men, **1.** 157; *Prometheus Unbound* of, quoted, **2.** 187; on the origin of the Pelasgi, **2.** 345; on the origin of the name of Rhegium, **3.** 25; speaks of " dog-headed " and other fabulous peoples, **3.** 191; on the " law-abiding " Scythians, **3.** 199; uses the poetic figure of " part with the whole," **4.** 37; on " Sacred Bura and thunder-smitten Rhypes " in Achaea, **4.** 225; on the geographical position of Aegina, **4.** 251; in his *Glaucus Pontius*, mentions Euboïs in Euboea, **5.** 15;

INDEX OF NAMES, PLACES, AND SUBJECTS

mentions the worship of Cotys among the Edonians, **5.** 105, and describes the worship of Dionysus, **5.** 107; in his *Niobê*, confounds things that are different, Mt. Sipylus with Mt. Ida, and places Adrasteia in Phrygia, **5.** 519; in his *Myrmidons*, on the Caïcus and Mysius Rivers, **6.** 139; in his *Persae* refers to Cissia, the mother of Memnon, **7.** 159

Aesepus River, the, in Asia, **5.** 413, 459, 461; borders on the Doliones, **5.** 499, 503; borders on the Troad, **6.** 3, 5, 9, 19, 23, 25, 27, 91; rises in a hill of Mt. Ida, **6.** 85; the Caresus empties into, **6.** 89; Palae-scepsis 30 stadia from, **6.** 91

Aesernia (Isernia) in Samnium, destroyed in the Marsic War, **2.** 415, 463

Aesis (Esino) River, the, once a boundary between Cisalpine Celtica and Italy, **2.** 331, 371; distance to, from Garganum, **3.** 133

Aesium, in Italy; geographical position of, **2.** 373

Aesyetes, tomb of, mentioned by Homer, **6.** 67, 75

Aethalia (Elba), isle between Italy and Corsica, **1.** 473; visible from Volaterrae, and contains iron-mines, **2.** 355; Portus Argoüs in, **2.** 357

Aethalöeis, the, a torrent in the territory of Scepsis, **5.** 115

Aethices, the, an Epeirote tribe; geographical position of Aethicia, the country of, **3.** 311; annexed to Thessaly, once lived on Mt. Pindus, are now extinct, **4.** 417

Aethicia (see Aethices, the)

Aethiopia, mentioned by Homer, **1.** 5; subject to inundations, **1.** 119; meaning of the term, **1.** 123; Ephorus on, **1.** 125; a desert country, **1.** 501; waters the land of Aegypt, **2.** 189; in many respects like India, **7.** 41; under guard of three Roman cohorts, **8.** 49; ex-tremities of, now reached by large fleets, **8.** 53; boundaries of, un-known, **8.** 209

Aethiopian merchandise, brought to Coptus, **8.** 119

Aethiopian women, some, arm for

battle, and wear copper ring through lip, **8.** 145

Aethiopians, the; position of, **1.** 9; "sundered in twain" by the Arabian Gulf, **1.** 111, 119, 129; by the Nile, **1.** 117; more parched than the Indians and divided into two groups, **1.** 395; the western, position of, **1.** 461; Homer quoted on, **3.** 191, **5.** 423; mentioned by Hesiod, **3.** 197; compared with the Indians, **7.** 21; explanation of black complexion and woolly hair of, **7.** 39; first subdued by Sesostris the Aegyptian, **7.** 313; weapons used by, **7.** 339; Homer on, **7.** 369; held as subjects the Megabari and the Blemmyes, **8.** 7; modes of life of, **8.** 9; do not use the Red Sea, **8.** 21; now disposed to peace, **8.** 135; once captured Syenê, Elephantinê, and Philae, and pulled down the statues of Caesar, but were repulsed and subdued by Petronius, **8.** 137; their weapons of war, **8.** 139; pardoned by Augustus for their attacks, **8.** 141; life, food, and worship of, **8.** 143; weapons and dress of, **8.** 145; religion, atheism, and customs among, **8.** 147

"Aethiopic" Zone, the, of Posei-donius, **1.** 371

Aetna, Mt., the region of, inhabited by Cyclopes, **1.** 73; the eruptions of, make the land suited to the vine, **2.** 453; Typhon lies beneath, **2.** 457; eruptions of, **3.** 25; the rivers flowing from, have good harbours at mouths, **3.** 63; ash-dust from, has a quality suited to the vine, **3.** 71; regions round, overrun by Eunus, **3.** 85; description of eruptions of, **3.** 87-91; holds in fetters the giant Typhon, **6.** 177

Aetna, the new name given to Catana (*q.v.*) by Hiero, **3.** 67; but later given to city at foot of Mt. Aetna (now Santa Maria di Licodia), **3.** 69, 87

Aetolia, promontories of, formerly islands, **1.** 221; acquired by Dio-medes, **3.** 305; Mt. Corax (Var-dusia) in, **3.** 327; bounded by the Acheloüs River, **4.** 17; named after Aetolus, **4.** 103; deserted lands of,

well adapted to horse-raising, **4.**
229; borders on Thessaly, **4.** 395;
description of, **5.** 23–31; divided
into two parts, the "Old" and
"Epictetus," **5.** 27; various places
in, **5.** 63; "Epictetus" assigned to
Calydon, **5.** 65; settled by the
Curetes, **5.** 85; now included within
a Roman Province, **8.** 215

Aetolian Catalogue, the, in Homer, **4.**
385

Aetolians, the, colonised Temesa in
Bruttium, **3.** 17; a Greek people,
4. 5; under Oxylus returned with
the Heracleidae, **4.** 91; drove the
Epeians out of Elis, **4.** 103; the
country of, never ravaged, according
to Ephorus, **4.** 367; were awarded
Naupactus in Western Locris by
Philip, **4.** 385; once powerful, **4.** 389;
by Homer always spoken of under
one name, **4.** 393; the Curetes belonged to, **4.** 395; helped the
Romans to conquer the Macedonians at Cynoscephalae in Thessaly,
4. 445; dispute of, with the Acarnanians, **5.** 57; tribe of, now reduced
to impotence, **5.** 65; powerful for a
time, **5.** 67; were never subject to
any other people, according to
Ephorus, **5.** 75, 79; with Aetolus,
founded the earliest cities in Aetolia,
5. 77; akin to the Eleians, **5.** 79

Aetolians, The Polity of the, by
Aristotle, **3.** 289

Aetolus, son of Endymion, from Elis;
Ephorus' account of, **4.** 101, 103;
with the Epeians took up abode in
Aetolia but were destroyed by the
Aeolians, **4.** 369; drove the Curetes
out of Aetolia and founded earliest
cities there, and statue of, at Therma
in Aetolia, **5.** 77, 79, 83

Aexoneis, the Attic deme, **4.** 271

Aexonici, the Attic deme, **4.** 271

Afranius, one of Pompey's generals;
defeated at Ilerda in Iberia by
Julius Caesar, **2.** 99

Afsia (see Ophiussa)

Agaeus, colonised the region about
Actê in Argolis after the return of the
Heracleidae, **4.** 235

Agamedes and Trophonius, built the
second temple at Delphi, **4.** 361

Agamemnon, from ignorance of geo-

graphy blundered in attacking
Mysia, **1.** 35; breastplate of, **1.** 145;
summoned Diomedes and Alcmaeon
to the Trojan War, **3.** 305; promised
to Achilles seven cities on the
Messenian and Asinaean Gulfs, **4.**
109, one of these being Pedasus
(Methonê, now Modon), **4.** 111; the
dominions of, **4.** 167; the men of,
sent to collect sailors, cursed
Methonê, **4.** 177; "found Menestheus standing still," **4.** 255;
received an oracle at Delphi, **4.** 347,
349; won over Diomedes, but not
Alcmaeon, to join the Trojan
expedition, **5.** 71; wished to remain
behind at Troy, according to
Athenê, **5.** 105; Cleues and Malaüs,
descendants of, founded Phry-
conian Cymê in Asia, **6.** 7; led 1000
ships against Troy, according to
Fimbria the Roman quaestor, **6.**
55; laid a curse on Ilium, **6.** 83;
Chryseïs presented to, **6.** 121; said
to have built a temple near Ephesus,
6. 233

Agapenor, founded Paphus in Cypros,
6. 381

Agatharcides, Peripatetic philosopher
and historian, native of Cnidus, **6.**
283; fellow-citizen of Ctesias, on the
origin of the name of the Erythraean ("Red") Sea, **7.** 351

Agathê, on the Arauris River, founded
by the Massaliotes, **2.** 183

Agathocles, son of Lysimachus, slain
by his father, **6.** 165

Agathocles, one of the successors of
Alexander and father of Lysimachus, **6.** 163

Agathocles (tyrant of the Siciliotes
at Syracuse, b. about 361 B.C.—d.
289 B.C.), conquered Hipponium in
Bruttium and built naval station
there, **3.** 19; served as general of the
Tarantini (about 300 B.C.), **3.** 115

Agathyrnum (Capo d'Orlando), in Sicily,
30 Roman miles from Tyndaris, **3.**
57

Agdistis, Mother (see Rhea); the
famous temple of, in Pessinus in
Galatia, **5.** 471

Agesilaüs, Lacedaemonian king,
father of the Archidamus who served
as commander for Tarentum, **3.** 115

INDEX OF NAMES, PLACES, AND SUBJECTS

INDEX OF NAMES, PLACES, AND SUBJECTS

Deuriopes on the Erigon River, 3. 311

Alalcomenian Athenê, the, mentioned by Homer, 4. 331

Alalcomenium (see Alalcomenae) in Boeotia, 30 stadia from Ocaleê and 60 from Haliartus, 4. 321

Alatri (see Aletrium)

Alazia, a city near the Odrysses River, 5. 407, now deserted, 5. 409

" Alazones," an emendation to, in the Homeric text, 5. 405; the Odrysses River flows through country of, 5. 409

Alazonia, near Scepsis in Asia, 5. 411

Alba Fucens, on the Valerian Way, 2. 403, 415; near the Marsi, 2. 423; used by the Romans as a prison, 2. 425

Alba Longa, on Mt. Albanus (Monte Cavo), founded by Ascanius, 2. 379; rule of, extended to the Tiber, 2. 381; lived in harmony with the Romans, but was later destroyed, except the temple, and its inhabitants were adjudged Roman citizens, 2. 387, 389

Alban wine, the, 2. 399

Albania in Asia, invaded by Pompey, 5. 187; bounded on the north by the Caucasus, 5. 207, 209; has fertile territory, 5. 217; the pass from, into Iberia, 5. 221; northern side of, protected by the Caucasian Mountains, and bounded on the south by Armenia, 5. 223; produces remarkable crops, 5. 225; extent of coast of, 5. 245; has a temple of Selenê, 5. 431

Albanians, the Asiatic, are excellent subjects, but from neglect by the Romans sometimes attempt revolutions, 3. 145; more inclined to the shepherd's life than the Iberians, 5. 223; neglect the soil but have remarkable crops, 5. 225; detailed description of, 5. 227–231; sent forth an army of 88,000 against Pompey, 5. 227; the king, priest, and worship of, 5. 229; extremely respectful to old age, 5. 231; geographical position of, 5. 269; take pride in their cavalry, 5. 331

Albanus, Lacus Laco di Albano), 2. 423

Albanus, Mt. (Monte Cavo), 2. 379, 411, 421, 423

Albian Mountain (Mt. Velika), the, in the land of the Iapodes in Italy; a part of the Alps, 2. 264, 3. 255, 259

Albienses, the, occupy the northerly parts of the Alps, 2. 269

Albingaunum (Albenga) in Italy; inhabitants of, called Ligures Ingauni, 2. 263

Albioeci, the, occupy the northerly parts of the Alps, 2. 269

Albis (Elbe) River, the, revealed to geographers by the Romans, 1. 51; the, in Germany, flows nearly parallel to the Rhenus, 3. 155; parts beyond wholly unknown, 3. 171

Albula Waters (La Solfatara), the, 2. 417

Alcacer-do-Sal in Iberia (see Salacia)

Alcaeus, the poet; wrongly refers to the Cuarius River as the " Coralius," 4. 323, 329; threw away his arms in battle, 6. 77, but later slew Phrynon the Athenian general, 6. 77; calls Antandrus a city of the Leleges, 6. 101; native of Mitylenê, 6. 141; author of Stasiotic poems, 6. 143; interpreted by Callias, 6. 147; on the " Carian crest," 6. 301

Alcestis, " fair among women," 1. 165

Alchaedamus, king of the Rhambaean nomads, an ally of the Syrian Bassus, 7. 253

Alcmaeon, son of Amphiaraüs, founded Argos Amphilochum on the Ambracian Gulf, 3. 305; with Diomedes destroyed the Aeolians, 4. 369; refused to join the Trojan expedition, 5. 71; according to Ephorus, king of Acarnania before the Trojan War, 5. 73

Alcmaeonis, the; an epic poem on the deeds of Alcmaeon, authorship unknown, 5. 35

Alcman of Sardis (fl. about 625 B.C.), deals in fables, 1. 157; founder of Dorian lyric poetry, used the poetic figure of " part with the whole," 4. 37; on the Carystian wine, 5. 11; on the Erysichaeans in Acarnania, 5. 65; on the " Andreia " at Sparta,

INDEX OF NAMES, PLACES, AND SUBJECTS

INDEX OF NAMES, PLACES, AND SUBJECTS

at, **8.** 27, 39; advantages of site of, **8.** 29–31, 53–55; shape, and dimensions, and buildings, of, **8.** 33–35; Alexander buried at, **8.** 35; Antony slew himself at, **8.** 39, 43; the streets of, **8.** 41; the several successors of Alexander at, **8.** 43–47; Pompey slain near, **8.** 47; present and past governments at, **8.** 49–53; diversions of people at, **8.** 65; full of the bird called " ibis," **8.** 151; about 10,000 stadia from Meroë and 13,000 from the torrid zone, **8.** 157; parallel of latitude of, as compared with the Great Syrtis, **8.** 199

Alexandrians, the; one tribe of, were Greeks in origin, **8.** 51

Alexandrium, a stronghold in Syria, destroyed by Pompey, **7.** 291

Alexarchus, son of Antipater, founded Uranopolis on isthmus of Athos, **3.** 357

Alicudi (see Ericussa)

Alinda in Caria, where Queen Ada resided, **6.** 285

Aliveri (see Tamynae)

Alizonium in the Troad, a place fabricated by Demetrius, **6.** 89

Alizonius River, the, in Asia, empties into the Cyrus River, **5.** 219, 229

Allifae (Alife), in Samnium, **2.** 415

Allitrochades, son of Androcottus, king of Palimbothra in India, **1.** 265

Allobroges, the, formerly a militant people, **2.** 199; geographical position of, **2.** 231; subject to the praetors sent to Narbonitis, **2.** 271

Allotrigans, the; a tribe in Iberia of no importance, **2.** 77

Alluvium, the, of the Nile, **1.** 131

Almonds, the, in Media, **5.** 317

"Alobê," the Homeric "Alybê" emended to, by some, **5.** 405, 407

"Alopê," the Homeric "Alybê" emended to, by some, **5.** 405, 407, **6.** 91

Alopê (near Melidoni) in Epicnemidian Locris, **4.** 381

Alopê, in the country of the Opuntian Locrians, damaged by earthquake, **1.** 225

Alopê in Ozolian Locris, **4.** 387

Alopê in Phthiotis, Thessaly, **4.** 387;

subject to Achilles, **4.** 401; historians in doubt about, **4.** 409

Alopecia, an island in Lake Maeotis, **5.** 195

Alopeconnesians, the; earlier founders of Aenus on the Melas Gulf, **3.** 373

Alopeconnesus, on the Melas Gulf, **3.** 373

Alorium in Laconia, where is the temple of the Heleian Artemis, **4.** 75

Alorus, in Macedonia, **3.** 339; a Bottiaean city, and identified (?) with Thessaloniceia, **3.** 341, 345

Alphabet, the, of the Turditanians, **2.** 13

Alpheius (Ruphia) River, the, "floweth in wide stream through the land of the Pylians," **4.** 21, 31, 87; the course of, **4.** 47, 49; so named, it is said, because its waters cure leprosy, **4.** 61; flows past Thryum, **4.** 71, and past Olympia, **4.** 87; receives the Enipeus, **4.** 99, and the Erymanthus, **4.** 101; marvellous circumstance pertaining to, **3.** 75, 93, **4.** 231; once inundated the land round the temple at Olympia, **4.** 233

Alponus, tower at, collapsed because of earthquake, **1.** 225

Alps, the, form a boundary of Celtica, **1.** 491; the source of various rivers, **2.** 223; general description of country and peoples of, **2.** 263–295; begin at Vada Sabata (now Vado), **2.** 263, 329, 427; stretch as far as the Albian Mountain (Mt. Velika), **2.** 265; the source of the Rhodanus and the Rhenus, **2.** 273, 283, 289; size and height of, **2.** 293, 299; description of base of, **2.** 303; begin at Ocelum, **2.** 329

Alps, the Julian (see Ocra, Mt.)

Alsium (Palo), a small town between Cossa and Ostia, **2.** 363

"Alsos," the Greek word, means a "sacred grove," but is used by the poets of any "sacred precinct," even if bare of trees, **4.** 329

Altes, the Homeric; "lord of the Leleges" in the Troad, **6.** 17, 151; Pedasus subject to, **6.** 99

Althaemenes the Argive, with Dorians founded ten cities in Crete, **5.** 143,

chariot (" harma ") near where his present temple is, the chariot itself being drawn empty to Harma, 4. 295; father of Alcmaeon, 5. 71; father of Amphilochus, 6. 233; Greek prophet and ruler, 7. 289

Amphictyonic Council, the, used to convene at Onchestus, 4. 329

Amphictyonic League, a kind of, connected with the temple of Poseidon on Calauria, 4. 173, 175

Amphictyonic League, the, was organised by the peoples who lived near Delphi, convened twice a year at Pylae (Thermopylae), and was first administered by Acrisius, 4. 357

Amphictyonic Rights, the, first proclaimed by Acrisius, 4. 357

Amphictyons, the, forbade the levying of taxes on those who visited the temple at Delphi, but for a time were successfully resisted by the Crisaeans and the Amphissians, 4. 353; built the present temple at Delphi, 4. 361; instituted equestrian and gymnastic contests with a crown as prize, 4. 361; rased Amphissa to the ground, 4. 385; performed sacrifices twice a year at Thermopylae, 4. 393

Amphidolia; the Margalae in, 4. 71

Amphidolis in Elis, where the people hold a monthly market, 4. 41

Amphigeneia, the Homeric, subject to Nestor, 4. 71; near the Hypsöeis River, where is the temple of Leto, 4. 73

Amphilochi, an ancient city in Iberia named after the Greek hero Amphilochus, 2. 83

Amphilochians, the, a barbarian tribe, now hold part of the country above Acarnania and Aetolia, 3. 289; at Argos Amphilochicum on the Ambracian Gulf, are Epeirotes, 3. 307; border on Thessaly, 4. 395; situated north of the Acarnanians, 5. 25

Amphilochus, son of Ampiaraüs and brother of Alcmaeon, died at Amphilochi in Iberia, 2. 83; gave the name Inachus to a river in the land of the Amphilochians, 3. 79; Amphilochian Argos named after, 5. 73; accompanied Calchas to the temple of Apollo Clarius in Asia, 6.

233; led from Troy the ancestors of the present Pamphylians, 6. 325; with Mopsus, founded Mallus in Cilicia, and died in duel with Mopsus there, 6. 353; other accounts of death of, 6. 355

Amphimalla in Crete, 5. 123

Amphinomus, and his brother Anapias, who saved their parents from doom at Aetna, 3. 69

Amphinomus, in the *Odyssey*, refers to the "tomouroi of great Zeus" at Dodona, 3. 315

Amphion, the husband of Niobê, 4. 113; with his brother Zethus said to have lived at Eutresis before reigning at Thebes, 4. 323

Amphipolis (Ennea Hodoi, now Neochori), on the Strymon River, founded by the Athenians, 3. 359; by Paulus made one of the four capitals of Macedonia, 3. 369

Amphiscian circles, the, 1. 367, 369

Amphiscians, the, 1. 509; term defined, 1. 517

Amphissa (Salona) in Western Locris, not mentioned by Homer, lies in the Crisaean Plain, and was destroyed by the Amphictyons, 4. 385

Amphissians, the, from Ozalian Locris, restored Crisa, dealt harshly with foreigners, and cultivated the holy Crisaean Plain, but were punished by the Amphictyons, 4. 353

Amphistratus, charioteer of the Dioscuri, 5. 203

Amphitryon, expedition of, to Cephallenia with Cephalus, 5. 47, 57; established Cephalus as master of the islands about Taphos, 5. 67

Amphius, son of Merops and Trojan leader, 6. 25

Amphrysus River, the, in Thessaly, flows close to walls of Halus, 4. 409, through the Crocian Plain, 4. 421

Amulius (see Amollius)

Amyclae (Tchaouchi), where is the temple of Apollo, 4. 125; given to Philonomus by the Heracleidae, 4. 133

Amyclaeum, the, of Apollo, at Amyclae in Laconia, 3. 109

Amycteres, the, a people in India, 7. 97

Amymonê, mother of the mythical Nauplius, 4. 153

INDEX OF NAMES, PLACES, AND SUBJECTS

236

INDEX OF NAMES, PLACES, AND SUBJECTS

INDEX OF NAMES, PLACES, AND SUBJECTS

463; founded Antigonia in the Troad, **6.** 53; transferred the Cebrenians and Scepsians to Antigonia (now called Alexandreia), 6. 65, 105; reassembled the Smyrnaeans in New Smyrna, **6.** 245; Eumenes revolted from, **6.** 343

Antilibanus, Mt., in Syria, **7.** 213; with Mt. Libanus forms Coelê-Syria, **7.** 261, 265

Antilochus, monument of, near Sigeium in the Troad, **6.** 61

Antimachus of Colophon (fl. about 425 B.C.), author of an epic poem entitled *Thebaïs* and an elegiac poem entitled *Lydê,* on the Epeians and Cauconians, **4.** 55; *apocope* in, **4.** 131; calls Dyme "Cauconian," **4.** 225; spells Thespiae "Thespeia," **4.** 315; on the goddess Nemesis, **6.** 31

Antimenidas, brother of Alcaeus, native of Mitylenê, fought on the side of the Babylonians, and slew a giant, **6.** 141

Antimnestus, founder of Rhegium in Italy, **3.** 21

Antiocheia on the Maeander, description of, **6.** 189; the road through, **6.** 309

Antiocheia in Margiana, founded by Antiochus Soter, **5.** 279

Antiocheia, the Mygdonian (see Nisibis)

Antiocheia, the, near Pisidia; temple of Mên Ascaeus near, **5.** 431; temple of Mên in territory of, **5.** 433; once held by Amyntas, **5.** 477; lies to the south of Phrygia Paroreia, on a hill, set free by the Romans, has a Roman colony, and once had a priesthood of Mên Arcaeus (Ascaeus?), **5.** 507

Antiocheia in Syria, **7.** 241; metropolis of Syria, and a great city, **7.** 243; inland voyages to, on the Orontes, **7.** 245; the plain of, **7.** 247

Antiocheians, the, in Syria worship Triptolemus as a hero, **7.** 243; hold a general festival at the temple of Apollo and Artemis at Daphnê, 7. 245

Antiochian War, the, in Asia, **6.** 317

Antiochis, daughter of Achaeus and mother of Attalus I., **6.** 165

Antiochus Epiphanes (reigned 175–164 B.C.), dedicated the Olympium

at Athens, **4.** 265 (see footnote 1); father of the Alexander (Balas) who was defeated by Demetrius Nicator, **6.** 169; founded one of the cities of the Antiocheian Tetrapolis, **7.** 243

Antiochus the Great (king of Syria 223–187 B.C.), conquered by the Romans, **3.** 143, **5.** 325, 337, **6.** 53; fought by Eumenes, **6.** 167; attempted to rob the temple of Belus among the Elymaeans, but was slain in the attempt, **7.** 223; fought Ptolemy IV at Rhaphia, **7.** 279

Antiochus Hierax, had a quarrel with his brother Seleucus Callinicus, **7.** 259

Antiochus the philosopher, native of Ascalon in Phoenicia, **7.** 277

Antiochus the Macedonian (b. about 358 B.C.), father of Seleucus Nicator; Antiocheia named after, **7.** 241

Antiochus Sidetes (reigned in Syria, 137–128 B.C.), son of Demetrius Soter, forced Diodotus Tryphon to kill himself, **6.** 327

Antiochus Soter (king of Syria 280–261 B.C.), founded Antiocheia in Margiana, **5.** 279; made the inhabitants of Celaenae move to Apameia, **5.** 509; conquered by Eumenes II near Sardeis, **6.** 165

Antiochus of Syracuse (fl. about 420 B.C.), author of a *History of Sicily* and *The Colonising of Italy,* of which only fragments are extant; on the Opici and Ausones, **2.** 435; on the founding of Elea in Italy by the Phocaeans, **3.** 5; on the country of the Brettii in Italy, **3.** 11; on the Napetine (Hipponiate) Gulf, **3.** 13; on the founding of Rhegium, **3.** 21; says the Siceli and Morgetes inhabited southern Italy in earlier times, **3.** 23; on the founding of Croton, **3.** 43; on Siris and Heracleia in Italy, **3.** 51; on Metapontium, **3.** 51, "first called Metabum," **3.** 53; on the founding of Taras (Tarentum), **3.** 107

Antiopê, the daughter of Nycteus, who founded Hysiae, **4.** 297

Antiparos (see Oliaros)

Antipater Derbetes, the pirate, once possessed Derbê, **5.** 349; slain by

INDEX OF NAMES, PLACES, AND SUBJECTS

INDEX OF NAMES, PLACES, AND SUBJECTS

INDEX OF NAMES, PLACES, AND SUBJECTS

INDEX OF NAMES, PLACES, AND SUBJECTS

Homer and Hesiod, **4**. 157; says there is no " Nisa" in Boeotia, **4**. 299; on "Samos" and "Samê" in Homer, **5**. 39; on the island Asteria (Homeric Asteris), **5**. 51; on certain places in Aetolia, **5**. 63; on the Erysichaeans in Acarnania, **5**. 65; on the Hyantes in Aetolia, **5**. 81; entitled to call Polybius to account, **5**. 83; his *Marshalling of the Trojan Forces* reviewed by Strabo, **5**. 413–423; on the Greek use of the term " barbarian," **6**. 303; says Homer enumerates all Trojan allies from Asia as from peninsula outside isthmus between Sinopê and Issus, **6**. 357; his work on Chorography, *A Description of the Earth*, **6**. 359; on the Galatians, **6**. 361; identifies things that are not alike, **6**. 371, 373

Apollodorus the Pergamenian, author of a work on *Rhetoric* and leader of the Apollodoreian sect, **6**. 171

Apollonia in Cyrenaea, a naval station, **8**. 201; now a dependency of Cyrenê, **8**. 203

Apollonia in Illyria, longest day at, has 15 equinoctial hours, **1**. 513; on the Aoüs River; an exceedingly well-governed city, founded by the Corcyraeans and Corinthians, and 10 stadia from the river and 60 from the sea, **3**. 265; 535 Roman miles, by the Egnatian Way, to Cypsela, **3**. 293; 7320 stadia from Byzantium, or, according to Polybius, 7500 stadia, **3**. 379; whither went many of the inhabitants of Dyspontium in Elis, **4**. 101; fountains of asphalt at, **7**. 295

Apollonia, site of, apparently, near Lake Bolbê in Crusis; destroyed by Cassander, and its inhabitants transferred to Thessaloniceia, **3**. 343

Apollonia, to the east of Pergamum on an elevated site, **6**. 171

Apollonia on Rhyndacus, near Lake Apolloniatis in Asia, **5**. 501

Apollonia, between the mouths of the Strymon and Nestus Rivers, **3**. 355; destroyed by Philip, **3**. 359

Apollonia in Syria, near Apameia, **7**. 253

Apollonia Pontica (Sizeboli), in Thrace,

founded by the Milesians, a greater part of which was founded on a certain isle, whereon was the colossal statue (work of Calamis) which was carried off to the Capitolium at Rome by Lucullus, **3**. 277; the coast at, called Thyniae, **5**. 375

Apollonias, near Apameia Cibotus, **5**. 477, 505

Apolloniatis (by the ancients called Sitacenê), in Assyria, or Babylonia, **5**. 309, **7**. 193

Apolloniatis, Lake, in Asia, **5**. 501

Apollonides (according to Apollonius Rhodius wrote a *Periplus of Europe*), says Scilurus the king of the Cimmerian Bosporus had 80 sons, **3**. 235; on the large army of Atropatian Media, **5**. 303; on certain insects in the snow on the Caucasian Mountains, **5**. 323

Apollonis of Cyzicus, mother of Eumenes II, **6**. 167

Apollonis, a city 300 stadia from both Sardeis and Pergamum; named after the wife of Attalus I, **6**. 171; seized by Aristonicus, **6**. 247

Apollonium, Cape, near Itycê (Utica) in Libya, **8**. 183

Apollonius Cronus, the Cyrenaean, teacher of Diodorus the dialectician; nickname of, transferred to his pupil, **6**. 291; teacher and philosopher, native of Cyrenê, **8**. 205

Apollonius Malacus of Alabanda, taught rhetoric at Rhodes (about 120 B.C.), **6**. 281; ridicules his native city, **6**. 299

Apollonius Molon of Alabanda (rhetorician, orator, ambassador to Rome, 81 B.C., and teacher of Cicero and Julius Caesar); speech of, at Rome, entitled *Against the Caunians*, **6**. 267; taught rhetoric in Rhodes, **6**. 281, 299

Apollonius, the epic poet, who wrote the *Argonauts*; though an Alexandrian, was called a Rhodian, **6**. 281

Apollonius the physician, born at Citium in Cypros, **6**. 379

Apollonius "Mys" (" Mouse"), the physician, fellow pupil of Heracleides the Herophileian physician and native of Erythrae in Asia, **6**. 243

Apollonius the Stoic philosopher, best

INDEX OF NAMES, PLACES, AND SUBJECTS

recesses, **7.** 277, 309; separates the Arabians from the Troglodytes, **7.** 355; borders on Arabia, **8.** 3; now navigated by large fleets, **8.** 53

Arabian merchandise, brought to the emporium Coptus, **8.** 119

Arabian "Scenitae" ("Tent-dwellers"), the, now called "Malians" by some writers; country of, borders on Mesopotamia, **7.** 203; occupy certain parts of Mesopotamia, **7.** 233; moderate in exaction of tribute, **7.** 235; border on Syria, **7.** 239; keep herds of all kinds, especially camels, **7.** 301

Arabian tribes, the, in Judaea, **7.** 281

Arabians, the; well-to-do and even rich, **1.** 145; much like the Armenians and Syrians, **1.** 153; unknown to Homer, **3.** 191; some of, who crossed over with Cadmus, settled in Euboea, **5.** 13; the Mesenian, country of, borders on Babylonia, **7.** 203; would not send ambassadors to Alexander, **7.** 211; in part give ear to the Romans and in part to the Parthians, **7.** 235, 237; less civilised than the Syrians, **7.** 255; those in Syria, **7.** 263, 265; desert of, **7.** 307; discussed at length by Artemidorus, **7.** 341; separated from the Troglodytes by the Arabian Gulf, **7.** 355; not very good warriors on land or sea, **7.** 355; by some identified with the Homeric Erembians, **7.** 371

Arachosia, a part of Ariana, **5.** 277, 279

Arachoti, the, in Asia; geographical position of, **5.** 269, 271, **7.** 141; road through country of, **7.** 143, 145

Arachthus River (see Aratthus)

Aracynthus (Zygos), Mt., in Aetolia, **5.** 27

Aradians, the; seaboard of, in Phoenicia, **7.** 255; history of, **7.** 257, 371; navigate the Jordan and Lycus Rivers, **7.** 261

Aradus, an island in the Persian Gulf, said to have been colonised by the Phoenician Aradus, **7.** 303

Aradus (Ruad), the island, off Phoenicia, **7.** 255; description and history of, **7.** 257, 259

Araethyraea (the Homeric Araethyreê,

q.v.), the country now called Phliasia, **4.** 205

Araethyreê (see Araethyraea), the Homeric, **4.** 185

Aragus River, the, empties into the Cyrus, **5.** 217

"Arambians" (see Erembians), name of one of the three Arabian tribes, **7.** 371

"Aramaeans," name of one of the three Arabian tribes, **7.** 371; applies to Syrians, **7.** 373

Arammaeans, the; racial likeness of to other peoples, **1.** 153

Arar (Saône) River, the, rises in the Alps and joins the Rhodanus at Lugdunum, **2.** 199, 223; navigable, **2.** 211; claimed as private property by both the Sequani and the Aedui, **2.** 225

Ararenê in Arabia, a desert country and ruled by King Sabos, **7.** 361

Aratthus (or Arachthus, now Arta) River, the, rises in Mt. Tymphê and flows past Ambracia, **3.** 303; empties into the Ambracian Gulf, **3.** 309, 311

Aratus, most illustrious tyrant of Sicyon and general of the Achaean League, **4.** 207; set free the Peloponnesus from tyrants and brought the League to the height of its power, **4.** 217

Aratus of Soli in Cilicia (b. about 315 B.C.), the astronomical poet, author of the *Phaenomena*, **6.** 341, of whose works there remain only two short poems and some recently discovered fragments; on the constellations, **1.** 11; on where "the extremities of east and west join each other," **1.** 397; apocopê in, **4.** 131; on the goat that nursed Zeus, **4.** 223; wrongly says that Mt. Dictê is near Mt. Ida in Crete, **5.** 139; calls Pholegandros "Iron" Island, because of its ruggedness, **5.** 161; in his *Catalepton* mentions the poverty of the isle Gyaros, **5.** 167

Arauris (Hérault) River, the, rises in the Cemmenus Mountain, **2.** 183

Arausio (Orange), **2.** 197

Araxenê in Armenia; bees and honey in, **1.** 273; has an abundance of honey, **5.** 251

INDEX OF NAMES, PLACES, AND SUBJECTS

Araxene Plain, the, in Armenia, very fertile, **5.** 321

Araxes River, the, the mouth of, near that of the Cyrus, **5.** 225, 265; course of, **5.** 187, 305, 321, 327; origin of name of, and description of, **5.** 335

Araxes River, the, in Persis, **7.** 165

Araxus (Kalogria), Cape, opposite Acarnania, **4.** 15, 17; distant 1030 stadia from the isthmus of Corinth, **4.** 19; the beginning of the sea-board of Elis, **4.** 25; 1030 stadia from the isthmus of Corinth, **4.** 227

Arbaces, the empire of, **7.** 195

Arbela, the Babylonian city, **7.** 195; the battle near, **7.** 197; the victory of Alexander at, foretold by oracle, **8.** 117

Arbelus, the son of Athmoneus and founder of Arbela in Assyria, **7.** 197

Arbies, the, a tribe in Ariana, **7.** 129

Arbis River, the, in Ariana, **7.** 129

Arbo, one of the Liburnides, **3.** 259

Arcadia, the home of Pelasgus, father of the Pelasgi, **2.** 345; lies in the interior of the Peloponnesus, **4.** 15; well-known cities in, **4.** 21; description and history of, **4.** 227–233

Arcadian breed of horses, the, are most excellent, **4.** 229

Arcadian colony, Rome an, **2.** 385

Arcadian tribes, the, **4.** 227

Arcadians, the, thought to have been admitted as colonists in the land of the Peucetii, **3.** 127; wholly mountaineers, **4.** 7; by some thought to be one of the three tribes in Triphylia, **4.** 23; fought the Pylians, **4.** 67; held the priesthood of the Heleian Artemis at Helus in Laconia, **4.** 75; sided with the Messenians in the Messenian War, **4.** 95, 121; called Berethra (" Pits ") " Zerethra," **4.** 231

Arcesilaüs of Pitanê in Aeolis (b. about 316 B.C.), founder of the Middle Academy of Philosophy; eminent at Athens, **1.** 53; fellow-student of Zeno under Polemon, **6.** 131

Arceuthus River, the, in Syria, **7.** 247

Archedemus the Stoic philosopher, native of Tarsus, **6.** 347

Archelaüs, grandson of Orestes, first

to lead the Aeolians across to Asia, **6.** 7

Archelaüs I, father of the Archelaüs who was priest at Comana; honoured by Sulla and the Roman Senate, **5.** 437; father of the Archelaüs who married Berenicê, carried on war with Sulla (86 B.C.) and was later honoured by the Romans, **8.** 45

Archelaüs II, son of the Archelaüs who was honoured by the Roman Senate, appointed priest at Comana, **5.** 435; reigned over Aegypt six months but was slain in battle, **5.** 437; pretended son of Mithridates and priest of Comana in Pontus, married Queen Berenicê, **8.** 45; slain by Ptolemy Auletes, **8.** 47

Archelaüs, last king of Greater Cappadocia, given kingdom and other territory by Antony (36 B.C.), **5.** 345, 349, 371; spent most of his time in Cilicia Tracheia, **5.** 361; the miners of, near Galatia, **5.** 369; married Queen Pythodoris, and appointed king of Lesser Armenia, **5.** 427; resided on the isle Elaeussa, **6.** 337; received Cilicia Tracheia from the Romans, **6.** 339

Archelaüs the natural philosopher, disciple of Anaxagoras, **6.** 245

Archelaüs, the, of Euripides, quoted on the Pelasgians, **2.** 345

Archemachus, the Euboean (fl. not later than the third century B.C.), wrote works (now lost) on the *History of Euboea* and *Metonymies* (*Changes in Names*); says the Curetes settled at Chalcis, but later migrated to Aetolia, **5.** 85

Archianax of Mitylenê, built a wall round Sigeium with stones taken from ancient Ilium, **6.** 75

Archias of Corinth, helped Myscellus to found Croton, **3.** 43; founded Syracuse, **3.** 71, 4. 199; landed at Zephyrium on way to Syracuse, **3.** 73

Archias of Thurii, the commander sent by the Macedonian Antipater to arrest Demosthenes on the island Calauria, **4.** 175

Archidamus III, king of Sparta, born about 400 B.C., lost his life in 338

247

INDEX OF NAMES, PLACES, AND SUBJECTS

248

INDEX OF NAMES, PLACES, AND SUBJECTS

6. 77; ancestor of Pylaeus the Pelasgian, **6.** 153; slew Peisander, the son of Bellerophon, in the Trojan War, **6.** 191; asses sacrificed to, in Carmania, **7.** 153

Aretas, Arabian ruler, kinsman of King Obodas, received Aelius Gallus in a friendly way, **7.** 359

Aretê, daughter and successor of Aristippus the Cyrenaïc philosopher, **8.** 205

Arethusa, a sacred spring in Chalcis in Euboea; fountains of, stopped up by earthquakes, **1.** 215, **5.** 21

Arethusa, the fountain in Sicily; mythical story of, **3.** 75, 77

Arethusa (Rentina), near the Strymon River and Lake Bolbê, **3.** 361

Arethusa in Syria, has a good government, **7.** 253, 255

Arezzo (see Arretium)

Argaeus Mountain (Mt. Erdjias), the, in Cappadocia; southern side of, 3000 stadia farther south than the Pontus, **1.** 275; has forests all round it, **5.** 363

Arganthonium, Mt., above Prusias in Asia, the scene of the myth of Hylas, who was carried off by the nymphs, **5.** 457

Arganthonius, king of Tartessus in Iberia, **2.** 59

Argeadae, the, became powerful in Thrace, **3.** 331; destroyed Abydon (the Homeric "Amydon") on the Axius River, **3.** 341

Argennum, Cape, in Asia, near Erythrae, **6.** 241

Argestes, the wind, **1.** 105; called Sciron by the Athenians, **4.** 245

Argilus, on the Strymonic Gulf, **3.** 355

Arginussae Islands, the, **6.** 133

Argissa, the Homeric, subject to Polypoetes, **4.** 437; the present Argura, on the Peneius River, **4.** 439

Argive Heraeum, the (see Heraeum, the Argive), 40 stadia from Argos, **4.** 151

Argives, the; the Homeric, **1.** 129; dispute of, with the Lacedaemonians, about Thyreae, **1.** 245; were allies of the Messenians, **4.** 121; city of, described, **4.** 159; laid waste most of the neighbouring cities because of their disobedience, **4.** 171;

paid dues for the Nauplians at the temple of Poseidon on Calauria, **4.** 175; once colonised Aegina, **4.** 181; lost Thyreae to the Lacedaemonians, **4.** 183; joined the Achaean League, and came under Roman dominion, **4.** 185; after the Battle of Salamis utterly destroyed Mycenae, **4.** 187; said to have founded Tralleis in Asia Minor, **6.** 257; founded Aspendus in Pamphylia, **6.** 325, Tarsus in Cilicia, **6.** 345, Curium in Cypros, **6.** 379; sent Triptolemus to Asia in quest of Io, **7.** 243

Argo, the ship of Jason; Portus Argöus in Aethalia named after, **2.** 357; despatched from Iolcus by Pelias, **4.** 423

Argolic breed of horses, the, is most excellent, **4.** 229

Argolic Gulf, the, follows Maleae and extends to Cape Scyllaeum (Skyll), **4.** 15, 149

Argonauts, the, wanderings of, **1.** 75; visited the island Aethalia, **2.** 357; the Minyans descendants of, **2.** 63; were called Minyans, **4.** 335; Mopsus the Lapith sailed with, **4.** 453; founded the temple of Mother Dindymenê in territory of Cyzicus, **5.** 501

Argonauts, The, by Apollonius, **6.** 281

Argos, subterranean reservoirs at, **1.** 87; the Pelasgians originated at, **2.** 345; 26 stadia from Temenium and 40 from the Argive Heraeum, **4.** 151; the various meanings of the word in Homer, **4.** 155; description of, **4.** 159; well supplied with water, according to Hesiod, and acropolis of, was founded by Danaüs, **4.** 163; name applied also to the whole of Greece, **4.** 163, and to the whole Peloponnesus, **4.** 135, 165; history of, as compared with Mycenae, **4.** 167; Cenchreae on road from, to Tegea, **4.** 185; fame and later history of, **4.** 185; fell to the Pelopidae and then to the Heracleidae, **4.** 187; added to the Achaean League by Aratus, **4.** 217; called "Inacheian" after the Inachus River, **4.** 225; colonised by Temenus and Cissus after the return

249

INDEX OF NAMES, PLACES, AND SUBJECTS

of the Heracleidae, **4.** 235; the birthplace of Hera, **4.** 331

Argos, a lofty stronghold near the Taurus Mountain, founded by Cissus, **5.** 149, 357

Argos Hippium (Arpino), in Apulia (see Argyrippa), **2.** 319

Argos, the Pelasgian, in Thessaly, subject to Achilles, **4.** 401, 403

Argos Amphilochicum, on the Ambracian Gulf; founded by Alcmaeon, the son of Amphiaraüs, who so named it after his brother Amphilochus, **3.** 79, 305, **5.** 73; belongs to the Acarnanians, **5.** 25

Argoüs, Portus, in Aethalia, **2.** 357

Argura (Kremnos) on the Peneius River, the Homeric Argissa, **4.** 439

Argyria, near Scepsis in Asia, **5.** 411, **6.** 91

Argyrippa (Arpino) in Apulia; in early times one of the two largest Italiote (Greek) cities, " at first called Argos Hippium, then Argyrippa, and now Arpi," **3.** 129

Argyro-castro, on the Viosa River (see Damastium)

Argyrusci (Aurunci?), the, overthrown by the Romans, **2.** 387

Aria, a part of Ariana; mild climate, fertility, and superior vintage of, **1.** 273; description of, **5.** 277, 279; the mountains bordering on, **5.** 299

Ariana (see Aria), called Section (" Sphragis ") Second of Asia, **1.** 293; shape of, **1.** 295, 317; a vast country, **1.** 497; 6000 stadia from the Hyrcanian (Caspian) Sea, **5.** 259; once mastered by the Greeks, **5.** 279; Bactriana the ornament of, **5.** 281; borders on the Indus River, **7.** 15; description of, **7.** 129–143; boundaries of, **7.** 141–143; possesses a part of Mt. Paropamisus, **7.** 147

Arians, the; racial likeness of to other peoples, **1.** 153; called " refined " by Eratosthenes, **1.** 249

Ariarathes the King (died 220 B.C.), the first man to be called " king of the Cappadocians," annexed Cataonia to Cappadocia, **5.** 347; dammed up the Melas River in Cappadocia and formed isles in it, **5.** 363; and also dammed up the Carmalas, but

in each case had to pay enormous damages, **5.** 365

Aricia in Latium, on the Appian Way, **2.** 387, 421

Aricini in Italy (see Rhacci)

Aridaeus (also spelled " Arrhidaeus "), made the expedition with Perdiccas to Aegypt, but departed thence to Macedonia, **8.** 37

Arii, the, in Asia; geographical position of, **7.** 143–145

Arima, the mountains, in Cilicia, **6.** 177

Arimaeans, the; the Syrians now called, **6.** 177

Arimaspian Epic, The; Aristeas of Proconnesus the author of, **6.** 33

Arimaspians, the, a Scythian one-eyed people, **1.** 79, **5.** 245

Arimi, the Homeric; variant accounts of home of, **6.** 175, 177, **5.** 423; scene of myth of, in Phrygia Catacecaumenê, **5.** 517, and in Syria, **7.** 245, 373

Ariminum (Rimini), in Italy, **2.** 301, 305, 327, 337, 369, 371

Ariobarzanes, chosen king by the Cappadocians by consent of the Romans, **5.** 371

Arion the citharist, of Methymna in Lesbos; the myth of, told by Herodotus, **6.** 145

Arisba, a city in Lesbos, occupied by Methymnaeans, **6.** 39

Arisbê (or Arisba) in the Troad, mentioned by Homer, **6.** 37, 39, 41; colonised by Milesians, **6.** 207

Arisbus River, the, in Thrace, **3.** 383, **6.** 39, 41

Aristarcha, priestess of the Ephesian Artemis at Massalia, **2.** 173

Aristarchus of Samothrace (fl. about 155 B.C.); grammarian and critic, and librarian at Alexandria; misjudges Homer, **1.** 113, 121, 133; his reading of Homer's passage in regard to rising and setting of Hyperion, **1.** 397; contemporary of Crates of Mallus and of Demetrius of Scepsis, **6.** 113; teacher of Menecrates of Nysa, **6.** 263

Aristeas of Proconnesus (of whom all accounts are uncertain), author of *The Arismaspian Epic*, **1.** 79; " a charlatan," **6.** 33; reputed teacher of Homer, **6.** 219

INDEX OF NAMES, PLACES, AND SUBJECTS

at Coloê in Asia, **6.** 173; "Arte-meas" (goddess of "safety and soundness"), **6.** 207; Tauropolus, temple of, on the isle Icaria, **6.** 221; Munychia, temple of, at Pygela in Asia, **6.** 223; the Ephesian, temple of, at the harbour Panormus near Ephesus, **6.** 223: description and history of, **6.** 225–229; said to have been born at Ortygia above Ephesus, **6.** 223; Mt. Coracius in Asia sacred to, **6.** 237; Leucophryenê, temple of, at Magnesia on the Maeander, in some respects superior even to that at Ephesus, **6.** 251; Cyndyas, temple of, near Bargylia in Caria, **6.** 289; Pergaea, temple of, near Pergê in Pamphylia, **6.** 323; the Sarpedonian, temple and oracle of, in Cilicia, **6.** 357; called Azara, temple of, among the Elymaei, robbed by the Parthian king, **7.** 223; temple of, at Daphnê in Syria, **7.** 245; Tauropolus, oracle of, on the isle Icarus in the Persian Gulf, **7.** 303

Artemisia, sister and wife of Mausolus, erected the Mausoleum at Halicarnassus, **6.** 283; became queen of the Carians, but died of grief for her husband, **6.** 285

Artemisium (Nemus Dianae), the, to the left of the Appian Way, **2.** 421

Artemisium, Cape and temple, in southern Asia Minor, **6.** 265

Artemita, in Babylonia, the home of Apollodorus, is 8000 stadia from Hyrcania, **5.** 291; a noteworthy city 500 stadia from Seleuceia on the Tigris, **7.** 219

Artemita, one of the Echinades Islands, joined to continent by earthquake, **1.** 221

Artis in Lebedos, seized by Andropompus, founder of Lebedos, **6.** 199

Arum (*maculatum*?), a vegetable in Maurusia, **8.** 163

Arupini, a city of the Iapodes, **2.** 287, **3.** 259

Arvacans, the, the most powerful of the four divisions of the Celtiberians in Iberia; the valour of, **2.** 103

Arvales Fratres (see Vol. II, p. 383, footnote 3)

Arverni, the, in Celtica, **2.** 211; a tribe in Aquitania, which once had the Vellavii included within their boundaries, **2.** 217; situated on the Liger, and marshalled tremendous army against Julius Caesar, **2.** 219; extent of domain of, **2.** 221; a conspicuous tribe, **2.** 231; the number of the, **2.** 241

Arx, the, on Capitoline Hill, **2.** 383

Arxata, on the Araxes River in Armenia, **5.** 325

Asander (usurped the throne of the Bosporus in 47 or 46 B.C. after killing King Pharnaces and also Mithridates of Pergamon), fortified the Chersonesus against the Scythians, **3.** 245, **5.** 201, **6.** 169

Asbestos, produced in Carystus in Euboea, **5.** 11

Asbystians, the, who live near Carthage, **1.** 503

Asca in Arabia, captured by Aelius Gallus, **7.** 361

Ascalon in Phoenicia, **7.** 277

Ascania, an Asiatic territory partly Phrygian and partly Mysian; mentioned by Homer, in two different senses, **5.** 459, 461, **6.** 371, 373

Ascania in Europe, whence the Phrygians crossed to Asia, **6.** 371

Ascanian Lake, the, in Asia, **5.** 459; poetic references to, **5.** 465; mentioned by Alexander the Aetolian, **6.** 373

Ascanius, the son of Aeneias, founded Alba on Mt. Albanus, **2.** 379; the descendants of, **2.** 381; said, with Scamandrius, to have founded Scepsis, **6.** 105; variant accounts of, **6.** 107

Ascanius, the, who, with Palmys and Morys, led forces "from deep-soiled Ascania" (the Mysian Ascania, near Nicaea), **5.** 461

Ascanius, the, who, with Phorcys, "led the Phrygians from Ascania," **5.** 459

Ascanius River, the, in Asiatic Mysia, **6.** 373

Asclepiadae, the; the places in

INDEX OF NAMES, PLACES, AND SUBJECTS

Thessaly subject to, according to Homer, **4**. 433

Asclepiades of Myrlea on the Propontis (fl. in first century B.C.), historian, grammarian, and teacher of grammar in Turditania; on Odysseia and Athenê's temple in Iberia, and on memorials of wanderings of Odysseus in Iberia, **2**. 83; on the Igletes, in Iberia, **2**. 119

Asclepiades, the physician, of Prusa; a native of Bithynia, **5**. 467

Asclepïeium, the; famous temple in Cos, **6**. 287

Asclepïeium, the, in the Troad, founded by Lysimachus, **6**. 89

Asclepius, the remarkable ivory image of, made by Colotes, at Cyllenê in Elis, **4**. 25; temple of, at Gerenia in Messenia, **4**. 113; famous temples of, at Epidaurus, Triccê, and on Cos, **4**. 177; temple of, 40 stadia from Dymê and 80 from Patras, **4**. 219; earliest and most famous temple of, at Triccê in Thessaly, **4**. 429; the statue of, at Epidaurus, brought to Italy by oracle of the Sibyl, **5**. 471; said to have been born in Triccê in Hestiaeotis in Thessaly, **6**. 249; grove of, in Phoenicia, **7**. 267; temple of, on acropolis of Carthage, burnt up by wife of Asdrubal, **8**. 185

Ascrê, native city of Hesiod, on a high and rugged hill about 40 stadia from Thespiae, and ridiculed by Hesiod, **4**. 315, 317, **6**. 161; "Arnê" in the *Iliad* ignorantly emended to "Ascrê" by Zenodotus, **4**. 331

Asculum Picenum (Ascoli Piceno), in Picenum, well fortified by nature, **2**. 429

Asdrubal (Hasdrubal), son-in-law and successor (reigned 229–221 B.C.) of Hamilcar Barcas, founded New Carthage, **2**. 87; wife of, burnt up the temple of Asclepius and herself along with it when Carthage was captured (by Scipio, 146 B.C.), **8**. 185

Asea (also called Asia), a village in the territory of Megalopolis, whence flows the Eurotas, **3**. 93, **4**. 47, 199

Ash-dust, the, from Aetna, makes the soil suitable for the vine, **3**. 69, 71

Asia in Arcadia (see Asea)

"Asia," perhaps applied to "Melonia" by Homer, **6**. 179

Asia, revealed to geographers by Alexander, **1**. 51; shape of, as compared with Europe and Libya, **1**. 467; bounded by the Nile, **1**. 485; divisions of, **1**. 495; subject to rulers appointed by the Romans, **3**. 145; "wheat-producing," **3**. 207; separated from Europe by the Cimmerian Bosporus, **3**. 239; Corinth on the direct route from, to Italy, **4**. 189; consecrated to Dionysus, **5**. 109; borders on Europe along the Tanaïs River, and is bisected by the Taurus range, **5**. 183; description of the northern division of, **5**. 185; shape and dimensions of eastern portion of, **5**. 289; whole of, once ruled by Greater Media, **5**. 307; now largely subject to the Romans, **8**. 211; in part a consular Province, **8**. 215

Asia (Minor), called "Asia" in the special sense of the term, **1**. 483; defined as the part of Asia this side the Taurus, **5**. 295, 347; or Asiatic peninsula; discussion of boundaries of, **6**. 359-365

"Asiarchs," the, in Tralleis, **6**. 255

Asiatic peninsula, the (Asia Minor); discussion of boundaries of, **6**. 359–365

Asiatic Stathmi, The, written apparently by a certain Amyntas who accompanied Alexander, **7**. 141

Asidigis, now Medina Sidonia (see Baetis)

Asii, the, in Asia, helped to take away Bactriana from the Greeks, **5**. 261

Asinaean Gulf (see Messenian Gulf), the, named after the Messenian Asinê, **4**. 109, 113

Asinê, the Hermionic, in Argolis, **4**. 113, 153, 171, 173, 181

Asinê in Laconia, **4**. 127

Asinê (Koron, or Koroni), in Messenia, **4**. 109; the Asinaean (Messenian) Gulf named after, **4**. 113

Asinius Pollio (76 B.C.–A.D. 4), orator, poet, historian, and consul (40 B.C.); wrongly says the Rhenus is 6000 stadia long, **2**. 227

Asioneis (or Esioneis), the, in Asia;

257

INDEX OF NAMES, PLACES, AND SUBJECTS

a notable city, **6**. 129; supplied Persia with wheat, **7**. 185

Assyria, borders on Persia and Susiana, **7**. 193

Assyrians, the; racial likeness of, to other peoples, **1**. 153; revere the Chaldaean philosophers, **7**. 289

Asta in Iberia, **2**. 17; purposely built near estuary, **2**. 31

Astaboras River, the; a branch of, empties into the Arabian Gulf, **7**. 319; joins the Astapus River near Meroê, **7**. 321, **8**. 145; flows into the Nile, **8**. 5

Astacenê Gulf, the, in the Propontis, **5**. 455

Astaceni, the, a tribe in India, **7**. 47

Astacus (near Dragomesto) in Acarnania, **5**. 61

Astacus, on the Astacenê Gulf in the Propontis; founded by Megarians and Athenians, and later by Doedalsus, but was rased to the ground by Lysimachus, and its inhabitants were transferred by Nicomedes to Nicomedeia, **5**. 455

Astae, the, in Thrace, plunder all who are cast ashore in Salmydessus, **3**. 279; in whose territory is Calybê, city of Philip's villains, **3**. 285; Bizyê the royal seat of, **3**. 369

Astapus River, the, joins the Astaboras near Meroê, **7**. 321, **8**. 145; flows into the Nile, **8**. 5

Astasobas River, the, joins the Nile near Meroê, **7**. 321, **8**. 145

Astêeis River, the, in Asia, whence the founders of Smyrna set out, **6**. 203

Asteria (the Homeric Asteris), no longer an isle, **1**. 221; between Ithaca and Cephallenia, **5**. 51

Asteris, the Homeric (see Asteria)

Asterium in Thessaly, subject to Eurypylus, **4**. 433; lies near Arnê and Aphetae, **4**. 437

Asteropaeus, son of Pelegon, one of the leaders who made the expedition to Troy, **3**. 363

Astigis, in Iberia, **2**. 21

Astrologers, the Chaldaean (see Genethlialogists), **7**. 203

Astronomers, the Sidonian, **7**. 269; those at Aegyptian Thebes, reckoned the year at 365¼ days, **8**. 125

Astronomy, in relation to geography, **1**. 233; fundamental to geography, **1**. 423, 429; discussion of the *Climata* appropriate to, **1**. 503; treated in a poem by Alexander of Ephesus, **6**. 231; the chief concern of the Chaldaean philosophers, **7**. 203; invented by the Phoenicians, **7**. 271; engaged in by Aegyptian priests, **8**. 9; the school of, at Heliupolis, **8**. 83

Asturia, traversed by the Melsus River, **2**. 121

Asturians, the, in Iberia; geographical position of, **2**. 77, 121; home of some of, on west of Celtiberians, **2**. 103

Astyages, Greater Media deprived of rulership over Asia by Cyrus in time of, **5**. 307; conquered by Cyrus at Pasargadae, **7**. 169

Astypalaea, ancient city of the Coans, in Cos; people of, changed abode to the present Cos, **6**. 287

Astypalaea, Cape, in Caria, **6**. 289

Astypalaea (Hagios Nikolaos), Cape, in Attica, **4**. 271

Astypalaea, one of the Sporades Islands in the Carpathian Sea, **5**. 175

Astypalaeans, the, of Rhoeteium, the first to settle Polium on the Simöeis River in the Troad, **6**. 83

Astyra, above Abydus, once had important gold mines, **6**. 45, 369; had the temple of Astyrene Artemis and the Palisade of Achilles, **6**. 129

Astyra on the Gulf of Adramyttium, has a precinct sacred to Artemis, **6**. 103

Asylum-precinct, the, at Daphnê in Syria, **7**. 245

Atabyris, Mt., highest mountain in Rhodes, sacred to Zeus Atabyrius, **6**. 279

Atagis River, the, **2**. 285

Atalanta, the island (Talantonisi), near Euboea, rent asunder by earthquake, **1**. 225; opposite Opus in Locris, **2**. 379

Atalanta, an isle near Peiraeus, **4**. 259, 379

Atargatis, the Syrian goddess, worshipped at Bambycê in Mesopotamia, **7**. 235

INDEX OF NAMES, PLACES, AND SUBJECTS

"Atargatis," barbarian name of Athara, **7.** 373

Atarneïtae, the; coast of, **6.** 121

Atarneus, a city in Asia, **6.** 5, 103; abode of the tyrant Hermeias, **6.** 131

Atarneus-below-Pitanê, a place in Asia, opposite the island Eleussa, **6.** 131

Atax (Aude) River, the, rises in the Cemmenus Mountain, **2.** 183; traffic on, **2.** 211

Ateas (Anteas?, Atheas?), who ruled over most of the barbarians about the Cimmerian Bosporus, waged war with Philip of Macedonia, **3.** 227

Ategua in Iberia, where the sons of Pompey were defeated, **2.** 21

Atella (Sant' Arpino), in Campania, **2.** 461

Atellanae Fabulae (see Mimes)

Ateporix, of the family of Galatian tetrarchs, assigned additional territory by the Romans, **5.** 443

Aterno-Pescara River, the (see Aternus River)

Aternum (Pescara), in Italy, **2.** 431

Aternus (Aterno-Pescara) River, the; boundary between the countries of the Vestini and the Marrucini, **2.** 431

Atesinus River, the, **2.** 285

Atesis River, the (see footnote 4, Vol. II, p. 285)

Athamanes, the, a barbarian tribe, hold part of the country above Acarnania and Aetolia, **3.** 289, 5. 23; an Epeirote tribe, **3.** 307; destroyed the Aenianians, **4.** 389; are now extinct, **4.** 393; border on Thessaly, **4.** 397; annexed to Thessaly, **4.** 415; country of, a refuge of the Perrhaebians, **4.** 439

Athamantis (see Teos)

Athamas, founded Halus in Thessaly, **4.** 409; first founder of Teos, **6.** 199

Athara, by barbarians called "Atargatis," but by Ctesias "Derceto," **7.** 373

Atheas (see Ateas)

Atheists, the, among the Aethiopians, **8.** 147

Athenae Diades in Euboea, founded by the Athenians, **5.** 9

Athenaeum, the, at Ephesus, **6.** 225

Athenaeum, Cape (Punta della Campanella), **2.** 435; where is a sanctuary built by Odysseus, **2.** 455

Athenaeus, son of Attalus I and brother of Eumenes II, remained a private citizen, **6.** 167

Athenaeus, Peripatetic philosopher, contemporary of Strabo, statesman, native of Seleuceia in Cilicia, came to sad end, **3.** 383, 6. 335

Athenaïs the prophetess, contemporary of Alexander the Great, native of Erythrae in Asia, **6.** 243; declared the divine descent of Alexander, **8.** 117

Athenê; sanctuary of, on the Strait of Capreae, **1.** 83; temple of, in Iberia, is sign that Odysseus wandered thither, **2.** 53, 83; altar of, on the Circaeum in Italy, **2.** 393; the wooden image (xoanon) of, at Siris, in Italy, opens and closes its eyes, **3.** 49; called "the Trojan" at Rome and other places, **3.** 49, 51; temple of, in country of the Salentini in Iapygia, **3.** 117; temple of, at Luceria in the country of the Daunii, **3.** 129; the Parthenos, **3.** 231 (see footnote 8); in the guise of Mentor in the *Odyssey* proposes to visit the Cauconians, **4.** 45, 57, 59; famous temple of, at Scillus near Olympia, **4.** 51; the Nedusian, temple of, on the Nedon River, and also at Poeäessa, **4.** 115; the Alean, temple of, in Tegea, **4.** 229; Polias, the priestess of, eats only foreign cheese, **4.** 257; the temple of (the Erechtheium), on the Acropolis at Athens, and the ivory statue of, in the Parthenon, by Pheidias, **4.** 261; Athens named after, **4.** 265; the Itonian, temple of, near Coroneia, **4.** 323, and at Itonus in Thessaly, **4.** 421, 433; the Alalcomenian (mentioned by Homer), temple of, near Alalcomenae, where they say she was born, **4.** 331; Agamemnon wished to propitiate, before leaving Troy, **5.** 105; called the mother of the Corybantes by the Prasians, **5.** 111; the Nedusian, temple of, on Ceos, **5.** 169; small temple of, at the present Ilium, **6.** 51; Glaucopis, **6.** 77; hated Ajax, **6.** 81; wooden image of, at present Ilium, stands

INDEX OF NAMES, PLACES, AND SUBJECTS

upright, but the Homeric was seated (as at various places to-day), **6.** 83; priestess of, at Pedasa in Caria, grows a beard when misfortune is imminent, **6.** 119; saved Augē and her son Telephus, **6.** 135; temple of, near Smyrna, **6.** 203; colossal statue of, at temple of Hera on Samos, **6.** 215; born from the head of Zeus, **6.** 277; famous temple of, at Lindus in Crete, **6.** 279; temple of, at Sidē in Pamphylia, **2.** 449; temple of, among the Elymaeans, robbed by the Parthian king, **7.** 223; Cyrrhestis, temple of, near Heracleia in Syria, **7.** 247; temple of, at Saïs in Aegypt, **3.** 67

Athenians, the; dispute of, with Boeotians about Oropus, **1.** 245; fond of letters, not by nature, but by habit, **1.** 395; colonised Neapolis, **2.** 449; destroyed the rebuilt Sybaris in Italy, and founded Thurii, **3.** 47; re-founded Cardia on the Melas Gulf, **3.** 373; regarded as an indigenous people, **4.** 7; rebuilt the Messenian Pylus as a fortress against the Lacedaemonians, **4.** 109; captured 300 Lacedaemonians on Sphacteria, **4.** 111; rivalled by the inhabitants of Aegina in the seafight at Salamis, **4.** 179; divided Aegina by lot among Athenian settlers but lost it to the Lacedaemonians, **4.** 181; joined Eurystheus in expedition against Iolaüs, **4.** 187; ancestors of the Ionians, **4.** 207; turned over their government to Ion the son of Xuthus, and sent a colony of Ionians to occupy the Aegialus in the Peloponnesus, **4.** 209; called the wind Argestes "Sceiron," **4.** 245; voluntarily received Melanthus the king of Messenia as their king, **4.** 249; once in strife with the Megarians for Salamis, but now hold it, **4.** 253; wont to despatch 400 ships on expeditions, **4.** 261; history of the forms of government of, **4.** 269, 271; hold Haliartus, as a gift from the Romans, **4.** 325; conquered by Philip at Chaeroneia, **4.** 333; the road taken by, on the Pythian procession to Delphi, **4.** 367; fought the Macedonians in the Lamian War, **4.** 413; 2000, from the deme of the Histiaeans, colonised Histiaea (Oreus) in Euboea, **5.** 7; founded Athenae Diades in Euboea, **5.** 9; said to have founded Chalcis and Eretria before the Trojan War, **5.** 13; always hospitable to all things foreign, especially foreign religious rites, **5.** 109; once slew most of the inhabitants of Melos from youth upwards, **5.** 163; now hold Delos, **5.** 167; once besieged Ceos, **5.** 169; under Athenocles colonised Amisus, **5.** 395; with the Megarians founded Astacus on the Propontis, **5.** 455; under Phrynon the Olympian victor seized Sigeium in the Troad, **6.** 75; Adramyttium a colony of, **6.** 103; ordered slaughter of all Mitylenaeans from youth up, but rescinded decree, **6.** 145; with Menestheus founded Elaea in Asia in Trojan times, **6.** 159; fined Phrynichus the tragic poet 1000 drachms because of his play on *The Capture of Miletus by Dareius*, **6.** 209; sent Pericles and Sophocles the poet to capture Samos, and allotted land to 2000 Athenians there, **6.** 219

Athenocles, and Athenians, colonised Amisus in Cappadocia Pontica, **5.** 395

Athenodorus of Canana near Tarsus (about 74 B.C.–A.D. 7), pupil of Poseidonius, friend of Strabo, learned scientist; on the tides, **1.** 19, 203, **2.** 147; teacher of Julius Caesar and for a time ruled over Tarsus, **6.** 349, 351; praises the government of the Petraeans in Arabia, **7.** 353

Athenodorus Cordylion, lived with Marcus Cato; native of Tarsus, **6.** 347

Athens, parallel of latitude through, **1.** 241, 253; distance of parallel of, from Meroê, **1.** 255; parallel of, perceptibly different from that of Rhodes as shown by sun-dial, **1.** 333; rivalled by Massalia as a centre of learning, **2.** 179; once inhabited by Pelasgi, **2.** 347; occupied by Maleos the Pelasgian, **2.** 365; belonged to a kind of Amphictyonic

INDEX OF NAMES, PLACES, AND SUBJECTS

League of seven cities, **4.** 175; connected with the Peiraeus by walls 40 stadia long, which were torn down by the Lacedaemonians and by Sulla, **4.** 261; description of, **4.** 261–263; named after Athenê—and the Theseium and other things have myths connected with them, **4.** 265; the different forms of government at, **4.** 267, 269; captured by Sulla, pardoned by him, and to this day is free, and held in honour by the Romans, **4.** 271; a part of, called "Pelasgicon," after the Pelasgians who were driven there from Thebes, **4.** 283; the commotion at, when Elateia was captured, **4.** 373; Codrus the king of, **6.** 199; the *Ephebi* at, **6.** 219

Athens in Boeotia, on the Triton River, **4.** 305; founded by Cecrops, and submerged by Lake Copaïs, **4.** 307

Athletes, the great, among the Crotoniates, **3.** 45

Athmoneus, father of the Arbelus who founded Arbela, **7.** 197

Athos, Mt., lies west of Lemnos, **3.** 353; description of, **3.** 355, 357; the cities around, colonised by the Eretrians, **5.** 13; Cheirocrates (Deinocrates?) proposed to fashion in likeness of Alexander the Great, **6.** 227

Athribis in Aegypt, **8.** 71

Athrula in Arabia, captured by Aelius Gallus, **7.** 361

Athymbradus, the Lacedaemonian, founded a city in Asia Minor, **6.** 261

Athyras River, the, empties into the Propontis, **3.** 379

Atintanes, the, an Epeirote tribe, **3.** 307

Atlantic, the; formerly not connected with the Mediterranean, **1.** 183; its bed lower, **1.** 189

Atlantis, the Island (or Continent), once existed, **1.** 391

Atlas, daughter of (Calypso), on Ogygia, **1.** 95

Atlas, the mountain in Libya, by the barbarians called Dyris, **8.** 157; extends through the middle of Maurusia and is inhabited, **8.** 159; about 5000 stadia in length, **8.** 165

Atmoni, the, a Bastarnian tribe, **3.** 221

Atmosphere; the temperature of, subject to three broad differences, **1.** 369

Atrax, in Thessaly, near the Peneius River, **3.** 337, **4.** 433, 439, 445

Atrebatii, the, a Celtic tribe; geographical position of, **2.** 233

Atreus the king, discovered that the sun revolves in direction opposite to revolution of the heavens, **1.** 87; the sons of, **4.** 167

Atria (Adria), in Italy, once an illustrious city, **2.** 317

Atropates, king of Atropatian Media, successfully resisted the Macedonians, and his descendants are still in power, **5.** 303

Atropatian Media; power and description of, **5.** 303; often plundered by the Armenians and Parthians, attained the friendship of Caesar, but pays court to the Parthians, **5.** 305

Atropatii, the, in Asia, border on Greater Media, **5.** 309

Atropenê, borders on Armenia, **5.** 317

Attaleia in Pamphylia, founded by, and named after, Attalus II (Philadelphus), **6.** 323

Attalic kings, the; the line of, failed, **3.** 145; Philotaerus, the founder of family of, born at Ticium in Bithynia, **5.** 381; caused the retirement of Prusias from Phrygia Hellespontica and called it Phrygia "Epictetus," **5.** 457; built up the temple of Mother Agdistis at Pessinus in Galatia, **5.** 471; gave part of territory of Priapus to the Parians, **6.** 31; built up the library at Pergamum, **6.** 111; had a naval station at Elaea, **6.** 159; long reigned at Pergamum, **6.** 163–169

Attalus, younger brother of Eumenes and Philotaerus, and father of Attalus I, **6.** 165

Attalus I (reigned 241–197 B.C.), son of Attalus the younger brother of Philotaerus and cousin of Eumenes I, transferred the Gergithians of the Troad to Gergitha near the sources of the Caïcus River, **6.** 139; first to be proclaimed king of Pergamum, after conquering the Galatians, fought with the Romans against

INDEX OF NAMES, PLACES, AND SUBJECTS

Philip, and died in old age, **6.** 165, 167

Attalus II (Philadelphus), son of Attalus I and brother of Eumenes II, embellished Pergamum, appointed guardian of Attalus III (Philometor), and reigned at Pergamum for 21 years (159–138 B.C.), **6.** 167; helped Alexander the son of Antiochus to defeat Demetrius the son of Seleucus, fought with the Romans against the Pseudo-Philip, made an expedition against Thrace, slew Prusias, and left the empire to his nephew Attalus III, **6.** 169; deceived in regard to the mole he had built at Ephesus, **6.** 229; settled the Dionysiac artists between Teos and Lebedus, **6.** 237; founded Attaleia in Pamphylia and sent a colony to the neighbouring Corycus, **6.** 323

Attalus III (Philometor), reigned only five years (138–133 B.C.) and left the Romans his heirs, **6.** 169

Attasii, the, a tribe of the Sacae and Massagetae in Asia, **5.** 269

Attea in Asia, **6.** 103

" Attes hyes " (see " Hyes attes ")

" Atthis," and " Attica," derived from Atthis the son of Cranaüs, **4.** 265

Atthis, the son of Cranaüs, gave name to " Atthis " (Attica), **4.** 265

Atthis (Attica), the *Land of*, the histories of, **2.** 347, **4.** 247

Attic dialect, the ancient; the same as the Ionic, **4.** 5

Attic people, the, of ancient times, called Ionians, **4.** 5

Attic Tetrapolis, the, **4.** 175

Attica (see Atthis), once held by the Thracians under Eumolpus, **3.** 287; the Tetrapolis of (or Marathonian Tetrapolis), founded by Xuthus the son of Hellen, **4.** 209; once held by the Ionians, **4.** 245; in early times called Ionia and Ias, and was divided up between the sons of Pandion, **4.** 247; invaded by the Heracleidae, **4.** 249; " the sanctuary of the gods," **4.** 263; once called " Ionia," after Ion, **4.** 207; has 170, or 174, demes, **4.** 263; in earlier times called " Acticê," " Mopsopia " and " Ionia," **4.** 267;

people of, settled by Cecrops in 12 cities, but later by Theseus united into one city, Athens, **4.** 267; demes of, in the interior, too tedious to recount, **4.** 275; the rivers of, **4.** 275, 277; Plataeae on the confines of, **4.** 325; people of, akin to the Trojans, **6.** 95

Aturia, a region in Assyria, **7.** 193, 195; plains of, surround Ninus, **7.** 197

Atys, the Lydian, whose son Tyrrhenus colonised Tyrrhenia in Italy, **2.** 337

" Auases," the Aegyptian word for " oases," **1.** 501

Aude River, the (see Atax)

Aufidus (Ofanto) River, the, **2.** 395 (where " Aufidus " is an error for " Ufens "); distance from, to Barium, **3.** 127

Augaeae in Laconia, the Homeric " Augeiae," **4.** 131

Augê, mother of Telephus; myth of, **6.** 135

Augeiae in Laconia; name now spelled Aegeae, **4.** 131

Augeiae in Locris, the Homeric, no longer existent, **4.** 131, 383

Augeias (or Augeas), the king of the Epeians, **4.** 29, **5.** 59; slain by Heracles, **4.** 39, 91; a foe of Neleus, **4.** 83; by some called king of Pisatis, **4.** 95

Augila, in the interior of Libya, a four days' journey from Automala, **8.** 209

Augusta in Sicily (see Xiphonia)

Augusta Emerita, in the country of the Turdulians in Iberia, **2.** 61, 121

Augusta Praetoria (Aosta), founded by Augustus, **2.** 281

Augustonemetum (see Nemossus)

Augustus Caesar (see Caesar Augustus)

Aulis, rightly called " rocky " by Homer, **3.** 189; mentioned by Homer in connection with Hyria; the Aeolic fleet despatched to Asia from, by the sons of Orestes, **4.** 283; a rocky place, a village of the Tanagraeans, and its harbour only large enough for 50 ships, and therefore the large harbour was probably the naval station of the Greeks, **4.** 289; Hyria situated near, **4.** 295, 313

INDEX OF NAMES, PLACES, AND SUBJECTS

INDEX OF NAMES, PLACES, AND SUBJECTS

important cities in, **7**. 219; temples in, robbed by the king of Parthia, **7**. 223; now subject to the Parthians, **7**. 233; produces the caryotic palm, **8**. 133

Babylonian Memoirs, the, on the straightforward character of the Scythians, **3**. 201

Babylonian women, all, have intercourse with a foreigner, **7**. 227

Babylonians, the; philosophers, not by nature, but by training and habit, **1**. 395; once fought by the Cossaei and Elymaei, **5**. 309; assisted in battle by Antimenidas the brother of Alcaeus, **6**. 141; customs of, described, being in general like those of the Persians, **7**. 225-229; wont to attack the Medes and the Armenians, **7**. 225

Babylonians, certain, withdrew to a certain stronghold, called Babylon, in Aegypt, **8**. 85

Babyrsa, a strong fortress in Armenia, **5**. 327

Bacchae, The, of Euripides, quoted, **7**. 9

Bacchae, the, ministers of Dionysus, **5**. 87, 97, 101, 103

Bacchiadae, the, tyrants of Corinth for 200 years, overthrown by Cypselus, **4**. 189

Bacchic chase, the; a custom of the kings in India, **7**. 93

Bacchic festival, a kind of, called the "Sacaea," in Cappadocia, **5**. 265

"Bacchus," another name of Dionysus, **5**. 105

Bacchylides, nephew of Simonides, from Iulis in Ceos, **5**. 169; wrongly says that the Caïcus River flows from Mt. Ida, **6**. 137

Bactra (also called Zariaspa), 3870 stadia from Alexandreia in Bactria, **5**. 271, 281

Bactria (or Bactriana, *q.v.*), description and history of, **5**. 279-285; the Greek kings and empire of, **5**. 281

Bactriana (or Bactria, *q.v.*), knowledge of, increased by the Parthians, **1**. 51; produces everything but olive-oil, **1**. 275; once occupied by the Sacae, **5**. 263; geographical position of, **5**. 269; revolted from the kings of

Syria and Media, **5**. 273; by the Greeks caused to revolt from the Syrian kings, **7**. 5; produces rice, **7**. 29; geographical position of, **7**. 145

Bactrians, the, in Asia; strange customs of, **5**. 281; speak the same language as the Arians, **7**. 143; possess a part of Mt. Paropamisus, **7**. 147

Badas River, the, in Syria, **7**. 159

Baenis (or Minius, now Minho) River, the; the largest river in Lusitania, but rises, according to Poseidonius, in Cantabria, **2**. 69

Baetera, a city near Narbo, on the Orbis River, **2**. 183

Baetica, in Iberia, named after the Baetis River, **2**. 13; whither runs the road from Italy, **2**. 95; traversed by the Baetis River, **2**. 101; the property of the Roman people, **2**. 119; governed by a praetor, and bounded on the east by the region of Castalo, **2**. 121

Baetis (Asidigis ?, Italica ?), a town in Iberia; colonised by Caesar's soldiers, **2**. 21

Baetis River (Guadalquivir), the, in Iberia; course and size of, **2**. 13; twofold division of outlet of, **2**. 17; flows through Turdetania, **2**. 19; has large population along its shores, and is navigable 1200 stadia, to Corduba, **2**. 23; said to rise in "Silver Mountain" (*q.v.*), but, according to Polybius, in Celtiberia, and identified with the ancient "Tartessus," **2**. 49; parallel to the Tagus for a distance, **2**. 65; rises in the Orospeda Mountain, and flows through Oretania into Baetica, **2**. 101

Baetorix, father of Deudorix (Theodoric) and brother of Melo, **3**. 161

Baeturia in Iberia, contains arid plains along the Anas, **2**. 25

Baetylus (see Oetylus)

Bagadania (Bagadaonia ?), in Cappadocia, lies at the foot of the Taurus, **5**. 367

Bagadaonia, between the Argaeus Mountain and the Taurus Range, produces fruit-trees, **1**. 275

"Bagas," a Paphlagonian name used in Cappadocia, **5**. 415

INDEX OF NAMES, PLACES, AND SUBJECTS

INDEX OF NAMES, PLACES, AND SUBJECTS

INDEX OF NAMES, PLACES, AND SUBJECTS

Strabo probably means Bion of Abdera, a philosopher and mathematician who flourished about 400 B.C.; on the winds, **1.** 107

Bion, the Borysthenite philosopher (fl. about 250 B.C.); highly esteemed by Eratosthenes, **1.** 53; emulated by Ariston of Ceos, **5.** 169

Bisa, a spring in Elis, **4.** 97

Bisaltae, the, in Thrace; geographical position of, **3.** 331; over whom Rhesus reigned, **3.** 359, 361

Bisons (aurochs), the, in India, **7.** 123

Bistonian Thracians, the, ruled over by Diomedes, **3.** 365

Bistonis, Lake (Bourougoel), in Thrace, submerged the cities on its shores, **1.** 221; has a circuit of about 200 stadia, **3.** 365, 367

Bithynia in Asia; Pompey added eleven states to, **5.** 373; the most westerly land on the right as one sails from the Propontis into the Euxine, **5.** 373; the extent of coast of under the Romans, **5.** 375; the Sangarius River flows through part of, **5.** 379; borders on Paphlagonia, **5.** 383; seized by Mithridates Eupator, **1.** 449; detailed description of, **5.** 455–467; boundaries of, **5.** 455, 459; Nicaea, the metropolis of, **5.** 463; has produced several noted scholars, **5.** 465, 467; with other territories, now a praetorial Province, **8.** 215

Bithynians, the, are in origin a Thracian tribe, **3.** 177; formerly Mysians, received their name from the Thracian Bithynians, **5.** 375; not mentioned by Homer, **6.** 363

Bithynium in Bithynia, **5.** 463

Bituitus, commander of the Arverni; carried on war against Maximus Aemilianus and Domitius Ahenobarbus, **2.** 221

Bituriges "Cubi," the, a tribe in Aquitania, **2.** 217

Bituriges "Vivisci," the, in Celtica, **2.** 215

Bizonê (Kavarna), on the Euxine, mostly engulfed by earthquakes, **1.** 199, **3.** 277

Bizyê (Viza) in Thrace, the royal seat of the Astae, **3.** 369

Black Forest, the (see Hercynian Forest)

Blaênê in Paphlagonia, **5.** 449

Blascon (Brescon), Isle of (now connected with mainland of France), **2.** 181

Bleminatis, a district of Laconia, **4.** 47

Blemmyes, the, subject to the Aethiopians, **8.** 7; situated to the south of Aegypt, **8.** 135

Blera, a town in Italy, **2.** 365

Blesinon, a town in Corsica, **2.** 359

Blest, the abode of the, near Maurusia, **1.** 7; placed by Homer in the far west, **2.** 55; also called Isles of the Blest, **2.** 57

Boagrius River (also called Manes), in Locris, the; course of changed by earthquake, **1.** 225; flows past Thronium, **4.** 381

Boar, a peculiar animal like a, in the Alps, **2.** 289

Boars, the wild, in the Scythian marshes, **3.** 249

Bocalia River (see Bocarus River)

Bocarus River, the, now called Bocalia, in Salamis, **4.** 253

Bocchus, kings of house of, held Maurusia in Libya, being friendly to the Romans, **8.** 169

Bodensee (see Constance, Lake of)

Boea (Vatika) in Laconia, **4.** 129

Boebê, on Lake Boebeïs in Thessaly, now a village belonging to Demetrius, **4.** 425, 433

Boebeïs, Lake, in Thessaly, **4.** 397; near Pherae, **4.** 425; near Ormenium, **4.** 433; mentioned by Homer, **4.** 445; in the Dotian Plain, **4.** 449, 453, **6.** 251

Boenoa (see Oenoê in Elis)

Boeoti in Laconia (see Thalami)

Boeotia, once occupied by the barbarian Aones, Temmyces, and Hyantes, **3.** 287; once occupied by the Leleges, according to Aristotle, **3.** 289; lies on the Crisaean Gulf, **4.** 195; forms an isthmus on the third peninsula of Greece, **4.** 243; detailed description and history of, **4.** 277–341; has fertile soil, good harbours and borders on three seas, **4.** 279; in early times inhabited by barbarians, **4.** 281; carried on war

269

INDEX OF NAMES, PLACES, AND SUBJECTS

with the Lacedaemonians under Epameinondas, almost gained the supremacy of Greece, fought with the Phocians and with the Macedonians, and is now in bad plight, **4.** 287; the dire results of earthquakes in, **4.** 301, 303; once ruled by Cecrops, being then called Cecropia, **4.** 307

Boeotian cities, the, are now, except Thespiae and Tanagra, only ruins or names, **4.** 319

Boeotians, the; dispute of, with Athenians, about Oropus, **1.** 245; naturally not fond of letters, **1.** 395; once called "Syes" ("swine"), according to Pindar, **3.** 287; once called Aonians, devastated Attica, **4.** 267; mostly under the command of the Phoenicians and the house of Cadmus, **4.** 283; war of, with the Thracians, **4.** 283–287; advised by the oracle at Dodona to commit an act of sacrilege, burnt by the priestess herself, **4.** 285; took possession of Orchomenus and Coroneia after the Trojan War, **4.** 323; conquered by Philip at Chaeroneia, **4.** 333; in the Trojan War, **4.** 407; call locusts "pornopion," **6.** 127

Boeotus, son of Melanippê the prisoner by Poseidon, at Metapontium, **3.** 53

Boerebistas, king of the Getans (see Byrebistas)

Boethus the Sidonian, Aristotelian philosopher and friend of Strabo, **7.** 271

Boethus, of Tarsus, bad poet and bad citizen, in power by favour of Antony for a time at Tarsus, **6.** 349

Boetylus (see Oetylus)

Boeüm, city of the Dorian Tetrapolis, **4.** 387

Boeüm, Mt., in Orestis, from which, according to some, one can see both the Aegaean Sea and the Ambracian Gulf, **3.** 327

Bogiodiatarus, by Pompey presented with Mithridatium in Pontus, **5.** 469

Bogus, king of Maurusia in Libya about 110 B.C.; neighbour to Aethiopians and visited by Eudoxus of Cyzicus, **1.** 383; urged by Eudox-

us to make expedition to India, **1.** 383, 389; ally of Antony, put to death at Methonê by Agrippa, **4.** 111; went up against the western Aethiopians, **8.** 165; kings of house of, held possession of Maurusia, being friendly to the Romans, **8.** 169

Bohemia (see Boïhaemum)

Bohemians, the; Forest of (see Gabreta Forest)

Böhmer Wald, or Forest of the Bohemians (see Gabreta)

Boïhaemum (cp. Bohemia), the domain of Marabodus, **3.** 155, 157

Boii, the, migrated across the Alps from Transalpine Celtica, **2.** 235; geographical position of, **2.** 281; one of the largest Celtic tribes, and driven out of Italy by the Romans, **2.** 311; opposed by the Cenomani in Roman battles, **2.** 323; the desert of, borders on the Lake of Constance, **3.** 165; in earlier times dwelt in the Hercynian Forest, **3.** 169; a Celtic tribe, **3.** 179, 253; destroyed by the Getans, **3.** 211; subdued by the Dacians, **3.** 253; virtually destroyed in wars with the Macedonians and the Romans, **3.** 263

Bolbê (Beschikgoel), Lake, **3.** 361

Bolbitine mouth of the Nile, the, **8.** 65, 67

Bologna in Italy (see Bononia)

Bolsena (see Volsinii)

Bolsena, Lake, near Volsinii, **2.** 367

Bombyces, the, a kind of reed-flute, **5.** 107

Bomians, the, in Aetolia, **5.** 29

Bonones, son of Phraates IV, sent by his father as hostage to Rome, **7.** 237, 239

Bononia (Bologna), not far from Ravenna, **2.** 327

Böos Aulê ("Cow's Stall"), a cave in Euboea, where Io is said to have given birth to Epaphus, **5.** 5

Boosura in Cyprus, **6.** 381

Bordeaux (see Burdigala)

Boreas the North Wind, snatched up Oreithyia, the daughter of Erechtheus, **1.** 105, **3.** 175

Boreium, Cape, with Cephalae forms the mouth of the Great Syrtis, **8.** 201

Borkum the island (see Burchanis)

Bornfornello in Sicily (see Himera)

INDEX OF NAMES, PLACES, AND SUBJECTS

Borrama, a fortress on Mt. Libanus, 7. 263

Borsippa, a city in Babylonia, sacred to Apollo and Artemis, noted for its linen and large bats, 7. 203

Borsippeni, the, a tribe of the Chaldaean philosophers, 7. 203

Borysthenes (now in ruins, near Nickolaiev), also called Olbia, a great emporium, founded by the Milesians, 3. 221

Borysthenes (Dnieper) River, the; meridian through mouth of, 1. 233, 269; the parallel through mouth of, same as that through Britain, 1. 237; distance of mouth of, from equator, 1. 269; where the vine does not grow or is unproductive, 1. 275; flows between the Tanaïs and the Ister into the Euxine, 1. 413; mouth of, the northerly point of the Mediterranean, 1. 483, and 3800 stadia north of Byzantium and 34,100 stadia north of equator, 1. 515; not mentioned by Homer, 3. 189; navigable for 600 stadia, and cities on, 3. 221

Bos, the, a fish indigenous to the Nile, 8. 149

Bosmorum, a grain smaller than wheat, grown in India, 7. 21, 29

Bosporians, the, about Lake Maeotis (Sea of Azov), now subject to the Romans, 3. 145, 237, 239, 247; all subject to potentates of Cimmerian Bosporus so called, 5. 199

Bosporus, the Cimmerian (Strait of Kertch), Homer's knowledge of, 1. 73; promontory in region of, 1. 417; home of the Cimmerians, 2. 51; named after the Cimbri, who made an expedition thither, 3. 169; the kings of, 3. 201; so named because the Cimmerians once held sway there, 3. 237; the kingdom of, situated partly in Asia, and it separates Europe from Asia, 3. 239; named after the Cimmerians, 5. 197; not mentioned by Homer, 5. 419; Mithridates the Pergamenian and Asander, the kings of, 6. 169

Bosporus, the Thracian; formerly non-existent, and how formed, 1. 183, 191; current does not change as at the Euripus and Strait of Sicily, but sometimes stands still, 1. 205; where empties the Euxine, 1. 481

Botrys, a stronghold of robbers at foot of Mt. Libanus, 7. 263

Botteia (or Bottiaea, *q.v.*), city of the Bottiaeans, named after Botton the Cretan, 3. 331

Bottiaea (see Botteia), in Macedonia, colonised by Cretans, 3. 121

Bottiaean city, a, Alorus (identified with Thessaloniceia?), 3. 341, 345

Bottiaeans in Macedonia, the; were colonists from Crete, 3. 111; once held much of Macedonia, 3. 329; Alorus a city of, and, they used to occupy Lower Macedonia, 3. 341

Botton, the Cretan, who, with the Bottiaeans, settled in Macedonia, 3. 329; the city Botteia named after, 3. 331

"Boulai"; the meaning of the word in Homer, 3. 317

Boulogne (see Itium)

Bourougoel (see Bistonis, Lake)

Bovianum (Bojano), a Samnite city, 2. 463

Bow, the, used by the Gauls, 2. 243; used by the Amazons, 5. 233; used by the Indians, 7. 117; used in Persia, 7. 181; those used by the people at Endera in Aethiopia are made of reeds, 7. 321; that of the Elephantophagi requires three persons to shoot it, 7. 325; used in battle by the Negrani in Arabia, 7. 361; four cubits long, used by the Aethiopians, 8. 145; used by the Pharusians and Nigritae in Libya, 8. 169

Bowls, made out of leaves in Aegypt, 8. 59

Box-tree, the, in India, 7. 97

Box-wood, the best, grows in the territory of Amastris in Paphlagonia, 5. 387

Boxus, of Persian descent, traces origin of name of Erythraean ("Red") Sea to a certain Persian Erythras, 7. 351

Bracciano, Lake (see Sabata)

Brachmanes (Brahmans), the, in India; life and tenets of, 7. 99–103; engage in affairs of state, 7. 115; derided by the Pramnae, 7. 123

271

INDEX OF NAMES, PLACES, AND SUBJECTS

INDEX OF NAMES, PLACES, AND SUBJECTS

2. 227; expedition of Julius Caesar to, 2. 229; distance from, to mouths of rivers in Celtica, 320 stadia, 2. 231; an island near, on which sacrifices are made similar to those in Samothrace to Demeter and Corê, 2. 251; detailed description of, 2. 253-259; shape and dimensions of, 2. 253; products, exports, and physique of inhabitants of, 2. 255; conquered by Julius Caesar, 2. 257; islands near, 2. 259

Britannic (British) Islands, the; outside the Pillars, 1. 493

Britomartis, fled from violence of Minos, 5. 139; the temple of, at Cherronesus in Crete, 5. 143

Britons, the, taller than the Celti, make no cheese, and have no experience in agriculture, 2. 255; chieftains of, won friendship of Augustus and dedicated offerings in the Capitolium, 2. 257; readily submit to heavy duties on imports and exports, 2. 259

Briula in Asia, near Nysa, 6. 261

Brixia (Brescia), in Italy, 2. 311

Bromius, another name of Dionysus, 5. 101

Bronze vessels, found at Corinth, sold at high price at Rome, 4. 203

Brothers, Monuments of the Seven (mountain-peaks in Libya), 8. 165

Bructeri, the, defeated by Drusus in a naval battle on the Ems River, 3. 155; live near the ocean, 3. 159; captives from, led in triumphal procession at Rome, 3. 163

Brundusium (see Brentesium)

Brutii, the (see Bretii)

Bruttium (see Brettii, the), description of, 3. 11-49

Brutus, Decimus (b. about 84 B.C.); his flight from Mutina (43 B.C.), 2. 279

Brutus, D. Junius (consul 138 B.C.), surnamed Callaïcus (from victory over Callaïcans); subjected Lusitanians in Iberia, 2. 63; campaign of, in Iberia, ended at Baenis (Minho) River, 2. 69, 77

Brutus, M. (and Cassius), defeat of, at Philippi (42 B.C.), 3. 363

Bruzzano, Capo (see Zephyrium, Cape)

Bryanium, a populous city on the Erigon River, 3. 311

Brygi (or Brigi, q.v.), the, an Illyrian tribe, 3. 307; are the same people as the Bryges and Phrygians, 5. 403, 405

Bubali (apparently the antelope *bubalis*), in Maurusia in Libya, 8. 163

Bubastus, near the Delta of Aegypt, 8. 79

Bubon in Phrygia, 6. 193

Buca (Termoli), on the coast of the Frentani, 3. 135

Bucephalia, a city founded by Alexander in India, 7. 49

Bucephalus, favourite horse of Alexander, killed in India, 7. 49

Buchetium, a small town of the Cossopaeans in Thesprotia, 3. 301

Bucolopolis in Phoenicia, 7. 275

Budorus, Mt., in Salamis, 5. 9

Budorus River, the, in Euboea, 5. 9

Bull, a, led the way for Sabine colonists, 2. 465

Bull-fights, the, at Memphis in Aegypt, 8. 89

Bulls, the wild, in Aethiopia, 7. 337

Buprasis, the territory of Buprasium, occupied by Cauconians, 4. 55

Buprasium in Elis, mentioned by Homer, 4. 35, 37, 39; separated from Dymê by the Larisus River, 4. 225

Bura, engulfed because of earthquake, 1. 99, 219; one of the twelve cities in which the Achaeans settled, 4. 219; about 40 stadia above the sea, swallowed up by an earthquake, 4. 221

Burchanis (called by the Romans Fabaria; now Borkum), the island, subjugated by Drusus, 3. 159

Burdigala (Bordeaux), emporium of the Bituriges, 2. 215

Busiris, a city in Aegypt, maligned as inhospitable, 8. 69

Busiris, the tyrant or king in Aegypt who never existed, 8. 69

Bustards, numerous in Iberia, 2. 107

Buthrotum (Butrinto), on Pelodes Harbour in Epeirus, has Roman settlers, 3. 299

Buticê, Lake, in Aegypt, 8. 67

INDEX OF NAMES, PLACES, AND SUBJECTS

INDEX OF NAMES, PLACES, AND SUBJECTS

Cadmilus, son of Hephaestus and Cabeiro, and father of three Cabeiri, **5.** 115

Cadmus, with the Phoenicians, occupied the Cadmeia at Thebes, fortified it, and left the dominion to his descendants, **3.** 287, **4.** 281, 283; the descendants of, ruled over the Enchelii, **3.** 307; some Arabians who crossed over with, settled in Euboea, **5.** 13; source of wealth of, **6.** 369

Cadmus of Miletus (fl. about 550 B.C.), supposed author of a work *On the Foundation of Miletus*; earliest writer of Greek prose, **1.** 65

Cadmus, Mt., in Greater Phrygia, whence the Lycus and Cadmus Rivers flow, **5.** 511

Cadmus River, the, in Greater Phrygia, **5.** 513

Cadurci, the, a tribe in Aquitania, **2.** 217

Cadusii, the, in Asia; extent of coast of, **5.** 245; geographical position of, **5.** 249, 251, 259, 269; mountaineers in Atropatian Media, **5.** 305; have a strong army, **5.** 307; border on Greater Media, **5.** 309

Caecias, the wind, **1.** 107

Caecuban Plain, the, produces fine wine, **2.** 389

Caecuban wine, the, **2.** 399

Caelium, Mt., joined by walls to Rome by Ancus Marcius, **2.** 401

Caeni, the, in Thrace, defeated by Attalus II, **6.** 169

Caenys, Cape (Cape Cavallo), **3.** 21; with Cape Pelorias forms the Strait of Sicily, **3.** 55

Caepio, Quintus (consul 106 B.C.), seized Delphian treasures at Tolosa and met unhappy end, **2.** 207

Caepio, Tower of, in Iberia, compared with that of Pharos in Aegypt, **2.** 17

Caeratus, the earlier name of Cnossus in Crete, **5.** 129

Caeratus River, the, in Crete, flows past Cnossus, **5.** 129

Caere (Caerea, now Cervetri), in Italy, formerly called Agylla, **2.** 341

Caerea (see Caere)

Caeretani, the, in Tyrrhenia; conquered the Galatae, **2.** 339; saved the refugees from Rome, but were ill-treated by the Romans, and dedicated at Delphi "the treasury of the Agyllaei," **2.** 341; Pyrgi the port-town of, **2.** 365

Caeretanian Springs (Bagni del Sasso?), the, **2.** 341

Caesar Augusta (formerly Salduba, now Sarragossa), in Iberia; on the Iberus River, **2.** 61, 97, 103

Caesar, Augustus (63 B.C.–A.D. 14); soldiers of, colonised Baetis in Iberia, **2.** 21; subdued Cantabrians and their neighbours, **2.** 79; territory of, in Iberia, **2.** 121; administration thereof, **2.** 123; his division of Transalpine Celtica into four parts, **2.** 165; naval station of (Forum Julium), in Celtica, **2.** 191; temple of, at Lugdunum in Celtica, **2.** 223; his friendship with British chieftains, **2.** 257; builder of roads and subduer of brigands, **2.** 275; his subjection of the Salassi, **2.** 279; founded Augusta Praetoria (Aosta), **2.** 281; vanquished the Iapodes, **2.** 287; constructive measures of, at Rome, **2.** 403; embellisher of Rome, **2.** 407; the Mausoleum of, **2.** 409; personal owner of island of Capreae (Capri), **2.** 459; ejected Pompey Sextus from Sicily and colonised Rhegium, **3.** 27, 67; restored Syracuse, **3.** 75, and also Catania and Centoripa, **3.** 79; subdued the Cantabrians, and at last Transalpine and Cisalpine Celtica, and Liguria, **3.** 143; held as hostages the children and grandchildren of Phraates IV of Parthia, and administered the empire as a father, **3.** 147; favoured Marabodus the German, **3.** 157; would not allow his generals to cross the Albis River, **3.** 159; presented by the Cimbri with the most sacred kettle in their country, **3.** 165; sent an expedition against the Getans, **3.** 213; has worn out the Iapodes, **3.** 259; set on fire five Dalmatian cities, **3.** 261; founded Nicopolis in honour of his victory over Antony, and dedicated the squadron of ten ships, as first fruits of his victory, at the naval station near Actium, **3.** 301; transferred

INDEX OF NAMES, PLACES, AND SUBJECTS

Caesar, Tiberius (Roman emperor A.D. 14–37); placed three legions over certain tribes in Iberia, **2**. 79; subjugated the Carni and Norici, **2**. 283; makes Augustus the model for his own administration and is assisted by his sons Germanicus and Drusus, **3**. 147; used an island in the Lake of Constance as a base of operations in his naval battle with the Vindelici, **3**. 163; saw the sources of the Ister at a day's journey from the Lake of Constance, **3**. 165; made Greater Cappadocia a Roman province, **5**. 349; restored places damaged by earthquakes, **5**. 517; Marcus Pompey of Mitylenê one of best friends of, **6**. 145; recently restored Sardeis, after the earthquakes, **6**. 179; sent by Augustus from Samos to Armenia, **8**. 141

Caesareia in Libya (see Iol)

Caesarium, the, at Alexandria, **8**. 39

Caesena, on the Aemilian Way, **2**. 327

Caïcus River, the, in Asia, **5**. 487; the Mysians settled above sources of, **5**. 489; geographical position and extent of, **6**. 5; outlets of, **6**. 103, 133; Teuthrania lies this side of **6**. 135; does not flow from Mt. Ida **6**. 137; borders on demain of Eurypylus, **6**. 153; flows past Pergamum, **6**. 169; Plain of, about the best land in Mysia, **6**. 169; Plain of, created by silt, **7**. 23

Caïetanus Sinus (Caïetan Kolpos; see Caïetas, Gulf of)

Caïta (Gaëta), in Italy, **2**. 397

Caïtas, the Gulf of, in Italy, **2**. 397; borders on the Caecuban Plain, **2**. 399

Calabrians (see Galabrii), the; country of, comprises one of the two parts of Iapygia, **3**. 103

Calacheuê, in Assyria, **7**. 193

Calaguris, a city of the Vasconians, in Iberia, where Sertorius fought, **2**. 99

Calamine, obtained from Cyprian copper, **2**. 107

Calamis (fl. at Athens about 450 B.C.), made the colossal statue of Apollo in the temple of Apollo on the Apollonian isle in the Euxine, which was carried off to Rome by Lucullus, **3**. 277

Calanus, the Indian sophist, accompanied Alexander to Persis and perished on funeral pyre, **7**. 7, 109, 111; different accounts of, **7**. 119, 121

Calasarna in Leucania, **3**. 11

Calatia (Galazze), on the Appian Way, **2**. 461, **3**. 125

Calauria (Poros), the isle, in the Myrtoan Sea, **1**. 477; four stadia from the mainland and has a circuit of 130 stadia, **4**. 153; had an asylum sacred to Poseidon, and was given in exchange by Leto to Poseidon for Delos, **4**. 173

Calbis River, the, in the Peraea of the Rhodians, **6**. 265

Calchas, the seer; the temple of, in Daunia; description of worship at, **3**. 131; founded Selgê in Pisidia, **5**. 481; story of contest, grief, and death of, **6**. 233, 235; led from Troy the ancestors of the Pamphylians, but, according to Callinus, died at Clarus, **6**. 325; contest of, with Mopsus, **6**. 353

Caledonian boar, the, **4**. 197

Calendar, the, of the astronomers at Heliupolis, **8**. 85; and at Aegyptian Thebes, **8**. 125

Calenian wine, **2**. 437

Cales (Calvi), the city of the Caleni, in Campania, **2**. 413, 461

Caleti, the, in Celtica; geographical position of, **2**. 211, 233

Callaïcans, the, in Iberia; geographical position, and military prowess of, **2**. 65; by some formerly called Lusitanians, **2**. 67; modes of life of, **2**. 77; some of, live on west of the Celtiberians, **2**. 103; have no god, **2**. 109; formerly called Lusitanians, **2**. 121

Callaïcia, settled by companions of Teucer, **2**. 83

Callas (Xeropotamos) River, the, in Euboea, **5**. 7

Callatis (Mangalia), on the Euxine, **3**. 273, 277; colonised by Heracleia Pontica, **5**. 379

Calliarus in Locris, now a beautifully tilled plain, **4**. 383

Callias, the interpreter of Sappho and

277

INDEX OF NAMES, PLACES, AND SUBJECTS

Alcaeus, a native of Lesbos, **6.** 147

Calliconê, a hill near Ilium, mentioned by Homer, **6.** 69

Callidromus, Mt., above Thermopylae, **4.** 389

Callimachus of Cyrenê (fl. about 250 B.C.), Greek poet and grammarian, librarian at Alexandria, cataloguer of the library, and said to have written about 800 works, in prose and verse. Only 6 hymns, 64 epigrams and some fragments are extant; names Gaudas (Gozo) and Corcyra as scenes of wanderings of Odysseus, **1.** 163; on traces of expedition of Jason in the Mediterranean, **1.** 169; on Pola in Italy, **2.** 323; "makes a pretence of being a scholar," but calls Gaudos the "Isle of Calypso" and Corcyra "Scheria," according to Apollodorus, **3.** 193; on Theras the founder of Thera, **4.** 63; records the measurements of Pheidias' image of Zeus in temple at Olympia, **4.** 89; in his *Collection of the Rivers*, on the foul waters of the Eridanus at Athens, **4.** 265; in his *Iambics*, calls Aphroditê Castnietis wisest of all Aphroditês, and is highly praised by Strabo for his learning, **4.** 431; wrongly says that Britomartis leaped into Dictê, **5.** 139; in the islands Thera and Anaphê, **5.** 161; an epigram of, in regard to a poem of Creophilus the Samian, **6.** 219; comrade of the poet Heracleitus, **6.** 285; on the Dromus of an Aegyptian temple, **8.** 81; a native of Cyrenê, **8.** 205

Callinus the elegiac poet, on the Teucrians, **6.** 95; says that the Trerans captured Sardeis, **6.** 179; calls the Ephesians "Smyrnaeans," **6.** 201; refers to the Magnetans and their war against the Ephesians, **6.** 251; on the capture of Sardeis by the Cimmerians, **6.** 253; says that Calchas died at Clarus near Colophon, **6.** 325

Calliopê, by some called the mother of the Corybantes by Zeus, **5.** 113

Callipidae, the, a tribe of Scythians beyond the Borysthenes River, **5.** 405

Callipolis (Gallipoli), 40 stadia distant from Lampsacus in Asia, **3.** 377, **6.** 35

Callipolis (now Strumitza?), a city in Macedonia, **3.** 361

Callipolis in Sicily, no longer inhabited, **3.** 83

Callistê, the earlier name of Thera (*q.v.*)

Callisthenes of Olynthus, pupil of Aristotle, accompanied Alexander on his Asiatic expedition, wrote an account of the same, and also a history of Greece in ten books, of which only fragments remain; calls Tyrtaeus an Athenian, **4.** 123; seized and imprisoned at Cariatae in Bactriana, **5.** 283; wrongly follows Herodotus in his account of the Araxes River, **5.** 335; in his *The Marshalling of the Trojan Forces*, defines the geographical position of the Cauconians in Asia, **5.** 377; on origin of name of Adrasteia in the Troad, **6.** 29; helped to annotate a recension of Homer, **6.** 55, 57; on the home of the Homeric Arimi, **6.** 177; on the capture of Sardeis by different peoples, **6.** 179; says that Phrynichus was fined 1000 drachmas by the Athenians because of his play on *The Capture of Miletus by Dareius*, **6.** 209; says that Trojan Cilicians founded Thebê and Lyrnessus in Pamphylia, **6.** 323; had false notions about the Halizones, **6.** 369; on the cause of the risings of the Nile, **8.** 19; dramatically describes visits of Alexander to temple of Ammon and oracle of Apollo among the Branchidae, **8.** 115

Cailydium, Cleon's strongest stronghold on the Mysian Olympus, **5.** 497

Calpas River, the, flows between Chalcedon and Heracleia Pontica, **5.** 379

Calpê (Gibraltar), description of, **2.** 15; distant from Gadeira about 750 stadia, **2.** 17, 129; from New Carthage, 2200 stadia, **2.** 79; by some regarded as one of the Pillars of Heracles, **2.** 135

Calybê (or Cabylê; now, apparently

INDEX OF NAMES, PLACES, AND SUBJECTS

Tauschan-Tépé on the Tounja River), where Philip settled the worst people in his kingdom, 3. 285

Calycadnus River, the, near the Seleuceia in Pieria (in Syria); the Arimi live near, 6. 177, 333, 335

Calydna (see Tenedos)

Calydnian Islands, the, among the Sporades, 5. 175, 177, 179; near Tenedos, 6. 93

Calydon (near Kurtaga) in Aetolia, 4. 385; mentioned by Homer, 5. 15; once an ornament to Greece, 5. 27, 29, 63; "steep" and "rocky," 5. 65, 75; region around subject to Oeneus, 5. 85

Calymna, one of the Sporades Islands, 5. 177; mentioned by Homer, 5. 179

Calymnian honey, the, particularly good, 5. 179

Calynda, in the Peraea of the Rhodians, 6. 265

Calypso, daughter of Atlas, lived in Island of Ogygia, 1. 95

"Camarae," the name of boats of Asiatic pirates, 5. 203

Camari (see Coroneia)

Camarina (Torre de Camarana) in Sicily, 20 Roman miles from Agrigentum, 3. 59; a colony of the Syracusans, 3. 81

Camarinum, in Umbria, 2. 369

Cambodunum (Kempten), a city of the Vindelici, 2. 281

Cambysenê, a waterless and rugged country through which leads the pass from Iberia into Albania, 5. 229, 323

Cambyses (king of Persia, 529–522 B.C.), destroyed the temples of the Cabeiri and Hephaestus in Memphis, 5. 115; succeeded his father Cyrus, but was deposed by the Magi, 7. 189; conquered Aegypt, 8. 19; ruthlessly outraged temples and obelisks when in Aegypt, 8. 79; overwhelmed in a wind-storm in Aethiopia, 8. 139

Cameirus, son of Cercaphus, 6. 275

Cameirus, a city in Rhodes, mentioned by Homer, 6. 273; origin of name of, 6. 275; position of, 6. 279

Camel-breeders, the, in Persis, 7. 155

Camel-drivers, the, in Mesopotamia, 7. 235; in Arabia, 7. 357

Camel-merchants, the, in earlier times travelled only by night, 8. 121

Camelopards, the, in southern Aethiopia; description of, 7. 337; found in western Aethiopia, 8. 163

Camels, used by the Aorsi in Asia, 5. 243; those of the Arabian Scenitae, 7. 301; the wild, in Arabia, 7. 343; afford all means of livelihood to a certain tribe in Arabia, 7. 345

Camertes, the, 2. 373

Camici in Sicily, the royal residence of Cocalus, where Minos is said to have been murdered, 3. 85

Camisa, an ancient fortress in Cappadocia Pontica, 5. 441

Camisenê in Greater Cappadocia; the Halys River rises in, 5. 393; by Pompey joined with Zelitis and Culupenê into one state, 5. 441

Campania, once held by the Ausones and the Osci, but now by the Latini, 2. 395; description of, 2. 433–471; the fertility of, 2. 435; produces the best wines, and has notable cities, 2. 437, 461; ravaged by the Samnitae, 2. 463

Campanian Phlegra, the (see Phlegraean Plain), 3. 119

Campanians, the, readily submitted to the Samnitae, 2. 463, and instantly to Hannibal, 2. 467; under Roman discipline now preserve their old-time reputation, 2. 469; have become Romans, 3. 9

Campsiani (or Campsani), the, live near the ocean, 3. 159; captives from, led in triumphal procession at Rome, 3. 163

Campus of Agrippa, the, at Rome (see 2. 406, footnote 5)

Campus Flaminius, at Rome (see 2. 406, footnote 5)

Campus Martius, the, at Rome; description of, 2. 407–409; the Villa Publica in, 2. 463

Camuni, the, a tribe of the Rhaeti, 2. 281

Canae in Aeolis, colonised from Dium in Euboea, 5. 9

Canae (or Canê), Cape; geographical position of, 6. 5; with Cape Lectum forms a large gulf, 6. 13, 105, 133

279

INDEX OF NAMES, PLACES, AND SUBJECTS

INDEX OF NAMES, PLACES, AND SUBJECTS

281

INDEX OF NAMES, PLACES, AND SUBJECTS

Homer, **5**. 421, **6**. 59, 87; source of, **6**. 89

Caria, a part of the Cis-Halys country, **1**. 497; colonised by Ionians from Athens, **4**. 211; now occupied by the Ionians, **5**. 509; has numerous tombs, fortifications, and traces of the Leleges, **6**. 119, 121

Carians, the, in Ionia; emigrations of, **1**. 227; by some identified with the Leleges, but with them occupied the whole of what is now called Ionia, **3**. 289; seized Epidaurus, **4**. 175; devastated Attica, **4**. 267; formerly islanders, settled on the mainland by aid of the Cretans, **5**. 491; by some confused with the Lycians, **5**. 495; a different people from the Leleges; **6**. 117; formerly lived in the Troad, but later migrated to Caria in the region of Halicarnassus, and with the Leleges invaded Greece, **6**. 119; in Trojan battles, **6**. 151; occupied parts of Asiatic coast in early times, but were driven out by the Ionians, **6**. 199; once inhabited Samos, **6**. 215; once inhabited Ephesus, **6**. 225; certain places occupied by, **6**. 249, 255; as brothers worship the Carian Zeus with the Lydians and Mysians, **6**. 293; once called Leleges, lived in the islands, and were subject to Minos, **6**. 301; first to be called "barbarians," **6**. 303; barbarous element in language of, **6**. 305; roamed throughout Greece, serving on expeditions for pay, **6**. 307; by the poets confused with other peoples, **6**. 315; tribes of, mentioned by Homer, **6**. 361

Cariatae in Bactriana, destroyed by Alexander, **5**. 283

Carides (shrimps and the like), found in the Indus River, **7**. 81

Carmalas River, the, flows round Dastarcum in Greater Cappadocia, **5**. 357; dammed up by Ariathres, **5**. 365

Carmania, the desert of, **7**. 145; description of, **7**. 151–155; very productive, **7**. 153; language and customs of, like those of the Medes and Persians, **7**. 155; abounds in palm-trees, **7**. 201; encircled on the north by Persis, **7**. 219

Carmanian vine, the, bears huge clusters of grapes, **7**. 153

Carmanians, the, a warlike people, **7**. 153; language and customs of, like those of the Medes and Persians, **7**. 155

Carmel, Mt., in Phoenicia, **7**. 275

Carmenta the nymph (see Carmentis)

Carmentis (Carmenta), the mother of Evander, worshipped by the Romans, **2**. 387

Carmo, in Iberia, **2**. 21

Carmylessus in Lycia, **6**. 317

Carna (or Carnana) in Arabia, **7**. 311

Carneades (b. about 213 B.C.), the best of the Academic philosophers, born at Cyrenê, **8**. 205

Carneates, Mt., a part of Mt. Celossus, **4**. 205

Carni, the; live near the recess of the Adriatic, **2**. 283, in Transpadana, **2**. 323; geographical position of, **3**. 165; possess Tergeste, **3**. 255; border on the Istrians, **3**. 257

Carnus in Phoenicia, naval station of the isle Aradus, **7**. 255

Carnutes, the, in Celtica, a conspicuous tribe, **2**. 231

Carob-tree, the (see *Ceratia*)

Carpasia in Cyprus, **6**. 377

Carpasian Islands, the, off Cyprus, **6**. 377, 379

Carpathian Sea, the; extent of, **1**. 477, **5**. 173, 175, 6. 375

Carpathos (the Homeric "Crapathos"), one of the Sporades Islands, **5**. 175, 179; description of, **5**. 177

Carpentras (see Aeria)

Carpetania in Iberia, borders on Turdetania, **2**. 19; coursed by the Tagus River, **2**. 65

Carpetanians, the, in Iberia; geographical position of, **2**. 13, 65, 67, 103

Carrara marble, quarries of (see Marble)

Carretanians, the, live on Celtic side of the Pyrenees, but are of Iberian stock and cure excellent hams, **2**. 101

Carrhae, a city in Assyria, **7**. 231

Carrot (see *Staphylini*)

Carseoli, on the Valerian Way, **2**. 415

Carsuli (Capella San Domiano), in Italy, **2**. 373

Carta, a city in Hyrcania, **5**. 251

INDEX OF NAMES, PLACES, AND SUBJECTS

INDEX OF NAMES, PLACES, AND SUBJECTS

271; 500 stadia from Rhagae and 1260 from Hecatompylus, **5.** 273; adjacent to Media, **5.** 295; the mountains at, **5.** 299; belong to Media, **5.** 301

Caspian (or Hyrcanian) Sea, the, **1.** 255, 265; one of the four large gulfs, **1.** 467; forms a part of the exterior ocean, **1.** 495; opens into the Northern Ocean, **3.** 371; borders on the Northern Ocean, **5.** 187; position and dimensions of, **5.** 243, 245; resembles an open sea, **5.** 249

Caspianê in Asia, belongs to the Albanians, **5.** 227; annexed to Armenia, **5.** 325

Caspians, the, in Asia; geographical position of, **5.** 269; starve to death all over seventy years of age, **5.** 283, 293

Caspius, Mt. (see Caucasus), about 1800 stadia from the Cyrus River, **5.** 269

Cassander, husband of Thessalonicê the daughter of Philip, rased 26 cities on the Thermaean Gulf and founded Thessaloniceia, **3.** 343, 347; restored Potidaea after its destruction, **3.** 349; reigned ten years over Macedonia, reduced Athens but treated it with great kindness, **4.** 269

Cassandra; the violation of, **3.** 49; was unknown to Homer, **6.** 79; hand of, sought by King Idomeneus, **6.** 81

Cassia, abundant in the country of the Sabaeans in Arabia, **7.** 349; produced from marshes, **7.** 365

Cassia, pseudo-, the, in Aethiopia, **7.** 333

Cassiepeia, the constellation; star on the neck of, on the arctic circle, 1400 stadia north of the Pontus, **1.** 515

Cassiopê (or Cassopê, now Cassopo), a harbour, and cape, of Corcyra, 1700 stadia from Brundusium, **3.** 299

Cassius (and Brutus), defeat of, at Philippi, **3.** 363; besieged Laodiceia in Syria, **7.** 249

Cassopaeans, the Thesprotian; a barbarian tribe, now hold part of the country above Acarnania and

Aetolia, **3.** 289; country of, extends to the recess of the Ambracian Gulf, **3.** 297, 303

Cassopê, Cape (see Cassiopê)

Cassiterides ("Tin," now Scilly) Islands, lie to the north of the Artabrians, **1.** 461; outside the Pillars, **1.** 493; number, description, and history of, **2.** 157

Castabala in Cilicia, assigned by the Romans to the predecessors of Archelaüs, **5.** 349; where is the temple of the Perasian Artemis, **5.** 359, 361

Castalo (Cazlona), in Iberia, above Corduba, **2.** 25; has lead mines, **2.** 47; a powerful city, **2.** 65; through which runs the main road, **2.** 97

Castanet, the, used in worship of Mother Rhea, **5.** 101, 105

Casteggio (see Clastidium)

Castel Franco (see Pandosia)

Castellaccio (see Collatia)

Castellamare della Brucca (see Elea)

Castellum Firmanorum (Porto di Fermo), in Picenum, **2.** 429

Castes, the, in Iberia in Asia, **5.** 221; discussion of the seven in India, **7.** 67–83

Casthanaea, a village at foot of Mt. Pelion, near which the Persian fleet was destroyed by a tempest, **4.** 451

Castiglione (see Gabii)

Castor, and Pollux (see Dioscuri)

Castor, father of Deïotarus, the last king of Paphlagonia, **5.** 453

Castor, medicinal, derived from beavers in Iberia and the Euxine, **2.** 107

Castration of horses, by the Scythians and Sarmatians, **3.** 249

Castrum Novum, in Picenum, **2.** 429

Casystes, a harbour near Erythrae in Asia, **6.** 241

Cat, the, worshipped by the Aegyptians in common with various other creatures, **8.** 109

Catabathmus, by later writers added to Aegypt, **8.** 23, 55; region round, destitute of water, **8.** 155; eastern boundary of Cyrenaea, **8.** 205

Catakolo, Cape (see Ichthys, Cape)

Catalogue of Ships, the, of Homer,

287

INDEX OF NAMES, PLACES, AND SUBJECTS

Cenchrius River, the, near Ephesus, **6**. 223

Cenomani, the, live in Transpadana, and used to help the Romans in their battles, **2**. 323

Census, the Roman, in Iberia, **2**. 131; of Patavium in Italy, **2**. 313

Centaurs, certain of the, washed off poison in the Anigrus River and gave it an offensive odour, **4**. 61; tomb of, on Taphiassus, a hill in Aetolia, **4**. 385; driven to the land of the Aethices on Mt. Pindus, **4**. 417; forced from Mt. Pelion by Peirithoüs, **4**. 439

Centoripa (or Centuripae, now Centorbi) in Sicily, restored by Augustus, **3**. 79; lies above Catana, **3**. 81, near the town Aetna, **3**. 87

Ceos, the city, on Ceos, lies 25 stadia from the sea, **5**. 169

Ceos, the island, one of the Cyclades, once ruled by the Eretrians, **5**. 17; Simonides and other famous men natives of, **5**. 169

Cephalae, Cape, forms the western boundary of the Great Syrtis, being 5000 stadia from Carthage, **8**. 195

Cephallenia, the island, off the Corinthian Gulf, **1**. 477; not more than eighty stadia from Cape Chelonatas, **4**. 27 ("eight" there is an error for "eighty")

Cephallenians, the; with Odysseus at Troy, **4**. 255; Laertes lord over, **5**. 31, 33; all subjects of Odysseus so called, **5**. 35; by some called "Taphians" and Teleboans, but were subject to Odysseus, **5**. 47

Cephaloedis (Cephaloedium) in Sicily, **3**. 81

Cephaloedium (or Cephaloedis, now Cephalu), in Sicily, 30 Roman miles from Alaesa, **3**. 57, 81

Cephalon, native of Gergithes in the territory of Cymê, **6**. 37

Cephalus, the son of Deïoneus, said to have leaped off Cape Leucatas into the sea, **5**. 33; expedition of, to Cephallenia, **5**. 47; an exile from Athens, reigned over Taphos and Cephallenia, **5**. 61; said to have gained the mastery over Acarnania, and to have been the first to leap off Cape Leucatas, **5**. 67

Cephisia, one of the twelve cities in Attica settled by Cecrops, **4**. 267

Cephissis (or Hylicê), Lake, near Lake Copaïs, and between Thebes and Anthedon, is filled from Lake Copaïs through subterranean channels, **4**. 309

"Cephissis Lake"; the name applied by Pindar to Lake Copaïs, **4**. 323

Cephissus, the fountain, at Apollonia near Epidamnus, **4**. 375

"Cephissus," the name of six different rivers, **4**. 375

Cephissus River, the, in Attica; description of course of, **4**. 275, 277, 375

Cephissus River, the, in Boeotia, empties near Larymna, **4**. 297; supplies Lake Copaïs, goes underground, and issues forth again near Upper Larymna (Larma), **4**. 305; the sources (at Lilaea in Phocis) and course of, **4**. 307, 309, 373; receives the waters of the Pindus River near Lilaea, **4**. 387

Cephissus River, the, in Salamis, **4**. 375

Cephissus River, the, in Scyros, **4**. 375

Cephissus River, the, in Sicyon, **4**. 375

Cephissus River, the; Parapotamii in Phocis situated on, **4**. 373; winding course of, described by Hesiod, **4**. 375

Cepi, near the Cimmerian Bosporus, **5**. 199

Ceprano (see Fregellae)

Ceramus, a town near Cnidus, **6**. 283

Cerasus in Cappadocia Pontica, **5**. 399

Cerata ("Horns") Mountains, the, between Megaris and Attica, **4**. 257

Ceratia (carob or locust tree), the, found in abundance in Aethiopia, **8**. 145

Ceraunia (apparently an error for "Cerynia"), situated on a high rock near Aegium in Achaea, **4**. 223

Ceraunian Mountains, the; distance from to Corcyra, Leucas, and the Peloponnesus, **1**. 405; with Cape Iapygia bar the mouth of the Ionian Gulf, **3**. 117; voyage from, to Brundisium, **3**. 125; where the Ionian Gulf and the Adriatic begin, **3**. 267, 277, 299, 307; in Asia, a part of the Caucasian Mountains so called, **5**. 223, 233

INDEX OF NAMES, PLACES, AND SUBJECTS

INDEX OF NAMES, PLACES, AND SUBJECTS

Chalcideis in Ionia, a place near the isthmus of the Chersonesus of the Teïans and Erythraeans, 6. 239

Chalcidians, the, and Cumaeans (from Euboea) founded Cumae in Italy, 2. 437; colonised Neapolis, 2. 449; founded Rhegium in Italy, 3. 21; founded Naxus in Sicily, 3. 65; became powerful in Thrace, 3. 331; possess Stageira the native city of Aristotle, 3. 359; enlarged the circuit of their walls in time of Alexander the Great, 5. 13; praised by oracle as best fighters of all, 5. 21; founded Euboea in Sicily but were driven out by Gelon, 5. 23

Chalcidic earth, by the Cyziceni mixed with grain to preserve it, 5. 501

Chalcidicê in Syria, 7. 255

Chalcis in Euboea, 670 stadia from Cape Sunium, 4. 289; and Corinth, called by Philip "the fetters of Greece," 4. 391; largest city in Euboea, 5. 11; said to have been founded by the Athenians before the Trojan War, and many colonies sent out by, 5. 13; now called the metropolis of the Euboeans, 5. 17; Aristotle sojourned and died at, 5. 19

Chalcis (also called Hypochalcis), a small city in Aetolia, mentioned by Homer, 4. 385, 5. 15, 29

Chalcis, the "rocky," in Elis, mentioned by Homer, 5. 15

Chalcis, an acropolis in Syria, 7. 253, 263

Chalcis, Mt., in Aetolia, by Artemidorus called Chalcia, 5. 63; perhaps two mountains with this name in Aetolia, 5. 29, 63

Chalcis River, the, and settlement, in Triphylia, 4. 49; Telemachus sailed past, 4. 77, 79

Chaldaeans, the, in Babylonia; attained pre-eminence through superior knowledge, 1. 87; honoured Heracles and Nabocodrosor, 7. 7; philosophers in Babylonia and elsewhere—and names of famous men among, 7. 203; revered by the Assyrians, 7. 289; certain exiled, live at Gerrha in Arabia, 7. 303

Chaldaeans, the, in Cappadocia Pontica; Trapezus and Pharnacia in Cappadocia Pontica, 5. 399, 423;

in ancient times called Chalybes, 5. 401, 403; subject to Lesser Armenia and later to Mithridates, 5. 425; now ruled by Queen Pythodoris, 5. 427; to this day are teachers of the Greeks, 8. 85

Chalk; Cameirus in Rhodes white with, 6. 275

Chalon-sur-Saone (see Cabyllinum)

Chalonitis; the Tigris River reappears near, 5. 329; a region in Assyria, 7. 193

Chalybê (see Alybê)

Chalybians, the, in Cappadocia, lost territory to the Armenians, 5. 325; now called Chaldaeans, 5. 401; not mentioned by Homer, 6. 363

Chalymonian wine, the, in Syria, used by the Persians, 7. 185

Chamaecaetae, the, live north of the Caucasus, 5. 241

Chamaerops humilis (?), a tree found near New Carthage, 2. 155

Chamanenê (or Chammanenê), one of the ten prefectures of Cappadocia, 5. 349, 369

Chanes River, the, empties into the Cyrus River, 5. 219

Chaones, the, a famous Epeirote tribe, and once ruled over the whole Epeirote country, 3. 297

Charadra in Laconia, founded by Pelops, 4. 113

Charadrus, a fortress in Cilicia, 6. 331

Charax, a town in Corsica, 2. 359

Charax, an emporium of the Carthaginians on the Great Syrtis, 8. 199

Charaxus, brother of Sappho, lover of the famous courtesan Doricha, and wine-exporter, 8. 93

Char-dagh (see Scardus, Mt.)

Chardak, Ghieul, a lake between Laodiceia and Apameia, emits a filthy odour, 5. 517

Chares the Lindian, made the Colossus of Helius at Rhodes, 6. 269

Chares River, the, flows near Dioscurias, 5. 215

Charilaüs, the son of Polydectes, reigned as king at Sparta, 5. 153

Charimortus, Pillars and Altars of, in Aethiopia, 7. 335

Chariots, used in Britain and Celtica, 2. 255

INDEX OF NAMES, PLACES, AND SUBJECTS

Charmides, the father of Pheidias the great sculptor, **4.** 89

Charmoleon of Massalia, host of Poseidonius in Liguria, **2.** 113

Charmothas Harbour, the, in the Arabian Gulf; description of, **7.** 345

Charon of Lampsacus (lived about 460 B.C.), on the boundaries of the Troad, **6.** 9; the historian (author of a *Persian History* and *Annals of the Lampsaceni*, **6.** 37

Charondas, ancient lawgiver of Catana; laws of, used by the Mazaceni in Cappadocia, **5.** 367

Charonia (or Plutonia, *q.v.*), the, at Acharaca in Nysaïs, near Magnesia and Myus, and at Hierapolis in Phrygia, **5.** 513

Charonium (cp. Plutonia), the, near Thymbria in Caria, a sacred cave which emits deadly vapours, **6.** 211; at Acharaca near Nysa in Caria, **6.** 259

Charybdis, a monstrous and destructive deep, **3.** 67, 77, 159; infested by brigands, **1.** 73; substantially correct account of, given by Homer, **1.** 91

Charybdis, a chasm in Syria into which the Orestes flows, **3.** 93

Chatramotitae, the, in Arabia, **7.** 311

Chatramotitis in Arabia, produces myrrh, **7.** 311

Chatti, the, an indigent German tribe, **3.** 159; captives from, led in triumphal procession at Rome, **3.** 161, 163

Chattuarii, the, an indigent German tribe, **3.** 159; captives from, led in triumphal procession at Rome, **3.** 163

Chaubi, the, a German tribe near the ocean, **3.** 159

Chaulotaeans, the, in Arabia, **7.** 309

Chazenê, in Assyria, **7.** 193

Cheese, on island near Gades, made of milk mixed with water, **2.** 133; not made in Britain, **2.** 255; made in the Alps, **2.** 283; made in Attica, not touched by priestess of Athenê Polias, **4.** 257; the Salonian, from Salon in Bithynia, **5.** 463; used by the Aethiopians, **8.** 143; and by the Masaesylians, **8.** 189

Cheimerium, Cape, in Epeirus, **3.** 299

Cheirocrates (Deinocrates?), completed the restoration of the temple of Artemis at Ephesus, and proposed to Alexander to fashion Mt. Athos in his likeness, **6.** 227

Chelidonia in Phrygia; the road through, **6.** 309

Chelidonian Isles (Khelidonia), the, at the beginning of the coast of Pamphylia, **5.** 295; off Lycia, form the beginning of the Taurus, **6.** 263, 319; 1900 stadia from Cyprus, **6.** 377

Chelonatas, Cape, the most westerly point of the Peloponnesus, **4.** 25; lies 180 stadia from Cephallenia, **5.** 51

Chelonophagi ("Turtle-eaters"), the, in Aethiopia, **7.** 329

Chersicrates, left by Archias to colonise Corcyra, **3.** 71, after driving out the Liburnians, **3.** 73

Chersiphron, first architect of the temple of Artemis at Ephesus, **6.** 225

Cherso Island (see Apsyrtides)

Chersonesus, a stronghold slightly to the west of Alexandria, **8.** 57

Chersonesus in Crete, the seaport of Lyctus, has the temple of Britomartis, **5.** 143

Chersonesus, the Great (the Tauric Chersonese, now the Crimea), **3.** 225, 229, 231, 233; similar to the Peloponnesus in size and shape, and ruled by the potentates of the Bosporus, **3.** 241; mostly level, exceedingly fertile, yielding thirty-fold, paid enormous tribute to Mithridates, and supplied the Greeks with grain and fish, **3.** 243; the isthmus of, fortified by Asander against the Scythians, **3.** 245

Chersonesus Heracleotica (or Heracleia) in the Crimea, **3.** 231

Chersonesus, the Little, a part of the Great Chersonesus (the Crimea), **3.** 233

Chersonesus, the New, a city on the Little Chersonesus in the Crimea, **3.** 233; subject to the present day to the potentates of the Bosporus, **3.** 233; the wall of, and the salt-works near, **3.** 247

Chersonesus, the Old, in the Crimea now in ruins, **3.** 233

INDEX OF NAMES, PLACES, AND SUBJECTS

Chersonesus, near Saguntum, in Iberia, **2.** 91

Chersonesus in Syria (see Apameia)

Chersonesus, the Thracian; one of the European promontories, **1.** 417; northern limit of Macedonia, **3.** 333; so called from its shape ("Hand-island"), **6.** 41

Chersonesus, Cape, in Crete, **8.** 205

Cherusci, the, an indigent German tribe, **3.** 159; captives from, led in triumphal procession at Rome, **3.** 161, 163

Chiana River, the (see Clanis)

Chians, the, say the Thessalian Pelasgians were their founders, **6.** 157; claim Homer, **6.** 243

Chiliocomum, a plain near Amaseia in Cappadocia Pontica, **5.** 447

Chimaera, a ravine in Lycia, scene of myth of Chimaera, **6.** 317, 3 19

Chios, the Aegaean isle, **1.** 477; Homer lived in, **5.** 153; image of Athenê in, **6.** 83; founded by Egertius, **6.** 201; produces excellent wine, **6.** 215, 287; description and famous men of, **6.** 243; at one time had a fleet, and attained to liberty and to maritime empire, **6.** 245

Chiusi (see Clusium)

Chiusi, Lake, near Clusium, **2.** 369

Chlamys, a; inhabited world shaped like, **1.** 435, 447, 455, 457, 463; also Alexandria in Aegypt, **8.** 33

Chloris, the mother of Nestor, from Minyeian Orchomenus, **4.** 63

Choaspes River, the, in India, **7.** 45

Choaspes River, the, in Susis; course of, **7.** 159, 161, 163, 175

"Choenicides," the name given by the natives to certain rock-cavities on the coast near Sinopê in Paphlagonia, **5.** 389

Choerilus, of Samos, the epic poet (fl. towards the end of the fifth century B.C.), author of an epic poem (exact title uncertain) based on the Persian Wars; his *Crossing of the Pontoon-Bridge* (apparently a sub-title of that poem), quoted on "the sheep-tending, law-abiding Sacae, of Scythian stock," **3.** 207; mentions the epitaph of Sardanapallus at Anchialê in Cilicia, **6.** 341

Choerus, the, a fish indigenous to the

Nile, **8.** 149; the crocodile afraid of, **8.** 153

Chonians, the, formerly held a part of Leucania, **3.** 7; Petelia (Strongoli) the metropolis of, **3.** 9; took their name from the city Chonê, **3.** 11; an Oenotrian tribe, **3.** 13; once possessed Siris, **3.** 49

Chorasmii, the, a tribe of the Sacae and Massagetae in Asia, **5.** 269

Chordiraza in Assyria, **7.** 231

Chorenê in Parthia, **5.** 273

Chorographer, the (alluding to the Map of Agrippa?), **2.** 359, 363; on the distance round the Tarantine Gulf, **3.** 39; on the distances between the Liparaean Islands, **3.** 103; on the distances between Brundisium, Garganum, and other places, **3.** 133

Chorography (see Chorographer), the, on the circuit of Sicily, in miles, **3.** 57–59; appropriate function of, **5.** 83

Chorzenê, annexed to Armenia, **5.** 323, 325

Chrysa, the Old, in the plain of Thebê, mentioned by Homer, **6.** 95; had the temple of Smynthian Apollo, **6.** 121

Chrysa, the present, in the Troad, on a rocky height above the sea; also has a temple of Sminthian Apollo, **6.** 93; with an image of Apollo that has a mouse at the foot, **6.** 95; temple of Sminthian Apollo transferred to, **6.** 125

Chryseïs, captured by Achilles and presented to Agamemnon, **6.** 121; lived at the Old Chrysa, **6.** 125

Chryses, the Homeric; lived at the old Chrysa, **6.** 125

Chrysippus of Soli (fl. about 230 B.C.), the Stoic philosopher; a prolific writer, of whose works only a few fragments are extant; on the kings of the Bosporus, the house of Leuco, **3.** 201; succeeded Cleanthes as head of the Stoic school, **6.** 115, 339

Chrysocolla ("gold-solder"), found in the bladder of some people, **7.** 295

Chrysopolis, a village in Asia near the mouth of the Pontus, **5.** 455

Chrysorrhoas River, the, in Syria, **7.** 261

INDEX OF NAMES, PLACES, AND SUBJECTS

700 stadia to Cape Taenarum from, **5**. 125

Cimbri, the; the opulence of, **2**. 229; were withstood only by the Belgae, **2**. 241; live near the ocean, **3**. 159; a wandering and piratical folk, and stories about, **3**. 165, 167; customs of, **3**. 169; one of the best known German tribes, **3**. 171

Cimiata, a strong fortress in Paphlagonia used as base of operations by Mithridates Ctistes and his successors, **5**. 453

Cimiatenê in Paphlagonia, **5**. 453

Ciminian Lake (Lake Vico), the, in Italy, **2**. 367

Ciminius Mt., in Italy, **2**. 371

Cinolis, in Paphlagonia, **5**. 387

Cimmerian Bosporus (see Bosporus, Cimmerian), the, where empties Lake Maeotis, **1**. 481

Cimmerians, the; overran country from Cimmerian Bosporus to Ionia, **1**. 21; an historical people, **1**. 73; invasion of, **1**. 75; invaded Paphlagonia and Phrygia, **1**. 229; transferred by Homer to neighbourhood of Hades because they were hated by the Ionians, **2**. 51; priests at Avernus in Italy, **2**. 443; once held sway in the Cimmerian Bosporus, **3**. 237; once powerful, and the Cimmerian Bosporus named after, **5**. 197; once made an expedition against the Trojans, **5**. 413; the onsets of, in Asia, **5**. 495; captured Sardeis, **6**. 179, 253

Cimmericum ("the Cimmerian village," **5**. 195), in earlier times a city of great importance, **5**. 197

Cimmeris, the City of, an invention reported by Hecataeus, **3**. 191

Cimmerius Mountain (Aghirmisch-Dagh), the, in the Crimea, **3**. 237

Cimolian earth, the, **5**. 161

Cimolos (Kimolos), one of the Cyclades Islands, whence comes the "Cimolian earth," **5**. 161, 165

Cinaedi, the; dialect and mannerisms of, set forth by Sotades and Alexander the Aetolian, **6**. 253

Cindyê, in Caria, **6**. 289

Cineas the Thessalian (d. about 276 B.C.), friend and minister of Pyrrhus, tells a mythical story about the transfer of an oak tree and the oracle

of Zeus from Thessaly to Epeirus, **3**. 319, 321

Cingulum, Mt., in Italy, **2**. 371

Cinnamon, produced in India, **7**. 37; more abundant in the interior of Aethiopia, **7**. 333; produced in the country of the Sabaeans in Arabia, **7**. 347, 365

Cinnamon-producing country, the; position of, **1**. 235; most remote inhabited country to south, **1**. 269, 439, 505; geographical position of, relative to Meroê, Syenê, and equator, **1**. 507, **7**. 333, 351, **8**. 3

Cinolis, in Paphlagonia, **5**. 387

Cinyras, of Cypros, who presented Agamemnon with a breastplate, **1**. 145

Cinyras the tyrant; royal residence of, at Byblus in Syria, **7**. 263

Circaeum, the; in earlier times the southern boundary of Latium on the coast, **2**. 389; associated with the myth of Circê, **3**. 393

Circê, story of, **1**. 75; terrified Odysseus, **1**. 159; Aeaea the home of, **1**. 171; quest of abode of, by Jason, **2**. 357; the Circaeum in Italy the scene of myth of, **2**. 393; the tomb of, on the larger of the two Pharmacussae Islands off Attica, **4**. 259

Circei, the promontory (see Circaeum)

Circumcision, a Judaean rite, **7**. 285; practised by the Aegyptians and Troglodytes, **7**. 339, **8**. 153

Cirella (see Cerilli)

Cirphis, a city in Phocis, **4**. 343

Cirphis, Mt., in front of Delphi, beyond the ravine and Pleistus River, **4**. 351

Cirrha, near the Pleistus River in Phocis, 200 stadia from Aegium and 500 to Thaumaci, **4**. 233; on the sea about 80 from Delphi, but was destroyed by the Crisaeans, **4**. 343, 351

Cirta, royal residence of Masanasses and his successors, **8**. 169, 183

Cisamus (Kisamo Kasteli) in Crete, seaport of Aptera, **5**. 141

Cis-Halys country, the; description of, **1**. 497

Cispadana, geographical description of, **2**. 323; famous cities in, **2**. 325; used to be covered with marshes,

INDEX OF NAMES, PLACES, AND SUBJECTS

and could be traversed only with difficulty by Hannibal, 2. 329;

Cisses (the Homeric), apparently the ruler of Cissus in Macedonia, 3. 343, 349

Cissus, one of the cities destroyed by Cassander, 3. 343, 349

Cissus, father of Althaemenes and coloniser of Argos after the return of the Heracleidae, 4. 235, 5. 149

Cis-Tauran regions of Asia, the, 1. 495, 5. 189, 295

Cisterns, the, at Rome, 2. 405

Cisthenê, a deserted city with a harbour outside the Gulf of Adramyttium, 6. 103

Cisthenê, an island off Lycia, 6. 319

Citaris, the Median, 5. 313

Cithaeron, Mt., joins the mountains of Megara and Attica, bends into the plains and ends near Thebes, 4. 301, 313; Plataeae lies at foot of, 4. 325

Cithara (see Lyre), the; the Asiatic, 5. 109; played by Arion and Terpander, 6. 145

Citharists, and flute-players, played the accompaniment to the Pythian Nome at Delphi, 4. 363

Citharoedes, the, sang paeans at Delphi in honour of Apollo, 4. 361, 363

Citharus, the, a fish indigenous to the Nile, 8. 149

Citium in Cypros, home of Zeno the Stoic and Apollonius the physician, 6. 379

Citrum, the Roman name of Pydna (*q.v.*) in Macedonia, 3. 341

Cius, a companion of Heracles, founded the city of Cius in Asia, 5. 457

Cius (see Prusias, the city), 5. 453, 455

Civilisation, the development of, according to Plato, 6. 47, 49

Civita Tommasa (see Foruli)

Clanis (Chiana) River, the (see Liris River), sources of the, 2. 287; runs through Tyrrhenia, 2. 403

Clarus near Colophon in Asia, 6. 233, where the seer Calchas is said to have died, 6. 325

Clastidium (Casteggio), near the Aemilian Way, 2. 327

Claterna, on the Aemilian Way, 2. 327

Claudius, Publius Pulcher, Roman tribune, sent Marcus Cato to take Cypros away from King Ptolemy, 6. 385

Clautenatii, the; one of the boldest tribes of the Vindelici, 2. 281

Clazomenae, once an island, 1. 217

Clazomenae in Asia, founded by Paralus, 6. 201; the Old and New, 6. 245

Clazomenians, the, on Lake Maeotis; with Milesians founded Cardia, 3. 373; engage in fishing, 5. 195; live on an isthmus, 6. 239

Cleandria in the Troad, 6. 89

Cleandridas, an exile from Lacedaemon, served as general for the Thurii, 3. 51

Cleantacidae, the; tyrants of Mitylenê, 6. 143

Cleanthes, the Corinthian; famous paintings of, entitled the "Capture of Troy" and the "Birth of Athenê," in the temple of Artemis near the mouth of the Alpheius River, 4. 49

Cleanthes, the Stoic philosopher and successor of Zeno, a native of Assus, 6. 115

Cleides, the, two isles off Cypros, 6. 375, 377, 379, 383

Cleitarchus the historian, who accompanied Alexander the Great on his Asiatic expedition; on the saltrock in India, 2. 357; on the danger of the tides on the coast of Celtica, 3. 167; on the isthmus of Asia Minor, 5. 187; on the birds used in processions in India, 7. 123

Cleitor (Palaeopoli near Klituras) in Arcadia, no longer exists, 4. 229

Cleobulus, one of the Seven Wise Men, a native of Lindus in Rhodes, 6. 279

Cleochares, the rhetorician, a native of Myrleïa in Bithynia, 5. 467

Cleomachus the pugilist, imitated the dialect and mannerisms of the *cinaedi*, 6. 253

Cleombrotus, supposed founder of Heraea in Arcadia, 4. 21

Cleon, chieftain of bands of robbers on the Mysian Olympus in Strabo's time; useful to Antony, later joined Caesar's side, and even received the priesthood of Comana, 5. 497, 499

295

INDEX OF NAMES, PLACES, AND SUBJECTS

INDEX OF NAMES, PLACES, AND SUBJECTS

"between a deer and ram in size, white, swifter than they, and drinks through its nostrils," **3.** 249

Colossae, a town in Phrygia Epictetus, **5.** 505

Colossi, the two, at the Aegyptian Thebes; the marvellous story of, **8.** 123

Colossian wool, the, brings in splendid revenue, **5.** 511

Colossus, of Helius in Rhodes, the, one of the Seven Wonders of the world, **6.** 269; at Memphis in Aegypt, **8.** 89

Colossus of Zeus, the bronze, at Taras, second in size only to the colossus at Rhodes; and that of Heracles, **3.** 107

Colotes of Paros (fl. 444 B.C.), maker of the remarkable ivory image of Asclepius at Cyllenê in Elis, **4.** 25

Columna Rhteginorum, near Rhegium, **3.** 21; with Caenys and Pelorias forms the Strait of Sicily, **3.** 55

Colyttus, the Attic deme, **1.** 243, 247

Comana (El Bostan), in Greater Cappadocia, where is the temple of Enyo, who is called "Ma," **5.** 351, 353; the Pontic Comana copied after, **5.** 433; the priest at, serves for life, **5.** 359; patterned after the Comana in Greater Cappadocia, and consecrated to the same goddess (Enyo), **5.** 433; populous, wealthy, and, like Corinth, noted for its multitude of courtesans dedicated to Aphroditê, **5.** 439; priesthood of, once held by Cleon the pirate, **5.** 499; Archelaüs the priest of, **8.** 45

Comarus (Gomaro), the harbour, forms an isthmus 60 stadia in width with the Ambracian Gulf, **3.** 301

Comedy, took its structure from tragedy, **1.** 65

Comic poets, the Greek, ridicule the welcome accorded to foreign religious rites at Athens, **5.** 109

Comisenê, in Armenia, **5.** 323

Comisenê, in Parthia, **5.** 273

Commagenê, borders on the Euphrates, **5.** 297, 319; abounds in fruit-trees, **5.** 351; road through,

6. 311; a part of Syria, **7.** 239; now a Roman province, **7.** 241

Communism, the, of the Scythians, according to Ephorus, **3.** 207; includes wives and children, in the Platonic way, **3.** 197, 199

Comum (Como), at foot of the Alps, near Lake Larius, **2.** 227, 273; colonised with Greeks and Romans, **2.** 311, 313

Conchliae, shell-fish in the Nile, **8.** 149

Concordia, in Italy, **2.** 317

Coniacans (Coniscans?), the, in Iberia, now take the field for the Romans, **2.** 79

Coniaci, the, a tribe in eastern India, **7.** 17, 21

Conisalus, Attic deity similar to Priapus, **6.** 29

Coniscans (see Coniacans), the, took part in the Celtic expedition to Cantabria, **2.** 101

Conon, Altars of, in Aethiopia on the Arabian Gulf, **7.** 321

Consentia (Cosenza), in Bruttium; metropolis of the Bruttii, **3.** 17

Constance, Lake of (Bodensee), **3.** 162 (see footnote); a day's journey from the sources of the Ister, **3.** 165; "the lake which is near the country of the Vindelici, Rhaeti, and Taenii (Helvetii? or Toȳgeni?)," **3.** 253

Constantia in Iberia (see Cotinae)

Constantinople (see Byzantium)

Constellations, the; the Bear and Wain in Homer, Berenicê's Hair, and Canobus, **1.** 9; in the zenith, **1.** 45; the Little Bear, **1.** 507; the Great Bear, **1.** 509; Cassiepeia and Perseus, **1.** 515

Constitution, the, at Emporium in Iberia, a Greek and barbarian mixture, **2.** 93; the Spartan, drawn up by Eurysthenes and Procles, according to Hellanicus, **4.** 139; the Cretan, described, **5.** 145

Consular legatus, a, serves as governor of most of Caesar's territory in Iberia, **2.** 121; his duties, **2.** 123

Continents, the; divisions of, **1.** 243; wrongly named by Greeks, **1.** 245; three in number, **1.** 393, **8.** 155; and each measured by space between two meridians, **1.** 415

INDEX OF NAMES, PLACES, AND SUBJECTS

stadia, **2.** 23; through which runs
the main road, **2.** 97

Cordylê, the, a kind of fish in the
Euxine off Pharnacia, **5.** 403

Corê (Persephonê), Proserpina, sacrifices to, in Samothrace and in island
near Britain, **2.** 251; used to visit
neighbourhood of, to gather
flowers, **3.** 19; trampled under-
foot Minthê the concubine of Hades
in Triphylia, **4.** 51; worshipped
there, **4.** 53

Corebus, the Eleian, victor at Olympia in the first Olympiad, **4.** 93

Coressia in Ceos, **5.** 169

Coressus, Mt., near Ephesus, **6.** 203,
225

Corfinium (Pentima), whither the
Valerian Way runs, **2.** 415; the
metropolis of the Peligni, **2.** 431

Corfu (see Corcyra)

Corinth; a tyrant of, was betrothed
to, and murdered, Rhadinê of
Samus in Triphylia, **4.** 65; Cypselus, the tyrant of, dedicated the
Zeus of beaten gold at Olympia, **4.**
89; destroyed, but rebuilt by the
Romans, **4.** 121; once subject to
Agamemnon, **4.** 167; "wealthy,"
4. 185; description and history of,
4. 189–203; the "key" of the
Peloponnesus, **4.** 189; the temple
of Aphroditê at, with 1000 courtesans, **4.** 191; including Acrocorinthus, about 85 stadia in circuit, **4**
193; the two harbours of, **4.** 197;
rased to the ground by Mummius,
4. 199; pitied by Polybius, **4.** 201;
restored by Julius Caesar, **4.** 203; in
proverb called "beetle-browed," **4.**
205; added by Aratus to the
Achaean League, **4.** 217; colonised
by Aletes after return of Heracleidae, **4.** 235; persuaded the Heracleidae to make an expedition
against Attica, **4.** 249; and Calchis,
by Philip called "the fetters of
Greece," **4.** 391; Comana in Cappadocia Pontica likened to, because of
its multitude of courtesans, **5.** 439;
remained desolate about as long as
Carthage, **8.** 189

Corinth, Gulf of, water-level of,
thought to be higher than that of
the Acgaean Sea, **1.** 201, **3.** 297;

description of, and of cities on, **4.**
15–19; 2100 stadia in perimeter from
the Evenus to Cape Araxus, **4.** 17;
begins at mouth of the Achelöus
River, **4.** 25; Mychus Harbour considered by some the inmost recess
of, but the inmost is at Pagae and
Oenoê, **4.** 317

Corinth, Isthmus of; canal through
attempted by Demetrius, **1.** 201;
inscribed pillar erected on, as boundary between Ionia and the Peloponnesus, **2.** 139; distant 1030
stadia from Cape Araxus (Kalogria), **4.** 19; narrowest at the
"Diolcus," **4.** 155

Corinthia, extends from Sicyonia to
the isthmus, **4.** 15; lies on the
Crisaean Gulf, **4.** 195; the Nemea
River a boundary of, **4.** 207

Corinthians, the, with the Corcyraeans founded Apollonia (Pollina)
in Illyria, **3.** 265; founded Potidaea,
3. 349; Tenea revolted from, **4.**
199; sided with Philip and insulted
the Romans, but suffered the
destruction of Corinth by Mummius, **4.** 199; conquered at Chaeroneia by Philip, **4.** 333; dug canal
through isthmus of Leucas, **5.** 33

Coriscus, the Socratic philosopher,
native of Scepsis, **6.** 111

Cornel-wood, the, of which javelins
are made, **5.** 483

Cornelius Gallus (d. 26 B.C.), the first
man to be appointed praefect of
Aegypt, by Augustus, and took
Heröonpolis with only a few soldiers,
8. 135

Corneto (see Tarquinia)

Corocondamê, a village on the Cimmerian Bosporus, **5.** 197, 205

Corocondamitis, Lake, near the Cimmerian Bosporus, **5.** 199

Coronaeis, the; inhabitants of Coronê
in Messenê called, **4.** 325

Coronê (Petalidi) in Messenia, by some
writers identified with the Homeric
Pedasus, **4.** 117; inhabitants of,
called Coronaeis, **4.** 325

Coroneia (Camari) the Homeric, in
Boeotia; the Cephissus River flows
near, **4.** 307; lies near Lake
Copaïs, **4.** 321; description and
history of, **4.** 323; inhabitants of,

INDEX OF NAMES, PLACES, AND SUBJECTS

called Coronii, **4.** 325; Lebadeia lies near, **4.** 333

Coroneia in Phthiotis, subject to Achilles, **4.** 413

Coronii; the inhabitants of Coroneia in Boeotia called, **4.** 325

Coronis "the unwedded virgin," mother of Asclepius, mentioned by Hesiod, **4.** 449

Coropassus, a village in Lycaonia, **5.** 475; the road through, **6.** 309

Corpilians, the, live along the Hebrus River in Macedonia, **3.** 369, 383

Corpilicê (formerly Apsinthis, *q.v.*), **3.** 383

Corsica (see Cyrnus), one of the largest Mediterranean islands, **1.** 471

Corsicans, the, bestial character of, **2.** 359

Corsium, a relish like pepper, found in Aegypt, **8.** 149

Corsura the island, opposite the middle of the mouth of the Cartha-ginian Gulf, **8.** 189

Corybanteium, in the territory of the Alexandreians in the Troad; the Cabeiri worshipped at, **5.** 115

Corybantes (see Curetes), the, identi-fied with the gods worshipped in Samothrace, **3.** 371; by some represented as identical with the Curetes, **5.** 87, 89, 99, 103, 113, 115; attendants of Dionysus, **5.** 105; by some called "Phrygians," by others "Bactrians," by others, "Colchians," and by the Prasians "sons of Athenê and Helius," **5.** 111; by some called sons of Cronus and by others sons of Zeus, **5.** 113; derivation of the term, **5.** 115; by some thought to be offspring of the Idaean Dactyli, **5.** 119

Corybissa in the Troad; the Cabeiri worshipped at, **5.** 115

Corycian Cave, the, in Cilicia, near Cape Sarpedon, **4.** 345, **6.** 177, 337

Corycian Cave (Corycium), the; the best known and most beautiful cave on Parnassus, and sacred to the nymphs, **4.** 345

Corycus, Cape, in Cilicia, **6.** 337

Corycus, Cape, in Crete, 700 stadia from Cape Maleae, **4.** 127

Corycus, Mt., in Asia, near Erythrae; waters along coast of, a haunt of pirates, **6.** 241

Corycus, a town in Pamphylia, colonised by Attalus II, **6.** 323

Corycus, a tract of sea-coast in Lycia, **6.** 319

Corydalleis, the deme, in Attica, **4.** 259

Corydallus, Mt., in Attica, **4.** 259

Coryphantis, a village of the Mityle-naeans in Asia, **6.** 103

Coryphasium (Navarino), a fortress in Messenia, near the site of the Messe-nian Pylus, **4.** 33, 65; seven stadia from Mt. Aegaleum, and settled by some inhabitants of the Messenian Pylus, **4.** 109

Cos, the island; temple of Asclepius on, **4.** 177; produces excellent wine **6.** 215; people of, are Dorians, **6.** 271, 273; description of, and famous men of, **6.** 287, 289

Cos, the city, in the isle Cos; "city of Eurypylus," **5.** 175, 177; the "Meropian," **7.** 5, 57

Cosa (or Cossa, now Ansedonia), dis-tance from, to Poplonium, **2.** 347; geographical position of, **2.** 363

Cosa River, the, flows past Frusino, **2.** 411

Coscile River, the (see Sybaris River)

Coscinia in Asia, near Nysa, **6.** 261

Coscinii, the, in Caria; a river in country of, crossed many times by the same road, **6.** 27

Cosenza (see Consentia)

Cosmi, the, in Crete, are public officials like the Ephors in Sparta, **5.** 151, 159

Cossa (see Cosa)

Cossaea, near Babylonia, has a fairly good supply of timber for ships, **7.** 209; borders on Carmania, **7.** 221

Cossaean Mts., the, in Asia, about 1000 stadia from the Euphrates, **7.** 213

Cossaeans, the, in Asia; the moun-tainous country of, **5.** 301; a pred-atory people, **5.** 307, 309; joined the Elymaeans in war against the Babylonians and Susians, **7.** 221

Cossura (Pantellaria), isle between Sicily and Libya, **1.** 473; lies off Lilybaeum and Aspis, **3.** 103

Cossurus (see Cossura), the island and city, between Carthaginia and Sicily, **8.** 191

INDEX OF NAMES, PLACES, AND SUBJECTS

302

INDEX OF NAMES, PLACES, AND SUBJECTS

303

INDEX OF NAMES, PLACES, AND SUBJECTS

INDEX OF NAMES, PLACES, AND SUBJECTS

River and were defeated, **3**. 37; produced great athletes, **3**. 43; destroyed Sybaris, **3**. 47

Crown, a, the prize of victory at Olympia, **4**. 87, 93

Crows, the two fabulous, with white wings, in Celtica, **2**. 249; (or rather eagles), the two set free by Zeus, met at Delphi, **4**. 355; the two which guided Alexander to the temple of Ammon, **8**. 115

Crucifixion, practised by the Cantabrians, **2**. 115

Cruni (Baltchik), on the Euxine, **3**. 277

Cruni, a spring in Triphylia, **4**. 49

Cruni River, the; Telemachus sailed past the mouth of, **4**. 77, 79

Crusis in Mygdonia, in Macedonia; cities in, destroyed by Cassander the son-in-law of Philip, **3**. 343

Crystals, slabs of, found by the miners of Archelaüs near Galatia, **5**. 369; of all kinds, found in India, **7**. 119

Ctenus Limen ("Comb Harbour," now the Harbour of Sebastopol), with Symbolon Limen forms an isthmus, **3**. 233; equidistant from the New Chersonesus and Symbolon Limen, **3**. 235, 247

Ctesias of Cnidus in Caria (fl. in the fifth century B.C.); historian, physician to Artaxerxes, and author of a *Persian History* in 23 books; includes myths in his works, **1**. 159; tells incredible stories, **5**. 247; native of Cnidus, **6**. 283; on the size of India, **7**. 17; on the origin of the name of the Erythraean ("Red") Sea, **7**. 351

Ctesiphon, an important village or city near Seleuceia on the Tigris River, **7**. 219

Ctistae, the; Thracians who live apart from women and are dedicated to the gods, **3**. 179

Cuarius River, the, flows near Coroneia in Boeotia, and by Alcaeus wrongly called Coralius, **4**. 323, 329; named after the Cuarius in Thessaly, **4**. 421, 433

Cuculum, on the Valerian Way, **2**. 415

Cuirasses, the, in Sardinia, made of sheep-hide, **2**. 363

Culupenê, joined by Pompey into one state with Zelitis and Camisenê, **5**. 441

Cumae, in Campania, history of, **2**. 437, 439; the tunnel leading to, **2**. 441; smells of sulphur, **2**. 447

Cumaeans or Cymaeans, the Asiatic, ejected the Sidicini from Campania, and were themselves ejected by the Tyrrheni, **2**. 435; joint founders of Cumae in Italy, **2**. 437; with Mitylenaeans, founded Aenus on the Melas Gulf, **3**. 373; founded Sidê in Pamphylia, **6**. 325

"Cuneus" ("Wedge"); Latin name for country adjacent to the Sacred Cape of Iberia, **2**. 7

Cups, drinking-, of the Scythians made of skulls, **3**. 197

Curd-eaters (see Galactophagi)

Cures (Arci, near Corressa), in the Sabine country, **2**. 375

Curetes, the, held a part of Acarnania, according to Aristotle, **3**. 289; identified with the gods worshipped in Samothrace, **3**. 371; should be classified as Aetolians, **4**. 395; the Pleuronian, in Aetolia, **5**. 29; the various accounts of, **5**. 75, 83–99; first held Aetolia, but withdrew to Acarnania, **5**. 77, 83; settled at Chalcis, but migrated to Aetolia, **5**. 85; mentioned by Homer, **5**. 87; origin of the name of, **5**. 89, 91; helpers of Rhea in Crete, **5**. 97; also called "Corybantes," **5**. 99; Cretan ministers of Mother Rhea, **5**. 103; origin of, and "rearers of Zeus," **5**. 111; "Ministers of Hecatê," according to some, **5**. 113; identified with the Corybantes, **5**. 115; by some thought to be offspring of the Idaean Dactyli, **5**. 119; invented the war-dance, **5**. 147; on Mt. Solmissus near Ephesus, frightened Hera, and concealed from her the birth of Leto's children (Apollo and Artemis), **6**. 223; special college of, meets annually in the grove Ortygia, **6**. 225

Curias, Cape, in Cyprus, **6**. 379

Curites (Quirites), the title by which orators addressed the Romans, **2**. 375; consented to reign of Romulus, **2**. 385

INDEX OF NAMES, PLACES, AND SUBJECTS

INDEX OF NAMES, PLACES, AND SUBJECTS

Indian cattle with their large dogs, **7**. 323

Cynia, a lake in Aetolia, **5**. 63

Cynical mode of life, the, **3**. 181

Cynocephali (*Papio hamadryas*), the; sacred baboons in Aethiopia, **7**. 333, 337

Cynocephalus (*Simia hamadryas*, baboon), worshipped at Hermopolis, **8**. 111

Cynonpolis, on the Nile, where Anubis and dogs are worshipped, **8**. 109

Cynoscephalae in Thessaly, where Titus Quintius Flamininus conquered Philip the son of Demetrius, **4**. 445

Cynospolis in Aegypt, near Busiris, **8**. 69

Cynos-Sema, a place on the coast to the west of Alexandria, **8**. 57

Cynos-Sema, in Caria, **6**. 281

Cynos-Sema (by some called Hecabe's Sema), Cape, in the Thracian Chersonesus at the beginning of the Hellespont, **3**. 377, **6**. 59

Cynthus (Kastro), Mt., in Delos, **5**. 163

Cynuria, a region on the common border of Laconia and Argolis, **4**. 183

Cynus, damaged by earthquake, **1**. 225; the seaport of Opus in Locris, lies opposite Aedepsus in Euboea, at a distance of 160 stadia, **1**. 379; founded Canae in Asia Minor, **6**. 133

Cyparissëeis; territory of Cyparissia; geographical position of, **4**. 67, 73

Cyparissëeis River, the, **4**. 73

Cyparissia in Laconia, on the Laconian Gulf, **4**. 129

Cyparissia in Messenia, **4**. 109, 111, 117

Cyparissia in Triphylia; the territory of, seized by the Cauconians, **4**. 55; geographical position of, **4**. 67, 73

Cyparisson in Assyria, **7**. 197

Cyparissus in Phocis, the Homeric; origin of name, and geographical position of, **4**. 369

Cyphus in Thessaly, held by the Perrhaebians, **4**. 443

Cyphus, Mt., in Perrhaebia, **4**. 449

Cyprians, the, in earlier times ruled by tyrants, **6**. 383, but later by the Ptolemies of Aegypt, **6**. 385

Cypros, lies in both Issican and Pamphylian Gulfs, **1**. 483; the copper of, alone produces calamine, chalcanthite, and spodium, **2**. 107; according to an oracle will some day be joined to the mainland by silt from the Pyramus River, **5**. 355; one of the seven largest islands, **6**. 277; kings of, co-operated with the Cilician pirates, **6**. 329; description and history of, **6**. 373–385; dimensions of, **6**. 375; fertility of, **6**. 383; now a praetorian province, **6**. 385, **8**. 215; boats built in, by Alexander, **7**. 209; united with Aegypt by the Ptolemies, but separated from it by the Romans, **8**. 23

Cypsela (Ipsala), on the Hebrus (Maritza) River, 535 Roman miles from Apollonia (Pollina), **3**. 293, 329, 369; 3100 stadia from Byzantium, **3**. 379

Cypselus, tyrant of Corinth (reigned 655–625 B.C.); father of Gorgus the founder of Ambracia, **3**. 303; dedicated the Zeus of beaten gold at Olympia, **4**. 87, 89; overthrew the house of the Bacchiadae at Corinth, **4**. 189; with his son Gorgus dug canal through isthmus of Leucas, **5**. 33

Cyra in Sogdiana, the last city founded by Cyrus the Elder, destroyed by Alexander, **5**. 283

Cyrbantes, the, identified with the gods worshipped in Samothrace, **3**. 371; descent of, **5**. 115

Cyrbas, a comrade of the Curetes in Crete and founder of Hierapytna, **5**. 111

Cyrenaea, a fertile country, **1**. 501; a voyage of two days and nights from, to Cape Criumetopon in Crete, **5**. 125; seized by the Ptolemies, but separated from Aegypt by the Romans, **8**. 23, 55; the Euphrantas Tower the former boundary of, on the west, **8**. 199; now, with Crete, forms a Roman Province, **8**. 215

Cyrenaeans, the; Thera the metropolis of, **5**. 161

Cyrenaïc juice, the, from the silphium in Cyrenaea, **5**. 311

INDEX OF NAMES, PLACES, AND SUBJECTS

308

INDEX OF NAMES, PLACES, AND SUBJECTS

Dacians, the; wars against, **2**. 287; fought by the Boii, **2**. 311; a division of the Getans, on the west; called Daϊ in early times, **3**. 213; language of, the same as that of the Getans, **3**. 215; border on the Ister, **3**. 251

Daciёan Zeus; temple of, in Cappadocia, **5**. 357

Dactyl, the, suited to hymns of praise, **4**. 363

Dactyli, the Idaean (see Idaean Dactyli), identified with the gods worshipped in Samothrace, **3**. 371

Dactylopius Vitis, a vine-infesting insect (see *Pseudo-coccus Vitis*)

Daedala, mountain and city, boundary between Lycia and the Peraea of the Rhodians, **6**. 265, 311, 313, 317

Daedalus, father of Iapyx, after whom the Iapyges were named, **3**. 111; adventures of, in Crete, **5**. 131; father of Icarus—and flight and fall of, **6**. 221

Daёs of Colonae, on the temple of Cillaean Apollo, **6**. 123

Daesitiatae, the, a Pannonian tribe, **3**. 257

Dagger, a small, used by the Sardinians, **2**. 363; used in Maurusia in Libya, **8**. 167

Dalion River, the, in Triphylia, **4**. 53

Dalmatia, the Ardian (Dinara) Mountain in, **3**. 251; cut into two parts by the Ardian Mountain, **3**. 261; Pannonia extends to, **3**. 271

Dalmatians, the, had as many as 50 noteworthy settlements, carried on war against the Romans for a long time, redistribute their land every seven years, and use no coined money, **3**. 261

Dalmium (also spelled Delminium, and now, apparently, Duvno), in Dalmatia, once a large city, but reduced to a small city by Nasica (155 B.C.), **3**. 261

Damala (see Troezen)

Damascenē in Syria, **7**. 261, 265

Damascus in Syria, a noteworthy city, **7**. 265

Damasia, the acropolis of the Licatii, **2**. 283

Damastes of Sigeium, Greek historian, contemporary of Herodotus, works of, now lost, discredited by Strabo, **1**. 173; on the boundaries of the Troad, **6**. 9; on the length of Cypros, **6**. 383

Damastium (Tepeleni? or Argyrocastro? on the Viosa River), the silver mines at, **3**. 307

Damasus, an Athenian, founder of Teos, **6**. 201

Damasus Scombrus, famous orator, native of Magnesia on the Maeander, **6**. 257

Damegam (see Hecatompylus)

Damnameneus, one of the Idaean Dactyli, **5**. 117

Danaäns, the; the name given to all the Pelasgians by Danaüs, **4**. 163; all the Greeks so called by Homer, **5**. 495

Danaё, mother of Perseus, rescued at Seriphos, **5**. 171

Danaïdes, the, of Aeschylus, quoted, on the Pelasgi, **2**. 345

Danala (Podanala?), a stronghold of the Galatian Trocmi, where Pompey and Leucullus held their conference, **5**. 469, 471

Danaüs, an historical king, **1**. 87; the father of fifty daughters, settled in Argos, **2**. 345; founder of the acropolis of the Argives, was from Aegypt, **3**. 287; the daughters of, discovered the wells at Argos; named all Pelasgians " Danaäns," and was buried in the market-place at Argos, **4**. 163; descendants of, reigned at Argos, **4**. 165; father of Celaeno the mother of Celaenus by Poseidon, **5**. 515

Dance, the war-, invented by the Curetes in Crete, and the Pyrrhic by Pyrrhichus, **5**. 147

Dancing, in Bastetania in Iberia, where women dance with men, **2**. 75

Dandarii, the, a tribe of the Maeotae, **5**. 201

Danthaletae, the, a brigandish tribe in the neighbourhood of the Haemus Mountain, **3**. 275

" Danuvius " (see Ister) River, the; the term formerly applied to the stretch of the Danube from its sources to the cataracts, the rest of its course being called " Ister," **3**. 215

INDEX OF NAMES, PLACES, AND SUBJECTS

INDEX OF NAMES, PLACES, AND SUBJECTS

INDEX OF NAMES, PLACES, AND SUBJECTS

account of all the earthquakes in Greece, **1**. 223

Demetrius, son of Euthydemus the king of Bactria; far-reaching conquests of, **5**. 281

Demetrius Lacon, pupil of Protarchus the Epicurean, **6**. 289

Demetrius of Phalerum (b. about 350 B.C.), pupil of Theophrastus, philosopher, statesman, orator, historian, and author of works on numerous subjects; on the diligence of the miners at the silver-mines of Laurium, **2**. 43; placed over Athens by Cassander the king, and even improved its democratic form of government, as is made clear in his *Memoirs*, but after the death of Cassander was forced to go into exile, **4**. 269

Demetrius of Pharos, on joining the Romans in 229 B.C., was made ruler of most of Illyria instead of Queen Teuta; a native of Pharos, **3**. 261; adviser of Philip V, son of Demetrius, on Acrocorinthus and Ithomê, **4**. 119, 121

Demetrius, the father of Philip V, **5**. 457

Demetrius Poliorcetes (334–283 B.C.), son of Antigonus the king of Asia; noted general, admiral, and engineer; intended to cut canal through Isthmus of Corinth, **1**. 201; his complaints against the pirates of Antium, **2**. 391; rebuilt Sicyon on a hill above the sea, **4**. 207; founded Demetrias in Magnesia and settled in it the inhabitants of several neighbouring towns, **4**. 423, 425

Demetrius, the son of Rhathenus, the mathematician, native of Amisus, **5**. 399

Demetrius of Scepsis (b. about 205 B.C.), grammarian and author of a historico-geographical work, in 30 books, on the Trojan allies; was the cause of some of Apollodorus' mistakes, **1**. 165; transfers scene of Jason's wandering to Oceanus, **1**. 171; on results of earthquakes and volcanic eruptions, **1**. 215; says that Homer's Ephyra is in Elis, **3**. 315; on the Halizoni, **3**. 351; does not

believe that the canal across Athos was navigable, **3**. 357; on the dimensions of the Propontis and the Hellespont, and on certain distances, **3**. 379; on the Selleëis River and Oechalia, **4**. 31; on "the contrariness of the soil" in Triphylia, **4**. 53; on the confusion of Methonê (Methana in Argolis with Methonê in Macedonia), **4**. 177; emends the *Iliad* and says Phoenix was from Ormenium, **4**. 435; on the isle Asteria (the Homeric Asteris), **5**. 51; on the Cabeiri, **5**. 113; on the Curetes and the Corybantes, **5**. 115; on Calymnae, **5**. 179; on the Halizoni and the Chalybians, **5**. 405, 407, 409, 411; on the poor plight of the Ilium he visited when a lad, **6**. 53; on the territories of Ilium, Cebrenê, Scepsis, and the course of the Scamander, **6**. 65; on the sites of the present and the Homeric Ilium, **6**. 67, and quotes Hestiaea of Alexandreia in regard thereto, **6**. 73; accuses Timaeus of falsehood, **6**. 77; on Cotylus, a hill of Mt. Ida and the rivers rising there, **6**. 85; on the Rhesus and other Trojan rivers, **6**. 87; wrote a work of 30 books on the *Trojan Catalogue*, **6**. 91; thinks Scepsis was the royal residence of Aeneias, **6**. 105; wrote a commentary on *The Marshalling of the Trojan Forces*, born at about the same time as Crates and Aristarchus, **6**. 113; calls the inhabitants of Gargara "semi-barbarians," **6**. 117; inclined to place the Homeric Hydê in Mysia Catacecaumenê, **6**. 177; on the Asioneis, **6**. 179; borrowed stories from Callisthenes, **6**. 369

Demetrius the son of Seleucus, defeated by Attalus II and Alexander the son of Antiochus, **6**. 167

Demetrius, Lookouts of, in Aethiopia on the Arabian Gulf, **7**. 321

Democles of Pygela in Lydia (fourth or fifth century B.C.), of whom little is known; recorded earthquakes, **1**. 217

Democoön, bastard son of Priam, **6**. 19

Democracy, the, at Athens, **4**. 269

Democritus of Abdera (b. about 460

313

INDEX OF NAMES, PLACES, AND SUBJECTS

B.C.), celebrated philosopher, **1.** 3; traveller, and lecturer; lauds the virtue of not marvelling at things, **1.** 227; has his own method of "dieting upon disputation," **1.** 243, 245; does not believe that nothing floats on the Silas River in India, **7.** 67

Demosthenes the orator (about 383–322 B.C.), on the destruction of Olynthus, **1.** 465; committed suicide on the island Calauria, **4.** 175; on the naturally strategic position of Elateia in Phocis, **4.** 373; says Philip established Philistides as tyrant in Euboea, **5.** 7; refers to the Phrygian religious rites, reproaching Aeschines and his mother, **5.** 109

Demus, wrongly thought by some writers to be the name of a *place* in Ithaca, **3.** 193

Dendra (see Midea near Tiryns)

Denia (see Hemeroscopeium)

Derbê in Asia Minor, once belonged to Antipater Derbetes the pirate, **5.** 349; royal residence of Antipater, and in Strabo's time held by Amyntas, **5.** 477

Derbices, the, in Asia; geographical position of, **5.** 269; border on the Tapyri, **5.** 273; barbarous customs of, **5.** 293

"Derceto," Otesias' name for Athara, **7.** 373

Derdae, the, a tribe in India, **7.** 75

Derrhis, the Aegyptian harbour, **8.** 57

Derrhis, Cape, opposite Cape Canastraeum and Athos, **3.** 353

Derton (Tortona), near the Aemilian Way, **2.** 327; size and geographical position of, **2.** 329

Dertossa (Tortosa), on the Iberus River in Iberia, **2.** 91, 95

Despotiko (see Prepesinthos)

Deucalion, presented by Zeus with the Leleges, "peoples picked out of the earth," **3.** 291; father of Hellen the founder of the Hellenes, **4.** 209; said to have lived at Cynus in Locris, and his grave to be seen at Athens, **4.** 379; ruled over Thessaly, **4.** 405; named southern Thessaly after his mother Pandora, **4.** 453

Deucalion the isle, near Pyrrha in Thessaly, **4.** 423

Deudorix (Theodoric), the Sugambrian, led captive in triumph at Rome, **3.** 161

Deuriopes, the; all the cities of, on the Erigon, were populous, **3.** 311

Deuriopus, the territory, **3.** 307

Dia (Hebê), worshipped at Phlius and Sicyon, **4.** 205

Dia, an isle in the Arabian Gulf, **7.** 343

Dia (Scandia), the island, off Crete, **5.** 161

Diagesbes (Iolaës), the; a tribe of mountaineers in Sardinia, **2.** 361

Dialects, the four Greek, **4.** 5, **6.** 369

Diana, the goddess (see Artemis)

Dianae, Nemus, near the Appian Way, **2.** 421; Speculum (Lacus Nemorensis, now Lago di Nemi), **2.** 423

Dianium, the, in Iberia (see Hemeroscopeium)

Dicaea (now Kurnu?), in Thrace, near Lake Bistonis, **3.** 365, 367

Dicaearcheia (now Puteoli), visited by Eudoxus of Cyzicus, **1.** 381; receives exports from Turdetania, **2.** 35; the tunnel from, to Neapolis, **2.** 445; description of, **2.** 447, 457; where Italy is contracted into an isthmus, **3.** 135; large exports from Alexandria to, **8.** 31

Dicaearchus of Messenê in Sicily (fl. about 320 B.C.), peripatetic philosopher, pupil of Aristotle, historian, and geographer, **1.** 3; besides other works wrote a *Periegesis*, and he was the first to measure the altitude of mountains, a subject upon which he wrote a treatise; criticises ancient geographers, **1.** 399; has no faith in Pytheas, **1.** 401; thinks recess of Adriatic farther than Pillars from the Peloponnesus, **1.** 405; on the geographical position of the Pillars of Heracles, **2.** 137

Dice, played by soldiers of Mummius on celebrated paintings at Corinth, **4.** 201

Dictê (Lassithi), Mt., in Crete; Dictaean Zeus named after, **5.** 113, 139

Dictê, a place in the territory of Scepsis, **5.** 113

Dictynna, the temple of, in Crete, **5.** 141

Dictynnaean temple, the, on Mt. Tityrus in Crete, 5. 139

Dictys, drew to land in Seriphos the chest in which Perseus and his mother Danaê were enclosed, 5. 171

Didyma near Miletus; temple of Apollo near, presided over by Branchus, descendant of Machaereus the Delphian, 4. 361; robbed by Xerxes, 5. 285

Didyman Hills, the, at the Dotian Plain in Thessaly, 4. 449; mentioned by Hesiod, 6. 251

Didymê, the "Twin" city of Gades, 2. 131

Didymê (Salina), one of the Liparaean Isles, 3. 99

Diegylis, king of the Caeni in Thrace, defeated by Attalus II, 6. 169

Dilisé (see Delium in Boeotia)

Dinara, Mt. (see Ardian Mountain)

Dindymenê (Mother Rhea); named after Mt. Dindymus in Galatia, 5. 471; temple of, on Mt. Dindymus in territory of Cyzicus, founded by the Argonauts, 5. 501; temple of, at Magnesia on the Maeander, no longer in existence, 6. 251

Dindymus, Mt., in territory of Cyzicus, has a temple of Mother Dindymenê, which was founded by the Argonauts, 5. 501

Dindymus, Mt., in Galatia, 5. 471

Dio of Syracuse (b. about 410 B.C.), made an expedition against Dionysius the Younger, 3. 15

Diochares, the Gates of, near the Lyceium at Athens, 4. 267

Diocles in Pherae, visited by Telemachus, 4. 147

Diocopenê in Cappadocia Pontica, 5. 447

Diodorus the Elder, of Sardeis, called Zonas; a great orator, who many times pleaded the cause of Asia, and acquitted himself of the charge of trying to cause cities to revolt from King Mithridates, 6. 179

Diodorus the Younger, of Sardeis, friend of Strabo, author of historical treatises, and various poems, 6. 181

Diodorus, general in the Mithridatic War, slew the members of the city council of Adramyttium, and died

in disgrace at Amaseia in Pontus, 6. 129

Diodorus, nicknamed "Cronus," a native of Iasus in Caria, 6. 291

Diodorus the Dialectician, of Iasus in Caria, pupil of Apollonius Cronus of Cyrenê, 8. 205

Diodorus the grammarian, a native of Tarsus, 6. 351

Diodotus, the sculptor, by some said to have made the remarkable statue of Nemesis at Rhamnus, 4. 263

Diodotus the Sidonian philosopher, friend of Strabo, 7. 271

Diodotus Tryphon, gained the upper hand over Arsaces I, king of Parthia, 5. 275; caused Syria to revolt from the kings, responsible for the organisation of the Cilician gangs of pirates, forced by Antiochus the son of Demetrius to kill himself, 6. 327

Diogenes the Cynic, a native of Sinopê, 5. 391

Diogenes the philosopher and poet, a native of Tarsus, 6. 351

Diogenes the Stoic philosopher, a native of Seleuceia on the Tigris, but called "the Babylonian," 7. 219

Diolcus, the; the narrowest part of the Corinthian isthmus, 4. 13, 155, 197

Diomedeae (Tremiti), the; isles off the Italian coast in the Adriatic, 1. 475, 2. 319; mythical story about, 3. 129; off Cape Garganum, 3. 131

Diomedes, the Greek hero; his opinion of Odysseus, 1. 61; wanderings of, a traditional fact, 2. 55; temple of, in the recess of the Adriatic, 2. 317; the Islands and worship of, 2. 319, 321; founded Canusium and Argyrippa in Apulia; and story of early dominion of, in the regions of Apulia, the land of the Frentani, and the land of the Heneti, 3. 129; further stories about, 3. 131; with Alcmaeon acquired Acarnania and Aetolia, 3. 305; ruled over the Bistonian Thracians, 3. 365; the horses of, devoured Abderus, 3. 369; expeditions of, with Alcmaeon, and participant in the Trojan expedition, 4. 369, 5. 71

INDEX OF NAMES, PLACES, AND SUBJECTS

INDEX OF NAMES, PLACES, AND SUBJECTS

the coast of, **5.** 207; occupies the most easterly point of the Euxine, and is the common emporium of seventy tribes called Caucasians, **5.** 209, 211, 241

Diospolis in Cappadocia Pontica (see Cabeira)

Diospolis, or "City of Zeus" (see Thebes, the Aegyptian)

Diospolis, Little, on the Nile, **8.** 117

Diospolis, a, near Mendes in Aegypt, **8.** 69

Diotimus, son of Strombichus, the Athenian ambassador; contemporary of Damastes, and said to have sailed from Cilicia on Cydnus and Choaspes Rivers to Susa in 40 days, **1.** 175

Diotrephes, native of Laodiceia on the Maeander, teacher of Hybreas the greatest orator in Strabo's time, **6.** 191

Diphilus, the comic poet, contemporary of Menander, a native of Sinopê, **5.** 391

Dircê, the spring near Phara in Achaea, bearing the same name as that at Thebes, **4.** 227; the spring near Thebes, **4.** 313

Dirk, the, used by the Iberians, **2.** 107

Diseases, of animals, a cure-all for, at the temple of Podaleirius in Daunia in Italy, **3.** 131; cured by waters of Cytherius River in Elis, **4.** 99

Dithyramb, a, of Pindar, quoted, **5.** 99

Ditiones, the, a Pannonian tribe, **3.** 257

Dium, a city of Athos, **3.** 355, 357

Dium (Lithada), near Cape Cenaeum in Euboea, colonised Canae in Aeolis, **5.** 9

Dium (Malathria), in southern Macedonia, in the foot-hills of Olympus, **3.** 339

Diurnal period, the, **2.** 149

Dius, father of Hesiod, native of Cymê Phryconis in Asia, but moved to "wretched" Ascrê in Boeotia, **6.** 161

Dius, legendary hero of Metapontium, **3.** 53

Divination; juggling and magic closely related to, **5.** 121

Division, the Northern, of the inhabited world, **1.** 293, 351; the Southern, divided into Sections (Sphragides), **1.** 293

Dnieper River, the (see Borysthenes)

Dniester River, the (see Tyras)

Doberus, near the Strymon River, **3.** 361

Docimaea, a village in Phrygia, where is the quarry of "Docimaean" marble, **5.** 507

Docimaean Marble, the, **4.** 429

"Dodo," an apocopated form of "Dodona," **4.** 131

Dodona, seat of the oracle of Dodonaean Zeus (near what is now Dramisi), **3.** 17, 297; the oracle at, now virtually extinct, **3.** 313; once under the rule of the Thesprotians and later of the Molossians, **3.** 315; temple of, according to Suidas, was transferred from Dodona in Thessaly, **3.** 317; oracle of, transferred in accordance with an oracle of Apollo, **3.** 321, 323; the copper vessel and copper scourge ("scourge of the Corcyraeans") at, **3.** 325; the oracle at, advised the Boeotians to commit an act of sacrilege, **4.** 285; a tripod secretly dedicated at, every year, by the Boeotians, **4.** 287; oracle of Zeus at, consulted by Greek statesmen, **7.** 287

Dodona, "wintry," in Thessaly, held by the Perrhaebians, **4.** 443; the oracle at, **4.** 445, transferred to Dodona in Epeirus, **3.** 317. 321, 323

Doedalsus, a founder of Astacus on the Propontis, **5.** 455

Dog-fish (see Galeotae)

Dogs, hunting, produced by Britain, **2.** 255; in Bactria and Sogdiana, called "undertakers," **5.** 283; the brave, in India, **7.** 65, 67; the large hunting, among the Cynamolgi in Aethiopia, **7.** 323; worshipped at Cynonpolis on the Nile, **8.** 109; of the Aethiopians, are small, **8.** 143

Dolabella, captured and slew Trebonius, one of the murderers of Caesar, at Smyrna, **6.** 247; almost caused the ruin of Laodiceia in Syria and was killed there (43 B.C.), **7.** 249

Dolicha (see Dulichium)

Dolion, son of Silenus and Melia, lived

317

INDEX OF NAMES, PLACES, AND SUBJECTS

INDEX OF NAMES, PLACES, AND SUBJECTS

INDEX OF NAMES, PLACES, AND SUBJECTS

INDEX OF NAMES, PLACES, AND SUBJECTS

Eisach River, the (see footnotes 2 and 3 in Vol. II, p. 284)

Eisadici, the, live north of the Caucasus, **5**. 241

Elaea on the Caïcus River, **6**. 103, 105; seaport of the Pergamenians, **6**. 133; founded by Mnestheus and Athenians in Trojan times, **6**. 159

Elaea, a harbour in the Arabian Gulf, **7**. 319

Elaeus (see Eleus)

Elaeussa in Cilicia Tracheia, assigned to Archelaüs by the Romans, **5**. 349; a fertile isle, where Archelaüs spent most of his time, **5**. 361; 120 stadia from Rhodes, **6**. 265; eight stadia in circuit, **6**. 267; royal residence of Archelaüs, **6**. 337

Elaïtic Gulf, the, in Asia, **6**. 5, 103; receives the Caïcus River, **6**. 133; a part of the Gulf of Adramyttium, **6**. 133; formed by two promontories, **6**. 159

Elaïtis in Asia; geographical position of, **5**. 487

Elaphonisi (see Onugnathus)

Elara, the mother of Tityus, **4**. 371

Elarium, a cave in Euboea, named after Elara the mother of Tityus, **4**. 371

Elateia (Drakhmani); wall of, broken up by earthquake, **1**. 225; the largest city in Phocis, through which flows the Cephissus River, **4**. 307, 347; strategic position of, **4**. 349, 373; 120 stadia from harbour at Daphnus, **4**. 381

Elatovouno, Mt. (see Aenus)

Elatria, a small town in Thesprotia, **3**. 301

Elba, the isle (see Aethalia)

Elbe River, the (see Albis)

Elè (see Elea)

Elea (also called Hyelê and Elê, now Castellamare della Brucca), in Leucania, native city of Parmenides and Zeno, **3**. 3; the good government, prowess, and pursuits of the people of—and founded by Phocaeans from Asia Minor, **3**. 5

Electrides Islands, the; fabulous story of, **2**. 319

Electrum (see Amber), a residuum containing a mixture of silver and gold, **2**. 41; among the Ligures, **2**. 267

Eleës (Hales, now Alento) River, the, gave name to city Elea, **3**. 5

Eleia (see Elis)

Eleian sect, the, of philosophers, **4**. 251

Eleians, the, regarded as sacred to Olympian Zeus, **4**. 7; spoke the Aeolic dialect, **4**. 9; one of the three tribes in Triphylia, **4**. 23; discussion of Homer's statement in regard to, **4**. 35–43; a different people from the Epeians, **4**. 39; carried on war against the Pylians, **4**. 79, 81; credited with the magnificence and honour of the temple at Olympia, and invented the Olympian Games, **4**. 91; had charge of both the temple and the games until the 26th Olympiad, **4**. 93, and again in later times, and settled the inhabitants of Nestor's Pylus in Lepreum, **4**. 95; by oath declared a people sacred to Olympian Zeus, but overrun by Pheidon, **4**. 105, and later acquired both Pisatis and Triphylia, **4**. 107; were allies of the Messenians, **4**. 121; rhotacized the letter *s*, **5**. 17

Elements, the four, spherical, **1**. 205

Eleon, the Homeric, a town of Parnassus, where Amyntor ruled, according to Crates, but not so, according to Demetrius of Scepsis; emended to "Heleon" by some, **4**. 321, 435

Elephantiasis, cured by the water of the Anigrus River in Triphylia, **4**. 61

Elephantinê, the boundary between Aegypt and Aethiopia, **8**. 7; an island close to Syenê, with a city and a Nilometer, **8**. 127; once captured by the Aethiopians, **8**. 137

Elephantophagi ("Elephant-eaters"), the; description of manner of capturing elephants by, **7**. 325

Elephants, the, in Cinnamon-bearing country, **1**. 507; in Taprobanê (Ceylon), **7**. 21; possession of, in India, a royal privilege, **7**. 69, 87; description of the capture and taming of, in India, **7**. 71, 73; live

INDEX OF NAMES, PLACES, AND SUBJECTS

INDEX OF NAMES, PLACES, AND SUBJECTS

Engineering, a branch of mathematics, **1**. 201

England (see Britain)

Enianians, the Homeric (see Aenianians), **4**. 443

Eniconiae, a town in Corsica, **2**. 359

Enipeus, god of the Enipeus River in Elis, loved by Tyro, **4**. 99

Enipeus (Lestenitza) River, the, in Elis, now called the Barnichius, empties into the Alpheius, **4**. 99

Enipeus (Tsanarlis) River, the, in Thessaly (by some spelled "Eniseus"), flows from Mt. Othrys, **4**. 99; the course of, **4**. 405

"Eniseus" River, the (see Enipeus River), the, in Thessaly, **4**. 99

Enispê, windy, the Homeric, now deserted, **3**. 385, **4**. 229

Enna in Sicily, where is the temple of Demeter, **3**. 81; taken by Eunus, **3**. 85; lies midway between Syracuse and Eryx, **3**. 87

Ennea Hodoi (see Amphipolis)

Ennius (b. 239 B.C.), the Roman poet, born at Rodiae, **3**. 119

Enopê, the Homeric, **4**. 109; by some identified with Pellana (now Zugra), and by others with Gerenia, **4**. 115

Enos (see Aenus)

Enotocoetae, the, in India, sleep in their ears, **7**. 95

Enydra in Phoenicia, **7**. 255

Enyo (Goddess of War), also called "Ma"; the temple of, at Comana in Greater Cappadocia—and the priest of, ranks next to the king, **5**. 351, 353, 357; temple of, also at Comana in Cappadocia Pontica, **5**. 433

Eordi, the, in Macedonia, through whose country the Egnatian Way passes, **3**. 295, 307

Eoubes (see Olbia)

Epacria, one of the twelve cities in Attica settled by Cecrops, **4**. 267

Epameinondas, conquered the Lacedaemonians in the Battle at Mantineia, but lost his life therein, **4**. 229; all but gained the supremacy of Greece for Thebes, **4**. 281, 287; defeated the Lacedaemonians at Leuctra, **4**. 335

Epeians, the, lived in Elis, **4**. 19; one of the three tribes in Triphylia,

4. 23; Otus, a chief of the, **4**. 25; discussion of Homer's statement in regard to, **4**. 35–43; a different people from the Eleians, **4**. 39; extent of territory of, **4**. 55; "held sway in Elis," according to Homer, **4**. 77; conceived a contempt for Neleus, **4**. 81; many of, embarked for Troy, **4**. 83; joined by the Aetolians under Oxylus, **4**. 91; Salmoneus the king of, drove Aetolus out of Eleia, but the Epeians were later driven out by Oxylus, **4**. 103; with Aetolus took up their abode in Aetolia, but were destroyed by the Aeolians, **4**. 369; occupied the Echinades Islands, **5**. 49; and Oxeiae Islands, **5**. 59; with the Aetolians founded the earliest cities in Aetolia, **5**. 77, 81.

Epeirotes, the, live on the flank of the Greeks, **3**. 287; 70 cities of, destroyed by Paulus Aemilius, **3**. 293; consist of 14 tribes, **3**. 297, 333.

Epeirotic tribes, names of certain, **3**. 289; certain, now included within a Roman Province, **3**. 215

Epeirus, geographical position of, **3**. 249, 299; rugged, but in earlier times populous, **3**. 311; once held a part of Macedonia, **3**. 329

Epeius, born at Panopeus in Phocis, **4**. 371

Ephebeia, the, at Neapolis, **2**. 449

Ephebi, the, at Athens; Epicurus and Menander enrolled among, at the same time, **6**. 219

Ephesians, the; certain of, called Sisyrbitae, **6**. 201; exchanged Neapolis for Marathesium, **6**. 223; defeated by the Magnesians, according to Callinus, **6**. 251

Ephesium, the; the temple of the Ephesian Artemis at Massalia, **2**. 173

Ephesus, the Selinus River flows through, **4**. 223; said to have been founded by the Amazons, **5**. 237, and given its name by them, **5**. 407; the greatest emporium in Asia Minor, **5**. 509; the Caÿster Plain in territory of, **6**. 155; 320 stadia from Smyrna, **6**. 197; parts round,

3²5

INDEX OF NAMES, PLACES, AND SUBJECTS

in earlier times occupied by Carians, **6**. 199; founded by Androclus the Athenian, **6**. 199; also called Smyrna, and induced Smyrna to join the Ionian League, **6**. 201; ancient and present sites of, **6**. 203, 205; produces good wine, **6**. 215; the temple of Artemis there, **6**. 223–229; history and description of, **6**. 225–231; notable men of, **6**. 231; distances from, to various places, **6**. 309

Ephialtes the giant, myth of, 1. 69

Ephialtes, the traitor, conducted Persians by path at Thermopylae, **1**. 35

Ephors, the, in Sparta, **5**. 151

Ephorus of Cymê in Aeolis, pupil of Isocrates, and author of a history dating from the Dorian invasion to 340 B.C., the year of his death; a philosopher, **1**. 3; quotes the Tartessians about the Aethiopians, **1**. 121; his division of the regions of earth into four parts, **1**. 125; refers to temple and altar of Heracles on the Sacred Cape of Iberia, **2**. 7; his account of Celtica, **2**. 251; on the Pelasgians, **2**. 343, 345; on the Cimmerians, **2**. 443; wrongly calls Locri Epizephyrii a colony of the Locri Opuntii, **3**. 29; on the laws of the Locri Epizephyrii and the Thurii, **3**. 33; says the Iapyges once lived at Croton, **3**. 43; calls Daulius, the tyrant of Crisa near Delphi, coloniser of Metapontium, **3**. 53; says the voyage round Sicily takes five days and nights, **3**. 59; on the earliest Greek cities founded in Sicily, **3**. 65; says Iberians were the first barbarian settlers of Greece, **3**. 73; on the Messenian War and the founding of Tarentum, **3**. 111; says the Celti on the ocean suffer more from the tides than from wars, **3**. 167; his *Europe* cited on the different modes of life of the Scythians and the Sauromatae, **3**. 205; and on the frugality and communism of the Scythians, **3**. 207; says the Ister has only five mouths, **3**. 219; says Alcmaeon helped Diomedes to acquire Aetolia and

Acarnania, and founded Argos Amphilochicum, **3**. 305; on the Halizoni, **3**. 351 (see footnote 3); discusses topography of the continents in his *History*, **4**. 3; on the boundaries of Greece, **4**. 9; quoted at length on Aetolus, the Aetolians, the Epeians, the Eleians, the Pisatans, Oxylus, the Heracleidae, Olympia, and Elis in general, **4**. 101–107; on the division of Messenia by Cresphontes into five city-states, **4**. 117; on the conquest of Laconia by Eurysthenes and Procles, the Heracleidae, **4**. 133; censures Hellanicus for ascribing the Spartan Constitution to Eurysthenes and Procles and for ignoring Lycurgus, **4**. 139; on the oracle about the exchange of Delos for Calauria and Delphi for Cape Taenarum, **4**. 173; says that silver was first coined in Crete, by Pheidon, **4**. 181; names the colonisers of the peoples who settled in the Peloponnesus after the return of the Heracleidae, **4**. 235; on the fertility, harbours and commerce of Boeotia, **4**. 279; and on the cause of its failure to gain the supremacy in Greece, **4**. 281; a noteworthy historian, but inserts myths about Apollo and others, thus confounding history and myth, **4**. 363–369; on the shipbuilding at Naupactus in Western Locris, **4**. 385; thinks that the cities Alyzia and Leucas in Acarnania were named after the two sons of Icarius, Alyzeus and Leucadius, **5**. 35; denies that the Acarnanians joined the Trojan expedition, **5**. 71; says that Alcmaeon was king of Acarnania before the Trojan War, **5**. 73; says the Aetolians had never been subject to any other people, **5**. 75; rightly signifies the kinship between the Eleians and the Aetolians, but displays inconsistencies in his discussion of the Aetolians and the Curetes, **5**. 79, 81; on King Minos, **5**. 131; on the good laws of Crete, **5**. 133; on the 100 cities in Crete, **5**. 143; on the Cretan constitution, **5**. 145; on the Cretan institutions, **5**. 147–153; on why Lycurgus went

326

INDEX OF NAMES, PLACES, AND SUBJECTS

to Crete, **5.** 151; says Cytorum was named after Cytorus the son of Phrixus, **5.** 387; on the abode of the Amazons, **5.** 405; on the boundaries of Aeolis in Asia, **6.** 9, 79; on "many-fountained Ida," **6.** 11; author of the *History* and a work on *Inventions*, a native of Cymê Phryconis in Asia, **6.** 161; ridiculed for his references to his countrymen, **6.** 163; tells the history of Miletus, **6.** 205; says that the Asiatic peninsula (Asia Minor) was inhabited by 16 tribes, **6.** 361, 367; misjudged by Apollodorus, **6.** 363; placed the Homeric Halizones in the interior, **6.** 365

"Ephyra," the earlier name of Cichyrus in Thesprotia, **3.** 301; nine cities so named, **3.** 339

Ephyra, an Aetolian village, **4.** 29

Ephyra, the, "in the inmost part of Argos", **4.** 165

Ephyra, the Corinthian (Korakou?), **4.** 27

Ephyra (Palaea Larissa), another name of Crannon in Thessaly, **3.** 335, 337

Ephyra (apparently the Homeric), on the Selleëis River in Elis, 120 stadia from the city Elis, **3.** 315; **4.** 27

Ephyra, a Sicyonian village, **4.** 29

Ephyra, the Thesprotian, **4.** 27, 29; whence the sons of Thessalus invaded Thessaly, **4.** 455

Ephyra, the Thessalian, **4.** 27

Ephyri, the Aetolian, Perrhaebian and Thesprotian, **4.** 29; the Homeric, "from Thrace," **4.** 447

"Ephyri," in earlier times the name of the Crannonians in Thessaly, **4.** 447

Epicarus (see Epidaurus)

Epicharmus of Cos (about 540–483 B.C.), the comic poet; *apocopê* in, **4.** 131

Epicnemidian Locrians (see Locrians), the, named after Mt. Cnemis, **4.** 343; **4.** 377; the territory of, **4.** 381; progenitors of the Ozolian Locrians, **4.** 387

Epicteti (Privy-councillors), the, at Ephesus, **6.** 225

Epicteti, the Phrygian, live about the Mysian Olympus, **5.** 499

Epicurus, "in a sense a Lampsacenian"; Metrodorus of Lampsacus a comrade of, **6.** 37; grew up in Samos and Teos, and became an *ephebus* at Athens, **6.** 219

Epidamnus (Durazzo) in Illyria; the distance from, to Thessaloniceia, **1.** 409; voyage from, to Brundisium, **3.** 125; founded by the Corcyraeans and now called Dyrrachium, **3.** 265; 535 Roman miles, by the Egnatian Way, to Cypsela (Ipsala) on the Hebrus (Maritza) River, **3.** 293; whither went many of the inhabitants of Dyspontium in Elis, **4.** 101

Epidaurian breed of horses, the, is most excellent, **4.** 229

Epidaurians, the, once colonised Aegina, **4.** 181

Epidaurus (once called Epicarus, now Epidavra), on the Saronic Gulf, **4.** 153; settled by emigrants from Tiryns, **4.** 171; belonged to a kind of Amphictyonic League, **4.** 173, 175; seized by Carians, **4.** 175; famed for its temple of Asclepius, and has a circular coast of 15 stadia, **4.** 177

Epidaurus Limera in Laconia, **4.** 151

Epidavra (see Epidaurus)

Epigoni, the; expedition of, against Thebes, **3.** 305, **4.** 283, **5.** 71; captured Thebes, **4.** 333

Epigram, an, of Callimachus, in regard to a poem of Creophilus the Samian, **6.** 219

Epimenides the Cretan wizard, said to have been from Phaestus, **5.** 141

Epistrategi (in, in Aegypt, **8.** 53

Epistrophus, the Homeric, leader of the Halizones, **5.** 403, 407, 409; slain by Achilles at Lyrnessus, **6.** 15, 121, 151

Epitalium in Macistia, the present name of the Homeric Thryum, **4.** 49, 71, 73

Epithets in Homer, **1.** 57, 91, 133

Epizephyrian Locrians (see Locrians), the, were colonists from the Ozolian Locrians, **4.** 387

Epopeus (Epomeo), Mt., on Pithecussae; shaken by earthquake, cast forth fire, **2.** 459

Epopis, a hill in Italy, on the brow of

327

INDEX OF NAMES, PLACES, AND SUBJECTS

which Locri Epizephyrii is situated,
3. 29

Eporedia (Ivrea), a Roman colony in
Italy, **2.** 279

Equator, the; the limit of the
southerly peoples, **1.** 231; geographical position of, **1.** 279;
divides earth into two hemispheres,
1. 371; region of, temperate, according to Eratosthenes and Polybius, **1.** 373; distance from, to pole,
one-fourth of earth's largest circle,
1. 429; measures 250,000 stadia,
according to Eratosthenes, **1.** 437;
distance from, to Cinnamon-bearing
country and Syenê, **1.** 507; between
which and tropic circle shadows fall
in both directions, **1.** 509; distance
from, to the tropic, $\frac{4}{60}$ of the greatest
circle, **1.** 521

Equestrian rank, the, a praefect of,
governs certain of the Ligures, **2.**
271; from men of, in Luca, the
Roman Senate recruits its ranks, **2.**
329

Equinoctial hours, the; meaning of,
1. 283 (footnote 4); at Meroê and
other places, **1.** 507, 509, 511, 513,
515, 517

" Equinoctial rising " of the sun, the;
a variable term, **1.** 415

Equinoctial signs, the, **2.** 153

Equinoctial west, the; the Tagus
River flows towards, **2.** 65

Equinoxes, the, **1.** 287, 291, **2.** 151

Erae in Asia, near Erythrae, **6.** 239

Erana (Kuriaki) in Messenia, by some
said to have been called Arenê in
earlier times, by the same name as
the Pylian Arenê, **4.** 69; wrongly
identified by some with the Homeric
Arenê, **4.** 117

Erasinus River, the, which flows from
Arcadia to the coast near Bura, **3.**
93, **4.** 161

Erasinus River, the, near Brauron in
Attica, **4.** 163

Erasinus (or Arsinus) River, the, in
Argolis, flows underground from the
Stymphalian Lake, **4.** 161, 231

Erasinus River, the, near Eretria, **4.**
163

Erasistratean school of medicine, the,
at Smyrna, **5.** 519

Erasistratus the physician (fl. in the

first half of the third century B.C.),
from Iulis in Ceos, **5.** 169; the
Erasistrateian school of medicine at
Smyrna, **5.** 519

Erastus, the Socratic philosopher,
native of Scepsis, **6.** 111

Erato, the clear-voiced muse, **4.** 65

Eratosthenes of Cyrenê (about 276–
194 B.C.), learned Alexandrian
scholar; geographer and philosopher, **1.** 3; on the aim of a poet,
1. 23, 55, 57; on additions to geographical knowledge, **1.** 49; his
wide knowledge of geography, **1.** 51;
never saw Athens, according to
Polemon, but in fact studied under
Zeno there, **1.** 53; his treatises *On
the Good* and his *Studies in Declama-
tion* show superficiality, **1.** 55; says
" Homer never lets fall an inappropriate epithet," **1.** 57; on limitations of Homer's knowledge, **1.** 59;
misrepresents Homer, **1.** 67, 81, 97;
on Hesiod's geography, **1.** 85; on
Aeolus, king of the winds, **1.** 87; on
the original level of the Mediterranean, **1.** 141; relies too much on
poor authorities, *e.g.* Damastes, **1.**
173; believed Gulf of Issus most
easterly point of Mediterranean, and
believes fabulous stories told about
northern parts of the Adriatic, and
even mentions an island Cerne, **1.**
175; on the shape of the earth and
its changes, **1.** 179; explains find-
ing of oyster-shells and salt-marshes
2000 or 3000 stadia from sea, **1.** 181;
does not confirm doctrine of Archi-
medes on the sphericity of liquid
bodies, **1.** 201; on changes about
Mt. Casius and Gerrha, **1.** 207; does
not believe in uniform level of the
seas, **1.** 209; on the Hyperboreians,
1. 229; reviser of geography, **1.** 231,
253, 267; on Iernê, **1.** 237; says
parallel through Athens is less than
200,000 stadia in circuit, **1.** 241; on
the division of the continents, **1.**
243; diets upon disputation, **1.** 245;
opposes dividing mankind into two
groups, Greeks and barbarians, **1.**
249; divides inhabited world into
two parts by line parallel to equator,
1. 253; discredited by Hipparchus,
1. 257; had access to library at

INDEX OF NAMES, PLACES, AND SUBJECTS

Alexandria, **1.** 259; quotes epigram from temple of Asclepius at Pantica-paeum, **1.** 277; discredits Deï-machus, **1.** 285; misrepresented by Hipparchus, **1.** 293; his divisions of Asia, **1.** 297; says the Tigris and Euphrates flow from Armenia south-wards and enclose Mesopotamia, **1.** 305; makes illogical divisions, **1.** 315, 319; divides inhabited world into two parts by the Taurus Range and the Mediterranean, **1.** 317; mis-takes of, in regard to promontories in the Mediterranean, **1.** 353; also in regard to distances, **1.** 355; entirely ignorant of Iberia, Celtica, Ger-many, and Britain, **1.** 357; calls country under equator temperate, **1.** 371; criticises ancient geo-graphers, **1.** 399; believes certain stories of Pytheas, being ignorant of western and northern Europe, **1.** 401, 409; his errors in estimates of distances corrected by Polybius, **1.** 409; says the Galati (Gauls) in-habit the country as far west as Gades, **1.** 411; his measurement of the earth, **1.** 437, 505; on the dis-tance from Rhodes to Alexandria, **1.** 483; wrongly makes the Issican Gulf the most easterly point of the Mediterranean, **1.** 485; says parallel through Lysimacheia passes through Mysia, Sinopê and certain other places, **1.** 513; on distances between parallels of Meroê, the Hellespont and the mouth of the Borysthenes, **1.** 517; contradicted by Artemi-dorus on statements regarding "Tartessis," "Blest Isle," tides, and other things, **2.** 49; wrongly says that Tarraco in Iberia has a roadstead, **2.** 91; on the geographi-cal position of the Pillars of Heracles, **2.** 137; incorrect when he says that neither Cyrnus (Elba) nor Sardo is visible from mainland, **2.** 357; says Homer was unacquainted with dis-tant places, **3.** 189, 195; petty criticisms of, borrowed by Apollo-dorus of Athens, **3.** 193; cites Hesiod in regard to the Scythian "Hippemolgi" (" Mare-milkers "), **3.** 197; makes some false hear-say statements in regard to Ister River

and other things, **3.** 269; saw the ruins of Helicê after it was sub-merged, **4.** 215; on the Anias River in Arcadia, **4.** 231; says the distance from Cyrenaea to Cape Criumetopon is 2000 stadia, **5.** 125; divided up the inhabited world as a whole by means of certain natural boundaries, **5.** 183; says the Caucasus is called "Caspius" by the natives, **5.** 209; on the Caspian Sea, **5.** 245; on the Oxus River, **5.** 253; says that Alex-ander built his fleet out of fir-wood in India, **5.** 257; on the geographical position of various Asiatic peoples, **5.** 269; gives the distances between various places in Asia, **5.** 271; divides Asia into "Northern" and "Southern," and into "Sphrag-ides," **5.** 301; Strabo's criticism of, **5.** 329; certain distances given by, on way to India, same as those of Artemidorus, **6.** 311; on the copper and silver mines in Cypros, **6.** 383; on the expeditions of Heracles and Dionysus to India, **7.** 9; gives a trustworthy account of India, **7.** 15–17; on the cause of the summer rains in India, **7.** 19; on the fertility of India, **7.** 31; on certain countries in Asia, **7.** 141; on the dimensions of Persis, **7.** 155, 157; discusses the lakes near Arabia, **7.** 211; on the Dead Sea, **7.** 297; describes the Persian Gulf, **7.** 301, 303, 305; opinions of, concerning Arabia, **7.** 309, 349; on the course of the Nile River, **8.** 3–7; says that expulsion of foreigners is a custom common to barbarians, **8.** 69; calls Tinx "Lixus," **8.** 159; statements of, concerning western Libya, disputed by Artemidorus, **8.** 169–171; native of Cyrenê, great philosopher and mathematician, **8.** 205

Eratyra, a district near Elimeia (*q.v.*), **3.** 307

Erechtheus, the daughter of, married Xuthus, **4.** 209

Eregli (see Perinthus)

Erekli (see Heracleia Pontica)

Erembians (Arabian Troglodytes?), the, mentioned by Homer, **1.** 5, 139, 151, **3.** 191, **7.** 369; either Arabians, or Troglodytes, or Arambians, **7.** 371

329

INDEX OF NAMES, PLACES, AND SUBJECTS

" Eremni " (" Black "), not applicable to the Arabians, **7.** 373

Eressus in Lesbos, the home of Theophrastus and Phanias, the Peripatetic philosophers, **6.** 145

Eretria, now a market-place at Athens, said to have colonised Eretria in Euboea, **5.** 15

Eretria in Euboea; across the strait 40 stadia from Oropus, **4.** 289; second largest city in Euboea, **5.** 11, 17; said to have been founded by the Athenians before the Trojan War, and many colonies sent out by, **5.** 13; by some said to have been colonised from Triphylian Macistus by Eretrieus, and in earlier times called Melaneïs and Arotria, **5.** 15; destroyed by the Persians but rebuilt, **5.** 17; the school of Eretrian philosophers at, **5.** 19

Eretria in Phthiotis, subject to Achilles, **4.** 413; near the Pharsalus in Thessaly, **5.** 15

Eretrian sect, the, of philosophers, **4.** 251

Eretrians, the, in Euboea, were colonists from the Attic deme of the Eretrians, **5.** 7; now hold the territory of Carystus, **5.** 11; once powerful, ruling over several islands, and rhotacised the letter *s*, **5.** 17; were carried off by the Persians, and said to have settled in Gordyenê in Asia, **7.** 233

Eretum (near Grotta Marozza), a village, **2.** 375; at the junction of the Salarian and Nomentane Ways, **2.** 377, 417

Erginus, tyrant of Orchomenus in Boeotia, received tribute from the Thebans, **4.** 335

Ericaceae, the botanical term, **3.** 99, footnote 6

Erichthonius, an original founder in both the Trojan and Attic tribes, **6.** 95

Ericodes (or Ericussa), distance from, to Phoenicodes, **3.** 103

Ericussa (Alicudi), one of the Liparaean Isles, named from its plant " heather," **3.** 99

Eridanus River, the, at Athens, **4.** 267

Eridanus, the, in Italy, a mythical river, **2.** 319

Erigon River, the, receives many streams from the Illyrian Mountains and empties into the Axius River, **3.** 311, 339, 341, 345; " the river in Thrace that is now called Rheginia," **3.** 371

Eriko (see Oricum)

Erimokastron (see Thespeia)

Erineus, the home of the poet Tyrtaeus, **4.** 123; a city of the Dorian Tetrapolis, **4.** 387; subject to Achilles, **4.** 413

Erineus, in the Troad, mentioned by Homer, **6.** 67; lies below the ancient Ilium, **6.** 71

Erymanthus River, the, empties into the Alpheius, **4.** 101; forms a boundary of Arcadia, **4.** 101

Erymnae in Thessaly, **4.** 451

Erysichaeans, the, a people in the interior of Acarnania, **5.** 65

Erytheia, the ancient, identified with Gadeira and called " Blest Isle," **2.** 49; scene of the adventures of Geryon, **2.** 133; necessity of bleeding animals at, **3.** 69

Erythini, " the lofty," in Paphlagonia (now called Erythrini), mentioned by Homer, **5.** 377, 387

" Erythra " (" Red "), name given by some to Erythraean Sea—and explanation of, **7.** 349

Erythrae, the Homeric, in Boeotia, by some writers regarded as subject to the Plataeans, **4.** 315, 321

Erythrae (Ritri) in Ionia, a colony of the Erythrae below Mt. Cithaeron, **4.** 297; founded by Cnopus, bastard son of King Codrus, **6.** 201, 239

Erythraean (Red) Sea, the, unknown to Homer, according to Apollodorus, **3.** 191; origin of name of, **7.** 349–351

Erythraeans, the, at Mimas, worship Heracles Ipoctonus, **6.** 127

Erythras, a harbour near Erythrae in Asia, **6.** 241

Erythras the king, a certain Persian, or son of Perseus, after whom, according to certain writers, the Erythraean (" Red ") Sea was named, **7.** 305, 351

Eryx, a city in Sicily, seized by Aeneias, **6.** 109

330

INDEX OF NAMES, PLACES, AND SUBJECTS

331

INDEX OF NAMES, PLACES, AND SUBJECTS

Tigris encloses Mesopotamia, **1**. 305; description of course of, **5**. 297, 319, 321; the Zeugma on, **5**. 307; empties into the Red Sea (!), **5**. 327; borders on Mesopotamia and empties into the Persian Gulf, **5**. 329; confused with the Halys, **5**. 363; distance to, from Mazaca, **5**. 365; separates Acilisenê from Lesser Armenia, **5**. 425; the road leading to, from the coast, **6**. 311; mouth of, 3000 stadia from Babylon, **7**. 163; flows through Babylon, **7**. 199; navigable to Babylon, and rises to flood-tide at beginning of summer, **7**. 205; Polycleitus on, **7**. 213; distances from, to the Tigris, **7**. 229

Euphronius, the Alexandrian grammarian (fl. in the third century B.C.), author of the *Priapeia* and calls Priapus "the Orneatan," **4**. 205

Euręeis River, the, in the territory of Scepsis, **5**. 115

Euripides, the tragic poet; the *Bacchae* of, defective in geographical accuracy, **1**. 99; the *Phaëthon* of, quoted on Aethiopia, **1**. 123; lays blame of Trojan War on Zeus, **2**. 189; the *Archelaüs* of, quoted on the Pelasgians and Danaans, **2**. 345; in his *Ion* and *Rhadymanthys* calls "Euboea" the island "a neighbouring city to Athens," **4**. 97, 99; in his *Aeolus*, on the kingdom of Salmoneus in Elis, **4**. 99; describes Laconia and Messenia, making several false statements, **4**. 141, 143; says Danaüs decreed that all Pelasgians should be called Danaäns, **4**. 163; uses the terms "Mycenae" and "Argos" synonymously, **4**. 187; on the Acrocorinthus, **4**. 193; associates the sacred rites in honour of Mother Rhea with those of Dionysus, **5**. 101; the *Palamedes* of, quoted, **5**. 103; contradicted by Demetrius of Scepsis in regard to worship of Mother Rhea, **5**. 113; on the "sickly plight" of "things divine" when a country is devastated, **5**. 213; says certain barbarous tribes in the Caucasus lament new-born babes and bury their dead with joy,

5. 291; on the myth of Augê and her child Telephus, **6**. 135; wrong in regard to Marsyas, **6**. 137; took entire course of Anaxagoras, **6**. 245; on the expedition of Dionysus to Asia, **7**. 9; on the oracle at Delphi, **7**. 287

Euripus, the, at Rome, **6**. 37

Euripus, the, at Chalcis; changes current seven times a day, **1**. 205, **4**. 291; caused by earthquake, **1**. 223; spanned by bridge two plethra long, **4**. 281; description of, **4**. 289; 530 stadia from Thermopylae, **4**. 393; included by Chalcidians within the walls of Chalcis in time of Alexander the Great, **5**. 13

Euromus in Caria; geographical position of, **6**. 209, 291

Europe; maximum distance from, to Libya, **1**. 403, 409; length of, **1**. 411 ("Iberia" on that page is an error for "Libya"); runs out into several promontories, **1**. 417; the most irregular in shape of the three continents, **1**. 467; general description of, **1**. 485–493; blessed by nature, **1**. 487; abounds with cattle, but wild animals scarce, **1**. 489; Iberia the first part of, **2**. 3; eastern parts and boundaries of, **3**. 151; separated from Asia by the Cimmerian Bosporus, **3**. 239; borders on Asia along the Tanaïs River, **5**. 183; perhaps larger than Libya, **8**. 155; almost the whole of, held by the Romans, **8**. 211

Europus in Media (see Rhaga in Media)

Europus (called by Homer "Titaresius") River, the, marks the boundary between Macedonia and Thessaly, **3**. 311, 335, **4**. 443

Eurotas (Iri) River, the, flows from the territory of Megalopolis, **4**. 47; empties between Gythium and Acraeae, **4**. 129; marvellous circumstances pertaining to, **3**. 93, **4**. 231

Eurus, the wind, **1**. 105

Eurycleia; nurse of Odysseus; statue of, in the temple of Artemis at Ephesus, **6**. 229

Eurycles, ruler of the Lacedaemonians, took Cythera as his own private property, **4**. 127; abused

333

INDEX OF NAMES, PLACES, AND SUBJECTS

the friendship of Julius Caesar, 4. 137, and was banished, 4. 139

Eurycydeium, the, a sacred precinct in Triphylia, 4. 59

Eurydicê, the mother of Philip the son of Amyntas, 3. 309

Eurylochus, drove the serpent called Cychreides out of Salamis, 4. 253

Eurylochus the Thessalian, destroyed the Phocian Crisa in the Crisaean War (about 595 B.C.), 4. 351

Eurymedon, the Athenian general, on the second Sicilian expedition (425 B.C.), rebuilt the Messenian Pylus, 4. 111

Eurymedon River, the, flows from the Selgic mountains into Pamphylia, 5. 485, 6. 325

Eurypon the son of Procles, the Lacedaemonian ruler, 4. 141

Eurypontidae, the; descendants of Eurypon, the Lacedaemonian ruler, 4. 141

Eurypylus, son of Euaemon; the domain of, in Thessaly, 4. 407, 413, 421, 433, 435, 437

Eurypylus, son of Telephus; Cos the island of, 5. 175; country of, sacked by Achilles; slain by Neoptolemus, 6. 15; domain of, 6. 21, 135, 137

Eurysthenes, and Procles, the Heracleidae, took possession of, and reorganised, Laconia, 4. 133, 235; drew up the Spartan Constitution, according to Hellanicus, 4. 133

Eurystheus, succeeded Sthenelus as king of Mycenae, 4. 185; death and burial of, 4. 187

"Eurystheus' Head," at Tricorynthus, where the head of Eurystheus was buried, 4. 187

Eurytanians, the, in Aetolia, 5. 17, 29

Eurytion, the neat-herd of Geryon, 2. 49

Eurytus, the Homeric, the Oechalian, 4. 31, 71, 433; the son of, met Telemachus at Pherae, 4. 145

Eusebeia near the Taurus (see Tyana)

Euthydemus, king of the Bactrians, caused Bactriana to revolt from the kings of Syria and Media, 5. 275; father of the Demetrius who made many conquests in Asia, 5. 281

Euthydemus of Mylasa in Caria, great orator, wealthy, and thought worthy

of the foremost honour in Asia, 6. 295

Euthymus, the Locrian pugilist, fought Polites at Temesa in Bruttium, 3. 15

Eutresis, the Homeric, a small village of the Thespians, where Zethus and Amphion are said to have lived before reigning over Thebes, 4. 323

Euxine Sea, the (or Pontus, q.v.), formerly had no outlet at Byzantium, and has shallow waters, 1.183; dimensions and shape of, 1. 479; beavers of, yield castor of superior medicinal quality, 2. 107; called "Axine" ("Inhospitable") in Homer's time, 3. 189; divided into two seas by the strait between Capes Criumetopon and Carambis, 3. 235; visible from Haemus Mountain, 3. 251; Dioscurias occupies the most easterly point of, 5. 209; numerous colonies of Miletus on, 6. 207

Euxynthetus, lover of the Cretan Leucocomas, 5. 139

Evander, mythical Arcadian founder of Rome, 2. 385

Evanthes, founder of Locri Epizephyrii in Italy (about 700 B.C.), 3. 29

Evenus (formerly called Lycormas, now Fidari) River, the, in Aetolia, empties into the sea, 3. 311, 4. 15, 5. 29; 630 stadia from Mt. Chalcis and 670 from Actium, 5. 63

Evenus River, the, flows past Pitanê in Mysia in Asia, 6. 131

Evergetae, the, in Asia, visited by Alexander, 7. 145

Evergreens, the, abundant in Armenia, 5. 323; found in India, 7. 97, and in Gordyaea, 7. 233

"Evoe saboe," a cry uttered in the ritual of Sabazius and the Mother, 5. 109

Excision, a Judaean rite, 7. 285; a rite of the Aegyptians, 8. 153

Exedra, the, of the Museum at Alexandria, 8. 35

Exitanians (see "Sex" and "Hexi"), the city of the, in Iberia, 2. 81, 135

F

Fabaria the island (see Borkum)

Fabius Maximus Cunctator (consul 233 and 228 B.C., and appointed dic-

INDEX OF NAMES, PLACES, AND SUBJECTS

tator 217 B.C.), removed the colossal statue of Heracles from Tarentum to Rome, 3. 107

Fabius the historian (the Quintus Fabius Pictor, who fl. about 220 B.C., oldest Roman annalist, and wrote his work in Greek, or possibly the Fabius Pictor, a later annalist, who wrote his work in Latin); on the wealth of the Sabini, 2. 377

Falerii, a town in Italy, 2. 365

Falernian wine, the, 2. 399, 437

Faliscum, Aequum, in Italy, 2. 365, 367

Famine, because of mice, or rats, in Cantabria, 2. 113; avoided in Italy by unfailing supply of millet in Cisalpine Celtica, 2. 331; among the Sabini, 2. 465

Fanary, Cape (see Parthenium)

Fanum Fortunae (see Fortune, Temple of)

Fasces, the Roman; the use of, transferred from Tarquinia, 2. 339

Faustulus, the swineherd who reared Romulus and Remus, 2. 381

Faventia (Faenza), on the Aemilian Way, 2. 327

Fawns, the, in India, 7. 125

Felicudi (see Phoenicaceae)

Fennel (see *Hippomarathi*)

Fennel (Marathon) Plain, the, in Iberia, 2. 95

Feodosia (see Theodosia)

Ferentinum, a town in Italy, 2. 365; on the Latin Way, 2. 411

Fermo (see Firmum Picenum)

Feronia (Sant' Antimo), at the foot of Mt. Soracte; remarkable sacred rites at, 2. 367

Ferrajo, Porto, in Aethalia (Elba) (see Argoüs)

Ferrets, Libyan, bred for the destruction of hares, 2. 35; in Maurusia, as large as cats, 8. 163

Festi, a former boundary of Roman territory, 2. 383

Fidari River, the (see Evenus River)

Fidenae (Serpentara) near Veii, 2. 365, 383

Fig; the "Antiocheian" dried, produced in great quantities at Antiocheia on the Maeander, 6. 189; the *sycamorus* in Aegypt like a, 8. 149

"Fig-tree, Under the" (now Galata),

a harbour five stadia from the Horn of the Byzantines, 3. 281

Fig-tree, the, in Hyrcania; productivity of, 1. 273, 5. 251; a tree in Celtica like, whose sap is deadly, 2. 251

Fig-trees, wild, abundant below the ancient site of Ilium, 6. 71

Filibedjik (see Philippi)

Fimbria, Roman quaestor (86 B.C.), slew the consul Valerius Flaccus in Asia, assumed command of the Roman army, and ruined Ilium, but was overthrown by Sulla, 6. 55

Finisterre, Cape (see Nerium)

Fire, worshipped by the Persians, 7. 175

Firmum Picenum (Fermo), in Picenum, 2. 429

Fish; caught in the ice at the Strait of Kertch, 3. 225; the skins of, used as wraps and bed-covers in Pharusia in Libya, 8. 169

Fish-salting industry, the, in Turdetania and about the Pontus, 2. 15, 33; at New Carthage, 2. 89; in Elea in Italy, 3. 5; on Lake Lychnidus, 3. 309; at Zuchis in Libya, 8. 195

Flaminian Way, the, 2. 367, 371

Flamininus, Titus Quintius, conquered Philip the son of Demetrius and king of Macedonia at Cynoscephalae in Thessaly, 4. 445

Flaminius, Gaius, the Elder (consul 223 and 217 B.C.), conquered by Hannibal, 2. 369

Flaminius, Gaius, the Younger (consul with Marcus Lepidus 187 B.C.), the builder of the Flaminian Way, from Rome to Ariminum, 2. 331

Flax, sown in rainy seasons in India, 7. 21

Fleece, the golden; an explanation of the origin of myth of, 5. 215

Flute, the, used by the Illyrian Dardanians, 3. 265; invented by Seilenus and Marsyas and Olympus, 5. 103, 105; the "bombyces," 5. 107; the Berecyntian and Phrygian, 5. 109

Flute-players, and citharists, played the accompaniment to the Pythian Nome at Delphi, 4. 363

Flute-reed, the, produced by a marsh in Boeotia, 4. 325

335

INDEX OF NAMES, PLACES, AND SUBJECTS

INDEX OF NAMES, PLACES, AND SUBJECTS

of the Celti; once seized Roman territory, **2.** 311, in Cispadana, **2.** 323; destroyed by the Romans, **2.** 325

Gaius Julius, son of Eurycles the Lacedaemonian ruler, **4.** 139

Galabrii, the, a Dardanian tribe in Illyria, thought to be the ancestors of the Italian Calabrians; have an ancient city, **3.** 265

Galactophagi (" Curd-eaters "), the Homeric, are wagon-dwelling Scythians and Sarmatians, **3.** 179, 181, 189, 195, 197, 205, 209, 243, **5.** 419; by Apollodorus called a fabrication of Homer, **5.** 423

Galata, the Harbour of (see " Fig-tree, Under the ")

Galatia; in Greater Phrygia, a territory seized by Tectosages from Celtica, who were "Galatians" (Gauls), **2.** 205; description and history of, **5.** 467–473; has three tribes, **5.** 467, 471; has a Council and twelve Tetrarchs, **5.** 469

Galatians (Gauls), the; emigrations of, **1.** 227; inhabit country as far west as Gades, according to Eratosthenes, **1.** 411; rank their mines with those of the Turditanians, **2.** 41; language and physique of, **2.** 163; trained by the Massaliotes to write Greek, **2.** 179; as a whole, by the Greeks called " Celti," **2.** 211; the fourteen tribes of, between the Garumna and Liger, **2.** 213; in common dedicated temple to Augustus at Lugdunum, **2.** 223; the Cisalpine, accorded civic rights by the Romans, **2.** 299; defeated Rome (390 B.C.), **2.** 339, 341; captured Rome, **3.** 141; the " Genuine " (*i.e.* Germans), **3.** 153; the Scordiscan, **3.** 169; in Asia, extent of territory of, **5.** 345; in Asia, given over to the hereditary Tetrarchs by Pompey, **5.** 373; some of, settled in Paphlagonia, **5.** 383; overran the country subject to the Attalic and Bithynian kings in Asia Minor, and finally, by voluntary cession, received the present Galatia, **5.** 469; occupied a part of Greater Phrygia, **5.** 485; onsets of, in Asia Minor, **5.** 495; who crossed over to Asia, found Ilium lacking in walls,

6. 53; conquered by Attalus I, **6.** 167; tribe of, said by Apollodorus to be more recent than the time of Ephorus, **6.** 361, 367

Galatic Gulf (Gulf of Lyons), the, on the southern side of Celtica, **1.** 491, **2.** 5, 181, 215

Galatic Gulfs, the two, **2.** 119

Galatic (Gallic, or Celtic) race (the Gauls, the); the traits and habits of, **2.** 237–249; are war-mad, **2.** 237; are akin to the Germans, **2.** 239; the armour of, **2.** 241; structure of the homes of, **2.** 243; have three sets of men who are held in particular honour, **2.** 245; barbaric customs of, **2.** 247

Galatic tribes, the, beyond the Rhenus and Celtica, **3.** 151, 153

Galaxidi (see Oeantheia)

Galazze (see Calatia)

Galeotae, the; a kind of fish caught in the Strait of Messina, also called sword-fish and dog-fish, **1.** 87

Galepsus, between the mouths of the Strymon and Nestus Rivers, **3.** 355; rased to the ground by Philip, **3.** 359

Galilee, **7.** 281

Gallesius, Mt., between Ephesus and Colophon, **6.** 233

Galli, the (priests of Cybelê), eunuchs at the Plutonium at Hierapolis in Phrygia, **6.** 187

Gallia Aquitanica (see Aquitania)

Gallia Belgica, **2.** 167 (footnote 2)

Gallia Lugdunensis, **2.** 167 (footnote 1), 223 (footnote 3)

Gallia Narbonensis (see Narbonitis)

Gallikos River (see Echedorus River)

Gallipoli (see Callipolis)

Gallo, Cape (see Acritas)

Gallo-Graecia, a part of Phrygia in Asia Minor, ceded to the Galatae, **1.** 497, **5.** 469

Gallus, Aelius (see Aelius Gallus)

Gallus, Cornelius (see Cornelius Gallus)

Gallus River, the, which rises at Modra in Phrygia Hellespontica, joins the Sangarius, **5.** 379

Gamabrivii, the, an indigent German tribe, **3.** 159

Gambarus, competent ruler in Syria, **7.** 255

Games, the Actian, at Nicopolis in

INDEX OF NAMES, PLACES, AND SUBJECTS

Greece, **3**. 305; the Eleutherian, at Plataea, where the victor received a crown, **4**. 327; the Nemean, **4**. 187; the Olympian, **4**. 87, 91–95; the Pythian, **4**. 361; the quinquennial, at Neapolis near Alexandria in Aegypt, **8**. 41

Gandaris in India, subject to Porus, **7**. 53

Gandaritis, a district in India, **7**. 45

Gangamê, an instrument with which fish are caught in the ice at the Strait of Kertch, **3**. 225

Ganges, the city, in India, **7**. 125

Ganges River, the, in India, **7**. 17; has many tributaries, and is the largest river in India, **7**. 19; largest of all rivers, **7**. 61, 63; course of, **7**. 125

Gangitis, a stone found in Gordyaea which is avoided by reptiles, **7**. 233

Gangra, a small town and fortress in Paphlagonia, residence of Morzeus, **5**. 453

Ganymede, snatched away either at Harpagia or at the Dardanian Promontory in the Troad, **6**. 27, 59

Garabuza, Cape (see Cimarus)

Garamantes, the, in Libya; geographical position of land of, **8**. 195, 207, 209

Gardiki (see Larisa Kremastê)

Gardinitza (see Opus in Locris)

Garescus in Macedonia, one of the cities destroyed by Cassander, **3**. 343, 361

Gargano (see Garganum)

Garganum (Gargano), the promontory, in Apulia, **3**. 131; distance from, to Brundisium, **3**. 133; the deep gulf at, **3**. 135

Gargara in Aeolis in Asia; territory of, **6**. 13, 99; on the Gulf of Adramyttium, **6**. 103, 115; founded by the people of Assus, **6**. 117

Gargarians, the, live on the borders of the Amazons, **5**. 233; cohabit with the Amazons, and live in Themiscyra, **5**. 235

Gargarum, a place high up on Mt. Ida, **6**. 13

Gargarus, Mt., the Homeric, a summit of Mt. Ida, **6**. 11

Gargettus (near Garito in Attica),

where the headless body of Eurystheus was buried, **4**. 187

Garindaeans, the, in Arabia, coast of, **7**. 343

Garmanes (Sramans), the, in India, **7**. 99; life and tenets of, **7**. 103

Garonne River, the (see Garumna)

Garsaüïra, a town on the borders of Lycaonia, said once to have been a metropolis, **5**. 359

Garsaüra in Cappadocia, near Soatra, **5**. 475; the road through, **6**. 309

Garsauritis, one of the ten prefectures of Cappadocia, **5**. 349

Garumna (Garonne) River, the, navigable and empties into the ocean, **2**. 211; approximately parallel to the Pyrenees, **2**. 213; whence is one of the four passages to Britain, **2**. 253

Gascogne, Gulf of, **1**. 491 (footnote 2)

Gastuniotikos River, the (see Peneius River, the, in Elis)

"Gasys," a Paphlagonian name used in Cappadocia, **5**. 415

Gaudos, **3**. 103; called the Isle of Calypso by Callimachus, **3**. 193

Gaugamela ("Camel's House"), a village in Aturia, where Dareius was conquered and lost his empire, **7**. 197

Gauls, the (see Galatic race, Celti, and Galatians)

Gaza, in Phoenicia, harbour and city, **7**. 277; sandy country of, **7**. 279

Gazaca (near Leilan), royal summer residence of kings of Atropatian Media, **5**. 305

Gazacenê in Cappadocia; Paphlagonian names prevalent in, **5**. 417

Gazaeans, the, a tribe in Syria, **7**. 239

Gazelles (see Deer), the, in the Scythian plains, **3**. 249; many, in Gazelonitis in Cappadocia Pontica, **5**. 393; in India, **7**. 125; horns of, used as weapons by the Simi in Aethiopia, **7**. 325; in Arabia, **7**. 343; abound in Maurusia in Libya, **8**. 163

Gazelon, a city in Gazelonitis in Cappadocia Pontica, **5**. 395

Gazelonitis in Cappadocia Pontica, fertile, level, and has gazelles and fine sheep, **5**. 393; Paphlagonian names prevalent in, **5**. 417; boundaries of, **5**. 443

INDEX OF NAMES, PLACES, AND SUBJECTS

339

INDEX OF NAMES, PLACES, AND SUBJECTS

INDEX OF NAMES, PLACES, AND SUBJECTS

Gomphi (Palaeo-Episkopi), a stronghold in Thessaly, **4.** 431

Gonnus, a Perrhaebian city, **4.** 443

Gonoessa, the Homeric, **4.** 185

Gorbeus, on the Sangarius River, in Galatia, royal residence of Castor the son of Saocondarius, where Deïotarus, Castor's father-in-law, slew him and his own daughter, **5.** 473

Gordium, on the Sangarius River in Galatia, **5.** 473; home of Cleon and by him enlarged into a city, which he named Juliopolis, **5.** 497

Gordius, the king, once lived on the Sangarius River, **5.** 473

Gordus in the Troad, **6.** 89

Gordyaea, borders on the Tigris, **5.** 299; borders on Babylonia, **7.** 203; places in, assigned to Tigranes by Pompey, **7.** 231; very productive, and a haunt of lions, **7.** 233

Gordyaean Mountains, the, in Asia, **5.** 299

Gordyaeans, the, by the ancients called Carduchians; subject to the king of Armenia, and later to the Romans, **7.** 231

Gordyenê in Asia, stadia through, still unmeasured, **1.** 303; geographical position of, **5.** 321; said to have been settled by Gordys the son of Neoptolemus, **7.** 233

Gordys, son of Triptolemus, said to have settled in Gordyenê in Asia, **7.** 233, 243

Gorgipia, in the Syndic territory, near the Cimmerian Bosporus, **5.** 199

Gorgon, the myth of, **1.** 69

Gorgons, the; home of, an invention, **3.** 191

Gorgus, the son of Cypselus the tyrant of Corinth, founded Ambracia, **3.** 303; with his father dug canal through isthmus of Leucas, **5.** 33

Gorgus, the mining expert, on the gold and silver mines in India, **7.** 53

Goritza (see Demetrias)

Gortyn (see Gortyna)

Gortyna (or Gortyn), one of the three famous cities in Crete, **5.** 127; at one time took precedence over Cnossus, **5.** 129; description of,

5. 137; 800 stadia from Cydonia, **5.** 139

Gortynia in Macedonia (see Gortynium)

Gortynians, the; war of, against the Cnossians, **5.** 135

Gortynium (or Gortynia) in Macedonia, **3.** 325

Gorys, a city in India, **7.** 45

Goths, the (see Butones)

Governor, the, at Alba, a young noble, **2.** 379

Graces, the; temples of, at Orchomenus, **4.** 337

Graea, the Homeric, in Boeotia, near Oropus, by some identified with Tanagra, **4.** 183, 293, 319

Graecia, Magna, in Italy, occupied by Greeks, **3.** 7

Grain, abundance of, exported from Turdetania in Iberia, **2.** 33; not produced in territory of Massalia, **2.** 175

Granicus River, the, in the Troad, **6.** 5; where Alexander utterly defeated the satraps of Dareius, **6.** 27; rises in a hill of Mt. Ida, **6.** 85, 87

Grape-vine, the; productivity of, in Hyrcania, **1.** 273; does not grow or else does not bear fruit about the Borysthenes or in the part of Celtica on the ocean, **1.** 275; buried during winter in southern districts of Celtica and about Bosporus, **1.** 275, 277; the wild, in India, **7.** 97

Grapes, produced in the territory of Massalia, **2.** 175; abundant in the land of the Sabini, **2.** 375; bunches of, two cubits (in length?) in Margiana, **5.** 279; abundant in Themiscyra, **5.** 397; among the Sydracae in India, fall off before they ripen because of excessive rains, **7.** 11

Gras, great-grandson of Orestes, with Aeolians occupied Lesbos, **6.** 7

Grass, used as food by the Aethiopians, **8.** 143

Grass-hoppers (*tettigae*), the, on the Halex River in Bruttium, **3.** 33

Gravisci, a small town in Italy between Cossa and Ostia, **2.** 363

Gravity, the centre of, **1.** 27, 41; the law of, **1.** 425

INDEX OF NAMES, PLACES, AND SUBJECTS

343

INDEX OF NAMES, PLACES, AND SUBJECTS

INDEX OF NAMES, PLACES, AND SUBJECTS

and rises in Camisenê in Greater Cappadocia, **5.** 393

Hamadan (see Ecbatana)

Hamaxia in Cilicia Tracheia, **6.** 331

Hamaxitans, the; territory of, **6.** 101

Hamaxitus, below Lectum in the Troad, **6.** 93, 97; where the mice attacked the Teucrians, **6.** 95

Hamilcar (see Barcas Hamilcar)

Hams, excellent, cured in Cantabria and country of the Carretanians, **2.** 101

Hannibal, crossed the Alps by the pass leading through the country of the Taurini, **2.** 293; campaign of, against the Romans, **2.** 323; crossed marshes of Cispadana only with difficulty, **2.** 329; forced to choose the more difficult pass, **2.** 369; expedition of, **2.** 447; besieged the Praenestini at Casilinum, **2.** 461; lavishly entertained by the Campani, **2.** 467; joined by the Picentes, **2.** 471; crushed the Brettii at Temesa, **3.** 15; destroyed Terina, **3.** 17; enslaved Tarentum, **3.** 117; devastated Apulia, **3.** 135; invaded Italy at time when the Romans were fighting the peoples about the Padus, during the second Carthaginian War, **3.** 141; founded Artaxata in Armenia for King Artaxias, **5.** 325; welcomed by Prusias after defeat of Antiochus, **5.** 457

Harbour, the Great, and the Eunostus, at Alexandria, **8.** 27, 37–39

Harbours, the treatises on, **4.** 3

Harbours, The, by Timosthenes, admiral of Ptolemy II, **4.** 363

Hares (see Rabbits), the burrowing, in Turdetania; very destructive, both there and elsewhere, **2.** 33, 35

Harma in Attica, near Phylê, **4.** 293

Harma in Boeotia, to be distinguished from the Harma in Attica; the proverb about, and said to be the place where Amphiaraüs and Adrastus fell, **4.** 295; one of the "Four United Villages," **4.** 301, 321

Harmatus, the promontory, with Hydra forms the Elaïtic Gulf, **6.** 159

Harmonia, the wife of Cadmus; the tomb-stone of, **1.** 169; descendants of, ruled over the Enchelii, **3.** 307

Harmozi, Cape, in Carmania, **7.** 301

Harmozicê, a fortified city on the Cyrus River, **5.** 221

Harpagia in the Troad, where, according to some, Ganymede was snatched away, **6.** 27

Harpagus, general of Cyrus the Great, captured Phocaea in Asia Minor (about 540 B.C.), **3.** 5

Harpalus, the Macedonian general, slain by Thibron, one of his officers, **8.** 203

Harvests, the, in Masaesylia in Libya, marvellous, **8.** 179

Hasdrubal (see Asdrubal)

Hawk, the, worshipped by the Aegyptians, **8.** 109; a peculiar kind of, worshipped at Philae, **8.** 131

Hawk Island, the, in the Arabian Gulf, **7.** 331

Hawks, the City of (Hieraconpolis), on the Nile, south of Thebes, **8.** 127

Heavens, the, revolve round the earth, **1.** 425; discussion of, **8.** 99–101

Hebê (see Dia), worshipped at Phlius and Sicyon, **4.** 205

Hebrus (Maritza) River, the, in Thrace, 535 Roman miles from Apollonia, **3.** 293, 329; navigable for 120 stadia, to Cypsela, **3.** 369; has two mouths, **3.** 373, 375; 3100 stadia distant from Byzantium, **3.** 379

Hecabê, sister of the Phrygian Asius, **6.** 41

Hecabê's Sema, or Tomb (see Cynos-Sema)

Hecataeus of Miletus (b. about 540 B.C.), geographer and philosopher, **1.** 3; left a geographical work, **1.** 23, which was entitled *Periegesis* and embodied about all that was known on the subject in his time; wrote poetic prose, **1.** 65; on the Inachus River, **3.** 79; calls the "City of Cimmeris" an invention, **3.** 191; calls the Aöus River "Aeas," saying that "the Inachus and the Aeas flow from the same place, the region of Lacmus" (*i.e.* Lacmon, a height of Pindus), **3.** 265; says the Peloponnesus was inhabited by barbarians before the time of the Greeks, **3.** 285; distinguishes between the Eleians and the Epeians, **4.** 39; in his *Circuit of the Earth*, discusses the Alazones at length, and

INDEX OF NAMES, PLACES, AND SUBJECTS

348

INDEX OF NAMES, PLACES, AND SUBJECTS

INDEX OF NAMES, PLACES, AND SUBJECTS

Heracleides, the Herophileian physician, native of Erythrae in Asia, 6. 243

Heracleides of Pontus (b. about 380 B.C.); pupil of Plato and Aristotle, and author of numerous works on a variety of subjects, including certain *Dialogues* mentioned by Strabo; makes a certain Magus say that he had circumnavigated Libya, 1. 377, 385; on the submersion of Helicê, 4. 215; Platonic philosopher, 5. 371; on the sacred mice round the temple of Sminthian Apollo at Chrysa, 6. 95

Heracleiotic (or Canobic) mouth, the, of the Nile, 8. 13, 63

Heracleitus the poet, comrade of Callimachus, native of Halicarnassus, 6. 285

Heracleitus of Ephesus (about 535–475 B.C.), founder of metaphysics and called " dark philosopher " because of the obscurity of his writings; on " the Bear " in Homer, 1. 11, 6. 231

Heracleium, the, near Canobus, in Aegypt, 8. 65

Heracleium in Crete, the seaport of Cnossus, 5. 129

Heracleium (Temple of Heracles), the, at Gades; behaviour of spring in, 2. 143, and wells in, 2. 145

Heracleium, near Lake Maeotis, 5. 197

Heracleium, the, in Sicily, 75 Roman miles from Lilybaeum, 3. 57

Heracleium in Syria, 7. 247, 255

Heracleium, Cape (Capo Spartivento), last cape of Italy, 3. 27

Heracleotae, the ; city of (Chersonesus Heracleotica or Heracleia), in the Crimea, 3. 231

Heracleotis, a district in the territory of the Ephesians, revolted from the Ephesians, 6. 233

Heracles, son of Zeus and Alcmenê ; invaded Iberia, 1. 7; wise from travel, 1. 31; mythical labours of, 1. 69; Pillars of, 22,500 stadia distant from Cape Malea, 1. 93; long journeys of, 1. 177; Pillars of, at end of inhabited world on west, 1. 253, and distance from, to Peloponnesus, 1. 403, to Strait of Sicily and

to Sacred Cape, 1. 407, to Massalia and the Pyrenees, 1. 409, and lie in the equinoctial west, 1. 411, and width and length of strait at, 1. 469, and at most westerly point of Mediterranean, 1. 485; temple and altar of, on the Sacred Cape of Iberia, 2. 7; said to have founded Calpê in Iberia, 2. 15; expedition of, in quest of kine of Geryon and apples of the Hesperides, 2. 57; certain companions of, colonised Iberia, 2. 83; temple of, on the isle of Gades, and twelve labours of, 2. 133; different theories as to site of Pillars of, 2. 135–143; wont to erect pillars at limits of his expeditions, 2. 139; pillars of, in India, no longer to be seen, 2. 141; informed by Prometheus of route from Caucasus to the Hesperides, 2. 187; temple of, built by Aemilianus at confluence of the Rhodanus and Isar Rivers, 2. 197; " Monoecus," temple of, on Port of Monoecus (Monaco), 2. 267; Atys the Lydian, a descendant of, by Omphalê, 2. 337; some children of, settled in Sardinia, 2. 361; Harbour of, at Cosa in Italy, 2. 363; entertained by Evander, mythical founder of Rome, and destined to become a god, 2. 385; temple of, at Tibur, 2. 417; Fortress of (Herculaneum), 2. 451; completed mound at Gulf Lucrinus, 2. 445; the Harbour of (Tropea), in Bruttium, 3. 19; the colossal bronze statue of, taken by Fabius Maximus from Tarentum to the Capitolium at Rome, 3. 107; drove out the Leuternian Giants, 3. 119; defeated the giants in Pallenê (Kassandra) the Macedonian peninsula, 3. 351; connected a hollow place in Thrace with the sea and thus created Lake Bistonis, 3. 365; the voyage of, from Troy, 3. 381; father of Tlepolemus of Ephyra, 4. 27; joined by the Epeians against Augeias, 4. 39; temple of, in Triphylia, 4. 65; ravaged the Pylian country, slaying all the twelve sons of Neleus except Nestor, 4. 81, 85; humbled the Eleians, 4. 91; by some said to have

INDEX OF NAMES, PLACES, AND SUBJECTS

been the first to contend in the Olympian Games and win the victory, **4.** 93; captured cities in Elis, **4.** 105; brought up Cerberus from Hades near Cape Taenarum, **4.** 127; drove the birds away from the Stymphalian Lake, **4.** 161; said to have driven out the Dryopians, **4.** 173; the sons of, **4.** 187; the painting of, in torture in the robe of Deïaneira, **4.** 201; slew Erginus the tyrant of the Orchomenians, **4.** 335; the hot waters of, at Aedepsus in Euboea, **4.** 379; death of, on Mt. Oeta, **4.** 387; hot waters near Thermopylae sacred to, **4.** 389; funeral pyre of, **4.** 391; captured Oechalia, **4.** 433; ancestor of Thessalian kings, **4.** 455; killed the ferryman Nessus at the Lycormas (Evenus) River in Aetolia, **5.** 29; defeated the river-god Acheloüs and thus won the hand of Deïaneira, **5.** 57; drained Paracheloïtis, **5.** 59; harbour and precinct of, in Acarnania, from which latter the "Labours of Heracles," by Lysippus, was carried to Rome, **5.** 61; the last of the giants destroyed by, lie beneath the isle Myconos, **5.** 171; slew the giants who attacked Aphrodite at Phanagoreia near the Cimmerian Bosporus, **5.** 201; reputed expedition of, to India, **5.** 239; Pillars of, 30,000 stadia from Issus, **5.** 289; Hylas, a companion of, carried off by the nymphs from Mt. Arganthonium in Asia, and Cius, a companion of, founded Cius, **5.** 457; not honoured by the Ilians, because he sacked their city, **6.** 61, 63; ruined Augê the mother of Telephus, **6.** 135; colossal statue of, in Samos, **6.** 215; father of Thessalus, **6.** 273; expedition of, to India, **7.** 7–13; worshipped by Indian philosophers, **7.** 97; temple of, on the Heracleium in Aegypt, **8.** 65; the City of, near the Nile, holds in honour the ichneumon, **8.** 107; said to have visited the temple of Ammon, **8.** 115; worshipped at Meroë, **8.** 147; altar of, on the Emporicus Gulf in Libya, **8.** 161; took Indian natives with him to

Libya, **8.** 169; a kind of temple of, in Cyrenaea, **8.** 207

Heracles, one of the Idacan Dactyli, not the son of Zeus and Alcmenê, said by some to have been the first to contend in the Olympian Games and win the victory, **4.** 93

Heracles, Island of (see Scombraria)

Heracles Cornopion ("Locust-killer"), worshipped by the Oetaeans, **6.** 127

Heracles Ipoctonus ("Ips-slayer"), worshipped by the Erythraeans in Mimas, **6.** 127

Heracleidae, the, brought back the Dorians, **4.** 7; the return of, after the Trojan War, **4.** 9, 91, 107, 175; guided back to the Peloponnesus by Oxylus, **4.** 103; under Eurysthenes and Procles seized Laconia, **4.** 133; succeeded the Pelopidae at Mycenae and Argos, **4.** 187; held all the Peloponnesus except Achaea, **4.** 211; invaded Attica, but were defeated, and founded Megara, **4.** 251; as some think, built their fleet at Naupactus, **4.** 385; returned to the Peloponnesus from the Dorian Tetrapolis, **4.** 387; once inhabited Rhodes, **6.** 273

Heraea (near Aianni) in Arcadia, settled either by Cleombrotus or Cleonymus from nine communities, **4.** 21; no longer exists, **4.** 229

Heraeum, the Argive, 40 stadia from Argos, **4.** 151, and common to Argos and Mycenae, and contains remarkable statues made by Polycleitus, **4.** 165, 167 (see footnote 1)

Heraeum, the, on the isle Samos, **6.** 213

Hérault River, the (see Arauris)

Herculaneum (see Heracles, Fortress of), **2.** 451

Hercynian (Black) Forest, the; near the sources of the Ister, **2.** 287; geographical position of, **3.** 155; description of, **3.** 163, 165

Herdonia (Ordona), on the mule-road between Brundisium and Beneventum, **3.** 123

Hermae, the, between Syenê and Philae; description of, **8.** 131

Hermaea, the promontory and city on the coast of Carthaginia, **8.** 183, 191

351

INDEX OF NAMES, PLACES, AND SUBJECTS

Hermagoras, contemporary of Cicero, and author of *The Art of Rhetoric*; a native of Temnus in Asia, **6.** 159

Hermeias the tyrant of Assus, pupil and benefactor of Aristotle, hanged by the Persians, **6.** 117

Hermes, a man without arms, sent to Augustus by King Porus in India, **7.** 127

Hermes; the god of travel, **1.** 401; numerous shrines of, in Elis, **4.** 49; at Aegyptian Thebes honoured as the patron of astronomy, **8.** 125

Hermionê (also spelled "Hermion," now Kastri) in Argolis, **4.** 153; an important city, and near it is the "short-cut" descent to Hades, **4.** 171; seized by the Carians, **4.** 175; belonged to a kind of Amphictyonic League, **4.** 175; mentioned by Homer, **4.** 181; added to the Achaean League by Aratus, **4.** 217

Hermionic Gulf, the, next to the Argolic Gulf, extends to Aegina and Epidauria, **4.** 15, 149; begins at the town Asinê in Argolis, **4.** 153

Hermocreon, builder of the huge altar at Parium in the Troad, **5.** 171, **6.** 29

Hermodorus, the most useful man in Ephesus, according to Heracleitus, but was banished; said to have written certain laws for the Romans, **6.** 231

Hermonassa in Cappadocia Pontica, **5.** 399

Hermonassa, near the Cimmerian Bosporus, **5.** 199

Hermonax (site unknown), a village at the mouth of the Tyras, **3.** 219

Hermondori, the, a tribe of the Suevi, **3.** 157

Hermonthis, city above Aegyptian Thebes, where Apollo and Zeus are worshipped and a sacred bull kept, **8.** 127

Hermupolis, an, in Aegypt, near Butus, on an island, and another in the Sebennytic Nome, **8.** 67, 69, 73

Hermus River, the, mentioned by Homer, **5.** 421; course of, **6.** 5, 13; deposited the land of Larisa Phriconis, **6.** 157; flows past the territory of Smyrna, **6.** 159; the Plain of, **6.** 171; the Pactolus and Hyllus empty into, **6.** 173; marks

a limit of the Ionian seaboard, **6.** 197; Plain of, created by silt, **7.** 23

Hernici, the, in Latium, **2.** 379; overthrow of, **2.** 387; cities of, founded by the Romans, **2.** 415

Hero, the Tower of, near Sestus, whence passage is taken across to Abydus, **6.** 43

Herod (Hyrcanus?), appointed to the priesthood of Judaea by Pompey, **7.** 299

Herod the Great; surnamed Samaria "Sebastê" (in honour of Augustus), **7.** 281; palace of, at Jericho, **7.** 291; slinked into the priesthood of Judaea, and was later given the title of king by Antony and also by Augustus, **7.** 299

Herodotus, the "Father of History" (about 484–425 B.C.); calls Aegypt "the gift of the Nile," **1.** 111, 131, **5.** 357, **7.** 23; includes myth in his *History*, **1.** 159; on the silting-up process, **1.** 221; on the Hyperboreians, **1.** 229; on the circumnavigation of Libya, **1.** 377, 385; on King Arganthonius in Iberia, **2.** 59; says Hyria in Iapygia was founded by Cretans, **3.** 121; on the straightforward character of Idanthyrsus the Scythian king, against whom Dareius made his expedition, **3.** 199, 201; says the Melas River was not sufficient to supply Xerxes' army, **3.** 373; says the Asopus flows through a deep gorge south of Trachin and empties near Thermopylae, **4.** 391; says there were temples of the Cabeiri at Memphis in Aegypt, **5.** 115; tells incredible stories, **5.** 247; wrong in regard to the Araxes River, **5.** 335; on the prostitutes in Lydia, **5.** 341; meaning of, on "the country this side the Halys River," **5.** 347; by "White Syrians" means "Cappadocians," and defines the course of the Halys River, **5.** 383; foists certain names of peoples on us, **5.** 405; on the Milyae in Asia, **5.** 491; on the Pedasians in Caria, **6.** 119; tells a myth about the Lesbian Arion, the citharist, **6.** 145; on the several rivers that empty near Phocaea, **6.** 173; says the

INDEX OF NAMES, PLACES, AND SUBJECTS

mound and tomb of Alyattes at Sardeis were built mainly by prostitutes, **6.** 177, 179; native of Halicarnassus, but called the Thurian because he took part in the colonisation of Thuria, **6.** 283, 285; on the origin of the Pamphylians, **6.** 325; talks much nonsense about the Nile and other things, **8.** 133; says that the Aegyptians knead mud with their hands, but suet for bread-making with their feet. **8.** 151

Heröonpolis, on the isthmus at the Arabian Gulf, **7.** 309, **8.** 71, 79; revolted but was subdued by Cornelius with only a few soldiers, **8.** 135; parallel of latitude the same as that of the Great Syrtis, **8.** 199

Herophileian school of medicine, the, at Carura, on the confines of Phrygia and Caria, established in Strabo's time by Zeuxis, **5.** 519

Herophilus, the great physician and surgeon, born at Chalcedon and lived at Alexandria in the reign of Ptolemy I; school of medicine of, called "Herophileian," established at Carura in Strabo's time, **5.** 519

Herostratus, set on fire the temple of Artemis at Ephesus, **6.** 225

Herpa, a small town in Sargarausenê in Cappadocia, **5.** 357; greatly damaged by the overflow of the Carmalas River, **5.** 365

Herphae in Cappadocia; the road through, **6.** 311

Hesiod of Ascrê in Boeotia (fl. in the eighth century B.C.), father of Greek didactic poetry. Extant works under his name are *Works and Days*, *Theogony*, and *The Shield of Heracles*. His knowledge of the scene of the wanderings of Odysseus, **1.** 85; knows of mouths of the Nile, **1.** 107; his mythical epithets and fabulous stories, **1.** 157; on the origin of the Pelasgians, **2.** 345; invented fabulous men, "half-dog," and "long-headed," **3.** 191; calls the Scythians "Hippemolgi" ("Mare-milkers"), **3.** 197; in his *Circuit of the Earth* mentions the Galactophagi ("Curd-eaters"), **3.** 205; on the Leleges, **3.** 291; on Dodona and the Pelasgians, **3.** 313;

on the Peirus River in Elis, **4.** 43; *apocopê* in, **4.** 131; calls the Greeks as a whole "Hellenes" and "Panhellenes," **4.** 157; calls Argos "well-watered," **4.** 163 (footnote 1); mentions a Helicê in Thessaly, **4.** 215; on the sacred serpent called "Cychreides," **4.** 253; ridicules Ascrê, his native city, **4.** 315, 331; describes the winding course of the Cephissus River in Phocis, **4.** 375; on the Dotian Plain in Thessaly, **4.** 449; on the origin of Nymphs, Satyrs and the Curetes, **5.** 109, 111; stories of, more credible than those of certain historians, **5.** 247; a native(?) of Cymê Phriconis in Asia, but moved to the "wretched" (he calls it) Ascrê in Boeotia, **6.** 161; on the contest between Calchas and Mopsus, **6.** 233, 235; on the origin of the Magnesians on the Maeander, **6.** 251; says that Amphilochus was slain by Apollo at Soli, **6.** 355

Hesionê, daughter of Laomedon; the myth of the liberation of, by Heracles, **6.** 63

Hesperian (Western, Ozolian) Locrians (see Locrians), the, **4.** 343; not specifically mentioned by Homer, **4.** 385

Hesperides, the; home of, an invention, **3.** 191

Hesperides, Harbour of the, in Libya, **8.** 201

Hesperus the star, engraved on the public seal of the Hesperian, or Ozalian, Locrians, **4.** 343

Hestiaea of Alexandreia, author of a work on Homer's *Iliad* and quoted by Demetrius of Scepsis; on the site of ancient Troy, **6.** 73, 75

Hestiaeotis (or Histiaeotis), one of the four divisions of Thessaly, **4.** 397; geographical position of, **4.** 399, 417, 429, 431, 443; "in earlier times called Doris, colonised Crete," according to Andron, **5.** 127

Heteroscian circles, the, **1.** 367, 369

Heteroscians, the, **1.** 509; term defined, **1.** 517

Hexamili, between the Melas Gulf and the Propontis (see Lysimacheia)

"Hexi" (see "Sex"), the name of the city of the Exetanians in Iberia, according to Pomponius Mela, **2**. 81 (footnote 4)

Hiberus (Ebro) River, the (see Iberus)

Hicetaon, the Homeric, father of Melanippus, who pastured kine in Percotê, **6**. 19, 21

Hides, abundant in Sicily, **3**. 87 ; sold by Asiatic nomads at Tanaïs, **5**. 193.

Hidrieis, the, in Caria, not mentioned by Homer, **6**. 363

Hidrieus, second son of Hecatomnos the king of the Carians, married his sister Ada, and became ruler of the Carians, **6**. 285

Hiera, Cape, in Lycia, **6**. 319

Hiera (see Thermessa)

Hieraconpolis (see Hawks, City of)

Hierapetra in Crete (see Hierapytna)

Hierapolis in Mesopotamia (see Bambycê)

Hierapolis, in Phrygia, near Mt. Mesogis, opposite Laodiceia, where are the hot springs and the remarkable Plutonium, **6**. 187 ; water at, remarkably adapted to dyeing of wool, **6**. 189

Hierapolitic marble, the, **4**. 429

Hierapytna in Crete, founded by Cyrbas, **5**. 111, 123 ; named after Pytna, a peak of Mt. Ida, **5**. 113

Hierapytnians, the, rased Prasus to the ground, **5**. 139

Hieratica byblus (papyrus), the, **3**. 61

Hierax (see Hawk), the, in Aegypt, tame like a cat as compared with those elsewhere, **8**. 151

Hiericus (Jericho), in Judaea, **7**. 281 ; description of, **7**. 291

Hierisos on the isthmus of Athos (see Acanthus)

Hiero (tyrant of Syracuse 478–467 B.C.), colonised Pithecussae (Ischia), **2**. 457 ; colonised Catana and changed its name to Aetna, **3**. 67 ; after his death declared founder of the new Aetna at foot of Mt. Aetna, **3**. 69

Hierocepia in Cypros, **6**. 383

Hierocepis in Cypros, **6**. 381

Hierocles the orator, a native of Alabanda in Caria, **6**. 299

Hieroglyphics, the, in regard to Sesostris the Aegyptian, **7**. 313

Hieron, benefactor of Laodiceia, **5**. 511

Hieron (Temple), the Chalcedonian; 3500 stadia from, to Sinopê, 2000

to Heracleia Pontica, and 700 to Cape Carambis, **5**. 391; lies at the mouth of the Pontus, **5**. 455

Hieron Oros (" Sacred Mountain ") on the Propontis, discharges asphalt into the sea at a place opposite Proconnesus (Isle of Marmora), **3**. 377

Hieronymus of Cardia, historian of the first fifty years after Alexander's death ; his description of Corinth, **4**. 191 (see footnote 4) ; on Thessaly, **4**. 453 ; on the dimensions of Crete, **5**. 123

Hieronymus, Peripatetic and historian (about 290–230 B.C.), a native of Rhodes, **6**. 279 (see references to Hieronymus of Cardia ; especially **4**. 191 and footnote 4, and Pauly-Wissowa, *s.v.*)

Hiketides, the, of Aeschylus (see *Suppliants*)

Himera (Bonfornello) in Sicily ; no longer settled, **3**. 83 ; the hot springs at, **3**. 91

Himera River, the, in Sicily, 18 Roman miles from Cephaloedium, **3**. 57

Hipparchus of Nicaea in Bithynia (fl. about 150 B.C.), the famous astronomer and geographer ; discovered the precession of the equinoxes, and was the first to outline a system of latitudes and longitudes ; regarded Homer as founder of geography, **1**. 5 ; on the tides, **1**. 19 ; wrote treatise *Against Eratosthenes*, **1**. 23 ; on eclipses, **1**. 23 ; praised by Strabo, **1**. 53 ; on extent of Homer's knowledge, **1**. 59 ; notes Homer's accuracy in geography, **1**. 101 ; says strait at Byzantium sometimes stands still, **1**. 205 ; on the levels of the Mediterranean and Red Seas, **1**. 209 ; plots celestial phenomena of inhabited places, **1**. 233 ; on certain parallels of latitude, **1**. 237 ; contradicts Eratosthenes on certain distances and discredits Patrocles, **1**. 257, 279 ; had access to library at Alexandria, **1**. 259 ; does not raise proper objections to the ancient maps, **1**. 267, 345 ; follows Pytheas concerning certain parallels and meridians, **1**. 269 ; on the sun,

INDEX OF NAMES, PLACES, AND SUBJECTS

1. 281; trusts Pytheas, **1.** 283; tries to correct Eratosthenes, **1.** 289; makes false assumptions, **1.** 291; unfair to Eratosthenes, **1.** 293. 301; would correct Eratosthenes' "Third Section," **1.** 305; his arguments against Eratosthenes "childish," **1.** 315; calls India four-sided and rhomboidal, **1.** 317; captious about the rough estimates of Eratosthenes, **1.** 325; again censured by Strabo for fault-finding, **1.** 335; rightly censures Eratosthenes, **1.** 357; Third Book of, approved by Strabo, **1.** 361; accepts Eratosthenes' measurement of the earth, **1.** 437; an authority on longitudes and latitudes, **1.** 503; on the measurement of the earth, **1.** 505; on the relative positions of the Cinnamon-bearing country, Syenê, and the equator, **1.** 507; referred to by Strabo as authority on northernmost regions of Europe and on further astronomical matters, **1.** 517; wrote treatises on *Physics* and *Mathematics*, **4.** 3; Strabo's criticism of, **5.** 329; native of Nicaea in Bithynia, **5.** 467

Hippeis (Knights), the, in Crete and Sparta, **5.** 151

Hippemolgi ("Mare-milkers"), Homer's, are wagon-dwelling Scythians and Sarmatians, **3.** 179, 181, 187, 189, 195, 197, 205, 243, **5.** 419; by Apollodorus called a fabrication, **5.** 423

Hippi, the, lie off Erythrae in Asia, **6.** 239

Hippobatae ("Knights"), the, in power at Chalcis, **5.** 13

Hippocampus, a, in hand of Poseidon, in the strait at Helicê, **4.** 215

Hippocles of Euboea (the Euboean Cymê), joint founder of Cumae in Italy, **2.** 437

Hippocoön, banished Tyndareus and Icarius from Lacedaemon, **5.** 69

Hippocorona, in the territory of Adramyttium, **5.** 113

Hippocoronium in Crete, **5.** 113

Hippocrates, the physician, a native of Cos, **6.** 289

Hippocrenê (see Hippucrenê)

Hippodrome, the, at Alexandria, **8.** 41

Hippomarathi (horse-fennel), found in Maurusia, **8.** 163

Hipponax of Ephesus (fl. 546–520 B.C.), the iambic poet, one of the Seven Wise Men, used the poetic figure of "part with the whole," **4.** 37; on a place called Smyrna that belonged to Ephesus, **6.** 201; on Bias, **6.** 211; a native of Ephesus, **6.** 231

Hipponiate (Napetine) Gulf, the, in Bruttium, **3.** 13

Hipponium (or Vibo Valentia, now Bivona near Monteleone), in Bruttium, founded by the Locrians, **3.** 17; naval station of, **3.** 19

Hippopotamus, the, found in India, according to Onesicritus, **7.** 21, 79; found in a lake near Cape Deirê in Aethiopia, **7.** 331

Hippos, the two, one near Itycê, and the other farther from Cirta, towards Tretum, **8.** 183

Hippothoüs, led the Pelasgians in the Trojan War, **2.** 345; **6.** 153; fell in the fight over Patroclus, **6.** 155

Hippotion, father of the Homeric Morys, **5.** 461

Hippucrenê (or Hippocrenê), the spring opened on Helicon by the winged horse Pegasus, **4.** 195, 319

Hippus River, the, empties into the Phasis, **5.** 211, 219

Hirê, "grassy," the Homeric, **4.** 109; the present site of, **4.** 115

Hirpini, the, a Samnite tribe; origin of name of, **2.** 467

Hispalis in Iberia, on the Baetis River, colony of the Romans and famous trade-centre, **2.** 21; about 500 stadia from the sea by boat, **2.** 25

Hispania; term now used synonymously with "Iberia," **2.** 119

Hispellum in Italy, **2.** 373

Histiaea (later called Oreus) in Euboea, the history of, **5.** 7

Histiaeans, the, in Euboea, forced to migrate to Thessaly by the Perrhaebians, **4.** 429; later called the Oreitae, were colonists from the Attic deme of the Histiaeans, **5.** 7

Histiaeotis (see Hestiaeotis) in Euboea, **5.** 7; in Thessaly, **5.** 9

Historians; the Greek and Roman, compared, **2.** 117; the early, in-

355

INDEX OF NAMES, PLACES, AND SUBJECTS

clude myths in their histories, **4.** 39

Historical Sketches, the, of Strabo, discussed Parthian usages at length, **5.** 277

History, the work entitled, by Polybius, and that by Ephorus, on the topography of the continents, **4.** 3

History, the, of Strabo, discussed Parthian usages at length, **5.** 277

History, importance of terrestrial, **1.** 29; aim of, **1.** 91; wishes for the truth, **5.** 235; that of the Persians, Medes, and Syrians untrustworthy, **5.** 247

Hog-meat, the finest, shipped from territory of the Sequani to Rome, **2.** 225

Hogs, the, in Celtica, run wild, **3.** 243; great supply of, in Cisalpine Celtica, **2.** 331

Holmi in Cilicia, **6.** 333

Holmi in Phrygia, the road through, **6.** 309

Homer, geographer and philosopher, **1.** 3; founder of geography, **1.** 5; quoted on movements of heavenly bodies, **1.** 5, 7; on people of the west, on Zephyrus, and on the Elysian Plain, **1.** 7; on the Aethiopians, and on the Bear and Wain, **1.** 9; makes Oceanus surround inhabited world and knows about the tides, **1.** 13, 159; knows the Mediterranean, **1.** 19; the Cimmerian Bosporus, **1.** 21; inserts an element of myth, **1.** 21, 23, 59, 65, 71, 73, 79, 135, 171; on Heracles' " great adventures," **1.** 31; on the rotundity of the earth, **1.** 43; speaks of bards as disciplinarians, **1** 57; his epithets appropriate, **1** 57, 91, 133; the limitations of his knowledge, **1.** 59; adorns Odysseus with every excellence, **1.** 61; an expert in the art of rhetoric, **1.** 63; based works on historical facts, **1.** 73; called " *The* Poet," **1.** 77; places scene of wanderings of Odysseus in the region of Sicily and Italy, **1.** 79; but, according to Eratosthenes, not so, **1.** 85; places the scene, in fancy, on Oceanus, **1.** 93; uses myth for a useful purpose, **1.** 97; the poet *par excellence,* **1.** 99; on the winds, **1.**

105; knew of mouths of the Nile, of Thebes, of Aethiopia, and of the isle Pharos, **1.** 109; means " Scythians " by his term " Nomads," **1.** 121; on the geographical position of Aethiopia, **1.** 125; on the cranes and pygmies, **1.** 127, 263; his fondness for knowledge, **1.** 131; did not know India, **1.** 143; uses figures of speech, **1.** 147; on Sidon, **1.** 149; on Jason's expedition, **1.** 171; quoted on the purgation of seas, **1.** 195, 197; on the cold and hot springs of Scamander, **1.** 215; on Nericus in Leucas, **1.** 219; on Arnê and Mideia, **1.** 221; present absence of his cave and grotto in Ithaca due to physical changes, **1.** 221; the isle of Asteris, **1.** 221; censured by Eratosthenes, **1.** 243; quoted on " amputation," **1.** 315; caused the wall of the Achaeans to disappear, **1.** 393; his reason for dividing Aethiopians into two groups, **1.** 395; probably knew nothing about India, **1.** 397; a riddle attributed to, **2.** 45; man of many voices and of wide information, probably knew much of Iberia and the far west, and of the far north, **2.** 51–59; named Tartarus after Tartessis in Iberia, and transferred the Cimmerians to the neighbourhood of Hades, **2.** 51; modelled his " Planctae " after the " Cyaneae " (" Symplegades "), and in general transferred *Iliad* and *Odyssey* from domain of historical fact to the realm of myth, **2.** 51; on the wanderings of Odysseus and other heroes, **2.** 55; on the Elysian Plain, **2.** 55; obtained wide information from the Phoenicians, **2.** 57; transferred scene of his mythical account of wanderings of Odysseus to the Atlantic, **2.** 85; on the breed of wild mules in the land of the Heneti, **2.** 309; says that the Pelasgi colonised Crete, and calls Zeus Pelasgian, **2.** 345; again on the Pelasgi, **2.** 345; not wont to fabricate wholly on his own account, **2.** 357; the Necyia of, **2.** 441; on the Cimmerians, **2.** 445; thought by some to mean Temesa in Italy by

INDEX OF NAMES, PLACES, AND SUBJECTS

"Tamassus," 3. 17; Islands of Aeolus of, 3. 19; scourged by Zollus (surnamed Homeromastix, "Scourge of Homer"), 3. 79; hinted at the truth when he called Aeolus "steward of the winds," 3. 97, 99; on "the Mysians, hand-to-hand fighters," 3. 177, 181, 187, 189, 209; on the Hippemolgi, Galactophagi, and Abii, 3. 179, 181, 195, 197, 205, 209; accused of ignorance of distant places by Apollodorus and Eratosthenes, but conceded accurate knowledge of places near by, never using an inappropriate epithet, 3. 189-199; placed the wanderings of Odysseus in Oceanus, 3. 193; wrongly reproached by Eratosthenes and Apollodorus for ignorance of geography, though he knew Greece and also regions remote, 3. 195; correctly describes the Scythians and other similar tribes, 3. 199, 205; knew of the potter's wheel (*Iliad* xviii. 600), 3. 207; did not invent the "Galactophagi" and the "Abii," 3. 209, 243, 245; invokes "Zeus, Dodonaean, Pelasgian," and describes the people (the Selli) of Dodona, 3. 313; the *Odyssey* of, quoted on the "tomouroi of great Zeus" at Dodona; the proper interpretation of his words "themistes" and "boulai," 3. 317; calls the Europus River "Titaresius," 3. 335; by "Phlegyae" means the Gyrtonians, 3. 335, 337; calls Abydon on the Axius River "Amydon," 3. 341, 343, 345; calls the Axius River "water most fair," 3. 343, 345; on Iphidamas, "whom Cisses reared," 3. 343, 349; on the "Sinties" (*i.e.* "Sinti") in Lemnos, 3. 367; invoked as witness by some writers in regard to the extent of the Hellespont, 3. 381, 383; on "Rhipe, Stratie, and windy Enispe," all now deserted, 3. 385, 4. 229; the first author to discuss Greece, 4. 3; calls the land of the Epeians Elis, 4. 19; knew of Pylus, both land and city, 4. 21; his words not to be contradicted, 4. 25; mentions Cyllene in Elis, 4. 25; apparently means by "Ephyra"

the city in Elis (five citations), 4. 27, 29; distinguishes between places bearing the same name by appropriate epithets, 4. 29; means by "Pylus" the Triphylian Pylus, 4. 31, 33, 57; divides the Eleian country into four parts, 4. 35; often by a poetic figure names a part with the whole, 4. 37; a case of *hyperbaton* in, 4. 41; on Athene's visit to the Cauconians, 4. 45, 57; mentions Helus near Sparta, 4. 47; means by "Pylus" (Nestor's home) the "Lepreatic (or Tryphylian) Pylus" and calls it "emathöeis," 4. 51; means that Telemachus found the Pylians offering sacrifice at the temple of the Samian Poseidon, and says the Cauconians came as allies of the Trojans, 4. 55; refers to the Eleian, not the Triphylian Cauconians, 4. 57; on Arene and Pylus, 4. 61; prolongs the Pylian Sea to the seven cities promised by Agamemnon to Achilles, 4. 67; his fame and knowledge, 4. 69; on the country that was subject to Nestor, 4. 71, 73; according to his statements the Pylus of Nestor could not lie on the sea, 4. 75; on the return voyage of Telemachus from Sparta, 4. 77; only the Triphylian Pylus could be the Pylus of Nestor, according to his account, 4. 77-87; his characterisation of Zeus followed by Pheidias in making the great image at Olympia, 4. 89; "alone has seen, or alone has shown the likenesses of the gods" (*e.g.* in his descriptions of Zeus and Hera), 4. 91; does not mention the Olympian Games, but certain funeral games in Elis, 4. 93; calls Lesbos the "city of Macar," 4. 97; most of the Pylian districts mentioned in his *Catalogue* thought to be Arcadian, 4. 101; on the seven cities promised by Agamemnon to Achilles, 4. 109; on the city Helus in Laconia, 4. 129; *Catalogue* of, quoted on Messe, 4. 129; calls Laconia "Achaean Argos," 4. 137; on the journey of Telemachus to Sparta via Pherae (Pharis), 4. 145; his

357

INDEX OF NAMES, PLACES, AND SUBJECTS

epithets applied to Lacedaemon, **4.** 147; assigns the Argolic Gulf to Argolis, **4.** 153; uses the word "Argos" in various senses, **4.** 155, 163, 165; calls the Peloponnesians "Achaeans" in a special sense, nowhere speaks of "barbarians," and thinks of all Greeks as "Hellenes," **4.** 157; cases of *hyperbaton* and *synaloepha* in, **4.** 161; on certain cities subject to Argos, **4.** 167, 169; on Aegina, **4.** 179; mentions some places in their geographical order, **4.** 181, but others not, **4.** 183; on the places subject to Mycenae and Agamemnon, **4.** 185; appropriately calls Cleonae "well-built," **4.** 187; mentions the sacrifice of a bull to the Heliconian Poseidon in Ionia, and hence is supposed to have lived after the Ionian colonisation, **4.** 213; does not mention Olenus in Achaea, **4.** 219; mentions the Aegae in Achaea and that in Euboea, **4.** 221; calls Mt. Scollis "the Olenian Rock," **4.** 225; on Rhipê, Stratiê, and Enispê, **4.** 229; on "Athens, well-built city," **4.** 245; said to have been interpolated by Peisistratus, or Solon, in favour of the Athenians, **4.** 255; does not enumerate the Orchomenians with the Boeotians, but calls them "Minyae," **4.** 283; on Nisa and Anthedon, **4.** 299; mentions Copae on Lake Copaïs, **4.** 305; on "grassy" Haliartus and the sources of the Cephissus River in Phocis, **4.** 307; mentions Lake Cephissis, meaning Lake Hylicê, **4.** 309; makes the first syllable of Hylê long at one time and short at another, and names places in Boeotia in their geographical order, **4.** 311; discussion of the various places in Boeotia in the order in which they are mentioned by, **4.** 313–341; on the wealth of the temple at Delphi ("rocky Pytho"), **4.** 359; mentions Daulis and Cyparissus, **4.** 369; says the Phaeacians led Rhadamanthys into Euboea to see Tityus, **4.** 371; does not know Elateia in Phocis, **4.** 373; says that Patroclus

came from Opus in Locris, **4.** 379; other places in Locris mentioned by, **4.** 383–387; does not expressly mention the Western Locrians, **4.** 385; on the Thessalians and Aetolians, **4.** 393; divides Thessaly into ten parts, or dynasties, **4.** 399 (see footnote 2); on the dynasty of Achilles, **4.** 399, of Phoenix, **4.** 401, 415, of Protesilaüs, **4.** 405, 419, of Eumelus, **4.** 423, of Philoctetes, **4.** 405, 425, of Eurypylus, **4.** 433, of Polypoetes, **4.** 437, of Guneus, **4.** 443; mentions Cape Geraestus, **5.** 11; on Chalcis in Aetolia and Chalcis in Elis, **5.** 15; says "Achilles alone knew how to hurl the Pelian ashen spear," **5.** 21; mentions Olenus and Pylenê in Aetolia, **5.** 29; mentions the "rock Leucas," **5.** 31; mentions Crocyleia and Aegilips, **5.** 33; Strabo's interpretation of references of, to the domain of Odysseus, **5.** 37–55; his description of Ithaca, **5.** 41–47; his Cephallenia not to be identified with Dulichium or Taphos, **5.** 47, 49; on the islands "Asteris" and "Samos" (Samothrace), **5.** 51; on other Aegaean isles, **5.** 53; on the domain of Meges, **5.** 59; on the subjects of Mentes, **5.** 61; on places in Aetolia, **5.** 65; on the Aetolians and Acarnanians, **5.** 67; means that the "Curetes" were Aetolians, **5.** 75; on the Calydonian boar, **5.** 87; on the Phaeacian "betarmones," **5.** 117; praises Cnossus above the rest of the cities in Crete, **5.** 127, 129; says Minos held converse with Zeus every ninth year, **5.** 131; calls Minos the first son of Zeus and "guardian o'er Crete," **5.** 133; calls Gortyn (Gortyna) in Crete "well-walled," **5.** 137; mentions Phaestus and Rhytium in Crete, **5.** 141; speaks of Crete as at one time "possessing 100 cities" and as at another "possessing 90 cities," **5.** 143; said to have been visited by Lycurgus in Chios, where he was living, **5.** 153; buried on the isle Ios, according to some writers, **5.** 161; mentions some of the Sporades Islands, **5.** 175, 177, 179;

INDEX OF NAMES, PLACES, AND SUBJECTS

quoted in reference to the remarkable soil of Albania in Asia, **5.** 225; stories of, more credible than those of certain historians, **5.** 247; speaks of the Aegyptian Pharos as "being out in the open sea," **5.** 357; interpolated by Callisthenes, **5.** 377; mentions the Sangarius River, which flows between Chalcedon and Heracleia Pontica, **5.** 379; his "Eneti" the most notable tribe of the Paphlagonians, **5.** 381; mentions certain places in Paphlagonia, **5.** 377, 387, 403, 405; certain emendations to text of, **5.** 407; certain interpolations in text of, **5.** 409, 411; his accurate knowledge of the Euxine and other regions averred by Strabo, **5.** 417–423; mentions Libya and the wind called Lips, **5.** 419; Smyrna by most writers called the birthplace of, **5.** 421; on Phorcys and Ascanius, leaders of "the Phrygians from Ascania" in Phrygia, **5.** 459; on another Ascanius who led forces from the Ascania near Nicaea—and names various places in Asia Minor, **5.** 461; makes the Pelasgians allies of the Trojans, **5.** 491; on Batieia in the Trojan Plain, **5.** 493; says that Rhodes and Cos were inhabited by Greeks before the Trojan War, and uses terms "Trojans," "Danaans," and "Achaeans" in broad sense, **5.** 495; leaves us to guess about most things, **6.** 3; on the extent of the sway of the Trojans, **6.** 5, 7, 9, 13; distinguishes between Ilium (the city) and Troy (the Troad), and names cities sacked by Achilles, **6.** 15, 17; on the homes of Briseïs, Chryseïs, Andromachê, and others, **6.** 17; on the Trojan leaders in the Trojan War, **6.** 19, 21; makes Aeolis and the Troad one country, **6.** 23; names various places in the Troad, **6.** 23, 25, 33, 35; on the peoples led by Asius the son of Hyrtacus, **6.** 37, 39; on another Asius, uncle of Hector, **6.** 41; on Aeneias, leader of the Dardanians, **6.** 45; suggests the different stages in the progress of civilisation, **6.** 49; the Ilium of,

much in dispute, **6.** 51; Alexander the Great preserved the "Recension of the Casket" of, **6.** 55, 57; on certain rivers in the Troad, **6.** 59; says that Heracles once sacked Ilios, **6.** 63; on a bastard son of Priam, **6.** 65; names places in the Troad, **6.** 67, 69; on Erineus (near Ilium) and on the cowardice of Hector, **6.** 71; cited in regard to site of ancient Ilium, **6.** 73, 75; knows not of the violation of Cassandra, **6.** 79; expressly states that Ilium was wiped out, **6.** 81; says the wooden image of Athenê at Ilium was in a sitting posture, **6.** 83; calls Ida "many-fountained," **6.** 85; on the two springs of the Scamander, and on other rivers, **6.** 87; *Trojan Catalogue* of, a little more than 60 lines, discussed by Demetrius in 30 books, **6.** 91; on Sminthian Apollo, **6.** 93; indicates the origin of the Teucrians, **6.** 95; on Pedasus, city of the Leleges, in Asia, **6.** 99; says Aeneias fled from Achilles to Lyrnessus, **6.** 105; says Aeneias was wroth at Priam, **6.** 107; in disagreement with those who make Aeneias leave Troyland, but some emend the text, **6.** 109; on the Leleges, Carians, Paeonians, and Cauconians, **6.** 117; on Chryseïs, Briseïs, and others, **6.** 121; on Chrysa, Thebê, and Cilla, **6.** 125; on King Eurypylus, son of Telephus, and the Ceteians, **6.** 135, 137; does not include Leleges, Cilicians, and others, in the *Trojan Catalogue*, **6.** 149, 151; on the Pelasgians and their leaders, **6.** 153; by some said to have been born at Cymê Phriconis in Asia, **6.** 161; on various peoples and places in Lydia, **6.** 175; perhaps referred to "Meionia" as "Asia," **6.** 179; on the Solymi, **6.** 191; on the "mountain of the Phtheires," **6.** 209; said once to have been entertained by Creophylus of Samos, and by some called pupil of Creophilus, by others of Aristeas the Proconnesian, **6.** 219; according to some, a native of Colophon, **6.** 237; claimed by Chios, **6.** 243; shrine of, at Smyrna,

INDEX OF NAMES, PLACES, AND SUBJECTS

6. 245; especially claimed by Smyrna, **6.** 247; on the "Asian meadow" (Leimon), **6.** 261; Rhodes and Cos in existence in time of, but not Halicarnassus and Cnidus, **6.** 273; on the Carians "of barbarian speech," **6.** 301; the "Solymi" of, not Lycians but Milyae, **6.** 321, 323; on the Cilicians in the Troad, **6.** 357; in his *Catalogue* names the various Trojan allies, **6.** 361; does not mention the Pamphylians and various other tribes, **6.** 363, 367, 369; misunderstood by Apollodorus, **6.** 371, 373; on the worship of Dionysus on Mt. Nysa, **7,** 9, 11; on the war between the pygmies and the cranes, **7.** 95; knows nothing about the empires of the Medes and Syrians, **7.** 187; does not mention Tyre, **7.** 267; on the skill of the Sidonians in beautiful arts, **7.** 269; on the oracle of Zeus at Dodona and his conversations with Minos in Crete, **7.** 287; says Persephonê granted reason to Teiresias after his death, **7.** 289; on the Aethiopians, Sidonians, and Erembians, **7.** 369, 371; on the Nile, "heaven-fed river," **8.** 21; cited in regard to Alexandria, **8.** 35; on where Helen got her "goodly drugs," **8.** 63; on the nods of Zeus, **8.** 115; on the Aegyptian Thebes, **8.** 121; Meninx (Jerba), in the Little Syrtis, regarded as "the land of the Lotus-eaters" of, **8.** 193

Homereium, the, at Smyrna, a quadrangular portico with shrine and statue of Homer, **6.** 245

Homeric Catalogue of Ships, The; the work of Apollodorus of Athens on, **3.** 187; most Pylian districts mentioned in, thought to be Arcadian, **4.** 101; writers on, have supplied Strabo with materials, **4.** 341

Homeridae, the, in Chios; mentioned by Pindar, **6.** 243, 245

Homolê (see Homolium in Magnesia)

Homolium, a city in Macedonia and Magnesia close to Mt. Ossa, **3.** 337, **4.** 449, 453

Homonadeis, the, in Pisidia; the country of, invaded by Amyntas, **5.** 477, 479, 481

Honey; in Hyrcania, drips from leaves of trees, as also in Matianê (in Media) and in Sacasenê and Araxenê (districts of Armenia), **1.** 273; exported from Turdetania, **2.** 33; produced in the Alps, **2.** 283; the "Hyblaean," at Megara Hyblaea in Sicily, **3.** 65; superior in Sicily, **3.** 85; excellent, at Brundisium, **3.** 121; the best, produced on Mt. Hymettus, **4.** 275; in the Sporades Islands, rivals that of Attica, **5.** 179; in Colchis, generally bitter, **5.** 211; abundant in Hyrcania, in Matianê in Media, and in Sacasenê and Araxenê in Armenia, **5.** 251; a crazing kind of mixture of, made by the Heptacomitae in Asia Minor, **5.** 401; yielded by the palm-tree, **7.** 215; abundant in Arabia, **7.** 311

Hoop-trundling, at Rome, **2.** 407

Horizon, change of, **1.** 45

Hormina (or Hyrmina), a mountain promontory near Cyllenê in Elis, **4.** 41

Horn, the, of the Byzantines, a gulf resembling a stag's horn, **3.** 281, 283

Horse, a white, sacrificed to Diomedes by the Eneti, **2.** 321

Horse-meat, eaten by the Scythian Nomads, **3.** 243

Horse-race, a, instituted by Romulus in honour of Poseidon (Neptune), **2.** 385

Horse-raising, in Aetolia, Acarnania, and Thessaly, **4.** 229

Horses, good qualities of, determined by training as well as by locality, **1.** 395; in Iberia, trained to climb mountains and to obey promptly, and swift, like those of Parthia, **2.** 107; superior, bred by the Eneti, **2.** 309, but practice now discontinued, **2.** 321; which drink from the Sybaris River in Italy are made timid, **3.** 47; excellent, in neighbourhood of Mt. Garganum in Apulia, **3.** 131; small, in region of Lake Maeotis, **3.** 225; castrated in Scythia and Sarmatia, **3.** 249; the breed of, in Arcadia, Argolis, and Epidauria, is most excellent, **4.** 229; the, of the Amazons, **5.** 233; the Nesaean, originated either in Greater Media or in Armenia, **5.** 311,

INDEX OF NAMES, PLACES, AND SUBJECTS

20,000 being sent annually from Armenia to the Persian king, **5**. 331; those in Parthia, **5**. 311; in India, possession of, a royal privilege, **7**. 69, 87; certain, in India, have one horn and the head of a deer, **7**. 93; scarce in Carmania, **7**. 153; more than 30,000 kept at royal stud at Apameia in Syria, **7**. 251; not found at Nabataea in Arabia, **7**. 369; the, in Masaesylia, are small, but quick, and obedient, **8**. 167; raised in great numbers between the seaboard and Getulia, **8**. 197

Horses, stunted (see Ginni)

Hortensius, married Marcia the wife of Marcus Cato, **5**. 273

Hot springs, the, in Pithecussae, a cure for gall-stones, **2**. 459

Hungarians, the (see Urgi)

Hya (see Hyampolis)

Hyacynthian Festival, the, in the temple of Amyclaean Apollo in Laconia, **3**. 109

Hyameitis, one of the five capitals of Messenia, **4**. 119

Hyampeia on Parnassus, not the same as Hyampolis, **4**. 373

Hyampolis (near Vogdhani) in Phocis, lies above the territory of Hyampolis, **4**. 341; later called Hya by some, whither the Hyantes of Boeotia were banished, is far inland and not to be confused with Hyampeia on Parnassus, **4**. 373

Hyantes, the, lived in Boeotia in earlier times, **3**. 287, **4**. 281; founded a city Hya in Phocis, **4**. 283; banished from Boeotia to Hyampolis in Phocis, **4**. 373; left Boeotia and settled in Aetolia, **5**. 81

Hyarotis River, the, in India, **7**. 35, 47, 51

Hybla in Sicily (see Megara Hyblaea)

Hyblaean honey, the, at Megara Hyblaea in Sicily, **3**. 65

Hybreas of Mylasa in Caria, greatest orator in Strabo's time, **6**. 191; remarkable career of, **6**. 295-297; provoked Labienus, withdrew to Rhodes, but returned and resumed power, **6**. 297

Hybrianes (Agrianes?), the, **3**. 275

Hydara, a stronghold built by Mithridates, **5**. 425

Hydarnes, one of the "Seven Persians," **5**. 337

Hydaspes River, the, in India, **7**. 5, 25, 47, 49, 55, 57

Hydatos-Potamoi (see Seleuceia in Pieria, in Syria)

Hydê, the Homeric, at foot of Mt. Tmolus in Lydia, **4**. 309; reputed home of the Homeric "Tychius, the best of workers in hide," and by some identified with Sardeis, **6**. 175

"Hydê," an incorrect reading, for "Hylê" in Boeotia, in Homer, **4**. 309, 311

Hydra (see Lysimachia), Lake, in Aetolia, **5**. 65

Hydra, the monster, poisoned certain of the Centaurs, **4**. 61; killed by Heracles at the lake called Lernê, in Argolis, **4**. 151, 163

Hydra, the promontory, with Harmatus forms the Elaïtic Gulf, **6**. 159

Hydraces, the, a tribe in India, summoned as mercenary troops by Cyrus. **7**. 9

Hydrelus, the Lacedaemonian, founded a city in Asia Minor, **6**. 261

Hydruntum (see Hydrus)

Hydrus (or Hydruntum, now Otranto), in Iapygia, **3**. 119

Hydrussa the island, off Attica, **4**. 271

Hyelê (see Elea)

"Hyes attes," a cry uttered in the ritual of Sabazius and the Mother, **5**. 109

Hylas; Mt. Arganthonium in Asia the scene of myth of, **5**. 457

Hylê, the Homeric (Hydê not being the correct reading), in Boeotia on Lake Cephissis (Hylicê), **4**. 309, 311, 321

Hylicê (the Homeric Cephissis), Lake, **4**. 309

Hyllus the eldest son of Heracles, adopted by Aegimius the king of the Dorian Tetrapolis, **4**. 387

Hyllus (now called Phrygius) River, the, mentioned by Homer, **5**. 421; empties into the Hermus, **6**. 173

Hylobii, the, in India, a sect of the Garmanes in India, **7**. 103

Hymettus, Mt., one of the most famous mountains in Attica, has marble quarries and produces the

INDEX OF NAMES, PLACES, AND SUBJECTS

best honey (especially the kind called " acapniston," near the silver mines), **4**. 275

Hypaepa, on the slopes of Mt. Tmolus, near Sardeis, **6**. 179

Hypaesia, wherein was the city Arenê, in Triphylia, **4**. 63

Hypana, a small Triphylian city, **4**. 53

Hypanis (Bog) River, the, flows between the Tanaïs and the Ister into the Euxine, **1**. 413; not mentioned by Homer, **3**. 189; near the Borysthenes, **3**. 221

Hypanis (Gharra) River, the, in India, said to have been crossed by Menander, king of Bactria, **5**. 279, **7**. 5, 25, 47, 55, 57, 63

Hypanis (Kuban) River, the; the Anticeites so called by some, **5**. 199; said to have been conducted over the country of the Dandarians by Pharnaces, **5**. 201

Hypasians, the, a tribe in India, **7**. 25, 47

Hypatus, Mt., in Theban territory near Teumessus and the Cadmeia, **4**. 327

Hypelaeus, a fountain near Ephesus, **6**. 203, 225

Hyperbaton, cases of, in Homer, **4**. 41, 161

Hyperboles, **1**. 133, 137, 151

Hyperboreans, the, **1**. 229, **3**. 175, **5**. 245; reputed to live 1000 years, **7**. 97

Hypereia, a spring in Thessaly, **4**. 405, 433; in the middle of the city of the Pheraeans, **4**. 437

Hyperesia, the Homeric Hyperesiê, **4**. 185; belonged to the Achaean League, **4**. 207

Hypernotians, the, **1**. 229

Hypnos (" Sleep "), the Homeric, came to Mt. Ida, **6**. 11

Hypocremnus in Asia, between the Erythraeans and the Clazomenians, **6**. 213

Hypothebes, the Homeric; meaning of the term, **4**. 327

Hypsicrates (contemporary of Julius Caesar, and author of historical and geographical treatises, of which the exact titles are unknown), says that Asander fortified the isthmus of the Tauric Chersonesus against

the Scythians, **3**. 245; on the home and habits of the Amazons, **5**. 233

Hypsöeis River, the, in Micistia, **4**. 73

Hyrcania, knowledge of, increased by the Parthians, **1**. 51; mild climate and fertility of, **1**. 273; geographical position of, **5**. 249, 261, 293; remarkable fertility of, **5**. 251; rivers in, **5**. 253; marvellous stories about, **5**. 257; 8000 stadia from Artemita in Babylonia, **5**. 291; Parthian kings reside in, in summer, **7**. 219

Hyrcanian Plain, the, whither the Persians brought Hyrcanian colonists, **6**. 185

Hyrcanian Sea (see Caspian Sea), the; distance from, to the ocean on the east, is about 30,000 stadia, **5**. 289

Hyrcanians, the; extent of coast of, on the Caspian Sea, **5**. 245; paid tribute to the Persians and Macedonians, **5**. 271; border on the Tapyri, **5**. 273, 293

Hyrcanium, a stronghold in Syria, destroyed by Pompey, **7**. 291

Hyrcanus, son of King Alexander of Judaea, overthrown by Pompey, **7**. 289

Hyria, the Homeric, near Aulis, **4**. 181; now belongs to Tanagra, but in earlier times belonged to Thebes, and is the scene of the myth of Hyrieus and of the birth of Orion, **4**. 295

Hyria in Iapygia, founded, according to Herodotus, by Cretans, must be identified with Uria or Veretum, **3**. 121

Hyrieans, the Boeotian, colonised Hysiae in Parasopia, **4**. 297

Hyrieus; Hyria the scene of the myth of, **4**. 295

Hyrmina (see Hormina)

Hyrminê in Elis, a small town, no longer in existence, **4**. 35, 39

Hyrtacus, father of Asius the Trojan leader, **6**. 19, 37

Hysiae, a village in Argolis, unknown to Homer, **4**. 183; mentioned in connection with Hyria in Boeotia, **4**. 297

Hysiae, in Boeotia, in the Parasopian country near Erythrae, called

INDEX OF NAMES, PLACES, AND SUBJECTS

INDEX OF NAMES, PLACES, AND SUBJECTS

Iconii, the, geographical position of, **2**. 195, 271

Iconium (Konia), capital of Lycaonia, **5**. 475

Icos, the isle off Magnesia, **4**. 427

Ictinus, builder of the Parthenon, and of the temple of Demeter at Eleusis, **4**. 257, 261

Ictumuli, a village near Placentia in Italy, **2**. 333

Ida, Mt., in Crete, scene of revels in honour of Dionysus and his mother, **5**. 103, 113; highest mountain in Crete, 600 stadia in circuit, **5**. 125

Ida, Mt., in the Troad; the city Dardania lies at the foot of, **3**. 173; iron first worked on, by the Idaean Dactyli, **5**. 117; lies above the Propontis, **5**. 497; extent of, **6**. 9; description of, **6**. 9, 11; Zeleia on farthermost foot-hill of, **6**. 25; borders on the Trojan Plain, **6**. 65; the two spurs of, **6**. 67; rightly called "many-fountained," **6**. 85; by some said to have been named after Mt. Ida in Crete, **6**. 95; timber from, marketed at Aspaneus, **6**. 103

"Idaea," an epithet of Rhea (*q.v.*)

Idaean Dactyli, the, identified with the gods worshipped in Samothrace, **3**. 371; by some represented as identical with the Curetes, **5**. 87, 89; discussion of, **5**. 117–119

Idaean Gulf (see Adramyttium, Gulf of), the, **6**. 13

Idaean Mother, the (see Cybelê)

Idanthyrsus the Scythian king, against whom Dareius made his expedition, **3**. 199, 201 (see p. 200, footnote 1); overran Asia as far as Aegypt, **7**. 9

Ideëssa, the present name of the City of Phrixus in Iberia, **5**. 215

Idiologus, the, a Roman official in Aegypt, **8**. 49

Idomeneus, the grandson of Minos; slew Phaestus from Tarnê in Lydia, **4**. 331; enemies of, said to have destroyed ten cities in Crete, **5**. 143; mentioned by Homer, **5**. 145; king of Crete, slew Othryoneus, and sought the hand of Cassandra, **6**. 79

Idomeneus, the able Lampsacenian and friend of Epicurus, **6**. 37

Idubeda, the mountain, in Iberia; geographical position of, **2**. 97,

101; forms the eastern boundary of Celtiberia, **2**. 103

Idumaeans (see Nabataeans), the, a tribe in Syria, **7**. 239; joined the Judaeans, **7**. 281

Iernê (Ireland), **1**. 235; inhabitable only after a fashion, **1**. 237; remotest northern part of inhabited world, **1**. 271, 505; scarcely habitable, **1**. 279; inhabitants of, complete savages, **1**. 443; description of, **2**. 259; inhabitants of, said to be cannibals, **2**. 259, 261

Igletes, the, in Iberia, **2**. 119

Ignatia (see Egnatia)

Iguvium (Gubbio), in Italy, geographical position of, **2**. 373

Ilan-Adassi in the Euxine (see Leucê)

Ilasarus, king of the Rhammanitae in Arabia, **7**. 361

Ilerda (Lerida), in Iberia; geographical position of, and where Sertorius fought his last battles and the generals of Pompey were defeated by Julius Caesar, **2**. 99

Ilergetans, the, in Iberia; districts of, near the Iberus, **2**. 99

Iliad, The, of the Casket, acquired by Alexander, **6**. 55, 57

Iliad, Homer's, transferred to realm of myth, **2**. 53

Ilians, the, befriended by Alexander, **6**. 55, and by Julius Caesar, **6**. 57; offer sacrifice to the four heroes, Achilles, Aias, Patroclus, and Antilochus, but do not honour Heracles, **6**. 61; village of, 30 stadia from the present Ilium, on the site of the ancient Ilium, **6**. 69; the stretch of coast now subject to, **6**. 79; the present, assert that Ilium was never destroyed nor deserted, **6**. 79

Ilibirris, river and city of, in Celtica; river of, rises in the Pyrenees, **2**. 183

Iliocolonê, in the territory of Parium, **6**. 35

Ilios, the Homeric (see Ilium)

Ilipa, on the Baetis River in Iberia; silver plentiful in region of, **2**. 25; about 700 stadia from the sea, **2**. 155

Ilissus River, the, in Attica; description of course of, **4**. 277

Ilium (the city Troy) in the Troad,

INDEX OF NAMES, PLACES, AND SUBJECTS

thenes, **1.** 249; better developed and less parched than the Aethiopians, **1.** 395; probably unknown by Homer, **1.** 397; compared with the Aethiopians and Aegyptians, **7.** 21, 41; fond of adornment, but ignorant of value of gold and silver in their country, **7.** 53, 55; lead a simple life, **7.** 87; habits and traits of, **7.** 89–91; beliefs of, **7.** 103; customs and laws of, **7.** 115; write on closely woven linen, **7.** 117; worship Zeus, the Ganges River, and local deities, **7.** 121; revere the Gymnosophists, **7.** 289; present large commerce of, with the Aegyptians, **8.** 53

Indians, certain, accompanied Heracles to Libya and remained there, **8.** 169

Indicetans, the, in north-eastern Iberia; four tribes of, **2.** 81; united with the Emporitans, **2.** 93

Indus River, the, in India, **7.** 11; forms the boundary between Ariana and India, **7.** 15, 17; has many tributaries, **7.** 19, 43, 55, 57; changed its bed because of earthquake, **7.** 31, 47; largest of all rivers except the Ganges, **7.** 61; the fish and *Carides* found in, **7.** 81; course of, **7.** 143

Infantry, the, of the Iberians, **2.** 107

Inhabited world, the, (see World)

Iniada (see Thynias)

Inn River, the (see footnote 4, Vol. II, p. 285)

Innessa, a hilly district at foot of Mt. Aetna, **3.** 69

Inscription, the, on the pillar at the boundary between Ionia and the Peloponnesus, **4.** 247; at Thermopylae, on the pillar erected by the Lacedaemonians, **4.** 393

Insubri (see Symbri), the, one of the largest tribes of the Celti, once seized Roman territory, **2.** 311; geographical position of, **3.** 165

Intemelii, the, in Italy, **2.** 265

Intemelium, Albium, in Italy, **2.** 265

Interamna (Terni), in Italy; geographical position of, **2.** 373

Interamnium (Termini), on the Liris River, **2.** 413

Intercatia in Iberia, mentioned by Polybius, **2.** 103

Interocrea (Antrodoco), in the Sabine country, **2.** 375

Inundations; Aegypt and Aethiopia subject to, **1.** 119; in Iberia, at flood-tides, **2.** 27

Io, said to have given birth to Epaphus at Böos Aulê (" Cow's Stall ") in Euboea, **5.** 5; the island Euboea probably so named in honour of, **5.** 7; quest of, by Triptolemus, **6.** 345; disappeared first in Tyre, **7.** 243

Iol (Caesarea), on the coast of Masaesylia in Libya, rebuilt by Juba the father of Ptolemy, **8.** 179

Iolaës, the (see Diagesbes)

Iolaüs, with some of children of Heracles, settled in Sardinia, **2.** 361; expedition of Eurystheus against, **4.** 187

Iolcus (Volo) in Thessaly, the home of Jason; inhabitants of, and hence the Argonauts, called Minyae, **4.** 335; in early times rased to the ground, and lies seven stadia from Demetrias, **4.** 423, 435; now a village belonging to Demetrias, **4.** 425

Iolcus, the name of the shore adjoining Demetrias in Thessaly, **4.** 425

Ion, the son of Achaeus, conquered the Thracians under Eumolpus their leader, and reigned over the Athenians, reorganised their government, and at his death left their country named Ionia after himself, **4.** 209; father of Ellops, **5.** 7

Ion of Chios, the tragic poet (fl. about 440 B.C.); his *Omphalê* quoted, on the Euripus, **1.** 223; *apocopê* in, **4.** 131; native of Chios, **6.** 243

Ion, the, of Euripides, refers to Euboea the island as a " city," **4.** 97

Ion River, the, on which lies the city Oxineia, **3.** 311

Ionaeum, the, a sacred precinct in Triphylia, **4.** 59

Ionia (Achaea), in the Peloponnesus, occupied by the Achaeans from Laconia, **4.** 133, 211; subject to Agamemnon, **4.** 167; once called Aegialus, or Aegialeia, **4.** 207, 209

Ionia (Attica), the southern boundary of, on Isthmus of Corinth, **2.** 139,

INDEX OF NAMES, PLACES, AND SUBJECTS

near Crommyon, **4.** 247; named after Ion the son of Xuthus, **4.** 265

Ionia in Asia, a part of the Cis-Halys country, **1.** 497; invaded by the Cimmerians, **2.** 51; the whole of what is now so called, used to be inhabited by Carians and Leleges, **3.** 289; Phocaea the beginning of, **6.** 5; length of coast of, about 800 stadia, **6.** 197, 309

Ioniades Nymphs, the, in Elis, who cured diseases with the waters of the Cytherius River, **4.** 99

Ionian cities, the twelve, joined by Smyrna, **6.** 201

Ionian colonisations, the, in Asia, supposed to have taken place before Homer's time, **4.** 213, **6.** 5; took place four generations after Aeolian, **6.** 7; Androclus leader of, **6.** 199

Ionian Gulf, the, the name of the lower part of the Adriatic, **1.** 475, being named after Ionius, an Illyrian from the isle of Issa (Lissa), **3.** 29, 267; at Apollonia distant 7320 stadia from Byzantium, or, according to Polybius, 7500 stadia, **3.** 379

Ionian League, the, in Asia, **6.** 201

Ionian migration, the, known by Homer, **5.** 51

Ionians, the; migrations of, **1.** 227; colonised Siris in Italy, **3.** 49; all sprang from the Attic people—colonised Ionia in Asia, **4.** 5; mastered the Aegialeia (Aegialus) in the Peloponnesus, and changed its name to Ionia, **4.** 7, 207, but were later driven back to Athens by the Achaeans, and then sent forth to colonise Caria and Lydia, **4.** 209, 211; requested statue of Poseidon at Helicè, but the people refused and their city was submerged by Poseidon, **4.** 215; fled for refuge to Helicè, but were driven out, **4.** 219; in early times held both Attica and Megaris, **4.** 245; often had disputes with the Peloponnesians about the boundary on the isthmus, **4.** 251

Ionians, the, in Achaea, **4.** 7, 137, 167, 215, 217, 219

Ionians, the, at Argos and Epidaurus, **4.** 175

Ionians, the, in Asia, hated the Cimmerians, because of their invasion of Ionia, **2.** 51; worshipped the Delphinian Apollo, **2.** 173; sprang from the Ionians of Attica, **4.** 5; founded cities on the Scythian seaboard, and changed name of "Axine" Sea to "Euxine," **3.** 189; expelled the Carians and the Leleges from what is now called Ionia, **3.** 289; sprang from the Ionians (*i.e.* the Attic people), **4.** 5; still worship the Heliconian Poseidon and offer the Pan-Ionian sacrifices, **4.** 213; called "tunic-trailing" by Homer, **5.** 89; once held mastery in Asia Minor, after the Trojan War, **5.** 463; now occupy Caria, **5.** 509; royal seat of, established at Ephesus, **6.** 199; celebrate the *Alexandreian Games* at a sacred precinct above Chalcideis, **6.** 239

Ionic dialect, the; the same as the ancient Attic, **4.** 5

Ionic laws, the; used at Massalia, **2.** 175

Iopè (Jaffa) in Phoenicia, Jerusalem visible from, **7.** 275

Ios (Nios), the island, where, according to some, Homer was buried, **5.** 161

Iphicrates, besieged Stymphalus in Arcadia, **4.** 233

Iphicrates, on the animals in western Aethiopia, **8.** 163; on the large species of reed and asparagus there, **8.** 165

Iphidamas, the Homeric, "whom Cisses reared," **3.** 343, 349

Iphigenia, the supposed temple of, in the land of the Taurians, **3.** 231 (see footnote 8); with Orestes, thought to have brought sacred rites in honour of Artemis Tauropolus to Comana in Cappadocia, **5.** 353, 359

Iphigeneia in Tauris, the, of Euripides, where "Argos" and "Mycenae" are used synonymously, **4.** 187

Iphitus (perhaps identical with son of Eurytus), celebrated the Olympian Games after they had been discontinued, **4.** 105

Iphitus, the son of Eurytus, met Telemachus at Pherae in Messenia, **4.** 145

INDEX OF NAMES, PLACES, AND SUBJECTS

INDEX OF NAMES, PLACES, AND SUBJECTS

near the Hercynian Forest, 3. 163;
not mentioned by Homer, 3. 189, 5.
419; contains an island called Peucê
("Pine"), 3. 201, 207; the name
formerly applied only to the stretch
of the Danube from the cataracts to
the Euxine Sea, 3. 215; the island
Peucê in, 3. 217, 223; geographical
divisions formed by, 3. 251, 253, 271,
285; once called the "Matoas," *i.e.*,
in Greek, "Asius," and then its
name was changed to "Danubis"
or "Daüsis," 3. 385, 387; 3200 stadia
from Thessaloniceia, 4. 233; largest
of all rivers except the Ganges and
the Indus, 7. 61

Isthmian Games, the, not mentioned
by Homer, 4. 93 (and footnote); a
source of great advantage to the
Corinthians, 4. 189, and used to be
celebrated by them, 4. 197

Isthmian Poseidon, the; temple of,
4. 197

Isthmus, the Aegyptian; description
of, 3. 13; between Pelusium and
the Arabian Gulf, 10,000 stadia in
breadth, 8. 71; between Coptus and
Berenicê, 8. 119–121

Istria, the geographical position of,
2. 299; entire distance along coast
of, 3. 257

Istrians, the; seaboard of, 2. 323; the
first people on the Illyrian seaboard,
3. 257

Isus in Boeotia near Anthedon, a
sacred place containing traces of a
city, 4. 299

Italian promontory, the; mentioned
by Eratosthenes, 1. 353

Italian seaboard, the, on the Adriatic,
is harbourless, but abounds with
the olive and the vine, 3. 271

Italians, certain tribes of the, wont to
overrun Celtica and Germany, 2.
281

"Italians," the; earlier scope of the
term, 3. 13

Italica in Iberia (identified with
Baetis, *q.v.* and also footnote 2. 20),
near the Baetis River, 2. 21

Italiotes, the, are autonomous with
the "Latin right," 2. 271; treated
cruelly by certain brigandish tribes,
2. 283; given equality of civic
rights by the Romans, 2. 299; the

oracle given out to, near Laüs in
Italy, 3. 5; borrowed most of their
usages from the Achaeans (of the
Achaean League), 4. 211

Italy, a treatise on, by Antiochus of
Syracuse, 3. 11

Italy; promontory of, 1. 417; whole
length of, traversed by the Apen-
nines, 1. 491; form and dimensions
of, 1. 493; described in detail, 2.
299, 3. 147; First Portion of, 2.
299–333; Second Portion of, 2.
333–335; Third Portion of, 2. 335–
369; Ombrica (Umbria) in, 2. 369–
373; formerly bounded by the
Aesis and Rubicon Rivers, but now
by the Alps, 2. 371; the Sabini in,
2. 375–377; an excellent nurse of
animals and fruits, 2. 375; Latium
in, 2. 377–425; Picenum in, 2. 427–
429; the Vestini, Marsi, Peligni,
and Marrucini in, 2. 429–433; the
Frentani in, 2. 433; Campania in,
2. 433–471; Leucania in, 3. 1–15,
49–55; Bruttium in, 3. 11–48;
the Old (Oenotria), 3. 13, 103; Sicily
and other islands of, 3. 55–103;
Iapygia in, 3. 103–127; Apulia in,
3. 127–136; its isthmus, 3. 135; its
favourable geographical position,
its climate, its productivity, 3. 137;
its rivers, lakes, health-resorts,
brave people, and wise government,
3. 139; its various conquests and
eventual supremacy, 3. 139–147;
boundary of, now advanced to
Pola, an Istrian city, 3. 257; Corinth
on the direct route from, to Asia, 4.
189

Italy Cispadana, description of, 2.
307–333; filled with rivers and
marshes, 2. 309; the inhabitants of,
2. 311; the cities of, 2. 313; comprises country as far as Genoa, 2.
323; famous cities in, 2. 325;
fertility of country of, 2. 331

Italy Transpadana, 2. 307, 323

Ithaca (Ithaki or Leucade?), the
Homeric, lies "towards the dark-
ness," *i.e.* towards the north, 1. 125;
absence now of Homer's cave and
grotto there due to physical changes,
1. 221; distance from, to Corcyra,
1. 409; lies off Corinthian Gulf, 1.
477; "Demus" not the name of a

INDEX OF NAMES, PLACES, AND SUBJECTS

place in, **3**. 193; return of Telemachus to, **4**. 77; "sunny" and "rugged," subject to Odysseus, **5**. 35; Odysseus dwelt in, **5**. 39; description of, **5**. 41–47

Ithaca-Leucas Problem, The; a statement of, *Appendix* **5**. 523–527, and a *Partial Bibliography*, **5**. 529–530

Ithacans, the, were friends of the Acarnanians, **5**. 67

Ithomê, the acropolis of Messenê in Messenia, **3**. 113, **4**. 107; one of the two strategic points in the Peloponnesus, according to Demetrius of Pharos, **4**. 119, 121

Ithomê (called Thomê), "rocky," in Thessaly, **4**. 429, 431

Itium (or Itius, now almost certainly Boulogne), Port, whence Julius Caesar sailed to Britain, **2**. 253

Itonian Athenê, the; temple of, in plain before Coroneia, **4**. 323, and in Thessaly, **4**. 433

Itonus in Thessaly, about 60 stadia from Halus, **4**. 409; temple of Itonian Athenê at, **4**. 421

Ituraeans, the, in Syria, **7**. 253, 263, 265

Itycê (Utica) in Libya, where Jugurtha slew Adarbal, **8**. 181; served Romans as metropolis and base of operations, **8**. 183

Itymoneus, slain by Nestor, **4**. 81

Iulis in Ceos, home of Simonides and Bacchylides, **5**. 169

Iulius, descendant of Aeneias and ancestor of Julius Caesar, **6**. 57

Ivory, exported from Taprobanê to India, **1**. 271; abundant among the Sabaeans and Gerrhaeans in Arabia, **7**. 349

Ivory chains and necklaces, imported to Britain from Celtica, **2**. 259

Ivrea (see Eporedia)

Ivy, grows on Mt. Merus in India, **7**. 11, 97

Ixia, a stronghold in Rhodes, **6**. 279

Ixion, the Lapith, reigned in Gyrton, in Thessaly, **3**. 335, 337; with his son Peirithoüs, humbled and ejected the Perrhaebians, **4**. 437, 439

J

Jackal, the (see Lycus)

Jackals (see Wolves)

Jaffa (see Iopê)

Jason, the expedition of, **1**. 75; kinsman of Achilles, **1**. 165; wanderings and sanctuaries of, in Armenia and Media, **1**. 167, 177; traces of expedition of, in Crete and Italy, **1**. 169, 171; return voyage of, on a mythical Ister that emptied into the Adriatic, **1**. 213; voyage of, through the "Symplegades" (Cyaneae), **2**. 53; visited the island Aethalia (Elba), **2**. 357, 359; built temple of Argoan Hera in Leucania, **3**. 3; despatched on his expedition from Iolcus by Pelias, **4**. 423; expedition of, to Colchis and Media, **5**. 213, 391; went far beyond Colchis, **5**. 231, 239; memorials of, in Media and Armenia, **5**. 315, 333; constructed outlet for the Araxes River in Armenia, **5**. 335; the Armenians and the Medes in a way the descendants of, **5**. 337

Jasonia (temples dedicated to Jason), in Armenia and Media, **5**. 231, 315

Jasonium, Cape, in Cappadocia Pontica, **5**. 399

Jasonium, Mt., above the Caspian Gates, named after Jason, **5**. 315

Javelin, the, used by the Iberians, **2**. 107; by the Amazons, **5**. 233; by the Indians, **7**. 117; by the Maurusians in Libya, **8**. 167

Javelins, the styracine, **5**. 483

Jerba, the isle (see Meninx)

Jericho (see Hiericus)

Jerusalem, visible from Iopê, **7**. 275, 281; the temple at, **7**. 281; kingdom of Moses at, **7**. 283–285; revered as a holy place even by robbers, **7**. 285; seized by Pompey, **7**. 291

Jewish fashion, the, of mutilation, practised by the Creophagi in Aethiopia, **7**. 323

Jews, the, in Aegypt; 500 of, led by Aelius Gallus into Arabia, **7**. 357

Jordan River, the, in Syria, navigable, **7**. 261

Juba I, father of King Juba of

INDEX OF NAMES, PLACES, AND SUBJECTS

INDEX OF NAMES, PLACES, AND SUBJECTS

374

375

INDEX OF NAMES, PLACES, AND SUBJECTS

377

INDEX OF NAMES, PLACES, AND SUBJECTS

Leonidas, the Spartan general, defeated at Thermopylae, **1.** 37, **4.** 393; soldiers of, dressed their hair before the battle, **5.** 89

Leonides the Stoic, native of Rhodes, **6.** 279

Leonidi (see Prasiae)

Leonnatus, comrade of Alexander the Great, lost his life in the Lamian War, **4.** 413

Leonnorius, leader of the Galatae, or Celts, in their expedition to Asia, **5.** 469

Leonteus, the able Lampsacenian, friend of Epicurus, **6.** 37

Leontinê, inhabited by Cyclopes, **1.** 73

Leontines, the, founded Euboea in Sicily, **3.** 83

Leontopolis in Phoenicia, **7.** 267; in Aegypt, **8.** 69

Leopard, the, found in Maurusia in Libya, **8.** 163

Leopards, the, in India, **7.** 123; fierce in southern Aethiopia, **7.** 335; in Arabia, **7.** 343; in Aethiopia, **8.** 145

Leosthenes, the Athenian general, lost his life in the Lamian War, **4.** 413

Lepenu (see Stratus)

Lepidotus, the (a scale-fish), worshipped by the Aegyptians, **8.** 109; indigenous to the Nile, **8.** 149

Lepidus, Marcus (consul with Gaius Flaminius 187 B.C.), the builder of a second Aemilian Way, from Ariminum to Aquileia, **2.** 331

Lepontii, the, geographical position of, **2.** 273; a tribe of the Rhaeti, **2.** 281

Lepra Actê (Mt. Prion), near Smyrna, **6.** 201

Lepreatic Pylus, the (see Triphylian Pylus); by Homer called "emathöeis," **4.** 51

Lepreum (near Strovitzi); the Cauconians about, **4.** 45; lies south of the Triphylian Pylus, 40 stadia from the sea, **4.** 53; seized by the Cauconians, **4.** 55; settled by the Eleians with inhabitants of Nestor's Pylus, **4.** 95

Lepreus, ruler of the Arcadian Cauconians, a harsh ruler and a bad man, **3.** 385

Leprosy, cured by the water of the Anigrus River in Triphylia, **4.** 61

Leptis (see Neapolis near the Great Syrtis)

Lerida (see Ilerda)

Lerius (Lero), the island; has a temple of Lero, **2.** 193

Lernê, Lake, in the Argolis, where is laid the scene of the killing of the Hydra by Heracles, **4.** 151; "a Lernê of ills," and near a spring called Amymonê, **4.** 163

Lernê River, the, in Argolis, **4.** 151

Lero (see Lerius)

Leros, one of the Sporades Islands, **5.** 173; mentioned by Homer, **5.** 179; colonised by Milesians, **6.** 207

Lesbian wine, the, exported to Aegypt, **8.** 93

Lesbians, the, founded Sestus and Madytus, **3.** 379; once laid claim to most of the Troad, and possess most of the settlements there now, **6.** 65, 67

Lesbocles of Mitylenê, contemporary of Strabo, **6.** 143

Lesbos, formerly called Issa, **1.** 223; the Aegaean isle, **1.** 477; called "Pelasgia," **2.** 345; by Homer called "city of Macar," **4.** 97, **5.** 421; geographical position of, **6.** 5; once occupied by Gras, great-grandson of Orestes, **6.** 7; sacked by Achilles, **6.** 15; description and history of, **6.** 139–147; metropolis of the Aeolian cities, **6.** 139; home of Sappho and famous men, **6.** 141, 143, 147; equidistant (about 500 stadia) from Tenedos, Lemnos, and Chios, **6.** 149; produces excellent wine, **6.** 215, 287; one of the seven largest islands, **6.** 277

Lestenitza River, the (see Enipeus River)

Lethaeus River, the, in Gortyna in Crete, **5.** 137, **6.** 249

Lethaeus River, the, which empties into the Maeander, not mentioned by Homer, **5.** 421, **6.** 249

Lethaeus (Lathon?) River, the, in western Libya, **6.** 249

Lethaeus River, the, near Triccê in Hestiaeotis in Thessaly, **6.** 249

Lethê (Forgetfulness), the River of, in Iberia; by some called the Limaeas and by others Belion, **2.** 69; why so called, **2.** 71

378

INDEX OF NAMES, PLACES, AND SUBJECTS

INDEX OF NAMES, PLACES, AND SUBJECTS

INDEX OF NAMES, PLACES, AND SUBJECTS

INDEX OF NAMES, PLACES, AND SUBJECTS

Syrtis, **2.** 85; used as food by the Aethiopians, **8.** 143; "a kind of plant and root," **8.** 171

Lotus-eaters, the, in northern Libya, **2.** 83, and also in the isle of Meninx, **2.** 85; "certain migrants" in western Libya, "who feed on lotus," **8.** 171; in the isle of Meninx in the Little Syrtis—the Homeric Lotus-eaters, **8.** 193

Luca, above Luna, in Italy, an important city, now in ruins, **2.** 329

Lucani, the (see Leucani)

Lucania (see Leucania)

Lucotocia, the city of the Parisii, **2.** 233

Lucrinus, Gulf (Lake Lucrino), the, **2.** 439, 441, 445, 447

Lucullus (see Leucullus)

Lucumo (Lucius Tarquinius Priscus), the son of the Corinthian Demaratus who colonised Tarquinia in Italy, and made king by the Senate and the people (615 B.C.), **2.** 339

Ludias, Lake, near Pella in Lower Macedonia, whence flows the Ludias River, **3.** 341

Ludias River, the; the course of, **3.** 339; flows from Lake Ludias, **3.** 341, 345

Luerio River, the, borders on the country of the Sallyes (Celtoligues), **2.** 269

Luerius, chieftain of the Arverni; rich and extravagant, **2.** 221

Lugdunum Convenarum (St. Bertrand de Comminges), in Aquitania, **2.** 217

Lugdunum (Lyon) in Celtica, lies at the end of the Cemmenus Mountain, **2.** 165; geographical position of, **2.** 199, 223; an acropolis and important centre, **2.** 289

Lugeum, a marsh (now Lake Zirknitz), whence there is a pass leading over Mt. Ocra to Tergeste, **3.** 255

Lugii, the, a German tribe, ruled by Marabodus, **3.** 157

Luna, in Italy; the mountains above, **2.** 329; the distance from, to Ostia and to Pisa, **2.** 347; city and harbour (Bay of Spezia), **2.** 349

Lupiae (Lecce) in Iapygia, **3.** 121

Lupias River, the, **3.** 159

Lusitania in Iberia, coursed by the Tagus River, greatest of the Iberian nations, and boundaries of, **2.** 65;

length of, to Cape Nerium, 3000 stadia, and breadth much less, **2.** 67; largest rivers in, **2.** 69; thirty different tribes in, between the Tagus and Artabria, finally subdued by the Romans, **2.** 71; meaning of the term in strict sense, **2.** 121

Lusitanians, the, in Iberia; some of, transferred by the Romans, **2.** 13; subjected by Brutus, **2.** 63; most of, now called Callaïcans, **2.** 65; traits, arms, customs, habits, and religious rites of, **2.** 71–79; eat only one meal a day, **2.** 73; offer hecatombs, like the Greeks, **2.** 75; marry in same way as Greeks, and expose the sick in the same way as the Aegyptians, **2.** 77; now more tractable, and in part civilised, under Roman influence, **2.** 77–79; armour of, **2.** 107; under jurisdiction of praetorian legatus, **2.** 121

Lusonians, the, in Iberia; geographical position of, **2.** 103

Lux Dubia (see Phosphorus)

Luxor (see Thebes, the Aegyptian)

Lycaeus (Diophorti) Mt., in Arcadia (see Lyrceius, Mt.), compared with the Alps, **2.** 293; where Rhea, mother of Zeus, caused a spring to break forth, **4.** 67; the temple of Zeus Lycaeus near, **4.** 229; a famous mountain, **4.** 231

Lycaon, the son of Pelasgus, **2.** 345

Lycaon, son of Priam, ransomed by Euneos, **1.** 151, **6.** 17, 19, 23; grandson of Altes, **6.** 153

Lycaonia in Asia, **1.** 497, **5.** 345; plateaus, of cold and bare of trees, grazed by wild asses, and have extremely deep wells, **5.** 473, 475; once held by Amyntas, **5.** 477; the road through, **6.** 309; not mentioned by Homer, **6.** 369

Lycaonians, the, not mentioned by Homer, **5.** 423

Lycastus in Crete, no longer exists, **5.** 143

Lyceium, the, at Athens, has a myth connected with it, **4.** 265; near the sources of the Eridanus, **4.** 267; the Ilissus River rises above, **4.** 277

Lychnidus (Ochrida), on the Candavian Way, **3.** 293, where are salt-fish establishments, **3.** 309

INDEX OF NAMES, PLACES, AND SUBJECTS

"Lychnite" (Tourmaline?) stones, the, said to be found in Masaesylia in Libya, 8. 177

Lychnus, the, a fish indigenous to the Nile, 8. 149

Lycia, 4000 stadia from Alexandria, 1. 93; a part of the Cis-Halys country, 1. 497; colonised by the Cauconians, 3. 385; home of the Cyclopes who helped to build the walls of Tiryns, 4. 169; the Homeric, in which Zeleia was situated, was subject to Pandarus, 5. 461; discussion of, 5. 491–495; origin of name of, 5. 491; the present, separated from the country of the Cibyrans by a ridge of the Taurus, 6. 265; description of, 6. 311–323

Lycians, the, were Trojans, according to Homer, 5. 37, 423; two groups of, the Trojan and that near Caria, 5. 491; the same as the Homeric "Solymi"(?), 5. 493; by some confused with the Carians, 5. 495, 6. 315; in the Troad, were led by Pandarus, 6. 19, held Zeleia, 6. 23, and "fight in close combat," 6. 45; in southern Asia Minor, captured Sardeis, 6. 179; continued to live in a decent and civilised way, 6. 313; by Homer made a different people from the Solymi, but by others said once to have been called "Solymi," and later "Termilae," and still later named after Lycus the son of Pandion, 6. 323, 361

Lycomedes the King, with Polemon captured Arsaces at Sagylium, 5. 445

Lycomedes, king of the isle Scyros, and father-in-law of Achilles, 4. 427

Lycomedes, priest of Comana in Cappadocia Pontica, 5. 437

Lycoreia, above the temple at Delphi, where the Delphians lived in earlier times, 4. 351

Lycormas River (see Evenus River)

Lyctians, the, in Crete, possess Minoa, 5. 123

Lyctus (or Lyttus, *q.v.*) in Crete, at one time, with Gortyna, took precedence over Cnossus, 5. 129; Cherronesus the seaport of, 5. 143; institutions at, 5. 149

Lycupolis, a, in the Sebennytic Nome in Aegypt, 8. 69

Lycurgus, the Edonian, identified with Dionysus, 5. 107; mentioned by Homer, 7. 11

Lycurgus, the lawgiver, responsible for the Laconian supremacy, 4. 137; wrongly ignored by Hellanicus, who ascribes the Spartan Constitution to Eurysthenes and Procles, 4. 139; a member of the house of the Eurypontidae, 4. 141; sixth in descent from Procles, 5. 149; for a time reigned as king at Sparta, sojourned in Crete and Aegypt, and then returned home as law-giver, 5. 153; often consulted the Pythian priestess at Delphi, 7. 287

Lycurgus, a work on, by Pausanias, one of the Eurypontidae, 4. 141

Lycurgus the orator (b. about 396 B.C.), agrees that the Homeric Ilium was wiped out, 6. 83

Lycus, son of King Pandion, received Euboea from his father, 4. 247, 249; named the Lycians after himself, 5. 493; banished from home and settled in Lycia, 6. 323

Lycus, the (*Canis lupaster*, jackal), worshipped at Lycopolis, 8. 111

Lycus (wrongly called the "Thermodon" by Eratosthenes) River, the, empties into the Euxine, 5. 327; rises in Armenia and joins the Iris River in Cappadocia Pontica, 5. 397, 429

Lycus River, the, between Ninus and Arbela, 7. 195, 197

Lycus River (Tchorouk Sou), the, in Phrygia, joins the Maeander, 5. 511

Lycus River, the, in Syria, navigable, 7. 261, 263

Lydia, The History of, by Xanthus, 5. 517

Lydia, a part of the Cis-Halys country, 1. 497; whence Tyrrhenus colonised Tyrrhenia in Italy, 2. 337; colonised by Ionians from Athens, 4. 209

Lydian Gate, the, at Adramyttium, 6. 127

Lydian language, the; no trace of, now left in Lydia, 6. 193

Lydians, the, caused flight of certain Ionians to Italy, 3. 49; once held the mastery after the Trojan War, 5. 463; confused with other peoples in Asia, 5. 487, 495; Gyges the king of, 6. 41; once held Adramyttium,

384

INDEX OF NAMES, PLACES, AND SUBJECTS

6. 127; by Homer and others called
" Meïonians," **6.** 173, by some later
writers, " Maeonians," **6.** 173, 185;
seized Cabalis, **6.** 191; rased Old
Smyrna to the ground, **6.** 245;
certain places occupied by, **6.** 249,
255; as brothers worship the
Carian Zeus with the Carians and
Mysians, **6.** 293; by the poets
confused with other peoples, **6.** 315;
were conquered by the Persians, **7.**
187

" Lydus," the name given a Lydian
slave in Attica, **3.** 213

Lydus, son of Atys the Lydian, **2.** 337

Lygaeus, grandfather of Penelopê, **5.**
69

Lygdamis, king of the Cimmerians,
captured Sardeis, but lost his life
in Cilicia, **1.** 229

Lyncestae, the; the country of
(Lyncestis), in western Macedonia,
through which the Egnatian Way
passes, **3.** 295; became subject to
Arrabaeus the Bacchiad, **3.** 309

Lyncestis, country of the Lyncestae,
through which the Egnatian Way
passes, **3.** 295

Lyncus, in Upper Macedonia, **3.** 309

Lynx (or Lixus) in Maurusia, **8.** 159,
161, 165, 171; fabulous tomb of
Antaeus and a skeleton 60 cubits
long near, **8.** 171

Lyon (see Lugdunum)

Lyon, Gulf of (see Galatic Gulf)

Lyrceium, a village in Argolis, unknown to Homer, **4.** 183

Lyrceius, Mt., near Cynuria in
Arcadia, where rises the Cephissus
River, **4.** 159 (see footnote 2), 159,
375

Lyre (see Cithara), the seven-stringed,
instead of the four-stringed, first
used by Terpander, **6.** 147

Lyrnessus in Pamphylia, founded by
Trojan Cilicians, **6.** 323, 357

Lyrnessus in the Troad, sacked by
Achilles, **6.** 15; Aeneias fled from
Achilles to, **6.** 105; home of
Briseïs, **6.** 121

Lysias, a town in Phrygia, **5.** 505

Lysias, a stronghold in Syria, destroyed
by Pompey, **7.** 253, 291

Lysimacheia (Hexamili), in the middle
of the isthmus between the Melas

Gulf and the Propontis, founded
(309 B.C.) by Lysimachus, **3.** 373,
375

Lysimachia, in Aetolia, has now disappeared, **5.** 65

Lysimachia, Lake, in Aetolia, once
called Hydra, **5.** 65

Lysimachus, one of Alexander's
generals and successors, obtained
Thrace as his portion, assuming
title of king in 306 B.C.; taken
captive and released by Dromi-
chaetes the Getan king (about
291 B.C.), **3.** 203, 217; once used
Cape Tirizis as a treasury, **3.** 279;
founded Lysimacheia (on Gallipoli),
3. 373; changed the name of Antigonia in the Troad to Alexandreia,
6. 53; permitted the Scepsians to
return home from there, **6.** 65, 105;
founded the Asclepieium in the
Troad, **6.** 89; destroyed Astacus, **5.**
455; founded Nicaea, naming it
after his wife, the daughter of
Antipater, **5.** 463; Pergamum the
treasure-hold of, **6.** 163; slew his
son Agathocles, overthrown by
Seleucus Nicator, and at last slain
by Ptolemy Ceraunus, **6.** 165;
built a wall round the present
Ephesus, and named it after his
wife Arsinoê, **6.** 225; re-assembled
the Smyrnaeans in New Smyrna,
6. 245

Lysioedi, the, corrupters of Melic
poetry, **6.** 253

Lysippus of Sicyon, the great sculptor,
contemporary of Alexander the
Great; made a colossal bronze
statue of Heracles for Tarentum,
3. 107; " Labours of Heracles " of,
carried from Acarnania to Rome,
5. 61; made the " Fallen Lion,"
which Agrippa took from Lampsacus, **6.** 37

Lysis, accompanied the talk of the
Cinaedi with song, **6.** 253

Lyttus in Crete, by Homer called
Lyctus (*q.v.*), **5.** 129

M

Ma (*i.e.* Enyo), the temple of, at
Comana in Cappadocia, **5.** 351

Macae, Cape, in Arabia, **7.** 301, 305

385

INDEX OF NAMES, PLACES, AND SUBJECTS

"Macar, the city of," in Homer, means the island Lesbos, 4. 97

Macaria, a spring near Tricorynthus in Attica, 4. 187

Macaria Plain, the, on the Pamisus River, 4. 117

Maccaresa (see Fregena)

Macedon, name of an ancient chieftain of Macedonia, 3. 329

Macedonia (in earlier times called Emathia), 3. 329; geographical position of, 3. 249; now held by Thracians, 3. 287; according to some writers, extends from the Strymon (Struma) to the Nestus (Mesta), 3. 297; fortified against Greece by the Peneius River, where it flows through Tempê, 3. 325; a part of Greece, 3. 327, 4. 3; like a parallelogram in shape, 3. 327; boundaries of, 3. 329, 369, 4. 395, 399; coast of, extends from Cape Sunium to the Thracian Chersonese, 3. 333; the Epeirotic tribes annexed to, 3. 369; Thrace now called, 3. 349; much of, as now, occupied by the Paeonians, 3. 363; divided into four parts by Paulus, 3. 369; countries annexed to, 4. 415, 417; with the country next to Epeirus, now a praetorial Province, 8. 215

Macedonia, Lower, 3. 341, 4. 399

Macedonia, Upper (or Free), consisted of the regions about Lyncus, Pelagonia, Orestias, and Elimeia, 3. 309, 331, 4. 399

Macedonian Kings, the, molested Athens, but let its government remain democratic, 4. 269

Macedonians, the, upbuilders of Europe, 1. 489; under Alexander, believed that Heracles and Dionysus preceded them in expedition to India, 2. 141; sided with the Carthaginians, and hence the later conquest of them by the Romans, 3. 141; greatly reduced certain tribes of the Galatae, Illyrians, and Thracians, 3. 263; subdued by Paulus Aemilius, 3. 293; inhabit the districts between the Paeonian Mountains and the Strymon (Struma) River, 3. 295; subjugated the Epeirote cities, 3. 303; the empire of, broken up by

the Romans, 3. 309, 345; called their senators "peligones," 3. 323; gained the hegemony of Greece, 4. 137; revered the temple of Poseidon on Calauria, 4. 175; dissolved the Achaean League, 4. 211; reduced the Dorian Tetrapolis, 4. 389; war of, with the Athenians, near Lamia, 4. 413; for a time strongly resisted by the Aetolians and Acarnanians, 5. 67; once ruled over Hyrcania, 5. 253; gave the name "Caucasus" to all the mountains which follow in order after the country of the Arians, 5. 259; received tribute from the Parthians and Hyrcanians, 5. 271; imposed their own names on conquered places, 5. 285; overthrew the Persians and occupied Syria, 5. 307; once ruled over Armenia, 5. 337; allowed the two satrapies of Cappadocia to change to kingdoms, 5. 349; succeeded the Persians as masters in Asia, 5. 463; onsets of, in Asia, 5. 495; certain, live about Mt. Tmolus in Lydia, 6. 173; Stratoniceia in Caria a settlement of, 6. 297; once used Cyinda in Cilicia as a treasury, 6. 341; gave Ariana to the Indians, 7. 15; subdued the Persians, 7. 159, 187; planted the vine in Susis and Babylonia, 7. 173; conquered Dareius at Gaugamela near Arbela, 7. 197; seized Phoenicia, 7. 257; took possession of Aegypt, and attacked the Cyrenaeans, 8. 203

Macestus River, the, in Asia, flows from Ancyra and empties into the Rhyndacus, 5. 503

Machaereus, a Delphian, slew Neoptolemus the son of Achilles, 4. 361

Machaerus, a stronghold in Syria, destroyed by Pompey, 7. 291

Macistia, in Triphylia, separated by a mountain from Pisatis, 4. 49; where is the temple of Leto, 4. 73

Macistians, the, used to have charge of the temple of Poseidon at Samicum, 4. 49; revere Hades, 4. 51

Macistus, the Triphylian, said to have colonised Eretria in Euboea, 5. 15

Macistus (or Platanistus, now Khaiaffa) in Triphylia, seized by the Cauconians, 3. 23, 4. 55

INDEX OF NAMES, PLACES, AND SUBJECTS

Macra River, the (see Macras River)

"Macraeones," the, in Iberia, 2. 57

Macras (or Macra), the plain, in Syria, where was seen the huge fallen dragon, 7. 261, 263

Macras (Macra) River, the, the boundary between Tyrrhenia and Liguria, 2. 351

Macri Campi, on the Aemilian Way, 2. 327

Macris ("Long"), the ancient name of Euboea, 5. 3

Macron Teichos ("Long Wall") on the Propontis, 3. 377

Macrones, the, in Cappadocia Pontica, 5. 399

Macropogones, the, in Asia, 5. 191

Macynia, a small city in Aetolia, 5. 29, 63; founded after the return of the Heracleidae, 5. 31

Macyperna, the naval station of Olynthus, 3. 351

Madaris (matara), a kind of javelin used by the Gauls, 2. 243

Madys the Scythian chief, who overran parts of Asia Minor, conquering Cyaxares (623 B.C.); his expeditions, 1. 227

Madytus (Maïtos), where Xerxes' pontoon-bridge was built, 3. 377; founded by the Lesbians, 3. 379

Maeander River, the, receives the waters of the Marsyas and Lethaeus Rivers, 5. 421; the course of, 5. 509, 511; territory near, subject to earthquakes, 5. 513; alters the boundaries of countries on its banks, and is subject to fines, 5. 517; the Lethaeus empties into, 6. 249; 1180 stadia from Physcus and 80 from Tralleis, 6. 309; Plain of, created by silt, 7. 23

Maeandrius, on the Eneti, 5. 415

Maecenê, in Arabia, on the borders of Babylonia, 7. 307

Maenaca (the present site of Almunecar) in Iberia, not to be confused with Malaca (Malaga), 2. 81

Maenalus, a city in Arcadia, no longer exists, 4. 229

Maenalus, Mt. (Apanokhrepa), a famous mountain in Arcadia, 4. 231

Maenoba in Iberia, purposely built near estuary, 2. 31

Maeonians, the, are the same people

as the Mysians and the Meïonians, 5. 405, 487, 6. 173; now called Lydians, 6. 155

Maeotae, the, on Lake Maeotis, 5. 191; though farmers, are no less warlike than the nomads, 5. 195; names of various tribes of, 5. 201

Maeotis, Lake (Sea of Azov), made known to geographers by Mithridates, 1. 51; severe frosts at, 1. 277; receives waters of the Tanaïs, 1. 413, 5. 193; circumference of, 9000 stadia, 1. 481; a boundary of Europe, 3. 151; marsh-meadows of, roamed by Scythian nomads, 3. 223; coldness of region of, and description of animals there, 3. 225; mouth of, called the Cimmerian Bosporus, 3. 239; dimensions of, 3. 241; Alopecia and other islands in, 5. 195; the mouth of, 5. 197; often freezes over, 5. 199; not mentioned by Homer, 5. 419

Magadis, a barbarian musical instrument, 5. 109

Magi, the; attained pre-eminence through superior knowledge, 1. 87; among the Parthians, compose a part of the Council, 5. 277; attend the Persian kings as counsellors, 7. 119; live an august life, 7. 157; on guard at the tomb of Cyrus at Pasargadae, 7. 167; the Persian superintend the sacrifices, 7. 175, 177, in Cappadocia, called "Pyraethi," 7. 177; certain barbarian customs of, 7. 183, 185; deposed Cambyses the son of Cyrus, 7. 189

Magic, closely related to religion and divination, 5. 121

Magna Graecia (see Graecia, Magna)

Magnesia in Caria, near the Maeander, colony of Cretans and Thessalian Magnesians; given by Xerxes to Themistocles to supply him with bread, 6. 211; description and famous natives of, 6. 249–255; 140 stadia from Tralleis, 6. 309

Magnesia in Lydia, 5. 421; at the foot of Mt. Sipylus, ruined by earthquakes, 5. 487, 515; has been set free by the Romans, and has been damaged by recent earthquakes, 6. 159

Magnesia in Thessaly; the boundaries

INDEX OF NAMES, PLACES, AND SUBJECTS

of, according to present historians, **4**. 407; description and history of, **4**. 423, 425; most of, annexed to Macedonia, **4**. 427; indistinctly mentioned by Homer, **4**. 415, 417; Hieronymus on, **4**. 453

Magnesians, the, in Caria, near the Maeander River, settled in the Antiocheia near Pisidia, **5**. 507; descendants of the Magnesians in Thessaly, utterly destroyed by the Trerans, **6**. 251

Magnesians (or Magnetans), the, in Thessaly; geographical position of, **4**. 395, 427, 447, 449; Homolium belongs to, **4**. 449, 451; colonised Magnesia on the Maeander River, **6**. 211, 251

Magnetans, the (see Magnesians)

Magnetis in Macedonia, **3**. 349

Magnopolis in Phanaroea in Cappadocia Pontica (see Eupatoria)

Magoedi, the, corrupters of Melic poetry, **6**. 253

Magus, a circumnavigator of Libya, according to Heracleides, and a visitor at court of Gelo, **1**. 377

Maïtos (see Madytus)

Makri, Cape (see Serrhium, Cape, in Thrace)

Makriplagi, Mt. (see Gerania)

Makronisi the island (see Helenê)

Malaca (now Malaga) in Iberia, bears the stamp of a Phoenician city, **2**. 81

Malaga (see Malaca)

Malaria (?), the disease, **2**. 315

Malathria in southern Macedonia (see Dium)

Malatia (see Melitina)

Malaucêne (see Durio)

Malaüs, descendant of Agamemnon, founded Phriconian Cymê in Asia, **6**. 7

Malea (or Maleae, q.v.) Cape, distant 22,500 stadia from Pillars of Heracles, **1**. 93; promontory ending in, **1**. 417

Maleae, Cape, 670 stadia from Cape Taenarum, **4**. 127, 129, 149, 151, 155; the sea beyond, hard to navigate, **4**. 189; the distance from, to the Ister River, **4**. 233, 235

Maleos, the Pelasgian king, **2**. 365

Malia, Mt. (see Aegaleum)

Malia, southernmost promontory of Lesbos, **6**. 139

Maliac Gulf, the, next to the Opuntian Gulf, **3**. 353, **4**. 381; has about the same length as the territory of Achilles, **4**. 407; enumeration of cities near, that were subject to Achilles, **4**. 413, 417, and cities on coast of, that were subject to Achilles, **4**. 417, 419

Malian War, the; Styra in Euboea destroyed during, **5**. 11

Malians, the Arabian, **7**. 233

Malians, the, in Thessaly; geographical position of, **4**. 395; subject to Achilles, **4**. 413, 449

Malli, the, a tribe in India, **7**. 57

Mallus in Cilicia, founded by Amphilochus and Mopsus, **6**. 353; birthplace of Crates the grammarian, **6**. 355

Malotha, a village in Arabia, **7**. 363

Malta (see Melitê)

Malus, in the Troad, **6**. 89

Malvasia (see Minoa the island)

Mamaüs River, the, flows past the Lepreatic Pylus, **4**. 51

Mamertine wine, the, made at Messenê in Sicily, rivals the best of the Italian wines, **3**. 67

Mamertini, the, a tribe of the Campani, settled at Messenê in Sicily, **3**. 65; got control of the city, **3**. 67

Mamertium, in Bruttium, **3**. 35

Mandanis, the Indian sophist, commended Alexander, **7**. 111; refused to visit Alexander, **7**. 121

Mandilo, Cape (see Geraestus)

"Manes," a name given Phrygian slaves in Attica, **3**. 213; a name used in Cappadocia, **5**. 415

Manes River, the (see Boagrius River, the, in Locris), **4**. 381

Mangalia (see Callatis)

Manius Aquillius (consul 129 B.C.), organised a province in Asia, **6**. 249

Mantianê, a large lake in Armenia; next to Lake Maeotis in size, **5**. 327

Mantineia (Palaeopoli) in Arcadia, settled by Argive colonists, **4**. 21; made famous by the Battle of Mantineia, but no longer exists, **4**. 229, 335

Manto, daughter of Teiresias the prophet and mother of Mopsus by Apollo, **4**. 453, **6**. 233, 353

Mantua, in Italy, **2**. 311

INDEX OF NAMES, PLACES, AND SUBJECTS

INDEX OF NAMES, PLACES, AND SUBJECTS

391

INDEX OF NAMES, PLACES, AND SUBJECTS

393

of the same workmanship as the Labyrinth, **8.** 111–113

Memnonium, the; name of the acropolis of Susa, **7.** 159

Memoirs, the Aegyptian, Babylonian, and Indian, on the straightforward character of the Scythians, **3.** 201

Memphis in Aegypt; temples of the Cabeiri and Hephaestus in, destroyed by Cambyses, **5.** 115; "royal residence of the Aegyptians," keeps the sacred bull Apis, **8.** 73, 87; distance from, to Thebaïs, **8.** 75; a curious kind of hall at, **8.** 83; description of, **8.** 87–89

Men, mythical, who are "half-dog," or "long-headed," or "pygmies," or "web-footed," or "dog-headed," or "have eyes in their breasts," or "one-eyed," invented by the poets, **3.** 191

Mēn (see Mēn Ascaeus), the temple of, in the country of the Antiocheians (at Saghir?), **5.** 433

Mēn Arcaeus (Ascaeus?), the priesthood of, at Antiocheia near Pisidia, **5.** 507

Mēn Ascaeus; temple of, near the Antiocheia that is near Pisidia, **5.** 431

Mēn of Carus; temple of, in place of same name, between Carura and Laodiceia, **5.** 431, 519

Mēn of Pharnaces, the temple of, at Cabeira in Cappadocia Pontica, **5.** 431

Menander the comic poet, of Athens (b. 342 B.C.); on the polygamy of the Thracians and Getans, **3.** 183; on the money and time spent by women on religious observances, **3.** 183, 185; says that Sappho the poetess was the first to leap off Cape Leucatas into the sea, **5.** 33; on a certain law in the isle Ceos, **5.** 169; says that the isle Samos "produces everything but birds' milk," **6.** 215, 217; became an *ephebus* at Athens, **6.** 219

Menander, king of Bactria; far-reaching conquests of, **5.** 279–281

Menapii, the, live on both sides of the Rhenus near its mouths, **2.** 231; border on the Marini, **2.** 253; fogs among, **2.** 257

Mendê, a city on Pallenê, **3.** 351

Mendes in Aegypt, where Pan and a he-goat are worshipped, **8.** 69

Mendesian mouth of the Nile, the, **8.** 65, 71

Menecles, the orator, teacher of Apollonius Malacus and Apollonius Molon, **6.** 281, 299

Menecrates of Elaea, a disciple of Xenocrates; opinions of, approved by Demetrius of Scepsis, **5.** 407; in his *Circuit of the Hellespont* discusses the Halizones, **5.** 409; regards the Mysians as Lydian in origin, **5.** 489; in his work on the *Foundings of Cities* discusses the Pelasgians in Asia, **6.** 157

Menecrates, pupil of Aristarchus and native of Nysa in Asia, **6.** 263

Menedemus, founder of the Eretrian sect of philosophers, **4.** 251, **5.** 19

Menelaüs, the brother of Ptolemy I; the Menelaïte Nome in Aegypt named after, **8.** 65

Menelaïs, a city in Aegypt, **8.** 73

Menelaüs, the Greek hero, destined for Elysian Plain, **1.** 7; travelled much, and hence a wise man, **1.** 29; traveller and braggart, **1.** 111; wanderings of, **1.** 137, 139; the prophecy uttered to, by Proteus, **1.** 141; wealthy palace of, **1.** 143; sojourned in Sidon, **1.** 149; wanderings of, a traditional fact, **2.** 55, 359; domain of, included Messenia, **4.** 87; accompanied to Troy by men of Pherae (Pharis), **4.** 109; also held Messenia as subject at time of Trojan War, **4.** 107, 109; palace of, at Sparta, visited by Telemachus, **4.** 147, 149; came into possession of Laconia, **4.** 167; in haste to return home from Troy, **5.** 105; said to have been entertained in Aegypt by King Thon, **8.** 63; took captive Trojans with him, who settled in Arabia, **8.** 95–97

Menelaüs Harbour, in Cyrenaea, **8.** 207

Menestheus, port and oracle of, in Iberia, **2.** 17; Greek charioteer at Troy, **4.** 255; with Athenians, founded Elaea in Asia in Trojan times, **6.** 159

INDEX OF NAMES, PLACES, AND SUBJECTS

Menesthles, the Homeric, leader of the Meïonians, **6.** 175

Meninx (Jerba), the island, land of the Lotus-Eaters, **1.** 91, **8.** 193

Menippus, the satirist, native of Gadaris in Phoenicia, **7.** 277

Menippus, surnamed Catocas, of Stratoniceia in Caria, applauded by Cicero above all Asiatic orators he had heard, **6.** 299

Menlaria, in Iberia, where were establishments for salting fish, **2.** 15

Mennaeus, father of Ptolemaeus the ruler of certain places in Syria, **7.** 253

Menodorus of Tralleis, contemporary of Strabo; learned, august, grave, priest of Zeus Larisaeus, slain by Dometius Ahenobarbus, **6.** 257

Menodotus the Pergamenian, of the family of Galatian tetrarchs, and father of the famous Mithridates the Pergamenian, **6.** 169

Menoetius, the father of Patroclus, lived at Opus in Locris, **4.** 379

Menon, sent by Alexander to the gold mines in Armenia, **5.** 329

Mentana (see Nomentum)

Mentes, the king of Taphos, **5.** 49; the subjects of, in the Trojan War, **5.** 61

Mentor, impersonated by Athenê in the *Odyssey*, **4.** 45, 57

Merenda (see Myrrhinus)

Meridian, the, through Meroê and Alexandria, **1.** 233

Meridians, the; graphic representation of, **1.** 463

Mermadalis (see Mermodas) River, the, flows between the countries of the Amazons and certain Scythians, **5.** 233

Mermodas (Mermadalis?) River, the, flows through the country of the Amazons and into Lake Maeotis, **5.** 235

Meroê, the city; geographical position of, **8.** 5; so named by Cambyses, **8.** 19; greatest royal seat of the Aethiopians, **8.** 143; about 10,000 stadia from Alexandria and 3000 from the torrid zone, **8.** 157

Meroê, largest of islands in Nile, residence of the king, metropolis of the

Aethiopians, **1.** 119; lies opposite southern capes of India, about 15,000 stadia distant from parallel of Athens, **1.** 255, 439; distance from, to Hellespont, **1.** 257; longest day at, has 13 equinoctial hours, **1.** 509; region of, gets no rain, **7.** 29; ruled by a queen, and a fifteen days' journey from the Arabian Gulf, **7.** 321; course of the Nile with reference to, **8.** 3; a rather large island, **8.** 5; so named by Cambyses, **8.** 19; description of, **8.** 143; worship and customs of inhabitants of, **8.** 147

Meropis, the Land of, an invention reported by Theopompus, **3.** 191

Merops of Percotê, father of two Trojan leaders, **6.** 21, 25

Merops, Aethiopian king, **1.** 123

" Merotraphes," an epithet of Dionysus, **7.** 9

Merus, Mt., in India, **7.** 11

Mesembria (Mesivri), on the Euxine, in Thrace, founded by the Megarians, **3.** 279

Mesivri (see Mesembria)

Mesoga, a city in India, **7.** 47

Mesogis, Mt.; geographical position of, **6.** 183, 185, 255; produces excellent wine, **6.** 215

Mesola in Messenia, by some identified with the Homeric Hirê, **4.** 115; by Cresphontes made one of the Messenian capitals, **4.** 119

Mesopotamia, like a galley in shape, **1.** 299, 305; enclosed by the Tigris and Euphrates, **1.** 305, 499, 5. 297, 317, 319; description of, **7.** 229; became subject to the Romans, **7.** 231; parts of, occupied by the Arabian Scenitae, **7.** 233

Messapia, the Greek name for Iapygia, **3.** 103; forms a sort of peninsula, **3.** 105

Messapius, Mt., near Anthedon, named after Messapus, who emigrated to Iapygia and called it Messapia, **4.** 299

Messapus, after whom Mt. Messapius in Boeotia and Messapia in Italy were named, **4.** 299

Messê, the Homeric, by some considered an apocopated form of Messenê, **4.** 129

396

INDEX OF NAMES, PLACES, AND SUBJECTS

Messeïs, a spring in Thessaly, **4.** 405

Messenê, the country (see Messenia)

Messenê, the city, capital of Messenia, whose acropolis was Ithomê, captured after a war of nineteen years, **3.** 113; not yet founded in time of Trojan War (founded by Epameinondas 369 B.C.), **4.** 107; like Corinth, **4.** 119; destroyed by the Lacedaemonians, but rebuilt by the Thebans and by Philip the son of Amyntas, **4.** 121

Messenê in Sicily, once ruled by Micythus, **3.** 5; 30 Roman miles from Tauromenium, **3.** 59; geographical position of, **3.** 63; founded by the Peloponnesian Messenians, and formerly called Zancle, **3.** 65; used by the Romans as a base of operation against the Carthaginians, and by Pompey Sextus against Augustus, **3.** 67

Messenia, the country, in the Peloponnesus, once called Messenê; bounded on the north by the Neda River, **4.** 67; the "Aulon" of, **4.** 75; classified as subject to Menelaüs, **4.** 87; detailed description of, **4.** 107-123, 141-149; a part of Laconia and subject to Menelaüs at time of Trojan War, at that time called Messenê, **4.** 107, 149; contained the seven cities promised by Agamemnon to Achilles, **4.** 109, 115; Pylus the naval station of, **4.** 111; divided by Cresphontes into five cities, **4.** 119; four wars of, against the Lacedaemonians, **4.** 121, 123; lauded for its streams and fertility by Euripides and Tyrtaeus, **4.** 141, 143; people of, incited the Heracleidae to invade Attica, **4.** 249

Messenian (or Asinaean) Gulf, the, **4.** 15, 109; begins at Cape Acritas, **4.** 113

Messenian War, the, **3.** 107, 111

Messenian Wars, the, as described by Tyrtaeus, **4.** 121, 123

Messenians, the Peloponnesian, who were charged with outraging the maidens at Limnae, and were cofounders of Rhegium, **3.** 23; an advantage of, in the Messenian War, **3.** 111; geographical position

of, **4.** 15; pretend a kinship with the Pylians, **6.** 199

Messenians, the, in Sicily, **3.** 21

Messinê, the Strait of; the reverse currents at, **1.** 85

Messoa, a ward of Sparta, **4.** 129

Mesta River, the (see Nestus River)

Metabus, legendary hero of Metapontium (Metabum), **3.** 53

Metagonium in Libya, country of a nomadic tribe, **2.** 137

Metagonium, the promontory in Maurusia in Libya, a waterless and barren place, **8.** 165; lies opposite to New Carthage, not to Massalia, **8.** 167; about 6000 stadia from Tretum, **8.** 173

Metapontium (Torre di Mari), settled by Pisatae from the Peloponnesus, **2.** 351; borders on country of the Tarantini, **3.** 13, 103, 105; history of, **3.** 51-55

Metapontus, son of Sisyphus and legendary hero of Metapontium, **3.** 53

Metaurus (Marro) River, the, in Bruttium, **3.** 19

Metellus Balearicus (consul 123 B.C.), subjugated the Balearic Islands and founded their cities, **2.** 125; colonised them with 3000 Romans, **2.** 127

Metempsychosis, a doctrine of the Druids in Gaul, **2.** 245 (see footnote)

Meteor, the, which fell at Aegospotami during the Persian War, **3.** 19

Methana (Megalokhorion), a stronghold between Troezen and Epidaurus, **4.** 177

Methonê in the Hermionic Gulf, near which a mountain was cast up by a volcanic eruption, **1.** 219

Methonê (Eleutherokhori) in Macedonia, lies about 40 stadia from Pydna, **3.** 341; where Philip had his right eye knocked out, **3.** 339, 345, **4.** 177; rased to the ground by Philip, **4.** 425

Methonê (Modon) in Messenia; the people of, called Phthians, **3.** 385; identified with the Homeric Pedasus, and is the place where Agrippa put to death Bogus the king of the Maurusians during the war of Actium (31 B.C.), **4.** 111; by some

397

INDEX OF NAMES, PLACES, AND SUBJECTS

209; the Old and the New, **6.** 205; noted for its colonisations, **6.** 207; taken by force by Alexander, **6.** 209; about 100 stadia from Heracleia and 30 from Pyrrha, **6.** 211

Miletus in Crete, no longer exists, **5.** 143; Sarpedon from, founded Miletus in Asia, **5.** 491

Milk, used by Scythian nomads, **3.** 223; and by the Aethiopians, **8.** 143, and Masaesylians, **8.** 189

Milk, mare's-, used by the Scythian and other nomads, **3.** 197

Millet, grown in Aquitania, **2.** 215; used as food by people near the Frigid Zone, **2.** 261; produced in great quantities in Cisalpine Celtica, **2.** 331; grown in Campania, **2.** 437; and spelt, the food of the Iapodes, **3.** 259; abounds in Themiscyra, **5.** 397; sown in rainy seasons in India, **7.** 21; used for food in Aethiopia, **8.** 143

Milo, the great athlete, from Croton in Italy; story of, **3.** 45

Miltiades, utterly destroyed the Persian army at Marathon, **4.** 273

Milya, the mountain-range extending from the pass at Termessus to Sagalassas and the country of the Apameians, **6.** 193

Milyae (once called Solymi), the, not mentioned by Homer, **5.** 423, **6.** 363; in Lycia, named " Termilae " by Sarpedon, but later named Lycians by Lycus, **5.** 491, 493; to be identified with the Homeric " Solymi," **6.** 323

Milyas, in Pisidia, laid waste by Alexander, **6.** 321

Mimallones, the; ministers of Dionysus, **5.** 97

Mimes (Atellanae Fabulae), **2.** 395

Mimnermus of Colophon (fl. about 625 B.C.), the elegiac poet; on Jason's quest of the golden fleece, **1.** 171; in his *Nanno*, says that Colophon was founded by Andraemon of Pylus, **6.** 199; on the Smyrnaeans, **6.** 203; a native of Colophon, **6.** 235

Mimosa Nilotica, the, a tree in Arabia, **7.** 309

Minaeans, the, in Arabia, take their aromatics to Palestine, **7.** 311, 343

Mincius (Mincio) River, the, **2.** 293

Mines, the, in Cisalpine Celtica, now neglected, **2.** 333; numerous in Italy, **3.** 139; at Cabeira in Cappadocia Pontica, **5.** 429; about Mt. Sipylus, source of wealth of Tantalus and the Pelopidae; those about Thrace and Mt. Pangaeus, source of wealth of Cadmus; those of gold, at Astyra near Abydus, source of wealth of Priam, **6.** 369; those round Mt. Bermius, source of wealth of Midas, and those in Lydia, source of wealth of Gyges, Alyattes, and Croesus, **6.** 371; of copper, gold, and precious stones on the island Meroë in the Nile, **8.** 143; of *smaragdus* (emerald), between Coptus and Berenicê in Libya, **8.** 121

Minius River, the (see Baenis)

Minoa (Settia), in Crete, a city of the Lyctians, **5.** 123

Minoa (Malvasia) in Laconia, a stronghold, **4.** 151

Minoa in Megaris, **4.** 151

Minoa, Cape, in Megaris, **4.** 245

Minos, king of Crete; maritime supremacy of, **1.** 177; by Homer placed in the Elysian Plain in the far west, **2.** 57; murdered at the palace of Cocalus in Camici in Sicily, **3.** 85, 109; voyage of, to Sicily, **3.** 121; drowned Scylla, **4.** 173; excellent law-giver, and lord of the sea, **5.** 129; held converse with Zeus, but by some writers represented as a harsh tyrant, **5.** 131; by Homer called first son of Zeus and " guardian o'er Crete," **5.** 133; united three cities into one metropolis, **5.** 141; violent towards Britomartis, **5.** 139; published laws to the Cretans as from Zeus, **5.** 153; Sarpedon the coloniser, a brother of, **5.** 491; the Carians once subject to, **6.** 301; held converse with Zeus every nine years and received decrees from him, **7.** 287

Minotaur, the, in Greek tragedy, **5.** 131

Mint, garden-, called " Hedyosmos "; found in Triphylia, **4.** 51

Minteius River (see Minyeius)

Minthê (Alvena), Mt., near the Triphylian Pylus, named after a concubine of Hades, **4.** 51

399

INDEX OF NAMES, PLACES, AND SUBJECTS

INDEX OF NAMES, PLACES, AND SUBJECTS

401

INDEX OF NAMES, PLACES, AND SUBJECTS

Taurus into Pamphylia, **6.** 325; founded Mallus in Cilicia, died in duel with Amphilochus there, **6.** 353, 355

Mopsus the Lapith who sailed with the Argonauts, after whom Mopsium in Thessaly was named, **4.** 453

Morals, the, of the barbarians, corrupted by " our mode of life," **3.** 199

Morava River (see Margus)

Morenê in Asia; a part of, subject to Cleon, **5.** 499

Morgantium (or Murgantia), in Sicily, took its name from the Morgetes, **3.** 23; settled by the Morgetes, **3.** 73

Morgetes, the, inhabited southern Italy in earlier times, **3.** 23; settled in Morgantium in Sicily, **3.** 73

Morimenê, one of the ten prefectures of Cappadocia, **5.** 349; the temple of Venasian Zeus in, **5.** 359

Morini, the, in Celtica; geographical position of, **2.** 233; from whose coast some sail to Britain, **2.** 253; fogs among, **2.** 257

Moron (Al-Merim), a city on a mountain near the Tagus River in Iberia, about 500 stadia from the sea, used as base of operations by Brutus, **2.** 63

" Mortuaries," the, found at Corinth, sold at high price at Rome, **4.** 203

Morys (the Homeric), son of Hippotion, led forces from Ascania, **5.** 461

Morzeus; Gangra in Paphlagonia the royal residence of, **5.** 453

Moschian country, the, held partly by the Colchians, partly by the Iberians, and partly by the Armenians, **5.** 213, 215

Moschian Mountains, the, in Asia Minor, **5.** 209, 299; joined by Mt. Scydises above Colchis, **5.** 401

Moschians, the, in the Mithridatic War, **5.** 207

Moses, an Aegyptian priest; his tenets, and his kingdom at Jerusalem, **7.** 283–285; revered as ruler and prophet, **7.** 289

Mosyhoeci (see Heptacomitae), the, lost territory to the Armenians, **5.** 325

Mouse, the, carved at foot of image of

Apollo at Chrysa in the Troad, **6.** 95; the *mus araneus* worshipped at Athribis, **8.** 111

Mudania on the Propontis (see Myrlea)

Muga River, the (see Clodianus)

Mugilones, the, a German tribe, ruled by Marabodus, **3.** 157

Mulberry-tree (see Sycaminus, the Aegyptian)

Mule, a, tows the boat on the canal alongside the Appian Way, **2.** 397

Mules, superior, bred by the Eneti in Italy, **2.** 309; the famous Reate-breed of, in the Sabine country, **2.** 375; wild, in Eneti (or Enetê?), **5.** 417; in Arabia, **7.** 343

Mules, stunted (see Ginni)

Mulius, the Epeian spearman, slain by Nestor, **4.** 29

Mullets, the " dug," in Celtica, **2.** 183

Mummius, Leucius, the consul (who destroyed Corinth by fire in 146 B.C.), **4.** 121, 199; personally indifferent to works of art, **4.** 201, 203

Munda in Iberia, where the sons of Pompey were defeated, **2.** 21; a capital city; distance from, to Carteia, **2.** 23; the battle at, **2.** 97

Mundas (Mondego) River, the, in Iberia; affords short voyages inland, **2.** 67

Munychia, the hill at Peiraeus; description and history of, **4.** 259, 261

Murgantia in Sicily (see Morgantium)

Murviedro in Spain (see Saguntum)

Musaeus, the musician, called a Thracian, **5.** 109; a prophet often consulted, **7.** 289

Muses, the, met Thamyris the Thracian singer at Dorium, **4.** 71; temple of, on Mt. Helicon, dedicated by Thracians, **4.** 319; are goddesses in a special sense, and preside over the choruses, **5.** 95; worship of, Thracian in origin, **5.** 107, 109

Museum, the, at Alexandria, **8.** 35

Music, in education, **1.** 55; at Neapolis, **2.** 449; brings one in touch with the divine, **5.** 93; our system of education based on; and made synonymous with philosophy by Plato and the Pythagoreians, **5.** 95; all, regarded as Thracian and Asiatic in origin, **5.** 107

INDEX OF NAMES, PLACES, AND SUBJECTS

INDEX OF NAMES, PLACES, AND SUBJECTS

Nabataeans (or Idumaeans), the, in Arabia Felix, **7.** 309; also dwell on islands near the coast of the Arabian Gulf, **7.** 343; often overran Syria, **7.** 351; promised to co-operate with the Romans, **7.** 355; customs of, **7.** 367; have the same regard for their dead as for dung, and worship the Sun, **7.** 369

Nabiani, the; a nomadic tribe between Lake Maeotis and the Caspian Sea, **5.** 243

Nablas, a barbarian musical instrument, **5.** 109

Nabocodrosor, in great repute among the Chaldaeans, and led an army to the Pillars of Heracles, **7.** 7, 9

Nabrissa, in Iberia, estuary at, **2.** 17; purposely built on estuary, **2.** 31

Naburianus, a famous Chaldaean philosopher, **7.** 203

Nacolia, a city in Phrygia Epictetus, **5.** 505

Nagidus in Cilicia, lies opposite Lapathus in Cypros, **6.** 333, 377

Nahr-el-Asi River, the, in Syria (see Orontes River)

Naïdes, the; ministers of Dionysus, **5.** 97

Nanno, the, of Mimnermus, **6.** 199

Nantuates, the, live on peaks of the Alps, **2.** 273

Nao, Capo (see Lacinium, Cape)

Naos, the, of an Aegyptian temple, **8.** 81

Napata in Aethiopia, royal residence of Queen Candacê, captured and destroyed by Petronius, **8.** 139

Napê in the plain of Methymnê, ignorantly called Lapê by Hellanicus, **4.** 383

Napetine Gulf, the (see Hipponiate Gulf)

Naphtha (liquid asphalt), a fountain of, **7.** 197; produced in great quantities in Susis, **7.** 215; inflammable, **7.** 217; produced in Gordyaea, **7.** 233

Naples (see Neapolis)

Nar (Nera) River, the, flows through Narnia, **2.** 371; through Umbria to the Tiber, **2.** 403

Narbo (Narbonne); distance from, to Strait of Sicily and to Pillars of Heracles, **1.** 403; approximately on same parallel as Massalia, **1.** 407; situated on the Galatic Gulf, **1.** 491; certain distances from, **2.** 171; description of, **2.** 181, 183; the most important naval station in Celtica, **2.** 201; traffic inland from, on the Atax River, **2.** 211; most populous city in Celtica, **2.** 223

Narbonitis in Celtica, the province of, **2.** 165, 193; produces the same fruits as Italy, **2.** 167; description of, **2.** 169–193; praetors sent to, **2.** 271; the road to, **2.** 291; now a praetorial Province, **8.** 215

Narcissus the Eretrian, the monument of, near Oropus, **4.** 293

Nard, produced in India, as in Arabia and Aethiopia, **7.** 37, 365

Nard plants, the, in India, **7.** 133

Narenta River, the (see Naro River)

Narna (Narni), through which the Nar (Nera) River flows, **2.** 371

Narni (see Narna)

Naro (Narenta) River, the, in Dalmatia, **3.** 261

Narthacium, subject to Achilles, **4.** 413

Narthecis, an isle off Samos, **6.** 213

Narwhals, cause of large size of, **2.** 37

Narycus, the home of Aias in Locris, king of the Opuntians, **4.** 381

Nasamones, the, a tribe in Libya, **8.** 199, 207

Nasica, P. Cornelius Scipio, reduced Dalmium in Dalmatia to a small city and made its plain a mere sheep pasture (155 B.C.), **3.** 261

Natiso River, the, near Aquileia, **2.** 317

Nature, and Providence; discussion of the work of, in regard to the earth and heavens, **8.** 99

Nauclus, bastard son of Codrus, second founder of Teos, **6.** 201

Naucratis, above Schedia in Aegypt, founded by the Milesians, **8.** 67, 73; imported Lesbian wine, **8.** 93; Doricha the famous courtesan sojourned at, **8.** 95

Naulochus, in Thrace, a small town of the Mesembriani, **3.** 279

Naupactus in Western Locris, near Antirrhium, still survives, but now belongs to the Aetolians, **4.** 385

Nauplia (or Nauplïeis), the naval

405

INDEX OF NAMES, PLACES, AND SUBJECTS

station of the Argives, **4.** 151; near the Cyclopeian caverns, **4.** 153, 169; inhabitants of, withdrew to Messenia, **4.** 171; belonged to a kind of Amphictyonic League of seven cities, **4.** 175

Nauplians, the; dues of, at temple of Poseidon on Calauria, paid by the Argives, **4.** 175

Naupliëis (see Nauplia)

Nauplius, the founder of Nauplia, **4.** 151, whom Strabo confuses with Nauplius the son of Poseidon and Amymonê, **4.** 153 (see footnote 1)

Nauportus (Ober-Laibach); imports to, **2.** 287; a settlement of the Taurisci, 350 stadia from Aquileia, **3.** 255

Naustathmus, in Cyrenaea, **8.** 205

Navigators, taught how to steer course in straits by Danaüs, **1.** 85

Naxians, the, founded Callipolis in Sicily, **3.** 83; always shared in the misfortunes of the Syracusans, but not always in their fortunes, **3.** 87

Naxos, one of the Cyclades Islands, **5.** 165, 169

Naxus (on Capo di Schiso) in Sicily, no longer existent, **3.** 63; founded by Theocles the Athenian and some Chalcidians, **3.** 65; founded at about the same time as Syracuse, **3.** 71

Nea, a village near Scepsis in Asia, **5.** 411; between Polichna and Palaescepsis (Aenea Comê?), **6.** 91

Neaethus (Neto) River, the, in Italy; origin of name of, **3.** 41

Neandria, incorporated into Alexandreia in the Troad, **5.** 113, **6.** 93

Neandrians, the, in the Troad; territory of, **6.** 101

Neanthes of Cyzicus (fl. in third century B.C.), voluminous writer on historical subjects, though only a few fragments are extant; credits Argonauts with erecting sanctuary of Cybelê near Cyzicus, **1.** 165

Neapolis in Asia, once belonged to the Ephesians, but now to the Samians, **6.** 221, 223

Neapolis, a fort in the Crimea (site unknown), built by Scilurus and his sons, **3.** 247

Neapolis (formerly called Phazemon) in Cappadocia Pontica, so named by Pompey, **5.** 443

Neapolis (Kavala) in Macedonia, marks the limit of the Strymonic Gulf, **3.** 353, 359

Neapolis (Naples); description of, **2.** 449–451, 457; Gulf of, called "Crater," **2.** 435; tunnel from, to Dicaearchia, **2.** 445; now non-Greek, **3.** 7

Neapolis, on the eastern coast of Carthaginia, **8.** 191

Neapolis (also called Leptis), a city near the Great Syrtis, **8.** 195

Neapolitans, the, once held Capreae, **2.** 459

Neapolitis in Cappadocia Pontica, **5.** 443

Nearchus, admiral under Alexander the Great; (in 325 B.C.) made expedition from the mouth of the Indus to the Persian Gulf; an abstract of his voyage is contained in Arrian's *Indica.* He was discredited by Strabo, **1.** 263; on the Bears, **1.** 291; on four predatory tribes in Asia, **5.** 309; on the ambition of Alexander when in India, **7.** 7; on the size of India, **7.** 19; on the alluvial deposits of various rivers, **7.** 23; on the rains in India, **7.** 27; on the cotton in India, **7.** 33; attributes the risings of the Nile and the rivers in India to the summer rains, **7.** 41; on the mouths of the Indus River in India, **7.** 59; on the capturing of elephants in India, and on the antlions there, **7.** 75; on the vicious reptiles in India, **7.** 77; on the sophists in India, **7.** 115, and on the skill of the Indians in handiwork, **7.** 117; on the Arbies in India, **7.** 129; commander of Alexander's fleet, **7.** 133, 135; difficult voyage of, in the Persian Gulf, **7.** 149; his account thereof, **7.** 151; on the language and customs of the Carmanians, **7.** 155; on the seaboard of Persis, **7.** 161; found no native guides on voyage from India to Babylonia, **7.** 173; navigated the Persian Gulf, **7.** 303, 305, 307

INDEX OF NAMES, PLACES, AND SUBJECTS

(Lisbon), 2. 67; the end of western and northern sides of Iberia, and inhabited by Celtic people, 2. 67

Nero, Mt. (see Aenus)

Neroassus (see Nora)

Nervii, the, a Germanic tribe in Celtica, 2. 231

Nesaea, a district in Hyrcania, 5. 253

Nesaean horses, the, in Media, 5. 311; in Armenia, 5. 331

Nesson, the son of Thessalus; both Thessaly and Lake Nessonis named after, 4. 455

Nessonis, Lake, in Thessaly, 4. 397; the Peneius flows into, 4. 439; not mentioned by Homer, 4. 445; named after Nesson the son of Thessalus, 4. 455

Nessus, the Centaur; tomb of, on Taphiassus, a hill in Aetolia, 4. 385

Nessus the ferryman, killed by Heracles at the Lycormas (Evenus) River in Aetolia, 5. 29

Nestor, son of Neleus, travelled much, 1. 29; on the wanderings of Menelaüs, 1. 139; accompanied by Pisatae to Troy, 2. 351; companions of, founded Metapontium in Italy, 3. 51; called by Homer "the Gerenian" after "Gerena" in Messenia, according to some writers, 3. 193, 4. 33, 85; ruler of Triphylian Pylus, 4. 19, 21, not of the Pylus of Coelê Elis, 4. 23; slew Mulius the Epeian spearman, son-in-law of Augeas, 4. 29; "the Gerenian," claimed by three different Pyluses, 4. 33, 113; lived in the Lepreatic, or Triphylian Pylus, according to Homer (Strabo says), 4. 51, 57; Chloris the mother of, from Minyeian Orchomenus, 4. 63; the subjects of, 4. 71, 75, 87; various proofs of his having lived at the *Triphylian* Pylus, 4. 77–87; his recital to Patroclus of the war between the Pylians and Eleians proves it, 4. 79, 81; descendants of, sided with the Messenians in the Messenian War, 4. 95; not mentioned by Homer as going forth to battle at Troy, 4. 401; knew nothing about affairs in Crete after he set out for Troy, 5. 145; founded temple of Nedusian Athenê on

Ceos on his return from Troy, 5. 169; by the more recent poets called a Messenian, 6. 199

Nestus (Mesta) River, the; the northern boundary of Macedonia, 3. 297, 355, 357, 363, 365, 367

Netium (Noja), on the mule-road between Brundisium and Beneventum, 3. 123

Neto River, the (see Neaethus)

New Carthage (Cartagena), famous silver-mines at, 2. 47; founded by Hasdrubal, 2. 87; a powerful city, 2. 89; where the consular governor administers justice in winter, 2. 123; has a tree from the bark of which woven stuffs are made, 2. 155

Nibarus, Mt., in Asia, extends as far as Media, 5. 321; a part of the Taurus, 5. 335

Nicaea, daughter of Antipater, and wife of Lysimachus; Nicaea, the metropolis of Bithynia, named after, 5. 463

Nicaea (Antigonia), metropolis of Bithynia, on the Ascanian Lake, first founded by Antigonus the son of Philip, who called it Antigonia, and later by Lysimachus, who changed the name to that of his wife, 5. 463; description of, 5. 463–465

Nicaea, a city in India founded by Alexander, 7. 49

Nicaea in Locris, 4. 383; a fort near Thermopylae, 4. 389

Nicaea (Nice), founded by the Massaliotes, 2. 175, 191; subject to the Massaliotes, belongs to Province of Narbonitis, 2. 193

Nicander (lived about 185–135 B.C.), poet, grammarian, and physician, and author of the *Theriaca*; on the two kinds of Aegyptian asps, 8. 151

Nicatorium, Mt., near Arbela, so named by Alexander after his victory over Dareius, 7. 197

Nice (see Nicaea)

Nicephorium in Assyria, 7. 231

Nicias, contemporary of Strabo, native of Cos, reigned as tyrant over the Coans, 6. 289

"Nicias, the Village of," to the west of Alexandria, 8. 57

Nicolaüs Damascenus, on the embassy

INDEX OF NAMES, PLACES, AND SUBJECTS

from India to Augustus Caesar, **7.** 125, and on the gifts sent to Augustus, **7.** 127

Nicomedeia in Bithynia, about 300 stadia from the Sangarius River, **5.** 379; lies on the Astacene Gulf and was named after Nicomedes I, the Bithynian king (264 B.C.), **5.** 455

Nicomedes, the son of Prusias, king of Bithynia; incited against his father by Attalus II, **6.** 169; forces of, utterly destroyed by Mithridates, **5.** 449, 455; fought against Aristonicus, **6.** 247

Niconia (near Ovidiopol), on the Tyras River, **3.** 219

Nicophorium at Pergamum, planted with a grove, **6.** 169

Nicopolis in Acarnania; Anactorium an emporium of, **5.** 25

Nicopolis, near Alexandria, greatly honoured by Augustus because of his victory there, **8.** 43

Nicopolis in Lesser Armenia, founded by Pompey, **5.** 425

Nicopolis in Cilicia, on the Gulf of Issus, **6.** 357

Nicopolis Actia (near Prevesa) in Epeirus, founded by Augustus in honour of his victory over Antony, **3.** 301; a populous and wealthy city, **3.** 303; Actian Games celebrated near, and it has several dependent settlements, **3.** 305

Nicostratê, mother of Evander, mythical founder of Rome; skilled in divination, **2.** 385

Nigritae (or Nigretes?), the, and the Pharusians, said to have destroyed 300 Tyrian cities on the western coast of Libya, **8.** 161; use bows and scythe-bearing chariots, **8.** 169

Nikaria (see Icaria)

Nile (Aegyptus) River, the; mouths of, **1.** 107; boundary between two continents, **1.** 119, 129, 243, 415; "heaven-fed," **1.** 133; cataracts of, impassable for ships, **1.** 139; alluvial deposits of, **1.** 193; fed by rains from mountains of Aethiopia, **1.** 375; navigated by Eudoxus of Cyzicus, **1.** 377; nearly on the same meridian as the Tanaïs, **1.** 415; by its overflows causes Lake Mareotis to lose its baneful qualities, **2.** 315;

flows underground for a distance near its sources, **3.** 93; risings of, unknown to Homer, according to Apollodorus, **3.** 189; the silting up of, like that of the Pyramus River, and Aegypt called by Herodotus the "gift" of, **5.** 357; produces huge creatures, **7.** 37; largest of all rivers except the Ganges, Indus, and Ister, **7.** 61; certain fish found in, **7.** 79; confusion in boundaries of lands caused by, gave rise to science of geometry, **7.** 271; joined by the Astaboras, **7.** 319; joined by the Astasobas near Meroê, **7.** 321; position and description of, **8.** 3–5; effects like results in Aegypt and Aethiopia, **8.** 7; confuses boundaries, rising as high as 14 cubits, **8.** 11; forms the Delta, **8.** 13–15; filled from summer rains in Aethiopia, **8.** 17–21; timely risings of, **8.** 31; mouths of, **8.** 65 ff.; canals of, **8.** 75 ff.; level of, marked by Nilometer, **8.** 11, 127; has numerous islands, **8.** 133; by Herodotus foolishly said to rise near Syenê, **8.** 133; names of fish indigenous to, **8.** 149; the fish and crocodiles in, **8.** 153; sources of, by some thought to be near the extremities of Maurusia, **8.** 161

Nilometer, the, in Aegypt, **8.** 11, 13; construction and utility of, **8.** 127

Nîmes (see Namausus)

Nineveh (see Ninus)

Ninia, a city in Dalmatia, set on fire by Augustus, **3.** 261

Ninus (Nineveh), the city, founded by Ninus, **1.** 319; wiped out after the overthrow of the Syrians (608 B.C.), **7.** 193, 195; surrounded by the plains of Aturia, **7.** 197

Ninus, husband of Queen Semiramis and founder of Nineveh, called a Syrian, **1.** 319

Niobê, the, of Aeschylus, quoted, **5.** 519

Niobê, given in marriage to Amphion by her brother Pelops, **4.** 113; the home of, in Phrygia, **5.** 487

Nios (see Ios)

Niphates, Mt., a part of the Taurus, **5.** 299, 301, 305, 321

Nisa in Boeotia, the Homeric, no-

INDEX OF NAMES, PLACES, AND SUBJECTS

Notium in Chios, a shore suited to anchoring of vessels, **6**. 243

Notu-ceras, Cape, in southern Aethiopia, **7**. 333

Notus, the wind, **1**. 105, 125; does not blow in Aethiopia, **1**. 229

Novum Comum (see Comum)

Nubae, the, a large tribe in Libya, divided into several kingdoms, **8**. 7; situated to the south of Aegypt, **8**. 135

Nuceria (Nocera) Alfaterna, on the Sarnus River in Campania, **2**. 453, 461

Nuceria (Nocera) Camellaria, where the wooden utensils are made, **2**. 373

Nuestra Senora de Oreto (see Oria)

Numa Pompilius, successor of Romulus as king of Rome, came from Cures in the Sabine country, **2**. 375, 385

Numantia (Garray, near Soria) in Iberia, on the Durius River, **2**. 69, 101; renowned city of the Arvacans, **2**. 103

Numantini, the (see Nomantini)

Numidians, the (see Nomades in Masaesylia), **1**. 503

Numitor, joint ruler of Alba with Amulius, and later sole ruler, **2**. 381

Nuts, abundant in Themiscyra, **5**. 397; the food of the Heptacomitae, **5**. 401

Nycteus, father of Antiopê, and from Hyria in Boeotia founded Hysiae, **4**. 297

Nycticorax (night-crow), the, in Aegypt, of a peculiar species, **8**. 151

Nymphaeum, the, near Apollonia in Illyria; a rock that gives forth fire, and has beneath it springs of warm water and asphalt, with a mine of asphalt on a hill near by, **3**. 267

Nymphaeum (Kalati), a city in the Crimea, **3**. 237

Nymphaeum, the, in Syria, a kind of sacred cave, **7**. 249

Nymphaeum, Cape (see Athos), **3**. 353

Nymphs, grotto of, in island of Ithaca, no longer to be seen, because of physical changes, **4**. 49; temples of, in the neighbourhood of the Alpheius River, **4**. 49; are ministers of Dionysus, **5**. 97;

origin of, **5**. 111; called Cabeirides, worshipped in Samothrace, **5**. 115

Nysa in Caria, near Mt. Mesogis; territory of, on the far side of the Maeander, **6**. 185; description of, **6**. 257; famous natives of, **6**. 263; the road through, **6**. 309

Nysa, a village in Helicon, substituted by some editors for the Homeric "Nisa," **4**. 301

Nysa in India, said to have been founded by Dionysus, **7**. 11

Nysa, Mt., in India, sacred to Dionysus, **7**. 9, 11

Nysaei, the, a tribe in India, **7**. 47

O

Oak (the stunted oak, *Quercus coccifera*), grows at bottom of (Mediterranean) sea (?) and on dry land in Iberia, **2**. 37

Oak-tree, the sacred, at Dodona, **3**. 315, 317; transplanted from Thessaly, **3**. 321; revered because it was thought to be the earliest plant created and the first to supply men with food, **3**. 323

Oaracta, an isle in the Persian Gulf, ruled over by Mazenes, **7**. 305

Oases, the, in Libya; called "Auases," **1**. 501; three of, classed as subject to Aegypt, **8**. 23; their geographical position, **8**. 113

Obelisks, the, at Heliupolis and Thebes; two of, brought to Rome, **8**. 79

Ober-Laibach (see Nauportus)

Obidiaceni, the, a tribe of the Maeotae, **5**. 201

Obodas, king of the Nabataeans in Arabia, cared little about public affairs, **7**. 357, 363

Observatory, astronomical, of Eudoxus at Cnidus, **1**. 461; in Aegypt, **8**. 85

Obulco, through which runs the main road, **2**. 21; and where Julius Caesar arrived in 27 days from Rome, **2**. 97

Ocaleê (or Ocalea) in Boeotia, midway between Haliartus and Alalcomenium, 30 stadia from each, and near Lake Copaïs, **4**. 321

Ocean, the, movement of, subject to periods like those of the heavenly

INDEX OF NAMES, PLACES, AND SUBJECTS

bodies and in accord with the moon, **2.** 149; the Northern, **3.** 153

Oceanus, surrounds inhabited world, **1.** 5–19; extends along entire southern seaboard, **1.** 127; lies between the northern and southern hemispheres, **1.** 429

Ocelas, a companion of Antenor, founded Opsicella in Iberia, **2.** 83

Ocelum (Avigliana) in north-western Italy, the road to, **2.** 171, 327

" Ochê," a former name of Euboea, **5.** 7

Ochê (Hagios Elias), Mt., the largest mountain in Euboea, **5.** 7

Ochrida, Lake (see Lychnidus)

Ochus River, the; traverses Hyrcania, **5.** 253; oil found near, by digging, **5.** 285; different views as to identity of, **5.** 285, 287

Ochyroma, an acropolis above Ialysus in Rhodes, **6.** 279

Ocra (Alpis Julia, now Nanos), Mt., almost joins the Albian Mountain (Mt. Velika), **2.** 265, 287, 303; between Aquileia and Nauportus, **3.** 255

Ocricli (Otricoli), on the Flaminian Way, **2.** 367; near the Tiber, **2.** 371

Octavia, sister of Caesar and mother of Marcellus, **6.** 351

Ocypodes, the, in India, run faster than horses, **7.** 95

Odeium, the, at Athens, **4.** 265

Odessus (Varna), in Thrace, founded by the Milesians, **3.** 279, 369

Odius, the Homeric, leader of the Halizones, **5.** 403, 407, 409

Odomantes, the, in northern Greece, over whom Rhesus ruled, **3.** 359

Odomantis in Armenia; Artaxias the king of, **5.** 325

Odrysae, the, neighbours of the Bessi in Thrace, and by some defined as extending from the Hebrus to Odessus, **3.** 369, 371

Odrysses River, the, near Alazia, flows out of Lake Dascylitis through Mygdonia, **5.** 409

Odysseia, a city in Iberia, is sign that Odysseus wandered thither, **2.** 53, 83

Odysseium, a stream issuing from Lake Ismaris in Thrace, **3.** 367

Odysseus, as characterised by Homer, **1.** 61, 63; wanderings of, an historical fact, **1.** 73; the historical scene of his wanderings, **1.** 79, 85, 93; the wanderings of, to Italy, Sicily, Iberia, and other places, a traditional fact, signs of, **2.** 53–55; memorials of, in temple of Athenê at Odysseia in Iberia, **2.** 83; scene of wanderings of, transferred by Homer to the Atlantic, **2.** 85; transferred by Homer to Oceanus, **2.** 357, 359; a sort of bowl once belonging to, to be seen on the Circaeum in Italy, **2.** 393; visited the oracle of the dead at Avernus, **2.** 441; Baius, a companion of, **2.** 447; built a sanctuary of Athenê on the Cape of Sorrento, **2.** 455; Draco a companion of, **3.** 5; Polites a companion of, **3.** 15; wanderings of, placed by Homer in Oceanus, **3.** 193; went to Ephyra " in search of a man-slaying drug," **4.** 27; had the Cephallenians at his side at Troy, **4.** 255; all subjects of, called Cephallenians by Homer, **5.** 35, 49; Cephallenia subject to, **5.** 47, 49; in the *Odyssey* speaks of "the ninety cities " in Crete, **5.** 143; came in contact with no Greeks in his wanderings, **5.** 145; the feigned story of, to Eumaeus, about Ilium, **6.** 73; returned Chryseïs to her father, **6.** 125, 127; altar of, in Meninx, land of the lotus-eaters, **8.** 193

Odyssey, the, of Homer (see Homer)

Oeantheia (Galaxidi) in Western Locris, **4.** 387

Ocaso (Oyarzun) in Iberia at the western end of the Pyrenees, **2.** 99

Oechalia in Aetolia, near the Eurytanians, **5.** 17

Oechalia in Euboea, destroyed by Heracles, **5.** 17

Oechalia, whence Thamyris the Thracian came, **4.** 71, **5.** 17; " now called Andania " (now Sandani), **4.** 75, 115; " city of Eurytus," by historians placed in three different countries, **4.** 31, 433

Oechalia, the Trachinian, **5.** 17

Oechalia, near Triccê, **5.** 17

Oedanes River, the, in India, **7.** 125

Oedipus, said to have been reared by Polybus at Tenea, **4.** 199

Oeneiadae, Old and New, in Acarnania, **5.** 25, 61

412

INDEX OF NAMES, PLACES, AND SUBJECTS

413

INDEX OF NAMES, PLACES, AND SUBJECTS

INDEX OF NAMES, PLACES, AND SUBJECTS

INDEX OF NAMES, PLACES, AND SUBJECTS

Ophelas (or Ophellas) of Pella in Macedonia, ruler of Cyrenê (322–308 B.C.) and a historian; wrote a *Circumnavigation of Libya*, but added a number of fabrications, 8. 159

Ophians, the, in Aetolia, 5. 29

Ophiodes, an island in the Arabian Gulf; topaz found in, 7. 317

Ophiogeneis ("Serpent-born"), the, in the Troad; mythical story of, 6. 31

Ophiussa (Afsia), one of the Pityussae; description of, 2. 125

Ophiussa, an earlier name of Rhodes, 6. 273

Ophiussa, on the Tyras River, 3. 219

Ophlimus, Mt., in Asia, protects Phanaroea on the west, 5. 429

Ophrynium in the Troad, near which is the sacred precinct of Hector, 6. 59

Opici, the, once lived in Campania and are also called Ausones, 2. 435; ejected by the Sabini, 2. 465

Opis (to be identified, apparently, with Seleuceia); the village, about 200 stadia distant from the Euphrates, 1. 305; on the Tigris River, 5. 329; the Tigris River navigable to, 7. 205

Opisthomarathus in Phocis, near Anticyra, 4. 369

Opitergium (Oderzo) in Italy, 2. 317

Opsicella in Iberia, founded by Ocelas, a companion of Antenor, 2. 83

Opuntian Locrians, the, named after their metropolis Opus, 4. 343

Opuntians, the, in Elis, claim kinship with the Locrian Opuntians, 4. 379

Opuntians, Polity of the, by Aristotle, 3. 289

Opus (near Gardinitza), damaged by earthquake, 1. 225; the metropolis of the Epicnemidian Locrians, 4. 341; the pillar dedicated by, at Thermopylae; 15 stadia from the sea and 60 from Cynus its seaport; by Homer called the home of Patroclus, 4. 379

Oracle, the, of Zeus, at Dodona, deceived Alexander the Molossian, 3. 17; founded by the Pelasgians, now virtually extinct, 3. 313; given

out to the Tyrians on the founding of Gades, 2. 135; regarded by Poseidonius as a Phoenician lie, 2. 137; of the dead at Avernus, 2. 441, 443, 445; given out at Delphi to Archias, founder of Syracuse, and to Myscellus, founder of Croton, 3. 71; to Phalanthus, coloniser of Tarentum, 3. 109; in regard to the exchange of Delos for Calauria and Delphi for Cape Taenarum, 4. 173; "Blest is Corinth, but Tenea for me," 4. 199; ordering Xenophon to buy a plot of land for Artemis in Elis, 4. 223; at Dodona, advised the Boeotians to commit sacrilege, 4, 285; in regard to flashes of lightning through Harma, 4. 293; at Delphi, personally consulted by Agamemnon, 4. 347; of Apollo, on Mt. Ptoüs, 4. 329; of Trophonian Zeus at Lebadeia, 4. 333; at Delphi, described, 4. 353, the most truthful of all oracles, 4. 355; consulted by Croesus and other foreigners, 4. 357; devised by Apollo to help mankind, 4. 365; of Abae, in Phocis, 4. 369; given out to people of Aegium, meaning that the Chalcidians are the best of all fighters, 5. 21; for sleepers, at Aniaricê in Asia, 5. 251; in regard to the Pyramus River, 5. 355; of the Sibyl, requiring the Romans to bring to Italy certain statues from Galatia and Epidaurus, 5. 471; of Apollo Actaeus at Adrasteia, abolished, as also that at Zeleia, 6. 29; to the Teucrians, to remain "where the earth-born should attack them," 6. 95; at Ammon, and those of Sibylla, 8. 113

Oracles, the, at Delphi, given out in words, but, at the temple of Ammon and other places, mostly by nods and signs, 8. 115

Orange, in France (see Arausio)

Oratory, the Asiatic style of, initiated by Hegesias, 6. 253

Orbelus, Mt. (Perim-dagh), on the northern boundary of Macedonia, 3. 329

Orbis River, the, rises in the Cemmenus Mountain, 2. 183

416

INDEX OF NAMES, PLACES, AND SUBJECTS

Orcaorci, a town in Galatia; region of, cold and bare of trees, grazed by wild asses, and has extremely deep wells, 5. 473, 475

Orcheni, the, a tribe of the Chaldaean philosophers, 7. 203

Orchistenê, in Armenia, has a large cavalry, 5. 323

Orchomenians, the, called by Homer "Minyae," joined the Thebans and helped the Thebans to drive out the Pelasgians and the Thracians, 4. 283; Homer gives catalogue of, separating them from the Boeotians, 4. 335; Lake Copaïs dry ground and tilled in time of, 4. 339; emigrated when the waters overflowed the plain, 4. 341; Mt. Acontius lies near, and the Cephissus River flows through, 4. 375

Orchomenus (Kalpaki), the Arcadian, "abounding in flocks," 4. 29; no longer exists, 4. 229

Orchomenus (Skripu), the Boeotian, "Minyeian," 4. 29, 175; Chloris the mother of Nestor came from, 4. 63; the site of, 4. 305, 333; a fissure in the earth opened up near, admitting the Melas River, and the Cephissus River flows near, 4. 307; occupied by the Boeotians after the Trojan War, 4. 323; by Homer called "Minyeian," and extremely wealthy, 4. 335, 339

Orchomenus near Carystus in Euboea, 4. 341

Ordona (see Herdonia)

Oreitae, the, a tribe in Asia, 7. 129

Oreitae, the, in Euboea, formerly called Histiaeans; Philistides the tyrant of, 5. 7; fought by the Ellopians, 5. 9

Oreithyia, snatched up by Boreas the North Wind, 3. 175

Ores, found in mountains between the Anas and Tagus Rivers, 2. 25

Orestae, the, an Epeirote tribe, 3. 307, 327, 341; annexed to Macedonia, 4. 417

Orestes, son of Agamemnon, said to have occupied Orestias and left it bearing his name, and to have founded a city which he called Argos Oresticum, 3. 307; Tisamenus the son of, powerful king of Achaea,

4. 211; sons of, despatched the Aeolian fleet from Aulis to Asia, 4. 283; with Iphigeneia, thought to have brought sacred rites in honour of Artemis Tauropolus to Comana in Cappadocia, 5. 353, 359; first leader of the Aeolian colonisations, but died in Arcadia, 6. 7

Orestes, the, of Euripides, where "Argos" and "Mycenae" are used synonymously, 4. 187

Orestias, occupied by Orestes and so named by him, 3. 307; used to be called a part of Upper Macedonia, 3. 309; geographical position of, 3. 325; said to have been the earlier name of Pelagonia, 3. 363

Oretania, borders on Turdetania, 2. 19; cities of, Castalo and Oria, very powerful, 2. 65; mountain-chain in, 2. 81; traversed by the Baetis, 2. 101

Oretanians, the, in Iberia; geographical position of, 2. 13, 65, 81, 103; extend almost to Malaca, 2. 105

Oreus (Histiaea in early times, now Oreï) in Euboea; walls and houses of, collapsed because of earthquake, 1. 223; Philistides the tyrant of, and site and history of, 5. 7, 9

Oria, a district of Histiaeotis in Euboea, 5. 7

Oria (see Uria)

Oria (now, apparently, Nuestra Senora de Oreto), in Iberia; a powerful city, 2. 65

Oricum (Erico), in Illyria, 3. 267

Orion, the; the bird in India that has the sweetest voice, 7. 123

Orion, reared at Oreus in Euboea, 5. 9

Ormenium (or Orminium) in Thessaly; territory of, now regarded as belonging to Magnesia, 4. 407; inhabitants of, transferred to Demetrias, 4. 423; a village at the foot of Mt. Pelion, 27 stadia from Demetrias and 20 from Iolcus, 4. 433, and the home of Phoenix, 4. 435

Ormenus the king, grandfather of Phoenix; the different accounts of, 4. 435

Orminium (see Ormenium)

Ornaments, barbaric, of women in Iberia, 2. 109, 111

Orneae in Argolis; unknown to

Homer, and bears the same name as the city between Corinth and Sicyon, **4.** 183

Orneae near Corinth, now deserted, formerly well peopled and had a highly revered temple of Priapus, **4.** 205, **6.** 27

Orneiae, the Homeric (see Orneae), **4.** 185

Ornithes (" Birds "), City of (Ornithopolis), between Tyre and Sidon, **7.** 271

Ornithopolis (see Ornithes)

Oroatis River, the, in Persis, **7.** 155; about 2000 stadia from the Pasitigris, **7.** 163

Orobiae, or Orobia, in Euboea, now Rovias (destroyed by a tidal wave 426 B.C.), near Aegae, **4.** 297; where was an oracle of Apollo Selinuntius, **5.** 7

Orodes, the Parthian king, surnamed " Arsaces," **7.** 63, 237 (footnote 3)

Orontes, descendant of Hydarnes, once held Armenia, **5.** 337

Orontes River (Nahr-el-Asi), the (formerly called Typhon), flows underground for a distance between Apameia and Antiocheia, **3.** 93; 1130 stadia from Orthosia, **6.** 333; course of, **6.** 357; in Syria, **7.** 243; course of, **7.** 245, 247, 249, 251; sources of, **7.** 265

Oropus, on the common boundary of Attica and Boeotia; has often been disputed territory, **1.** 245, **4.** 273; across the strait 40 stadia from Eretria, **4.** 289, 291; temple of Amphiaraüs and monument of Narcissus near, **4.** 293

Oros, Hieron (see Hieron Oros)

Orospeda, the mountain, in Iberia; geographical position of, **2.** 97

Orpheus, lived at Pimpleia in southern Macedonia; wizard, musician, and soothsayer, **3.** 339; Thamyris the Thracian like, **3.** 357; the rites of, originated among the Thracians, **5.** 105; a Thracian himself, **5.** 109; a prophet often consulted, **7.** 289

Orphic arts, the, **5.** 121

Orris-root (see Iris, the Selgic)

Orthagoria in Thrace, **3.** 367

Orthagoras, says the isle Ogyris lies 2000 stadia from Carmania, **7.** 305

Orthanês, Attic deity similar to Priapus, **6.** 29

Orthê, the Homeric, subject to Polypoetes, **4.** 437; by some called the acropolis of the Phalannaeans, **4.** 439

Orthopolis, a city in Macedonia, **3.** 361

Orthosia in Caria, **6.** 261

Orthosia in Phoenicia, **7.** 255, 259, 265; 3650 stadia from Pelusium and 1130 from the Orontes River, **7.** 281

Orthosia in Syria, 3900 stadia from Pelusium, **6.** 333

Ortilochus, the home of, in Pherae, visited by Telemachus, **4.** 147

Orton (Ortona), the port-town of the Frentani, **2.** 433

Ortospana in Asia; geographical position of, **5.** 271

" Ortygia," name of nurse at travail of Leto, **6.** 223

Ortygia, a grove above Ephesus, said to be the scene of the travail of Leto, whose nurse was named " Ortygia," **6.** 223

Ortygia, the earlier name of Rheneia, the desert isle near Delos, **5.** 167

Ortygia, the island off Syracuse, **3.** 75, 79

Osca (Huesca), in Iberia; geographical position of, and where Sertorius was killed, **2.** 99

Oscan tribe, the Sidicini an, **2.** 435

Osci, the; country and dialect of, **2.** 395; have disappeared, **2.** 413; the mountains of, **2.** 435; once held Herculaneum and Pompeii, **2.** 453

Osimo (see Auxumum)

Osiris, the asylum of, in Aegypt, **8.** 73; mythical story of, **8.** 75; same as the bull Apis, **8.** 87; rites at temple of, **8.** 117

Osismii (Ostimii), the, live on a promontory in Celtica, **2.** 237

Ossa, Mt., in Greece, broken off from Olympus, **1.** 223; neighbourhood of, once inhabited by the Aenianians, **1.** 227; compared with the Alps, **2.** 293; belongs to Thessaly, **3.** 335; held by Demetrias, **4.** 393, 425; split off from Mt. Olympus by earthquakes, **4.** 397; the Dotian Plain lies near, **4.** 449; the voyage along coast of, long and rough, **4.** 451

INDEX OF NAMES, PLACES, AND SUBJECTS

distance from, to Criumetopon in Crete and to Strait of Sicily, **1.** 407; one of the three capes of Sicily, **3.** 55, 57; 50 Roman miles from Camarina and 36 from Syracuse, **3.** 59; 4000 stadia from the Alpheius, **3.** 61; 4600 stadia from Cape Taenarum, **4.** 127

Pacorus (eldest son of Orodes the king of Parthia, with Labienus overran Syria and part of Asia Minor, but was defeated in 39 B.C. by Ventidius, a legate of Antony. Again invaded Syria but fell in battle there); reverses of, **7.** 237; killed by Ventidius, **7.** 247

Pactolus River, the, rises in Mt. Tmolus, **5.** 421; once brought down quantities of gold-dust, **6.** 173

Pacton, a boat made of withes, used at Philae, an isle in the Nile, **8.** 131

Pactyë on the Propontis, **3.** 373, 375, 377

Pactyes, Mt., in the territory of Ephesus, **6.** 249

Padua (see Patavium)

Padus (Po) River, the, **2.** 271; the largest of all European rivers except the Ister, **2.** 227, 271, 273, 295, 307, 309, 311, 313, 327, 329, 435

Paean, the, to Apollo, originated at the slaying of the Python by Apollo at Delphi, **4.** 127

Paeanismos, the, of the Thracians, called *titanismos* by the Greeks, **3.** 363

Paeans, the Cretic, invented by Thales, **5.** 147; adopted at Sparta, **5.** 151

Paeonia, boundaries of, **3.** 251, 275, 325, 333; land of, contains gold nuggets, **3.** 355; the Axius and Strymon Rivers flow from, **3.** 361; traditions about, **3.** 363

Paeonians, the, in Asia, mentioned by Homer, **6.** 117; in Trojan battles, **6.** 151

Paeonians, the, a Thracian tribe, lived in Amphaxitis, *i.e.* on both sides of the Axius River, **3.** 331, 333, 341, 345; in early times, as now, occupied much of Macedonia, **3.** 363

Paerisades (see Parisades)

Paeseni, the, in the Troad, changed their abode to Lampsacus, **6.** 35

Paestan Gulf, the (see Poseidonian Gulf)

Paesus (or Apaesus), a city and river between Parium and Lampsacus, **6.** 35; former colonised by Milesians, **6.** 207

Pagae (Psatho), a stronghold in Megaris, nearly 530 stadia from Peiraeus, **4.** 197, 243; situated in the inmost recess of the Corinthian Gulf, **4.** 317

Pagasae (Angistri) in Thessaly, seaport of Pherae, and 90 stadia from it, **4.** 423

Pagasitic Gulf, the; position of, on the Aegaean, **3.** 353, **4.** 425, 433

Pago, one of the Liburnides, **3.** 259

Pagrae, a stronghold near Antiocheia in Syria, **7.** 247

Palacium, a fort in the Crimea (site unknown), built by Scilurus and his sons, **3.** 247

Palacus, son of Scilurus, a prince in the Tauric Chersonese, assisted by the Roxolani in his war against Mithridates, **3.** 223, 235

"Palae," apparently a native Iberian word for "nuggets," **2.** 41

Palaea in Asia, 130 stadia from Andeira, **6.** 131

Palaea, a town in Cypros, **6.** 379

Palaea-Akhaia (see Olenus in Achaea)

Palaebyblus (Old Byblus) in Syria, **7.** 263

Palaeo-Episcopi (see Gomphi)

Palaeo-Episcopi (see Tegea)

Palaeokastro in Euboea (see Eretria)

Palaeokastro (see Lilaea in Phocis)

Palaeokastro near Navarino (see Pylus, the Messenian)

Palaeokastro (see Thuria)

Palaeopoli near Klituras (see Cleitor)

Palaeopoli (see Mantineia)

Palaepaphos in Cypros, where is a temple of the Paphian Aphroditê, **6.** 381

Palaephaetus, author of a work *On Incredible Things*; opinions of, approved by Demetrius of Scepsis, **5.** 407; on the Homeric Halizones, **5.** 409

Palaepharsalus in Thessaly; Pompey fled from, to Aegypt, **8.** 47

Palaerus in Acarnania, **5.** 25, 61

Palaescepsis (Old Scepsis), in the

INDEX OF NAMES, PLACES, AND SUBJECTS

Troad, **6.** 89, 91, 101; lay near the highest part of Mt. Ida, but its inhabitants were removed to the present Scepsis, 60 (260?) stadia lower down, **6.** 105

Palaestine, whither Minaeans and Gerrhaeans convey their aromatics, **7.** 343

Palamedes, The, of Euripides, quoted, **5.** 103

Palamedes, the son of Nauplius, **4.** 151

Palatium, the, walled by the first founders of Rome, **2.** 399; the works of art on, **2.** 409

Paleis, a city in Cephallenia, **5.** 47, 49, 51

Palermo (see Panormus)

Palestrina (see Praeneste)

Palibothra (or Palimbothra) in India, on the Ganges River, **7.** 17, 125; description of, **7.** 63

Palici, the, territory of, in Sicily, has craters that spout up water, **3.** 91

Palinthus (Plinthus ?), the name of the tomb of Danaüs at Argos, **4.** 163

Palinuro, Cape (see Palinurus)

Palinurus (Palinuro), Cape of, in Italy, **3.** 5

Paliurus, in Cyrenaea, **8.** 207

Pallades, or *pallacides* ("dedicated maidens"), the, at Aegyptian Thebes, **8.** 125

Pallantia (Palencia), in Iberia, belongs to the Arvacans, **2.** 103

Pallas, "breeder of giants," son of King Pandion, received southern Atthis (Attica) from his father, **4.** 247, 249

Pallenē (in earlier times called Phlegra, but now Kassandra), the Macedonian peninsula, **3.** 349; where the Trojan women set on fire the ships of their Greek captors, **3.** 351; colonised by the Eretrians, **5.** 13

Palm, the; most abundant in Babylonia, at Susa, and on the coast of Persis and Carmania, **7.** 201; 360 uses of, **7.** 215; limited cultivation of, by Judaeans, in order to increase revenues, **8.** 61; in general not of good species in Aegypt, though good in Judaea, **8.** 133; found in abundance in Aethiopia, **8.** 145

Palma, a city on the larger of the Gymnesiae, **2.** 125

Palm-trees, great grove of, in Plain of Jericho, **7.** 291; abundant in region of Cape Deirê in Aethiopia, **7.** 331; excellent grove of, near Cape Poseidium on the Arabian Gulf, **7.** 341

Palms, the sweet-smelling, in Arabia, **7.** 347

Palmys, the Homeric, led forces from Ascania, **5.** 461

Paltus in Syria, where Memnon was buried, **7.** 159, 255

Pamboeotian Festival, the, held at the temple of Athenê near Coroneia, **4.** 325

Pamisus (Mavrozumenos) River, the, flows in Messenia, and is not the boundary between Laconia and Messenia, as Euripides says, **4.** 87, 117, 143

Pamisus River, the, a torrential stream flowing near the Laconian Leuctrum, **4.** 119

Pamisus (or Amathus) River, the, in Triphylia, flows past the Lepreatic Pylus, **4.** 21, 31, 51, 119

Pamphylia in Asia; the Chelidoniae Islands at beginning of coast of, **5.** 295; borders on Lycia, **6.** 311; description of, **6.** 323–325

Pamphylian Sea, the, **1.** 481; boundaries of, **6.** 375

Pamphylians, the, in Asia, not mentioned by Homer, **5.** 423, **6.** 363; do not wholly abstain from piracy, **5.** 481; engaged in piracy, and gained mastery of the sea as far as Italy, **6.** 313; said to be descendants of the peoples led from Troy by Calchas and Amphilochus, **6.** 325

Pan, the god, worshipped at Mendes in Aegypt, **8.** 69; and at Meroê, **8.** 147

Panaenus, the painter, assisted his uncle Pheidias in making the image of Zeus in the temple at Olympia, and also made many paintings therefor, **4.** 89

Panaetius the philosopher; Apollonius of Nysa the best of disciples of, **6.** 263; native of Rhodes, **6.** 279; reputed to have been pupil of Crates of Mallus, **6.** 355

Panaria (see Euonymus)

421

INDEX OF NAMES, PLACES, AND SUBJECTS

Panchaea, the Land of, an invention reported by Euhemerus, **3.** 191

Pandareus (see Pandarus), the Homeric, said to have been from Lycia, **6.** 317

Pandarus, the Homeric; Lycia subject to, **5.** 461; "glorious son of Lycaon" and leader of the Lycians in the Trojan War, **6.** 19; worshipped at Pinara in Lycia, and identified with the Homeric Pandareus, **6.** 317

Pandateria (Ventotene), small island opposite Minturnae in Italy, **1.** 473, **2.** 399

Pandion, king of Atthis (Attica), **4.** 247; father of the Lycus who settled in Lycia, **5.** 493, **6.** 323

Pandion, the king, in India, sent gifts to Augustus Caesar, **7.** 5

Pandora, the mother of Deucalion; southern Thessaly named after, **4.** 453

Pandosia (Castel Franco or Anglona?), in Bruttium; a strong fortress, where Alexander the Molossian was killed, **3.** 17

Pandosia (Kastri) in Thesprotia, **3.** 17, 301

Paneium (Sanctuary of Pan), the, at Alexandria; description of, **8.** 41

Pangaeum (Pirnari), Mt., near Philippi in Macedonia, has gold and silver mines, **3.** 355, 363; mines at, source of wealth of Cadmus, **6.** 369

"Panhellenes," critics in dispute about meaning of term, **4.** 157

Pan-Ionian festival, the, at Panionium in Asia, **6.** 221

Pan-Ionian sacrifices, the, in Asia Minor, **4.** 213

Panionium, the, on the seaboard of the Ephesians, where the Pan-Ionian festival is held, and where sacrifices are performed in honour of the Heliconian Poseidon, **6.** 221

Panitza River (see Inachus, in the Argolid)

Panna, a Samnite city, **2.** 463

Pannonia, description of, **3.** 253

Pannonians, the; country of, **2.** 289; names of tribes of, and position of territory of, **3.** 257, 271

Panopeans, the; boundary of territory of, **4.** 373

Panopeus (or Phanoteus, *q.v.*) in Phocis, lies above the territory of Orchomenus, **4.** 341; near Lebadeia, native land of Epeius, and scene of the myth of Tityus, **4.** 371

Panopolis, an old settlement of linen-workers, **8.** 111

Panormo (see Panormus)

Panormus, the harbour, near Ephesus, where is a temple of Ephesian Artemis, **6.** 223

Panormus (Panormo), the seaport of Oricum (Eriko), in Illyria, **3.** 267; a large harbour at centre of the Ceraunian Mountains, **3.** 299

Panormus (Palermo) in Sicily, 35 Roman miles from the Himera River, **3.** 57; has a Roman settlement, **3.** 81

Pans, the, with wedge-shaped heads, **1.** 263; attendants of Dionysus, **5.** 105

Pantaleon, the Pisatan general, who joined the Messenians in the Second Messenian War, **4.** 123

Pantellaria (see Cossura)

Panticapaeum (Kertch), the metropolis of the Bosporians; the frosts at, **1.** 277; a colony of the Milesians, long ruled as a monarchy, **3.** 237; the greatest emporium, **3.** 239; founded by the Greeks, **5.** 197; metropolis of the European Bosporians, **5.** 199

Panxani, the; a nomadic tribe between Lake Maeotis and the Caspian Sea, **5.** 243

Panypertatê, meaning of, in Homer as applied to Ithaca, **5.** 41, 43

Paphlagonia, the Heneti of, settled a colony in Italy, **2.** 235, 307; the Cauconiatae in, identified with the Cauconians who came as allies of the Trojans, **4.** 55; borders on Cappadocia, **5.** 345; certain parts of, once held by Mithridates Eupator, **5.** 371; certain places in, **5.** 449–453; Deïotarus, son of Castor and surnamed Philadelphus, the last king of, **5.** 453

Paphlagonian kings, the; line of, failed, **3.** 145

Paphlagonians, the, not mentioned by Homer, **3.** 189; the Eneti (or Heneti) the most notable tribe of,

INDEX OF NAMES, PLACES, AND SUBJECTS

INDEX OF NAMES, PLACES, AND SUBJECTS

summer at Ecbatana and in Hyrcania, **7**. 219

Parthian War, the, **5**. 437

Parthians, the; have added to knowledge of geography, **1**. 49; geographical position of, **1**. 499; have now yielded to the pre-eminence of the Romans, **3**. 145; have sent to Rome the trophies of their former victory, **3**. 147; the supremacy of, disclosed more geographical knowledge, **5**. 247; once ruler over Hyrcania, **5**. 253; Hecatompylus the royal seat of, **5**. 273; the Council of, described, **5**. 277; wrested the satrapies Turiva and Aspionus away from Eucratides, **5**. 281; use Ecbatana as summer-residence for their kings, **5**. 303, 307; wont to plunder Atropatian Media, **5**. 305; joined Labienus against Mylasa in Caria, **6**. 297; got possession of region on far side of the Euphrates, **6**. 329, 331; give the surname " Arsaces " to all their kings, **7**. 63; geographical position of, **7**. 145; now rule over the Persians, **7**. 159; present empire of, **7**. 173, 233; now rule over the Medes and Babylonians, but never once over the Armenians, **7**. 225; friendly towards the Romans, but defended themselves against Crassus, and later sent to Augustus the trophies of their victory, **7**. 237

Parthica, The, of Apollodorus, **7**. 5

Parthini, the, an Illyrian tribe, **3**. 307

Partridge, the, famous painting of, at Rhodes, by Protogenes, **6**. 269, 271; larger than a vulture, sent to Augustus by King Porus in India, **7**. 127

Partridges, the, in India, as large as geese, **7**. 95

Paryadres, Mt., in Asia, **5**. 209, 299; geographical position of, **5**. 319, 401; contained several fortified treasuries of Mithridates, **5**. 425; protects Phanaroea, **5**. 429

Parysatis, by barbarians called Pharziris, **7**. 373

Pasargadae, royal palace, treasures, and tombs at, **7**. 159; description of tomb of Cyrus at, **7**. 165

Pasiani, the, in Asia, helped to take away Bactriana from the Greeks, **5**. 261

Pasitigris River, the; the name of the Tigris River at its outlets, **7**. 161, 163

Passo di Civita (see Teanum Apulum)

Patala, a notable city in India, **7**. 59

Patalenê in India, occupied by Euthydemus the king of Bactria, **5**. 281; similar to the Delta of Aegypt, **7**. 19, 25; is an island, **7**. 57

Patara in Lycia, has a temple of Apollo; by Ptolemy Philadelphus named the Lycian Arsinoê, **6**. 317

Patarus, founder of Patara in Lycia, **6**. 317

Patavium (Padua), like Gadeira, has 500 knights, **2**. 131; an important city, **2**. 313; region of, produces wool of medium quality, **2**. 333

Pateischoreis, the, a tribe in Persis, **7**. 157

Patmos, the isle, **5**. 173

Patrae (Patras), made up of seven communities, **4**. 23; member of a new league after the dissolution of the Achaean League, **4**. 211; one of the 12 Achaean cities, **4**. 219; where the Romans settled a large part of the army after the Battle of Actium; a very populous city, and has a fairly good anchoring-place, **4**. 225

Patraeus, a village on the Cimmerian Bosporus, **5**. 197, 199

Patras (see Patrae)

Patrocles (about 312–261 B.C.); Macedonian general under Seleucus I and Antiochus I, explorer, author of geographical treatises now lost, and regarded as trustworthy by Strabo, **1**. 259, 261, 265; on the distance from the southern capes of India to the Caucasus Mountains, **1**. 255; discredited by Hipparchus, **1**. 257, 261; governor in the Orient, **1**. 281; on the Cadusii and the Caspian Sea, **5**. 251; on the Oxus River, **5**. 253; says the mouths of the Oxus and Iaxartes Rivers are 80 parasangs distant from one another, **5**. 287; on the possible voyages from India to Hyrcania, **5**. 289; on the length of India, **5**. 17

425

INDEX OF NAMES, PLACES, AND SUBJECTS

INDEX OF NAMES, PLACES, AND SUBJECTS

427

INDEX OF NAMES, PLACES, AND SUBJECTS

INDEX OF NAMES, PLACES, AND SUBJECTS

429

INDEX OF NAMES, PLACES, AND SUBJECTS

intermingled with the Lapiths, according to Simonides, **4.** 445; lived about Mt. Pelion and the Peneius, **4.** 447; little or no trace of, now preserved, **4.** 449; carried off the Histiaeans of Euboea into Thessaly, **5.** 9

Persea, a luscious fruit in Aethiopia, **7.** 331; the tree in Aethiopia, **8.** 145, and in Aegypt, **8.** 149

Persephonê (see Corê), the festival of, **1.** 377; endowed Teiresias with reason after his death, **7.** 289

Persepolis, 4200 stadia from Susa, **7.** 157; royal palace, treasures, and tombs at, **7.** 159; second only to Susa, **7.** 165

Perseus, king of Macedonia, overthrown by Paulus Aemilius, **3.** 143, 293, 345; captured by Paulus, **3.** 369; rased Haliartus to the ground, **4.** 129; son of Philip V the son of Demetrius II, **5.** 457; fought by the Romans and Eumenes II, **6.** 167

Perseus, the ancient, father of Helius, **4.** 129; founded Mycenae, **4.** 185; rescued by Dictys at Seriphos, **5.** 171; father of Erythras, **7.** 351; the Watchtower of, in Aegypt, **8.** 67; said to have visited the temple of Ammon, **8.** 115

Perseus, the constellation; star on the right elbow of, slightly to north of arctic circle, at 1400 stadia north of the Pontus, **1.** 515

Persia, geographical position of, **1.** 499; annual tributes paid to, by Cappadocia and Media, **5.** 313

Persian battle, the, at Marathon, **4.** 263; near Plataeae, **4.** 287

Persian fleet, the, destroyed at Cape Sepias in Magnesia, **4.** 451

Persian Gates, the, passed through, by Alexander, **7.** 163

Persian Gulf (or Persian Sea), the; one of the four large gulfs, **1.** 467; the Euphrates and Tigris Rivers empty into, **5.** 297; spouting whales in, **7.** 149; can be crossed in one day at its mouth, **7.** 155; borders on Babylonia, **7.** 203; description of, **7.** 301–303; borders on Arabia, **8.** 3

Persian Letters, the, on the straightforward character of the Scythians, **3.** 201

Persian Sea (see Persian Gulf)

Persian War, the; meteor fell at Aegospotami during, **3.** 377; the sea-fight at Salamis in time of, **4.** 179

Persians, the; blundered from ignorance of geography, **1.** 35; 300,000 wiped out by the Greeks at Plataeae, **4.** 325; for a time withstood by Leonidas at Thermopylae, **4.** 393; most of customs of, imitated by the Siginni, **5.** 293; overthrown by the Macedonians, **5.** 307; once ruled over Armenia, **5.** 337; sacred rites of, followed by the Medes and Armenians, **5.** 341; divided Cappadocia into two satrapies, **5.** 349; once held mastery in Asia Minor after Trojan War, **5.** 463; onsets of, in Asia, **5.** 495; hanged Hermeias the pupil and friend of Aristotle, **6.** 117; built an arcade of white marble on Mt. Tmolus near Sardeis, **6.** 173; named the "Hyrcanian Plain" and the "Plain of Cyrus," **6.** 185; once captured Miletus, **6.** 209; hanged Polycrates the powerful tyrant of Samos (522 B.C.), **6.** 217; said to have deposited treasures in the temple of Artemis at Ephesus, **6.** 227; once ruled over Ariana, **7.** 15, 129; language and customs of, used by the Carmanians, **7.** 155; country, customs, and history of, **7.** 155–189; established royal seat of their empire at Susa, **7.** 157; now subject to the king of the Parthians, **7.** 159; once collected tributes from all Asia, **7.** 163; conquered by Alexander, **7.** 165, 169; customs and worship of, **7.** 175–187; the hegemony of, over Asia, lasted 250 years, **7.** 189; overthrew the Medes, **7.** 195; ruined Babylon, **7.** 199; constructed cataracts in the Euphrates and Tigris to prevent navigation, **7.** 205; seized Phoenicia, **7.** 257; used Ptolemaïs in Phoenicia as base of operations against Aegypt, **7.** 271; revere the Magi and other diviners, **7.** 289; wont to guide ambassadors treacherously, **8.** 71

Persica, The, of Baton the Sinopean, **5.** 391

INDEX OF NAMES, PLACES, AND SUBJECTS

431

INDEX OF NAMES, PLACES, AND SUBJECTS

432

INDEX OF NAMES, PLACES, AND SUBJECTS

INDEX OF NAMES, PLACES, AND SUBJECTS

435

INDEX OF NAMES, PLACES, AND SUBJECTS

INDEX OF NAMES, PLACES, AND SUBJECTS

INDEX OF NAMES, PLACES, AND SUBJECTS

Phthiotis, one of the four divisions of Thessaly, **4.** 397, 409, 411, 413, 419, 421, 423, 429

Phycus (Ras-al-Razat), Cape, in Cyrenaca, 3000 stadia from Cape Taenarum, **4.** 127, **8.** 201

Phylacè in Phthiotis, subject to Protesilaüs, and about 100 stadia from Thebes, **4.** 411, 421

Phylè, deme of Attica, whence Thrasybulus brought back the popular party to Peiraeus and Athens, **4.** 263; borders on Tanagra, **4.** 293

Phyleus, brought the corselet of Meges from Ephyra (Homer), **4.** 27; son of Augeas and father of Meges, **5.** 49, 59

Phyllus in Thessaly, where is the temple of Phyllian Apollo, **4.** 421

Physa, the, a fish indigenous to the Nile, **8.** 149

Physcus, in the Peraea of the Rhodians, 850 stadia from Lagina, **6.** 267, 307; 1180 stadia from the Maeander, **6.** 309

Physicians, the hiring of, at Massalia, **2.** 179; commend the Lagaritan wine, **3.** 49; the, in India, **7.** 103, 105

Physics, the principles of, introduced by Eratosthenes into geography, **1.** 233; division of earth into five zones in harmony with, **1.** 369; views of Poseidonius on, **1.** 397; fundamental to astronomy and geography, being a science which postulates nothing, and one of the three most important, **1.** 423; teachings of, in regard to the earth, **1.** 425

Physics, the treatises on, by Poseidonius and Hipparchus, **4.** 3

Pianosa, the island (see Planasia)

Piasus, ruler of the Pelasgians, honoured at Phriconian Larisa, and violated his daughter Larisa, but was killed by her, **6.** 157

Picentes, the; country of, extends to the Silaris River, **2.** 469; ejected by the Romans, **2.** 471

Picentia (Vicenza), capital of the Picentes, **2.** 471

Picentine country, the (Picenum), **2.** 373

Picentini, the; colonists from the Sabini, **2.** 377, 427; a small offshoot (Picentes) of, on the Poseidonian Gulf, **2.** 469

Picenum, description of, **2.** 427–433

Picrum Hydor, a river in Cilicia, **6.** 337

Pictae, the Inns of (Ad Pictas), on the Latin Way, **2.** 411

Pictones, the, a tribe in Aquitania, **2.** 215, 217

Picus (" Woodpecker "), a, led the way for colonisers of Picenum, **2.** 427

Pieria (see Pieris), in Thrace, **3.** 331, 335, 341, 345, 363; the Muses worshipped at, **5.** 107

Pierians, the, a Thracian tribe, inhabited Pieria and the region about Olympus, **3.** 331; dedicated places to the Muses, **4.** 319

Pieris, the land of Pieria in Macedonia, consecrated by Thracians to the Muses, **4.** 319

Pigeons (see Doves), the sacred, at Dodona, **3.** 323

Pikes, used as weapons by some of the Aethiopians, **8.** 139

Pillars, the, of Heracles (see Heracles); the strait at, 120 stadia long, and 60 wide where it is narrowest, **8.** 165

Pilus, the Median, **5.** 313

Pimoliseně in Cappadocia Pontica, **5.** 447

Pimolitis in Cappadocia, **5.** 417

Pimpla; the Muses were worshipped at, **5.** 107

Pimpleia, a village in southern Macedonia, where Orpheus lived, **3.** 339; consecrated by Thracians to the Muses, **4.** 319

Pinara in Lycia, member of the Lycian League, **6.** 315; a large city, **6.** 317

Pinarus River, the, in Cilicia, **6.** 355

Pindar, the lyric poet, of Thebes; a proverb quoted from, **1.** 85; on offering hecatombs, **2.** 75; on the " Gates of Gades," meaning the " Pillars of Heracles," **2.** 137, 143; on the caverns and fire beneath the region of Italy and Sicily, **2.** 457; calls Hiero the founder of Aetna, **3.** 67; on the Alpheius River and the fountain Arethusa, **3.** 75; says the Boeotian tribe was once called Syes (" Swine "), **3.** 287; on the

INDEX OF NAMES, PLACES, AND SUBJECTS

439

INDEX OF NAMES, PLACES, AND SUBJECTS

INDEX OF NAMES, PLACES, AND SUBJECTS

founding cities as far as possible from the sea, 3. 205; in his *Phaedrus* lauds the fountain above the Lyceium from which the Ilissus flows, 4. 277; calls philosophy "music," 5. 95; mentions the "Bendideian" rites, 5. 109; on the three stages in civilisation, 6. 47, 49; teacher of Hermeias the tyrant, 6. 117; comrade of Eudoxus of Cnidus, 6. 283; on the immortality of the soul and the judgments in Hades, 7. 103; says that King Minos received his laws from Zeus every nine years, 7. 287; on the Nile and the Aegyptian Delta, 8. 13; spent 13 years with the priests at Heliupolis, 8. 83; learned some of their doctrines, 8. 85

Pleiad, the; the setting of, 8. 153

Pleiades, the, the setting of, in India, 7. 25, 27

Pleiades, the seven daughters of Atlas; the scene of the story of, a cave in Triphylia, 4. 59

Pleias, the; contains a list of the seven Pleiades, *i.e.* the seven great tragic poets, 6. 353

Pleistus River, the, flows in the ravine in front of Delphi, 4. 351

Plemyrium, a city in India, 7. 45

Plentuisans, the; some unknown tribe in Iberia which "now takes the field for the Romans," 2. 79

Pleraei, the, live about the Naro River in Dalmatia, 3. 261; situated near the island Black Corcyra, 3. 263

Pleuron in Aetolia, Old and New, once an ornament to Greece, 5. 27, 63; held the level country, 5. 65; Thestius the king of, 5. 69; mentioned by Homer, 5. 75; subject to Agrius, and occupied by the Curetes, 5. 85

Pleutaurans, the; a tribe in Iberia of no importance, 2. 77

Plinthinê, a place on the coast to the east of Alexandria, 8. 57

Plinthus (see Palinthus)

Plough, a wooden, used in Albania in Asia, 5. 225

Plumbaria, a small island off eastern Iberia, 2. 89

Plutiades the philosopher, a native of Tarsus, 6. 351

Pluto, jokingly confused with Plutus (the god of riches), 2. 43

Plutonia, the, where rise mephitic vapours, 2. 443

Plutonium, the, at Hierapolis in Phrygia; detailed description of, 6. 187; at Acharaca in Caria, 6. 259

Plutus (see Pluto)

Plynus Harbour, the, in Cyrenaea, 8. 207

Pneuentia, in Picenum, 2. 429

Pnigeus, a village on coast of Aegypt, 8. 57

Podaleirius, the temple of, in Daunia, whence flows a stream that is a cure-all for diseases of animals, 3. 131

Podanala (see Danala)

Podarces, marshal of the forces of Philoctetes at Troy, 4. 407

Poeäessa, temple of Athena Nedusia at, 4. 115

Poecilê, the colonnade called, at Athens, 4. 265 (see footnote 2)

Poecilê in Cilicia, 6. 337

Poedicli, the (see Peucetii)

Poeëessa in Ceos, 5. 169

Poemandrians, the; another name of the Tanagraeans, 4. 293

Poeninus (Pennine Alps), the; the road through, 2. 277, 289, 291

Poet, the aim of the, 1. 23, 55

Poetry, a kind of elementary philosophy, 1. 55; compared with prose, 1. 65; the source and origin of style, 1. 65; used in disciplining every period of life, 1. 71; that of Homer greatest of all, 1. 99; aim of, 1. 137; myths appropriate to, 3. 315; as a whole, laudatory of the gods, 5. 95

Pogon, the harbour of Troezen, 4. 173

Pola, or Polae, an Italian city, built by Colchians, 1. 169, 2. 323; an Istrian city, now included within the boundaries of Italy, 3. 257

Polae in Italy (see Pola)

Pole, the north; the limit of the northerly peoples, 1. 231; distance from, to equator, a fourth part of earth's largest circle, 1. 429; is the most northerly point of the sky, 5. 45

Polemon (d. 273 B.C.), eminent

441

INDEX OF NAMES, PLACES, AND SUBJECTS

Athenian philosopher, and teacher of Zeno and Arcesilaüs, **6.** 131

Polemon of Troas, the famous Periegete (fl. about 200 B.C.); among other works wrote one on Athens. His works, now lost, were rich with information for travellers and students of art and archaeology; says that Eratosthenes the geographer never saw even Athens, **1.** 53; wrote four books on the " dedicatory offerings on the acropolis at Athens alone," **4.** 263

Polemon I, son of Zeno the rhetorician of Laodiceia, possessed Iconium in Lycaonia, **5.** 475; thought worthy of a kingdom by Antony and Augustus, **5.** 511; became king of the Cimmerian Bosporus (about 16 B.C.); sacked the city Tanaïs because of its disobedience, **5.** 193; caught alive and killed by the Aspurgiani, **5.** 201; married Queen Pythodoris and acquired Colchis, **5.** 213, 427

Polemon II, assists his mother, Pythodoris the queen, **5.** 427

Polentia (Polenzo), a city on the larger of the Gymnesiae, **2.** 125

Poles, the; elevations of, **1.** 45

Policastro (see Pyxus)

Polichna in the Troad, enclosed by walls, **6.** 89, 91; near Palaescepsis, **6.** 105

Polichnê in Megaris, **4.** 255

Polieium (see Siris)

Polisma (see Polium)

Polites, a companion of Odysseus; hero-temple of, near Temesa in Bruttium, **3.** 15

Polites, the Trojan sentinel, **6.** 75

Polities, the, of Aristotle, of which only fragments remain, on the Leleges of Ionia, and their conquests and settlements in Greece, **3.** 289

Polium (now Polisma) in the Troad, **6.** 83

Pollina (see Apollonia in Illyria)

Pollux, and Castor (see Dioscuri)

Polyandrium, the, at Thermopylae, where five pillars with inscriptions were dedicated to the fallen, **4.** 379, 393

Polyanus, Mt., in north-western Greece, **3.** 311

Polybius of Megalopolis in Arcadia (b. about 204 B.C.); author of *Histories* in 40 books, of which only the first five are extant in complete form, and of a geographical treatise, which is thought to be identical with the 34th book of his *Histories*; a philosopher, **1.** 3; praised by Strabo, **1.** 53; on the mythical element in Homer, **1.** 73; holds correct views about the wanderings of Odysseus and about King Aeolus, **1.** 85; divides the earth into six zones, **1.** 367; wrongly defines some zones by arctic circles, **1.** 371; calls country at equator temperate, **1.** 373; discredits Pytheas, **1.** 399; on certain distances in the Mediterranean basin, **1.** 401; on certain distances in the Sicilian Sea and the Adriatic Gulf, **1.** 405; makes false calculations, **1.** 407; corrects Eratosthenes' estimates of distances, **1.** 409; on the length of the Tagus River, **1.** 411; introduces new method in estimating length of three continents, **1.** 415; makes serious errors in regard to Europe and in his description of Libya, **3.** 251; says the Turdulians (in Iberia) are neighbours of the Turdetanians on the north, **2.** 13; on the food (acorns) of the tunny-fish, **2.** 39; on the silver-mines at New Carthage, **2.** 47; says the Baetis and the Anas rise in Celtiberia, **2.** 49; on the civility of the Iberian Celti, **2.** 59; on Intercatia and Segesama in Iberia, **2.** 103; says Tiberius Gracchus destroyed 300 cities in Celtiberia, **2.** 105; on the geographical position of the Pillars of Heracles, **2.** 137; on the behaviour of a spring in the Heracleium at Gades, **2.** 143, 147; says the Rhodanus has only two mouths, **2.** 189; censures Pytheas for his falsehoods about Britain, **2.** 215; adds the Oxybii and Decietae to the Ligures, **2.** 265; on a peculiar animal in the Alps, **2.** 289; on a gold mine near Aquileia, **2.** 291; on the size and height of the Alps, **2.** 293; on the distance by land and sea from Iapygia to the Strait of

INDEX OF NAMES, PLACES, AND SUBJECTS

INDEX OF NAMES, PLACES, AND SUBJECTS

Euxine); peoples beyond, unknown, **3.** 173; forty rivers empty into, **3.** 189; " left parts " of, extend from the Ister to Byzantium, **3.** 285, 327

Ponza (see Pontia)

Poplar-trees, the Heliades changed into, **2.** 319

Poplonium (or Populonia, near Piombino), distance from, to Cosa, **2.** 347; visited by Strabo, **2.** 355

" Pordalis," an indecent name, **6.** 149

Pordoselenê (Poroselenê?), near Lesbos, **6.** 147

" Pornopion," the name of a certain month among the Aeolians in Asia, **6.** 127

Poros, the isle (see Calauria)

Poroselenê (see Pordoselenê)

Porsinas, the king of Clusium (Chiusi) in Tyrrhenia, tried to restore Tarquinius Superbus to the throne, **2.** 339

Porta Collina, at Rome, **2.** 377

Porthaon, the Homeric, father of " Agrius, Melas, and Oeneus, who lived in Pleuron and steep Calydon," **5.** 75

Porticanus, the country of, in India, **7.** 59

Porto di Fermo (see Castellum Firmanorum)

Portugal (a part of ancient Iberia, *q.v.*)

Porus, the king, captured by Alexander and presented with a large part of India by Alexander, **7.** 5; country of, has about 300 cities, **7.** 49, 51

Porus, the Indian; country of, in India, called Gandaris, **7.** 25; a relative of the Porus whom Alexander captured, **7.** 51

Porus, ruler of 600 kings in India, wished to be a friend of Augustus Caesar, sending ambassadors and gifts to him, **7.** 127

Poseidium, the, at Alexandria, containing a temple of Poseidon, **8.** 39

Poseidium, a small town in Syria near Laodiceia, **7.** 249, 255

Poseidium, Cape, in Arabia, **7.** 341

Poseidium, Cape, in Chios, **6.** 241, 243

Poseidium, Cape (Punta della Licosa), promontory in Leucania, **3.** 3

Poseidium, Cape, of the Milesians;

end of coast of Ionia, **6.** 197, 205, 263, 291; altar on, erected by Neleus, **6.** 199

Poseidium, Cape, on the isle Samos, has a temple of Poseidon, **6.** 213

Poseidium (Cape Scala), the, in Thesprotia, **3.** 299

Poseidium, Cape, north of Euboea in Thessaly; position of, in the Aegaean, **3.** 353

Poseidon; Asphalius, temple of, on new volcanic isle, **1.** 215; according to Homer, halted his horses at the Euboean Aegae, whence, probably, the Aegaean Sea took its name, **4.** 221; a horse-race instituted in honour of, by Romulus, **2.** 385; numerous temples of, on capes in Elis, **4.** 49; temple of the " Samian " at Samicum in Triphylia, **4.** 49, 59, 63, where Telemachus found the Pylians offering sacrifices, **4.** 53; temple of, on Cape Taenarum, **4.** 127; father of the mythical Nauplius, **4.** 153; the Isthmian, temple of, on the Isthmus of Corinth, **4.** 155, 197; Troezen in Argolis sacred to; asylum in Calauria, sacred to; gave Leto Delos for Calauria, and Apollo Delphi for Cape Taenarum, **4.** 173, 175; the Heliconian, temple of, at Helicê, submerged by tidal wave, **4.** 213, 215; sacred precinct of, at Onchestus, **4.** 329; notable temple of, on Cape Geraestus in Euboea, **5.** 11; great temple of, on the island Tenos, **5.** 173, and on the island Nisyros, **5.** 177; worshipped in Phrygia, in the interior— and explanation thereof, **5.** 515; destroyed Aias (Ajax), **6.** 81; temple of, on Cape Poseidium in Samos, **6.** 213; the Heliconian, sacrifices to, at Panionium in Asia, **6.** 221; temple of, at Alexandria, **8.** 39

Poseidonia (Pesto) in Leucania, **2.** 469, **3.** 3; people of, conquered by the people of Elea, **3.** 5

Poseidonia, Gulf of, in Leucania, **2.** 299, 305, 469

Poseidonia, the earlier name of Troezen in Argolis, **4.** 173

Poseidonius of Apameia in Syria (b. about 130 B.C.), author of a history in 52 books, now lost, and

445

INDEX OF NAMES, PLACES, AND SUBJECTS

a geographical and astronomical scholar of peculiar value to Strabo and other later scientific writers; philosopher, 1. 3; on the tides, 1. 15, 19, 203; praised by Strabo, 1. 53; on the winds, 1. 107; on the Erembians, 1. 151; on the Syrians and kindred peoples, 1. 153; on the silting-up process, 1. 199; on the partial destruction of Sidon by an earthquake, 1. 215; his treatise on Oceanus and his discussion of the zones, 1. 361; estimates circumference of earth at 180,000 stadia, 1. 365; his "Aethiopic" and "Scythico-Celtic" zones, 1. 371; on the oblique motion and celerity of the sun at equator, 1. 375; believes the ocean flows in a circle round the inhabited world, 1. 385; philosopher and master of demonstration, 1. 391; thinks migration of Cimbrians was caused by inundation of sea, and approves of division of inhabited world into three continents, 1. 393; would emend Homer's text, 1. 395; views of, on physics, 1. 397; imitates Aristotle, 1. 399; says Cnidus lies on same parallel as Rhodes and Gades, 1. 461; on the Periscians, Amphiscians, and Heteroscians, 1. 517; on sunsets in Iberia, 2. 9; made observations of the sun on visit to Gades (Cadiz), 2. 11; on the east winds of the Mediterranean, 2. 31; praises extravagantly quantity and quality of silver and gold ores in Turdetania, 2. 41–47; says Aristotle wrongly attributes tides to "high and rugged coasts" of Maurusia and Iberia, 2. 67; says the Baenis (Minius) River rises in Cantabria, 2. 69; on Odysseia and Athenê's temple in Iberia, 2. 83; says Marcus Marcellus exacted tribute of 600 talents from Celtiberia, but denies that the country had 300 cities, 2. 105; on three by-products of Cyprian copper, on Iberian crows, and on Celtiberian and Parthian horses, 2. 107; on the fortitude of women in some countries, notably in Liguria at child-birth, 2. 113; on the Pillars of Heracles, 2. 137;

on two wells in the Heracleium at Gades, 2. 145; on the causes of the tides, 2. 147–151; on a peculiar tree (*Dracaena Draco* ?) in Iberia, 2. 155; on the origin of the large stones in Stony Plain in Celtica, 2. 185; on the treasures found at Tolosa, 2. 207; on the width of the isthmus between Narbo and the ocean, 2. 209; on barbaric customs of the Gauls, 2. 247; on a certain isle off the mouth of the Liger where no male sets foot, 2. 249; on quarrying stones in Liguria, 2. 335; says the circuit of Sicily is 4400 stadia, 3. 57; on the geographical position of the three capes of Sicily, 3. 59, 61; on the effects of the eruptions of Aetna, 3. 69; on Syracuse, Eryx, and Enna, 3. 87; on a submarine eruption between Hiera and Euonymus, 3. 101; on the expedition of the Cimbri to the region of Lake Maeotis, 3. 169; on the Homeric Mysians, 3. 177, 179, 195; would emend "Mysi" to "Moesi" in Homer, 3. 181; says Scilurus, the king of the Bosporus, had 50 sons, 3. 235; says the earth poured into the trenches at the mine of asphalt near Apollonia in Illyria changes to asphalt, and describes the asphaltic vine-earth at the Pierian Seleuceia (Kabousi) and in Rhodes (where he was Prytanis), which kills the insects on infected vines, 3. 267; known by Strabo (?), 3. 383 (see footnote 6); wrote treatises on *Physics* and *Mathematics*, 4. 3; more accurate in matter of distances than Polybius, 5. 83; on the width of the isthmuses (1) between Colchis and the mouth of the Cyrus River, (2) between Lake Maeotis and the Ocean, and (3) between Pelusium and the Red Sea, 5. 187; wrote a history of Pompey, 5. 189; on the earthquakes round Rhagae, 5. 273; on the Council of the Parthians, 5. 277; on bricks in Iberia that float on water and are used to clean silver, 6. 133; sojourned and taught in Rhodes, 6. 279; on the springs of naphtha in Babylonia, 7. 217;

INDEX OF NAMES, PLACES, AND SUBJECTS

says that Seleucis in Syria was divided into four satrapies, **7.** 241; most learned of all philosophers in Strabo's time, native of Apameia, **7.** 255; on the huge dragon seen in Syria, **7.** 261; says that the ancient dogma about atoms originated with Mochus the Sidonian, **7.** 271; on the sorcerers about the Dead Sea, **7.** 295; on the fragrant salts in Arabia, **7.** 351; emends the Homeric "Erembians" to "Arambians," and says that the Arabians consist of three tribes, **7.** 371; on the cause of the risings of the Nile, **8.** 19; on the breadth of the isthmus between Pelusium and Heröonpolis, **8.** 71; amused by the apes on the coast in Maurusia, **8.** 163; says that the rivers in Libya are "only few and small," and discusses the effect of the sun on different regions, **8.** 175–177

Potamia in western Paphlagonia, **5.** 453

Potamon of Mitylenê, contemporary of Strabo, **6.** 143

Potamus, the Attic deme, north of Cape Sunium, **4.** 271

Potentates, the, subject to the Romans, **8.** 213

Potidaea (later called Cassandreia, now Kassandra), founded by the Corinthians, **3.** 349

"Potistra" (see "Pistra")

Potniae near Thebes, scene of the myth of the Glaucus who was torn to pieces by the Potnian mares, **4.** 313; by some identified with the Homeric Hypothebes, **4.** 327

Potnian mares, the, which tore Glaucus to pieces, **4.** 313

Practius (see Practius River), a supposed place in the Troad, **6.** 39; mentioned by Homer, **6.** 37

Practius River, the, in the Troad, **6.** 9, 19, 23, 39

Praefect, a, of equestrian rank, sent to govern certain Ligures, **2.** 271

Praefect, the, of Aegypt, has the rank of king, **8.** 49

Praefects, the; in Iberia, reside at Tarraco, **2.** 91; sail up the Nile in cabin-boats, **8.** 63; the Nilometers

useful to, in determining revenues, **8.** 129; hold as personal property a certain island in the Nile, **8.** 133; sent by the Romans to the Provinces, **8.** 211

Praeneste (Palestrina), between the Latin and Valerian Ways, **2.** 415; description of, **2.** 417–419

Praenestine Way, the, **2.** 415

Praenestini, the, 540 in number, who long held out against Hannibal at Casilinum, **2.** 461

Praetor, a, governs Baetica, **2.** 121

Praetor nocturnus, the, a local official in Alexandria, **8.** 49

Praetorian legatus, a, administers justice to the Lusitanians, **2.** 121

Praetors, the Roman, insulted by the Lacedaemonians, **4.** 137; sent by Augustus to all "Provinces of the People," **8.** 213

Pramnae, the, a sect of philosophers in India, **7.** 123; life and habits of, **7.** 125

Prasia (or Prasiae), a deme on the eastern coast of Attica, **4.** 271

Prasiae (Prasto, near Leonidi), in Argolis, belongs to the Argives, **4.** 151; belonged to a kind of Amphictyonic League of seven cities, **4.** 175

Prasians, the, in the Argolis; dues of, at temple of Poseidon on Calauria, paid by the Lacedaemonians, **4.** 175

Prasians, the, in Crete, called the Corybantes sons of Athenê and Helius, **5.** 111; country of, **5.** 139

Prasii, the, superior to all other tribes in India, **7.** 63

Prasto (see Prasiae)

Prasus in Crete, where is the temple of the Dictaean Zeus, **5.** 127; lies 60 stadia above the sea and was rased to the ground by the Hierapynians, **5.** 139

Praxander, founded Lapathus in Cypros, **6.** 377

Praxiphanes the philosopher, native of Rhodes, **6.** 279

Praxiteles, the great sculptor (b. about 390 B.C.); the "Eros" of, at Thespiae, brought fame to that city, **4.** 319; works of, filled whole of altar in temple of Artemis at Ephesus, **6.** 229

INDEX OF NAMES, PLACES, AND SUBJECTS

INDEX OF NAMES, PLACES, AND SUBJECTS

449

INDEX OF NAMES, PLACES, AND SUBJECTS

285-247 B.C.); Timosthenes the admiral of, writer on *Harbours* and composer of melody of the Pythian Nome, **4.** 363; Arsinoë, wife and sister of, founded the city Arsinoë in Aetolia, **5.** 65; Philotera named after sister of, **7.** 315; sent Eumedes to the hunting-grounds for elephants, **7.** 319; much interested in the sciences, **8.** 17-19; succeeded Ptolemy Soter, and was succeeded by Euergetes, **8.** 43; built the road from Coptus to Berenicê on the Red Sea, **8.** 119

Ptolemy III, Euergetes, succeeded Ptolemy Philadelphus and was succeeded by Philopator, **8.** 43

Ptolemy IV, Philopator or Tryphon (reigned 222-205 B.C.); partly walled Gortynia, **5.** 137; fought Antiochus the Great at Rhaphia, **7.** 279; son of Agathocleia, succeeded Euergetes and was succeeded by Epiphanes, **8.** 43

Ptolemy V, Epiphanes, succeeded Philopator and was succeeded by Philometor, **8.** 43

Ptolemy VI, Philometor (reigned 181-146 B.C.); conquered Alexander Balas in Syria (146 B.C.), but died from a wound (fell from his horse), **7.** 247; succeeded Epiphanes and was succeeded by Euergetes II (Physcon), **8.** 43

Ptolemy VII, Euergetes II, Physcon (reigned 146-117 B.C.); received favourably Eudoxus of Cyzicus, **1.** 377; succeeded by his wife Cleopatra, **1.** 379; his scarcity of competent pilots, **1.** 387; knew nothing about India, **1.** 397; succeeded Philometor and was succeeded by Ptolemy Lathurus, **8.** 43; sent masses of people against soldiers, thus causing their destruction, **8.** 51

Ptolemy VIII, Lathurus, succeeded Ptolemy Euergetes II (Physcon) and was succeeded by Auletes, **8.** 43

Ptolemy IX, Auletes (reigned 80-58 B.C. and 55-51 B.C.); illegitimate son of Ptolemy VIII, Lathurus; banished by the Aegyptians (58 B.C.), but restored to the throne by Gabinius the proconsul, **5.** 437;

father of Cleopatra and brother of Ptolemy the king of Cypros, **6.** 385; successor of Ptolemy Lathurus and father of Berenicê and Cleopatra, **8.** 43; the reign of, **8.** 45-47; worst king of all, but received large revenues, **8.** 53

Ptolemy, last king of Cypros (reigned 80-57 B.C.), younger brother of Ptolemy IX, Auletes; being deposed, and refusing to surrender to Marcus Cato, committed suicide, **6.** 385

Ptolemy, grandson of Antony and Cleopatra and son of Juba the Younger, succeeded to the throne of Maurusia, **8.** 169

Ptolemy "Cocces" and "Pareisactus," from Syria, plundered the gold sarcophagus of Alexander, **8.** 37

Ptoüs (Skroponeri), Mt., in Boeotia; the oracle of Apollo on, **4.** 329

Publicans, Roman, worked the gold mines in the land of the Salassi, **2.** 277

Pulse, sown in the winter season, **7.** 21

Purple, the marine, used for dyeing, **6.** 189; the Tyrian, most beautiful of all, **7.** 269

Purple-fish of huge size at Carteia, **2.** 37

Puteoli (see Dicaearchia); origin of name of, **2.** 447

Pydna (Citrum, now Kitros), a Pierian city, **3.** 339, 341, 345, 359

Pygela, a town in Asia, founded by Agamemnon, has a temple of Artemis Munychia, **6.** 223

Pygmies, the, slaughtered by cranes, **1.** 127; explanation of reputed size of, **8.** 143

Pylae, boundary between Cilicia and Syria, **6.** 357

Pylae (see Thermopylae), **4.** 11; the Amphictyonic League convened at, twice a year, **4.** 357

Pylaean Assembly, the, of the Amphictyons at Thermopylae, **4.** 393

Pylaemenes, the descendants of, given by Pompey the kingship over certain of the Paphlagonians, **5.** 371; the leader of the Eneti of the Paphlagonians in the Trojan War, **5.** 381

Pylaeus, scion of Ares, ruler of the Pelasgians at Larisa Phryconis, **6.**

INDEX OF NAMES, PLACES, AND SUBJECTS

153; leader of the Lesbians in the Trojan War, **6.** 157

Pylaeus, Mt., in Lesbos, **6.** 157

Pylagorae (*i.e.* Assembly-men), the, of the Amphictyonic League, sacrificed to Demeter, **4.** 357

Pylaic (Peliac?) Festal Assembly, the, near Demetrias in Thessaly, **4.** 425 (see footnote 2)

Pylenê, the Homeric, in Aetolia, later moved and called Proschium, **5.** 29; only traces of, left, **5.** 65

Pylian Sea, the, prolonged by Homer to the seven cities promised by Agamemnon to Achilles, **4.** 67

Pylians, the, in the Peloponnesus, fought the Arcadians, **4.** 67; pretend a kinship with the Messenians, **6.** 199

Pylon, a place on the Candavian Way which marks the boundary between Illyria and Macedonia, **3.** 293, 295

Pylus, the city in Elis, not yet founded in Homer's time, **4.** 21, and not the Homeric Pylus, **4.** 23; lies between the outlets of the Peneius and Selleëis Rivers, **4.** 31; the land of, cannot be the Homeric Pylus of Nestor, **4.** 79, 83

Pylus, the Messenian (Palaeokastro near Navarino), wrongly claims Nestor, and so most recent writers, **4.** 33; near the isle Protê (Prodano), **4.** 69; according to Homer's account, cannot be the Pylus of Nestor, **4.** 79, 83; lies at foot of Mt. Aegaleum (Malia), was torn down, but later built up by two Athenian generals, **4.** 109; the naval station of the Messenians, **4.** 111; one of the five capitals of Messenia, **4.** 119

Pylus, the Triphylian (or Lepreatic), the land of Nestor, through which the Alpheius flows, **4.** 21; extends as far as Messenê and is the Homeric Pylus, both land and city, **4.** 23, 49, 57, 75; by Homer called "emathöeis," **4.** 51; about 400 stadia from the Messenian Pylus, **4.** 75; nowhere touches Messenia or Coelê Elis, and lies more than 30 stadia from the sea, **4.** 75; further proofs of its being the Homeric Pylus, **4.** 77–87

Pyraechmes, the Aetolian champion,

defeated Degmenus the Epeian champion, **4.** 103

Pyramid, the, at the Labyrinth; the tomb of King Imandes (Mandes?), **8.** 105 (see footnote 1)

Pyramids, the, of Gizeh, visible from the ridge at the stronghold called Babylon, **8.** 87; description of, **8.** 89–95; the Labyrinth comparable to, **8.** 103

Pyramus River, the, has added much land to Cilicia, **1.** 195; flows through Cataonia, **5.** 353, **6.** 353; detailed description of, **5.** 353–355

Pyrasus, the Homeric (see Demetrium)

Pyrenees, the; distance from, to Massalia and to the Pillars, **1.** 409; separate Iberia and Celtica, **1.** 489; parallel to the Rhine, and at right angles to the Cemmenus, **1.** 491; form boundary between Iberia and Celtica, **2.** 5, 119, distant 1600 stadia from the Iberus River, **2.** 81; occupied by some of the Emporitans, **2.** 95; well-wooded on Iberian side, but bare, and has glens, on Celtic side, **2.** 101; shortest distance from, to the Rhenus, **2.** 253

Pyrgetans, the; last of the Triphylians, border on the Cyparissians, first of the Messenians, **4.** 67

Pyrgi (San Severa), in Italy, a small town between Cossa and Ostia, **2.** 363; the port-town of the Caeretani, **2.** 365

Pyrgi, on the Neda River in Triphylia, **4.** 67

"Pyrigenes" ("Fire-born"), an epithet of Dionysus; origin of term, **6.** 183

Pyriphlegethon River, the, **2.** 443

Pyrrha, wife of Deucalion; grave of, at Cynus in Locris, **4.** 379; Pyrrha, later called Melitaea, in Thessaly, named after, **4.** 405; Thessaly named "Pyrrhaea" after, **4.** 453

Pyrrha, the promontory on the Gulf of Adramyttium, where is the Aphrodisium, **6.** 103

Pyrrha in Ionia, about 30 stadia from Miletus, and 50 from mouth of Maeander River, **6.** 211

Pyrrha in Lesbos, rased to the ground, **6.** 145

Pyrrha, Cape, in Thessaly, **4.** 423

INDEX OF NAMES, PLACES, AND SUBJECTS

INDEX OF NAMES, PLACES, AND SUBJECTS

and other countries, **5.** 213, 427, 431, 441, 443; daughter of Pythodorus of Tralleis, **6.** 257

Pythodorus of Tralleis, contemporary of Strabo, native of Nisa, friend of Pompey, father of Queen Pythodoris, and very wealthy, **5.** 427, **6.** 257

Pytholaüs, Cape of, in Aethiopia, **7.** 331; Pillars and Altars of, **7.** 335

Python, according to Ephorus, a cruel man known as the Dragon, slain by Apollo, **4.** 367

Pytna, a peak of Mt. Ida in Crete, **5.** 113

Pyxus (Buxentum, now Policastro), in Leucania, colonised from Messenê in Sicily, **3.** 5

Q

Quaestor, a, serves as assistant to a praetor in governing Baetica in Iberia, **2.** 121; the, at Nemausus, a Roman citizen, **2.** 203

Quarries of stone, the, near Tibur, **2.** 417, and near Tunis, **8.** 191

Quarry, the, above Cape Amphialê in Attica, **4.** 257

Quirinal Hill, the, walled by the first founders of Rome, but easy to capture, **2.** 399

" Quirites," the, origin of term, **2.** 375

R

Rabbits (see Hares), the, in the Gymnesiae no longer a pest, **2.** 129

Rafina (see Halae Araphaenides)

Rain, no, in Babylonia, at Susa, and in Sitacenê, **7.** 201

Rains, the cause of, at the equator, **1.** 373

Ram, a, never sacrificed at the oracle of Phrixus, **5.** 213

Rams, in Turdetania, bought at a talent apiece, **2.** 33

Rasa near Olympia (see Scillus)

Ras-al-Razat (see Phycus)

Rat (?), a, sold for 200 drachmae at Casilinum, **2.** 461 (footnote 3)

Ravenna, in Umbria, **2.** 301, 327; largest city in the marshes; description of, **2.** 313, 315, 337; where the Ombrici (Umbri) begin, **2.** 369

Reate (Rieti), a Sabine city, **2.** 375

Red-rust, often ruins crops in Triphylia, **4.** 53

Red Sea (see Arabian Gulf and Erythraean Sea), the, **1.** 119, 123, **8.** 7; once extended to Gerrha, **1.** 185, 207, 209; thought by Dareius I to lie at a higher level than Aegypt, **8.** 77; probably once confluent with the Mediterranean, **8.** 99; the road from Coptus to, **8.** 119-121

Reed, the kind of, used for flutes, produced by a marsh in Boeotia, **4.** 325; the, in India, are tremendous in size, **7.** 93; uses of, on the Euphrates, **7.** 205, 207; in Lake Gennesaritis, **7.** 261; abundant in the country of Coracius in Aethiopia, **7.** 321; in country of the Sabaeans in Arabia, **7.** 347

Reed-roots, used as food by the Aethiopians, **8.** 143

Reeds, in western Aethiopia, whose joints each hold eight *choinices*, being like those in India, **8.** 165

Reggio d'Emilia (see Regium Lepidum)

Regis Villa, between Ossa and Gravisci, where once was a palace of Maleos the Pelasgian, **2.** 365

Regium Lepidum (Reggio nell' Emilia), on the Aemilian Way, **2.** 311, 327

Religion, chiefly supported by women, **3.** 183; the, of the Greeks and barbarians, **5.** 93

Remi, the, a notable tribe in Celtica, **2.** 233

Remus (Romus), the story of, **2.** 381; slain as result of a quarrel, **2.** 383

Rentina (see Arethusa)

Reptiles (see Serpents and Snakes), the deadly, in Albania in Asia, **5.** 229; with wings like bats, in India, **7.** 65; numerous and vicious in India, **7.** 77, 79; in Gordyaea, avoid a certain stone called Gangitis, **7.** 233; on the isthmus between Pelusium and Heröonpolis, **8.** 71

Republic, Plato's, cited on founding cities as far as possible from the sea, **3.** 205

Resin, produced in the Alps, **2.** 283

Revolutions, the, of the heavenly bodies, **1.** 425

INDEX OF NAMES, PLACES, AND SUBJECTS

Rhetia, mother of the Cyrbantes, by Apollo, **5.** 115

Rhetoric, definition of, **1.** 61; Homer an expert in, **1.** 63

Rhetoric, a work on, by Apollodorus the Pergamenian, **6.** 171

Rhetoric, The Art of, by Hermagoras of Temnus, **6.** 159

Rhine River, the (see Rhenus River)

Rhinoceros, the, in southern Aethiopia; description of, **7.** 335

Rhinoceros, the (see " *Rhizeis*," **8.** 163)

Rhinocolura in Phoenicia, the lakes and pits near, **7.** 211; origin of name of, **7.** 279; receives aromatics from Leucê Comê in Arabia, **7.** 359

Rhipae (see Rhipê)

Rhipaean Mountains, the mythical, **3.** 175, 191

Rhipê, the Homeric (perhaps also called Rhipae), now deserted, **3.** 385, **4.** 229

Rhium, in Messenia, by Cresphontes made one of the five capitals of Messenia, **4.** 117, 119

Rhium (Rion), Cape, at the entrance of the Corinthian Gulf, **4.** 17, 241

Rhizeis (rhinoceros?), found in western Aethiopia, **8.** 163

Rhizo (Risano), on the Rhizonic Gulf, **3.** 263

Rhizonic Gulf (Gulf of Cattaro), the, in Illyria, **3.** 257, 263

Rhizophagi (" Root-eaters "), the, in Aethiopia, **7.** 321

Rhizus in Thessaly, now a village belonging to Demetrias, **4.** 425, 451

Rhodanus (Rhone) River, the, formerly called the boundary between Celtica and Iberia, **2.** 117; a navigable river, **2.** 167; empties into the Galatic Gulf, **2.** 181; controversy as to number of mouths of, **2.** 189; the largest river in Celtica, **2.** 195; joins the Cemmenus Mountain and the Isar River, **2.** 197; passes through Lemenna Lake, **2.** 199; navigable, **2.** 211; borders on the land of the Sallyes, **2.** 269; traverses Lake Lemenna, **2.** 273; rises in the Alps, **2.** 291; flows through Lake Lemenna, **3.** 77

Rhodaspes, son of Phraates IV, sent by his father as hostage to Rome, **7.** 237, 239

Rhodes, about 4000 stadia from Alexandria, **1.** 93, 323; parallel of, perceptibly different from that of Athens as shown by sun-dial, **1.** 333; distance from, to various points, **1.** 407, 447, 483; longest day at, at about centre of, has 14½ equinoctial hours, **2.** 357; the colossus of, **3.** 107; ledges of rock in, **1.** 513; has asphaltic earth which cures the infested vine, **3.** 267; the nine Telchines lived in, some accompanying Mother Rhea thence to Crete, **5.** 111; type of adornment of, like that of Cyzicus, **5.** 501; the city, terraced like Munychia at Peiraeus, **4.** 259; description and history of, **6.** 269–281; maritime supremacy of, **6.** 269; government of, not democratic but beneficent, **6.** 271; earlier names of, **6.** 273; the present city, founded in the time of the Peloponnesian War, **6.** 275; colonies of, **6.** 277; notable men of, **6.** 279, 281

Rhodians, the, erected temple on new volcanic isle, **1.** 215; thought by some to have founded Siris and Sybaris in Italy, **3.** 51; city of, terraced like Munychia at Peiraeus, **4.** 259; worship Apollo " Erythibius," **6.** 127; fleet of joined the Romans against Philip, **6.** 167; the Peraea (Mainland) of, **6.** 191, 263, 265, 311; friends to the Romans and Greeks, **6.** 269; take care of their poor people, and are Dorians in origin, **6.** 271; even in early times sailed far and wide, and founded several cities, **6.** 277; famous men among, **6.** 279; unfriendly to the Syrians, **6.** 329

Rhodius River, the, mentioned by Homer, **5.** 421; empties between Abydus and Dardanus, and is mentioned by Homer, **6.** 59, 87; source of, **6.** 89

Rhodopê, Mt. (Despoto-Dagh), compared with the Alps, **2.** 293; a boundary of Paeonia, **3.** 251; borders on the country of the Bessi, **3.** 275; on northern boundary of Macedonia, **3.** 329; position of, with reference to the Strymon River, **3.** 361; the

INDEX OF NAMES, PLACES, AND SUBJECTS

INDEX OF NAMES, PLACES, AND SUBJECTS

in Laconia, **4.** 139; extravagance of, in the importation of marble from Laconia, **4.** 143; joined by Tenea against Corinth, **4.** 199; all Greece became subject to, **4.** 201; wished to destroy some Greek states and preserve others, **4.** 217; settled a large part of the army at Patrae after the Battle of Actium, **4.** 225; leave Athens free and hold it in honour, **4.** 269, 271; became lords of all by their intercourse with mankind, and by applying themselves to training and education, **4.** 281; annexed Upper Larymna to Larymna, **4.** 305; gave Haliartus to the Athenians, **4.** 325; completely defeated the forces of Mithridates at Chaeroneia, **4.** 333; found the Dorian Tetrapolis virtually extinct, **4.** 389; under Titus Quintius Flamininus, conquered Philip the son of Demetrius at Cynoscephalae in Thessaly, **4.** 445; strongly resisted and tricked by the Acarnanians, **5.** 67, 73; broke up the piracy of the Cilicians, **5.** 133; Lagetas, great-uncle of Strabo, betrayed kingdom of Mithridates Eupator to, **5.** 135; now rule Crete, **5.** 159; made Delos a great commercial centre, **5.** 167; the supremacy of, disclosed more geographical knowledge, **5.** 247; a marriage-custom among, **5.** 273; received large tribute from Tigranes the king of Armenia, **5.** 331; now rule over Armenia, **5.** 341; assigned an eleventh prefecture to predecessors of Archelaüs, and to Archelaüs still further territory, **5.** 349; allowed the Cappadocians and others to collect large damages from Ariathres, **5.** 365; jurisconsults of, expound the law, **5.** 367; conquered Antiochus and began to administer affairs of Asia, **5.** 369; granted autonomy to Cappadocia, **5.** 371; made various different administrative changes in Asia Minor through their prefects, **5.** 373; occupied Heracleia Pontica, **5.** 379; boundaries of the Pontic Province of, **5.** 385; colonised Sinopê, **5.** 391; pulled down part of the walls of Kainon Chorion in Cappadocia Pontica, **5.** 429; assignments of territory by, in Cappadocia Pontica, **5.** 443; gave freedom to the Prusians in Asia, **5.** 457; succeeded the Macedonians as masters in Asia, **5.** 463; have united into one province all the country subject to Amyntas, **5.** 469; made famous the temple of Mother Agdistis at Pessinus in Galatia, **5.** 471; subdued Lycaonia and Cilicia, **5.** 475; gave Isaura to Amyntas, **5.** 477; now hold Pisidia, **5.** 485; honoured Cyzicus, giving it further territory, **5.** 503; set free Antiocheia near Pisidia from its kings, and gave Eumenes II his kingdom in Asia, **5.** 507; export great monolithic pillars of Synnadic marble from Phrygia, **5.** 507; found the present Ilium to be only a village when they expelled Antiochus from Asia, **6.** 53; under Fimbria, in the time of the Mithridatic War, ruined Ilium, **6.** 55; regard Aeneias as their original founder, **6.** 57; Attalus I and Rhodian fleet fought on side of, against Philip, and by Eumenes II against Antiochus the Great and Perseus, **6.** 167; assisted by Attalus II against the Pseudo-Philip, **6.** 169; left as heirs of Attalus III, and proclaimed his empire a Roman province, **6.** 169; confused the boundaries of Lydia, Phrygia, and Caria by making their own administrative divisions, **6.** 183; restored revenues to Artemis at Ephesus, **6.** 233; restored the Caunians in Asia to the Rhodians, **6.** 267; the Rhodians friendly to, **6.** 269; remitted to the Coans 100 talents of the appointed tribute in return for the *Aphroditê Anadyomenê* of Apelles, **6.** 289; left the Lycians in Asia free, **6.** 315; gave Telmessus in Lycia to Eumenes II, **6.** 317; became rich after the destruction of Carthage and Corinth, and used many slaves, **6.** 329; finally overthrew the Cilicians, **6.** 331; gave Cilicia Tracheia to Archelaüs, **6.** 339; proclaimed Tarcondimotus in Cilicia king, **6.** 355; took possession

INDEX OF NAMES, PLACES, AND SUBJECTS

of Cypros, **6.** 385; took the cities in Gordyaea by force, **7.** 231; hold certain parts this side the Euphrates, **7.** 235; rule over part of the Arabians, **7.** 237; seized Phoenicia, **7.** 257; re-built Berytus (Beyrout), **7.** 263; broke up band of robbers in Syria, **7.** 265; granted autonomy to the Tyrians, **7.** 269; revere the Tyrrhenian nativity-casters, **7.** 289; now rule over the Syrians, Sabaeans, and Sabataeans, **7.** 351; now well acquainted with Arabia, **7.** 353; certain of, in Aegypt, led by Aelius Gallus into Arabia, **7.** 357; killed 10,000 men in battle in Arabia but lost only two men, **7.** 361; reduced Aegypt to its former geographical limits, **8.** 23; have organised and regulated Aegypt, **8.** 51; now satisfied with the oracles of Sibylla only and with the Tyrrhenian prophecies, having neglected the oracles at Ammon and elsewhere, **8.** 113; call the Maurusians "Mauri," **8.** 157; supplied with large tables of one piece of wood by Maurusians, **8.** 161; destroyed Zama in Libya, **8.** 173; administration of Libya by, **8.** 179–181; used Itycê (Utica) as Libyan metropolis after destruction of Carthage, **8.** 183; booty received by, in the last Punic War, from the Carthaginians, **8.** 185; proclaimed part of the Carthaginian territory a Province, **8.** 187; destroyed various cities in Carthaginia, **8.** 191; acquired Cyrenê, **8.** 203; occupy the best and best known ports of Libya, and conquests and ascendancy of, in general, **8.** 209–221; division of dependencies of, into Provinces, **8.** 213

Rome; commercial dealings of, with Turdetania, **2.** 31; once appealed to by people of Gymnesian Islands for new place of abode when plagued by hares, **2.** 35; obtains large revenues from silver-mines at New Carthage, **2.** 47; journey from, to Obulco in Iberia made by Julius Caesar in 27 days, **2.** 97; receives supplies of meat from Celtica, **2.** 243; exports to, from Patavium, **2.** 313; largely dependent

upon Cisalpine Celtica for meat and grain, **2.** 331; adopted various Tarquinian usages, **2.** 339; captured by the Galatae, **2.** 341; imports (Carrara) marble, **2.** 349; erected buildings of Persian magnificence, **2.** 353; imports slaves from Corsica, **2.** 359; exports from Tyrrhenia to, **2.** 367; founded by Romulus and Romus (Remus), **2.** 381; site of, not naturally adapted to a city, **2.** 383, 399; an older, and fabulous, account of founding of, **2.** 385–387; detailed description of, **2.** 399–409; its walls, **2.** 399; depended mainly on arms and valour, not walls, **2.** 401; its sources of supplies, **2.** 403; its roads, sewers, aqueducts, and service-pipes, **2.** 405; its Campuses, Games, and buildings, **2.** 407; its tombs, its Capitolium, its Palatium and its Forum, **2.** 409; the Thurii took refuge in, **3.** 47; has reproduction of temple of Venus Erycina from Eryx in Sicily, **3.** 81; route to, from Greece and Asia, via Brundisium, **3.** 123; distant 360 Roman miles from Brundisium, **3.** 125; the history of, **3.** 139–147; captured by, and regained from, the Gauls, **3.** 141; dominion of, over the Argives, **4.** 185; the temple of Ceres in; obtained the best of the works of art found by Mummius in Corinth, **4.** 201; prefers the Scyrian marble to all others, **4.** 429; wooden image of Athenê at, in a sitting posture, **6.** 83; full of learned men from Tarsus and Alexandria, **6.** 353

Romulus, the story of, **2.** 381–385; the Asylum of, **2.** 383; the prowess of, **2.** 387

Romus (see Remus)

Roots, used for food by the Masaesylians, in Libya, **8.** 189

Roussillon, Castel (see Ruscino)

Rovias (see Orobia)

Roxolani, the, the most northerly of the Bastarnians; beyond Germany, **3.** 173; under Tasius waged war with the generals of Mithridates Eupator, **3.** 223

Roxolanians, the; most remote of the Scythians, **1.** 441

INDEX OF NAMES, PLACES, AND SUBJECTS

INDEX OF NAMES, PLACES, AND SUBJECTS

INDEX OF NAMES, PLACES, AND SUBJECTS

INDEX OF NAMES, PLACES, AND SUBJECTS

INDEX OF NAMES, PLACES, AND SUBJECTS

INDEX OF NAMES, PLACES, AND SUBJECTS

INDEX OF NAMES, PLACES, AND SUBJECTS

to have unearthed a skeleton 60 cubits long near Lynx in Maurusia, **8.** 171

Servilius, Publius Isauricus, an acquaintance of Strabo, subjugated Isaura in Lycaonia and destroyed most of the strongholds of pirates on the sea, **5.** 475; demolished Isaura and wiped out piracy, **6.** 315; seized various places in Lycia and Pamphylia, **6.** 339

Servius Tullius, legendary king of Rome, joined Esquiline and Viminal Hills to Rome, **2.** 401

Sesamê, sown in rainy seasons in India, **7.** 21

Sesamê-oil, used in Babylonia, **7.** 215; used instead of olive-oil in Nabataea in Arabia, **7.** 369

Sesamus in Paphlagonia, one of the four places incorporated into Amastris, **5.** 385

Sesarethii, the (see Enchelii)

Seschio River, the (see Ausar)

Sesithacus, son of Segimerus and chieftain of the Cherusci, led captive in triumph at Rome, **3.** 161

Sesostris (Rameses II, king of Aegypt about 1333 B.C.), abandoned building canal through Aegyptian isthmus, **1.** 141; expeditions of, to remote lands, **1.** 227; advanced as far as Europe, **7.** 7, leading his army from Iberia to Thrace and the Pontus, but did not reach India, **7.** 9; remarkable exploits of, **7.** 313; built a temple of Isis on a mountain near the Arabian Gulf, **7.** 319; travelled over the whole of Aethiopia, **8.** 19; said to have been the first to cut the canal that empties into the Red Sea and the Arabian Gulf, **8.** 77

Sessa (see Suessa Aurunca)

Sestias, Cape, in the Thracian Chersonesus, where Xerxes' pontoon-bridge was built, **3.** 377

Sestus (Boghaly), 80 stadia from Aegospotami, **3.** 377; a colony of the Lesbians 30 stadia from Abydus, **3.** 379; at end of seaboard of the Propontis, **6.** 5; the voyage to, from Byzantium, **6.** 13; mentioned by Homer, **6.** 37; best of the cities in the Chersonesus, and by the Romans assigned to the same governor as Abydus, **6.** 41; length of pontoon-bridge at, **6.** 43; mistress of the strait, **6.** 45

Set, the Aegyptian god, **8.** 75 (see footnote 2)

Setabis in Iberia, the road through, **2.** 95

Setia (Sezze), territory of, marshy and unhealthful, **2.** 389; between the Latin and Appian Ways, and produces an expensive wine, **2.** 413

Setinian wine, the, **2.** 399

Setium, Mt. (Cape de Cette), divides the Galatic Gulf into two gulfs, **2.** 181

Settia in Crete (see Minoa)

Seusamora, a fortified city on the Aragus River, **5.** 221

Seuthes, king of the Odrysae, **3.** 371

Sewers, the, at Rome, **2.** 405

" Sex " (see " Hexi "), the name of the city of the Exitanians in Iberia, according to Ptolemaeus, **2.** 81 (footnote 4)

Sextius, Titus, one of Caesar's legates in Gaul and at the time of Caesar's death (44 B.C.) governor of Numidia; defeated the Sallyes and founded Aquae Sextiae (now Aix), **2.** 177

Sezze (see Setia)

Sheep, a, sacrificed at only one place in Aegypt, **8.** 73

Sheep, the, in Celtica have rough and flocky wool, **2.** 241; in Sardinia grow goat-hair instead of wool, **2.** 363; in neighbourhood of Mt. Aetna, choke from fatness, **3.** 69; excellent, about Mt. Garganum in Apulia, **3.** 131; large, in the region of Lake Maeotis, **3.** 225; which drink from a certain river in Euboea turn white and from another black, **5.** 21; the skin-clad, in Gazelonitis in Cappadocia Pontica, yield soft wool, **5.** 393; in Lycaonia, numerous but have coarse wool, **5.** 475; of the Laodiceians, noted for softness and raven-black colour of their wool, **5.** 511; fattened on date-stones in Babylonia, **7.** 215; in Arabia, are white-fleeced, **7.** 369; of the Aethiopians, are small, **8.** 143, and have hair like that of goats, **8.** 145; in certain parts of

INDEX OF NAMES, PLACES, AND SUBJECTS

Libya brought up on milk and meat, **8.** 197

Sheep-skins, worn by Aethiopians, **8.** 145

Shell-fish, of huge size at Carteia, **2.** 37; fattened in pools by the Ichthyophagi in Aethiopia, **7.** 329

Shepherds, a certain tribe of Arabian, **7.** 233

Shield, the Lusitanian; description of, **2.** 71; a long oblong, used by the Gauls, **2.** 243; a bronze, used by the Ligures, **2.** 267; a small leather, used by the Sardinians, **2.** 363; a light, used by the Amazons, **5.** 233

Shields, the, of the Aethiopians, **8.** 139; made of elephant-skin in Maurusia, **8.** 167; of the Carthaginians, given up to the Romans, **8.** 187

Ships, the structure of, the of the Belgae, **2.** 235; timber suitable for building, among the Ligures, **2.** 265; of the Carthaginians, **8.** 187

Shoes, like drums, worn by the Caucasians, **5.** 241

Sibae, the, a tribe in India, said to be descendants of Heracles and his followers, **7.** 11, 57

Sibini, the, a German tribe, ruled by Marabodus, **3.** 157

Sibyl, the Cumaean; oracle of, required the Romans to bring the statue of Mother Agdistis from Galatia and that of Asclepius at Epidaurus, **5.** 471; the Erythraean, native of Erythrae in Asia, **6.** 241; oracles of, suffice the Romans, **8.** 113; the Erythraean Athenaïs like, **8.** 117

Sicani, the, in Sicily, **3.** 73

Siceli, the (the indigenous inhabitants of Sicily), inhabited southern Italy in earlier times, **3.** 23, 73

Sicilian (Ausonian) Sea, the; extent of, **1.** 473, 475; borders on Sicily, **2.** 305, **3.** 63

Sicilian War, the, between the Romans and the Carthaginians, **3.** 67

Siciliotes (Sicilian Greeks), the, **3.** 19

Sicily, touched three times by Odysseus, **1.** 93; deep waters of, **1.** 183; broken off from Italy, or created by volcanic eruption, **1.** 199, 213;

explanation of strong currents in strait of, **1.** 201, where current changes twice a day, **1.** 205; a fragment broken off from district of Rhegium, **1.** 223; triangular in shape, **1.** 315; distance from, to Cape Pachynum and to Pillars of Heracles, **1.** 407; largest and best island in the Mediterranean, **1.** 471; caused to revolt by Pompey Sextus. **2.** 23, 439; betrays signs of Odysseus' wanderings, **2.** 53; Dionysius the tyrant of, **2.** 309, 365, 427; once a part of Magna Graecia, **3.** 7; rent from the continent by earthquakes, **3.** 25; detailed description of, **3.** 55–93; at first called Trinacria, and later Thrinacis, **3.** 55; its three capes and its dimensions, **3.** 55–63; its cities and rivers, **3.** 63–85; first colonised by Iberians, **3.** 73; its fertility, **3.** 85–87; Mt. Aetna in, **3.** 87–91; taken away from the Carthaginians by the Romans, **3.** 141; neighbourhood of, the scene of Odysseus' wanderings, **3.** 193; the second Athenian expedition to, **4.** 111; one of the seven largest islands, **6.** 277; now a praetorial Province, **8.** 215

Sicinos, one of the Cyclades Islands, **5.** 161

Sicyon (formerly called Aegiali and then Meconê), once subject to Agamemnon, **4.** 167; where Adrastus was king at the first, **4.** 185; famous for its artists, **4.** 203; rebuilt by Demetrius Poliorcetes on a hill "about 20 stadia (others say 12)" above the sea, **4.** 207; one of the twelve cities in which the Achaeans settled, **4.** 219; colonised by Phalces after the return of the Heracleidae, **4.** 235

Sicyonia, geographical position of, **4.** 15, 195; the Nemea River a boundary of, **4.** 207

Sicyonians, the, obtained from the Romans most of Corinthia, **4.** 201

Sidê, a stronghold in Sidenê in Cappadocia Pontica, **5.** 397

Sidê in Cilicia, 1600 stadia from Cypros, **6.** 375

Sidê, in Pamphylia, **5.** 479; where captives were sold at auction, **6.**

313; colony of the Cymaeans, **6.** 325

Sidenê in Cappadocia Pontica, 3000 stadia from Dioscurias, **1.** 485; a low-lying country, **1.** 193; subject to Themiscyra, **5.** 395; a fertile plain, **5.** 39?; borders on Pharnacia, **5.** 427

Sidenê in the Troad, on the Granicus River, now in ruins, **6.** 27; refuge of the tyrant Glaucias and destroyed by Croesus, **6.** 83

Sideros, Cape (see Samonium)

Sidicini, the, an Oscan tribe, once occupied Campania, **2.** 435

Sidon, two-thirds of, engulfed because of an earthquake, **1.** 215; longest day at, has 14¼ equinoctial hours, **1.** 511; belongs to the Phoenician Tripolis, **7.** 259; near Mt. Antilibanus, **7.** 261; description and history of, **7.** 267

Sidoni, the, a Bastarnian tribe, **3.** 221

Sidonians, mentioned by Homer, **1.** 5, **3.** 191, **7.** 369; makers of beautiful works of art, **1.** 151; skilled in many arts, in astronomy, mathematics, and seamanship, **7.** 269; famous men among, **7.** 271; discussion of, **7.** 371

Sifanto (see Siphnos)

Siga in Masaesylia in Libya, royal residence of Sophax, now in ruins, 1000 stadia from Maurusia, **8.** 173

Sigeium, Cape (Yeni-Scheher), in the Troad, **3.** 375, **6.** 61, 91

Sigeium in the Troad, now in ruins, **6.** 61, 67; a wall around built with stones from ancient Ilium, **6.** 75; has been rased to the ground by the Ilians, **6.** 79; received part of the territory of ancient Ilium, **6.** 85

"Sigelus's," the monument of Narcissus near Oropus so called, **4.** 293

Sigerdis, the kingdom of, in Asia, **5.** 281

Sigia, once the name of the site of Alexandreia in the Troad, **6.** 93

Siginni, the, in Asia, imitate the Persians in most of their customs, **5.** 293

Signia (Segni), between the Latin and Appian Ways, produces the Signine Wine, **2.** 413

Sigri, Cape (see Sigrium)

Sigrianê, in Asia, **5.** 313

Sigrium (Sigri), Cape, in Lesbos, **3.** 381, **6.** 139, 141, 145

Sila, Mt. (Aspromonte), in Bruttium, **3.** 35

Silaceni, the, in Asia, **7.** 223

Silanus the historian, on the behaviour of a spring at Gades, **2.** 145

Silaris (Sele) River, the, flows between Campania and Leucania, **2.** 469, **3.** 3; any plant let down into, turns to stone, **2.** 471

Silas River, the, in India, **7.** 67

Sileni, the, ministers of Dionysus, **5.** 87, 97

Silenus, father of the Dolion who dwelt on the Ascanian Lake, **5.** 465, **6.** 373

Silli ("Lampoons "), the, of Xenophanes, **6.** 235

Silo (Pompaedius Silo)

Silphium, produced in zones beneath the tropics, **1.** 367; in Libya, **1.** 501; whence the " Medic juice," **5.** 311; in Asia, helpful in the digestion of raw food, **7.** 147; the Cyrenaean, **8.** 199, 203, 209

Silting-up, the, of the Rhodanus, **2.** 189; of the sea at the mouth of the Nile, unknown to Homer, according to Apollodorus, **3.** 189; at the mouths of the Cyrus River, **5.** 223; at the mouth of the Pyramus River, like that of the Nile, **5.** 355, 357; at the mouth of the Maeander, has made Prienê an inland city, **5.** 515

Silurus, the, a fish indigenous to the Nile, **8.** 149

Silva Gallinaria, on the Gulf of Cumae, where pirates assembled, **2.** 439

Silver, plentiful in regions of Ilipa and Sisapo in Iberia, **2.** 25; largest quantity and best quality of, in Turdetania, **2.** 39, 45; a composite part of " electrum," **2.** 41; " effloresces " from the soil in Artabria, **2.** 45; description of mines of, at New Carthage, **2.** 47; found mixed in small quantities with lead at mines at Castalo in Iberia, **2.** 47; produced in Britain, **2.** 255; first coined (in Crete) by Pheidon, **4.** 181; Alybê in Cappadocia "the birthplace of," **5.** 403, 405; cleaned with

INDEX OF NAMES, PLACES, AND SUBJECTS

Slaves, exported from England, 2. 255; in Rome, from Corsica, 2. 359; named by the Attic people after their countries (e.g. "Lydus"), or given names prevalent in their countries (e.g. "Midas"), 3. 213; sold by Asiatic nomads at Tanaïs, 5. 193

Sling, the, used by the Iberians, 2. 107; invented by the Aetolians, 4. 103

Slingers, the best, are the Gymnesians (in the Balearic Islands), 2. 125

Slings, used by the Gauls, 2. 243; used in Persia, 7. 181; used in battle by the Negrani in Arabia, 7. 361

Smaragdus (emerald?), the mines of, between Coptus and the Red Sea, 8. 121

Sminthi (see Apollo, Sminthian), means "mice," 6. 127

Sminthia; two places near Hamaxitus so called, others near Larisa, another near Parium, another in Rhodes, another in Lindus, and others elsewhere, 6. 97

Sminthian Apollo (see Apollo, Sminthian)

Sminthium, the temple of Apollo near Hamaxitus, 6. 97

Smyrna, an Amazon, after whom both Ephesus and Smyrna were named, 6. 201

Smyrna, said to have been founded by the Amazons, 5. 237; named by the Amazons, 5. 407; by most writers called the birthplace of Homer, but not mentioned by Homer, 5. 421; the Erasistrateian school of medicine at, 5. 519; 320 stadia from Ephesus, 6. 197; joined the Ionian League of twelve cities, 6. 201; formerly occupied by the Leleges, who were driven out by Smyrnaeans from Ephesus, who founded the ancient Smyrna 20 stadia from the present Smyrna, 6. 203; produces fine wine, 6. 215; discussion of the Old and the New, 6. 245, 247; various distances from, 6. 309

Smyrnaeans, the, from Ephesus, founded ancient Smyrna, were driven out by the Aeolians, fled to Colophon, but later returned, 6. 203; laid especial claim to Homer and had a bronze coin called "Homereium," 6. 247

Snails, the best in the world, caught at Linum in the Troad, 6. 33

Snakes (see Serpents, Vipers, Reptiles), that swallow oxen, 1. 263; a plague of, 2. 35; the small and deadly, in India, 7. 79; skins of, used as wraps and bed-covers in Pharusia in Libya, 8. 169

Soandum in Cappadocia, the road through, 6. 309

Soanes, the, hold the heights of the Caucasus above Dioscurias, and have a king and a council of 300 men, 5. 207, 215

Soatra in Lycaonia, has extremely deep wells and actually sells water, 5. 475

Socrates, in Plato's *Phaedrus*, disregards Sophocles' statement about Boreas, 3. 175

Socratic philosophers, the: Eucleides of Megara and Phaedon the Eleian, 4. 251

Soda, found in Lake Arsenè in Armenia, 5. 327

Sodom, once the metropolis of numerous cities about the Dead Sea, destroyed by eruptions of fire, water, and sulphur, 7. 297

Sogdiana in Asia, once held by the Greeks, 5. 281

Sogdiani, the, in Asia; geographical position of, 5. 269; strange customs of, 5. 281; speak the same language as the Arians, 7. 143

Soil, the, round Mts. Vesuvius and Aetna, burnt out and suited to the vine, 2. 453

Solfatara (see Albula Waters), 2. 449

Soli in Cilicia, 6. 311; Pompey, after breaking up all piracy, settled many pirates in, 4. 227; named Pompeïopolis by Pompey, 6. 315; founded by Achaeans and Rhodians —and names of famous natives of, 6. 339; founded by Phalerus and Acamas the Athenians, 6. 381

Solmissus, Mt., near Ephesus, where the Curetes frightened Hera when spying on Leto, 6. 223

476

INDEX OF NAMES, PLACES, AND SUBJECTS

INDEX OF NAMES, PLACES, AND SUBJECTS

478

INDEX OF NAMES, PLACES, AND SUBJECTS

hearsay, **1.** 451; ascended Nile with Aelius Gallus the Roman praefect, **1.** 455; quoted by Athenaeus as saying that he (Strabo) says that he knew Poseidonius, **3.** 383; not alien to Cnossus in Crete—and the history of relatives of, **5.** 133–137; distinguished ancestors of, **5.** 433, 435; took entire course of Aristodemus at Nysa in Asia, **6.** 263

Stratarchas, son of Dorylaüs the military expert, **5.** 135

Stratiê, the Homeric, now deserted, **3.** 385, **4.** 229

Stratius the priest, at Panticapaeum, **1.** 277

Strato of Lampsacus in Mysia in Asia Minor; became head of Peripatetic school of philosophy in 287 B.C.; called the "physicist," and praised by Eratosthenes for his explanation of physical changes of lands and seas, **1.** 181; prophesies silting up of whole Euxine Sea, **1.** 183; on the bed-levels of the Mediterranean and the Atlantic, **1.** 187; says that the bed of the Euxine is higher than that of the Propontis, **1.** 189

Strato, an isle in the Arabian Gulf, **7.** 319

Strato, the Tower of, in Phoenicia, **7.** 275

Stratocles, the Athenian archon (425 B.C.), went on the second Sicilian expedition (?), **4.** 111 (see footnote)

Stratocles the philosopher, native of Rhodes, **6.** 279

Straton the tyrant, put Amisus in Cappadocia Pontica in bad plight, **5.** 395

Stratonicê, daughter of King Ariathres, wife of Eumenes II, and mother of Attalus III, **6.** 167

Stratoniceia in Caria, a noteworthy city, **6.** 291; description and history of, **6.** 297–299

Stratonicus the citharist, utters a proverb on the city Assus, **6.** 115; on the paleness of the Caunians in the Peraea of the Rhodians, **6.** 267

Stratos, the earlier name of Dymê in Achaea, **4.** 225

Stratus (near Lepenu) in Acarnania,

on the Acheloüs River, **5.** 25; geographical position of, **5.** 27

Strombichus, father of the Athenian ambassador Diotimus, **1.** 175

Stromboli (see Strongylê)

Strongoli (see Petelia)

Strongylê (Stromboli), one of the Liparaean Isles, the home of Aeolus, "steward of the winds," **3.** 99

Strophades Islands, the, lie about 400 stadia off the Messenian Cyparissia, **4.** 111

Strovitzi (see Lepreum)

Struma River, the (see Strymon River)

Strumitza (see Callipolis in Macedonia)

Struthophagi ("Bird-eaters"), the, in Aethiopia; manner of capture of birds like ostriches by, **7.** 325

Strymon (Struma) River, the, **3.** 295, 297, 325, 331, 335, 355, 359, 363

Strymonic Gulf, the; position of, on the Aegaean, **3.** 353, 357, 363

Stubara, a populous city on the Erigon River, **3.** 311

Stura (see Styra)

Stymphalian Lake, the, in Arcadia, whence Heracles drove out the birds, **4.** 161; source of the Erasinus River, **4.** 231, 233

Stymphalides, the; name of the birds at the Stymphalian Lake, **4.** 161

Stymphalus in Arcadia, no longer exists, **3.** 93, **4.** 161, 229; once on the Stymphalian Lake, but now 50 stadia away, and why, **4.** 231 (see footnote 5); besieged by Iphicrates, **4.** 233

Styptic earth, a kind of, used in refining gold, **2.** 41

Styra (Stura) in Euboea, **5.** 9; destroyed in the Malian War by Phaedrus the Athenian general, **5.** 11

Styrax (or Storax) shrub, or tree, abundant in a certain region of Aethiopia, **7.** 329

Styrax-tree, the, abounds in the region of Mt. Taurus, **5.** 483

Styx River, the, at Avernus in Italy, **2.** 443

Styx River, the, in Rhodes, water

INDEX OF NAMES, PLACES, AND SUBJECTS

of, mixed with sulphur, poured by the Telchines upon animals and plants in order to destroy them, **6.** 275

Suchus, the sacred crocodile at Arsinoë, story of, **8.** 107

Sucro (Jucar) River, the, shallow, and geographical position of, **2.** 89, 105

Sudinus, a famous Chaldaean philosopher, **7.** 203

Suessa Aurunca (Sessa), the metropolis of the Volsci, captured by Tarquinius Superbus, **2.** 387

Suessa Pometia (site unknown), in Italy, **2.** 413

Suessiones, the, in Celtica, geographical position of, **2.** 233; bravest of the Belgae except the Bellovaci, **2.** 241

Suessula (Cancello), in Campania, **2.** 461

Suet, used for bread-making in Aegypt, **8.** 151

Suevi, the; the most powerful of the German tribes, **2.** 231; near whose country are the sources of the Ister, **2.** 287; some of the tribes of, dwell in the Hercynian (Black) Forest, **3.** 155; others outside the Forest, as far as the country of the Getae, **3.** 157; others on the Albis River, **3.** 173

Suez, Isthmus of (see Isthmus between Pelusium and Arabian Gulf)

Sugambri, the, a Germanic people, **2.** 231, **3.** 155; live near the ocean, **3.** 159; began the war with the Romans under Melo, **3.** 161; one of the best known German tribes, **3.** 171

Suicide, committed by Iberians, **2.** 115

Suidas, of whom little is known except that he wrote a *History of Thessaly* and a *History of Euboea*; says that the temple of Zeus at Dodona in Thesprotia was transferred from Thessaly, **3.** 317

Sulchi, a city in Sardinia, **2.** 361

Sulgas River, the, in Celtica, empties into the Rhodanus, **2.** 197

Sulla, L. Cornelius (138–78 B.C.), the dictator; withstood a siege in land of the Volaterrani for two years, **2.** 353; Roman dictator, **2.** 463; tore down the walls between Athens and Peiraeus, and captured Athens and Peiraeus, **4.** 261; punished its tyrant Aristion, but pardoned the city, **4.** 271; the Roman commander, used the disease-curing fountains in the Lelantine Plain in Euboea, **5.** 13; honoured Archelaüs the father of the priest Archelaüs, **5.** 437; overthrew Fimbria and arranged terms with Mithridates Eupator at Dardanus in the Troad, **6.** 55, 59; after capture of Athens carried off to Rome the libraries of Aristotle and Theophrastus, **6.** 113; tore down the Peiraeus, **6.** 275; fought by Archelaüs (86 B.C.), **8.** 45

Sulmon (Sulmona), in Italy, **2.** 431

Sulmona (see Sulmon)

Sulphur, the district of Baiae and Cumae full of, **2.** 447

Sulpicius Quirinius (see Cyrinius)

"Summer sunrise," a variable term, **1.** 415

Sun, the, revolves in opposite direction to movement of heavens, **1.** 87; rises from, and sets in, Oceanus, according to Homer, **1.** 5; revolution of, **1.** 115; ascent of, **1.** 283; oblique motion of, more rapid at equator, **1.** 375; revolves round earth in zodiac, **1.** 425; reaches maximum height of nine cubits (18°) in winter to peoples round southern parts of Lake Maeotis (Sea of Azov), **1.** 515; round parts north of Lake Maeotis, six cubits, **1.** 517; moves along circle parallel to the revolution of the universe, **1.** 517; false stories about, in Iberia, **2.** 9; visual rays from, refracted through vapour, **2.** 11; revolution of, measures one day and night, **2.** 149; hated and reviled by some of the Aethiopians, **8.** 147; passes quickly when it rises, but turns back slowly, according to Poseidonius, **8.** 175–177

Sun, the (Helius), worshipped by the Albanians in Asia, **5.** 229; the only god of the Massagetae in Asia, **5.** 265; worshipped by the Nabataeans in Arabia, **7.** 369

481

INDEX OF NAMES, PLACES, AND SUBJECTS

Sun-dial, the, evidence of, **1**. 43; relation of index of, to shadow, at Massalia, **1**. 237; differences of latitude observed by, **1**. 333; usefulness of, to geometricians in determining latitudes and longitudes, **1**. 429; casts no shadow at Syenê at summer solstice, **1**. 439; relation of index to shadow of, at Byzantium, the same as at Massalia, **1**. 443; shadows of, at Gades, the Pillars, the Strait of Sicily, and Rhodes agree, **1**. 459; yields correct distance from Rhodes to Alexandria, **1**. 483

Sunium, Cape, reaches almost as far south as Maleae, **1**. 353; the southern limit of the Macedonian coast, **3**. 333; the promontory of Attica, **4**. 239; 330 stadia from Peiraeus, **4**. 241; 300 stadia from Euboea, **4**. 275; lies nearly as far east as Cape Samonium in Crete, **5**. 121

Sunium, a noteworthy deme, near Cape Sunium, **4**. 271

Sunrise, winter, **1**. 125

Sunset, winter, **1**. 125

Sunshades, barbaric, used by women in Iberia, **2**. 107

Suppliants, the, of Aeschylus, quoted, on the Pelasgi, **2**. 345

Surena, the Parthian, captured and slew Crassus at Sinnaca, **7**. 231

Surrentine wine, the, **2**. 437

Surrentum (Sorrentum, now Sorrento) in Campania, **2**. 455

Susa, a notable city; said to have been reached from Cilicia by Diotimus in 40 days, **1**. 175; history and description of, **7**. 157–161; contained many Persian treasures, **7**. 169; gets no rain, **7**. 201; lies to the east of Babylon, **7**. 219

Susiana, position of, **1**. 499

Susians, the, once fought by the Cossaei and Elymaei, **5**. 309; were also called Cissians, after Cissia the mother of Memnon, **7**. 159

Susis, produces rice, **7**. 29; in a way, a part of Persis, **7**. 157; description of, **7**. 169–173; borders on Babylonia, **7**. 203

Sutri (see Sutrium)

Sutrium (Sutri), a city in Italy, **2**. 365

Swans, numerous in Iberia, **2**. 107

Swine, accepted as sacrifice by Aphroditê Castnietis, **4**. 431; not allowed to be brought into Comana in Pontus, **5**. 499

Sword (see Dirk and Dagger), a broad, used by the Indians, **7**. 117

Sword-fish (see Galeotae)

Swords; used in Persia, **7**. 183; used by the Negrani in Arabia, **7**. 361; used by some of the Aethiopians, **8**. 139; many given up by the Carthaginians to the Romans, **8**. 187

Syangela in Caria, **6**. 119

Sybaris, in Bruttium, founded by the Achaeans, **3**. 43, 45; once a powerful city, marshalling 300,000 men, **3**. 47; the, on the Teuthras River, founded by the Rhodians, according to some historians, **3**. 51, **6**. 277

Sybaris, a spring at Bura in Achaea; the Sybaris River in Italy said to have been named after, **4**. 223

Sybaris (Coscile) River, the, in Italy, **3**. 47; makes timid the horses that drink from it, **3**. 47; said to have got its name from the spring Sybaris at Bura in Achaea, **4**. 223

Sybaritae, the, erected fortifications on the sea near Paestum (Pesto), **2**. 469; Laüs in Leucania a colony of, **3**. 5; deposited offerings at treasure-house at Delphi, **4**. 359

Sybota (Syvota) Islands, the, off the coast of Epeirus, **1**. 475, **3**. 299

Sycaminopolis in Phoenicia, **7**. 275

Sycaminus, the Aegyptian (mulberry-tree), found in Aethiopia, **7**. 331; produces the *sycamorus* (like a fig), **8**. 149

Sycamorus, the (like a fig), found in Aegypt, **8**. 149

Sydracae, the, a tribe in India, said to be descendants of Dionysus, **7**. 11, 57

Sydrê (see Arsinoê in Cilicia)

Syedra (see Arsinoê in Cilicia)

Syenê (Assuan), belongs to Aegypt, **1**. 147; lies under summer tropic, **1**. 439; distance from, to Meroê and to equator, **1**. 439; distance

INDEX OF NAMES, PLACES, AND SUBJECTS

INDEX OF NAMES, PLACES, AND SUBJECTS

INDEX OF NAMES, PLACES, AND SUBJECTS

INDEX OF NAMES, PLACES, AND SUBJECTS

Teanum Apulum (Passo di Civita) in Apulia, where Italy is contracted into an isthmus, **3**. 135

Teanum Sidicinum (Teano) in Italy, a noteworthy city, **2**. 413, 459, 461

Tearco, the Aethiopian chief; his expeditions, **1**. 227; advanced as far as Europe, **7**. 7, even to the Pillars of Heracles, **7**. 9

Teate (Chieti), the metropolis of the Marrucini in Italy, **2**. 431

Tectosages, the, a tribe of the Volcae in Celtica; geographical position of, **2**. 203; once a powerful people, some of whom took possession of territory in Greater Phrygia now called Galatia, **2**. 205; border on the Aquitani, **2**. 213; one of the three tribes of the Galatians in Asia Minor, named after the Tectosages in Celtica, **5**. 467; possess the parts near Greater Phrygia, including Ancyra (now Angora, the Turkish capital), **5**. 471

"Tegea," accented on the penult, **4**. 169

Tegea (Palaeo-Episcopi) in Arcadia, settled from nine communities, **4**. 21; Cenchreae on road to Argos from, **4**. 183; an oracle perverted to apply to, **4**. 199; still endures, **4**. 229

Tegeatans, the, helped the Argives to destroy Mycene after the Battle of Salamis, **4**. 187

Teïans, the, abandoned their city Teos in the time of the Persians and migrated to Abdera, a Thracian city, **6**. 237

Teichius, a fort near Thermopylae, **3**. 391

Teichos, Macron (see Macron Teichos)

Teiresias, the seer; tomb of, at the foot of Mt. Tilphossius, near Alalcomenae in Boeotia, where he died at the time of the flight of the Thebans, **4**. 323; father of Manto the mother of Mopsus, **4**. 453; by Persephonê granted reason and understanding after his death, **7**. 289

Telamon, father of Teucer, **6**. 377

Telamon, the father of Aias (Ajax), **4**. 253

Telchines, the, represented by some as identical with the Curetes, **5**. 87, 89; reared Zeus in Crete, **5**. 111; in Rhodes, emigrants from Crete and Cypros, the first people to work iron and brass, and made Cronus' scythe, **6**. 275

Telchinis, an earlier name of Rhodes, **6**. 273

Teleboans (see Taphians), the, held a part of Acarnania, according to Aristotle, **3**. 289; the islands of, **5**. 59; all said to be pirates, **5**. 61; said once to have lived in Acarnania, **5**. 67

Teleboas, grandson of Lelex and founder of the Teleboae, had 22 sons, some of whom dwelt in Leucas, **3**. 289

Teleclus, king of the Lacedaemonians, killed by the Messenians, **3**. 111; colonised Poeäessa and other places in Laconia, **4**. 115

Telemachus, son of Odysseus, marvels at palace of Menelaüs, **1**. 143; thought by the wooers to have gone to Ephyra for deadly drugs, **4**. 29; found the Pylians offering sacrifice at the temple of the Samian Poseidon, **4**. 53; route of, from Pylus to Sparta, and return trip of, **4**. 57, 75–79; visited Diocles in Pherae (the Homeric Pharis) in Messenia, **4**. 145, and Menelaüs at Sparta, **4**. 147, **5**. 69

Telephus, king of the Mysians in Asia, **5**. 487, **6**. 23; from Arcadia, and adopted son of Teuthras, **5**. 491; father of Eurypylus, **6**. 15; myth of, **6**. 135

Telesia (near Venefrum), a Samnite city, **2**. 463

Telethrius, Mt., in Euboea, **5**. 7; Oreus situated at the foot of, **5**. 7

Tellenae, in Latium, **2**. 387

Telmessis, Cape, in Lycia, **6**. 317

Telmessus in Lycia, **6**. 317

Telos (Tilos), one of the Sporades Islands, **5**. 175

Tembrion, the Ionian coloniser of Samos, **5**. 53, **6**. 201

Temenium in Argolis, where Temenus was buried, lies 26 stadia from Argos, **4**. 151

Temenus, leader of the Heracleidae on their return to the Peloponnesus,

487

INDEX OF NAMES, PLACES, AND SUBJECTS

489

INDEX OF NAMES, PLACES, AND SUBJECTS

490

INDEX OF NAMES, PLACES, AND SUBJECTS

Theodosia (Feodosia or Kaffa) in the Crimea, **3**. 235; situated in a fertile plain and has a large harbour, **3**. 237

Theodosius, the mathematician, and his sons, natives of Bithynia, **5**. 467

Theology, borders on mythology, **5**. 119

Theomnestus, contemporary of Strabo, renowned harper, political opponent of Nicias, a native of Cos, **6**. 289

Theon Limen (God's Harbour) in Masaesylia in Libya, **8**. 173

Theophanes of Mitylenê (fl. about 62 B.C.; intimate friend of Pompey, and wrote a history of his campaigns), on the course of the Tanaïs River, **5**. 193; made the expedition with Pompey and tells where Amazons lived, **5**. 233; on certain insects in Armenia, **5**. 323; on the size of Armenia, **5**. 331; changed the spelling of "Sinoria" to "Synoria," **5**. 425; father of Marcus Pompey, contemporary of Strabo, historian, statesman, friend of Pompey, and most illustrious of all the Greeks, **6**. 143, 145

Theophilus, son of Tibius the cousin of Strabo's grandfather, slain by Mithridates, **5**. 435

Theophrastus the Peripatetic philosopher (d. 278 B.C.), teacher of Demetrius of Phalerum, who reigned at Athens by appointment of Cassander the king of Macedonia, **4**. 269; pupil of Aristotle, author of treatise *On Love*; on Leucocomas and Euxynthetus, **5**. 139; inherited the library of Aristotle, **6**. 111; disciple of Aristotle, native of Eressus in Lesbos, first named Tyrtamus, his name being changed by Aristotle, and most eloquent of Aristotle's disciples, **6**. 145

Theopompus of Chios (b. about 380 B.C.), pupil of Isocrates and historian of Greece (411–394 B.C.) and of Philip of Macedon (360–336 B.C.); professedly narrates myths in his histories, **3**. 191; on the "Land of Panchaea," an invention, **3**. 191; on the origin of the names "Ionian Gulf" and "Adriatic (Adrias) Gulf," **3**. 267; wrong on the length

of the Adriatic and Illyria, and makes a number of incredible statements, **3**. 269; says there were 14 tribes of the Epeirotes, **3**. 297; on the conquests and hospitality of the Lacedaemonians, **4**. 171; on Methonê in Macedonia and Methonê (Methana) in Argolis, **4**. 177; on the geographical position of Parapotamii, **4**. 373; on the Larisa between Elis and Dymê, **4**. 441; on Histiaea (Oreus) in Euboea, **5**. 7; says that Mariandynus ruled over part of Paphlagonia, took possession of the country of the Bebryces, and left the country named after himself, **5**. 375; on Amisus, **5**. 395; on the strait at Sestus, **6**. 45; on Mt. Mesogis in Asia, **6**. 185; native of Chios, **6**. 243

Theopompus of Cnidus, contemporary of Strabo, friend of Julius Caesar, **6**. 283

Thera (formerly called Callistê), the island, founded by Theras, a descendant of Polyneices, **4**. 63; metropolis of the Cyrenaeans and a colony of the Lacedaemonians, **5**. 161, **8**. 203

Therapnae, in the territory of Thebes, **4**. 315

Theras, son of Autesion, descendant of Polyneices, founded Thera, the mother-city of Cyrenê, **4**. 63

Therasia (Thirasia), the island, near Thera, **5**. 161

Theriaca, the, a poem on poisonous animals by Nicander, **8**. 151

Therikos (see Thoricus)

Therma (earlier name of Thessaloniceia, *q.v.*)

Therma in Aetolia; statue of Aetolus at, **5**. 77

Thermaean Gulf (Gulf of Saloniki), the, **3**. 297; receives the waters of the Haliacmon, **3**. 325; Alorus in inmost recess of, **3**. 341; cities on, destroyed by Cassander the son-in-law of Philip, **3**. 343, 345, 349; position of, on the Aegaean, **3**. 353, 381

Thermessa (or Hiera, now Vulcanello), one of the Liparaean Islands, **3**. 95

Thermodon (see Lycus) River, the;

INDEX OF NAMES, PLACES, AND SUBJECTS

silting-up at mouth of, **1**. 193; not mentioned by Homer, **3**. 189; flows through Themiscyra, **5**. 395

Thermopylae (or Pylae), treason of Ephialtes at pass of, **1**. 35; hot springs at, once ceased to flow because of earthquake, **1**. 223; the Amphictyonic League convened at, **4**. 357; memorial pillar at, dedicated by the Locrians, **4**. 379; Mt. Oeta highest at, **4**. 389; 15 stadia from the Asopus River, **4**. 391; Leonidas fought the Persians at, and is 40 stadia by land from the Trachinian Heracleia, and 70 by sea from Cape Cenaeum and 530 from the Euripus, **4**. 393, 395, 411, 417, 419

Theseium, the, at Athens, **4**. 263; has a myth connected with it, **4**. 265

Theseus, the legendary Attic hero; mythical deeds of, **1**. 69; long journeys of, and reputed to have visited Hades, **1**. 177; said to have colonised Brentesium, **3**. 121; slew the Crommyonian sow, **4**. 197; killed Sceiron and Pityocamptes the robbers, **4**. 245; snatched Helen at Aphidna, **4**. 263; incorporated the 12 cities in Attica into one city, Athens, **4**. 267; slew the Marathonian bull, **4**. 273; adventures of, in Crete, **5**. 131

Thesmophoria, the; celebration of, at Alponus, **1**. 225

Thespeia (or Thespiae, q.v., now Erimokastron), the Homeric, **4**. 183

Thespiae (or Thespeia), has held out fairly well to this day, **4**. 287; Creusa the naval station of, **4**. 299; geographical position of, **4**. 315; well known in earlier times because of the Eros of Praxiteles there, and still endures, **4**. 319

Thespians, the; the Homeric village Eutresis belonged to, **4**. 323

Thesprotians, the, a barbarian tribe, now hold part of the country above Acarnania and Aetolia, **3**. 287, 289, 297

Thessalian horses, the, praised as best in oracle, **5**. 21

Thessalians, the, had serfs called "Penestae," **5**. 377

Thessalians, the, said to have founded Ravenna in Italy, **2**. 315; are the most ancient composite part of the Greeks, **4**. 393

Thessaliotis, one of the four divisions of Thessaly, **4**. 397; geographical position of, **4**. 399, 421, 433

Thessalonicê, daughter of Philip and wife of Cassander, after whom Thessaloniceia was named, **3**. 343, 347

Thessaloniceia (in earlier times called Therma, now Saloniki); distance from, to Epidamnus, **1**. 409; whither runs the Egnatian Way from Apollonia (Pollina) in Illyria, **3**. 295; now the largest city in Macedonia, **3**. 297, 329, 333, 341, 347, 349, 369; named after Thessalonicê the daughter of Philip and wife of Cassander, **3**. 343; 260 stadia from the outlets of the Peneius and 3200 from the Ister, **4**. 233

Thessalus, the son of Haemon, Thessaly named after, **4**. 453

Thessalus, son of Heracles, and father of the two Coan leaders, Pheidippus and Antiphus, **6**. 273

Thessaly, once called "Haemonia," **1**. 169; certain parts of, now held by Thracians, **3**. 287; Pelasgiotis, where (at Scotussa) was the original temple of Dodonaean, or Pelasgian, Zeus, **3**. 319; well adapted to horseraising, **4**. 229; description and history of, **4**. 395–455; boundaries of, **4**. 395; wholly a plain except Pelion and Ossa, **4**. 397; divided into four parts, **4**. 397; divided into ten parts by Homer, **4**. 399; ruled by Deucalion, **4**. 405; the domain of Achilles in, **4**. 399–419; the domain of Phoenix in (the Dolopians), **4**. 401, 415 (cp. **4**. 435); the domain of Protesilaüs in, **4**. 405, 407, 411, 415, 419, 421; the domain of Philoctetes in, **4**. 405, 407, 425, 427, 451; the domain of Eurypylus in, **4**. 407, 413, 421, 433, 435, 437; the domain of Eumelus in, **4**. 423, 425, 437, 447, 451; the domain of Polypoetes in, **4**. 437;

INDEX OF NAMES, PLACES, AND SUBJECTS

Thynians, the Pontic, are in origin a Thracian tribe, **3.** 177

Thynians, the Thracian, gave their name to Thynias, the coast between Salmydessus and Apollonia Pontica, **5.** 375

Thynias (Iniada), Cape, on the Euxine, **3.** 279

Thyreae, possession of, disputed by Argives and Lacedaemonians, **1.** 245, 247; on the confines of Laconia and Argolis, not mentioned by Homer, **4.** 183

Thyrides (Kavo Grosso), **4.** 15, 113, 125

Thysa, daughter of Dionysus, mentioned by Euripides, **5.** 103

Thyssus, a city of Athos, **3.** 355, 357

Tiara, the Median, **5.** 313

Tibareni, the, in Asia; geographical position of, **5.** 319, 399, 423; subject to Mithridates Eupator, **5.** 371; subject to Lesser Armenia and later to Mithridates, **5.** 425; now ruled by Queen Pythodoris, **5.** 427

Tiber River, the, borders on Tyrrhenia, **2.** 335; navigable, **2.** 349; tributaries of, from Tyrrhenia, **2.** 367; silting-up of, at mouth of, **2.** 391; tributaries of, from Umbria, and elsewhere, **2.** 403

Tiberius (see Caesar, Tiberius)

Tiberius Gracchus (consul 177 B.C.), by Polybius said to have destroyed 300 cities in Celtiberia, **2.** 105

"Tibius," a name given Paphlagonian slaves in Attica, **3.** 213; a Paphlagonian name used in Cappadocia, **5.** 415

Tibius, cousin of Strabo's grandfather, slain by Mithridates, **5.** 435

Tibur (Tivoli), visible from Rome, **2.** 415; description of, **2.** 417-419

Tiburtine stone, the quarries of, near Tibur, **2.** 417

Ticinum (Pavia), in Italy, **2.** 327

Ticinus (Tessin) River, the, tributary of the Padus, **2.** 295, 327

Tides, the, understood by Homer, **1.** 13; thoroughly investigated by Poseidonius and Athenodorus, **1.** 19, 203; at the Strait of Messina, **1.** 85; caused by the rising and

sinking of the beds of the seas, **1.** 187; compared with currents at straits, and correspond to rising and setting of the moon, **1.** 203; inundations of, in Iberia, **2.** 27, 29; ebb and flow of, responsible for large size of oysters and cetaceans, **2.** 37; cast ashore quantities of acorns, **2.** 39; said by Eratosthenes to come to an end at the Sacred Cape, **2.** 49; form estuaries on west coast of Iberia, **2.** 63; wrongly explained by Aristotle, according to Poseidonius, **2.** 67; effect of, on a spring at Gades, **2.** 143, 153, and on wells there, **2.** 145; increase of, at time of the full moon, **2.** 257; behaviour of, at head of the Adriatic, **2.** 309; on the coast of the Cimbri, **3.** 165, 167

Tieium, the city of the Cauconians in Bithynia, **5.** 377; home of Philotaerus, head of the family of the Attalic kings, **5.** 381; further history of, **5.** 385; Bithynium lies above, **5.** 463

Tigers, the largest, twice as large as lions, found in the country of the Prasii in India, **7.** 65

Tigranes, king of Armenia 96-56 B.C.; father of Artavasdes; treasury of, near Artaxata, **5.** 327; paid large tribute to the Romans, **5.** 331; descendant of Artaxias, and king of Armenia properly so called, **5.** 337; the remarkable career of, **5.** 337; seized Syria and Phoenicia, **5.** 339; forced the Mazaceni to migrate to Mesopotamia and founded Tigranocerta with them, **5.** 367; sent Metrodorus back to Mithridates, **6.** 115; opposed all attacks successfully, **7.** 225; held the Gordyaeans in subjection, and favoured by Pompey, **7.** 231; slew Selenê, surnamed Cleopatra, **7.** 241; by Pompey shut off from Antiocheia in Syria, **7.** 249

Tigranocerta, lies below Mt. Masius, **5.** 299, **7.** 231; founded by Tigranes the king of Armenia, **5.** 339, 367

Tigris River, the, flows from Armenia southwards, and with the Euphrates encloses Mesopotamia, **1.** 305; flows underground for a distance near

INDEX OF NAMES, PLACES, AND SUBJECTS

its sources, 3. 93; description of course of, 5. 297; empties into the Red Sea (!), 5. 327; origin of name of, 5. 329; at its outlets is called " Pasitigris," 7. 161; navigable to Opis, or Seleuceia, 7. 205; Polycleitus on, 7. 213; distances from, to the Euphrates, 7. 229

Tigyreni, the, a tribe of the Helvetii, joined the Cimbri, 3. 169

Tilos (see Telos)

Tilphossa, a spring near Lake Copaïs, 4. 323; at the foot of Mt. Tilphossius, 4. 333

Tilphossium (see Tilphusium) in Boeotia, near Lake Copaïs, 4. 331

Tilphossius, Mt., in Boeotia, where rises the spring Tilphossa, 4. 323; lies above Alalcomenae, 4. 333

Tilphusium (Tilphossium?) in Boeotia, near Lake Copaïs, 4. 321

Timaeus (also called " Epitimaeus ") of Tauromenium (b. about 352 B.C. and lived 96 years), the historian, his greatest work being a history of Sicily from the earliest times to 264 B.C., in 38 books or more, of which only fragments remain; on the number of the mouths of the Rhodanus, 2. 189; on the results of earthquakes in the Pithecussae Islands, 2. 459; on the contest between Eunomus and Ariston at the Pythian Games, 3. 35; connects the fountain of Arethusa with the Alpheius River, 3. 75; accused of falsifying by Demetrius of Scepsis, 6. 77; on the means used to restore the temple of Artemis at Ephesus, 6. 227; on the size of the larger of the Gymnesian Isles, 6. 277

Timagenes, a rhetorician and historian from Alexandria, contemporary of Augustus and author of a history of his exploits; on the fate of consul Caepio's daughters, 2. 207; says that brass rained from the skies and was swept down by rivers, 7. 97

Timavi Fons (Timavo), the, empties into the Adriatic, 2. 319

Timavum, the name of a temple of Diomedes in the recess of the Adriatic, 2. 319, 323

Timavus (Timavo) River, the, in

Italy, 2. 319; runs underground for a distance, 3. 93

Timon the " Misanthrope," imitated by Antony at Alexandria, 8. 39

Timonitis in western Paphlagonia, 5. 451

Timonium, the name given by Antony to his royal lodge at Alexandria, 8. 39

Timosthenes of Rhodes (fl. about 280 B.C.), admiral under Ptolemy Philadelphus; on the winds, 1. 107; author of a work on Harbours, 1. 353; mistakes of, in regard to promontories in the Mediterranean, 1. 353; entirely ignorant of Iberia, Celtica, Germany, Britain, and other countries, 1. 357, 361; says that Calpê in Iberia was in ancient times called Heracleia, 2. 15; composed the melody of the Pythian Nome, and wrote a work on Harbours in ten books, 4. 363; wrongly says there are forty islands between Asia and Lesbos, 6. 147; wrongly says that the promontory Metagonium lies opposite Massalia, 8. 167

Timotheus Patrion, a native of Sinopê, 5. 391

Timouchos, the title of an Assemblyman at Massalia, 2. 175

Tin, is dug from the ground in Turdetania, not found on surface as among Artabrians; also found in the Cassiterides and the Britannic Islands, and exported to Massalia, 2. 45, 157; found in the country of the Drangae in Asia, 7. 145

Tingis (Tangier, see Tinx) in Maurusia; passage from, to Belon in Iberia, 2. 15

Tinos (see Tenos)

Tinx (Tingis), by some confused with " Lynx " and " Lixus " (q.v.), 8. 159; geographical position of, 8. 165

Tirizis (Kaliakra), Cape, in Thrace, once used as a treasury by Lysimachus, 3. 279

Tiryns " of the great walls "; acropolis of, now deserted, 4. 169; inhabitants of, migrated to Epidaurus, 4. 171

Tisamenus, son of Orestes, persuaded by Philonomus to emigrate with Achaeans in Laconia to Ionia (Achaea), 4. 133, 211, 235

INDEX OF NAMES, PLACES, AND SUBJECTS

497

INDEX OF NAMES, PLACES, AND SUBJECTS

INDEX OF NAMES, PLACES, AND SUBJECTS

Autariatae, **3**. 271; bordered on the Little Scordisci, **3**. 273

Tribocchi, the, a Germanic tribe in Celtica, **2**. 229

Tribute, collectors of, sent by the Romans to the Provinces, **8**. 211

Triccê (Trikala) in Thessaly, **3**. 311; has the famous temple of the Triccaean Asclepius, **4**. 113, 177; has the earliest and most famous temple of Asclepius, **4**. 429; a stronghold, **4**. 431, 433

Triclari, the, the Erigon River flows from the country of, **3**. 341

Tricorii, the; the geographical position of, **2**. 195, 271

Tricorynthus (Kato-Suli) in Attica, a city of the Marathonian Tetrapolis, where the head of Eurystheus was buried, **4**. 187, 209, 273

Tridentini, the; geographical position of, **2**. 273

Trieres, a kind of stronghold in Phoenicia, **7**. 259

Trieste (see Tergeste)

Trieterides ("Triennial Festivals"), the, in honour of Dionysus, **5**. 103

Trikala (see Triccê)

Trinemeis, the Attic deme, where rises the Cephissus River, **4**. 277

Triouto River, the (see Teuthras River)

Triphylia, a district of Elis, **4**. 23; traversed by the Alpheius, **4**. 47; "contrariness of the soil" in, **4**. 53; settled by the Minyans, **4**. 63; bounded on the south by the Neda River, **4**. 67; most parts of, border on Arcadia, **4**. 101; brought under the sway of the Eleians, **4**. 107

Triphylians, the, composed of three tribes, as the name indicates, **4**. 23; even name of, no longer in use, **4**. 95

Tripod, a, the prize of victory at the funeral games in Elis, **4**. 93, 95

Tripodes in Megaris, **4**. 255; now called Tripodiscium, near which is the present market-place of Megara, **4**. 257

Tripodiscium (see Tripodes)

Tripolis, the, in Phoenicia, **7**. 259, 261

Tripolitis, the Pelagonian, **3**. 307

Triptolemus, in quest of Io, founded Tarsus in Cilicia, **6**. 345; father of Gordys, **7**. 233; descendants of,

settled at Antiocheia in Syria by Seleucus Nicator, and he was worshipped there as a hero, **7**. 243

Tritaea (Kastritza), one of the twelve cities in which the Achaeans settled, **4**. 219

Tritaeans, the, in Elis, **4**. 41

Triton River, the, in Boeotia, on which Eleusis and Athens are situated, **4**. 307

Tritonias, Lake, near the Great Syrtis, **8**. 199

Troad, the, submerged by tidal wave, **1**. 217; a part of "Phrygia-on-the-Hellespont," **1**. 497; seized by the Phrygians after the Trojan War, **5**. 119; detailed description of, **6**. 3–149; divided into eight or nine domains, **6**. 5, 9; extent of, **6**. 7, 9; cities in, **6**. 15 ff.; Priam held sway over, **6**. 13; begins after the city Cyzicus, **6**. 23; once under the sway of King Gyges of Lydia, **6**. 41; now, for the most part, belongs to the Lesbians, **6**. 75, 77

Trocmi, the, in Galatia, a tribe of the Tectosages, **2**. 205; border on the territory of Amaseia, **5**. 449; one of the three tribes of the Galatians, **5**. 467; possess the parts near Pontus and Cappadocia, and have three walled garrisons, **5**. 469, 471

Troes (now called Xypeteones), a deme in Attica, **6**. 95

Troezen, the son of Pelops, came originally from Pisatis, **4**. 175

Troezen (near Damala) in Argolis, **4**. 153, 169, 177, 181; an important city 15 stadia from the sea, sacred to Poseidon, and once called Poseidonia, **4**. 173

Trogilian isle, the, off the Trogilian promontory, **6**. 213

Trogilian promontory, the, a kind of spur of Mt. Mycalê, **6**. 211, 213

Trogitis, Lake, in Lycaonia, **5**. 475

Troglodyte country, the; a desert country, **1**. 501

Troglodytes, the Arabian ("Erembians," mentioned by Homer), **1**. 5, 153, **7**. 371; near the western coast of the Euxine, **3**. 273; who live north of the Caucasus, **5**. 241; first subdued by Sesostris the Aegyptian, **7**. 313; life and habits of, **7**.

499

INDEX OF NAMES, PLACES, AND SUBJECTS

337–341; fight with stones, arrows, and daggers, **7**. 339; make merry over their dead, **7**. 341; separated from the Arabians by the Arabian Gulf, **7**. 355; the country of, **8**. 3, 7; large commerce of, with the Aegyptians, **8**. 53; situated to the south of Aegypt, **8**. 135; dig homes in the earth, **8**. 169

Trojan Forces, The Marshalling of the, by Demetrius of Scepsis; on the dimensions of the Propontis and the Hellespont, and on certain distances, **3**. 379

Trojan Mountain, the, in Arabia, **8**. 95

Trojan Plain, the, description of, **6**. 65

Trojan War, the; an historical fact, **1**. 73; left only a Cadmeian victory to the Greeks, **2**. 55; attributed by Euripides to Zeus, **2**. 189

Trojans, the, colonised Siris in Italy, **3**. 49; by Dardanus were taught the Samothracian Mysteries, **3**. 371; had the Cauconians as allies, **4**. 57; had no allies from beyond the Borysthenes in the Trojan War, **5**. 407; allies of, **5**. 413, 415, **6**. 357, 359; boundaries of, confused with those of the Dolíones and Mygdonians, **5**. 459; term used by Homer for all peoples who fought on Trojan side, **5**. 495; extent of sway of, **6**. 5; led by Hector, **6**. 19; have many names in common with the Thracians, **6**. 41; " fight in close combat," **6**. 45; cheered by Ares, **6**. 69; faint-heartedness of, **6**. 71; evidences of original kinship with the people of Attica, **6**. 95; closely related to the Leleges and Cilicians, **6**. 149; by poets confused with other peoples, **6**. 315

Tronto River, the (see Truentinus)

Tropea, the harbour, in Bruttium, **3**. 19

Trophonian Zeus (see Zeus, the Trophonian)

Trophonius, with Agamedes, built the second temple at Delphi, **4**. 361; Greek prophet and ruler, **7**. 289

Tropic, the summer, **1**. 289; must pass through Syenê, **1**. 439. 507;

is $\frac{1}{15}$ of a zodiacal sign from the horizon, **1**. 515

Tropic, the winter, **1**. 15, 287, 289

Tropic circle, the; between which and equator shadows fall in both directions, **1**. 509; relation of, to arctic circle, **1**. 519; distance of, from the equator $\frac{1}{60}$ of greatest circle, **1**. 521

Tropic circles, the, must not be used as boundaries of torrid zone, **1**. 371; terrestrial and celestial, **1**. 427

Troy, the city (see Ilium); called " the Simuntian," after the Simŏeis River, **4**. 225; captured by Paches the Athenian general (427 B.C.), **6**. 79

Troy (*i.e.* the Troad); broad use of term, **6**. 7; topography best marked by Mt. Ida, **6**. 9; whole domain of Priam so called, **6**. 13, 15; by Homer combined with Aeolis into one country, **6**. 23

Troy, a village in Arabia, an ancient settlement of captive Trojans, **8**. 95

Truentinus (Tronto) River, the, in Picenum, **2**. 429

Tryphon, surnamed Diodotus (see Diodotus Tryphon), usurper of the throne of Syria, reigned 142-139 B.C., used Apameia as base of operations, **7**. 251; career of, **7**. 253; rased Berytus to the ground, **7**. 263

Tsanarlis River, the (see Enipeus River in Thessaly)

Tubatii, the, captives from, led in triumphal procession at Rome, **3**. 163

Tuccis in Iberia, where the sons of Pompey were defeated, **2**. 21

Tuder (Todi), a well-fortified city in Italy, **2**. 373

Tullum, Mt.; a mountain lying above the Vindelici, **2**. 287

Tunic, the Median, **5**. 313

Tunics; long, worn by inhabitants of the Cassiterides Islands, **2**. 157; worn by the Gauls, **2**. 241; the Ligurian, **2**. 267

Tunics, ungirded, with long borders, worn in Libya, **8**. 167

Tunis (see Tynis)

Tunnel, the, from Avernus to Cumae, and that from Dicaearchia to Neapolis, **2**. 445, 451

INDEX OF NAMES, PLACES, AND SUBJECTS

INDEX OF NAMES, PLACES, AND SUBJECTS

INDEX OF NAMES, PLACES, AND SUBJECTS

INDEX OF NAMES, PLACES, AND SUBJECTS

505

INDEX OF NAMES, PLACES, AND SUBJECTS

INDEX OF NAMES, PLACES, AND SUBJECTS